Studies in Diversity Linguistics

Chief Editor: Martin Haspelmath

In this series:

1. Handschuh, Corinna. A typology of marked-S languages.
2. Rießler, Michael. Adjective attribution.
3. Klamer, Marian (ed.). The Alor-Pantar languages: History and typology.
4. Berghäll, Liisa. A grammar of Mauwake (Papua New Guinea).
5. Wilbur, Joshua. A grammar of Pite Saami.
6. Dahl, Östen. Grammaticalization in the North: Noun phrase morphosyntax in Scandinavian vernaculars.
7. Schackow, Diana. A grammar of Yakkha.
8. Liljegren, Henrik. A grammar of Palula.
9. Shimelman, Aviva. A grammar of Yauyos Quechua.
10. Rudin, Catherine & Bryan James Gordon (eds.). Advances in the study of Siouan languages and linguistics.
11. Kluge, Angela. A grammar of Papuan Malay.
12. Kieviet, Paulus. A grammar of Rapa Nui.
13. Michaud, Alexis. Tone in Yongning Na: Lexical tones and morphotonology.
14. Enfield, N. J (ed.). Dependencies in language: On the causal ontology of linguistic systems .
15. Gutman, Ariel. Attributive constructions in North-Eastern Neo-Aramaic.
16. Bisang, Walter & Andrej Malchukov (eds.). Unity and diversity in grammaticalization scenarios.
17. Stenzel, Kristine & Bruna Franchetto (eds.). On this and other worlds: Voices from Amazonia.

ISSN: 2363-5568

On this and other worlds

Voices from Amazonia

Edited by

Kristine Stenzel

Bruna Franchetto

Kristine Stenzel & Bruna Franchetto (eds.). 2017. *On this and other worlds: Voices from Amazonia* (Studies in Diversity Linguistics 17). Berlin: Language Science Press.

This title can be downloaded at: http://langsci-press.org/catalog/book/167
© 2017, the authors
Published under the Creative Commons Attribution 4.0 Licence (CC BY 4.0):
http://creativecommons.org/licenses/by/4.0/
ISBN: 978-3-96110-018-7 (Digital)
      978-3-96110-019-4 (Hardcover)
ISSN: 2363-5568
DOI:10.5281/zenodo.892102
Source code available from www.github.com/langsci/167
Collaborative reading: paperhive.org/documents/remote?type=langsci&id=167

Cover and concept of design: Ulrike Harbort
Typesetting: Rafael Nonato, Sebastian Nordhoff, Kristine Stenzel
Illustration: Auxiliadora Figueiredo, Cédric Yvinec, Estevão Socot, Lidia Sakyrabiar, Miguel Cabral Junior, Moisés Galvez Trinidade, Ozélio Sakyrabiar, Sebastian Nordhoff, Sepé Kuikuro
Proofreading: Ahmet Bilal Özdemir, Andreas Hölzl, Anne Kilgus, Bev Erasmus, Eitan Grossman, Ikmi Nur Oktavianti, Jean Nitzke, Jeroen van de Weijer, Ludger Paschen, Neele Harlos, Nick Williams, Prisca Jerono, Sandra Auderset, Steven Kaye
Fonts: Linux Libertine, Arimo, DejaVu Sans Mono
Typesetting software: X∃LATEX

Language Science Press
Unter den Linden 6
10099 Berlin, Germany
langsci-press.org
Storage and cataloguing done by FU Berlin

Language Science Press has no responsibility for the persistence or accuracy of URLs for external or third-party Internet websites referred to in this publication, and does not guarantee that any content on such websites is, or will remain, accurate or appropriate.

Contents

Acknowledgments v

Standard abbreviations used in this volume vii

1 Amazonian narrative verbal arts and typological gems
Bruna Franchetto & Kristine Stenzel 1

I Life, death, and the world beyond

2 Kuikuro
Bruna Franchetto, Carlos Fausto, Ájahi Kuikuro & Jamalui Kuikuro Mehinaku 23

3 Kalapalo
Antonio Guerreiro, Ageu Kalapalo, Jeika Kalapalo & Ugise Kalapalo 89

4 Marubo
Pedro de Niemeyer Cesarino, Armando Mariano Marubo Cherõpapa Txano & Robson Dionísio Doles Marubo 139

5 Trumai
Raquel Guirardello-Damian, Kumaru Trumai & Tarukuy Trumai 163

II Beginnings

6 Kotiria
Kristine Stenzel, Teresinha Marques, José Galvez Trindade & Miguel Wacho Cabral 189

7 Hup
Patience Epps, Isabel Salustiano, Jovino Monteiro & Pedro Pires Dias 277

Contents

8   Sakurabiat
Ana Vilacy Galucio, Mercedes Guaratira Sakyrabiar, Manoel Ferreira Sakyrabiar, Rosalina Guaratira Sakyrabiar & Olimpio Ferreira Sakyrabiar   331

III   Ancestors and tricksters

9   Kĩsêdjê
Rafael Nonato, Kujusi Suyá, Jamthô Suyá & Kawiri Suyá   355

10   Kwaza
Hein van der Voort, Edileusa Kwaza, Zezinho Kwaza & Mario Aikanã   387

11   Aikanã
Joshua Birchall, Hein van der Voort, Luiz Aikanã & Cândida Aikanã   405

12   Suruí of Rondônia
Cédric Yvinec & Agamenon Gamasakaka Suruí   439

13   Ka'apor
Gustavo Godoy & Wyrapitã Ka'apor   467

Index   481

Acknowledgments

Our heartfelt thanks go to all the master narrators, indigenous researchers, and academic scholars for their priceless contributions, patience, and hard work in bringing these narratives to light. We are also grateful to Martin Haspelmath and the Studies in Diversity Linguistics editorial board for their enthusiastic response to our proposal and encouragement throughout its development. Very special acknowledgment is due to Sebastian Nordhoff for his technical expertise and boundless patience as well as to Rafael Nonato and Gustavo Godoy for their generous assistance in many stages of the project. Finally, we are very grateful to the team of proofreaders who volunteered their time, aiding us with valuable suggestions and finishing touches.

Standard abbreviations used in this volume

1	first person	INS	instrumental
2	second person	INTJ	interjection
3	third person	INTR	intransitive
ABL	ablative	IPFV	imperfective
ABS	absolutive	IRR	irrealis
ADV	adverb(ial)	LOC	locative
ALL	allative	M/MSC	masculine
APPL	applicative	N	non-
AUX	auxiliary	NEG	negation/negative
BEN	benefactive	NMLZ	nominalizer/nominalization
CAUS	causative	NOM	nominative
CLF	classifier	OBJ	object
COM	comitative	OBL	oblique
COMPL	completive	PFV	perfective
COND	conditional	PL	plural
COP	copula	POSS	possessive
DAT	dative	PRF	perfect
DIM	dimunitive	PRS	present
DECL	declarative	PROG	progressive
DEF	definite	PROH	prohibitive
DEM	demonstrative	PROX	proximal/proximate
DIST	distal	PST	past
DISTR	distributive	PTCP	participle
DU	dual	PURP	purposive
DUR	durative	Q	question particle/marker
ERG	ergative	QUOT	quotative
EXCL	exclusive	RECP	reciprocal
F/FEM	feminine	REM	remote
FOC	focus	SBJ	subject
FUT	future	SBJV	subjunctive
GEN	genitive	SG	singular
IMP	imperative	TOP	topic
INCL	inclusive	TR	transitive
INDF	indefinite	VOC	vocative

Chapter 1

Amazonian narrative verbal arts and typological gems

Bruna Franchetto
Museu Nacional, Federal University of Rio de Janeiro, Brazil

Kristine Stenzel
Federal University of Rio de Janeiro, Brazil

1 Origins

This volume owes its development to a confluence of circumstances, not least of which is the veritable explosion of scholarship on Amazonian languages that has taken place over the last several decades. Though the description and analysis of the 300 or so still-existing languages spoken in Amazonia[1] is still far from comprehensive, repositories of linguistic and anthropological academic references, such as the *Etnolinguistica* web site, clearly reflect exponential growth in the field since the 1990s.[2] This same period of expanding academic focus on Amazonian languages also saw the rise of new language documentation efforts and

---

[1] Following Epps & Salanova 2013 "Amazonia" is understood here as comprising both the Amazon and Orinoco basins, covering parts of Brazil, Bolivia, Peru, Ecuador, Colombia, Venezuela, Suriname, and the Guianas. For more on the distribution and state of endangerment of Amazonian languages, see Moore 2008.

[2] http://www.etnolinguistica.org/. Of the 358 dissertations or theses on Amazonian languages on file as of May 2017, just 6 were written before 1980, the number jumping to 19 during the next decade and then to 41 during the 1990s (representing some 18 percent of the total on record). Between 2000 and 2010, contributions increased more than fourfold, to 170 (47 percent of the archive), and another 123 have been added in the last six years. We should note that researchers make their own academic works available on this site, so the numbers cited do not represent a fully comprehensive view of all scholarship.

Bruna Franchetto & Kristine Stenzel. 2017. Amazonian narrative verbal arts and typological gems. In Kristine Stenzel & Bruna Franchetto (eds.), *On this and other worlds: Voices from Amazonia*, 1–19. Berlin: Language Science Press.
DOI:10.5281/zenodo.1008775

the establishment of archives of cultural and linguistic materials in which languages of the region are well represented.[3] The interdisciplinary and highly collaborative nature of most new documentation projects in Amazonia[4] has in turn strengthened dialog between anthropologists and field linguists who recognize the narrative genre as a prime source of both cultural understanding and verbal artistry, especially when offered by knowledgeable and eloquent orators such as those whose voices are represented here. Thus, text analysis — a longstanding element of language documentation in classic Boasian terms — is itself making a welcome comeback.

Our idea to gather a set of narratives from recent documentation projects into an organized volume is a product of this renaissance.[5] However, as word of our initiative began to circulate, the response from interested colleagues quickly threatened to swell the project to near-Amazonian proportions, and we found ourselves forced to make difficult choices. Fully recognizing that our final selection is but a sample of the rich materials available, we can only hope to see more collections of this type organized in the future.

The narratives themselves led us to organize the volume into three broad themes that are highly significant for Amazonian ethnology and its recent developments. The first theme — *Life, death, and the world beyond* — refers to crucial cosmological dimensions and forces us to rethink notions such as death, the dead, life, embodiment, the soul, the spirit, and post-mortem destiny, which are often not well translated or are cannibalized by Western/non-indigenous concepts. The second theme — *Beginnings* — includes fragments of Amerindian philosophy, in which reflection on the origin of beings does not pass through *ex-nihilo* creation, there being no "genesis" in the Judeo-Christian vein. The third theme — *Ancestors and tricksters* — introduces us to a few members of the Amerindian repertoire of comic and crafty characters, and leads us to memories of historical events and into realms of relations, whether among relatives or between enemies, that lie at the heart of societal living, with all its fluid frontiers and rituals.

---

[3] The DoBeS archive (Volkswagen Foundation, Germany) has materials from 14 Amazonian languages; ELAR (Endangered Languages Archive, University of London/SOAS) over 40; AILLA (Archive of the Indigenous Languages of the Americas, University of Texas Austin) an additional 60. More than 80 languages are included in the documentation archive maintained at the Emilio Goeldi Museum (MPEG, in Pará, Brazil) and another 18 in Indigenous Languages Documentation Project (PRODOCLIN) archive at the Museum of Indigenous Peoples (Museu do Índio/FUNAI, Rio de Janeiro, Brazil).

[4] The "participatory" or "collaborative" paradigm is widely adopted in current documentation projects in Amazonia, which prioritize training of indigenous researchers and high levels of community involvement (see Franchetto & Rice 2014; Stenzel 2014).

[5] As is the *Texts in the Indigenous Languages of the Americas* series, a recently re-established yearly supplement to the *International Journal of American Linguistics*.

1 Amazonian narrative verbal arts and typological gems

2 A contribution to Amazonian ethnology

Each chapter of this book presents a single narrative, an ever-present and much appreciated genre among almost all Amazonian peoples. Each embodies a unique rendition offered by a specific narrator, in circumstances and settings that vary widely: some were offered in a village, town, or intimate home setting in response to a specific request, one was recorded during a community language workshop (Kotiria), others in the course of everyday activities or within the context of a ritual.[6] As we contemplate these diverse settings, we are reminded that the act of narration is never monologic: there is always an audience, there are always interlocutors and "what-sayers". Narration is itself both a communicative and formative act. It not only transmits collective or individual memories, weaving the continuity of a people, clan, sib, or family, but also establishes the limits of social and antisocial behavior (and their consequences), revealing transformations, original and potential, creative or destructive.

At the same time, we can extract from these narratives mythical structures comparable to others in and beyond the Americas, following the paths of Levi Strauss's *esprit humain*. Through narratives, thought is molded, instruction and knowledge are transmitted and refined. The Ka'apor and Kuikuro narratives, for instance, exemplify diffused bits and pieces of pan-Amazonian mythology, crossing frontiers between genres, peoples, and regions. Scatological and obscene, the Ka'apor narrative finds parallels in the oral traditions of many Amazonian groups. The Kuikuro narrative is not only an element of the Upper-Xinguan network, in which peoples of distinct origins and languages share rituals, myths, discourses and each other, but is also a unique female rendition of a narrative heard before only in masculine voices. Feminine voices resound in the Trumai, Hup, Kwaza, and Kotiria narratives as well.

A classic theme in Amazonian mythology, the origins of crucial cultural items – such as songs, rituals, and cultivated plants — are often viewed as gifts or as bounty seized in encounters involving confrontation or alliance between enemies or occupants of "other" worlds. In the Sakurabiat narrative, for example, the origin of corn involves knowledge captured by great shamans from neighboring groups.

The Kalapalo and Trumai live in the same Upper Xingu regional multilingual cultural system, occupying distinct niches due to different degrees of adaptation and incorporation into the system. A comparison of the Kalapalo and Trumai narratives is particularly interesting because both describe funerary rituals and practices, recounting the origins of the Trumai chanted lamentations and some

---

[6]Links to the audio or video renditions are provided in each chapter.

of the Kalapalo songs performed during the Xinguan mortuary ritual. A Kalapalo man married to a Snake-Woman acquires the songs from his father-in-law; the Trumai people receive their chanted lamentations from the Smooth-billed Ani, a bird. Likewise, the origins of places, such as the Kotiria sacred cemeteries, and elements of the natural environment, such as the Deer's Tomb Constellation of the Hup narrative, lie in similar transformational fluidity and transposition of boundaries between this and other worlds.

Metamorphosis is a pervasive and relevant theme in Amerindian shamanic thought and contemporary Lowland South American ethnology. It evidences communication and change of perspectives between humans and non-humans, between the living and the dead, between blood relatives and affines, us and "others", a challenge to the irreducible and naturalized distinctions in Western thought. Translation, understood in its most ample sense, is a necessary but not mechanical mediation, since translation itself moves, modifies, and creates. In "The death-path teachings", two Marubo spirit-shamans, able to cross the world of spirits and dead people, connect exoteric knowledge with instructive speech. Likewise, a Kuikuro woman travels, still alive, to the upside-down world of the dead and there converses with them and hears their "twisted" words.

Narrative events occur in what is for us a remote "past" or mythological *illo tempore*, or better yet, as one Kuikuro chief puts it, a time "when we were all hyper-beings" speaking the same "language" or making ourselves understood through languages. It was or still is a time, a dimension out of time, or between times, peopled by ancestors and "monstrous" beings, such as the clumsy people-eater *Khátpy* of the Kĩsêdjê narrative. Indeed, the terms "myth" or "mythological narratives", and "history" or "historical narratives" are frequently used to define or at least suggest what might be considered narrative sub-genres. However, as the Kotiria narrative shows, this is a more-than-fluid frontier where the supposedly self-evident opposition between regimes of memory crumbles.

This fluidity is nowhere clearer than in comparative analysis of evidentials and/or epistemic markers used in narratives, markers that take more into account than the mere qualification of source of information. Such elements may be manipulated by the narrator, sensitive to the occasion and audience, to mark voices of authority. Evidentials or epistemic markers — crucial and often obligatory — first of all define the epistemological status of narrative speech, as we see in the use of the Ka'apor reportative, but above all, reveal ambiguities and porous boundaries. Is the Kuikuro narrative a "myth" about the inverted life of the dead or a "memory" of a live woman's journey to another world and return to narrate what she saw to fellow members of the living world? The narrator tempers her own assertions with markers typical of "historical" facts transmitted through collective memory and with the non-certainty of events not directly and visually witnessed, marking that is impossible in "mythical" narratives, which speak of origins, indistinctions among species, and transformations. The Suruí narrative vividly evokes episodes from a not-too-distant past — though still prior to times known by adults today — replete with battles between neighboring peoples, yet in this narrative we observe the "deletion of non-witnessed evidentiality" characteristic of "myths".

3 Narrative verbal artistry

To narrate is not just to verbally express an account in prosaic form. As we have noted, the act of narration is a performance, whether public or private, offered to interlocutors and audiences and open for evaluation, criticism, and praise. The narrator is often a "master" in the art of oration, a specialist of "good and beautiful speech", recognized as such and fully aware of his or her role in the chain of transmission of abilities and content. The master's artistic skills include manipulation of distinct protagonists' perspectives, balancing of repetitions with nuanced variation, control of the necessary detours from the advancing storyline, full command of all the varied means of capturing and holding the listeners' attention. Such mastery is evident in the Marubo narrative genre *yoã vana*, distinct from the sung narrative genre *saiti vana*, but both highly poetic performances. Cesarino's division of lines in the written text attempts to reproduce, if only partially, the dramatic effect produced by the rhythm of the oral performance and by thoughts-utterances whose understanding requires careful exegesis.

Similarly, the "masters" of the Kuikuro and Kalapalo narratives share like abilities and the narratives themselves reveal similar structures: formulaic openings and closings, scenes, blocks, parallelisms; movement verbs and logophoric connectives mark sequences and the development of events and actions. In the Hup and Kotiria narratives, skilled use of tail-head linking strategies guarantee sequential cohesion. Even more impressive is the Kwaza narrator's domination of anticipatory switch-reference marking as she constructs the narrative, in van der Voort's words, as "one long sentence, each chained clause being either in a subordinate mood or in a cosubordinate mood."

The rarity, or near absence, of indirect reported speech in Amazonian narratives draws our attention to the preponderance of direct reported speech, observed throughout the volume. Our narrators are masters in performance of such speech, leading us to wonder about other possibilities of embedding and recursive structures. In fact, we are dealing not only with cited dialogues, but also the expression of inner thoughts, which take the form of images, perceptions, emotions, plans. For instance, almost half of the Kuikuro and Kalapalo narratives is animated by dialogues between the characters, with a predominance of verbal forms inflected by performative modes (imperative, hortative, imminent future), as well as epistemic markers that modulate the attitudes and communicative intentions of the interacting characters. Cesarino mentions "the extensive use of reported speech, which allows the (Marubo) narrator to shift between voices." Last but not least, we highlight the "embedded quotations of successive narrators of the events" in the Surui narrative, as Yvinec observes.

These are but a few of the many and varied narrative discourse structures resources present in this volume, calling our attention to the richness and diversity of narrative verbal artistry in Amazonia.

4 A host of typological gems

This volume not only introduces us to a rich panorama of narrative styles and cultural themes, it also demonstrates the astounding genetic and structural diversity of Amazonian languages. Although not all recent research on Amazonian languages has been fully explored and incorporated into typological databases,[7] the picture that is emerging is one of much greater structural diversity within the Amazonian basin than was previously supposed. Indeed, the impetus to define a set of recognizably distinct "Lowland Amazonian" linguistic features (Payne 1990; Dixon & Aikhenvald 1999; Aikhenvald 2012) wanes in light of empirical evidence underscoring vast regional diversity (van der Voort 2000; Campbell 2012; Epps & Salanova 2013). Additionally, analyses such as Birchall's (2014) work on argument coding patterns in South American languages suggest that broader Western/Eastern South American perspectives may actually be more significant to understanding patterns of structural similarity and difference than earlier assumptions of an Andean/Lowland Amazonian dichotomy (see also O'Connor & Muysken 2014).[8]

This debate is far from concluded, and as research continues to pour in, it is certain to bring new insights into deep genetic relationships, pre-historical movements and patterns of contact, as well as contemporary areal phenomena,

---

[7]Such as such as the *World Atlas of Linguistic Structures* (WALS) http://wals.info/ and its more recently organized counterpart, (SAILS) *South American Indigenous Language Structures* http://sails.clld.org/.

[8]Other chapters in the same volume focus on specific typological features, including OV order, nominalization as a subordination strategy, post-verbal negation, and use of desiderative morphemes, that appear to characterize South American languages as a whole.

1 Amazonian narrative verbal arts and typological gems

Figure 1: Peoples and languages represented in this volume

all of which serving to refine our typological profiles. For the moment, suffice it to say that even the small selection of languages in our volume clearly shows that there is no easy answer to the question: "What does an *Amazonian language* look like?"

The twelve languages in this volume come from a variety of geographic locations within Amazonia, and include three linguistic isolates and members of the Carib, East Tukano, Nadahup, Jê, Tupi, and Pano families — only a fraction of the more than four dozen distinct genealogical units that compose the Amazonian linguistic landscape (Epps & Salanova 2013: 1). Three regions characterized by longstanding and systemic cultural and linguistic interaction are also represented by different subsets of these languages. Kotiria and Hup are spoken in the Upper Rio Negro region of northwestern Amazonia in the Brazil-Colombia borderlands (see Aikhenvald 2002, Aikhenvald 2012: 73–84, Epps & Stenzel 2013), and the Guaporé-Mamoré region of Southern Rondônia and northeastern Bolivia is represented by Kwaza, Aikanã, and Sakurabiat (Crevels & van der Voort 2008). Indeed, the chapters by Epps and van der Voort in this volume discuss features that support characterization of these two regions as "linguistic areas" in which contact and multilingual practices have led to structural similarities among genetically unrelated languages. The third multilingual system, represented by Kuikuro, Kalapalo, and Trumai, is the Upper Xingu in central Brazil (Franchetto 2011). The chapters by Franchetto, Guerreiro, and Guirardello-Damian, point out that, in contrast to the Upper Negro and Guaporé-Mamoré regions, in the Upper Xingu context, multilingualism emerges and is evidenced primarily as a component of Xinguan ritual arts.

Kuikuro and Kalapalo are actually variants of a single language, baptized by Franchetto as the "Upper Xingu Carib Language". Though viewed as *dialects* for the linguist, they are *languages* for their speakers for two substantive reasons. First, because within the Upper Xingu multilingual regional system, they are diacritics of local political identities. Secondly, because attributing the status of "language" to both establishes their equal value, counterbalancing the tendency for indigenous languages labeled as "dialects" to be viewed as having an inferior or marginal existence. We have strategically opted to present the Kuikuro and Kalapalo narratives in sequence so that the reader can appreciate the obvious similarities between the syntax of the two languages as well as the differences — sometimes quite subtle — in morphology and lexicon. Unfortunately, the written medium masks a crucial dimension of dialectal difference occurring on the prosodic level, where Kuikuro and Kalapalo clearly exemplify the notion of words "dancing to the beats of different drummers". Equally strategic is the sequencing of the Kwaza and Aikanã narratives, versions of the same story offered by speakers of two language isolates in the same multilingual region.

A broad overview of the twelve languages reveals a handful of common structural features, including agglutinative and preferentially suffixing morphology, as well as predominantly head-final constituent order (the exception being the relatively free word order of Kwaza). However, a closer look shows interesting variations in clausal constituent ordering, including object-initial order, which first came to light in languages of the Carib family[9] and which can be seen in numerous lines of the Kuikuro and Kalapalo narratives, such as (1):

(1) *tüti ilü leha iheke*

    tüti   *i-lü*   *leha*   *i-heke*
    REFL.mother fight-PNCT COMPL 3-ERG

    'He fought with his own mother' [KUIKURO, line 243]

---

[9] Several Carib languages are analyzed as having OVS as the dominant order, and OVS is also found in some East Tukano, Tupi, Arawak languages (see Derbyshire 1999: 155; Campbell 2012: 273–275).

As a frequently occurring alternate order, OVS is found in many other Amazonian languages, including Kotiria, where known, non-focused subjects are sentence-final, as we see in (2).

(2) *"hiphiti a'ri phinitare naita yɨ'ɨ" nia.*

híphiti   a'rí   ~phídi-ta-re   ~dá-i-ta   yɨ'ɨ
everything DEM.PROX right.here-EMPH-OBJ get-M-INTENT 1SG
~dí-a
say-ASSERT.PFV

'"All of these things here I'm taking away," (*Dianumia Yairo*) said.' [KOTIRIA, line 242]

Another striking feature observed throughout the volume is the rampant use of derivational processes to create new lexical concepts, counterbalance parsimonious lexical class distinctions, and define contexts of complementation and subordination (van Gijn, Haude & Muysken 2011; Bruno et al. 2011). Some interesting examples of verbalizations are the derived forms for 'teaching' in Kalapalo (3), 'body painting (with genipapo)' in Kuikuro (4), and 'marrying' in Kotiria (5).

(3) *akihata iheke*

aki-ha-ta   i-heke
word-VBLZ-DUR 3-ERG

'He was teaching.' [KALAPALO, line 78]

(4) *engü isangatelü leha*

*engü is-**anga-te**-lü   leha*
then 3-jenipa-VBLZ-PNCT COMPL

'Then she was painted with genipapo' [KUIKUIRO, line 10]

(5) *phɨaro numia, phɨaro numia ti phapɨre namotia tire himarebɨ, tiaro numiapɨ bɨhkɨthurupɨre.*

phɨá-ro ~dúbí-á   phɨá-ro ~dúbí-á   ti=phá-pɨ-re
two-SG woman-PL two-SG woman-PL ANPH=time-LOC-OBJ
*~**dabó-tí**-á   tí-re   hí-~bare-bɨ   tiá-ro*
wife-VBZ-ASSERT.PFV ANPH-OBJ COP-REM.IPFV-EPIS three-SG
~dúbí-á-pɨ   bɨkɨ-thúrú-pɨ-ré
woman-PL-LOC ancestor-times-LOC-OBJ

'In those olden times, the custom was to marry two wives, two or even three.' [KOTIRIA, line 23]

A far vaster set of morphemes are employed in nominalizations, a small sample being the Sakurabiat 'hammock' in (6), the Kwaza 'olden times' in (7), and in (8), the Kĩsêdjê autodenomination.

(6) *Pɨbot nẽãrã setoabõ*

*pɨbot neara se-**top-ap**=õ*
arrive again 3COR-**lying.down-NMLZ**=DAT

'He arrived again at his own hammock.' [SAKURABIAT, line 15]

(7) *a'ayawɨ cwata unĩtetawata txarwa hakahĩ awɨ*

*a~a-ya-wɨ   cwa-ta   unĩteta-wa-ta   txarwa **haka-hĩ***
exist~exist-IOBJ-time ISBJ-CSO converse-ISBJ-CSO first **old-NMLZ**
a-wɨ
exist-time

'Speaking today about our olden times,' [KWAZA, line 55]

(8) *Kĩsêdjê*

kĩ   sêt-∅   jê
village burn-NMLZ PL

'The ones who burn villages' [KĨSÊDJÊ, line 2]

In Kuikuro and Kalapalo, there are locative, agent, non-agent, and instrument nominalizers, the latter used with the root *hü* (Kuikuro) / *hüti* (Kalapalo) 'to feel shy/respect/shame', in the derivation of terms for one's parents-in-law (9).

(9) *ihütisoho kilü*

*i-**hüti-soho** ki-lü*
3-**shame-INS** say-PNCT

'His father-in-law said.' [KALAPALO, line 130]

Aikanã has a nominalizer for actions (10), Kotiria one for reference to events/locations (11), and Sakurabiat one exclusively used for syntactic objects, seen in (12).

(10) *üre'apa'ine xarükanapɨire'ẽ kukaẽ*

üre-apa'i-ne   *xa-rüka-napa-ire-'ẽ*   *kuka-ẽ*
hide-ACT.NMLZ-LOC 1PL-DIR:around-CLF:forest-almost-IMP tell-DECL

'"We will sneak around them," said Fox.' [AIKANÃ, line 25]

(11) *do'poto to hiro hia.*
do'pó-to to=hí-ro hí-a
origin/roots-NMLZ.LOC/EVNT 3SG.POSS=COP-SG COP-ASSERT.PFV
'It's his (Ñahori's) origin site.' [KOTIRIA, line 36]

(12) *Kʷai mariko kɨpkɨba 'a mariko sete*
kʷai mat **i-ko** kɨpkɨba 'a mat **i-ko** sete
stone ? OBJ.NMLZ-**ingest** tree fruit ? OBJ.NMLZ-**ingest** 3SG
'He only eats stone and fruit (as if he were not human).' (Lit. 'Stone is what he eats, and fruit is what he eats.') [SAKURABIAT, line 55]

Valence-increasing operators include the productively used transitivizing auxiliary of Marubo, shown in (13).

(13) *vanavanakwãi avai kayakãisho*
vana-vana-kawã-i **a-vai** kaya-kãi-sho
speak-speak-go-PROG AUX.TRNS-con leave-INC-SSSA
'Calling and calling she left' [MARUBO, line 16]

Marubo also has morphological causatives, as do Suruí, *-ma* in 'torching the house' in (14), Ka'apor, *-mu* in 'opening one's anus to fart' in (15), and Kuikuro, *-nhe* in 'moving the woman up' in (16).

(14) *""Eebo oyena G̃oxorsabapa yã" iyã" de.*
ee-bo o-ya-ee-na G̃oxor-sab-**ma**-apa a
ENDO-ADVERS 1SG-NWIT-ENDO-FOC Zoró-house-CAUS-burn SFM.NWIT
i-ya ∅-de
3SG-NWIT 3SG-WIT
'"""Thus I burnt down the Zoró's house.""'[10] [SURUÍ, line 42]

(15) *xape ai jumupirar te'e xoty je*
i-ʃapɛ ai ju-**mu**-piɾaɾ tɛʔɛ i-ʃɔtɪ jɛ
3-anus bad REFL-CAUS-open free 3-towards HSY
'Her disgusting asshole opened towards the boy.' [KA'APOR, line 21]

---

[10]Multiple sets of quotation marks in the Suruí narrative indicate layers of embedding in quoted speech, as Yvinec discusses in Footnote 8 of chapter 12.

(16) itükanhenügü letüha iheke itükanhenügü itükanhenügü
itüka-**nhe**-nügü   üle=tü=ha   i-heke itüka-**nhe**-nügü
3.move.up-TR-PNCT LOG=UNCR=HA 3-ERG 3.move.up-TR-PNCT
itüka-**nhe**-nügü
3.move.up-TR-PNCT
'Then, she moved her up, she moved her up, she moved her up' [KUIKURO, line 98]

Hup, on the other hand, has causative constructions formed with serialized roots, such as *k'ët-* 'stand', used repeatedly in (17) to indicate indirect or "sociative" causation.

(17) Yúp mah, yɨno yő' mah yúp, yúp hỗp tɨh k'ët wédéh, hỗp tɨh k'ët wèd, mòh tɨh k'ët wèd, nííy mah.
[.6em] yúp=mah,   yɨ-no-yő?=mah   yúp,   yúp   hỗp tɨh
       DEM.ITG=REP DEM.ITG-say-SEQ=REP DEM.ITG DEM.ITG fish 3SG
k'ët-wéd-éh   hỗp tɨh **k'ët**-wèd, mòh   tɨh **k'ët**-wèd, ní-íy=mah.
stand-eat-DECL fish 3SG **stand**-eat tinamou 3SG **stand**-eat be-DYNM=REP
'Having said that, it's said, he gave her fish to eat; he went on giving her fish to eat, to give her tinamous to eat, it's said.' [HUP, line 27, see also Footnote 10 in chapter 7.]

Valence-decreasing derivational processes include morphological intransitivizers in Sakurabiat (18), and Kuikuro (19), while (20) gives an example of the productive noun incorporation found in Trumai.

(18) Kɨrɨt sɨ̄it jãj etsɨgɨka
kɨrɨt sɨ̄it jãj   e-sɨgɨ-ka
child DIM tooth INTRVZ-drop-VBLZ
'(That's why) kids' teeth drop out.' [SAKURABIAT, line 44]

(19) luale utimükeĩtai
luale **ut**-imükeiN-tai
sorry 1.DTR-turn.face-FUT.IM
'"Sorry! I will turn my face back"' [KUIKURO, line 224]

(20) ina hen esak ji hen mal husa husa ke ine jik, det'a hen jaw aţu tsula nawan de.

ina	hen	esak	ji	hen
DISC.CON	then	hammock	PRAG.IN	then

mal husa husa ke   ine   ji=k
edge tie tie   DISLOC.ABS 3ANAPH.MASC PRAG.IN=ERG

det'a hen jaw   aṭu tsula   nawan de
well then human.being dead be.lying similar already

'Then he tied the hammock, it became very similar to a dead person lying.' [TRUMAI, line 10, see also note 13 in chapter 5].

The languages in our collection also vary significantly in the extent to which they employ bound morphology. (18) and (20) above clearly show the more analytical profiles of Sakurabiat and Trumai, contrasting with the distinctly synthetic morphology of languages such as Kwaza (21) and Suruí (22).

(21)   *tsɨwɨdɨte xareredɨnãiko adɨ'ata*

     tsɨwɨdɨte xarere-dɨnãi-ko   a-di-a-ta
     girl   crazy-manner-INS exist-CAUS-1PL.INCL-CSO

     'We let girls act crazy like that, in our present life.' [KWAZA, line 59]

(22)   *Omamõperedene.*

     o-ma-amõ-pere-de-na-e
     1SG-POSS-grandfather-ITER-WIT-FOC-SFM.WIT

     'My grandfather did that again and again.' [SURUÍ, line 47]

Highly complex verbal morphology is especially striking in Aikanã (23) and Kotiria, particularly in the latter's productive use of verb serialization to code aspectual, modal, and adverbial spatial/manner distinctions (24). Similar constructions with serialized roots are seen in Hup verbal words (25), one of the structural features likely diffused through centuries of language contact (Epps 2007).

(23)   *yãw'ẽ wikere xü'iaxanapetaka'ĩwãte kukaẽ*

     yãw'ẽ   wikere
     let's.go.IMP peanut

     xü'i-a-xa-nape-ta-ka-'ĩwã-te   kuka-ẽ
     dig-uproot-1PL-DIR:forest-REM.FUT-CLF:pieces-ADMON-PST tell-DECL

     '"Let's go digging up peanuts as planned," he told her.' [AIKANÃ, line 14]

(24) *pha'muri mahsa õre pha'muyohataa.*
~*pha'bú-rí*   ~*basá*   ~*ó-ré*
originate-NMLZ people DEIC.PROX-OBJ
~*pha'bú-yóhá-tá-a*
originate-go.upriver-come-ASSERT.PFV
'The origin beings appeared coming upriver here.' [KOTIRIA, line 15]

(25) *Yɨno yő' mah yúp, tɨhàn hɨd dö' híayáh.*
yɨ-no-yő?=mah   *yúp,*   *tɨh-àn*   *hɨd* ***dö?-hí**-ay-áh*
DEM.ITG-say-SEQ=REP DEM.ITG 3SG-OBJ 3PL **take-descend**-INCH-DECL
'Saying thus, it's said, they took (the baby deer) down.' [HUP, line 99]

Indeed, the narratives of this volume attest the rich means use to code movement and spatial relations in Amazonian languages (see also Bozzi 2013). A few languages employ locative postpositions or case markers with spatially specific semantics: inessive and allative markers in Kuikuro, Kalapalo and Aikanã, ablatives in Suruí and Sakurabiat, and the "provenence locative" marker in Marubo (26).

(26) *Vei Maya vei mai nãkõsh wenímarivi, shavo wetsa.*
Vei   Maya vei   mai nãkõ- **sh**   wení-ma-rivi shavo   wetsa
death Maya death land nectar- **LOC.PROV** rise-NEG-EMP woman other
'Vei Maya did not come from the Death-Land nectar; she is another woman.' [MARUBO, line 4]

Many more integrate detailed spatial or movement information in verbal morphology, through root serialization showing associated motion or direction (as seen in the Kotiria and Hup examples (24)–(25) above), or with bound directional/locational morphemes indicating notions such as 'outside', 'hither', 'close', etc., in Aikanã and Kwaza (27).

(27) *watxile karẽxu katsutyata xareyawata axehĩko tsadwɛnɛ*
watxile karẽxu   *katsu-tya ta* *xareya-wa-ta* *axe-hĩ-tya*
finally dry.heartwood cross-CSO CSO search-ISBJ-CSO find-NMLZ-CSO
*tsadwɛ-**nɛ***
onto.path-**DIR:hither**
'Later, crossing the dry log, they then searched and then got back onto the path.' [KWAZA, line 32]

1 Amazonian narrative verbal arts and typological gems

Directional auxiliaries, such as 'go uphill' in Trumai (28), are also commonly found. Similar directional verbs occur in Kotiria, e.g. 'go upriver' (in lines 225 and 253 of chapter 6), and Hup 'go upstream' (in lines 4 and 12 of chapter 7, among others).

(28) ka?ʃɨ ṭ'axer lahmin.

ka?ʃɨ ṭ'axer **lahmi**=n
walk poorly **go.uphill**=3ABS

'She left.' [TRUMAI line 3, see also Footnote 8 in chapter 5]

Sakurabiat uses verbal auxiliaries for associated movement and to indicate the body position of subjects (29), and has positional demonstratives that code the body position of other referents (30).

(29) Pɨ ke itoa enĩĩtse

pɨ   ke   i-**to**-a   eni=ese
lying DEM 3SG-AUX.LIE-THV hammock=LOC

'He (Arɨkʷajõ) was there just lying in the hammock.' [SAKURABIAT, line 3]

(30) Tamõ'ẽm porẽtsopega petsetagiat:

ta=bõ='ẽp   porẽsopeg-a pe=se-tak-iat
DEM.STAND=DAT=EMPH ask-THV   OBL=3COR-daughter-COL

'He just got there and asked to his daughters:' [SAKURABIAT, line 16]

Kuikuro, on the other hand, makes an interesting centripetal/centrifugal distinction in its imperative suffixes, the latter seen in (31).

(31) ouünko tuhipe kunhigake ika kigeke

o-uüN-ko   tuhi-pe   ku-ng-ingi-**gake**   ika   kigeke
2-father-PL   garden-NTM   1.2-OBJ-see-IMP.CTF   wood let's.go

'"Let's go see your father's old garden, let's go to cut wood!"' [KUIKURO, line 15]

Nearly half of the languages in the collection have switch-reference systems, with notable variation in terms of the contexts in which markers occur and the additional grammatical categories they may express. In Kotiria, overt switch-reference marking occurs only in contexts of clause subordination. In contrast, clause coordination is the relevant context in Kĩsêdjê, which has some 'different subject' forms that further indicate anticipatory subject agreement, and if third person, tense distinctions as well. Switch-reference markers in Kwaza and

Aikanã can signal a new foregrounded topic or important turn of events in discourse. As is the case with most languages in the Pano family, Marubo has a complex system in which switch-reference markers code distinctions of same and different subjects as well as simultaneous or sequential actions (see van Gijn & Hammond 2016).[11]

An even larger set of languages have grammaticalized markers with evidential and/or epistemic semantics. The complex systems of obligatory evidential marking in Hup and Kotiria have four or five categories that contrast hearsay/reported information with different subtypes of direct sensory (visual, non-visual) and indirect (inferred, presumed) evidential sources. Other languages, such as Suruí, have a basic witnessed/non-witnessed distinction, but can employ evidential markers pragmatically in discourse to prioritize focus on particular events over identification of source of evidence. Suruí evidential markers can also occur recursively with an utterance containing embedded quoted speech, as we see in (32), as can the Sakurabiat evidential *eba* (e.g. line 20 of chapter 8).

(32) ""*Nem, olobaka G̃oxoriyã*" *iyã*" *de*.
 nem o-sob-aka   G̃oxor-ya   i-ya   ∅-de
 INTJ 1SG-father-kill Zoró-NWIT 3SG-NWIT 3SG-WIT
 '""Well, a Zoró killed my father.""' [SURUÍ, line 3]

Trumai and Ka'apor typically make use of hearsay evidentials to indicate narratives as having a non-firsthand source of information, while Kuikuro and Kalapalo have a large number of optional evidential and epistemic markers that occur primarily in the quoted speech of narrative protagonists, indicating their attitudes and intentions in interaction.

Ergativity is a well-known feature of Amazonian languages (see Gildea & Queixalós 2010) and occurs in some form in nearly half of the languages in this volume. Fully ergative systems are seen in Kuikuro and Kalapalo, in which the morpheme (-)*heke* always marks the ergative argument, as in (1), (3) and (16) above, and absolutive arguments are formally unmarked. Trumai makes use of ergative clitics and absolutive bound pronouns, while ergative marking in Marubo — in keeping with patterns found throughout Panoan languages — involves suprasegmental nasality, easily observed in pronominal forms such as *e* '1SG.ABS' vs. *ẽ* '1SG.ERG' and *mato* '2PL.ABS' vs. *mã* '2PL.ERG'. Kĩsêdjê has a split system, with nominative-accusative alignment in main clauses and ergative-absolutive alignment in embedded clauses, as we see in (33).

---

[11]Other chapters in the same volume offer case studies of switch-reference systems in diverse Amazonian languages.

(33) Kôt hry jatuj khãm khutha.

  [**kôt**   hry j-atu-j   ] khãm **khu**-ta
   3.ERG trail E-stop-NMLZ   in   3-put.standing.SG

  'He put it down [where he had stopped making the trail].' [KĨSÊDJÊ, line 51]

Finally, Galucio describes the mixed system of Sakurabiat as "nominative-absolutive". Verbal prefixes index the subject of an intransitive verb or object of a transitive verbs (the absolutive argument), while transitive subjects (A) are obligatorily expressed as free pronouns. The same free pronominal forms can also be used as subjects in intransitive sentences, revealing nominative (S/A) alignment.

While on the topic of pronouns, we should note that eight of the twelve languages in this collection have an inclusive/exclusive distinction in their pronominal paradigms. In (34), we see that Trumai additionally marks a *dual* inclusive/exclusive value.

(34) "huk'anik, huta.kaʃ ka a huʔtsa kawa."

  huk'anik huta.kaʃ **ka**   a   huʔtsa kawa
  EXPR   later   1INCL DU   see   go

  '"Wait, later we are going to see her (i.e., take care of her)."' [TRUMAI, line 23]

Turning our attention very briefly to the "sounds" one hears in Amazonian voices, an overview of the phonological systems of the languages in our volume reveals the frequency of a high central vowel [ɨ], which occurs in ten of the twelve languages as a phoneme or commonly used allophone. As for consonants, Kuikuro has a unique uvular flap and for an Amazonian language, Trumai has an whoppingly large 23-consonant inventory that includes a lateral fricative, as well as ejectives and plosives that make a distinction between alveolar and dental points of articulation. Nasality (a suprasegmental feature in Hup and Kotiria), nasal-harmony or spreading processes (in Kotiria and Sakurabiat), tone (in Kotiria, Hup, and Suruí), and glottalic sounds — full glottal stops, glottalized and aspirated consonants, and laryngealized vowels — are other prominent phonological features. In Kĩsêdjê, infixed aspiration of voiceless plosives has a syntactic function, marking third person agreement, as seen in (35).

(35) Akwyn nen thẽn khatho.

  akwyn   ne=n   thẽ=n   k<**h**>atho
  back   be.so=&.SS   go.SG=&.SS   <3>come.out.SG

  'He came back and came out (of the forest).' [KĨSÊDJÊ, line 43]

Our tour of the fascinating structural features of Amazonian languages could go on an on, adding the noun classifiers of Kwaza and Kotiria, the "nominal tense" suffix of Kuikuro, the five-way past-tense distinction of Marubo, and the suppletive verbal forms of Kĩsêdjê — among others — to this initial collection of typological gems. However, we will stop here in the hope your curiosity has now been sufficiently sparked and you are ready to explore for yourself the delights, details, and discoveries our contributors have provided in the chapters that follow.

References

Aikhenvald, Alexandra Y. 2002. *Language contact in Amazonia.* Oxford: Oxford University Press.

Aikhenvald, Alexandra Y. 2012. *The languages of the Amazon.* New York: Oxford University Press.

Birchall, Joshua. 2014. Verbal argument marking patterns in South American languages. In Loretta O'Connor & Pieter Muysken (eds.), *The native languages of South America. Origins, development, typology,* 223–249. Cambridge: Cambridge University Press.

Bozzi, Ana Maria Ospina (ed.). 2013. *Expresión de nociones espaciales en lenguas amazónicas.* Bogotá: Instituto Caro y Cuervo/Universidad Nacional de Colombia.

Bruno, Ana Carla, Frantomé Pacheco, Francesc Queixalós, Stella Telles & Leo Wetzels. 2011. *La structure des langues amazoniennes II.* Special issue of Amerindia 35.

Campbell, Lyle. 2012. Typological characteristics of South American indigenous languages. In Verónica Grondona & Lyle Campbell (eds.), *The native languages of South America. Origins, development, typology,* 259–330. Berlin: Mouton de Gruyter.

Crevels, Mily & Hein van der Voort. 2008. The Guaporé-Mamoré region as a linguistic area. In Pieter Muysken (ed.), *From linguistic areas to areal linguistics,* 151–178. Amsterdam/Philadelphia: John Benjamins.

Derbyshire, Desmond. 1999. Carib. In Robert W. Dixon & Alexandra Y. Aikhenvald (eds.), *The Amazonian languages,* 23–64. Cambridge: Cambridge University Press.

Dixon, Robert W. & Alexandra Y. Aikhenvald. 1999. *The Amazonian languages.* Cambridge: Cambridge University Press.

Epps, Patience. 2007. The Vaupés melting pot: Tukanoan influence on Hup. In Alexandra Y. Aikhenvald & R. M. W. Dixon (eds.), *Grammars in contact: A cross-linguistic typology* (Explorations in linguistic typology 4), 267–289. Oxford: Oxford University Press.

Epps, Patience & Andrés Salanova. 2013. The languages of Amazonia. *Tipiti (Journal for the Anthropology of Lowland South America)* 11(1). 1–28.

Epps, Patience & Kristine Stenzel (eds.). 2013. *Upper Rio Negro. Cultural and linguistic interaction in northwestern Amazonia*. Rio de Janeiro: Museu do Índio/FUNAI. http://etnolinguistica.wdfiles.com/local--files/biblio%3Aepps-stenzel-2013/epps_stenzel_2013_upper_rio_negro.pdf.

Franchetto, Bruna (ed.). 2011. *Alto Xingu: Uma sociedade multilíngue*. Rio de Janeiro: Museu do Índio/FUNAI. http://www.etnolinguistica.org/index/xingu.

Franchetto, Bruna & Keren Rice. 2014. Language documentation in the Americas. *Language Documentation and Conservation* 8. 251–261.

Gildea, Spike & Francesc Queixalós (eds.). 2010. *Ergativity in Amazonia*. [typological studies in language 89]. Amsterdam/Philadelphia: John Benjamins.

Moore, Denny. 2008. Endangered languages of lowland tropical South America. In Matthias Brenzinger (ed.), *Language diversity endangered*, 29–58. Berlin: Mouton de Gruyter.

O'Connor, Loretta & Pieter Muysken (eds.). 2014. *The native languages of South America. Origins, development, typology*. Cambridge: Cambridge University Press.

Payne, Doris L. 1990. Morphological characteristics of lowland South American languages. In Doris L. Payne (ed.), *Amazonian linguistics: Studies in lowland South American languages*, 213–241. Austin: University of Texas Press.

Stenzel, Kristine. 2014. The pleasures and pitfalls of a 'participatory' documentation project: An experience in northwestern Amazonia. *Language Documentation and Conservation* 8. 287–306.

van der Voort, Hein. 2000. Introduction. In Hein van der Voort & Simon van de Kerke (eds.), *Indigenous languages of lowland South America*, 1–7. [Indigenous Languages of Latin America, 1]. Leiden: Research School of Asian, African, & Amerindian Studies (CNWS).

van Gijn, Rik & Jeremy Hammond (eds.). 2016. *Switch reference 2.0* (Typological Studies in Language 114). Amsterdam/Philadelphia: John Benjamins.

van Gijn, Rik, Katharina Haude & Pieter Muysken (eds.). 2011. *Subordination in native South American languages* (Typological Studies in Language 97). Amsterdam/Philadelphia: John Benjamins.

Part I

Life, death, and the world beyond

Chapter 2

Kuikuro

Bruna Franchetto
Museu Nacional, Federal University of Rio de Janeiro, Brazil

Carlos Fausto
Museu Nacional, Federal University of Rio de Janeiro, Brazil

Ájahi Kuikuro

Jamalui Kuikuro Mehinaku

1 Introduction

Anha ituna tütenhüpe itaõ, 'The woman who went to the village of the dead', is a narrative lasting roughly twenty minutes. It was registered by Bruna Franchetto and Carlos Fausto on the 23rd of November, 2004, in both audio and video formats, in *Ipatse*, the main Kuikuro village (Southern Amazonia, State of Mato Grosso, Brazil). Bruna Franchetto began her linguistic and anthropological research on the Upper Xingu Carib languages, particularly on the Kuikuro dialect, in 1977. Carlos Fausto began his anthropological research among the Kuikuro in 1998.

The storyteller was *Ájahi*, a woman who was around 65 years old at that time, a renown ritual specialist and expert singer of the female rituals of *Jamugikumalu* and *Tolo*.

Basic annotation of the recording – orthographic transcription and translation - was done by *Jamalui*, a Kuikuro researcher, using ELAN, with the assistance of Carlos Fausto. *Asusu* Kuikuro helped with the penultimate revision, carried out in June 2016. The annotated text has been revised more than once by Franchetto, who added the interlinear analysis.

Bruna Franchetto, Carlos Fausto, Ájahi Kuikuro & Jamalui Kuikuro Mehinaku. 2017. Kuikuro. In Kristine Stenzel & Bruna Franchetto (eds.), *On this and other worlds: Voices from Amazonia*, 23–87. Berlin: Language Science Press. DOI:10.5281/zenodo.1008774

Figure 1: Bruna Franchetto and *Ájahi* Kuikuro (Photo: *Takumã* Kuikuro, 2001)

The transcription line is orthographic. Kuikuro (alphabetic) writing was developed by indigenous teachers, in collaboration with Bruna Franchetto, in the 1990s. The correspondences between "letters" or groups of letters (digraphs and trigraphs) and symbols from the International Phonetic Alphabet (IPA), when different, are as follows: <ü> /ɨ/, <j> /ǰ/, <g> /ř/ (uvular flap), <ng> /ŋ/, <nh> /ɲ/, <nkg> /ŋg/; N represents a subspecified fluctuating nasal.

2 Kuikuro: people and language

Kuikuro is the name by which one of the dialects of the Upper Xingu Carib Language, in the Xinguan Southern Branch of the Carib family, is known (Meira & Franchetto 2005; Meira 2006). It is spoken by approximately 600 people, distributed in six villages in the region known as "Upper Xingu", in the headwaters of the Xingu river, Southern Amazonia, Brazil. They inhabit the southeastern region of the Xingu Indigenous Park, between the Culuene and the Buriti rivers, where they have lived since at least the second half of the 16th century. Archaeological, linguistic, and ethnological research all point to the upper Rio Buriti

Figure 2: Villages of the Upper Xingu people, Xingu Indigenous Land.

region as the homeland of the Kuikuros' ancestors. This region was occupied by Carib groups who had travelled from the west of the Rio Culuene, possibly in the 17th century. The denomination "Kuikuro" derives from the toponym for the place where, at the beginning of the 19th century, the first Kuikuro village (*Kuhi ikugu*, 'Needle Fish Creek') was erected as the residence of a recognized autonomous member of the Upper Xingu system. This toponym has been frozen as a permanent ethnonym since the first written ethnographic record by Karl von den Steinen at the end of the 19th century (von den Steinen 1894).

Upper Xingu Carib dialects are distinguished mainly by different prosodic structures (Silva & Franchetto 2011). The speakers of these varieties are part of the Upper Xingu Carib sub-system, which in turn is tied to the multilingual and multiethnic regional system known as the Upper Xingu. This comprises the drainage basin of the headwaters of the Xingu River, itself one of the largest southern tributaries of the Amazon. Thanks to the collaborative work of archaeologists, linguists, and anthropologists (Franchetto & Heckenberger 2001; Fausto, Franchetto & Heckenberger 2008; Franchetto 2011), we are beginning to understand the historical origins of this regional system. We can now confidently claim that this system was formed over the last four hundred years, incorporating people from different origins in a continuous and dynamic process. Speakers of languages belonging to the three major linguistic groupings in South America (Arawak, Carib, and Tupi) and one linguistic isolate (Trumai) created a unique social system that remains functional today.

Kuikuro should be considered a stable, albeit vulnerable, language/variety. Its stability derives from the protection of the Kuikuro territory over the last fifty years, the gradual and late start of formal schooling in the last twenty years, and a linguistic and cultural heritage that is highly valued, both internally and externally, since the Kuikuro are part of the Upper Xingu region, which has been constructed as a Brazilian national icon of "Indianness". Its vulnerability is due to a variety of factors including conflict between the indigenous language and the dominant language (Portuguese), schooling, the growing presence of written media and television, the increasing mobility of individuals and families between villages and towns, and prolonged stays in town. Another extremely relevant and ambiguous factor related to the preservation or weakening of the indigenous language is contact with missionaries, which has become increasingly intense. In contrast, initiatives that seek to strengthen the indigenous language have been put into effect by researchers (linguists and anthropologists) in participative documentation projects that including the production of videos via the training of indigenous filmmakers, publications and the supervision of indigenous researchers. This process needs to continue in order to effectively safeguard the indigenous language.

The morphosyntactic characteristics of Kuikuro can be summed up in the following generalizations:

- It is a highly agglutinative, head final, and ergative language.

- Any head constitutes a prosodic unit with its internal argument.

- A unique set of prefixal person markers indexes internal (absolutive) argument on verbs, nominals, and postpositions. Kuikuro, similar to many other Amerindian languages, makes a morphological distinction between first person plural inclusive and first person plural exclusive. The abbreviations '1.2' and '1.3' were chosen as glosses for first person plural inclusive and first person plural exclusive, respectively. The prefixed morpheme *ku-* (*kuk-* with nominal and verbal stems beginning with a vowel) is the phonological exponent of the abstract person features [ego&tu] or [actor&participant].The prefixed morpheme *ti-* (*tis-* with vowel-initial stems) is the phonological exponent of the abstract person features [ego&alter] or [actor&non-participant].

- There are no auxiliaries and there is no explicit agreement between verbs and their arguments.

- Argument nominals are bare, underdetermined for number and definiteness.

- The aspectual inflection of the Kuikuro verb includes three main suffixes: punctual (PNCT, an event or action seen as instantaneous, without inherent temporal duration), durative (DUR) and perfect (PRF). Tense is outside the verbal word.

The ubiquity of the clitic *ha* is noteworthy, a grammatical morpheme whose function and meaning are still under investigation. We have not yet defined a specific meta-linguistic gloss for it. It certainly marks an important component of the syntactic packaging of information, acting at the interface with discourse. In fast speech, *ha* cliticizes to the following word, while in slow speech it cliticizes to the preceding word. Kalin (2014) offers an interesting formal explanation of the same particle in Hixkaryana, a Northern Carib language.

The grammatical morpheme, possible cliticizable, *leha*, interpreted as a completive aspect, also occurs in most Kuikuro sentences. It "closes" main as well as secondary predications and is possibly responsible for the finiteness of the verbal word. Like the clitic *ha*, it can occur more than once in the same utterance. It is interesting to see the complementary positioning of *ha* and *leha* in lines 4 and 5, giving a semantically differentiating nuance whose subtlety we are still unable to grasp completely.

For more information on Kuikuro grammar, see, among other publications: Franchetto (1986; 2010; 2015); dos Santos (2007); Franchetto & Santos (2009; 2010); Lima, Franchetto & Santos (2013).

3 The narrative

Anha ituna tütenhüpe itaõ 'The woman who went to the village of the dead', offers a distinctively feminine version of the pan-xinguan and better-known narrative '*Agahütanga*, the trip of a living man to the village of the dead'. In the more – let us call it – "masculine" version, *Agahütanga* cries for a dead friend, who descends from the celestial world of the dead to take him on a journey of knowledge. During the journey, *Agahütanga* witnesses the fatal obstacles that can dissolve the dead into the nothingness of smoke. He manages to reach the celestial village, whose owner is a two-headed vulture, devourer of the dead, which is also where the stars that mark the seasonal calendar reside. *Agahütanga* returns to earth but was killed by a jealous and greedy enemy (and sorcerer).

Kuikuro and Kalapalo masculine versions of this narrative were published in Carneiro (1977) and Basso (1985: 91–140), respectively. Another Kuikuro version was recorded in 2003 by Carlos Fausto, and deposited (transcribed and translated), alongside the present version by *Ájahi*, in the Kuikuro digital archives hosted by the DoBeS (Documentation of Endangered Languages, Max Pank Institute of Psycholinguistics and VolkswagenStiftung) Program and by the ProDoclin (Program for the Documentation of Indigenous Languages, Museu do Índio, FUNAI, Rio de Janeiro). Two short Kamayurá (masculine) versions, both in Portuguese, were published in Villas Boas & Villas Boas (1970: 122–130) and Agostinho (1974: 200–201).

In *Ájahi*'s version, a woman is taken, by her dead mother-in-law and by her longing (a dangerous and virtually fatal feeling) for her dead husband, through the path of the dead (*anha*) to their celestial village. "Dead" is a possible and viable translation for the word *anha*. *Akunga* or *akuã* designates an animic principle that animates living beings, a shadow of a thing or person, or a double. The *akunga* of a dead person is *akungape*, an ex-*akunga*, the word receiving the suffix *-pe* that marks the nominal past tense or, better, the nominal terminative aspect. "The *akunga* remains inside the body of the deceased until the grave begins to be filled in; but then, feeling the weight of fresh earth being heaped upon it, it slips out of the body and abandons the grave. At about this point, the soul ceases to be called *akunga* and is referred to as añá [*anha*], the name it will bear from here on" (Carneiro 1977: 3).

Ájahi describes the astonishing village of the dead, pointing to the three essential elements of the structure of a true Xinguan village (lines 145-148). Beside the *hugogo*, the *kuakutu* (an Arawakan word) known, in Portuguese, as "men's house", is a small traditional house built in the middle of the plaza and is the place where only men gather daily for pleasure, shamanistic sessions, political discussions, body painting, sharing food, and ritual concentration. *Tajühe* is the third defining element of village architecture: the prototypical house of a big chief, much larger than the common houses, decorated internally and externally, including two "ears" (large triangular mats at the ends of the horizontal rod supporting the ceiling, twisted with moriche palm leaves (*Mauritia flexuosa*) fibers. Every house is a body, with a butt, belly, back, and earrings.

From the village of *anha*, the living visitor has to be upside down in order to see the world of the living. Hiding behind her mother-in-law, the woman sees her dead-husband's-soul and his dead-brother's-soul returning from a fishing

Figure 3: The Kuikuro village of *Ipatse* drawn by *Sepé* Kuikuro, 2006

trip. She sees him with another woman. In lines 81 and 171, *Ájahi* introduces this personnage: *Itsangitsegu*, the wife of the dead husband in the afterworld, the celestial village of the dead. *Itsangitsegu* is an *itseke* (a hyper-being or supernatural being), not a dead person. She is the *itseke* that gets the old dead who are weak, takes care of them, puts them in seclusion, and feeds them until they are raised up again. She is an *itseke* with only one breast and one buttock, but she is very generous and all women are jealous of her. *Itsangitsegu* is the mother of the twins Sun and Moon, the ancestors who created the human species. A character of a long and founding mythical saga, *Itsangitsegu* was killed by her mother-in-law Jaguar, and, after her death, was honored by Sun and Moon in the first *egitsü*, known as "Kwaryp", the great Xinguan intertribal ritual that marks the end of the mourning period after the deaths of chiefs and outstanding ritual specialists and singers.

In the afterworld, other words are used, referring to an inside-out world. The woman returns from this exceptional journey to the world of the living, but her fate on this side will be determined by the consequences of having dared to transpose an impassable frontier. It is impossible not to note the similarities between this narrative and the Greek myth of Orpheus and Eurydice: Orpheus crosses through the door to the world of the dead because of his devastating desire to have Eurydice, his dead wife, back. Hades, the god of the underworld, grants him the possibility of bringing her back to the world of the living, but if he turns to see his beloved, who is following him out of the underworld, he will lose her forever. Orpheus disobeys, and Eurydice is transformed into a statue of salt.

These are the most relevant linguistic and structural characteristics of the narrative. The text recurrently makes use of the suffix *–pe*, glossed as NTM ("nominal tense marker"), as in *kakisükope* (*k-aki-sü-ko-pe*, 1.2-word-POSS-PL-NTM), which can be loosely translated as 'our former words' or 'those which were our words', referring to the words of the living that the dead seek out and transform, in their language of the dead, into other words. In lines 128-141, *Ájahi* insists on the contrast/complementarity between the language of the dead and the language of the living. The suffix *-pe* here means that the dead are trying to recover their language (that they used when they were alive), but in this effort they only find synonyms in the language of the dead. *–pe* could also be analysed as a "nominal terminative aspect" and is attested for common nouns and proper names, as well as in possessed and absolute noun phrases, conveying the death/destruction/end of the referent(s), a change of form/identity of the referent(s), or a loss of functionality of the referent(s) (Franchetto & Santos 2009; Franchetto & Thomas 2016).

Another relevant aspect is the use of specific forms and expressions during verbal interaction between affinal relatives, particularly between mother-in-law and daughter-in-law. In these interactions, the use of the second person plural instead of the second person singular is obligatory, as in, for example, *emuguko* (*e-mugu-ko*, 2-son-PL), 'your son' (the woman speaking to her mother-in-law about her own husband, the son of the mother-in-law). The Kuikuro kinship term for one's parents-in-law is *hüsoho*, a nominalization (*-soho*) of the verbal stem *hü*, meaning 'to feel shy/respect'. So, *hüsoho* means, literally, 'made to feel shy/respect'.

Concerning the noteworthy traits of the narrative structure (see also Basso 1985; Franchetto 2003) we draw attention to the following:

- More than half of the text is a direct citation of dialogue between the characters, with a predominance of verbal forms inflected by performative modes (imperative, hortative, imminent future), interjections, as well as epistemic markers (including evidentials) that modulate the attitudes and communicative intentions of the interacting speakers. In Kuikuro there are several *verba dicendi*, such as the roots *ki* (say), *itagi* (talk), *aki* (language/word). Particularly interesting is the very frequent use of just the aspectual morphemes *tagü* (durative) and *nügü* (punctual) immediately at the end of the directly reported speech.

- The storyteller regularly marks the progressive development of the narrative by logophoric connectives (*lepe, ülepe*) and by movement verbs (for instance, *te*, 'to go'). This is how the textual units that we may equate to paragraphs are marked, grouping phrases/enunciations, the minimal textual units represented by the lines in the transcription.

- We have sought to keep most of the repetitions, which constitute the parallelistic characteristics of the narrative style, configuring its rhythm and, at times, changes of perspective before events that we would otherwise suppose to be understood as a single unit.

The narrative presented here is an example, in female voice, of the Kuikuro art of telling. Its apprehension is synergistically verbal and visual: the scenes succeed one another by movement through space-time, characters become animated one before another in their voice-bodies. Listeners are captured as if in a dream.

4 Anha ituna tütenhüpe itaõ
'The woman who went to the village of the dead'
'A mulher que foi para a aldeia dos mortos'[1]

(1) *tüma akinha ititüi*

  tü-ma akinha ititü-i
  Q-DUB story name-COP
  'Which is the name of the story?' (question by Bruna Franchetto)
  'Como é o nome da estória?' (pergunta de Bruna Franchetto)

(2) *anha ituna tütenhüpe itaõ*

  anha itu-na   tü-te-nhü-pe   itaõ
  dead place-ALL PTCP-go.PTCO-NANMLZ-NTM woman
  'The woman who went to the village of the dead, the woman'
  'A mulher que foi para a aldeia dos mortos, a mulher'

---

[1] Recordings of this story are available from https://zenodo.org/record/997443

(3) *anha ituna etelü*
    anha itu-na   e-te-lü
    dead place-ALL 3-go-PNCT
    'She went to the village of the dead'
    'Ela foi para a aldeia dos mortos'

(4) *inhope apünguha*
    i-nho-pe   apünguN=ha
    3-husband-NTM die.PNCT=HA
    'Her husband had died'
    'O esposo dela tinha falecido'

(5) *inhope apüngu leha*
    i-nho-pe   apünguN leha
    3-husband-NTM die.PNCT COMPL
    'Her husband died'
    'O esposo dela faleceu'

(6) *lepe inhaka leha itsagü*
    üle-pe   i-ngaka[2]   leha   i-tsagü
    LOG-NTM 3-instead.of COMPL 3.be-DUR
    'Then, she stayed in his place (she went into morning for him)'
    'Depois, ela foi ficando no lugar dele (foi ficando de luto por ele)'

(7) *hombei leha hombei leha itsagü*
    hombe-i   leha   hombe-i   leha   i-tsagü
    widow-COP COMPL widow-COP COMPL 3.be-DUR
    'A widow, she was widowed'
    'Enviuvou, ficou viúva'

(8) *ülepei leha itsagü leha hombe tamitsi*
    üle-pe-i   leha   i-tsagü   leha   hombe tamitsi
    LOG-NTM-COP COMPL 3.be-CONT COMPL widow longtime
    'After this, she remained widowed for a long time'
    'Depois disso, ela ficou viúva por muito tempo'

---

[2] The velar nasal palatalizes after the high front vowel, at the morphemic boundary (see Franchetto 1995).

(9) *ülepe leha aiha*

üle-pe leha aiha³
LOG-NTM COMPL done

'After this, done'

'Então, acabou' (o luto)

(10) *engü isangatelü leha*

engü is-anga-te-lü leha
then 3-jenipa-VBLZ-PNCT COMPL

'Then she was painted with genipapo'

'Então, ela foi pintada com jenipapo'

(11) *isangatelü leha ihombundaõ⁴ heke isangatelü leha*

is-anga-te-lü leha i-hombundaõ heke is-anga-te-lü leha
3-jenipa-VBLZ-PNCT COMPL 3-widow.COL ERG 3-jenipa-VBLZ-PNCT COMPL

'The brothers of her dead husband painted her'

'Os irmãos do falecido esposo pintaram-na'

(12) *lepene leha itsagü*

lepene leha i-tsagü
then   COMPL 3.be-CONT

'Then, she remained'

'Depois, ela ficou'

(13) *anhü tülimo heke ijimo⁵ ijimo ijimo*

anhü tü-limo heke i-limo i-limo i-limo
son REFL-children ERG 3-children 3-children 3-children

'"My dears!" (she said) to her children, children of this size, and this size, and this size'

'"Meus queridos!", (disse) para os seus filhos, filhos desse tamanho, desse tamanho e desse tamanho'

---

[3] The meaning of the particle *aiha* is here roughly translated as 'done'. *aiha* has a clear discursive function when it is used to close a block or scene of a narrative.

[4] This word could be the result of: *hombe(N)+(C)aõ* (widow+collective). The brothers-in-law of a woman are her potential sexual partners and potential spouses. Here, they are referred to as a group of associated "widowers" and they are responsible for important duties and functions towards the widow.

[5] At morphemic boundaries, the consonant /l/ palatalizes to [ɟ] after the high front vowel /i/.

(14) *anhü apa tuhipe kunhigake ouünko tuhipe*

    anhü apa   tuhi-pe   ku-ng-ingi-gake[6]   *o-uüN-ko   tuhi-pe*
    son father garden-NTM 1.2-OBJ-ver-IMP.CTF 2-father-PL garden-NTM

    '"My dears! Go to see the father's old garden, your father's old garden!"'
    '"Meus queridos! Vamos ver a roça que era do pai, a roça que era do pai de vocês!"'

(15) *ouünko tuhipe kunhigake ika kigeke*

    o-uüN-ko   tuhi-pe   ku-ng[7]*-ingi-gake   ika   kigeke*
    2-father-PL garden-NTM 1.2-OBJ-see-IMP.CTF wood let's.go

    '"Let's go see your father's old garden, let's go to cut wood!"'
    '"Vamos lá ver a roça que era do pai de vocês, vamos catar lenha!"'

(16) *ehe ijimo telü leha*

    ehe i-limo   te-lü   leha
    ITJ 3-children go-PNCT COMPL

    '"Yes!" her children went away'
    '"Sim!", seus filhos foram'

(17) *etelüko leha etelüko leha*

    e-te-lü-ko   leha   e-te-lü-ko   leha
    3-go-PNCT-PL COMPL 3-go-PNCT-PL COMPL

    'They went away, they went away'
    'Eles foram, eles foram'

---

[6] The inflectional morphemes of the imperative mood are sensitive to the directional egocentered kind of movement involved: centrifugal imperative (IMP.CTF, go to …), centripetal imperative (IMP.CTP, come to …), and imperative (IMP, no movement).

[7] The object marker *ng-*, prefixed to the verbal stem, is the spelled-out trace of the object (patient). Observe that the agent appears in absolutive case. See Franchetto (2010) and Franchetto & Santos (2010) for an analysis of this type of construction, which these authors called "de-ergativized", due to a special kind of downgraded transitivity. This construction characterizes relative or focus sentences, where the relativized or the focused argument is the object, as well as some sentences with the verb inflected for imminent future, imperative mood, or hortative mood.

(18) eh tigati leha kuigi andati leha
      eh tigati leha   kuigi   anda-ti leha
      ITJ there COMPL garden LOC-ILL COMPL
      'Yes, right to the garden'
      'Sim, direto para a roça'

(19) inhünkgo leha itsuhipüati leha tünho tuhipüati
      i-nhüN-ko   leha   i-tuhi[8]-püa[9]-ti   leha   tü-nho
      3.be-PNCT-PL COMPL 3-garden-ex.place-ILL COMPL REFL-husband
      tuhi-püa-ti
      garden-ex.place-ILL
      'They reached the place of the father's old garden'
      'Chegaram no lugar que tinha sido a roça dele'

(20) jatsitsü jatsitsü
      jatsitsü jatsitsü
      poor.man poor.man
      '"Poor man, poor man!" (the widow said)'
      '"Coitado, coitado!", (a viúva disse)'

(21) ige inhambalüila tinika ulimo uün etsujenügü uãke nügü iheke
      ige   inhamba-lü-i-la   tinika u-limo   uüN   etsuje-nügü uãke
      PROX eat-PNCT-COP-PRIV ADV   1-children father die-PNCT   PST
      nügü   i-heke
      say.PNCT 3-ERG
      '"My children's father died without eating this (the manioc from his garden)," she said'
      '"O pai dos meus filhos morreu sem se alimentar disto (da roça dele)", ela disse'

---

[8]The consonant /t/ palatalizes to [ts] after the high front vowel /i/ at morphemic boundaries (see Franchetto 1995)

[9]The suffix -püa is used to characterize a place where something was previously located (a village, a garden).

(22) *ige inhambangatüingi hõhõ ataiti uãke ulimo uüN heke*

ige inhamba-nga-tüingi hõhõ ataiti uãke u-limo uüN heke
DEM.PROX eat-AVD EMP IRR PST 1-children father ERG

'"My children's father could have eaten this"'
'"O pai dos meus filhos poderia ter se alimentado disto"'

(23) *iheke uãke tünhope heke*[10]

i-heke uãke tü-nho-pe heke
ele-*erg* pst REFL-husband-NTM ERG

'"It was him," (talking) about her dead husband'
'"Ele, faz tempo", (falando) do seu falecido esposo'

(24) *tita leha inilundagü inilundagü leha*

tita leha ini-luN-tagü ini-luN-tagü leha
there COMPL cry-VBLZ-DUR cry-VBLZ-CONT COMPL

'There she was crying, crying'
'Ficou lá chorando, chorando'

(25) *inhope tuhi heke isotünkgitsagü*

i-nho-pe tuhi heke is-otüN-ki-tsagü
3-husband-NTM garden ERG 3-sorrow-CAUS-DUR

'The garden of her dead husband was making her deeply sorrowful'
'A roça do falecido esposo fazia com que ela sentisse muita pena'

(26) *ülepe leha etelü indeha eitsüe*

üle-pe leha e-te-lü inde=ha e-i-tsüe
LOG-NTM COMPL 3-go-PNCT here=HA 2-be-IMP.PL

'Then she went away, "Stay here!" (she said to her own children)'
'Depois ela foi, "Fiquem aqui!", (ela falou para seus filhos)'

(27) *tülimo ngondilü leha iheke*

tü-limo ngondi-lü leha i-heke
REFL-children leave-PNCT COMPL 3-ERG

'She left her children there'
'Ela deixou seus filhos lá'

---

[10] See Franchetto (2010) for a description and analysis of the coexisting functions and meanings of the postposition *heke*, as a case (ergative) marker of the external argument of a "transitive verb", and as a perspective locative.

(28) *ilaha utetai*

    ila=ha   u-te-tai
    there=HA 1-go-FUT.IM

    "'I am going that way'"
    "'Eu vou para lá'"

(29) *ilaha nhingadzetai ige nhigüintsai*

    ila=ha   ng-ingaNtse-tai   ige   ng-igüiN-tsai
    there=HA OBJ-look-FUT.IM PROX OBJ-surround-FUT.IM

    "'I'll have a look and take a walk (around the garden)'"
    "'Vou dar uma olhada nisso e vou dar uma volta nisso (na roça)'"

(30) *lepe leha etelü leha igüinjüi leha*

    üle-pe   leha   e-te-lü   leha   iguiN-jü-i   leha
    LOG-NTM COMPL 3-go-PNCT COMPL surround-PNCT-COP COMPL

    'Then she went away and took a walk around (the garden)'
    'Depois ela foi-se e deu uma volta (na roça)'

(31) *üle hata ah nügü iheke ukugesube ukugesube*

    üle   hata   ah   nügü   i-heke   ukuge=sube ukuge=sube[11]
    LOG when ITJ PNCT 3-ERG people=EP   people=EP

    'Meanwhile, "Ah!" she said, "Is it people? Is it people?"'
    'Enquanto isso, "Ah!", ela disse, "Será que é gente? Será que é gente?"'

(32) *tübeki ekisei nügü iheke*

    tü=beki ekise-i   nügü i-heke
    Q=EP   3.DIST-COP PNCT 3-ERG

    "'Who can that person be?" she said'
    "'Quem será aquela pessoa?", ela disse'

(33) *lepe leha isinügü leha etuhupüngenügü*

    üle-pe   leha   is-i-nügü   leha   et-uhupünge-nügü
    LOG-NTM COMPL 3-come-PNCT COMPL 3DTR-disguise-PNCT

    'Then she came back and disguised herself'
    'Depois ela voltou e disfarçou'

---

[11] *sube* and, in the following line, *beki* are clitic particles expressing a feeling of surprise, fear and dramatic curiosity.

(34) *ijopenümi leha ihüsoho einhügü leha*
i-lope-nümi   leha i-hüsoho   ei-nhügü   leha
3-come.toward-PNCT.COP COMPL 3-mother.in.law come-PNCT COMPL
'Her mother-in-law came toward her'
'A sogra vinha em sua direção'

(35) *ijopenümi leha kagahuku akata leha*
i-lope-nümi   leha kagahuku akata   leha
3-come.toward-PNCT.COP COMPL fence   along.inside COMPL
'Toward her along on the inside of the fense'
'Na direção dela acompanhando a cerca (da roça) por dentro'

(36) *aka nügü iheke uãki eitsako nügü iheke*
aka nügü i-heke uã-ki e-i-tsa-ko   nügü i-heke
ITJ PNCT 3-ERG Q-INS 2-be-DUR-PL PNCT 3-ERG
'"Wow!" she (the mother-in-law) said to her: "What are you doing here?" she said to her'
'"Nossa!", ela disse: "O que vocês estão fazendo aqui?", ela disse'

(37) *eh nügü iheke inde muke utetagü emuguko tuhipe ingiale*
eh nügü i-heke inde muke u-te-tagü e-mugu-ko tuhi-pe   ingi-ale
ITJ PNCT 3-ERG here EP   1-go-DUR 2-son-PL garden-NTM see-while
'"Yeah!" she (the woman) said to her, "I'm walking here looking at your son's old garden"'
'"Sim!" ela disse "estou indo por aqui olhando a roça que foi do teu filho"'

(38) *uinilale nügü iheke uinilale utetagü inde*
u-inilu-ale nügü i-heke u-inilu-ale u-te-tagü inde
1-cry-while PNCT 3-ERG 1-cry-while 1-go-DUR here
'"Crying," she said to her, "I'm going here crying"'
'"Chorando", ela lhe disse, "estou indo por aqui chorando"'

(39) *ehẽ nügü iheke einilundako kahegei*
ehẽ nügü i-heke e-iniluN-ta-ko=kaha ege-i
ITJ PNCT 3-ERG 2-cry-DUR-PL=EP   DIST-COP
'"Yes," she (the mother-in-law) said, "you are really crying"'
'"Sim", ela (sogra) disse, "você está chorando mesmo"'

(40) *elimo uünkoi ailene inatagü*[12]

　　e-limo　　uüN-ko-i　　ailene inata-gü
　　2-children father-PL-COP feast　nose-POSS

　　'"Your children's father used to be the first of the feast"'
　　'"O pai dos seus filhos era sempre o primeiro da festa"'

(41) *kogetsi epetsakilü kogetsi epetsakilü*

　　kogetsi　　epetsaki-lü kogetsi　　epetsaki-lü
　　tomorrow adorn-PNCT tomorrow adorn-PNCT

　　'"One day he adorned himself and the other day he adorned himself (also)"'
　　'"Um dia se enfeita, outro dia se enfeita (também)"'

(42) *ilango gitse elimo uünkoi*

　　ila-ngo　　　gitse e-limo　　　uüN-ko-i
　　there-NMLZ EP　 2-children father-PL-COP

　　'"Your children's father was so"'
　　'"O pai dos seus filhos era assim"'

(43) *tingakugui gitse etengatohokoi inhaka nügü iheke*

　　tingakugu-i　gitse e-te-nga-toho-ko-i　　　　i-ngaka　　　nügü i-heke
　　weeping-COP EP　 2-go-HAB-INSNMLZ-PL-COP 3-instead.of PNCT 3-ERG

　　'"You will always be weeping for him," she (the mother-in-law) said'
　　'"Você ficará sempre lamentando por ele", ela (a sogra) disse'

(44) *ehẽ nügü iheke*

　　ehẽ nügü i-heke
　　AFF PNCT 3-ERG

　　'"Yes," she (the woman) said'
　　'"Sim", ela (a mulher) disse'

(45) *lepe inho ügühütuki leha isakihata leha iheke*

　　üle-pe　　i-nho　　ügühütu-ki　　leha　is-aki-ha-ta　　　　leha
　　LOG-NTM 3-husband way.being-INS COMPL 3-word-VBLZ-DUR COMPL
　　i-heke
　　3-ERG

　　'Then she was telling her about her husband's way of being'
　　'Depois ela ficou lhe contando sobre o jeito de ser do seu esposo'

---

[12] To be the first one is expressed as 'to be the nose (of something)': here, the nose of the feast.

(46) kigekeha
kigeke=ha
1.2.go.IMP=HA
'"Let's go!"'
'"Vamos!"'

(47) aminga akatsange uenhümingo eitigini einhani nügü iheke aminga
aminga   akatsange u-e-nhümingo e-itigi-ni e-inha-ni nügü i-heke
other.day INT   1-come-FUT   2-FIN-PL 2-DAT-PL PNCT 3-ERG
aminga
other.day

'"The day after tomorrow I'll come to you, to get you," she (the mother-in-law) said to her, "the day after tomorrow"'
"Depois de amanhã eu voltarei para vocês, para buscar vocês", ela (sogra) disse para ela, "depois de amanhã"

(48) kekeha egetüeha
keke=ha   egetüe=ha
1.2.go=HA go.IMP.PL=HA

'"Let's go," (the woman said). "You can go!" (the mother-in-law replied)'
'"Vamos!", (disse a mulher) "Podem ir", (respondeu a sogra)'

(49) etelü hõhõ ihüsoho telü leha anha telü leha[13]
e-te-lü   hõhõ i-hüsoho   te-lü leha anha te-lü   leha
3-go-PNCT EMPH 3-mother.in.law go-PNCT COMPL dead go-PNCT COMPL

'She went away, her mother-in-law went away, the dead one went away (but would be back soon)'
'Ela foi embora, a sogra foi embora, a morta foi embora (mas iria voltar logo)'

---

[13] As explained by the Kuikuro speakers, when someone says "*etelü hõhõ*" (she/he went away EMPHATIC), they are speaking about another person who went away with the intention of returning soon, the same day or the following day; when someone says "*etelü leha*" (she/he went away COMPLETIVE), they are speaking about someone who went away not knowing if they would come back.

(50) *anha hekisei ihoginhi leha isipe ihüsohope*

   anha=ha ekise-i   i-hogi-nhi   leha   isi-pe
   dead=HA 3.DIST-COP 3-find-ANMLZ COMPL mother-NTM
   i-hüsoho-pe
   3-mother.in.law-NTM

   'It was the dead one that found her, the one who had been the mother (of her husband), her deceased mother-in-law'
   'Era a morta aquela que a encontrou, a que tinha sido a mãe (do seu esposo), sua finada sogra'

(51) *lepe leha umm igiataka tünkgülü ihanügü iheke*[14]

   üle-pe   leha   umm igia=taka t-ünkgü-lü   iha-nügü i-heke
   LOG-NTM COMPL ITJ SO=EP   REFL-sleep-PNCT tell-PNCT 3-ERG

   'Then, (the woman remembered): "Umm, that was how she promised to sleep"'
   'Depois (a mulher lembrou): "Umm, foi assim que ela prometeu dormir"'

(52) *lepe leha anhü ika kigeke*

   üle-pe   leha   anhü ika   kigeke
   LOG-NTM COMPL son   wood 1.2.go.IMP

   "Then, (she said): "My dears! Let's go collect wood!"
   'Depois, (ela disse): "Queridos! Vamos buscar lenha!"'

(53) *etelü leha*[15]

   e-te-lü   leha
   3-go-PNCT COMPL

   'She went away'
   'Ela foi embora'

---

[14] The storyteller showed the fingers of her hand counting the number three; to 'sleep three' means a three day period of time.

[15] In a narrative, the expression of movement with the verb 'go' (root *te*) often means the movement of the narrative itself, from one scene to the following one.

(54) *etsutühügü ati leha inhügü*

etsu-tühügü   ati   leha   i-nhügü
promise.return-PRF when COMPL be-PNCT

'Then came the day she had promised to return'
'Chegou o dia em que ela tinha prometido voltar'

(55) *indeha eitsüe tülimo ngondingalü leha iheke inhondingalüko*

inde=ha e-i-tsüe   tü-limo   ngondi-nga-lü leha i-heke
here=HA 2-be-IMP.PL REFL-children leave-HAB-PNCT COMPL 3-ERG
i-ngondi-nga-lü-ko
3-leave-HAB-PNCT-PL

'"Stay here!" She used to leave her children, she often leaves them'
'"Fiquem aqui!" Ela costumava deixar seus filhos, ela costumava deixá-los'

(56) *indeha amanhetüe*

inde=ha amanhe-tüe
here=HA play-IMP.PL

'"Play here!"'
'"Brinquem por aqui!"'

(57) *lepe leha*

üle-pe   leha
LOG-NTM COMPL

'After this'
'Depois disso'

(58) *etelü leha egei isinümbata gehale ihüsoho enhümbata*

e-te-lü   leha   ege-i   is-i-nüN-hata   gehale i-hüsoho
3-go-PNCT COMPL DIST-COP 3-be-PNCT-when also   3-mother.in.law
eN-nhüN-hata
come-PNCT-when

'She went away when she (the mother-in-law) was coming back again'
'Foi, quando ela (a sogra) estava vindo novamente'

(59) *inhalü leha ingügijüi leha hüle iheke*

    inhalü[16] *leha ingügi-jü-i leha hüle i-heke*
    NEG COMPL give.lap-PNCT-COP COMPL CNTR 3-ERG

    'However, she (the mother-in-law) did not circle around anymore'
    'Ela (a sogra), porém, não deu mais voltas'

(60) *uhunügü leha iheke*

    uhu-nügü leha i-heke
    know-PNCT COMPL 3-ERG

    'She (the woman) already knew'
    'Ela (a mulher) já sabia'

(61) *lepe leha isinügü*

    üle-pe leha is-i-nügü
    then COMPL 3-be-PNCT

    'Then, she (the mother-in-law) arrived'
    'Então, ela (a sogra) chegou'

(62) *ande taka uetsagü akihalükoinha*

    ande taka u-e-tsagü akiha-lü-ko-inha
    here EP 1-arrive-PROG 2.tell-PNCT-PL-DAT

    '"Here I come to warn you" (the mother-in-law said)'
    '"Aqui chego para avisá-los" (disse a sogra)'

(63) *aminga akatsange elimo uünko telüingo haguna aminga*

    aminga akatsange e-limo uüN-ko te-lü-ingo hagu-na
    other.day INT 2-children father-PL go-PNCT-FUT bayou-ALL
    aminga
    other.day

    '"The day after tomorrow your children's father will go on a fishing trip"'
    '"Depois de amanhã o pai de seus filhos irá para a pescaria"'

---

[16] Kuikuro has two free grammatical forms to mark negation having scope on verbal or nominal phrases: *inhalü* is a kind of weak negation, and it always occurs with the non-verbal copula *-i* suffixed to the negated verb or nominal. *ahütü* is for stronger negations and it always occurs with the privative *-la* suffixed to the negated verb or nominal.

(64) *ülegote akatsange uenhümingo akihalükoinha ülegote*

üle-gote akatsange u-e-nhümingo akiha-lü-ko-inha üle-gote
LOG-when INT 1-arrive-PNCT.FUT tell-PNCT-PL-DAT LOG-when

'"When this happens, I'll come to warn you"'
'"Quando isso acontecer, eu virei avisá-la"'

(65) *eitigini etimbelüko ingitomi*

e-itigi-ni etimbe-lü-ko ingi-tomi
2-FIN-PL arrive-PNCT-PL see-PURP

'"To pick you up, so you'll see their arrival (from the fishing trip)"'
'"Para buscar você, de modo que veja a chegada deles (da pescaria)"'

(66) *esepe kae akatsange uenhümingo eitigini*[17]

ese-pe kae akatsange u-e-nhümingo e-itigi-ni
3.PROX-NTM LOC INT 1-arrive-PNCT.FUT 2-FIN-PL

'"After this (after four days), I'll come back to pick you up"'
'"Depois deste (depois de quatro dias), eu virei lhe buscar"'

(67) *isakihatagü gehale üleki ügühütuki hagunaha etelükoingoki*

is-akiha-tagü gehale üle-ki ügühütu-ki hagu-na=ha
3-tell-DUR also LOG-INS custom-INS bayou-ALL=HA
e-te-lü-ko-ingo-ki
3-go-PNCT-FUT-INS

'She (the mother-in-law) was also telling about that, about their way of being, about how they go on fishing trips'
'Ela (a sogra) também ficou contando sobre aquilo, sobre o jeito deles, sobre como eles vão para a pescaria'

(68) *kekeha nügü iheke etelüko leha*

keke=ha nügü i-heke e-te-lü-ko leha
1.2.IMP=HA PNCT 3-ERG 3-go-PNCT-PL COMPL

'"Let's go!" she said, they went away'
'"Vamos!", ela disse e foram embora'

---

[17] *Esepe kae* (after this one): the mother-in-law counts three fingers and indicates the fourth finger, the one after the third finger. The system of Kuikuro numerals is base 5, with counting beginning with the thumb and progressing to the little finger, thus completing a unit of 5. From 6 to 9 the numbers from 1 to 4 are repeated with the addition of the expression "made to cross to the other side". The number 10 closes another unit of 5. The same logic operates for the numbers from 11 to 15 (on the foot) and from 16 to 20 (crossing to the other side [the other foot]).

(69) *tetingugi leha atahaingalüko*
    tetingugi leha   at-ahaiN-nga-lü-ko
    each   COMPL 3DTR-separate-HAB-PNCT-PL
    'They separated, each walking to a different side at the same time'
    'Separaram-se, cada uma indo para um lado ao mesmo tempo'

(70) *lepe leha igia isünkgüpügü atai*
    üle-pe   leha   igia   is-ünkgü-pügü atai
    LOG-NTM COMPL so   3-sleep-PRF   when
    'After sleeping this way' (3)[18]
    'Depois de ter dormido assim' (3)

(71) *ika kigeke ailehüle üle tohoingo hüle*
    ika   kige-ke aileha=hüle   üle-toho-ingo   hüle
    wood go-IMP COMPL=CNTR LOG-INSNMLZ-FUT CNTR
    '"Let's go to collect wood!" It will be then that it happened'
    '"Vamos buscar lenha!" Será naquele momento que acontecerá'

(72) *ijopenümi gehale isinügü*
    ijope-nümi   gehale is-i-nügü
    come.toward-PNCT.COP also   3-be-PNCT
    'Once more she (the mother-in-law) came toward her'
    'Novamente ela (a sogra) veio em sua direção'

(73) *andetaka uetsagü akihalükoinha*
    ande=taka u-e-tsagü   akiha-lü-ko-inha
    now=EP   1-come-DUR tell-PNCT-PL-DAT
    '"I came here today to warn you"'
    '"Eu vim lhe avisar"'

(74) *ehe elimo uünko akatsange leha haguna ihaki nügü iheke*
    ehe e-limo   uüN-ko   akatsange leha   hagu-na   ihaki nügü i-heke
    ITJ 2-children father-PL INT   COMPL bayou-ALL far   PNCT 3-ERG
    '"All right, your children's father (is) really far away on the fishing trip," she said to her'
    '"Certo, o pai dos seus filhos (está) mesmo longe na pescaria", disse para ela'

---

[18] *Ájahi* indicates with the hand the number 3, meaning that three days elapsed.

(75) *igia akatsange isüngülüko inhatüi inhatüi*

igia akatsange is-üngü-lü-ko   inhatüi inhatüi
SO   INT   3-sleep-PNCT-PL five   five

'"They will sleep five (days), five (during the fishing trip)"'
'"Eles vão dormir cinco (dias), cinco (na pescaria)"'

(76) *esepe kae akatsange uenhümingo eitigini*

ese-pe   kae akatsange u-e-nhümingo   e-itigi-ni
3.PROX-NTM LOC INT   1-come-PNCT.FUT 2-FIN-PL

'"One after this, I'll really come back to pick you up"'
"Um depois deste, eu voltarei para lhe buscar"'

(77) *ingigokomi hõhõ ehekeni*

ingi-gokomi   hõhõ e-heke-ni
3.see-PURP.PL EMPH 2-ERG-PL

'"For you to see them"'
'"Para você vê-los"'

(78) *igiaha tingakügüi etelüko hinhe*

igia=ha tingakügü-i   e-te-lü-ko=hinhe
SO=HA   weeping-COP 2-go-PNCT-PL=NPURP

'"So you do not go around weeping for him"'
'"Para você não mais andar pranteando por ele"'

(79) *elimo uünko hüngüngü igelü hinhe ehekeni*

e-limo   uüN-ko   hüngüngü   ige-lü=hinhe   e-heke-ni
2-children father-PL feeling.lack carry-PNCT=NPURP 2-ERG-PL

'"For you to no longer carry such nostalgia for your children's father"'
'"Para você não carregar mais a saudade do pai dos seus filhos"'

(80) *epetsakinge inatagü sogitse tingakügüi gitse etengatohokoi gitse elimo uünko nügü iheke*

epetsaki-nge inata-gü   sogitse tingakügü-i   gitse
adorn-NMLZ noose-POSS EM   weeping-COP EM

e-te-nga-toho-ko-i   gitse e-limo   uüN-ko   nügü i-heke
2-go-HAB-INSNMLZ-PL-COP EM   2-children father-PL PNCT 3-ERG

'"He is the first to adorn himself; don't go around weeping for your children's father," she said to her'

"'Ele é o primeiro a se enfeitar; não ande sempre por aí pranteando o pai dos seus filhos", ela lhe disse'

(81) *tatoho ingakatalü sogitse elimo uünkoi gitse esei tingakugui eigengalüko heke*

    t-atoho   *ingakata-lü sogitse e-limo*   *uüN-ko-i*   *gitse*
    REFL-other.wife love-PNCT em   2-children father-PL-COP em
    ese-i   *tingakügü-i*   *e-ige-nga-lü-ko*   *heke*
    3.PROX-COP weeping-COP 2-take-HAB-PNCT-PL ERG

    '"He makes love with his other wife, your children's father is like this, while you are weeping"'
    '"Ele namora com a sua outra esposa (do outro mundo), assim é o pai dos seus filhos, enquanto você fica chorando"'

(82) *tahekasasai gele tatoho itinhündelü heke*

    tahekasasa-i gele t-atoho   *itinhünde-lü*   *heke*
    lying-COP   still REFL-other.wife lie.hammock-PNCT ERG

    '"He is always lying down in the hammock with his other wife"'
    '"Ele está sempre deitado na rede com a sua outra esposa"'

(83) *ilango gitse elimo uünkoi tühünitati ehekeni*

    ila-ngo   *gitse e-limo*   *uüN-ko-i*   *tü-hüni-tati*   *e-heke-ni*
    there-NMLZ EP   2-children father-PL-COP REFL-feel.lack-? 2-ERG-PL

    '"There, your children's father is like this, the one that you are missing"'
    '"Lá, o pai dos seus filhos é assim, aquele de quem você sente falta"'

(84) *eijatongoko itinhündelü heke gitse elimo uünko itsagü nügü iheke*

    eijatongo-ko itinhünde-lü heke gitse e-limo   *uüN-ko*   *i-tsagü nügü*
    2nd.wife-PL lie-PNCT   ERG EP   2-children father-PL be-DUR PNCT
    i-heke
    3-ERG

    '"Your children's father always lies down in the hammock with his second wife," she said to her'
    '"O pai dos seus filhos fica sempre deitado na rede com a sua segunda esposa", ela disse'

(85) üle heke leha ihitsü ingüngingükijü

üle heke leha   i-hi-tsü   ingüN-ki-nguN-ki-jü
LOG erg COMPL 3-wife-POSS eye-INS-VBLZ-INS-PNCT

'This made his wife think'
'Isso fez a esposa dele pensar'

(86) lepe leha etelüko leha etelü leha

üle-pe   leha   e-te-lü-ko   leha   e-te-lü   leha
LOG-NTM COMPL 3-go-COMPL-PL COMPL 3-go-PNCT COMPL

'After this, they went away, she went away'
'Depois, elas foram, ela foi'

(87) lepe leha engü leha ijimo telü leha haguna leha

üle-pe   leha   engü leha   i-limo   te-lü   leha   hagu-na   leha
LOG-NTM COMPL then COMPL 3-children go-PNCT COMPL bayou-ALL COMPL

'Then, her (mother-in-law's) children went on the fishing trip'
'Então, os filhos dela (da sogra) foram para a pescaria'

(88) igeitaka isünkgülüingo igeitaka

ige-i=taka   is-ünkgü-lü-ingo   ige-i=taka
PROX-COP=EP 3-sleep-PNCT-FUT PROX-COP=EP

'"Will she sleep so many nights?"'[19]
'"Será que ela irá dormir estas tantas noites?"'

(89) esepe kae itigi hüle isinügü

ese-pe   kae itigi   hüle   is-i-nügü
3.PROX-NTM LOC to.seek CNTR 3-come-PNCT

'But exactly on this day she (the mother-in-law) arrived to get her'
'Mas exatamente neste dia ela (a sogra) veio buscá-la'

(90) kekegeha nügü iheke

kekege=ha   nügü i-heke
let's.go=HA PNCT 3-ERG

'"Let's go," she said to her'
'"Vamos!", ela lhe disse'

---

[19] The widowed woman asks herself how many days will pass until her mother-in-law comes back to get her.

(91) *ande akatsege elimo uünko etimbelüingo nügü iheke*
 ande akatsege e-limo   uüN-ko   etimbe-lü-ingo   nügü i-heke
 now INT   2-children father-PL come-PNCT-FUT   PNCT 3-ERG

 '"Today your children's father will come," she said to her'
 '"Hoje o pai dos seus filhos vai chegar", disse a ela'

(92) *lepe leha etelü leha*
 üle-pe   leha   e-te-lü   leha
 LOG-NTM COMPL 3-go-PNCT COMPL

 'Then she went away'
 'Depois disso ela foi'

(93) *inde atsange eitsüe nügü iheke tülimo heke leha*
 inde atsange e-i-tsüe   nügü i-heke tü-limo heke   leha
 here INT   2-be-IMP.PL say 3-ERG REFL- children ERG COMPL

 '"Stay here!" she (the woman) said to her own children'
 '"Fiquem aqui!", ela (a mulher) disse para os seus filhos'

(94) *ilá kohõtsige utehesundagü ige nügü iheke*
 ilá   kohõtsige   u-tehesuN-tagü ige   nügü i-heke
 there walking.little 1-walk-PROG   PROX say 3-ERG

 '"I'm going there walking a little," she said to them'
 '"Eu vou para lá, passear um pouco", ela disse para eles'

(95) *lepe leha etelüko leha*
 üle-pe   leha   e-te-lü-ko   leha
 LOG-NTM COMPL 3-go-PNCT-PL COMPL

 'Then, they went away'
 'Depois disso, eles foram'

(96) *hakitsetse leha atamini ngika ngondilü ihekeni osiha ina eitsüe*
 haki-tsetse leha   ata-mini ngika ngondi-lü i-heke-ni osi=ha ina
 far-DIM   COMPL when-PL   them leave-PNCT 3-ERG-PL well=HA here
 e-i-tsüe
 2-be-IMP.PL

 'When they were not so far from the village, they left them (the children): "Stay here!"'

'Quando estavam pouco longe da aldeia, os (filhos) deixaram: "Fiquem aqui!"'

(97) *tüatsagati leha tüilü iheke*
tü-atsagati   leha   tüi-lü   i-heke
REFL-in.front COMPL put-PNCT 3-ERG
'She (the mother-in-law) put her in front of herself'
'Ela (a sogra) a colocou em sua frente'

(98) *itükanhenügü letüha iheke itükanhenügü itükanhenügü*
itüka-nhe-nügü   üle=tü=ha   i-heke itüka-nhe-nügü
3.move.up-TR-PNCT LOG=UNCR=HA 3-ERG 3.move.up-TR-PNCT
itüka-nhe-nügü
3.move.up-TR-PNCT
'Then, she moved her up, she moved her up, she moved her up'
'Ela a fez subir, fez subir, fez subir'[20]

(99) *inegetüha ihhh kahü ijatüna tsitsi letsügüha inhünkgo leha*
inege=tü=ha   ihhh kahü ijatü-na   tsitsi   üle=tsügü=ha
this.side=UNCR=HA ID   sky armpit-AL almost LOG=UNCR=HA
i-nhüN-ko   leha
3-be-PNCT-PL COMPL
'On this side, *ihhh*, they reached almost to the limit of the sky (with the earth) and (there) they stayed'
'Deste lado, *ihhh*, chegaram quase no limite do céu (com a terra) e (lá) ficaram'

(100) *itükainjüko leha osiha etimükeĩtüe ah etimükeĩtüe*
itükaiN-jü-ko   leha   osi=ha   et-imükeĩ-tüe   ah
3-move.up-PNCT-PL COMPL well=HA 2.DTR-turn.face-IMP.PL ITJ
et-imükeĩ-tüe
2.DTR-turn.face-IMP.PL
'They moved up: "Well, turn your face (down), ah, turn your face (down)!"'
'Elas subiram; "Vire o rosto (para baixo), vire o rosto (para baixo)!"'

---

[20] *tü(ha)* and *tsügü(ha)* are clitics, epistemic/evidentials (EM), whose meaning is approximately: 'I, the speaker, cannot assume the truth of this information; people say it happened'.

(101) *tetimükeĩtü eh humbungaka leha*

    t-et-imükeĩ=tü   eh humbungaka leha
    PTCP-DTR-turn.face.PTCP=UNCR ITJ upside.down COMPL

    'With the face turned down, upside down'
    'Com o rosto virado (para baixo), de cabeça para baixo'

(102) *engü atühügü leha ngongoho atühügü leha*

    engü a-tühügü leha   ngongo-ho a-tühügü leha
    then be-PRF   COMPL earth-LOC be-PRF   COMPL

    'Then, the earth appeared (upside down)'
    'Então, a terra apareceu (de cabeça para baixo)'

(103) *ama üntepügü leha kahü alüpengine ige ige ugupongaha*

    ama ünte-pügü leha   kahü alüpengine ige   ugupo-nga=ha
    way down-PRF COMPL SKY   INE   PROX above-all=HA

    'The way down from the sky to above here'
    'O caminho que desce do céu até em cima daqui'

(104) *igeha kungongogu uguponga leha*

    ige=ha   ku-ngongo-gu   ugupo-nga leha
    PROX=HA 1.2[21]-earth-POSS above-ALL COMPL

    'Here above our earth'
    'Aqui em cima da nossa terra'

(105) *lepe leha etelüko*

    lepe leha   e-te-lü-ko
    then COMPL 3-go-PNCT-PL

    'Then, they went away'
    'Depois disso, elas foram'

(106) *anha engübeha tanginhügü ẽgipügati leha inhügü*

    anha engübeha tanginhü-gü   ẽgipügati   leha   i-nhügü
    dead EP   main.path-POSS at.top.head COMPL be-PNCT

    'They stayed right at the beginning of the main path of the dead'
    'Ficaram bem no começo do caminho principal dos mortos'

(107) üle ama gae geletügüha inginügü iheke

üle ama gae   geletügü=ha ingi-nügü   i-heke
LOG path on.edge ?=HA   3.bring-PNCT   3-ERG

'She (the mother-in-law) brought her right to the edge of the path'
'Ela (a sogra) a trouxe bem na beira do caminho'

(108) itsapügü itahiale leha itsapügü ingitüingiha anha heke

i-tapü-gü   itahi-ale   leha   i-tapü-gü   ingi-tüingi=ha anha heke
3-foot-POSS   erase-SIM   COMPL 3-foot-POSS   see-AVD=HA   dead ERG

'Erasing her footprints, for the dead not to see her footprints'
'Apagando as pegadas dela, para o morto não ver as pegadas dela'

(109) ihüsoho e-nhügü leha isingi

i-hüsoho   e-nhügü   leha   is-ingi
3-mother.in.law   come-PNCT   COMPL   3-after

'The mother-in-law was coming after her'
'A sogra vinha atrás dela'

(110) inhalütüha tütüte isingi inginümi iheke

inhalü=tü=ha   tütüte   is-ingi ingi-nümi   i-heke
NEG=UNCR=HA   hidden   3-after bring-PNCT.COP   3-ERG

'She (the mother-in-law) didn't bring her (daughter-in-law) hidden after her'
'Ela (a sogra) não trouxe (a nora) escondida atrás dela'

(111) teh titamingügi ekubetüha anha akapügüha

teh titamingügi   ekube=tü=ha   anha akapügü=ha
ITJ drawn   good-UNCR=HA   dead proper=HA

'Wow! (The path) was really beautiful, drawn properly for the dead'
'Poxa! Era bem bonito (o caminho) desenhado especialmente para os mortos'

(112) amaha simagüko tanginhü

ama=ha   is-ima-gü-ko   tanginhü
path=HA   3-path-POSS-PL   main.path

'The path, their path (of the dead), the main path'
'O caminho, o caminhos deles (dos mortos), o caminho principal'

(113) *tange itamingügüi leha teh*
 tange itamingü-gü-i   leha   teh
 pot   drawing-POSS-COP COMPL ITJ
 'It looked like the drawing on the small pots, beautiful!'
 'Parecia com a pintura da panelinha de barro, bem bonita!'

(114) *ama tepügü*
 ama te-pügü
 path go-PRF
 'The way of going (to the village of the dead)'
 'O caminho da ida (para a aldeia dos mortos)'

(115) *anha akapügütsügü*
 anha akapügü=tsügü
 dead proper=UNCR
 'Done especially for the dead'
 'Feito especialmente para os mortos'

(116) *ingiale ekugu igia tsügü tihü heke gele ingiale isita gele*
 ingi-ale ekugu igia=tsügü   tihü   heke gele ingi-ale is-ita   gele
 see-SIM really like.this=UNCR living ERG still see-SIM 3-be-CONT still
 'The living one was coming like this, looking, looking'
 'A viva estava vindo assim olhando, olhando'[22]

(117) *anha imagü*
 anha ima-gü
 dead path-POSS
 'The path of the dead'
 'O caminho dos mortos'

(118) *lepe leha etelüko leha*
 üle-pe   leha   e-te-lü-ko   leha
 log-NTM COMPL 3-go-PNCT-PL COMPL
 'Then, they went'
 'Depois elas foram'

---

[22] Only one who is dead can pass on the path of the dead, but in this case the woman was alive.

(119) *ngikaho letühα sinünkgo*

　　　ngikaho　　üle=tü=ha　　　is-i-nüN-ko
　　　back.door　LOG=UNCR=HA　3-be-PNCT-PL

　　　'At the back of the houses, there they stayed'
　　　'Atrás das casas, lá ficaram'

(120) *enüngo titage leha ogo²³ uguponga leha*

　　　e-nüN-ko　　　titage　　leha　ogo　　　　ugupo-nga leha
　　　enter-PNCT-PL straight COMPL platform on-ALL　　COMPL

　　　'They entered (into the house) directly, over the platform'
　　　'Entraram (na casa) direto, por cima do jirau'

(121) *timbuku²⁴ tüha üle hujati leha*

　　　timbuku=tü=ha　　　　üle　huja-ti　　leha
　　　cassava.piece=UNCR=HA LOG middle-ALL COMPL

　　　'Just in the middle of the pieces of dried cassava paste'
　　　'No meio dos pedaços de massa seca de mandioca'

(122) *ĩtsüi kuiginhu²⁵ hagatepügü*

　　　ĩtsüi kuiginhu　　　hagate-pügü
　　　lot　 cassava.flour　store-PRF

　　　'There was a lot of cassava flour stored there'
　　　'Tinha muito polvilho armazenado'

(123) *anha inhangoha kaküngi tsügüha anha inhango*

　　　anha inhango=ha　kaküngi tsügü=ha　anha inhango
　　　dead food=HA　　 much　　UNCR=HA　 dead food

　　　'There was a lot of the food of the dead, food of the dead'
　　　'Tinha muita comida dos mortos, comida dos mortos'

---

[23] The cassava paste is placed on an *ogo* – a platform built at the back of the house – to dry in the sun.

[24] The word *timbuku* refers to a particular form of the pieces of the dried cassava paste.

[25] The word *kuiginhu* refers to the cassava flour, the end product of women's long and heavy labor necessary to process the cassava (*Manihot esculenta*), which begins in the gardens with the digging up of the roots and goes through successive phases of withdrawal of the hydrocyanic acid (poisonous to humans), until the cassava paste is left to dry in the sun.

(124) *üle hata letü ihüsoho agapagatsita leha*

üle hata üle=tü   i-hüsoho   agapagatsi-ta leha
LOG while LOG=UNCR 3-mother.in.law sweep-DUR   COMPL

'Meanwhile her mother-in-law was sweeping'
'Enquanto isso, a sogra dela varria'

(125) *engüha egei uhupungetagü leha iheke uhutüingiha uhutüingi*

engü=ha ege-i   uhu-pu-nge-tagü²⁶ leha i-heke uhu-tüingi=ha
CON=HA   DIST-COP know-NEG-TR-DUR   COMPL 3-ERG know-AVD=HA

uhu-tüingi
know-AVD

'(The mother-in-law) was hiding (her daughter-in-law) so nobody knew, so nobody knew'
'(A sogra) estava escondendo (a nora) para ninguém saber, para ninguém saber'

(126) *üle hata tsügü gehale*

üle hata tsügü gehale
LOG while UNCR again

'Meanwhile, again'
'Enquanto isso, novamente'

(127) *túhagu²⁷ ingete anha kitagü üngahingo²⁸ kitagü*

túhagu iN-kete   anha ki-tagü üngahi-ngo   ki-tagü
strainer bring-IMP dead say-DUR circle.houses-NMLZ say-DUR

'"Bring *túhagu* (a sieve)" the dead one was saying, the one of the other house was saying'
'"Traga *túhagu* (peneira)!" dizia o morto, dizia o da outra casa'

(128) *itsatüeha itsatüeha kakisükope uhitsa leha kupeheni*

i-ta-tüe=ha   i-ta-tüe=ha   k-aki-sü-ko-pe
3-hear-IMP.PL=HA   3-hear-IMP.PL=HA   INCL-word-POSS-PL-NTM

---

[26] Literally, '(she) was making (her) unknown'.

[27] In the language of the dead, words are different (for the same referent): *túhagu* is the word of the dead for 'strainer', *angagi* in the language of the living.

[28] The adverb *üngahi* means 'along the circle of the houses' (the Xinguan village is typically an oval circle of houses) and here it is nominalized by the suffix *-ngo*, exclusive for adverbs and numerals.

uhi-tsa   leha   kupehe-ni
search-PROG COMPL 1.2.ERG-PL

"'Listen! Listen! They are trying to speak our former language'" (the mother-in-law was saying)
"'Ouça! Ouça! Eles estão tentando falar a nossa língua (quando vivos)'" (a sogra dizia)

(129) *egea akatsange kakisüko anügü leha*

egea   akatsange k-aki-sü-ko   a-nügü   leha
like.that INT   1.2-word-POSS-PL   be-PNCT COMPL

"'That's how our language is here'"
"'É assim que é a nossa língua aqui'"

(130) *kakisükope uhitsa leha igei kupeheni leha egea leha*

k-aki-sü-ko-pe   uhi-tsa   leha   ige-i kupehe-ni leha
INCL-word-POSS-PL-NTM search-DUR COMPL PROX 1.2-PL   COMPL

egea leha
SO   COMPL

'They were trying to speak our language (that was their language when alive)' (comment by *Ájahi*)
'Eles estavam tentando falar a nossa língua (que era a língua deles quando vivos)' (comentário de *Ájahi*)

(131) *igiatsetse unkgu uigiholotogu²⁹ ingete*

igia-tsetse   unkgu u-igiholoto-gu iN-kete
like.this-DIM small 1-griddle-POSS bring-IMP.CNTP

'It did not take too long, (she heard): "Bring my *igihitolo* (a clay griddle for cooking cassava bread)"'
'Não demorou muito, (ela ouviu): "Traga meu *igihitolo* (tacho)!"'

(132) *itsatüeha*

i-ta-tüe=ha
3-hear-IMP.PL=HA

'Listen to this!' (*Ájahi* says to the researcher)
'Ouça isto!' (*Ájahi* diz para o pesquisador)

---

[29] *Igiholoto* is the word for *alato* (the griddle pan for cooking cassava bread), in the language of the dead.

(133) *alato heke akatsege tagü iheke*
 alato heke akatsege tagü i-heke
 griddle ERG INT DUR 3-ERG

 'She said (referring to) *alato* (the griddle for cooking cassava bread in the language of living)'
 'Ela falou referindo-se a *alato*' (tacho na língua dos vivos)

(134) *ekü hüle egei angagi heke túhagu ingete ta iheke*
 ekü hüle ege-i angagi heke túhagu iN-kete ta iheke
 CON CNTR PROX-COP strainer ERG túhagu bring-IMP.CTP

 'But before it was the sieve she was talking about, (when she said) "Bring *túhagu*!"'
 'Mas antes era da peneira que ela estava falando, (quando disse) "Traga *túhagu*!"'

(135) *angagi heke tetunetohongoi heke*
 angagi heke t-et-une-toho-ngo-i heke
 strainer ERG REFL-DTR-sift-INSNMLZ-NMLZ-COP ERG

 '(Referring) to the sieve, that she used to sift (cassava paste) for herself'
 '(Referindo-se) à peneira, aquilo que serve para ela peneirar para ela mesma'

(136) *ikine ikitsomi tsügü hüle egei iheke tük*
 ikine iki-tsomi tsügü hüle ege-i i-heke
 cassava.bread make.cassava.bread-PURP UNCR CNTR DIST-COP 3-ERG
 tük
 IDEO

 'But for her to cook cassava bread, *tük*'
 'Mas para para ela fazer beiju, *tük*'

(137) *uigiholotogu ingete tatohoi iheke*
 u-igiholoto-gu iN-kete ta-toho-i i-heke
 1-griddle-POS bring-IMP.CNTP say-INS.NMLZ-COP 3-ERG

 '"Bring my *igiholoto* (griddle)," was what she meant to say'
 '"Traga meu *igiholoto* (tacho)!", era para ela dizer'

(138) itsatüeha nügü iheke
 i-ta-tüe=ha nügü i-heke
 3-hear-IMP.PL=HA say.PNCT 3-ERG
 '"Listen!" she said'
 '"Ouça!", ela disse'

(139) egea akatsange leha kakisükope leha
 egea akatsange leha k-aki-sü-ko-pe leha
 like.this INT COMPL 1.2-word-POSS-PL-NTM COMPL
 '"This is what our language is like here"' (the mother-in-law said)
 '"É assim que é a nossa língua aqui"' (a sogra disse)

(140) kakisükope elükugigatühügü leha
 k-aki-sü-ko-pe elükugi-ga-tühügü leha
 1.2-word-POSS-NTM reverse-DUR-PRF COMPL
 '"Our former language was reversed"'
 '"A nossa língua foi sendo invertida"'

(141) uhijüi leha kupehe ngiko itanügü kupehe
 uhijü-i leha kupehe ngiko ita-nügü kupehe
 search-COP COMPL 1.2.ERG thing call-PNCT 1.2.ERG
 '"We try to call things"'
 '"Nós tentamos chamar as coisas"'

(142) ta tsügü iheke
 ta tsügü i-iheke
 DUR UNCR 3-ERG
 'She was saying to her'
 'Dizia para ela'

(143) tumukugu hitsü akihatagü iheke
 tu-muku-gu hi-tsü aki-ha-tagü i-heke
 REFL-son-POSS wife-POSS word-VBLZ-DUR 3-ERG
 'She was telling her son's wife'
 'Ela contava para a esposa do seu filho'

(144) *ülepe igia ünkgu tinho tataheti teh*

üle-pe igia ünkgu tü-nho t-atahe-ti teh
LOG-NTM like.this little REFL-husband PTCP-spy-PTCP ITJ

'Shortly after, she spied on her husband (and said): "Wow! Beautiful!"'
'Pouco depois disso, ela espiou o esposo (e disse): "Nossa! Que bonito!"'

(145) *tahisügi*[30] *ekubekuletüha anha itu hugogo*[31] *teh*

tahisügi ekubeku=letü=ha anha itu hugogo teh
red really=UNCR=HA dead village plaza ITJ

'The plaza of the village of the dead was really reddish, beautiful!'
'A praça da aldeia dos mortos era bem avermelhada, muito bonita!'

(146) *tatsajo ületü tomogokombeke üne tepügü*

tatsajo üle=tü tomogokombeke üne te-pügü
all.together LOG=UNCR stuck.in.the.other house go-PRF

'The houses were one next to the other'
'As casas eram coladas umas às outras'

(147) *tepugopeti*

t-epugope-ti
PTCP-be.circle-PTCP

'In a circle'
'Em círculo'

(148) *hangakaki tajühe tsetsei kuakutu*

hanga-ka-ki tajühe tsetse-i kuakutu
ear-big-INS chief.house almost.same-COP men.house

'The *kwakutu* (men's house) was almost as the *tajühe* (chief's house) with big ears'
'O *kwakutu* (casa dos homens) era quase do tamanho da *tajühe* (casa do chefe) de orelhas grandes'

---

[30] The village plaza is qualified as reddish (*tahisügi*, root *hisu* 'red') because this is the typical color of most of the non-flood areas of central Brazil; the villages are always erected in these higher places.

[31] *Hugogo* is the village plaza, surrounded by the circle of houses.

(149) *tihü heke tsama ingitai iheke ahütüha apünguhügüila*
 tihü heke tsama ingi-tai i-heke ahütü=ha apüngu-hügü-i-la
 living ERG ? see-FUT.IM 3-ERG NEG=HA die-PRF-COP-PRIV
 'The living one, it was she who could see, she was not really dead'
 'A viva, era ela quem podia ver, não estava mesmo morta'

(150) *ülepe leha igia ungku giti ikühagatilü*
 üle-pe leha igia ungku giti ikühagati-lü
 LOG-NTM COMPL like.this little sun rise-PNCT
 'Shortly after, the sun came up'
 'Não demorou muito e o sol logo nasceu'

(151) *hü hü hü[32] aikobeha inhomo etimbelü*
 hü hü hü ai-ko-be=ha i-nho-mo[33] etimbe-lü
 hü hü hü DEM-PL-?=HA 3-husband-COLL come-PNCT
 '*Hü hü hü*, those, her husband and brothers-in-law, came'
 '*Hü hü hü*, aqueles, seu esposo e os cunhados, chegaram'

(152) *aindeko akatsange*
 ainde-ko akatsange
 DEM-PL INT
 'They are coming'
 'Eles estão vindo'

(153) *etihüĩtsüe etihüĩtsüe*
 et-ihüĩ-tsüe et-ihüĩ-tsüe
 2.DTR-stay.quite-IMP.PL 2.DTR-stay.quite-IMP.PL
 '"Don't move, don't move!"' (the mother-in-law says to her daughter-in-law hidden among the cassava balls)
 '"Não se mexa, não se mexa!"' (a sogra fala para a nora escondida entre as bolas de massa de mandioca)

---

[32] The fishermen shout as they approach the village.

[33] The collective of "husband" refers to the group composed by the husband and his brothers. These are a woman's potential sexual partners and spouses. The suffix *-mo* is a cognate of a common plural/collective suffix in other Carib languages.

(154) *elimo uünko ingilüpile atsange ketikaĩtsó*

    e-limo   uüN-ko   ingi-lü-pile   atsange ket-ikaĩ-tsó
    2-children father-PL see-PNCT-CONC INT   PROH-get.up-PROH

    '"Even if you see the father of your children, don't get up!"'
    '"Mesmo se você ver o pai dos seus filhos, não se levante!"'

(155) *ketikaĩtsó atsange*

    ke-tikaĩ-tsó   atsange
    PROH-get.up-PROH INT

    '"Don't really get up!"'
    '"Não se levante mesmo!"'

(156) *kakungakitüingi atsange elimo uünko enhügü kakungakitüingi*

    k-akunga-ki-tüingi atsange e-limo   uüN-ko   e-nhügü
    1.2-soul-VBLZ-AVD INT   2-children father-PL come-PNCT
    k-akunga-ki-tüngi
    1.2-soul-VBLZ-AVD

    '"Do not be alarmed by the arrival of the father of your children, do not be alarmed!"'
    '"Não se assuste com a chegada do pai dos seus filhos, não se assuste!"'

(157) *ülepe leha*

    üle-pe   leha
    LOG-NTM COMPL

    'After this'
    'Depois disso'

(158) *ẽnünkgo leha ihinhanoko ẽnügü pokü*

    ẽ-nüN-ko   leha   i-hinhano-ko   ẽ-nügü   pokü[34]
    3.enter-PNCT-PL COMPL 3-older.brother-PL enter-PNCT IDEO

    'They entered (the house), their older brother entered, *pokü*'
    'Eles entraram, o irmão mais velho deles entrou, *pokü*'

---

[34] Ideophone for the act of unloading weight from the back or from the head to the floor.

(159) *asankgu leha inhegikini itsangagüko*
 asankgu leha   inhegiki-ni i-kanga-gü-ko
 basket COMPL each.one-PL 3-fish-POSS-PL
 'Each had a basket (full of) fish'
 'Cada um tinha um cesto de peixe'

(160) *inhakagüki*[35] *hegei ütepügüko totsonkgitohokoki*
 inhakagü-ki=ha ege-i   ü-te-pügü-ko t-ot-konkgi-toho-ko-ki
 soap-INS=HA DIST-COP 3-go-PRF-PL REFL-DTR-INSNMLZ-PL-INS
 'They had already gone to look for *inhakagü* to wash themselves'
 'Já tinham ido buscar *inhakagü* para se lavar'

(161) *igia tuhugu tsügü nhakagü kamisatühügü*
 igia   tuhugu=tsügü inhakagü kami-sa-tühügü
 like.this amount=UNCR soap   tie-DUR-PRF
 'That's how they had tied the bundle of *inhakagü* roots'
 'Era assim que eles tinham amarrado o feixe de raízes de *inhakagü*'

(162) *isasankguguko ugupo itsangagüko ugupo*[36]
 is-asankgu-gu-ko ugupo i-kanga-gü-ko ugupo
 3-basket-POSS-PL on   3-fish-POSS-PL on
 'On their baskets, on their fishes'
 'Em cima do cesto deles, em cima dos peixes deles'

(163) *ai tüha ēnünkgo*
 ai=tü=ha   ẽ-nüN-ko
 then=UNCR=HA enter-PNCT-PL
 'Then, they entered'
 'Então, eles entraram'

(164) *ihinhanoko hotugui tüẽdinhüi*
 i-hinhano-ko   hotugu-i tü-ẽ-ti-nhü-i
 3-older.brother-PL first-COP PTCP-enter-PTCP-NANMLZ-COP
 'It was the older brother who entered first'
 'Foi o irmão mais velho que entrou primeiro'

---

[35] Root of an unidentified plant that when rubbed with water produces foam; it was used before industrialized soap became available.

[36] *Ájahi* remembered an old custom and showed to the listeners how old people used to manage and carry the traditional "soap".

(165) *ülepe ihisü ülepe isingingope ülepe aküpügüko tsügü hüle ekisei ihisükoi*

üle-pe   i-hi-sü   üle-pe   is-ingi-ngo-pe
LOG-NTM 3-younger.brother-POSS LOG-NTM 3-behind-NMLZ-NTM
üle-pe   aküpügü-ko=tsügü   hüle ekise-i
LOG-NTM 3.youngest-PL=UNCR CNTR 3.DIST-COP
i-hi-sü-ko-i
3-younger.brother-POSS-PL-COP

'Then the younger brother, then the one who comes after him, then the last one, that one, their younger brother'
'Depois o irmão mais novo, depois o que vem atrás dele, depois o último, aquele, o irmão mais novo deles'

(166) *ekiseiha ekisei ngisoi*

ekise-i=ha   ekise-i   ngiso-i
3.DIST-COP=HA 3.DIST-COP spouse-COP

'That one was the husband of that (woman)'
'Aquele era o esposo daquela (mulher)'

(167) *üẽnünkgo leha*

ü-ẽ-nüN-ko   leha
3-enter-PNCT-PL COMPL

'They entered'
'Eles entraram'

(168) *tünho ingilütü iheke ikühagatilü ikühagatilü*

tü-nho   ingi-lü=tü   i-heke ikühagati-lü
REFL-husband see-PNCT=UNCR 3-ERG 3.get.up.little-PNCT
ikühagati-lü
3.get.up.little-PNCT

'She saw her husband (and) got up a little, she got up a little'
'Ela viu o esposo e se levantou um pouco, se levantou um pouco'

(169) *tãuguila letüha titaginhu imbüa geleha ihüsoho heke apenügü*

tãuguila   üle=tü=ha   t-itaginhu   imbua   gele=ha
speaking.high LOG-UNCR-HA REFL-converse in.middle still=HA
i-hüsoho   heke ape-nügü
3-mother-in-law ERG tell.shut.up-PNCT

'While (her mother-in-law) was speaking loudly (with her son), still in the middle of the conversation, her mother-in-law told her to shut up'

'Enquanto (a sogra) falava alto (com o filho), ainda no meio da conversa, a sogra mandou ela se calar'

(170) üle lopenümi ületahüle ihitsü etikainjü itsikuoinjüinha
üle lope-nümi ületa=hüle i-hi-tsü et-ikaiN-jü
LOG stand.direction-PNCT.COP LOG=CNTR 3-wife-POSS 3.DTR-get.up-PNCT
i-tikuoĩ-jü-inha
3-hug-PNCT-DAT

'Going to meet him (the dead), the wife (of the dead) got up to hug him'
'Indo ao seu (do morto) encontro, a esposa (do morto) se levantou para abraçá-lo'[37]

(171) ikuilisale leha ipigagü kae
i-kuili-sale leha i-piga-gü kae
3-kiss-SIM COMPL 3-cheek-POSS on

'She kissed him on the cheeks'
'Beijou-o nas bochechas'

(172) akehenügü ületüha iheke mbokü
akehe-nügü üle=tü=ha i-heke mbokü[38]
take.house.corner-PNCT LOG=UNCR=HA 3-ERG IDEO

'She took him to the corner of the house (and) lay on top of him'
'Ela o levou para o canto da casa (e) deitou-se em cima dele'

(173) itsikaĩholü itsikaĩholü
i-tikaĩ-ho-lü i-tikaĩ-ho-lü
3-get.up-CF-PNCT 3-get.up-CF-PNCT

'She (the living wife) almost got up, she almost got up'
'Ela (a esposa viva) quase se levantou, quase se levantou'

(174) itsinhulukijü tsügüha Itsangitsegu heke
i-kinhulu-ki-jü tsügü=ha Itsangitsegu heke
3-jealousy-VBLZ-PNCT UNCR=HA itsangitsegu ERG

'She got jealous of *Itsangitsegu*'
'Ela ficou com ciúmes de *Itsangitsegu*'

---

[37] *Ájahi* refers here to *Itangitsegu*, the wife of the dead in the village of the dead.
[38] Ideophone that expresses the act of lying on someone (the sexual act).

(175) *Itsangitsegu hekisei ihitsüi Itsangitsegu atühügü*

Itsangitsegu=ha ekise-i   i-hi-tsü-i   Itsangitsegu a-tühügü
itsangitsegu=HA 3.DIST-COP 3-wife-POSS-COP itsangitsegu STAY-PRF

'That one was *Itsangitsegu*, *Itsangitsegu* had become his wife'
'Aquela era *Itsangitsegu*, *Itsangitsegu* tinha se tornado a esposa dele'

(176) *ülehinhe hüle egei*

üle-hinhe   hüle ege-i
LOG-NPURP CNTR DIST-COP

'It was because of her (that the living wife had been jealous)'
'Era por causa dela (que a esposa viva tinha ficado com ciúme)'

(177) *ketikaïtsó atsange ketikaïtsó*

ke-tikaï-tsó   atsange ke-tikaï-tsó
PROH-get.up-PROH INT   PROH-get.up-PROH

'"Do not get up, do not get up!"' (the mother-in-law said)
'"Não se levante, não se levante!"' (disse a sogra)

(178) *hum hum uãbeki kukanünkgo*

hum hum uã-beki kuk-a-nüN-ko
IDEO IDEO Q-EP   1.2-be-PNCT-PL

'"*Hum hum*, what's happening to us?"' (the dead said)
'"*Hum hum*, o que está acontecendo conosco?"' (os mortos disseram)

(179) *hum hum tihühokolo giketilübe nügü leha ihekeni*

hum hum[39] *tihühokolo gike-ti-lü=be   nügü leha i-heke-ni*
IDEO IDEO living   smell-VBLZ-PNCT=EP say COMPL 3-ERG-PL

'"*Hum*, I can smell a living person," they said'
'"*Hum*, estou sentindo cheiro de pessoa viva" eles disseram'

---

[39] At this moment, *Ájahi*, the storyteller, represents the dead character spitting on the ground, thus expressing nausea induced by the smell of the living. It is another example of inverted perspective, since the smell of the dead (rotten flesh) causes disgust in the living. In the next lines she repeats the gesture.

(180) *tihühokolo giketilübe hum ahijunu giketilübe*
 tihühokolo gike-ti-lü=be   hum ahijunu⁴⁰ gike-ti-lü=be
 living   smell-VBLZ-PNCT=EP IDEO annatoo smell-VBLZ-PNCT=EP
 '"A living person is giving off a smell, annatto is giving off a smell"'
 '"Uma pessoa viva está exalando cheiro, urucum está exalando cheiro"'

(181) *umüngi hekeha egei ta iheke umüngiha egei nhigatakoi ahijunui*
 umüngi heke=ha ege-i   ta   i-heke umüngi=ha ege-i
 annatto ERG=HA DIST-COP DUR 3-ERG annatto=HA DIST-COP
 i-ng-iga-ta-ko-i   ahijunu-i
 3-OBJ-name-CONT-PL-COP annatto-COP
 'It was annatto he was talking about, it was annatto that they called *ahijunu*' (clarification by *Ájahi*)'
 'Era do urucum que ele estava falando, era urucum o que eles chamavam de *ahijunu*' (esclarecimento de *Ájahi*)

(182) *hum tihühokolo giketilübe*
 hum tihühokolo gike-ti-lü=be
 IDEO living   smell-VBLZ-PNCT=EP
 '"Hum, a living person is giving off a smell"'
 '"Hum, uma pessoa viva está exalando cheiro"'

(183) *ülepe leha*
 üle-pe leha
 LOG-NTM COMPL
 'After this'
 'Depois disso'

(184) *tükangagüko inkgatilü leha ihekeni hugombonga*
 tü-kanga-gü-ko   inkgati-lü   leha i-heke-ni hugombo-nga
 REFL-fish-POSS-PL go.share-PNCT COMPL 3-ERG-PL plaza-all
 'They went to the middle of the plaza to share their fish'⁴¹
 'Eles levaram peixe para o centro da aldeia'

---

⁴⁰The dead smell the living, who give off the scent of annatto (*Bixa orellana*). A red pigment extracted from the seeds of this plant is used not only on ritual occasions, but almost daily, to paint the body and artifacts. In the language of the dead, however, annatto is called *ahijunu*, while in the language of the living it is called *umüngi*. Annatto is life.

(185) *etelüko*

    e-te-lü-ko
    3-go-PNCT-PL

    'They went'
    'Eles foram'

(186) *lepe enhügü leha*

    üle-pe   e-nhügü   leha
    LOG-NTM come-PNCT COMPL

    'Then they came back'
    'Depois voltaram'

(187) *igia unkgu kigeke tuãka kigeke tuãka*

    igia   unkgu kigeke   tuãka   kigeke   tuãka
    like.this little 1.2.go.IMP water.all 1.2.go.IMP water.ALL

    'It did not take long: "Let's take a bath! Let's take a bath!"'
    'Não demorou muito: "Vamos tomar banho! Vamos tomar banho!"'

(188) *ese heke inhakagü igelü ese heke nhakagü igelü tüẽgikini*

    ese   heke inhakagü ige-lü   ese   heke inhakagü ige-lü
    3.PROX ERG soap   carry-PNCT 3.PROX ERG soap   carry-PNCT
    tü-ẽgiki-ni
    REFL-each-PL

    'He took *inhakagü*, he took *inhakagü*, each one for himself'
    'Ele pegou *inhakagü*, ele pegou *inhakagü*, cada um deles para si mesmo'

(189) *inhakagü inügü leha ihekeni*

    inhakagü i-nügü   leha   i-heke-ni
    soap   bring-PNCT COMPL 3-ERG-PL

    'They brought *inhakagü*'
    'Eles trouxeram *inhakagü*'

---

[41] When men return from a collective fishing trip, during the performance of a ritual, they take much of what they have caught to the central plaza of the village, in front of or inside the men's house, to be divided and distributed to all houses and to the men gathered in the center.

(190) etelüko leha
e-te-lü-ko   leha
3-go-PNCT-PL COMPL
'They went'
'Eles foram'

(191) totsonkgilükoinha leha tüenkgügükope tijüinha tsügüha egei ütelüko
t-o-konkgi-lü-ko-inha   leha   tü-enkgü-gü-ko-pe
REFL-DTR-wash-PNCT-PL-DAT COMPL   REFL-bad.smell-POSS-PL-NTM
tijü-inha   tsügü=ha ege-i   ü-te-lü-ko
take.off-DAT UNCR=HA DIST-COP   3-go-PNCT-PL
'They went to wash themselves, to get rid of their bad smell (of fish)'
'Foram para se lavar, para tirar o seu cheiro podre de peixe'

(192) atütüila kukugeko ai
atütü-i-la   kukuge-ko ai
good-COP-PRIV 1.2-PL   IDEO
'"Unfortunately, we're not well!"' (the mother-in-law said)
'"Hélas, nós não (estamos) bem!"' (a sogra disse)

(193) Tisuge[42]
Tisuge
1.3
'"We"'
'"Nós"'

(194) igia agagenaha ketsüjenügü
igia   agage=naha k-etsüje-nügü
like.this AS=EP   1.2-DIE-PNCT
'When we die'
'Quando morremos'

---

[42]The dead mother-in-law alternates between use of first-person plural inclusive free pronoun *kukugeko* (in the preceding line) and the first-person plural exclusive free pronoun *tisuge*. This is an example of the shift of perspective from inclusive to exclusive pronouns (or vice-versa): with *kukuge(ko)* the addressee is included because her body will rot inevitably when she becomes *anha*; with *tisuge*, the speaker excludes the addressee, opposing the dead to the living.

(195) ülepe inhalüma jahetüha kukenkgügü etijüi

üle-pe   inhalü-ma jahe=tü=ha   kuk-enkgü-gü
LOG-NTM NEG-DUB quickly=UNCR=HA 1.2-smell-POSS

et-ijü-i
DTR-remove-PNCT-COP

'Our bad smell does not come out soon'
'Nosso mal cheiro não sai logo'

(196) itsatüe papa hõhõ ugikegü

i-ta[43]-tüe   papa hõhõ u-gike-gü
3-smell-IMP.PL ITJ   EMPH 1-smell-POSS

'"So, smell me!"'
'"Então, cheire-me!"'

(197) igia tühigüsi inatati

igia   tü-hi-gü-isi   inata-ati
like.this REFL-grandson.POSS-mother noose-ILL

'Like this, (she extended her hand) to the nose of the grandchildren's mother (her daughter-in-law)'
'Desse jeito, (levou a mão) ao nariz da mãe dos netos (sua nora)'

(198) igia ige tüilü iheke

igia   ige   tüi-lü   i-heke
like.this PROX do-PNCT 3-ERG

'Like this, she did it'
'Desse jeito ela fez'

(199) tühüseki isikegü

tühüseki i-gike-gü[44]
fetid   3-smell-POSS

'Quite stinky, her smell'
'Bastante fétido, o cheiro dela'

---

[43]The verbal root *ta* means all kind of perceptions through the senses, except for vision.
[44]After the high front vowel, at morphemic boundaries, the consonant /g/ is realized as [s] (Franchetto 1995).

(200)　*etelüko kigekeha kigekeha*

    e-te-lü-ko　　　kigeke=ha kigeke=ha
    3-go-PNCT-PL let.go=HA let.go=HA

    'They went away, "Let's go! Let's go!"'
    'Elas foram, "Vamos! Vamos!'

(201)　*üle hata tülimo ugutega hõhõ iheke*

    üle　hata　tü-limo　　　ugu-te-ga　　　hõhõ　i-heke
    LOG when REFL-children flat.bread[45]-VBLZ-DUR EMPH 3-ERG

    'Meanwhile she was making cassava flat bread for her own children'
    'Enquanto isso, ela estava fazendo beiju para os seus filhos'

(202)　*ikuguko ẽgiki tatute tülimo ugutelü iheke*[46]

    iku-gu-ko　　　　ẽgiki tatute tü-limo　　　ugu-te-lü　　　　i-heke
    3.beverage-POSS each all　　REFL-children flat.bread-VBLZ-PNCT 3-ERG

    'She made beiju for the cassava beverage of each of her own chidren'
    'Ela fez beiju para a bebida de mandioca de cada um dos seus filhos'

(203)　*üle onhati leha kanga hutita iheke ese oku uguponga ese oku uguponga tülimo ẽgiki*[47]

    üle　onhati　　　leha　　kanga huti-ta　　i-heke　　ese　　　oku　　ugupo-nga
    LOG inside.ILL COMPL fish　　take-DUR 3-ERG　　3.PROX drink on-ALL

    ese　　　oku　　ugupo-nga　　tü-limo　　　ẽgiki
    3.PROX drink on-ALL　　　REFL-children each

    'Inside this (cassava flat bread), she was putting the fish, one by one, and (she was putting beiju) on top of the beverage of one, on top of the beverage of another, (for) each one of her own children'
    'Ela colocou os peixes dentro do beiju, um por um, (e colocou beiju) sobre a bebida deste, sobre a bebida daquele, (para) cada um dos seus filhos'

(204)　*lepene tü hüle ütelüko*

    lepene=tü　hüle　ü-te-lü-ko
    then=UNCR CNTR 3-go-PNCT-PL

    'Then, however, they went'
    'Depois disso, contudo, elas foram'

---

[45] *Ugu* refers to a specific food, the cassava flat bread, called "beiju" in Brazilian Portuguese.

[46] *Iku* refers to a beverage made with thin, dried cassava flatbread mixed with water.

[47] The root *huti* means 'take one out of a set'.

(205) *tülimo kangagü hutita letü iheke*
  tü-limo   kanga-gü huti-ta   leha=tü   i-heke
  REFL-children fish-POSS take-DUR COMPL=UNCR 3-ERG
  'She was taking the fish of her own children, one by one'
  'Ela foi tirando os peixes dos seus filhos, um por um'

(206) *ese kangagü ese kangagü ese kangagü*
  ese   kanga-gü ese   kanga-gü ese   kanga-gü
  3.PROX fish-POSS 3.PROX fish-POSS 3.PROX fish-POSS
  'The fish of this one, the fish of this one, the fish of this one'
  'O peixe desse, o peixe desse, o peixe desse'

(207) *inkgatingalü letüha iheke egena*
  inkgati-nga-lü   üle=tü=ha   i-heke egena
  3.share-HAB-PNCT LOG=UNCR=HA 3-ERG there.all
  'In this way, she used to share (food) there (in the middle of the village)'
  'Ela sempre compartilhava (alimentos) para lá (no meio da aldeia)'

(208) *tühigüsi kangagüingoha egei*
  tü-higü-isi   kanga-gü-ingo=ha ege-i
  REFL-grandson-mother fish-POSS-FUT=HA DIST-COP
  'That will be the fish of the mother of her (the mother-in-law's) own grandchildren'
  'Aquilo será o peixe da mãe dos seus (da sogra) netos'

(209) *nhigelüingoha nhingütelüingoha ina*
  i-ng-ige-lü-ingo=ha   i-ng-ingüte-lü-ingo=ha   ina
  3-OBJ-take-PNCT-FUT=HA 3-OBJ-go.down-PNCT-FUT=HA here.ALL
  'That she (daughter-in-law) will take, that she will bring down here'
  'Que ela (nora) levará, que ela trará aqui em baixo'

(210) *kigekeha nügü iheke*
  kigeke=ha nügü i-heke
  let.go=HA say 3-ERG
  '"Let's go!" she (the mother-in-law) said'
  '"Vamos!", ela (a sogra) disse'

(211) *opü atsange elimo otomoko einhümingo opü*

      opü atsange e-limo   oto-mo-ko   ei-nhümingo opü
      ITJ INT   2-children master-COLL-PL be-PNCT.FUT ITJ

      '"Pay attention! The parents of your children will stay like this"'
      '"Preste atenção! Os pais dos seus filhos vão ficar assim"'

(212) *lepe leha etelüko leha*

      üle-pe   leha   e-te-lü-ko   leha
      LOG-NTM COMPL 3-go-PNCT-PL COMPL

      'Then, they went away'
      'Então, elas foram'

(213) *etelüko letü*

      e-te-lü-ko   leha=tü
      3-go-PNCT-PL COMPL=UNCR

      'They went away'
      'Elas foram'

(214) *tüimapüani itsapügü itahiale leha*

      tü-ima-püa-ni   i-tapü-gü   itahi-ale   leha
      REFL-path-NTM-PL 3-foot-POSS delete-SIM COMPL

      'Along their former way (of coming), erasing their footprints'
      'Por aquele que fora o seu caminho [de vinda], apagando as suas pegadas'

(215) *tanginhü ẽgipügati*[48]

      tanginhü   ẽgipügati
      main.path on.top.head

      'On top of the head of the main path'
      'No topo da cabeça do caminho principal'

(216) *aibeha ina ama humbugakainjü*

      aibe=ha ina   ama   humbugakaiN-jü
      CON=HA here path be.head.down-PNCT

      'Here, the path turns upside down'
      'Aqui o caminho fica de cabeça para baixo'

---

[48] 'On top of the head of the main path' means: 'Just at the end of the main path'.

(217) *osiha inaha eitsüe*

    osi=ha   ina=ha e-i-tsüe
    all.right=HA her=HA 2-be-IMP.PL

    '"All right, stay here!"' (the mother-in-law said to her daughter-in-law)
    '"Certo, fique aqui!"' (a sogra disse para a nora)

(218) *tütüki letüha inginügü iheke inatsüha ina leha kungongoguhonga*

    tütüki üle=tü=ha   ingi-nügü i-heke ina=tsü=ha   ina
    slowly LOG=UNCR=HA 3.bring-PNCT 3-ERG here=UNCR=HA here
    leha   ku-ngongo-gu-ho-nga
    1.2-earth-POSS-LOC-ALL

    'Very slowly, she was bringing her here on our land'
    'Bem devagar, ela a trazia aqui na nossa terra'

(219) *aiha*

    aiha
    done

    'Done'
    'Feito'

(220) *egetüeha egetüeha*

    ege-tüe=ha   ege-tüe=ha
    can.go-IMP.PL=HA can.go-IMP.PL=HA

    '"You can go, you can go!"' (the mother-in-law said to her daughter-in-law)
    '"Você pode ir, pode ir!"' (a sogra disse para a nora)

(221) *kegetimükeĩtó atsange kegetimükeĩtó atsange*

    keg-et-imükeĩ-tó   atsange keg-et-imükeĩ-tó   atsange
    PROH-DTR-turn.face-PROH INT   PROH-DTR-turn.face-PROH INT

    '"Do not turn your face back, do not turn your face back!"'
    '"Não vire o rosto para trás, não vire o rosto para trás!"'

(222) *eitsamini geleha*

    e-i-tsa-mini   gele=ha
    2-be-DUR-PURP.PL still=HA

    '"For you to stay alive"'
    '"Para você permanecer viva"'

(223) *jatsitsü üngelei atsütaka atehe egei uitigi sinügü üngelei*

jatsitsü üngele-i atsütaka atehe ege-i   u-itigi is-i-nügü
poor   3.   LOG-COP EP because DIST-COP 1-FIN 3-come-PNCT
üngele-i
3.LOG-COP

'"Poor thing! Because she is the only one who could come and get me, only she" (the woman, the daughter-in-law, was saying to herself)'
'"Coitada! Porque só ela é quem poderia vir me buscar, só ela" (a mulher, a nora) falava para si mesma'

(224) *luale utimükeĩtai*

luale ut-imükeiN-tai
sorry 1.DTR-turn.face-FUT.IM

'"Sorry! I will turn my face back"'
'"Desculpe! Eu vou virar meu rosto para trás"'

(225) *igiagage tetimükei uãhhhh etinhapehikilü*[49]

igia=agage   t-et-imükeiN.   uãhhhh et-inhapehiki-lü
like.this=same PTCP-DTR-face.turn.PTCP ITJ   3.DTR-wave.hand-PNCT

'When she (daugther-in-law) turned her face back, *uãhhhh*, the mother-in-law waved her open hand'
'Quando ela (a nora) olhou para trás, *uãhhhh*, a sogra acenou (para ela) com a mão aberta'

(226) *kegetimükeĩtó ukita titakegei*

keg-et-imükeiN-to   u-ki-ta   ti=taka=ege-i
PROH-DTR-turn.face-PROH 1-say-DUR CR=EP-DIST-COP

'"Don't turn your face back! I really meant it" (the mother-in-law said)'
'"Não vire seu rosto para trás! Eu eastava falando a verdade mesmo" (a sogra disse)'

---

[49] *Etinhapehikilü* means 'with the open hand'; with this gesture, the mother-in-law communicates to her daughter-in-law that she (the daughter-in-law) will die in five days time, after not many days, soon.

(227) *isünkgülü aküngiduingo ale hegeĩ*[50]
   is-ünkgü-lü aküngiN-tu-ingo ale=ha ege-i
   3.sleep-PNCT quantity-NMLZ-FUT ?=HA DIST-COP
   'This will be the number (of days) she was going to sleep'
   'Este é o número (de dias) que ela iria dormir'

(228) *ülepeha ahütüha elimo uünko etsote elimo uünko itajotelüingola ehekeni*
   üle-pe=ha ahütü=ha e-limo uüN-ko e-tsote e-limo
   LOG-NTM=HA NEG=HA 2-children father-PL come-when 2-children
   uüN-ko itajote-lü-ingo-la e-heke-ni
   father-PL swear-PNCT-FUT-PRIV 2-ERG-PL
   '"Later, when the father of your children comes, you can not swear at him" (the mother-in-law said)'
   '"Depois, quando o pai dos seus filhos vier, não poderá xingá-lo" (a sogra disse)'

(229) *itaginkgügikümingola nügü hõhõ i-heke*
   itagi-nkgügi-kü-mingo-la nügü hõhõ iheke
   speech-hard-?-PNCT.FUT-PRIV PNCT EMPH 3-ERG
   '"Without you talking harshly," she (the mother-in-law) said to her'
   '"Sem falar duro", (a sogra) disse a ela'

(230) *üngele akatsange ekise tengalü heke hokugeũ hokugeũ hokugeũ itigiha*
   üngele akatsange ekise te-nga-lü heke hokugeũ hokugeũ
   3.LOG INT 3.DIST go-HAB-PNCT ERG pauraque pauraque
   hokugeũ itigi=ha
   pauraque 3.FIN=HA
   '"It is he who always goes seeking (and saying): hokugeũ[51], hokugeũ, hokugeũ"'
   '"É ele mesmo que sempre anda buscando (dizendo): "hokugeũ, hokugeũ, hokugeũ"'

---

[50] *Ájahi*, the story-teller, showed her open hand to mean the number five: the daughter-in-law, the living one, will die in a few days: her destiny is sealed.
[51] *Anha* (the dead) may return to the living, announcing himself, behind the houses, as a common pauraque bird (*Nyctidromus albicollis*). It has a brownish and greyish plumage, and its singing sounds like a piercing scream, and is repeated in regular intervals for hours after dusk. *hokugeũ*, his name in Kuikuro, is an onomatopoeic noun; this is an ominous sign.

(231) aitüha isinügü kohotsi

ai=tü=ha   is-i-nügü   kohotsi
então=UNCR=HA 3-come-PNCT late.afternoon

'So, she (the living daugther-in-law) came (to the village) in the late afternoon'
'Então, ela (a viva) chegou (na aldeia) no final da tarde'

(232) ingitühügüko atai leha kohotsi ko ko hokugeũ

ingi-tühügü-ko atai   leha   kohotsi   ko ko hokugeũ
3.bring-PRF-PL when COMPL late.afternoon ko ko pauraque

'When it had already been brought, in the late afternoon, pauraque (sang) "ko ko"'
'Quando ela já tinha sido trazida, no final da tarde, bacurau (cantou) "ko ko"'

(233) eteke tingibataha uheke ehitsü anügü

e-te-ke   t-ingiN=hata=ha   u-heke e-hi-tsü   a-nügü
2-go-IMP PTCP-see.PTCP=HA 1-ERG   2-esposa-POSS be-PNCT

'"Go away! I've already seen how your wife is" (the living woman said)'
'"Vá embora! Eu já vi como é a sua esposa'

(234) heinongombe ihugu ehitsü heinongombe nhangatügü ehitsü

heinongombe i-hu-gu   e-hi-tsü   heinongombe inh-angatü-gü
with.half   3-ass-POSS 2-wife-POSS with.half   3-breast-POSS
e-hi-tsü
2-wife-POSS

'"Your wife (has) half an ass (one buttock), your wife has half (one) breast"'
'"A sua esposa (tem) meia (uma) nádega, sua esposa (tem) meia (uma) teta"'

(235) *mbüu itsuhünkginügü*[52] *leha etelü leha*

  mbüu itsu-hüN-ki-nügü leha e-te-lü leha
  IDEO sound-emit-VBLZ-PNCT COMPL 3-go-PNCT COMPL

  '*mbüu*, he stopped making the sound (of a pauraque) and went away'
  '*mbüu*, ele parou de emitir som (como bacurau) e foi embora'

(236) *lepetü tüti ilüinha leha*

  üle-pe-tü tüti i-lü-inha leha
  LOG-NTM-UNCR REFL.MOTHER fight-PNCT-DAT COMPL

  'Shortly after, he (the dead husband) (arrived) to fight with his own mother'
  'Logo depois, ele (o morto) (chegou) para brigar com a sua própria mãe'

(237) *ehigüsi ingitühügü itsagü nika uãke*[53] *eheke egei*

  e-hi-gü-isi ingi-tühügü i-tsagü nika uãke e-heke
  2-grandson-POSS-mother bring-PRF 3.be-DUR EP time.ago 2-ERG
  ege-i
  DIST-COP

  '"Did you really bring the mother of your grandchildren?" (the dead man said)'
  '"Você trouxe mesmo a mãe dos seus netos?" (o morto disse)'

(238) *uhupüngekela*[54] *hüle egei uãke tisitsagü*

  uhu-püngekela hüle ege-i uãke tis-i-tsagü
  know-? ADV DIST-COP time.ago 1.3-be-DUR

  '"We had realized this (the coming of the living woman)"'
  '"Nós tínhamos percebido isso (a vinda da mulher viva)"'

---

[52] *Mbüu* is an ideophone, whose meaning is a sudden and abrupt interruption of some event or action. The verbal stem *itsu-hüN-ki-* is formed by the roots *itsu* (sound vocalized by non-humans and some musical instruments), and *hüN* 'emit', and by the verbalizer *ki* 'take off, stop'.

[53] *Uãke*, in this line and in the following ones, is an adverb with temporal and epistemic values: it determines the interpretation of the event/action as having occurred before the speech time (past tense), and has an epistemic value of strong authority.

[54] We could not segment what follows the root *uhu*.

(239) tütomima uãke ehigüsi itigi etepügü tütomi
 tü-tomi=ma uãke e-hi-gü-isi itigi e-te-pügü tü-tomi
 Q-PURP=DUB time.ago 2-grandson-POSS-mother 3.FIN 2-go-PRF Q-PURP
 '"Why did you go to get the mother of your grandchildren? Why?"'
 '"Por que você foi buscar a mãe de seus netos? Por quê?"'

(240) ehinhão ingitahüngü ekuniküle uãke eheke nügü iheke
 e-hi-nhão ingi-ta-hüngü eku=niküle uãke e-heke nügü i-heke
 2-grandson-COLL see-DUR-NEG real-EP time.ago 2-ERG PNCT 3-ERG
 '"Do not you look after your grandchildren?" he said'
 '"Você não pensa nos seus netos?", ele disse'

(241) ehinhão inkgukitai atainipa hõhõ ehigüsi heke
 e-hi-nhão inkguki-tai atai=nipa hõhõ e-hi-gü-isi
 2-grandson-COLL raise-FUT.IM ?=EP EMPH 2-grandson-POSS-MOTHER
 heke
 ERG
 '"Let the mother of your grandchildren raise them!"'
 '"Deixe a mãe dos seus netos criá-los!"'

(242) utelüingo akatsige itigi nügü leha iheke
 u-te-lü-ingo akatsige itigi nügü leha i-heke
 1-go-PNCT-FUT INT 3.FIN PNCT COMPL 3-ERG
 '"I will really go to look for her," he said to her'
 '"Eu mesmo irei buscá-la" ele disse a ela'

(243) tüti ilü leha iheke
 tüti i-lü leha i-heke
 REFL.mother fight-PNCT COMPL 3-ERG
 'He fought with his own mother'
 'Ele brigou com a sua própria mãe'

(244) ülepe leha isiko enhügü gehale
 üle-pe leha isi-ko e-nhügü gehale
 LOG-NTM COMPL 3.mother-PL come-PNCT again
 'After this, their mother (deceased) came again (to the village of the daughter-in-law)'
 'Depois disso, a mãe deles voltou de novo (à aldeia da nora)'

(245) *ülepe ihatigi ngikahonga*
üle-pe   iha-tigi ngikaho-nga
LOG-NTM tell-FIN back.house-ALL
'To tell her behind the house'
'Para contar (a ela) atrás da casa'

(246) *ukita heke ande akatsange uetsagü nügü iheke ande akatsange uetsagü nügü iheke*
u-ki-ta   heke ande akatsange u-e-tsagü   nügü i-heke   ande
1-say-DUR ERG here INT   1-come-DUR PNCT 3-ERG   here
akatsange uetsagü   nügü iheke
INT   1-come-DUR PNCT 3-ERG
'"I'm saying that I really came here" she said to her (the daughter-in-law) "I came here" she said to her'
'"Estou dizendo que eu vim mesmo aqui", ela disse para ela (para a nora), "eu vim mesmo aqui", ela disse para ela'

(247) *tütomima elimo uünko itaginkgugita ehekeni*
tü-tomi=ma e-limo   uüN-ko   itaginkgugi-ta e-heke-ni
Q-PURP=DUB 2-children father-PL speak.hard-DUR 2-ERG-PL
'"Why were you speaking harshly to the father of your children?"'
'"Por que você falou duro para o pai dos seus filhos?"'

(248) *uita takege ihekeni leha uitagü eigepügüko hinhe*
u-i-ta   takege i-heke-ni leha u-i-tagü   e-ige-pügü-ko=hinhe
1-fight-DUR EP   3-ERG-PL COMPL 2-fight-DUR 2-take-PRF-PL=NPURP
'"They are fighting (with me), fighting (with me), because I took you (to the village of dead)"'
'"Eles estão brigando comigo, brigando, por que eu levei você (para a aldeia dos mortos)"'

(249) *isakisüpeko ihataleha egea leha ihata leha iheke*
is-aki-sü-pe-ko   iha-ta=leha   egea   leha iha-ta leha
3-word-POSS-NTM-PL tell-DUR=COMPL like.this COMPL tell-DUR COMPL
i-heke
3-ERG
'She was reporting their words, she was telling in this way'
'Ela estava relatando as palavras deles, contando assim'

(250) *ukipügüa leha ihata leha iheke*
  u-ki-pügü-a   leha   iha-ta   leha   i-heke
  2-say-PRF-like.this COMPL tell-DUR COMPL 3-ERG

  'The way I said it, she was telling (to the daughter-in-law)'
  'Do jeito que eu falei, ela estava contando (para a nora)'

(251) *tumukugu akisüpe ihata leha iheke*
  tu-muku-gu   aki-sü-pe   iha-ta   leha   i-heke
  REFL--son-POSS word-POSS-NTM tell-DUR COMPL 3-ERG

  'She was reporting the words of her son'
  'Ela estava relatando as palavras do filho'

(252) *ami atsange isitote ketitaginkgugito*
  ami   atsange is-i-tote   ket-itaginkgugi-tó
  other.day INT   3-come-when PROH-speak.hard-PROH

  '"The next time he comes, do not talk harshly with him!"'
  '"Da próxima vez que ele vier, não fale duro com ele!"'

(253) *ami ami akatsange eitigini leha isinümingo tükotui tükotui*
  ami   ami   akatsange e-itigi-ni leha   is-i-nümi-ingo
  other.day other.day INT   2-FIN-PL COMPL 3-come-PNCT-FUT
  tü-kotu-i   tü-kotu-i
  REFL-angry-COP REFL-angry-COP

  '"Next time, next time, he will come get you angry, angry"'
  '"Na próxima vez, na próxima vez, ele virá buscar você com raiva, com raiva"'

(254) *ehe lepei igei igei isünkgülü hata isünkgülü hata*
  ehe   üle-pe-i   ige-i   ige-i   is-ünkgü-lü   hata   is-ünkgü-lü
  AFF LOG-NTM-COP PROX-COP PROX-COP 3-sleep-PNCT when 3-sleep-PNCT
  hata
  when

  'Yes, then, she (the living woman) slept like this, she slept like this'[55]
  'Sim, então, ela (a viva) dormiu assim, dormiu assim'

---

[55] *Igei* ('it is this'): Ájahi is showing her open hand to mean five days (or nights).

(255)   teti

         t-e-ti
         PTCP-come-PTCP

         '(The dead husband) came'
         '(O esposo morto) veio'

(256)   kü kü hokugeũ etekebeha tüki nigei enhalü igei tüki nigei enhalü

         kü   kü   hokugeũ   e-te-ke=be=ha   tü-ki   nile-ige-i
         ONTP ONTP pauraque 2-go-IMP=EP=HA Q-INS EP-PROX-COP
         e-nha-lü   igei   tü-ki nige-i   e-nha-lü
         arrive-HAB-PNCT PROX-COP Q-INS EP-PROX-COP arrive-HAB-PNCT

         'The pauraque *kü kü* (sang). "Go away! Why do you always come? Why do you always come?" (the living woman said)'
         'O bacurau *kü kü* (cantou). "Vá embora! Por que você sempre vem? Por que você sempre vem?" (a esposa viva disse)'

(257)   tüki

         tü-ki
         Q-INS

         '"Why?"'
         '"Por quê?"'

(258)   ehitsütsapa itinhündeta heinongo nhangatügü

         e-hi-tsü=tsapa itinhüN-te-ta   heino-ngo i-ngangatü-gü
         2-wife-POSS=E lay.down-VBLZ-DUR half-NMLZ 3-breast-POSS

         '"Go to bed with your wife who only has one tit!"'
         '"Vá lá deitar com a sua esposa que só tem uma teta!"'

(259)   heinongo ihugu

         heino-ngo i-hu-gu
         half-NMLZ 3-buttock-POSS

         '"(And) just one buttock"'
         '"(E) só uma nádega"'

(260) tüendi tsürürü gitsitoho⁵⁶ atati uẽtigi leha

tü-eN-ti   tsürürü gitsi-toho   atati uẽ-tigi   leha
PTCP-enter-PTCP IDEO   urinate-INSNR ILL   wait-FIN COMPL

'He (the dead) entered: *tsürürü!* the place where people urinate, to wait'
'Ele (o morto) entrou *tsürürü!* no lugar onde se urina, para esperar'

(261) lepe leha itsagü leha

üle-pe   leha   i-tsagü leha
LOG-NTM COMPL 3-ERG   COMPL

'Then, he stayed (there)'
'Aí, ele ficou (lá)'

(262) koko bela leha kahugutilü leha koko tsitsi leha

koko=bela leha   k-ahuguti-lü   leha   koko tsitsi leha
night=EP COMPL 1.2-get.dark-PNCT COMPL night DIM COMPL

'Already at dusk, in the early evening'
'Já de noite, anoiteceu, no começo da noite'

(263) tütikaĩsitü gitsitoho atati tügitsilüinha

tü-tikaiN-si=tü   gitsi-toho   atati tü-gitsi-lü-inha
PTCP-get.up-PTCP=UNCR urinate-INSNMLZ ILL REFL-urinate-PNCT-DAT

'Having got up, to go to the place to urinate '
'Tendo ela se levantado, para ir ao local de urinar'

(264) isitsilü hata tük titsimbe eke atati leha inhügü

i-gitsi-lü   hata   tük   t-itsi=mbe   eke   atati leha
3-urinate-PNCT when   IDEO PTCP-bite.PTCP=EP   snake ILL   COMPL
i-nhügü
be-PNCT

'While she was urinating, *tük!* he had turned into a snake and he bit her'
'Enquanto ela estava urinando, *tük!* transformado em cobra ele a mordeu'

---

⁵⁶ *Gitsi-toho*, 'made for urinating': in the old days, there were bits of bamboo inside the house, into which people urinated. The dead husband has already turned into a snake and hides in the old urinal.

(265) *eke tük ige kaenga itsilü iheke*

    eke   tük   ige   kae-nga itsi-lü   i-heke
    snake IDEO PROX LOC-ALL 3.bite-PNCT 3-ERG

    'As a snake, he bit her here' (*Ájahi* shows the place)
    'Como cobra, ele a mordeu aqui' (*Ájahi* mostra o local)

(266) *hum pok pok pok*[57] *aletüha etelü leha*

    hum pok pok pok ale=tü=ha   e-te-lü   leha
    IDEO IDEO IDEO IDEO SIM=UNCR=HA 3-go-PNCT COMPL

    '"Hum," pok pok pok, she screamed and convulsed'
    '"*Hum*", *pok pok pok*, ela gritou e ficou se debatendo'

(267) *pok pok pok pok tük isotütitagü leha tütükibeletü apüngü leha apüngü*

    pok pok pok pok tük is-otüti-tagü   leha   tütüki=bele=tü
    IDEO IDEO IDEO IDEO IDEO 3-convulse-DUR COMPL slowly=EP=UNCR
    apüngü   leha   apüngü
    3.die.PNCT COMPL 3.die.PNCT

    'She was convulsing, and she died, she died slowly'
    'Ficou tendo convulsões, aos poucos foi morrendo'

(268) *itigi hegei inhotelü itigi*

    i-tigi=ha ege-i   i-nho   te-lü   itigi
    3-FIN=HA DIST-COP 3-husband go-PNCT 3.FIN

    'The husband went to get her'
    'O esposo foi buscá-la'

(269) *aiha*[58]

    aiha
    done

    'Ready'
    'Pronto'

---

[57] The ideophones transcribed as *hum* and as *pok* (repeated, iterative) is the cry of the woman and her spasms, respectively.

[58] The last four lines contain the formulas that every good storyteller must use to close her narrative: *áiha* ('ready/done'); *upügüha egei* ('that was the last/the end'); *uitsojigü*, an untranslatable word that the storytellers say use to frighten away sleep, since the listener would be in a state of sleep/dreaming, from which he must awaken.

(270) ai akatsange
 ai   akatsange
 ready INT
 'Truly ready'
 'Pronto mesmo'

(271) upügü hegei
 upügü=ha ege-i
 last=HA DIST-COP
 'That was the end'
 'Aquilo foi o final'

(272) uitsojigü nika kitse
 uitsojigü nika ki-tse
 uitsojigü EP   say-IMP
 'Say: *uitsojigü!*'
 'Diga: *uitsojigü!*'

Acknowledgments

Our first debt is to the Kuikuro for their commitment, generosity and longstanding hospitality. The following Brazilian institutions have been a fundamental support for conducting research among the Kuikuro since 1976: Fundação Nacional de Apoio ao Índio (FUNAI), Conselho Nacional de Desenvolvimento Científico e Tecnológico (CNPq), Museu Nacional (Universidade Federal do Rio de Janeiro). The DoBeS Program financed the Project for the Documentation of the Upper Xingu Carib Language or Kuikuro from 2001 to 2005. We would also like to thank Gustavo Godoy for his technical expertise and suggestions, to Kristine Stenzel for her many and wise revisions, and to Luiz Costa for the English translation of the Introduction.

Non-standard abbreviations

1.2	1st person plural inclusive	IMP.CTP.PL	plural centripetal imperative
1.3	1st person plural exclusive	IMP.CTF	centrifugal imperative
3.DIST	3rd person distal	IMP.CTF.PL	plural centrifugal imperative
3.PROX	3rd person proximal		
AFF	affirmative		
ANMLZ	agent nominalizer	INE	inessive
AVD	avoidance	INEL	inelative
CF	counterfactual	INSNMLZ	instrumental nominalizer
CNTR	contrastive		
CON	connective	ITJ	interjection
CONC	concessive	INT	intensifier
CR	certainty	LOG	logophoric
DIM	diminutive	3.LOG	3rd person logophoric
DTR	detransitivizer		
DUB	dubitative	NANMLZ	non-agent nominalizer
EMPH	emphatic		
EP	epistemic	NPURP	negative purposive
FIN	finality	NTM	nominal tense marker
FUT.IM	imminent future		
HA	ha particle	O	object
HAB	habitual	ONTP	onomatopoeia
HORT	hortative	PNCT	punctual
HORT.PL	plural hortative	PRIV	privative
ILL	illative	SIM	simultaneous
IMP.PL	imperative plural	UNCR	uncertainty
IMP.CTP	centripetal imperative	VBZL	verbalizer
IDEO	ideophone		

References

Agostinho, Pedro. 1974. *Kwarìp: Mito e ritual no Alto Xingu*. São Paulo: EDUSP.

Basso, Ellen B. 1985. *A musical view of the universe. Kalapalo myth and ritual performances*. Philadelphia: University of Pennsylvania Press.

Carneiro, Robert. 1977. The afterworld of the Kuikuru Indians. In Ronald K. Wetherington (ed.), *Colloquia in anthropology*, vol. 1, 3–15. Dallas: Fort Burgwin Research Center.

dos Santos, Gélsama M. F. 2007. *Morfologia Kuikuro: Gerando nomes e verbos.* Rio de Janeiro: UFRJ thesis.

Fausto, Carlos, Bruna Franchetto & Michael J. Heckenberger. 2008. Language, ritual and historical reconstruction: towards a linguistic, ethnographical and archaeological account of Upper Xingu society. In David K. Harrison, David S. Rood & Aryenne Dwyer (eds.), *Lessons from documented endangered languages,* 129–158. Amsterdam: John Benjamins Publishing Company (Typological Studies in Language 78).

Franchetto, Bruna. 1986. *Falar Kuikúro: Estudo etnolinguístico de um grupo caribe do Alto Xingu.* Rio de Janeiro: UFRJ thesis.

Franchetto, Bruna. 1995. Processos fonológicos em Kuikúro: Uma visão auto-segmental. In Leo Wetzels (ed.), *Estudos fonológicos das línguas indígenas brasileiras,* 53–84. Rio de Janeiro: Editora UFRJ.

Franchetto, Bruna. 2003. L'autre du même: Parallélisme et grammaire dans l'art verbal des récits kuikuro (caribe du Haut Xingu, Brésil). *Amerindia* 28. Paris: AEA, 213–248.

Franchetto, Bruna. 2010. The ergativity effect in Kuikuro (Southern Carib, Brazil). In Spike Gildea & Francesc Queixalós (eds.), *Ergativity in Amazonia,* 121–158. Philadelphia: John Benjamins Publishing Company, (Typological Studies in Language 89).

Franchetto, Bruna (ed.). 2011. *Alto Xingu: Uma sociedade multilíngue.* Rio de Janeiro: Museu do Índio/FUNAI. http://www.etnolinguistica.org/index/xingu.

Franchetto, Bruna. 2015. Construções de foco e arredores em Kuikuro. *Revista Virtual de Estudos da Linguagem-ReVEL* 10. 246–264.

Franchetto, Bruna & Michael J. Heckenberger (eds.). 2001. *Os povos do Alto Xingu. História e cultura.* Rio de Janeiro: Editora da UFRJ.

Franchetto, Bruna & Mara Santos. 2009. Tempo nominal em Kuikuro (Karib Alto-Xinguano). *Revista Virtual de Estudos da Linguagem-ReVEL.* Edição especial no 3. [www.revel.inf.br], 1–16.

Franchetto, Bruna & Mara Santos. 2010. Cartography of expanded CP in Kuikuro (Southern Carib, Brazil). In José Camacho, Rodrigo Gutiérrez-Bravo & Liliana Sánchez (eds.), *Information structure in indigenous languages of the Americas: Syntactic approaches,* 87–113. Ed. New York: De Gruyter Mouton, 2010, v. 1.

Franchetto, Bruna & Guillaume Thomas. 2016. The nominal temporal marker -pe in Kuikuro. In Thuy Bui & Ivan Rudmila-Rodica (eds.), *Proceedings of the Ninth Conference on the Semantics of Under-Represented Languages in the Americas. University of California, Santa Cruz (May 6-8, 2016).* 25–40. Amherst: GLSA

(Graduate Linguistics Student Association), Department of Linguistics, University of Massachussets.

Kalin, Laura. 2014. The syntax of OVS word order in Hixkaryana. *Natural Language and Linguistic Theory* 32. 1089–1104.

Lima, Suzi O., Bruna Franchetto & Mara Santos. 2013. Count/mass distinction in Kuikuro: On individuation and counting. *Revista Linguistica* 9(1). 55–88. https://revistas.ufrj.br/index.php/rl/article/view/4566.

Meira, Sérgio. 2006. A família linguística Caribe (Karíb). *Revista de Estudos e Pesquisas* 3(1/2). 157–174.

Meira, Sérgio & Bruna Franchetto. 2005. The Southern Cariban languages and the Cariban family. *International Journal of American Linguistics* 71 2(71). 127–192.

Silva, Glauber R. da & Bruna Franchetto. 2011. Prosodic distinctions between the varieties of the Upper-Xingu Carib language: Results of an acoustic analysis. *Amerindia* 35. La structure des langues amazoniennes II, 41–52.

Villas Boas, Orlando & Claudio Villas Boas. 1970. *Xingu: Os índios, seus mitos*. São Paulo: Editora Edibolso.

von den Steinen, Karl. 1894. *Unter den naturvolkern Zentral-Braziliens*. Berlin: Dietrich Reimer.

Chapter 3

Kalapalo

Antonio Guerreiro
University of Campinas, Brazil

Ageu Kalapalo

Jeika Kalapalo

Ugise Kalapalo

1 Introduction

Kalapalo is a dialectal variaton of the Upper Xingu Carib Language. The narrative presented in this chapter is around 12 minutes long and was recorded in 2010, with seventy-year-old *Ageu Kalapalo*. He tells us how a man named *Kamagisa*[1] married a Snake Woman and learned from his father-in-law a suite of songs of the Xinguan mortuary ritual (*egitsü*, broadly known as "Quarup"). When *Kamagisa* decided to move permanently to his wife's village, he performed a ritual for himself and taught the songs to another human singer. The events take place in *Hagagikugu*, an important historical site for the Kalapalo and Nahukua peoples. *Ageu* also explains how these same events are reflected in verses sung in Kamayurá, a Tupi-Guarani language (Tupian), an example of the inter-relatedness of history, narratives and music in the Xinguan multiethnic and multilingual network.

The Kalapalo are a Carib-speaking people who live in the southern region of the Xingu Indigenous Land, in northern Mato Grosso, Brazil. They are a population of over 700 people living in ten villages, but most of them are concentrated in

---

[1]*Ageu* calls him *Kamagisa*, but most people insist the character's correct name would be *Kumagisa*. We have decided to keep *Ageu*'s original pronunciation.

 Antonio Guerreiro, Ageu Kalapalo, Jeika Kalapalo & Ugise Kalapalo. 2017. Kalapalo. In Kristine Stenzel & Bruna Franchetto (eds.), *On this and other worlds: Voices from Amazonia*, 89–138. Berlin: Language Science Press. DOI:10.5281/zenodo.1008777

Aiha (their oldest and biggest village, with more than 270 people) and *Tankgugu*. Alongside the pressures they've been suffering from farming, illegal fishing and logging, as well as from the Brazilian government, the Kalapalo have been able to maintain their lifestyle, with their narratives (*akinha*) playing a very important part. As some say, *akinha* are neither "myths" nor "stories", but actual *history*: they tell about events that made the world the way it is today.

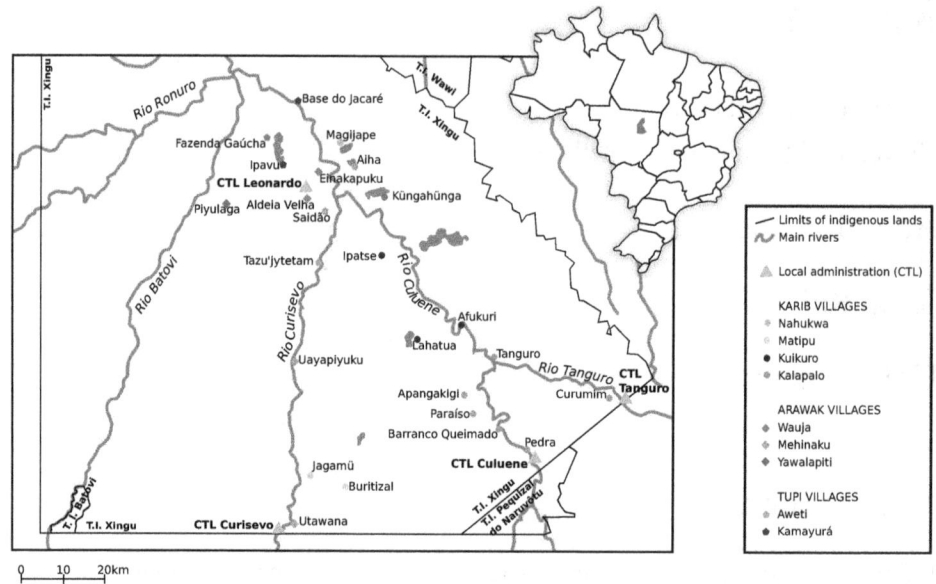

Figure 1: Upper Xingu villages, southern area of the Xingu Indigenous Land

The telling of *akinha* is a complex verbal art, and also a highly valued knowledge. Only a few people can be considered true "masters (or owners) of stories" (*akinha oto*). To be so, one must learn them from good storytellers, and tell them "beautifully" to others. A good story-telling involves several abilities, such as keeping a regular rhythm, making good use of parallelism to call the audience's attention to events or characters (Franchetto 2003), and giving details that make the listener actually "see" what is being told. The combination of these stylistic features may induce the listeners (especially children and younger people) into an almost dreamlike state, from which they must be "awakened" after an *akinha* ends so they do not get sleepy, lazy, or — what would be even worse — they do not keep thinking about the spirit-beings of which they might have heard, since it could cause them to be attacked by these dangerous beings.

Kamagisa's narrative brings together several issues of Xinguan thought: the problem of mortality; the possibility of metamorphosis of humans into spirit-beings, and vice-versa; the details demanded by ritual communication and action; and the multilingual character intrinsic to Xinguan life. Perhaps all these issues could be thought of as versions of an all-encompassing one: the problem of communication (and, thus, of *translation*) that imposes itself on the relations between different kinds of people, such as consanguines and affines, humans and non-humans, the living and the dead, fellow villagers and foreigners, etc.

The narrative was transcribed, translated, and analyzed using ELAN, with the help of *Jeika* and *Ugise Kalapalo*. The narrative is phonetically transcribed in the first line, and morphologically segmented in the second one. The third line presents the glosses, and the last two contain free translations in English and Portuguese. The transcription, morphological segmentation, and most glosses follow the works of Bruna Franchetto (1986; 2002; 2003), Ellen Basso (2012), Mara dos Santos (2007), Mutua Mehinaku (2010), and Aline Varela Rabello (2013). We thank Bruna Franchetto for her continuous help with the Kalapalo language.

Let's now follow *Kamagisa* on his unexpected journey to the world of the spirits.

2 *Kamagisa etsutühügü*

'*Kamagisa* sang for the first time'

'*Kamagisa* cantou pela primeira vez'[2]

(1) *ihaü̃ heke onta*

   i-haü̃   heke on-ta
   3-cousin ERG repudiate-DUR

   'His cousin was repudiating him.'

   'A prima dele o estava rejeitando.'

(2) *indzahatohoi indzahatohoi itsa*

   i-ndzaha-toho-i   i-ndzaha-toho-i   i-tsa
   3-fiancée-INS-COP 3-fiancée-INS-COP to.be-DUR

   'His fiancée, she was his fiancée.'

   'Sua noiva, ela era sua noiva.'

---

[2]Recordings of this story are available from https://zenodo.org/record/997435

(3) ah indisüi ijogu indisü
    ah   0-indi-sü-i   i-jo-gu   0-indi-sü
    EXPL 3-daughter-POSS-COP 3-mother's.brother-POSS 3-daughter-POSS
    'Ah, she was his daughter, his mother's brother's daughter.'
    'Ah, ela era filha dele, filha do irmão de sua mãe.'

(4) Kamagisa haũha ihaũ
    Kamagisa haũ-ha   i-haũ
    Kamagisa cousin-HA³ 3-cousin
    'Kamagisa's own cousin, his cousin.'
    'A própria prima de Kamagisa, sua prima.'

(5) ülepe hale egei
    üle-pe   hale ege-i
    LOG-NTM CNTR DIST-COP
    'Because of that ...'
    'Por causa disso ...'

(6) onta leha iheke tsuẽ ekugu onta iheke
    on-ta   leha i-heke tsuẽ ekugu on-ta   i-heke
    repudiate-DUR COMPL 3-ERG a.lot true repudiate-DUR 3-ERG
    'She was repudiating him, she was truely repudiating him a lot.'
    'Ela o estava rejeitando, ela o estava rejeitando demais.'

(7) ihitsü heke
    i-hitsü heke
    3-wife ERG
    'His wife did it.'
    'Sua esposa o fez.'

---

³Please see Franchetto's introduction to chapter 2 for discussion of the HA particle, found in both Kuikuro and Kalapalo.

(8) *ihaũ hekeha*
 i-haũ   heke-ha
 3-cousin ERG-HA
 'His cousin did so.'
 'Sua prima fez assim.'

(9) *inhalü etengalü embege etengalü inhalü*
 inhalü e-te-nga-lü   embege   e-te-nga-lü   inhalü
 NEG 3-go-HAB-PNCT tentatively 3-go-HAB-PNCT NEG
 'Nothing, in vain he used to go after her; he used to go after her, and nothing.'
 'Nada, ele tentava ir atrás dela em vão; ele tentava ir atrás dela, e nada.'

(10) *onta leha iheke leha*
 on-ta   leha   i-heke leha
 repudiate-DUR COMPL 3-ERG COMPL
 'She would readily repudiate him.'
 'Ela prontamente o rejeitava.'

(11) *üle hinhe leha etijakilü leha*
 üle   hinhe leha   et-ija-ki-lü   leha
 LOG PURP COMPL 3.DTR-hammock's.rope-VBLZ-PNCT COMPL
 'Because of that, he untied the ropes of his hammock.'
 'Por causa disso, ele desamarrou as cordas de sua rede.'

(12) *apokinenügü iheke leha tühitsü apokinenügü*
 apoki-ne-nügü   i-heke leha   tü-hitsü   apoki-ne-nügü
 drop-VBLZ-PNCT 3-ERG COMPL REFL-wife drop-VBLZ-PNCT
 'He left her, he left his own wife.'
 'Ele a deixou, ele deixou sua própria esposa.'

(13) *apokinenügü leha iheke*
 apoki-ne-nügü   leha   i-heke
 drop-VBLZ-PNCT COMPL 3-ERG
 'He soon left her.'
 'Ele logo a deixou.'

(14) *üle ineke hale egei*

üle   ineke hale   ege-i
LOG PURP CNTR DIST-COP

'Because that made him sad ...'

'Porque aquilo o deixou triste ...'

(15) *üle ineke hale egei tingunkgingu ineke Kakakugu heke sijatitselü eke heke beha*

üle   ineke hale   ege-i   t-ingunkgingu ineke Kakakugu heke
LOG PURP CNTR DIST-COP REFL-thought PURP Kakakugu ERG
s-ijati-tse-lü   eke   heke be-ha
3-offer-VBLZ-PNCT snake ERG AUG-HA

'... because that made him sad, because his thoughts made him sad, *Kakakugu* made him an offer, a big snake did so.'

'... porque aquilo o deixou triste, porque seus pensamentos o deixaram triste, *Kakakugu* fez uma oferta a ele, uma grande cobra o fez.'

(16) *eke helei Kakakugui*

eke   h-ele-i   Kakakugu-i
snake HA-3.DIST-COP Kakakugu-COP

'He is a snake, *Kakakugu*.'

'Ele é uma cobra, *Kakakugu*.'

(17) *ahütü kuge hüngü*

ahütü kuge   hüngü
NEG   human NEG

'He is not human.'

'Ele não é humano.'

(18) *itseke beja*

itseke beja
spirit EP

'A spirit, indeed.'

'Um espírito, de fato.'

(19) *itseke*
itseke
spirit
'A spirit.'
'Um espírito.'

(20) *itseke*
itseke
spirit
'A spirit.'
'Um espírito.'

(21) *jatsi jatsi jasu nügü iheke*
jatsi jatsi jasu   nügü i-heke
poor poor pitiful PNCT 3-ERG
'"Poor me, poor me, pitiful me," he [*Kamagisa*] said.'
'"Pobre de mim, pobre de mim, que pena de mim," ele [*Kamagisa*] disse.'

(22) *uonlü nika iheke nügü iheke*
u-on-lü   nika i-heke nügü i-heke
1-repudiate-PNCT EP   3-ERG PNCT 3-ERG
'"Is it true that she rejected me?" he said.'
'"Será verdade que ela me rejeitou?" ele disse.'

(23) *üle hinhe hale egei inhaha sinügü*
üle   hinhe hale ege-i   0-inha-ha s-i-nügü
LOG PURP CNTR DIST-COP 3-to-HA 3-come-PNCT
'Because of that he came to him.'
'Por causa disso ele veio até ele.'

(24) *Kakakugu suũ enügüha*
Kakakugu s-uũ   e-nügü-ha
Kakakugu 3-father come-PNCT-HA
'*Kakakugu*, her [*Kamagisa's* future wife] father, came.'
'*Kakakugu*, o pai dela [da futura esposa de *Kamagisa*], veio.'

(25) suũha tetinhü inha
s-uũ-ha   t-e-ti-nhü   0-inha
3-father-HA REFL-come-PTCP-NANMLZ 3-to
'Her father is the one who came to him.'
'O pai dela é quem veio até ele.'

(26) suũ enügü
s-uũ   e-nügü
3-father come-PNCT
'Her father came.'
'O pai dela veio.'

(27) ülepe
üle-pe
LOG-NTM
'Then ...'
'Então ...'

(28) aiha
aiha
done
'... done.'
'... pronto.'

(29) ingilabe lahale ingila itseke hisuũgü gele ukenübata egei
ingila-be   lahale ingila itseke hisuũ-gü gele uk-enü-bata   ege-i
before-AUG CNTR   before spirit kin-POSS ADV DU-stay-TEMP DIST-COP
'This was a long time ago, when we were still kin to the spirits.'
'Isso foi há muito tempo atrás, quando nós ainda éramos parentes dos espíritos.'

(30) ülepe
üle-pe
LOG-NTM
'Then ...'
'Então ...'

(31) *sinügü*
    s-i-nügü
    3-come-PNCT
    '... he came.'
    '... ele veio.'

(32) *Kamagisa inha etelü*
    Kamagisa inha e-te-lü
    Kamagisa to   3-go-PNCT
    'He went to *Kamagisa*.'
    'Ele foi até *Kamagisa*.'

(33) *ihumita hegei tindisü inha*
    i-humi-ta h-ege-i t-indi-sü inha
    3-send-DUR HA-DIST-COP REFL-daughter-POSS to
    'He was sending him to his daughter.'
    'Ele o estava enviando para sua filha.'

(34) *ẽ tindisü inha*
    ẽ t-indi-sü inha
    AFF REFL-daughter-POSS to
    'Yes, to his daughter.'
    'Sim, para sua filha.'

(35) *ülepe*
    üle-pe
    LOG-NTM
    'Then ...'
    'Então ...'

(36) *aiha*
    aiha
    done
    '... done.'
    '... pronto.'

(37) *igelü leha iheke leha*
 ige-lü   leha   i-heke leha
 take-PNCT COMPL 3-ERG COMPL
 'He soon took him.'
 'Ele logo o levou.'

(38) *Kamagisa hogijü iheke leha*
 Kamagisa hogi-jü   i-heke leha
 Kamagisa find-PNCT 3-ERG COMPL
 'He had already found *Kamagisa*.'
 'Ele já havia encontrado *Kamagisa*.'

(39) *kuge bejetsa atühügü leha*
 kuge   be-jetsa atühügü leha
 human AUG-EV become COMPL
 'He had already become just like a person.'
 'Ele já havia se tornado exatamente como uma pessoa.'

(40) *eke atühügü kugei leha*
 eke   atühügü kuge-i   leha
 snake become human-COP COMPL
 'The snake had already become a person.'
 'A cobra já havia se tornado uma pessoa.'

(41) *hm eingadzu inha etete nügü iheke*
 hm   e-ingadzu inha e-te-te   nügü i-heke
 EXPL 2SG-sister to   2SG-go-IMP PNCT 3-ERG
 'Hm, "Go to your sister," he said.'
 'Hm, "Vá para sua irmã," ele disse.'

(42) *eingadzu inha kete nügü iheke*
 e-ingadzu inha k-e-te   nügü i-heke
 2SG-sister to   DU-go-IMP PNCT 3-ERG
 '"Let's go to your sister," he said.'
 '"Vamos para sua irmã," ele disse.'

(43) *üngele kilüha*
 üngele ki-lü-ha
 3.LOG say-PNCT-HA
 'That one said so.'
 'Aquele é quem disse isso.'

(44) *Kakakugu kilüha*
 Kakakugu ki-lü-ha
 Kakakugu say-PNCT-HA
 '*Kakakugu* said so.'
 '*Kakakugu* disse isso.'

(45) *suũ kilüha*
 s-uũ   ki-lü-ha
 3-father say-PNCT-HA
 'Her father said so.'
 'O pai dela disse isso.'

(46) *ẽhẽ nügü iheke*
 ẽhẽ nügü i-heke
 AFF PNCT 3-ERG
 '"Yes," he answered.'
 '"Sim," ele respondeu.'

(47) *ẽhẽ nügü iheke*
 ẽhẽ nügü iheke
 AFF PNCT 3-ERG
 '"Yes," he answered.'
 '"Sim," ele respondeu.'

(48) *ngukuagi tsügüha inhüngü tadüponhokokinhü igia*
 ngukuagi   tsügüha iN-üngü t-adüponhoko-ki-nhü   igia
 cerrado.palm EP   3-home REFL-small.mound-INS-NANMLZ this.way
 'It seems that his house is a small *cerrado* palm called *ngukuagi*, that stands on a small mound like this.'

'Parece que a casa dele é uma pequena palmeira do cerrado chamada *ngukuagi*, que fica desse jeito em cima de um morrinho.'

(49) *uge uũpe kita ũāke*
 uge uũ-pe ki-ta ũāke
 1 father-NTM say-DUR EV.PST
 'My deceased father used to say:'
 'Meu finado pai costumava dizer:'

(50) *Kakakugu üngü hegei*
 Kakakugu üngü h-ege-i
 Kakakugu home HA-DIST-COP
 '"That's *Kakakugu*'s house."'
 '"Aquela é a casa de *Kakakugu*."'

(51) *inhüngü hegei*
 iN-üngü h-egei-i
 3-house HA-DIST-COP
 'That's his house.'
 'Aquela é a casa dele.'

(52) *inhüngü*
 iN-üngü
 3-house
 'His house.'
 'A casa dele.'

(53) *üle hujati*
 üle huja-ti
 LOG midst-ALL
 'Into the middle of that ...'
 'Para o meio daquilo ...'

(54) *ah etelü leha*
 ah e-te-lü   leha
 EXPL 3-go-PNCT COMPL
 '... ah, he readily went!'
 '... ah, ele foi prontamente!'

(55) *ngukuagi*
 ngukuagi
 cerrado.palm
 'Into the small *cerrado* palm.'
 'Para dentro da pequena palmeira do cerrado.'

(56) *ẽ inhüngü hegei Kakakugu*
 ẽ   iN-üngü h-egei-i   Kakakugu
 AFF 3-home HA-DIST-COP Kakakugu
 'Yes, that's his house, *Kakakugu's* house.'
 'Sim, aquela é a casa dele, a casa de *Kakakugu*.'

(57) *ülepe*
 üle-pe
 LOG-NTM
 'Then ...'
 'Então ...'

(58) *aiha*
 aiha
 done
 '... done'
 '... pronto'

(59) *ah tindisü tuponga leha ijatelü leha iheke*
 ah t-indi-sü   t-upo-nga   leha
 EXPL REFL-daughter-POSS REFL-above-ALL COMPL
 ija-te-lü   leha i-heke
 hammock's.rope-VBLZ-PNCT COMPL 3-ERG
 'Ah, he then tied his hammock just over his daughter's.'
 'Ah, então ele amarrou sua rede logo acima da de sua filha.'

(60) *ijatelü leha*
 ija-te-lü   leha
 hammock's.rope-VBLZ-PNCT COMPL
 'Tied his hammock.'
 'Amarrou sua rede.'

(61) *sangagübe teh ah sangatepügü*
 s-anga-gü-be   teh ah   s-anga-te-pügü
 3-genipapo-POSS-AUG ITJ EXPL 3-genipapo-VBLZ-PFV
 'She had a great *genipapo* painting - wow! - she was painted with *genipapo*.'[4]
 'Ela tinha uma linda pintura de jenipapo - uau! - ela estava pintada com jenipapo.'

(62) *indisüha*
 0-indi-sü-ha
 3-daughter-POSS-HA
 'His daughter was.'
 'A filha dele estava.'

(63) *indisü angatepügü*
 0-indi-sü   anga-te-pügü
 3-daughter-POSS genipapo-VBLZ-PFV
 'His daughter was painted with *genipapo*.'
 'A filha dele estava pintada com jenipapo.'

(64) *ülepe leha*
 üle-pe   leha
 LOG-NTM COMPL
 'Just after that ...'
 'Logo depois disso ...'

---

[4] *Genipapo* is the fruit of the *Genipa americana* tree. The Kalapalo extract from it a clear liquid used for skin painting, as well as for decorating ceramics and wooden benches. After the liquid oxidizes, it turns black, and may stay on the skin for several days. The liquid may be mixed with charcoal soot to make the painting even darker.

(65) *ah ihitsüi leha itsa leha*
    ah i-hitsü leha i-tsa   leha
    EXPL 3-wife COMPL to.be-DUR COMPL
    '... ah, she was already his wife.'
    '... ah, ela já era sua esposa.'

(66) *ihitsüi leha*
    i-hitsü-i   leha
    3-wife-COP COMPL
    'Already his wife.'
    'Já era sua esposa.'

(67) *ihitsüi leha itsa leha*
    i-hitsü-i   leha i-tsa   leha
    3-wife-COP COMPL to.be-DUR COMPL
    'She was already his wife.'
    'Ela já era sua esposa.'

(68) *aiha*
    aiha
    done
    'Done.'
    'Pronto.'

(69) *ingati beja inhalü ikungalü leha iheke leha*
    ingati   beja i-nha-lü   iku-nga-lü   leha i-heke
    lie.together EP   to.be-HAB-PNCT to.have.sex-HAB-PNCT COMPL 3-ERG
    leha
    COMPL
    'He always lay with her in his hammock, and he always had sex with her.'
    'Ele sempre se deitava com ela em sua rede, e ele sempre fazia sexo com ela.'

(70) ikungalü beja iheke leha
      iku-nga-lü   beja i-heke leha
      to.have.sex-HAB-PNCT EP 3-ERG COMPL
      'He always really had sex with her.'
      'Ele realmente sempre fazia sexo com ela.'

(71) ah ngikona tüilü iheke
      ah   ngiko-na t-üi-lü   i-heke
      EXPL thing-EP REFL-make-PNCT 3-ERG
      'Ah, who knows how he did it ...'
      'Ah, quem sabe como ele fazia isso ...'

(72) aiha
      aiha
      done
      'Done.'
      'Pronto.'

(73) sakihata iheke tita gisüki
      s-aki-ha-ta   i-heke tita   gi-sü-ki
      3-word-VBLZ-DUR 3-ERG mortuary.effigy song-POSS-INS
      'He was teaching him ... with songs of mortuary effigies.'
      'Ele o estava ensinando ... com cantos de efígies mortuárias.'

(74) tita gisüki
      tita   gi-sü-ki
      mortuary.effigy song-POSS-INS
      'Songs of mortuary effigies.'
      'Cantos de efígies mortuárias.'

(75) tita gisüki ah sakihata iheke
      tita   gi-sü-ki   ah   s-aki-ha-ta   i-heke
      mortuary.effigy song-POSS-INS EXPL 3-word-VBLZ-DUR 3-ERG
      'With songs of mortuary effigies... ah, he was teaching him.'
      'Com cantos de efígies mortuárias... ah, ele o estava ensinando.'

(76) *Kakakugu heke*
Kakakugu heke
Kakakugu ERG
'*Kakakugu* was.'
'*Kakakugu* estava ensinando.'

(77) *ah tindisü ngiso akihata iheke*
ah t-indi-sü ngiso aki-ha-ta i-heke
EXPL REFL-daughter-POSS husband word-VBLZ-DUR 3-ERG
'Ah, he was teaching his daughter's husband.'
'Ah, ele estava ensinando o marido de sua filha.'

(78) *akihata iheke*
aki-ha-ta i-heke
word-VBLZ-DUR 3-ERG
'He was teaching.'
'Ele estava ensinando.'

(79) *akihata iheke*
aki-ha-ta i-heke
word-VBLZ-DUR 3-ERG
'He was teaching.'
'Ele estava ensinando.'

(80) *etelü hõhõ tüti inha*
e-te-lü hõhõ tü-ti inha
3-go-PNCT EMPH REFL-mother DAT
'He went to visit his mother for a while.'
'Ele foi visitar sua mãe por um tempo.'

(81) *tüti inha hõhõ sinügü Kamagisa enügü*
tü-ti inha hõhõ s-i-nügü Kamagisa e-nügü
REFL-mother DAT EMPH 3-come-PNCT Kamagisa come-PNCT
'*Kamagisa* came to visit his mother for a while.'
'*Kamagisa* veio visitar sua mãe por um tempo.'

(82) tüti inha
   tü-ti   inha
   REFL-mother DAT
   'To his mother.'
   'Até sua mãe.'

(83) ihitsü ike leha
   i-hitsü ike leha
   3-wife with COMPL
   'With his wife.'
   'Com sua esposa.'

(84) ihitsü
   i-hitsü
   3-wife
   'His wife.'
   'Sua esposa.'

(85) tünho akuã leha teta leha
   tü-nho   akuã   leha   te-ta   leha
   REFL-husband shadow COMPL go-DUR COMPL
   'She was walking right behind her husband, like his shadow.'
   'Ela ia andando logo atrás de seu marido, como sua sombra.'

(86) inde giti atani etimbelüko
   inde giti atani et-imbe-lü-ko
   here sun TEMP 3.DTR-arrive-PNCT-PL
   'When the sun was here, they arrived.'
   'Quando o sol estava nessa posição, eles chegaram.'

(87) etimbelüko
   et-imbe-lü-ko
   3.DTR-arrive-PNCT-PL
   'They arrived.'
   'Eles chegaram.'

(88) *totomonaha*
 t-oto-mo-na-ha
 REFL-kin-PL-ALL-HA
 'To his kin.'
 'Nos seus parentes.'

(89) *totomo*
 t-oto-mo
 REFL-kin-PL
 'His kin.'
 'Seus parentes.'

(90) *tetuna beja*
 t-etu-na   beja
 REFL-village-ALL EP
 'To his own village, indeed.'
 'Para sua própria aldeia, de fato.'

(91) *Kamagisa etu leha*
 Kamagisa etu   leha
 Kamagisa village COMPL
 'They were already at *Kamagisa*'s village.'
 'Eles já estavam na aldeia de *Kamagisa*.'

(92) *Kamagisa etuna etimbelüko*
 Kamagisa etu-na   et-imbe-lü-ko
 Kamagisa village-ALL 3.DTR-come-PNCT-PL
 'They arrived at *Kamagisa*'s village.'
 'Eles chegaram na aldeia de *Kamagisa*.'

(93) *atibe Kamagisa enta nügü iheke*
 atibe Kamagisa e-nta   nügü i-heke
 ITJ   Kamagisa come-DUR PNCT 3-ERG
 '"There he comes, *Kamagisa*," they said.'
 '"Lá vem ele, *Kamagisa*," disseram.'

(94) *inhalü ihitsü ingilüi ihametijaõ heke*
 inhalü i-hitsü ingi-lü-i i-hameti-jaõ heke
 NEG 3-wife see-PNCT-COP 3-sister.in.law-PL ERG
 'His wife could not be seen by her sisters-in-law.'
 'Sua esposa não podia ser vista pelas cunhadas dela.'

(95) *inhalü ingilü ihekeni*
 inhalü ingi-lü i-heke-ni
 NEG see-PNCT 3-ERG-PL
 'They didn't see her.'
 'Elas não a viam.'

(96) *uendeha ike eteta*
 uende-ha ike e-te-ta
 there-HA 3.with 3-go-DUR
 'But she was there, she was going with him.'
 'Mas ela estava lá, ela estava andando com ele.'

(97) *ike eteta*
 ike e-te-ta
 3.with 3-go-DUR
 'She was going with him.'
 'Ela estava andando com ele.'

(98) *ihitsü tetaha*
 i-hitsü te-ta-ha
 3-wife go-PNCT-HA
 'His wife was going.'
 'Sua esposa estava andando.'

(99) *ülepe*
 üle-pe
 LOG-NTM
 'Then ...'
 'Então ...'

(100) *etimbelüko*
 et-imbe-lü-ko
 3.DTR-arrive-PNCT-PL
 '... they arrived.'
 '... eles chegaram.'

(101) *ahametigüko akongo aketsugei nügü iheke tingajomo heke*
 a-hameti-gü-ko   ako-ngo   akets=uge-i nügü i-heke t-ingajomo
 2-sister.in.law-POSS-PL with-NMLZ EV=1-COP PNCT 3-ERG REFL-sisters
 heke
 ERG
 '"I'm in the company of your sister-in-law," he said to his sisters.'
 '"Eu estou acompanhado de sua cunhada," ele disse para suas irmãs.'

(102) *ahametigüko akongo aketsugei*
 a-hameti-gü-ko   ako-ngo   akets=uge-i
 2-sister.in.law-POSS-PL with-NMLZ EV=1-COP
 '"I'm in the company of your sister-in-law."'
 '"Eu estou acompanhado de sua cunhada."'

(103) *itaginhitüe tsüha ahametigüko nügü iheke*
 itaginhi-tüe tsüha a-hameti-gü-ko   nügü i-heke
 greet-IMP.PL EP   2-sister.in.law-POSS-PL PNCT 3-ERG
 '"You may greet your sister-in-law," he said.'
 '"Vocês podem cumprimentar sua cunhada," ele disse.'

(104) *ẽ uhitseke geleha*
 ẽ   uhitseke gele-ha
 AFF in.vain ADV-HA
 '"Ok," they said in vain.'
 '"Tudo bem," elas disseram à toa.'

(105) *amago nika nügü ngapa iheke*
 amago nika nügü ngapa i-heke
 2PL   EP   PNCT EP   3-ERG
 '"Are you really here?" they may have said.'
 '"Você está mesmo aí?" talvez elas tenham dito.'

(106) shhh ekei bele itüinjü iheke
shhh eke-i   bele itüin-jü   i-heke
IDEO snake-COP CU   answer-PNCT 3-ERG
'"*Shhh*" - she answered in the snake's language.'
'"*Shhh*" - ela respondeu na língua das cobras.'

(107) üngele hekeha
üngele heke-ha
3.LOG ERG-HA
'That one did so.'
'Ela fez isso.'

(108) ihametigüko heke
i-hameti-gü-ko   heke
3-sister.in.law-POSS-PL ERG
'Their sister-in-law did.'
'A cunhada delas fez.'

(109) *Kakakugu indisü hekeha*
Kakakugu indi-sü   *heke-ha*
Kakakugu daughter-POSS ERG-HA
'*Kakakugu*'s daughter did so.'
'A filha de *Kakakugu* fez isso.'

(110) shhh ah nügü iheke
shhh ah   nügü i-heke
IDEO EXPL PNCT 3-ERG
'"*Shhh*," ah, she said!'
'"*Shhh*," ah, ela disse!'

(111) aiha
aiha
done
'Done.'
'Pronto.'

(112) *ah tihü hakilü hale iheke*
 ah   t-ihü   haki-lü   hale i-heke
 EXPL REFL-body reveal-PNCT CNTR 3-ERG
 'Ah, and then she revealed her body.'
 'Ah, e então ela revelou seu corpo.'

(113) *atsakilü lahale atütüi*
 a-tsaki-lü   lahale atütü-i
 3-appear-PNCT CNTR beautiful-COP
 'She appeared beautiful.'
 'Ela apareceu muito bonita.'

(114) *hm atsakilü leha*
 hm   a-tsaki-lü   leha
 EXPL 3-appear-PNCT COMPL
 'Hm, she appeared.'
 'Hm, ela apareceu.'

(115) *atsakilü leha*
 a-tsaki-lü   leha
 3-appear-PNCT COMPL
 'She appeared.'
 'Ela apareceu.'

(116) *kogetsi*
 kogetsi
 tomorrow
 'The next day ...'
 'No dia seguinte ...'

(117) *etinga inhalüko unditü ukugahipügü*
 etinga   i-nha-lü-ko   unditü   ukugahi-pügü
 lie.on.hammock be-HAB-PNCT-PL long.hair hang.dowards-PFV
 'When they lay down together, her hair was hanging downwards.'
 'Quando eles se deitaram juntos, o cabelo dela estava pendurado em direção ao chão.'

(118) ande leha ihametijaõ heke ingingalü leha
ande leha i-hameti-jaõ heke ingi-nga-lü leha
now COMPL 3-sister.in.law-PL ERG see-HAB-PNCT COMPL
'Now her sisters-in-law could already see her.'
'Agora suas cunhadas já podiam vê-la.'

(119) ihametijaõ
i-hameti-jaõ
3-sister.in.law-PL
'Her sisters-in-law.'
'Suas cunhadas.'

(120) aiha
aiha
done
'Done.'
'Pronto.'

(121) ülepe sinünkgo leha tetuna beha
üle-pe s-i-nü-nkgo leha t-etu-na beha
LOG-NTM 3-come-PNCT-PL COMPL REFL-village-ALL EV
'Then, they came back to their village.'
'Então, eles voltaram para sua aldeia.'

(122) tseta leha ihütisoho heke sakihata
tseta leha i-hüti-soho heke s-aki-ha-ta
there COMPL 3-shame-INS ERG 3-word-VBLZ-DUR
'There, his father-in-law was teaching him.'
'Lá, seu sogro o estava ensinando.'

(123) igeki beha
ige-ki beha
PROX-INS EV
'About this.'
'Sobre isso.'

(124) *tita gisüki*
 tita gi-sü-ki
 mortuary.effigy song-POSS-INS
 'About the songs of mortuary effigies.'
 'Sobre os cantos de efígies mortuárias.'

(125) *tita gisüki*
 tita gisü-ki
 mortuary.effigy song-POSS-INS
 'About the songs of mortuary effigies.'
 'Sobre os cantos de efígies mortuárias.'

(126) *aiha etsuhukilü leha inha leha*
 aiha etsuhuki-lü leha 0-inha leha
 done finish-PNCT COMPL 3-DAT COMPL
 'Done, it was finished for him.'
 'Pronto, estava tudo concluído para ele.'

(127) *hm untsi nügü iheke*
 hm untsi nügü i-heke
 EXPL uterine.nephew PNCT 3-ERG
 '"Hm, nephew," he said.'
 '"Hm, sobrinho," ele disse.'

(128) *etsuke hetsange hõhõ ihakitomi eheke nügü iheke*
 etsu-ke hetsange hõhõ i-haki-tomi e-heke nügü i-heke
 debut-IMP HORT EMPH 3-reveal-PURP 2-ERG PNCT 3-ERG
 '"You may sing for the first time, to reveal your songs," he said.'
 '"Você pode estrear, para revelar seus cantos," ele disse.'

(129) *nügü iheke*
 nügü i-heke
 PNCT 3-ERG
 'He said.'
 'Ele disse.'

(130) *ihütisoho kilü*
 i-hüti-soho   ki-lü
 3-shame-INS say-PNCT
 'His father-in-law said.'
 'Seu sogro disse.'

(131) *Kakakugu kilü beha*
 Kakakugu ki-lü   beha
 Kakakugu say-PNCT EV
 '*Kakakugu* said that.'
 '*Kakakugu* disse isso.'

(132) *etsuke hetsange hõhõ ah ihakitomi eheke nügü iheke*
 etsu-ke   hetsange hõhõ ah   i-haki-tomi   e-heke nügü i-heke
 debut-IMP HORT   EMPH EXPL 3-reveal-PURP 2-ERG PNCT 3-ERG
 '"You may now sing for the first time, ah, to reveal them," he said.'
 '"Você agora pode estrear, ah, para revelá-los," ele disse.'

(133) *ihakitomi nügü iheke*
 i-haki-tomi   nügü i-heke
 3-reveal-PURP PNCT 3-ERG
 '"To reveal them," he said.'
 '"Para revelá-los," ele disse.'

(134) *ah nügü iheke*
 ah   nügü i-heke
 EXPL PNCT 3-ERG
 '"Ah," he said.'
 '"Ah," ele disse.'

(135) *nügü iheke Kamagisa heke*
 nügü i-heke Kamagisa heke
 PNCT 3-ERG Kamagisa ERG
 'He said to *Kamagisa*.'
 'Ele disse para *Kamagisa*.'

(136) *atütüi beja itsalü leha iheke leha*
　　　atütü-i　　　beja　i-tsa-lü　　　 leha　 i-heke leha
　　　beautiful-COP EP　3-hear-PNCT COMPL 3-ERG COMPL
　　　'He had already listened to it really well.'
　　　'Ele já os havia escutado muito bem.'

(137) *itsalü leha atütüui ekugu leha*
　　　i-tsa-lü　　　 leha　 atütü-i　　　 ekugu leha
　　　3-hear-PNCT COMPL beautiful-COP true　COMPL
　　　'He listened to it really well.'
　　　'Ele os havia escutado muito bem.'

(138) *ülepe etimbelü tetuna*
　　　üle-pe　　et-imbe-lü　　　 t-etu-na
　　　LOG-NTM 2.DTR-come-PNCT REFL-village-ALL
　　　'Then he arrived in his village.'
　　　'Então ele chegou em sua aldeia.'

(139) *tikongoingo akihalü hõhõ iheke*
　　　t-iko-ngo-ingo　　　aki-ha-lü　　　 hõhõ i-heke
　　　REFL-with-NMLZ-FUT word-VBLZ-PNCT EMPH 3-ERG
　　　'First he taught the one who was going to be his singing companion.'
　　　'Primeiro ele ensinou aquele que seria seu companheiro de canto.'

(140) *ah tikongoingo akihalü engü beja otohongoingo beja iginhundote*
　　　ah　 t-iko-ngo-ingo　　　 aki-ha-lü　　　 engü beja otohongo-ingo
　　　EXPL REFL-with-NMLZ-FUT word-VBLZ-PNCT CON　EP　 other.similar-FUT
　　　beja igi-nhun-dote
　　　EP　song-VBLZ-ADV
　　　'Ah, he taught the one who was going to be his companion, his other, when he was to sing.'
　　　'Ah, ele ensinou aquele que seria seu companheiro, seu outro, quando ele fosse cantar.'

(141) *otohongoingo tsüha*
otohongo-ingo   tsüha
other.similar-FUT EV.UNCR
'That one who would be his companion.'
'Aquele que seria seu companheiro.'

(142) *üngele akihalü hõhõ iheke*
üngele aki-ha-lü   hõhõ i-heke
3.LOG word-VBLZ-PNCT EMPH 3SG-ERG
'First he taught him.'
'Primeiro ele o ensinou.'

(143) *üngele akihalü.*
üngele aki-ha-lü
3.LOG word-VBLZ-PNCT
'Taught him.'
'O ensinou.'

(144) *aiha etükilü*
aiha etüki-lü
done complete-PNCT
'Done, it was complete.'
'Pronto, estava completo.'

(145) *etükilü leha inha*
etüki-lü   leha   0-inha
complete-PNCT COMPL 3-DAT
'It was complete for him.'
'Estava completo para ele.'

(146) *otohongo inha*
otohongo   inha
other.similar DAT
'For his companion.'
'Para seu companheiro.'

(147) *osiha*
osi-ha
HORT-HA
'"Let's go."'
'"Vamos lá."'

(148) *osiha ai hale tüti heke nügü iheke*
osi-ha   ai   hale tü-ti   heke nügü i-heke
HORT-HA PURP CNTR REFL-mother ERG PNCT 3-ERG
'"Let's go," and then he said to his mother:'
'"Vamos lá," e então ele disse para sua mãe:'

(149) *ama*
ama
mother
'"Mother."'
'"Mãe."'

(150) *ah kupuke hõhõ nügü iheke*
ah   k-upu-ke   hõhõ nügü i-heke
EXPL DU-make.a.visual.imitation-IMP EMPH PNCT 3-ERG
'"Ah, make our image," he said.'
'"Ah, faça nossa imagem," ele disse.'

(151) *ah kupuke hõhõ nügü iheke*
ah   k-upu-ke   hõhõ nügü i-heke
EXPL DU-make.a.visual.imitation-IMP EMPH PNCT 3-ERG
'"Ah, make our image," he said.'
'"Ah, faça nossa imagem," ele disse.'

(152) *kupuke ah nügü baha iheke*
k-upu-ke   ah   nügü baha i-heke
DU-make.a.visual.imitation-IMP EXPL PNCT EV   3-ERG
'"Make our image," ah, that's what he said.'
'"Faça nossa imagem," ah, isso é o que ele disse.'

(153) ẽhẽ nügü iheke
ẽhẽ nügü i-heke
AFF PNCT 3-ERG
'"Yes," she said.'
'"Sim," ela disse.'

(154) isi heke tsüle togokige ihenügü togokibe bahale
isi heke tsüle togokige ihe-nügü togoki-be bahale
mother ERG EP cotton spin-PNCT cotton-AUG ADV
'Then his mother spun cotton, a lot of cotton.'
'Então sua mãe fiou algodão, muito algodão.'

(155) igia kugube sueletu sagagebe otohongo
igia kugu-be s-uele-tu s-agage-be otohongo
this.way true-AUG 3-girth-POSS 3-alike-AUG other.similar
'A roll was this big, and another one also had the same size.'
'Um rolo era grande desse jeito, e um outro tinha o mesmo tamanho.'

(156) tita etikoguingo hegei
tita etiko-gu-ingo h-ege-i
mortuary.effigy belt-POSS-FUT HA-DIST-COP
'This is what would become the effigy's belt.'
'Isso é o que se tornaria o cinto da efígie.'

(157) ege hungu jetsa inke tsapa akago heke tüita
ege hungu jetsa in-ke tsapa akago heke t-üi-ta
DIST similar EV see-IMP EP 3PL ERG REFL-make-DUR
'Like those, look those they are making.'[5]
'Como aqueles, veja aqueles que eles estão fazendo.'

(158) üle hunguingo hegei
üle hungu-ingo h-ege-i
LOG similar-FUT HA-DIST-COP
'It was meant to be like those.'
'Era pra ser como aqueles.'

---

[5] Ageu refers to the cotton belts some young men were making at a neighboring house.

(159) *üle hunguingo hegei*
 üle hungu-ingo h-ege-i
 LOG similar-FUT HA-DIST-COP
 'It was meant to be like those.'
 'Era pra ser como aqueles.'

(160) *isi ngihetanümi*
 isi ng-ihe-ta-nümi
 mother LOG-spin-DUR-PNCT.COP
 'What his mother was spinning.'
 'O que sua mãe estava fiando.'

(161) *isi ngihetanümi togokigeha*
 isi ng-ihe-ta-nümi togokige-ha
 mother LOG-spin-DUR-PNCT.COP cotton-HA
 'The cotton his mother was spinning.'
 'O algodão que sua mãe estava fiando.'

(162) *aiha*
 aiha
 done
 'Done.'
 'Pronto.'

(163) *togokige etükilü*
 togokige etüki-lü
 cotton complete-PNCT
 'The cotton was ready.'
 'O algodão estava pronto.'

(164) *osiha*
 osi-ha
 HORT-HA
 '"Let's go."'
 '"Vamos lá."'

(165) *aibeha*
 aibeha
 done
 'Done.'
 'Pronto.'

(166) *tita ikenügü ihekeni*
 tita   ike-nügü   i-heke-ni
 mortuary.effigy to.cut-PNCT 3-ERG-PL
 'They cut down a log for an effigy.'
 'Eles derrubaram uma tora para fazer uma efígie.'

(167) *tita ikenügü leha ihekeni*
 tita   ike-nügü   leha   i-heke-ni
 mortuary.effigy to.cut-PNCT COMPL 3-ERG-PL
 'They had already cut down a log for an effigy.'
 'Eles já tinham derrubado uma tora para fazer uma efígie.'

(168) *ületoho*
 üle-toho
 LOG-INS
 'To do that.'
 'Para fazer isso.'

(169) *tühutoho hegei*
 tü-hu-toho   h-ege-i
 REFL-imitation-INS HA-DIST-COP
 'That was his image.'
 'Aquela era sua imagem.'

(170) *agetsiha agetsi tita*
 agetsi-ha agetsi tita
 one-HA one mortuary.effigy
 'There was only one, one effigy.'
 'Havia apenas uma, uma única efígie.'

(171) ülepea higei ah titabe ige tüingalü higei
üle-pe-a   h-ige-i   ah   tita-be   ige
LOG-NTM-CAUS HA-PROX-COP EXPL mortuary.effigy-AUG PROX
t-üi-nga-lü   h-ege-i
REFL-make-HAB-PNCT HA-DIST-COP
'It's since this that we have been making effigies.'
'É desde então que nós temos feito efígies.'

(172) ülepeaha
üle-pe-a=ha
LOG-NTM-as=HA
'Since this.'
'Desde então.'

(173) aiha
aiha
done
'Done.'
'Pronto.'

(174) ülepebe
üle-pe-be
LOG-NTM-AUG
'Then.'
'Então.'

(175) ah inhegikaginenügü bele iheke
ah   inh-egikagi-ne-nügü   bele i-heke
EXPL 3-sing.closely-VBLZ-PNCT CU   3-ERG
'Ah, he sang behind the effigy.'
'Ah, ele cantou atrás da efígie.'

(176) angi taka kangaki etelüko inhalü hungube
angi taka kanga-ki e-te-lü-ko   inhalü hungu-be
INT ADV fish-INS 3-go-PNCT-PL NEG   similar-AUG
'Did they go fishing? It doesn't seem so ...'
'Será que eles foram pescar? Não parece que foram ...'

(177) ẽ kangaki muke etelüko
ẽ   kanga-ki muke e-te-lü-ko
AFF fish-INS ADV 3-go-PNCT-PL
'Yes, they must have gone fishing.'
'Sim, eles devem ter ido pescar.'

(178) kangaki hõhõ etelüko
kanga-ki hõhõ e-te-lü-ko
fish-INS EMPH 2-go-PNCT-PL
'First they went fishing.'
'Primeiro eles foram pescar.'

(179) ah ületohokibe
ah   üle-toho-ki-be
EXPL LOG-INS-INS-AUG
'Ah, to do so.'
'Ah, para fazer isso.'

(180) inhalü ihagitoguiha inhalü
inhalü i-hagito-gu-i-ha   inhalü
NEG   3-guest-POSS-COP-HA NEG
'He didn't have guests, no.'
'Ele não tinha convidados, não.'

(181) etsuta hale egea hale egei
etsu-ta   hale egea   hale ege-i
debut-DUR CNTR like.that CNTR DIST-COP
'He was just singing for the first time.'
'Ele estava apenas estreando.'

(182) hm etsuta
hm   etsu-ta
EXPL debut-DUR
'Hm, he was singing for the first time.'
'Hm, ele estava estreando.'

(183) *aiha*
 aiha
 done
 'Done.'
 'Pronto.'

(184) *ah iginhun leha*
 ah igi-nhun leha
 EXPL song-VBLZ COMPL
 'Ah, he started to sing!'
 'Ah, ele começou a cantar!'

(185) *nhagati bele ekü telü tita telü leha egea*
 nhaga-ti bele ekü te-lü   tita   te-lü   leha egea
 hole-ALL EV CON go-PNCT mortuary.effigy go-PNCT COMPL like.that
 'The effigy was put standing straight in a hole.'
 'A efígie foi colocada de pé em um buraco.'

(186) *üle egikagineta bele ihekeni*
 üle egikagi-ne-ta   bele i-heke-ni
 LOG sing.closely-VBLZ-DUR EV 3-ERG-PL
 'This is what they were siging about behind it.'
 'Era sobre isso que eles estavam cantando atrás dela.'

(187) *ah totohongo ake leha*
 ah t-otohongo   ake leha
 EXPL REFL-other.similar COM COMPL
 'Ah, together with his companion.'
 'Ah, junto com seu companheiro.'

(188) *tüngakihapügü ake tsüha*
 tüng-aki-ha-pügü   ake tsüha
 REFL-word-VBLZ-PFV COM EV.UNCR
 'With the one he taught.'
 'Com aquele que ele ensinou.'

(189) tüngakihapügü ake
tüng-aki-ha-pügü   ake
REFL-word-VBLZ-PFV COM
'With the one he taught.'
'Com aquele que ele ensinou.'

(190) ah iginhundako leha
ah   igi-nhu-nda-ko   leha
EXPL song-VBLZ-DUR-PL COMPL
'Ah, they were singing.'
'Ah, eles estavam cantando.'

(191) aiha akinügü leha
aiha aki-nügü   leha
done finish-PNCT COMPL
'Done, it was finished.'
'Pronto, estava terminado.'

(192) akinügü
aki-nügü
finish-PNCT
'It was finished.'
'Estava terminado.'

(193) ülepe
üle-pe
LOG-NTM
'Then ...'
'Então ...'

(194) kohotsi inhügü iginhuko leha
kohotsi inhügü igi-nhu-ko   leha
at.dusk become song-NMLZ-PL COMPL
'When dusk came, they were singing again.'
'Quando chegou o entardecer, eles estavam cantando novamente.'

(195) *ah iginhundako leha*
 ah igi-nhuN-da-ko leha
 EXPL song-VBLZ-DUR-PL COMPL
 'Ah, they were singing again.'
 'Ah, eles estavam cantando novamente.'

(196) *kohotsi*
 kohotsi
 at.dusk
 'At dusk.'
 'Ao entardecer.'

(197) *ülepe mitote*
 üle-pe mitote
 LOG-NTM at.dawn
 'And then at dawn ...'
 'E depois ao amanhecer ...'

(198) *aibeha inhügü gehale*
 ai-be-ha inhügü gehale
 HORT-AUG-HA become ADV
 '... ready, one more time.'
 '... pronto, mais uma vez.'

(199) *inhügü gehale*
 inhügü gehale
 become ADV
 'One more time.'
 'Mais uma vez.'

(200) *ah ta beja iheke*
 ah ta beja i-heke
 EXPL DUR EP 3-ERG
 'Ah, his words!'
 'Ah, suas palavras!'

(201) *Kamagisa kita leha*
 Kamagisa ki-ta   leha
 Kamagisa say-DUR COMPL
 'What *Kamagisa* was saying.'
 'O que *Kamagisa* estava dizendo.'

(202) *iginhundako leha*
 igi-nhun-da-ko   leha
 SONG-VBLZ-DUR-PL COMPL
 'They were singing.'
 'Eles estavam cantando.'

(203) *aiha*
 aiha
 done
 'Done.'
 'Pronto.'

(204) *aiha mitote*
 aiha mitote
 done at.dawn
 'Done, at dawn ...'
 'Pronto, ao amanhecer ...'

(205) *ah sitogupe onginügübe*
 ah   s-ito-gu-pe   ongi-nügü-be
 EXPL 3-fire-POSS-NTM bury-PNCT-AUG
 '... Ah, his fire was buried.'[6]
 '... Ah, seu fogo foi enterrado.'

---

[6] During the last night of a mortuary ritual, a fire is kept in front of the deceased's effigy. While it is kept burnig, the soul of the deceased is present among the living. At dawn, the fire is buried while a chief makes a speech exhorting the deceased to leave permanently to the village of the dead.

(206) *engü bejaha sitogupeha onginügü leha mitote*
 engü beja-ha s-ito-gu-pe-ha   ongi-nügü leha   mitote
 CON EP-HA 3-fire-POSS-NTM-HA bury-PNCT COMPL at.dawn
 'Yes, his fire was buried at dawn.'
 'Sim, seu fogo foi enterrado ao amanhecer.'

(207) *apungu baha egei leha*
 apungu baha ege-i   leha
 end   EV DIST-COP COMPL
 'That was the end.'
 'Aquilo foi o fim.'

(208) *apungu leha egei inhalü hale ikinduko*
 apungu leha ege-i   inhalü hale ikindu-ko
 end COMPL DIST-COP NEG CNTR wrestling-PL
 'That was the end, they didn't wrestle *ikindene*.'[7]
 'Aquilo foi o fim, eles não lutaram *ikindene*.'

(209) *inhalü hale ikinduko egea gele hegei gele*
 inhalü hale ikindu-ko   egea   gele h-ege-i   gele
 NEG CNTR wrestling-PL like.that ADV HA-DIST-COP ADV
 'They didn't wrestle *ikindene*, it was just like that.'
 'Eles não lutaram *ikindene*, foi só daquele jeito.'

(210) *tuhunügü gele*
 tu-hu-nügü   gele
 REFL-make.an.image-PNCT ADV
 'Just his image was made.'
 'Só sua imagem foi feita.'

---

[7] *Ikindene* is a combat sport practiced by all the peoples of the Upper Xingu, and it is considered one of the most important features of their regional society. Wrestling is the *climax* of the Quarup mortuary ritual, but, since *Kamagisa* didn't have any guests, his ritual also didn't have *ikindene*.

(211) *etsunügü gele Kamagisa etsunügü*

      etsu-nügü   gele Kamagisa etsu-nügü
      debut-PNCT ADV Kamagisa debut-PNCT

      'Just *Kamagisa*'s debut and self-image-making.'

      'Só a estreia e feitura da própria imagem de *Kamagisa*.'

(212) *ama*

      ama
      mother

      '"Mother."'

      '"Mãe."'

(213) *jeugagi je jeuga jeuga jeuga*

      [*Kamagisa* was singing in Kamayurá, a Tupi-Guarani language][8]

      [*Kamagisa* estava cantanto em Kamayurá, uma língua Tupi-Guarani]

(214) *ama jeuga ipugu inkgete umbüngaitsü tühügü hegei iheke*

      ama   jeuga   ipu-gu   i-nkgete   u-mbüngai-tsü tühügü
      mother macaw feather-POSS bring-IMP 1-armlet-POSS PFV
      h-egei   i-heke
      HA-DIST-COP 3-ERG

      '"Mother, bring my macaw feathers armlets," that's what he said.'

      '"Mãe, traga meus braceletes de pena de arara," é o que ele disse.'

(215) *hm Kamagisa kilü*

      hm   Kamagisa ki-lü
      EXPL Kamagisa say-PNCT

      'Hm, *Kamagisa* said.'

      'Hm, *Kamagisa* disse.'

(216) *ületse ingugiha isi heke indzüngaitsü inginügü*

      üle-tse   ingugi-ha   isi   heke i-ndzüngai-tsü ingi-nügü
      LOG-DIM decision.solution-HA mother ERG 3-armlet-POSS bring-PNCT

      'It was soon solved, and his mother brought his armlets.'

      'Isso logo se resolveu, e sua mãe trouxe seus braceletes.'

---

[8] Multilinguism in ritual language is discussed in the final section.

(217) *jahu ehe jahu e*

[*Kamagisa* was still singing in Kamayurá]

[*Kamagisa* ainda estava cantando em Kamayurá]

(218) *ama jahu puguha ulekugu inkgete*

ama	jahu	pugu-ha	u-leku-gu	i-nkgete
mother	oropendola	feather-HA	1-headdress-POSS	bring-IMP

'"Mother, bring my oropendola [*Psarocolius sp.*] feathers headdress."'[9]

'"Mãe, traga minha plumária de penas de xexéu [*Psarocolius sp.*]."'

(219) *leku heke ẽ ẽ hügeku heke*

leku	heke	ẽ	ẽ	hügeku	heke
headdress	ERG	AFF	AFF	headdress	ERG

'He was talking about a headdress called *leku*, yes, yes, about a headdress also called *hügeku*.'

'Ele estava falando de uma plumária chamada *leku*, sim, sim, sobre uma plumária também chamada de *hügeku*.'

(220) *Kamajula hegei*

Kamajula	h-ege-i
kamayurá	HA-DIST-COP

'That is in the Kamayurá language.'

'Aquilo está na língua Kamayurá.'

(221) *egea ta iheke kamajulai*

egea	ta	i-heke	kamajula-i
like.that	DUR	3-ERG	kamayurá-COP

'He was saying that in Kamayurá.'

'Ele estava dizendo aquilo em Kamayurá.'

(222) *kamajula*

kamajula
kamayurá

'In Kamayurá.'

'Em Kamayurá.'

---

[9]The oropendolas — *xexéu*, in Portuguese, and *kui*, in Kalapalo — are birds of the *Psarocolius* genus, whose tail feathers are highly esteemed for their vivid yellow tones.

(223) *Kamajula heke küngüa iganügü jahu nügü iheke*

Kamajula heke küngüa   iga-nügü   jahu   nügü i-heke
kamayurá ERG oropendola name-PNCT oropendola PNCT 3-ERG
'The Kamayurá call the oropendola "*jahu*," that's what they say.'
'Os Kamayurá chamam o xexéu de "*jahu*," isso é o que eles dizem.'

(224) *aiha*

aiha
done
'Done.'
'Pronto.'

(225) *apungu leha*

apungu leha
end   COMPL
'That was the end.'
'Aquele foi o fim.'

(226) *etsuhukilü leha*

etsuhu-ki-lü   leha
end-VBLZ-PNCT COMPL
'It was over.'
'Tinha acabado.'

(227) *etsuhukilü*

etsuhu-ki-lü
end-VBLZ-PNCT
'Over.'
'Acabado.'

(228) *ama nügü iheke*

ama   nügü i-heke
mother PNCT 3-ERG
'"Mother," he said.'
'"Mãe," ele disse.'

(229) *ama*

ama
mother
'"Mother."'
'"Mãe."'

(230) *uentomila aketsange uteta leha igei leha*

u-en-tomi-la   aketsange u-te-ta   leha ige-i   leha
1-wait-PURP-NEG INT   1-go-DUR COMPL PROX-COP COMPL
'"This is so that I'm never coming back, I am leaving."'
'"Isso é para que eu nunca mais volte, eu estou partindo."'

(231) *üle igakaho hegei etsuta*

üle igakaho h-ege-i   etsu-ta
LOG ahead   HA-DIST-COP debut-DUR
'Before that he sang for the first time.'
'Antes disso ele estreou.'

(232) *etsuta hegei*

etsu-ta   h-ege-i
debut-DUR HA-DIST-COP
'That was his first time singing.'
'Aquela foi a primeira vez dele cantando.'

(233) *ama*

ama
mother
'"Mother."'
'"Mãe."'

(234) *uenügüti hestange keiti*

u-e-nügü-ti   hetsange k-e-iti
1-come-PNCT-wish HORT   IMP.PROH-2SG-wish
'"You shall not want me to come back."'
'"Você não deve querer que eu volte."'

(235) *ah ahati heke seku ũãke utihunhetatühügü ũãke*

ah   a-hati   heke seku ũãke   u-ti-hu-nhe-ta-tühügü   ũãke
EXPL 2SG-niece ERG EP   EV.PST 1-throat-swell-VBLZ-DUR-PFV EV.PST

'"Ah, your niece made my throat swell with sadness in the past."'

'"Ah, sua sobrinha fez minha garganta ficar inchada de tristeza no passado."'

(236) *ah nügü leha iheke tüti heke*

ah   nügü leha   i-heke tü-ti   heke
EXPL PNCT COMPL 3-SG   REFL-mother   ERG

'Ah, he said so to his mother.'

'Ah, ele disse para sua mãe.'

(237) *üi üi üi isi honunda leha*

üi   üi   üi   isi   honu-nda leha
IDEO IDEO IDEO mother   cry-DUR   COMPL

'"Üi, üi, üi" - his mother was crying.'

'"Üi, üi, üi" - sua mãe estava chorando.'

(238) *kogetsi kogetsi leha egei sinügü etsutühügüngine*

kogetsi   kogetsi   leha   ege-i   s-i-nügü   etsu-tühügü-ngine
tomorrow   tomorrow   COMPL   DIST-COP 3-come-PNCT   debut-PFV-ALL

'On the next day, the day after he came, after he had sung for the first time.'

'No dia seguinte, no dia após sua vinda, depois que ele havia cantado pela primeira vez.'

(239) *etsutühügü*

etsu-tühügü
debut-PFV

'He sang for the first time.'

'Ele cantou pela primeira vez.'

(240)   *etsutühügüngine leha sinügü*
       etsu-tühügü-ngine leha   s-i-nügü
       debut-PFV-ALL   COMPL 3-come-PNCT
       'After he had sung for the first time, he came.'
       'Depois que ele havia cantado pela primeira vez, ele veio.'

(241)   *apungu ekugu leha inhalü leha totomona tünga tetuna etelüi leha*
       apungu ekugu leha   inhalü leha   t-oto-mo-na   t-ünga
       end   true COMPL NEG   COMPL REFL-kin-PL-ALL REFL-house
       t-etu-na   e-te-lü-i   leha
       REFL-village-ALL 3-go-PNCT-COP COMPL
       'He went away for good, he didn't ever come back to his kin, to his house, to his village.'
       'Ele foi embora de vez, ele nunca mais voltou para seus parentes, para sua casa, para sua aldeia.'

(242)   *inhalü leha*
       inhalü leha
       NEG   COMPL
       'Never again.'
       'Nunca mais.'

(243)   *apungui leha etelü*
       apungu-i leha   e-te-lü
       end-COP COMPL 3-go-PNCT
       'He went away for good.'
       'Ele foi embora de vez.'

(244)   *tsakeha*
       tsa-ke-ha
       listen-IMP-HA
       'Listen.'
       'Ouça.'

(245) *uitsajingugu kitseha*
    uitsajingugu ki-tse-ha
    ?   say-IMP-HA
    'Say "*uitsajingugu.*"'[10]
    'Diga "*uitsajingugu.*"'

(246) *upügü hegei*
    upügü h-ege-i
    last   HA-DIST-COP
    'This is the end.'
    'Este é o fim.'

3 Comments: alterity and translation

This *akinha*, 'story, narrative', is formally similar to all others the Kalapalo recount, and they share a narrative style with the Kuikuro, Matipu, and Nahukua, their Carib-speaking neighbors (Basso 1985; Franchetto 1986). An *akinha* stands apart from ordinary talk by means of stylistic resources that mark its "frontiers" to the listeners, usually beginning and ending with the word *tsakeha*, 'listen' (followed, in the end, by the expression *upügü hegei*, 'this is the end', when the narrator declares there's nothing left to be told). *Ageu* usually marks these "frontiers" when telling stories, but this one is an exception, since it begins without his calling any special attention to it. *Kamagisa's* story, like other narratives, is also internally divided into thematic blocks that may be identified by opening and closing lines, such as *ülepe*, 'then' and *aiha*, 'done'.

The first block (lines 1-28) tells how a hurtful event led to *Kamagisa's* separation from his kin, followed by his first contact with *Kakakugu*, an *itseke*, a powerful spirit-being. In the second block (lines 29-58), we are told about *Kamagisa's* displacement to the spiritual world, resulting (block 3, lines 59-68) in his marriage with *Kakakugu's* daughter (a Snake Woman). When, in the fourth block (lines 69-111), *Kamagisa* returns to his village accompanied by his new wife, she is still invisible to her affines, and speaks a language incomprehensible to humans. As they lie together and have frequent sexual relations, the Snake Woman's body becomes visible to her affines (block 5, lines 112-120), and, when *Kamagisa* returns

---

[10] We could never find a proper translation of this word. A nahukua man once said it would mean 'my little shin!', and explained that one should say so to avoid getting lazy after listening to a narrative.

to his father-in-law's village, he finishes his learning of a special knowledge. He learns songs that will lead him to ask his mother to 'make an image' for him (block 6, lines 121-162), a request followed by the description of important steps in the preparation of the *egitsü* mortuary ritual: the cutting of a special tree from which the effigy is made (block 7, lines 163-174), the temporal sequencing of the song performances (block 8, lines 175-203), a brief explanation of the musical language (block 9, lines 204-224), and, finally, a sad farewell to the human world (block 10, lines 225-246). A similar structure can be found in other narratives, in which a deception or fight with someone's kin may lead a character away from the human world, provoking his contact with Others (spiritual beings, enemies, or non-Indians) that will become the source of some special knowledge that he or she will transmit to humans.[11]

This narrative calls our attention to a trope, contained both in its title and its events. I've decided to translate *Kamagisa etsutühügü* as '*Kamagisa* Sang for the First Time' because this is the sense in which this expression is usually understood. More specifically, the verb *etsunügü* can be translated as 'to debut', as I've done in the glosses. However, *etsunügü* has also two other meanings closely related to the final scenes of the narrative: it can also mean 'to make an image of oneself' (such as a self-portrait, a *selfie* picture with a cell phone or, in this case, a mortuary effigy), and 'to set a date for leaving'. While debuting as a singer, Kamagisa also performed the other two actions. First, he made an image of himself, a *tita*, a mortuary effigy which is also called *kuge hutoho* ('made in order to imitate a person', or 'the image of a person'). By doing so, he revealed to his mother his intention to leave his kin and his village once and for all, since his feelings were deeply hurt by his former fiancée (his mother's brother's daughter, MBD). During the *egitsü*, or Quarup, the production and display of mortuary effigies is done in order for the dead to depart and leave their kin behind (Guerreiro 2011; 2015). Kamagisa, in this sense, was acting like a dead person, performing his own mortuary ritual. *Etsunügü*, then, combines different actions performed by *Kamagisa* in a single word — who, by making an effigy of himself, created both the context for revealing songs learned from the spirits and for his final departure.

---

[11] It is noteworthy that this narrative inverts several aspects of the myth of *Arakuni* as told by the Arawak-speaking Wauja. *Arakuni* is *loved* (not repudiated) by his *sister* (a forbidden woman, the opposite of a cross-cousin as a preferred spouse); instead of leaving of his own will, his mother is the one who *sends him away*; and finally, instead of marrying a spirit-being, *he becomes one himself* (a great snake). When leaving the human world, Arakuni sings until he is fully transformed into a spirit-being, and his chants are now part of the Quarup repertoire. I would like to thank Aristóteles Barcelos Neto for calling my attention to the relations between both narratives.

Figure 2: Kalapalo boy sitting nearby two mortuary effigies at Aiha.
Photo: Marina Pereira Novo

Kamagisa's story also introduces us to the multiethnic and multilingual composition of Xinguano rituals, and the means of translating myths into songs, songs into action, and action into creative or transformative social relations. The songs *Kamagisa* learned form a musical suite, or *gepa*, named after *Kamagisa's* village *Hagagikugu*. This village resulted from the fission of the Akuku, an ancient Carib-speaking people linguistically and sociopolitically closely related to the Kalapalo. Some say they were actual Kalapalo ancestors, as we can also see in the literature (Basso 2001). Others, however, insist the Akuku were a different people, more closely related to the Nahukua. In any case, *Kamagisa's* story tells about the origins of a suite of songs considered to be special Kalapalo knowledge, and that's why the Kalapalo are seen as their true 'owners' or 'masters' (*otomo*). However, most Kalapalo can't understand but a few words of it, since the songs are almost entirely in Kamayurá, a language of the Tupi-Guarani family. We're facing here a fairly common (and fascinating) situation in the Upper Xingu: we're talking about the origin myth of a suite of Kalapalo songs, sung mostly in a Tupi-Guarani language, and which plays a central role in a ritual with a probable Arawakan origin.

When interacting with different forms of alterity, the problem of communication comes to the fore, and *Kamagisa's* narrative shows how translations can be produced by several media: what one sings, even though it's not completely understood, may be translated into actions, that, in turn, can be translated into social relations. As Rafael Bastos (1983) already argued some time ago, this suggests that, if there is anything like a *lingua franca* in the Upper Xingu, it is their rituals and the communication system they compose from myths, musical and choreographic performances, and bodily decoration.

Acknowledgments

Writing of this chapter was made possible by financial support from the São Paulo Research Foundation (FAPESP) for the Young Researcher Project "Transforming Amerindian regional systems: the Upper Xingu case" (process number 2013/26676-0).

Non-standard abbreviations

AFF	affirmative	HORT	hortative
AUG	augmentative	IDEO	ideophone
CNTR	contrastive	INT	intensifier
COM	comitative	ITJ	interjection
CON	connective	LOG	logophoric
CU	cumulative effect	NANMLZ	non-agent nominalizer
DTR	detransitivizer	NMLZ	nominalizer
EP	epistemic	NTM	nominal tense marker
EMPH	emphatic	PNCT	punctual aspect
EV	evidential	PURP	purposive
EXPL	expletive	TEMP	temporal marker
HAB	habitual aspect	UNCR	uncertainty
HA	ha particle	VBLZ	verbalizer

References

Basso, Ellen B. 1985. *A musical view of the universe. Kalapalo myth and ritual performances*. Philadelphia: University of Pennsylvania Press.

Basso, Ellen B. 2001. O que podemos aprender do discurso kalapalo sobre a "história kalapalo"? In Bruna Franchetto & Michael Heckenberger (eds.), *Os povos do Alto Xingu: História e cultura*, 293–307. Rio de Janeiro: Editora da UFRJ.

Basso, Ellen B. 2012. *A grammar of Kalapalo, a Southern cariban language. Kalapalo collection of Ellen Basso. The Archive of the Indigenous Languages of Latin America: Www. Ailla. Utexas. Org. Media: Text. Access: Public.* Resource: KUI015R002.

Bastos, Rafael. 1983. Sistemas políticos, de comunicação e articulação social no Alto Xingu. *Anuário Antropológico* 81. 43–58.

dos Santos, Gélsama M. F. 2007. *Morfologia Kuikuro: Gerando nomes e verbos.* Rio de Janeiro: UFRJ thesis.

Franchetto, Bruna. 1986. *Falar Kuikúro: Estudo etnolinguístico de um grupo caribe do Alto Xingu.* Rio de Janeiro: UFRJ thesis.

Franchetto, Bruna. 2002. Kuikuro. Uma língua ergativa no ramo meridional da família karib (alto xingu). In Franciso Queixalós (ed.), *Ergatividade na amazônia i*, 15–44. Brasil: Centre d'études des langues indigènes d'Amérique (CNRS, IRD), Laboratório de Línguas Indígenas (Unb).

Franchetto, Bruna. 2003. L'autre du même: Parallélisme et grammaire dans l'art verbal des récits kuikuro (caribe du Haut Xingu, Brésil). *Amerindia* 28. Paris: AEA, 213–248.

Guerreiro, Antonio. 2011. Refazendo corpos para os mortos: As efígies mortuárias Kalapalo. *Tipití: Journal of the Society for the Anthropology of Lowland South America* 9(1). 1–29.

Guerreiro, Antonio. 2015. *Ancestrais e suas sombras: Uma etnografia da chefia Kalapalo e seu ritual mortuário.* Campinas: Editora da Unicamp.

Mehinaku, Mutua. 2010. *Tetsualü: Pluralismo de línguas e pessoas no Alto Xingu.* Rio de Janeiro: Museu Nacional/UFRJ thesis.

Rabello, Aline Varela. 2013. *Marcadores de modalidade epistêmica nas narrativas históricas Kuikuro.* Museu Nacional/UFRJ dissertation.

Chapter 4

Marubo

Pedro de Niemeyer Cesarino
University of São Paulo, Brazil

Armando Mariano Marubo Cherõpapa Txano

Robson Dionísio Doles Marubo

1 Introduction

The Marubo are Panoan-speakers from the Javari River Indigenous Reservation (Terra Indígena Vale do Javari, state of Amazonas, Brazil), who live along the headwaters of the Ituí and Curuçá Rivers, as well as in the cities of Cruzeiro do Sul (in the state of Acre) and Atalaia do Norte (Amazonas). Their population is currently estimated at 1,700. The Marubo were reasonably unaffected by the rubber trade that devastated vast portions of the Amazon region during the nineteenth and early twentieth centuries, including the Juruá river basin, where other Panoan-speakers still live. Far from the urban centers, their lands protected a society that was created at the turn of the twentieth century by an important chief and shaman, João Tuxáua, and his relatives (Ruedas 2001; Welper 2009). João Tuxáua was responsible for gathering a number of dispersed Panoan-speakers and creating a new society out of earlier cultural and linguistic traditions, adopting the language of one group – the Chai Nawavo – that now comprise the contemporary Marubo. In fact, earlier groups (whose names are always followed by *nawavo* or 'people', as in *Chai Nawavo* or 'Bird People' and *Vari Nawavo* or 'Sun People') became segments of Marubo social and kinship system. The Marubo continue to live in longhouses, which have been abandoned by other Panoan-speakers, such as the Kaxinawa, Katukina, Yaminawa, Sharanawa, and Shipibo-Conibo, but are also maintained by the Matis, Mayoruna, and Korubo: three other Panoan-speaking peoples from the Javari river basin.

Pedro de Niemeyer Cesarino, Armando Mariano Marubo Cherõpapa Txano & Robson Dionísio Doles Marubo. 2017. Marubo. In Kristine Stenzel & Bruna Franchetto (eds.), *On this and other worlds: Voices from Amazonia*, 139–162. Berlin: Language Science Press.
DOI:10.5281/zenodo.1008779

Figure 1: The Javari basin and location of the Marubo.

The Marubo preserve a very active ritual life characterized by the work of prayer-shamans (*kẽchĩtxo*) and spirit-shamans (*romeya*). Complex initiation and ritual knowledge transmission processes are ongoing, and involve the performance and instruction of verbal genera, such as curing songs (*shõki*), spirit songs (*iniki*), chiefly speeches (*tsãiki*), instructive speeches (*ese vana*), and mythical narratives (see Montagner 1985; 1996; Cesarino 2011; 2013, among others). The latter can be performed in two ways: narrated (*yoã vana*) with the special use of parallelism, rhythm, metaphors, and gestures, or sung (*saiti vana*), by use of constant melodic phrases (one for each story) and fixed meters. The vast *yoã vana*, a collection of mythical narratives, is the cornerstone of Marubo ritual knowledge; its episodes can be transferred to other verbal arts for ritual efficacy or counsel (see Cesarino 2011 for a detailed study). Prayer-shamans are responsible for verbal knowledge transmission and understanding, while spirit-shamans (who are also prayer-shamans) circulate through the realms of spirits and dead people that compose Marubo cosmology.

The research presented here was conducted with two spirit-shamans, Robson Dionísio Doles Marubo and Armando Mariano Marubo, as well as with other important prayer-shamans (Antonio Brasil Marubo, Lauro Brasil Marubo, and

Paulino Joaquim Marubo). The now deceased prayer-shaman, Armando, authored the narrative that follows, which connects a traditional narrative about the formation of the Death Path (*Vei Vai yoã*) with an instructive speech (*ese vana*) about eschatological conceptions. The narrative was performed and recorded at Alegria village (Upper Ituí river) in 2007, after three years of collaboration between author and researcher. The original audio digital recording was transcribed, reviewed, and translated with the help of Robson Dionísio, a shaman, bilingual researcher and schoolteacher. The complete literary translation of this narrative was published elsewhere in Portuguese (Cesarino 2012) and can be compared with a sung version of the Death Path narrative, also previously translated and published (Cesarino 2011: 303ff). The present version revises and adds details to the original narrative, including the unpublished interlinear segmentation.

The first part of Armando's narrative synthesizes the formation of the Death Path by *Vei Maya* and the tree spirits; the second part connects this narrative with the moral teachings involved in the journey along this dangerous path. This is the kind of teaching that Marubo youngers should attend to, so as to prepare themselves for the afterlife. The lines of narrative were divided according to rhythm and parallelism, in order to reproduce the dramatic effect, a prominent characteristic of the original oral performance, in the written version. One of the central features conveying this effect (which is also didactic) is the extensive use of reported speech, which allows the narrator to shift between voices, be it the voice of an ancestor (as in line 25) or of a generic dead person (as in line 71). It is also important to note that the first Portuguese translation, from which this detailed and segmented version is derived, was actually conceived to be literary rather than completely literal.

Linguistic data on the Marubo language was first obtained through Costa's (1992, 1998, 2000) preliminary phonological and morphological research, which I later revised and expanded for my ethnographic research and verbal arts translations. My research was also based on other linguistic studies of Panoan languages (Valenzuela 2003 for Shipibo-Conibo; Fleck 2003 for Matsés; Camargo 1995; 1996a,b; 1998; 2003; 2005 for Kaxinawá, among others), as well as on a revision of the orthographic conventions used for the Marubo language by the New Tribes Mission linguists since 1950. Despite the traits that it shares with other Panoan languages – such as agglutinative morphology, easily identifiable morpheme boundaries, the presence of ergative-absolutive case marking, and a complex switch-reference system that distinguishes same/different subjects and sequential/simultaneous actions – the classification of the Marubo language within the Panoan linguistic group is still being debated (Valenzuela 2003: 55).

The Marubo phonemic system, with orthographic conventions indicated by <>, is composed of fourteen consonants (p <p>, m <m>, v <v>, w <w>, t <t>, n <ñ>, s <s>, ts <ts>, ɾ <r>, ʃ <sh>, tʃ <tx>, ʂ < ch>, y < y >, k <k>) and four vowels (i <i>, ɨ (e), a <a>, u <o>).

2 The teachings of the Death-Path

Ensinamentos do Caminho-Morte

I. A história de Vei Maya

(1) *Txõtxõ Koro shavo, winin aká shavo,*

   Txõtxo Koro shavo   winin   aká   shavo
   bird   grey women erection AUX.TRNS women

   'Bird-women, seductive women,'
   'Mulheres-pássaro, as mulheres sedutoras,'

(2) *Atisho vei ooki vei oo atisho.*

   a-ti-sho   vei   oo-iki   vei   oo   a-ti-sho
   3DEM-NMLZ-SSSA death cry-VBLZ death cry 3DEM-NMLZ-SSSA

   'women of the death-cry, of the death-cry.'
   'aquelas que soltaram o grito-morte, aquelas do grito-morte.'

(3) *Aivo askásevi Vei Maya askásevi,*

   a-ivo   aská-sevi Vei   Maya aská-sevi
   3DEM-GENR SML-CON death Maya SML-CON

   'And her also, Vei Maya also,'
   'e também ela, Vei Maya também,'

(4) *Vei Maya vei mai nãkõsh wenímarivi, shavo wetsa.*

   Vei   Maya vei   mai nãkõ-sh   wení-ma-rivi shavo   wetsa
   death Maya death land nectar-LOC.PROV rise-NEG-EMP woman other

   'Vei Maya did not come from the Death-Land; she is another woman.'[1]
   'Vei Maya não surgiu do néctar da terra-morte, é outra mulher.'

---

[1] The narrator is saying that *Vei Maya* was not born in the Death-Land that she later created. 'Nectar' (*nãko*) is a shamanic term for a special transformational substance.

(5) *Aská akĩ, aská akĩ, isĩ akĩ,*
 aská a-kĩ   aská a-kĩ   isĩ   a-kĩ
 SML do-SSSA SML AUX.TRNS-SSSA strong AUX.TRNS-SSSA
 'Doing this, doing this, doing this strongly,'
 'Fazendo assim, fazendo assim, fazendo forte,'

(6) *aská akĩ, isĩ akĩ rishkikinã.*
 aská a-kĩ   isĩ   a-kĩ   rishki-ki-nã
 SML AUX.TRNS-SSSA strong AUX.TRNS-SSSA beat-ASS-FOC
 'doing this strongly, her husband beat her.'
 'fazendo assim, fazendo forte, [o marido] ia mesmo espancando.'

(7) *Awẽ amaĩnõ wetsarotsẽ a venemesh merasho rishkiti tenãi.*
 awẽ a-maĩnõ   wetsa-ro-tsẽ   a   vene-mesh mera-sho rishki-ti
 what AUX.TRNS-CON other-TOP-CON 3.DEM man-?   find-SSSA beat-INS
 tenã-i
 DIE-PST1
 'And doing so, the husband killed his other wife.'
 'E assim fazendo, o homem matou a sua outra mulher.'

(8) *Askámãi wetsarotsẽ, wetsa westí tsaopakea aivorotsẽ,*
 aská-mãinõ wetsa-ro-tsẽ,   wetsa westí tsao-pake-a
 SML-CON   other-TOP-CON other alone seat-DISTR-RLZ
 a-ivo-ro-tsẽ
 3.DEM-GENR-TOP-CON
 'But the other, the one who sat alone,'
 'Mas a outra, aquela que ficou sozinha sentada,'

(9) *aro awẽ vene rishkia.*
 a-ro   awẽ vene rishki-a
 3.DEM-TOP POSS man beat-RLZ
 'the husband beat.'
 'o marido nela bateu.'

(10) *Awẽ chinã naíai tsaõ,*
 awẽ chinã   naí-ai   tsaõ
 POSS thought sad-INCP seated.LOC
 'There she sat with a sad thought,'
 'Ficou sentada com o pensamento entristecido,'

(11) *vei ari kenai, vei ari kenai.*

   vei   a-ri   kena-i   vei   a-ri   kena-i
   death 3.DEM-REFL call-PROG death 3.DEM-REFL call-PROG

   'alone, calling for death, alone, calling for death.'
   'pela morte sozinha chamava, pela morte sozinha chamava.'

(12) *Vei Mayanã.*

   Vei   Maya-nã
   death Maya-FOC

   'This is Vei Maya.'
   'É Maya-Morte.'

(13) *Aivo vei ari kenaiti.*

   a-ivo   vei   a-ri   kena-i-ti
   3.DEM-GENR death 3.DEM-REFL call-PROG-PST5

   'The one that, in the old times, called for death.'
   'A que há tempos pela morte chamava.'

(14) *Aská akĩserotsẽ ari iniki vanai.*

   aská a-kĩ-se-ro-tsẽ   a-ri   iniki vana-i
   SML   AUX.TRNS-SSSA-EXT-TOP-CON 3.DEM-REFL song speech-PROG

   'This way she called, this way she sang for herself.'
   'Assim mesmo chamando, ela sozinha cantofalava.'

(15) *Ronorasĩ kenaiti.*

   rono-rasĩ kena-i-ti
   snake-COL call-PROG-PST5

   'She called for the snakes long ago.'
   'Chamava pelas cobras,'

(16) *Vanavanakwãi avai kayakãisho*

   vana-vana-kawã-i   a-vai   kaya-kãi-sho
   speak-speak-go-PROG AUX.TRNS-CON leave-INC-SSSA

   'Calling and calling she left'
   'falando e falando foi saindo,'

(17) *kayã nachima.*

　　kayã　　nachi-ma
　　river.LOC bathe-CAUS

　　'to bathe in the river.'
　　'foi banhar no rio.'

(18) *A nachia tsaosmãis, a rono anõ rakákawãs nachai.*

　　a　　　nachi-a　　tsao-se-mãinõs　a　　　rono　anõ raká-kawãs nacha-i
　　3.DEM bathe-RLZ seat-EXT-CON 3.DEM snake FIN lie-go　　　bite-PST1

　　'While she sat to bathe, a passing snake bit her.'
　　'Enquanto sentava-se para banhar, uma cobra que ali ficava a mordeu.'

(19) *Tenãseiti.*

　　tenã-se-iti
　　die-EXT-PST5

　　'And she died a long time ago.'[2]
　　'Morreu mesmo há muito tempo.'

(20) *Aská akaivo voshõ,*

　　aská aka-i-vo　　　　　　vo-shõ
　　SML AUX.TRNS-PROG-PL arrive.PL-DSSA

　　'And then they arrived.'
　　'E assim então eles chegaram,'

(21) *Shono Yove Nawavo pakeivo paraiki voshõ.*

　　Shono　　　　Yove Nawa-vo pake-i-vo　　para-iki
　　samaúma.tree spirit people-PL fall-PROG-PL come.down-VBLZ
　　vo-shõ.
　　arrive.PL-CON

　　'Samaúma Spirit-People were coming down, arriving.'
　　'O Povo-Espírito da Samaúma foi descendo, chegando.'

---

[2]There are at least three verbal forms for 'death' in the present text: *vopia*, 'to die in this world'; *veia*, a 'second possible death and/or transformation in the afterlife'; *tenãia*, 'to be physically injured to the point of death'.

(22) *Anosho chinãi,*
 ano-sho   chinã-i
 there-LOC.PROV think-PROG
 'And there she thought,'
 'E ali elá pensou,'

(23) *ato chinãmakĩ,*
 ato   chinã-ma-kĩ
 3PL.DEM think-CAUS-SSSA
 'about them she was thinking,'
 'Sobre eles ficou pensando,'

(24) *ato chinãmakĩ.*
 ato   chinã-ma-kĩ
 3PL.DEM think-CAUS-SSSA
 'About them she was thinking.'[3]
 'Sobre eles pensou.'

(25) *"Ramaro nokẽ chinã naíai, nõ neskái,*
 rama-ro nokẽ   chinã   naí-ai nõ   neská-ai
 now-TOP 1PL.GEN thought sad-INCP 1PL.GEN SML-INCP
 '"Now our thought saddened, so we became,'
 '"Agora que ficamos com o pensamento entristecido,'

(26) *noke neská akavo, noke.*
 noke   neská aka-vo   noke
 1PL.ABS SML   AUX.TRNS-PL 1PL.ABS
 'now we will do it this way.'
 'agora vamos fazer assim.'

---

[3] The Samaúma Spirit-People came down from the *Tama Shavá*, a dwelling in the tree canopies, a better world to which all the deceased were destined in ancient times, regardless of their moral qualities. *Vei Maya* is outraged with this common destiny and thus provokes an eschatological transformation. Samaúma (*ceiba petandra*) is one of the tallest Amazonian trees; its spirit-people are some of the most important in Marubo shamanism. The next two trees mentioned in the narrative could not be identified in Portuguese, but the Marubo used to call the *chai* tree with the regional term "envireira".

(27) *Txipo shavá otapa roai askátanivai ari shavámisvo.*

txipo shavá otapa roa-i   aská-ta-ni-vai a-ri
after time   come sorcery-PROG SML-ASS-?-CON 3.DEM-REFL
shavá-misi-ivo
live-POSSIB-GENR

'The future we will change, so that they might suffer.'
'A época que virá vamos transformar para que os outros sofram.'

(28) *Vei Vai arina shovimakĩ!*

Vei   Vai a-ri-na   shovi-ma-ki
death path AUX.TRNS-IMP-? make.built-CAUS-ASS

'Come and make the Death-Path!'
'Vamos, façam logo o Caminho-Morte!'

(29) *Vei Vai arina shovimakĩ!" ikiti.*

Vei   Vai a-ri-na   shovi-ma-ki   iki-ti
death path AUX-IMP-? make.built-CAUS-ASS say-PST5

'Come and make the Death-Path!" she commanded long ago.'
'Façam logo o Caminho-Morte!", disse ela há muito tempo.'

(30) *Askáka akátõsh tanamakinãnãi.*

aská-aka   aká-tõsho   tana-ma-iki-nãnã-i
SML-AUX.TRNS AUX.TRNS-CNS understand.decide-CAUS-ASS-RECP-PST1

'And they arranged everything amongst themselves.'
'Assim eles entre si tudo combinaram.'

(31) *Chai Yove Nawavo,*

Chai   Yove Nawa-vo
envireira.tree spirit people-PL

'Spirit People of the Envireira Tree,'
'Povo-Espírito da Envireira,'

(32) *Shono Yove Nawavo,*

Shono   Yove Nawa-vo
samaúma.tree spirit people-PL

'Spirit People of the Samaúma Tree,'
'Povo-Espírito da Samaúma,'

(33) *Tama Yove Nawavo,*
 Tama Yove Nawa-vo
 tree spirit people-PL
 'Spirit People of the Tama Tree,'
 'Povo-Espírito das Árvores,'

(34) *ati tanamakinãnãvaikis,*
 a-ti tana-ma-iki-nãnã-vaikis
 3.DEM-NMLZ understand.decide-CAUS-AUX-RECP-CON
 'they decided everything amongst themselves,'
 'são estes os que entre si tudo combinaram,'

(35) *awẽ vana anõkis akavo*
 awẽ vana anõ-ki-se aka-vo
 POSS speech FIN-ASS-EXT AUX.TRNS-PL
 'and obeyed her'
 'a ordem obedeceram e fizeram,'

(36) *Vei Vai shovimakĩ.*
 Vei Vai shovi-ma-kĩ
 death path make-CAUS-ASS
 'building the Death-Path.'
 'construíram o Caminho-Morte.'

(37) *Atiãro yora veiya roase,*
 atiã-ro yora vei-ya roa-se
 TEMP-TOP people die-PRF easy-EXT
 'At that time people died easily,'
 'Naquela época as pessoas morriam tranquilas,'

(38) *Vopitani tachikrãse,*
 vopi-ta-ni tachi-krã-se
 die-ASS-? arrive-DIR.C-EXT
 'died and arrived there [in the world in the tree canopies],'
 'faleciam e já chegavam [na Morada Arbórea],'

(39) *vopitani tachikrãseika.*
   vopi-ta-ni   tachi-krã-se-i-ka
   death-ASS-? arrive-DIR.C-EXT-PST1-?
   'died and really arrived there.'[4]
   'faleciam e já chegavam mesmo .'

(40) *Akámẽkirotsẽ ãtõ atovo,*
   aká-mẽkĩ-ro-tsẽ   ãtõ   ato-vo
   AUX.TRNS-CON-TOP-CON   3PL.DEM.ERG   3PL.ABS-PL
   'So it was, but then they made it,'
   'Assim era, mas ela ordenou e fizeram,'

(41) *Vei Vai aská akĩ shovimai akavo.*
   Vei   Vai   aská a-kĩ   shovi-ma-i   aka-vo
   death path SML AUX.TRNS-SSSA built-CAUS-PROG AUX.TRNS-PL
   'Death-Path they made.'
   'construíram o Caminho-Morte.'

(42) *Shovo Yove Nawavo aská vei chinãya shokoma,*
   Shovo   Yove Nawa-vo aská vei   chinã-ya   shoko-ma
   samaúma.tree spirit people-PL SML death thought-ATR.PERM live-NEG
   'Samaúma Spirit People do not live with death-thought,'
   'Povo-Espírito da Samaúma não vive assim com pensamento-morte,'

(43) *Tama Yove Nawavo vei chinãya shokoma,*
   Tama Yove Nawa-vo vei   chinã-ya   shoko-ma
   tree   spirit people-PL death thought-ATR.PERM live-NEG
   'Tama Spirit People do not live with death-thought,'
   'Povo-Espírito das Árvores não vive com pensamento-morte,'

(44) *Chai Yove Nawavo vei chinãya shokoma.*
   Chai   Yove Nawa-vo vei   chinã-ya   shoko-ma
   envireira.tree spirit people-PL death thought-ATR.PERM live-NEG
   'Chai Spirit People do not live with death-thought.'
   'Povo-Espírito da Envireira não vive com pensamento-morte.'

---

[4]In the world of the tree canopies.

(45) *Akámẽkĩtsẽ ãtõ ato vanaka,*
 aká-mẽki-tsẽ   ãtõ   ato   vana   aka
 AUX.TRNS-CON-CON 3PL.DEM.ERG 3PL.ABS speech AUX.TRNS
 'So they are, but she commanded,'
 'Assim mesmo são, mas ela os ordenou,'

(46) *chinãmakinãnãvaikis akavo,*
 chinã-ma-ki-nãnã-vaikis   aka-vo
 think-CAUS-ASS-RECP-CON   AUX.TRNS-PL
 'and they decided amongst themselves,'
 'eles pensaram entre si e então fizeram,'

(47) *a vai shovimakinã.*
 a   vai   shovi-ma-ki-nã
 3.DEM   path built-CAUS-ASS-FOC
 'and built that path.'
 'construíram aquele caminho.'

(48) *Atõ aská ati,*
 atõ   aská   a-ti
 3PL.DEM   SML   AUX-PST5
 'Long ago they made it,'
 'Assim há tempos fizeram,'

(49) *atõ aská atisho.*
 atõ   aská   a-ti-sho
 3PL.DEM   SML   AUX.TRNS-PST5-SSSA
 'Long ago they did it.'
 'assim há tempos eles fizeram.'

(50) *Akĩ vai roa aina, vai roakama,*
 a-kĩ   vai   roa   a-ina   vai   roaka-ma
 3.DEM-SSSA   path   arrange AUX.TRNS-CON.FIN path   good-NEG
 'The path they arranged, a bad path,'
 'Ajeitaram o caminho, caminho ruim,'

(51) *anõsh txipo kaniaivo askái shavánõ,*

   anõ-sh txipo kania-ivo askái shavá-nõ
   for-DAT after grow-GENR SML live-FIN

   'so that the youngsters might experience it,'
   'para que os depois nascidos padeçam,'

(52) *txipo kaniaivo anõ yostánõ.*

   txipo kania-ivo anõ yostá-nõ
   after grow-GENR for suffer-FIN

   'So that they suffer.'
   'Para que os depois nascidos sofram.'

II. A travessia

(53) *Wetsaro vei ikitai,*

   wetsa-ro vei   iki-ta-i
   other-TOP death COP-ASS-PST1

   'This one is dead,'
   'Um já está morrido,'

(54) *wetsaro vei ikitai,*

   wetsa-ro vei   iki-ta-i
   other-TOP death COP-ASS-PST1

   'this one is dead,'
   'outro já está morrido,'[5]

(55) *wetsaro vei matsá pakei,*

   wetsa-ro vei   matsá pake-i
   other-TOP death mud   fall-PST1

   'the other one has fallen in the death-mud,'
   'Outro caiu no lamaçal-morte,'

---

[5] The Portuguese "morrido" translates the difference between two possible deaths conceived by Marubo eschatology: the death of the carcass-body (*vopia*) and the death of the double (*veia*). The first is translated as 'morto' and the second one as 'morrido', thus mirroring a popular Brazilian expression that also distinguishes two kinds of death: "morte matada e morte morrida".

(56) *wetsaro vimi noiaivo,*
 wetsa-ro vimi noia-ivo
 other-TOP fruit like-GENR
 'the other, fond of fruit,'
 'outro, o fã de frutas,'

(57) *awẽ vimi amaĩnõ anosho atxitai.*
 awẽ vimi a-maĩnõ ano-sho atxi-ta-i
 POSS fruit AUX.TRNS-CON there-LOC.PROV stuck-ASS-PST1
 'became stuck in the fruit.'
 'come a fruta e ali mesmo fica preso.'

(58) *Akáakarasĩ aská atõ veikãse aya.*
 aká-aká-rasĩ aská atõ vei-kãia-se aya
 AUX.TRNS-AUX.TRNS-COL SML 3PL.DEM DIE-INC-EXT be
 'Doing this and that they keep dying there.'
 'Assim fazendo eles ali ficam morridos.'

(59) *Askámãi yora ese vanaya,*
 aská-mãinõ yora ese vana-ya
 SML-CON person wisdom speech-ATR.PERM
 'But the person with wise speech,'
 'Mas a pessoa de fala sabida,'

(60) *yora vanaya,*
 yora vana-ya
 person speech-ATR.PERM
 'the talkative person,'
 'a pessoa faladora,'

(61) *vana shatesmaivo yora,*
 vana shate-se-ma-ivo
 speech cut-EXT-NEG-GENR
 'the person of constant speech,'
 'a pessoa de fala firme,'

(62) *yora akáro aská:*

    yora   aká-ro   aská
    person DEM.GENR-TOP SML

    'this person is like this:'
    'esta é assim.'

(63) *aro na mai shavápashõ nishõ,*

    a-ro   na   mai shavá-pa-shõ   ni-shõ
    3.DEM-TOP DEM.PROX land dwelling-LOC-LOC.PROV live-DSSA

    'having lived in this land,'
    'Esta, tendo vivido nesta terra,'

(64) *wa shavo kai wetsa,*

    wa   shavo ka-i   wetsa
    DEM.DIST woman go-PROG another

    'with that woman,'
    'com aquela mulher,'

(65) *wa shavo kai wetsa,*

    wa   shavo ka-i   wetsa
    DEM.DIST woman go-PROG another

    'with that other woman,'
    'com aquela mulher,'

(66) *wa shavo kai wetsa, akama.*

    wa   shavo ka-i   wetsa   aka-ma
    DEM.DIST woman go-PROG another AUX-NEG

    'with that other woman, he didn't go.'
    'com aquela outra mulher não saía.'

(67) *Mato mã aĩ viá keská,*

    mato   mã   aĩ   viá   keská
    2PL.ABS 2PL.ERG woman take SML

    'Just like when you choose a woman,'[6]
    'Como vocês que escolhem as suas mulheres,'

---

[6]This is a reference to me (Cesarino) and monogamous white people.

(68) *a westí verõsho oĩa akavo,*

    a   westí   verõ-sho oĩa aka-vo
    3.DEM only.one eye-CON see AUX.TRNS-PL

    'person who looks with only one eye'[7]
    'pessoas que olham com apenas um olho,'

(69) *yoratsẽ Vei Maya vei akatĩpa,*

    yora-tsẽ   Vei   Maya vei   aka-tĩpa
    person-CON death Maya death AUX.TRNS-IMPOSS

    'this kind of person, Vei Maya cannot hold,'
    'esse tipo de pessoa Vei Maya não consegue pegar'

(70) *askárasĩ vei akatĩpa.*

    aská-rasĩ vei   aka-tĩpa
    SML-COL death AUX.TRNS-IMPOSS

    'this kind of person cannot die.'
    'pessoas assim não podem ficar morridas.'

(71) *Wa mai shavápashõ,*

    wa   mai shavá-pa-shõ
    DEM.DIST land dwelling-LOC-LOC.PROV

    '"In that land,'
    '"Na morada daquela terra,'

(72) *wa mai shavapashõ,*

    wa   mai shavá-pa-shõ
    DEM.DIST land dwelling-LOC-LOC.PROV

    'in that land,'
    'na morada daquela terra,'

(73) *wa shavo kai wetsa,*

    wa   shavo   ka-i   wetsa
    DEM.DIST woman go-PROG another

    'with that and that woman,'
    'com aquela mulher,'

---

[7] "Person who looks with only one eye" is a metaphor for those who search for only one women, as white people. The Marubo polygamy was once restricted to shamans and chiefs but nowadays is practised with more relaxed criteria, which produces this kind of criticism by elder shamans as Armando.

(74) wa shavo kai wetsa,

    wa   shavo ka-i   wetsa
DEM.DIST woman go-PROG another
'with that and that woman,'
'com aquela mulher,'

(75) ẽ yora onã shavorasĩ,

    ẽ   yora onã   shavo-rasĩ
1SG.GEN people know women-COL
'with my relatives' wives,'
'com mulheres conhecidas,'

(76) akĩ ichná kawãi ẽ niámarvi.

    a-kĩ   ichná kawã-i ẽ   niá-ma-rivi
AUX.TRNS-SSSA bad   go-PROG 1SG.ERG live-NEG-EMP
'I did not live by flirting.'
'eu não fiquei mesmo fazendo besteira.'

(77) ẽ oĩtivoivo,

    ẽ   oĩ-ti-vo-ivo
1SG.GEN see.choose-NMLZ-PL-GENR
'Only with my chosen one,'
'Apenas com a minha escolhida,'

(78) shavo ninivarãsh,

    shavo ni-ni-varã-sh
woman live-live-DIR.C-DSPA
'the woman that I brought to live with me,'
'A mulher que eu trouxe para viver comigo,'

(79) aivo shavo oĩ inishõ neskái.

    a-ivo   shavo oĩ i-ni-shõ   neská-i
3.DEM-GENR woman see AUX-ASSOC-DSSA SML-PST1
'only with this one I've lived.'
'por ter vivido apenas com ela é que fiquei assim.'

(80) *Vei kayapai ẽ neskámaĩnõ.*

    vei   kaya-pai   ẽ   neská-maĩnõ
    death true.principal-COMP 1SG.GEN SML-CON

    'An honest dead I now am.'
    'Por isso agora sou morto íntegro.'

(81) *Matõ neskánamãsh, ea vei akatĩpa ea.*

    matõ   neská-namã-sh ea   vei   aka-tĩpa   ea
    2PL.GEN SML-LOC-DSPA 1SG.ABS death AUX.TRNS-IMPOSS 1SG.ABS

    'In this place of yours, you cannot kill me."'
    'Por isso vocês aqui não podem, não podem me matar."'

(82) *Ikitõ awẽ ese vanase ainai,*

    iki-tõ   awẽ   ese   vana-se   a-ina-i
    say-CNS POSS wisdom speech-EXT AUX.INTR-MOV.up-PROG

    'His wise words he says ascending,'[8]
    'Assim ele vai então dizendo sua fala sabida,'

(83) *awẽ ese vanase vevo ashõ kai,*

    awẽ   ese   vana-se   vevo   a-shõ   ka-i
    POSS wisdom speech-EXT before AUX.TRNS-DSSA go-PR

    'with wise words he goes,'
    'tendo dito sua fala sabida ele avança,'

(84) *katsese vana ikitai tapi,*

    katsese   vana   iki-ta-i   tapi
    everything speech say-ASS-PROG go

    'speaking with everything he continues,'[9]
    'Falando com tudo ele segue,'

---

[8] This refers to the speech of a deceased person, who is crossing the path.

[9] He refers to all of the path's dangers, which the dead should know in their numerous forms (*shovia*). The person should acquire this knowledge during his/her life in order to face the challenges of the afterlife.

(85) *awá shao tapã vana ikitase,*

　　awá shao tapã　vana　iki-ta-se
　　tapir bone bridge speech say-ASS-EXT

　　'speaking with the tapir bone bridge,'
　　'com a ponte de osso de anta ele fala,'

(86) *awá shao tapã masotanáiri*

　　awá shao tapã　maso-taná-iri
　　tapir bone bridge upon-arranged-DIR

　　'with the sharp shell heap,'
　　'coma as cortantes conchas,'

(87) *pao shokoarasĩ vana ikitase*

　　pao　shokoa-rasĩ vana　iki-ta-se
　　shell heap-COL speech say-ASS-EXT

　　'above the tapir bridge he speaks,'[10]
　　'sobre a ponte de ossos de anta ele fala,'

(88) *vei yochĩrasĩ vanaainase*

　　vei　yochĩ-rasĩ vana-a-ina-se
　　death spirit-COL speech-REL-MOV.up-EXT

　　'speaking with the dead spirits he goes,'
　　'com todos os espectros-morte ele fala,'

(89) *vimirasĩ vanaainase.*

　　vimi-rasĩ vana-a-ina-se
　　fruit-COL speech-REL-MOV.up-EXT

　　'speaking with the fruits he goes.'[11]
　　'com os frutos todos ele fala.'

---

[10] A heap of shells that cut and kill the dead.
[11] Death-fruits (*vei vimi*) that he might eat instead of continuing his ascent.

(90) *Wa mai shavápashõ, vimi ichnárasĩ yaniakĩ niáma,*

    wa   mai shavá-pa-shõ   vimi ichná-rasĩ õsipa yania-kĩ
DEM.DIST land dwelling-LOC-LOC.PROV fruit bad-COL   varied feed-SSSA
niá-ma
live-NEG

'"In that land, I didn't live by eating bad and varied fruit,'
'"Naquela terra, não vivi me alimentando de ruins e fartos frutos.'

(91) *eri píti koĩ meramashõrivi ea anõ yanini.*

    e-ri   píti koĩ   mera-ma-shõ-rivi ea   anõ yani-ini
1SG-REFL food real.true find-CS-SSPA-EMP 1SG.ABS FIN feed-?

'I've worked to have my own real food.'
'Eu mesmo procurava comida de verdade para me alimentar.'

(92) *Aki ea anõ mato ea mã veikatĩpa.*

    a-ki   ea   anõ mato ea   mã   vei-aka-tĩpa
AUX-ASS 1SG.ABS FIN 2PL.ABS 1SG.ABS 2PL.ERG death-AUX.TRNS-IMPOSS

'That's how I've lived, so you cannot kill me."'
'É assim que sou, vocês não podem me matar!"'

(93) *A kaisa vanania.*

    a   kai-sa vana-ina
3.DEM go-? speech-MOV.up

'There he goes ascending and speaking.'
'Assim ele sobe falando.'

(94) *Vei shõparasĩ askásevi,*

    Vei   shõpa-rasĩ askásevi
death papaya-COL SML-CON

'With papaya-death also,'
'Com os mamãos-morte também,'

(95) *askárasĩ awe kẽvo anõ inã askásevi,*

    aská-rasĩ awe kẽ-vo   anõ inã   aská-sevi
SML-COL thing desire-PL FIN offer SML-CON

'with all the alluring things also,'
'com todas as coisas sedutoras também,'

(96) *askásevi askásevi vana akitase kãi,*

    aská-sevi aská-sevi vana-a-ki-ta-se   kãi
    SML-CON SML-CON speech-REL-SSSA-ASS-EXT go

    'with all the things he speaks and speaks,'
    'e também e também, com tudo ele vai mesmo falando.'

(97) *vanaarasĩ nokorivi,*

    vana-a-rasĩ   noko-rivi
    speech-RLZ-COL arrive-EMP

    'speaking with everything he arrives,'
    'Falando com tudo ele chega mesmo,'

(98) *ese vanase vevo oshõ kãi nokorivi.*

    ese   vana-se   vevo   o-shõ   kã-i   noko-rivi
    wisdom speech-EXT before come-DSSA go-PROG arrive-EMP

    'having walked with wise words he arrives.' [12]
    'tendo antes falado sabiamente ele chega mesmo.'

(99) *Askámaĩnõ wetsaro, awẽ ese vana keyonamãsho,*

    Aská-maĩnõ wetsa-ro   a-ivo   awẽ ese   vana   keyo-namã-sho
    SML-CON   other-TOP DEM-GENR POSS wisdom speech over-LOC-CON

    'But the other one, in that place where his speech failed,'
    'Mas aquele outro, naquele lugar mesmo em que sua fala sabida acabou,'

(100) *awẽ keyovãianamãsho atxitase.*

    awẽ keyo-vãia-namã-sho atxi-ta-se
    POSS over-INC-LOC-CON   hold-ASS-EXT

    'in that place where it failed he gets stuck.'
    'ali mesmo onde a fala acabou ele fica preso.'

(101) *Nokẽ shenirasĩ, ramama itivorasĩ,*

    Nokẽ   sheni-rasĩ   rama-ma i-ti-vo-rasĩ
    1PL.GEN forbear-COL now-NEG live-PST5-PL-COL

    'Our forbearers, those born long ago,'
    'Os nossos antigos, os antepassados de outros tempos,'

---

[12] Arrives at the end of the Death-Path, where he/she will find the ancient people.

(102) askásevi veikenaivorasĩ.
askásevi vei-ke-na-ivo-rasĩ
SML   death-COMPL-?-GENR-COL
'they also used to die.' [13]
'ficavam também morridos.'

(103) Rave nokoma, rave nokoa, Vei Naí Shavaya nokoma,
rave noko-ma   rave noko-ma   vei   naí shavaya noko-ma
part arrive-NEG part arrive-NEG death sky dwelling arrive-NEG
'Some didn't arrive, some didn't arrive, in the Death-Sky Dwelling they couldn't arrive,'
'Uns não chegavam, uns não chegavam, na Morada do Céu-Morte não chegavam.'

(104) ravero nokoai, ravero nokoma, ravero nokoai.
rave-ro   noko-ai   rave-ro   noko-ma   rave-ro   noko-ai
part-TOP arrive-INCP part-TOP arrive-NEG part-TOP arrive-INCP
'some arrived, some couldn't arrive, some arrived.'
'Uns chegavam, uns não chegavam, outros chegavam.'

(105) Akarivi
aka-rivi
AUX.TRNS-EMP
'That's how it happened.' [14]
'Assim mesmo é.'

---

[13] Meaning that they also used to die or become transformed along the path, because of their lack of knowledge and/or good moral behavior.

[14] The narrative continues with the exposition of other dangers of the path, giving the sequence of the history of *Vei Maya*, as well as with its moral speculations (see Cesarino 2012 for the complete version).

Non-standard abbreviations

ASS	assertive	INC	inchoative
ASSOC	associative	INCP	incompletive
ATR.PERM	attributive, permanent	LOC.PROV	provenance
ATR.TRNS	attributive, transitional	MOV.UP	movement up
CNS	consecutive	POSSIB	possibility
COMP	comparative	PST1	past (immediate)
CON	connective	PST2	past (months)
CON.FIN	connective of finality	PST3	past (years, decades)
DIR	direction	PST4	past (decades, centuries)
DIR.C	direction, centripetal		
DISTR	distributive	PST5	past (remote, narrative)
DSPA	different subject, previous action	RLZ	realized action
DSSA	different subject, simultaneous action	SML	similitive
		SSPA	same subject, previous action
EMP	emphatic		
EXT	existential predication	SSSA	same subject, simultaneous action
FIN	finality		
FUT	future	TEMP	temporal subordination
GENR	generic		
IMPOSS	impossible	VBLZ	verbalizer

References

Camargo, Eliane. 1995. Enunciação e percepção: A informação mediatizada em Caxinaua. *Bulletin de la Société Suisse des Américanistes* 59-60. 181–188.

Camargo, Eliane. 1996a. Des marqueurs modaux en Caxinaua. *Amerindia* 21. 1–20.

Camargo, Eliane. 1996b. Valeurs médiatives en caxinaua. In Zlatka Guentchéva (ed.), *Énonciation médiatisée*, 271–284. Louvain, Paris: Peeters.

Camargo, Eliane. 1998. La structure actancielle du Caxinaua. *La Linguistique* 34(1). 137–150.

Camargo, Eliane. 2003. Construções adjetivais e participais em Caxinauá (Pano). *Liames* 3. 39–51.

Camargo, Eliane. 2005. Manifestações da ergatividade em Caxinauá (Pano). *Liames* 5. 55–88.

Cesarino, Pedro de Niemeyer. 2011. *Oniska - poética do xamanismo na Amazônia*. São Paulo: Editora Perspectiva/ FAPESP.

Cesarino, Pedro de Niemeyer. 2012. Os relatos do Caminho-Morte: Etnografia e tradução de poéticas ameríndias. *Estudos Avançados* 26. 75–100.

Cesarino, Pedro de Niemeyer. 2013. *Quando a terra deixou de falar - cantos da mitologia Marubo*. São Paulo: Editora 34.

Costa, Raquel. 1992. *Padrões rítmicos e marcação de caso em Marubo (Pano)*. MA thesis: Federal University of Rio de Janeiro.

Costa, Raquel. 1998. Aspects of ergativity in Marubo (Panoan). *The Journal of Amazonian Languages* 1(2). 50–103.

Costa, Raquel. 2000. *Aspectos da fonologia Marubo (Pano): Uma visão Não-Linear*. Federal University of Rio de Janeiro dissertation.

Fleck, David W. 2003. *A grammar of Matses*. Rice University dissertation.

Montagner, Delvair. 1985. *O mundo dos Espíritos: Estudo etnográfico dos ritos de cura Marúbo*. University of Brasília dissertation.

Montagner, Delvair. 1996. *A morada das almas*. Belém: Museu Paraense Emílio Goeldi.

Ruedas, Javier. 2001. *The Marubo political system*. Tulane University dissertation.

Valenzuela, Pilar. 2003. *Transitivity in Shipibo-Konibo grammar*. University of Oregon dissertation.

Welper, Elena. 2009. *O mundo de João Tuxáua: transformação do povo Marubo*. Federal University of Rio de Janeiro dissertation.

Chapter 5

Trumai

Raquel Guirardello-Damian
University of Bristol, England and Museu Paraense Emílio Goeldi, Brazil

Kumaru Trumai

Tarukuy Trumai

1 Introduction

The story of the Smooth-billed Ani (a type of bird in the cuckoo family[1]) is a myth told by the Trumai people of the central region of Brazil. It was video recorded in 2000 by the author (Raquel Guirardello-Damian) and narrated by Kumaru Trumai, a middle-aged woman who has since died. She learned it from her father, Initiari, a great and respected storyteller. The myth was later transcribed and analyzed with the assistance of a young man, Tarukuy, who is bilingual in Trumai and Portuguese. The text is presented in its phonological form with IPA symbols, followed by English glosses and free translation. When necessary, comments are added in the footnotes.

2 The Trumai people and their language

The Trumai live in the "Xingu Indigenous Land", at the northern edge of the Upper Xingu area. The group originally came from another land, located to the southeast of the Upper Xingu (Murphy & Quain 1955), and it is assumed that they moved to the Xingu region in the first half of the 19th century due to attacks by another tribe, possibly the Xavante (Villas Boas & Villas Boas 1970). Their initial

---

[1]The smooth-billed ani (*Crotophaga ani*) is a breeding species that lives in several regions across the Americas. It is a black bird, known in Portuguese as *anu* or *anu preto*.

Raquel Guirardello-Damian, Kumaru Trumai & Tarukuy Trumai. 2017. Trumai. In Kristine Stenzel & Bruna Franchetto (eds.), *On this and other worlds: Voices from Amazonia*, 163–185. Berlin: Language Science Press. DOI:10.5281/zenodo.1008781

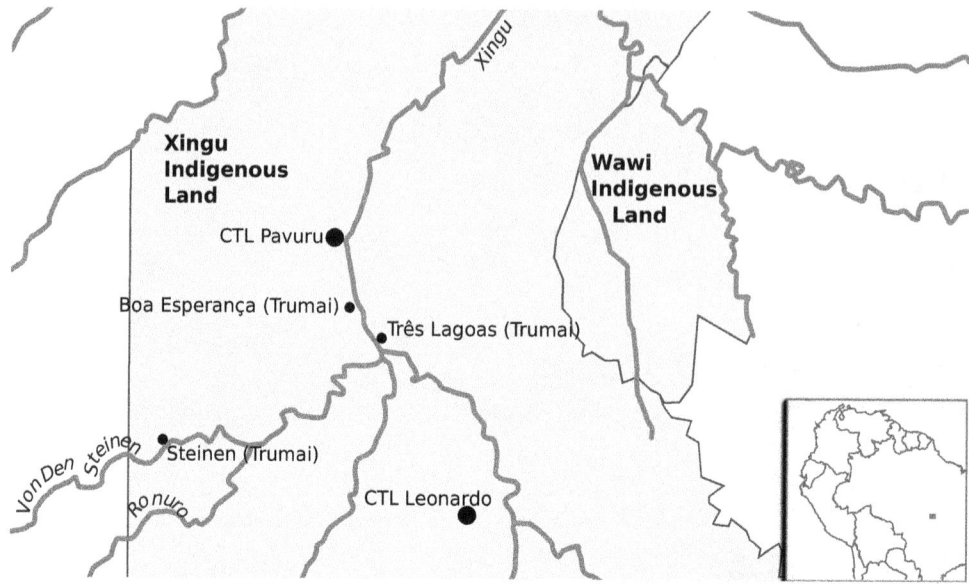

Figure 1: Trumai villages in the Xingu Indigenous Land.

contacts with the local groups were not peaceful and led to some conflicts. When von den Steinen (1940) visited the region, in the second half of the 19th century, the Trumai still did not have good relations with the Upper Xinguan tribes, but eventually became integrated to the new environment.

The Upper Xingu is a multilingual and multi-ethnic regional system. Several groups live in the area, having different languages and historical backgrounds. However, they also share many common cultural features, observed especially in the activities of daily survival, diet, mythology, and inter/intra village rituals (Galvão & Simões 1966). Such cultural homogeneity was developed through the interaction of various factors, such as the isolation of the region, physical proximity of the groups, commerce and intertribal marriages, and groups' influence on each other. The Trumai people are the least integrated into this system. Although they share several of the Upper Xingu cultural practices, they also keep some of their own original traditions – for example, they do not take part in the *Kwarup* ceremony, an important intertribal ritual, and they eat certain kinds of animals that are forbidden to other Upper Xinguan groups (Monod-Becquelin 1975; Monod-Becquelin & Guirardello 2001).

The location of the Trumai villages in the Xingu reserve changed several times after their arrival in the area. Nowadays, their population is concentrated mainly in three villages: *Boa Esperança*, *Três Lagoas* (with inhabitants from the former village known as *Terra Preta*), and *Steinen*. There are also families living in cities close to the reserve. The community has more than 100 individuals, but the number of Trumai speakers is reduced, being approximately 50. Levels of proficiency vary among individuals, with the older speakers exhibiting broader and deeper linguistic knowledge. Children do not learn the language anymore, speaking Portuguese (the national language of Brazil) or another Xinguan language instead. Various historical factors contributed to its endangerment (cf. Guirardello 1999, preface).

With regard to genetic linguistic affiliations, Trumai is considered an isolate language (Rodrigues 1986; Kaufman 1994). In relation to the Xingu area, Trumai seems to have a unique status, not only in terms of genetic affiliation, but also with regard to typological features. For instance, it has ejective stops, sounds not observed in the other languages of the region (Seki 2000; Fargetti 1992; Dourado 2001; Emmerich 1980). It also employs positional verbs in locative and existential constructions, another fact not attested in other Xinguan languages (Guirardello-Damian 2007). It also has three dative markers, a quite interesting typological characteristic.

Trumai has four open classes (nouns, verbs, adjectives, and adverbs) and little inflectional morphology, i.e., words usually consist of a single morpheme. For nouns, there are two important subdivisions: (i) alienably possessed versus inalienably possessed nouns, with a further subdivision between body parts and kinship terms; (ii) animate versus inanimate nouns. These distinctions are observed in various points of the grammar. Trumai has five verbal classes and the case system exhibits an ergative-absolutive alignment, manifested through markers on NPs or the use of postpositions. There are also ergative alignments in syntax (Guirardello-Damian 2010). The basic word order is SOV, but variations of order are possible depending on pragmatic factors; the variations observed in negative clauses are particularly noteworthy (Guirardello 1999).

With regard to the phonological system, Trumai has six vowels (/i/, /e/, /ɨ/, /a/, /u/, /o/) and twenty three consonants (/p/, /ṭ/, /t/, /d/, /k/, /ʔ/, /ṭ'/, /t'/, /k'/, /ts/, /ts'/, /f/, /s/, /ʃ/, /x/, /h/, /m/, /n/, /l/, /ɬ/, /ɾ/, /w/, /j/). The vowels /e/ and /o/ have two allophones in free variation: [e] and [ɛ], [o] and [ɔ] respectively (cf. Guirardello 1999: 1–6).

3 The topic of the narrative

The narrative presented here is related to issues of life and death. It explains the origins of the chanted cries and lamentations that the Trumai people perform when mourning somebody's death. The story happens in mythological times, when animals were like human beings, having their own villages, conducting daily survival activities, and being able to speak. Thus, the main character in the story, the Smooth-billed Ani, has anthropomorphic features. One day he decides to play a trick on his grandmother. While she is in the fields collecting firewood, he stages a big scene in her house, pretending that she has died. He then performs some actions and crying, showing that he is sad for her death. The crying was later imitated by others and became part of the Upper Xinguan traditions for expressing sorrow.[2]

Trumai funeral practices were first documented by the ethnologist Buell Quain, who lived among them in 1938, although his description is brief. Further research conducted by the anthropologist Emmanuel de Vienne obtained many more details and revealed that the practices can be quite elaborate. The next paragraphs give an overview of the information provided by Murphy & Quain (1955) and De Vienne (personal communication).

In the Trumai funerary ceremony, the classic division is between the ones who dig the hole for the grave (*owowas xotkenke wan* 'the hole diggers') and those who perform the crying (*watkanke wan* 'the ones who cry'). Ritual cries and lamentations begin from the moment of death. Close relatives cry by repeating the kinship term that bound them to the deceased person. The other relatives use the same formula, but also provide consolation to the close relatives by saying stereotyped expressions (e.g. "This is how it is, we cannot do anything"; "It is like this for us, humans"; "You have to be strong, because it happens to everyone"). The crying follows a particular melody and consists of the repetition of the vocative used to call the dead person (for example: *atseda* 'grandma', *ajej* 'grandpa', *atsiwe* 'mum', etc.). This vocative can be combined with expressions that convey compassion and sadness. In the myth below, we will see a concrete example of this.[3]

The ritual crying happens before and at the moment of burying the body. There is also the practice of "welcome in tears", which is a crying performed when relatives living far away arrive for the first time after the death, even several months later. The visitors start to cry loudly on their way to the village. The

---

[2] In a section about Trumai mythology, Murphy & Quain (1955: 73) apparently make a brief mention of this myth – although they refer to the smooth-billed ani as "crow", another black bird: "crow appeared as a trickster and, although not a creator deity, managed to bring forth new things in the process of his machinations."

[3] The tradition of executing ritual cries is also part of the death ceremonies of other Upper Xinguan tribes. For example, Guerreiro Júnior (2012: 441) describes the crying used in the funerary rituals of the Kalapalo people, which exhibits the same pattern as the Trumai one.

close relatives of the deceased person then come to welcome them in the central square of the village and they go together to the grave in order to cry. There are further ritual cries in secondary funerary rituals, such as the Javari festivity.

Burial takes place in the central area of the village, which has a circular shape. On the day of death, or the next day (if it is necessary to wait for the arrival of relatives), three or four men who are distant relatives from the deceased ask permission to dig the grave. These man must not have children under the age of two, otherwise the spirit of the deceased person may bring diseases to the child. They proceed as the crying and lamentations continue. First, they measure the body with a bamboo in order to determine the size of the grave, which is prepared in the shape of a hole. The bottom widens to form a tunnel where the corpse will be placed. Chiefs, both male and female, are given a special burial treatment, since their grave has a tunnel with two exits. Special funerary treatments for chiefs are observed in other Upper Xingu groups as well, such as the Kuikuro (Heckenberger 2003).

After finishing their job, the diggers return to the dead person's house and start the ceremonial crying, then announce that it is time to bury the body, which is painted and adorned with feathers by a distant relative. They wrap and tie a hammock around the body, starting with the feet. The face is protected by a fiber mat (*tuwawi*) to prevent it from coming into contact with the soil/earth. Personal objects are placed inside the hammock: cooking utensils for women, bows and arrows for men. The remaining possessions are broken and burned or used to "pay" visitors and diggers. Guided by a close relative, the diggers carry the body through the front door, walk around the house several times, and enter through the back door. They do the same action inside, before going to the grave. During this time, cries and demonstrations of deep sadness continue.

The corpse is "interred lying on its back in an extended position" (Murphy & Quain 1955: 90).[4] The feet are placed towards the east, so that the soul of the deceased person faces the direction it should go. A shaman performs a ritual prayer in order to prevent it from coming back. This prayer is performed in the grave and all the places where the deceased person used to go (house, garden plot, etc.). The following day, the diggers go fishing and take the fish to the deceased person's house. A close relative takes them to the grave, where a shaman performs a prayer and blows tobacco smoke on the fish. This food is meant for spirits, which

---

[4] According to another text recorded with a Trumai speaker, chiefs would be buried in a different way: male chiefs (*aek*) would be buried in a standing position, while female chiefs (*aek pekts'a*) would be buried in a seated position. However, this information was not confirmed by De Vienne's consultants, thus it is not clear if it refers to a practice currently followed by the Trumai or to some older tradition.

are expected to be present in large numbers around the grave. After this, the fish are shared and distributed to the whole village. A fire is placed on the grave for the next three or four days, the time necessary for the deceased person's soul to go away to the village of the dead.

Figure 2: A Trumai village, with its central area

4 General aspects of the narrative

Some of the procedures of the Trumai funerary practices – the ritual crying, the breaking and burning of the deceased's possessions, the wrapping of the body in a hammock – are observed in the narrative presented in the next section. As already mentioned, there are two central characters, the Smooth-billed Ani and his grandmother, with a third character appearing just briefly (his aunt). Events happen in chronological order, with one pause made by the narrator to make a comment about the Upper Xingu death rituals (lines 34-37).

With regard to the linguistic characteristics of the narrative, a visible feature is the use of kinship terms (*aɬahne* 'grandmother', *mako* 'aunt (mother's sister)', *doxo* 'grandchild') with their possessive marker (*tsi-* '3POSS'). The text also employs motion verbs and directional auxiliaries, such as *lahmi* 'go uphill'. The occurrence of *k(e)tsi* is particularly interesting. In daily conversations, this auxiliary is employed to describe motion towards the place where the speaker is, often generating the sense of 'come' or 'bring' (Guirardello-Damian 2012), but in the case of this narrative, *k(e)tsi* is employed when somebody moves towards the place where the main character and key actions are (lines 29-31) – in other words, this auxiliary can also be used for a place that is the focus of the attention of the speaker and listener.

The text has various instances of hearsay particles and ideophones, which is not surprising, since they are often found in narratives. It is worth mentioning that some Trumai ideophones are similar in shape to the ones in Kamayurá, another Xinguan language (Guirardello-Damian 2014). This is the case of the ideophone for "walking" observed in the text (cf. Footnote 22).

There are occurrences of direct speech in the narrative, but they do not configure dialogues properly speaking. The main character (Smooth-billed Ani) does not talk to anyone in particular; rather, he talks in order to be heard by people in the village. The other character (his grandmother) talks to herself, wondering what is happening in her house. In her speech (lines 40 and 45), we find the particle *apa*, which indicates uncertainty by the speaker and can be broadly translated as 'I wonder'. The aunt is the only character who talks to a specific addressee, and in her speech we can see the 2nd person pronoun (*hi* 'you') or the 1st person inclusive (*ka a* 'we two (inclusive)', which contrasts with *ha a* 'we two (exclusive)', *ka wan* 'we – more than two (inclusive)' and *ha wan* 'we – more than two (exclusive)').

As a final note, it is interesting to mention that all verbal classes are represented in the text, since it contains several action verbs. For example: **class 1 (intransitives)**: *kaʔfɨ* 'walk'; **class 2 (transitives)**: *husa* 'tie', *tsisi* 'burn'; *kiwa* 'abandon'; **class 3 (ditransitives)**: *tsitsu* 'put'; **class 4 (intransitives with two positions)**: *kuʔku* 'break', *huʔtsa* 'see', *faʔtsa* 'hear'; **class 5 (verbs with varied transitivity)**: *naha* 'cut/break' (for more information about the verbal classes, cf. Guirardello-Damian 2010). The text also includes the verbs for crying: *watkan* 'to weep' (i.e. to shed tears when one is sad) and *ora* 'to cry intensely, screaming' (as small children do when they fall. This term can also be used for the cries of certain animals, such as monkeys). In the narrative, the occurrence of *ora* is much higher than *watkan*, which makes sense, since the main character is trying to get attention and provoke a commotion as part of his trick, thus his crying needs to be intense.

5 trumaj wankaṭe dainṭ'a: kowow

'A Trumai narrative: the Smooth-billed Ani'

'Um mito Trumai: o Anu'[5]

(1) *trumaj wankaṭe dainṭ'a: kowow*

trumaj	*wan=kaṭe*	*dainṭ'a:*	*kowow*
trumai	PL=GEN	old.times.narrative	Smooth-billed.Ani

'A Trumai narrative: the Smooth-billed Ani'

'Um mito Trumai: o Anu'[6]

(2) *inis hen tsile hen, tsiɬahne de kaʔʃɨ lahmi kuṭ'aki de,*

inis	*hen*	*tsile*	*hen*	*tsi-aɬahne*		*de*
DISC.CON	then	hearsay	then	3POSS(KIN)-grandmother		pitiful

kaʔʃɨ	*lahmi*	*kuṭ'a=ki*	*de*
walk	go.uphill	garden.plot=DAT	already

'So, people say that his poor grandmother went walking to (her) garden plot,'

'Dizem que a coitada da avó dele foi caminhando para a roça,'[7]

(3) *kaʔʃɨ ṭ'axer lahmin.*

kaʔʃɨ	*ṭ'axer*	*lahmi=n*
walk	poorly	go.uphill=3ABS

'she left.'

'foi embora.'[8]

---

[5] Recordings of this story are available from https://zenodo.org/record/997451

[6] The term *daint'a* refers to both myths and historical narratives (i.e., facts from ancient times).

[7] Two comments with regard to this sentence: (i) *inis* occurs in the first position of a clause and is often followed by the adverb *hen* 'then'. It can be analyzed internally as a combination of two morphemes (the demonstrative pronoun *in* plus the temporal marker *-is*, which would be literally translated as 'in this situation/event'), but its main role is as a discourse connector, with the sense of 'and then'. Sometimes *inis* can be replaced by *ina*, another possible connector; (ii) The adjective *de* indicates pity for the person being mentioned. The speaker talks in a touching and tender way.

[8] When Trumai speakers express motion events, they often use directional auxiliaries to further specify the type of motion: uphill, downhill, upriver, downriver, towards the village, towards the river, and so on (for more detail, cf. Guirardello-Damian 2012).

(4) *husakwaʃ t'axeraɫ tsile api piṭan, kaʔʃɨ lahmin hen.*

    husa=kwaʃ   t'axer=a=ɫ   tsile   api piṭa=n
    tie=thing.for modest/poor=EP.VW=DAT hearsay grab go.out=3ABS
    kaʔʃɨ lahmi=n   hen
    walk go.uphill=3ABS then

    'She went out (of her house) taking a rope (to tie firewood), and she left.'
    'Saiu (da casa) levando uma corda (para amarrar lenha), e foi embora.'

(5) *kaʔʃɨ t'axer lahmin, kaʔʃɨ den lahmin.*

    kaʔʃɨ t'axer lahmi=n   kaʔʃɨ den   lahmi=n
    walk poorly go.uphill=3ABS walk AUX? go.uphill=3ABS

    'She left, she disappeared (in the distance).'
    'Foi embora andando e sumiu (na distância).'

(6) *ina hen tsiɫahne de kaʔʃɨ den lahmi hen.*

    ina   hen   tsi-aɫahne   de   kaʔʃɨ den lahmi hen
    DISC.CON then 3POSS(KIN)-grandmother pitiful walk AUX? go.uphill then

    'His poor grandmother went walking and disappeared.'
    'A coitada da avó foi caminhando e sumiu.'[9]

(7) *ina hen iji lat peʃ.kiwda=n ale de. kowow ji de.*

    ina   hen   iji   lat peʃ.kiwda=n   ale   de.
    DISC.CON then PRAG.IN lie go.running=3ABS hearsay already
    kowow   ji   de.
    Smooth-billed.Ani PRAG.IN already

    'Then he went (to her house) and started lying. He, the Smooth-billed Ani.'
    'Então ele foi (para a casa dela) e começou a mentir. Ele, o Anu.'[10]

---

[9] Note that the speaker describes the same action several times (the grandmother left, she left). Such repetition is part of a narration strategy, in order to make the description of events more elaborate and interesting to follow.

[10] This sentence contains instances of the morpheme *(i)ji*, which occurs in NPs. This morpheme has a unique nature and its function is not not entirely clear, but it seems to be linked to pragmatic information. It presents two forms: *ji*, which occurs in NPs containing an element (i.e., a noun, pronoun or pluralizer), and *iji*, which can occur by itself in a NP (but only Absolutive NPs). We could analyze *iji* as a pronominal form (i.e., a dummy pronoun) and *ji* as some sort of modifier, however this analysis has its own limitations (cf. Guirardello-Damian 2005: 281-285). For the present text, I will use 'PRAG.IN' as the gloss for this morpheme.

(8) ina hen tsiɬahne dekte sopʃatki daʔtsi.wawan ale, esak faxki de iji tsitsu de.

ina   hen tsi-aɬahne   de=kte   sopʃat=ki
DISC.CON then 3POSS(KIN)-grandmother pitiful=GEN firewood=DAT
daʔtsi.wawa=n ale,   esak   fax=ki   de   iji
gather=3ABS   hearsay hammock interior=DAT already PRAG.IN
tsitsu de
put   already

'He gathered his grandmother's firewood and put it in a hammock.'
'Ele juntou a lenha da avó e colocou dentro de uma rede.'[11]

(9) det'a det'a pits tsile, jaw pits' nawan de, esak faxki iji tsitsu le, jaw kuta nawan tsile.

det'a det'a pits   tsile   jaw   pits' nawan de
well well really/very hearsay human.being   foot similar already
esak   fax=ki   iji   tsitsu le   jaw   kuta nawan
hammock interior=DAT PRAG.IN put   hearsay human.being   head similar
tsile
hearsay

'Very perfectly, he put in the hammock a thing imitating a human foot, and (another) thing imitating a human head.'
'Bem direitinho, colocou na rede uma coisa imitando pé de gente, e (uma outra) coisa imitando uma cabeça.'

(10) ina hen esak ji hen mal husa husa ke ine jik, det'a hen jaw atu tsula nawan de.

ina   hen esak   ji   hen
DISC.CON then hammock PRAG.IN then
mal[12] husa husa ke[13]   ine   ji=k
edge   tie tie   DISLOC.ABS 3ANAPH.MASC PRAG.IN=ERG
det'a hen jaw   atu tsula   nawan de
well then human.being dead be.lying similar already

---

[11]There are three variants of the hearsay particle: *ale* (after a verb with the 3ABS enclitic), *le* (after a verb without the 3ABS enclitic), and *tsile* (in other positions).

[12]In this example, the noun *mal* 'edge/border' is incorporated in the verb ('He border-tied the hammock'). Trumai allows noun incorporation (cf. Guirardello-Damian 2005: 225-226).

[13]The particle *ke* appears when the Absolutive NP is not in its typical position, which is right before the verb. This occurs when the Absolutive NP or the verb is fronted in order to be highlighted (as in this example — the word for 'hammock' (*esak*) is fronted).

'Then he tied the hammock, it became very similar to a dead person lying.'
'Então ele amarrou a rede, ficou igualzinho a uma pessoa morta deitada.'

(11) *iji late ale de.*

    iji   lat=e   ale   de
    PRAG.IN lie=3ABS hearsay already

    'He was pretending (that his grandmother had died).'
    'Ele estava fingindo (que a avó tinha morrido).'

(12) *inis hen tsile iji oran ale:*

    inis   hen   tsile   iji   ora=n   ale
    DISC.CON then hearsay PRAG.IN cry=3ABS hearsay

    'Then he cried:'
    'Então chorou:'

(13) *"hele deke atseda iṭa fakdits? atseda iṭa ..."*

    hele deke atseda   iṭa   fakdits atseda   iṭa
    why EMPH grandmother(VOC) pitiful die   grandmother(VOC) pitiful

    '"Why has my poor grandma died? Poor grandma ..."'
    '"Por que a coitada da vovó morreu? Pobre vovó ..."'[14]

(14) *deṭ'a deṭ'a pits tsile tsiɬahne de faʃṭaki iji kuʔkukman: too!*

    deṭ'a deṭ'a pits   tsile   tsi-aɬahne   de
    well well really/very hearsay 3POSS(KIN)-grandmother pitiful
    faʃṭa=ki   iji   kuʔku=kma=n   too
    belongings=DAT PRAG.IN break=PERF=3ABS ID:BREAKING

    'Then he broke all of his grandmother's things: *too!*'
    'Então ele quebrou todas as coisas da avó: *too!*'

---

[14] When the interrogative word *hele* is combined with the particle *deke*, the question has a more emphatic tone.

(15) *ałaṯ pates kuʔkun ale, inałkaṯe murukuyu muṯ ṯ'axer, amusadipu muṯ tsile.*

   ałaṯ   pat=e=s   kuʔku=n   ale
   clay.pan small=EP.VW=DAT break=3ABS hearsay

   inał=kaṯe   murukuyu muṯ
   3ANAPH.FEM=GEN red.paint wrapping/container

   amusadipu muṯ   tsile
   resin   wrapping/container hearsay

   'He broke little clay pans, the basket with her red body paint, the basket for wax.'
   'Quebrou panelinhas de barro, o urucum dela, a cestinha para cera cheirosa.'[15]

(16) *deṯ'a deṯ'a pits tsile iji mapa mapa.*

   deṯ'a deṯ'a pits   tsile   iji   mapa mapa
   well well really/very hearsay PRAG.IN break break

   'He broke (everything) very well.'
   'Quebrou (tudo) bem direitinho.'[16]

(17) *iʔimasṯame tsile hen.*

   iʔimasṯame tsile   hen
   commotion hearsay then

   'It was a commotion.'
   'Foi uma agitação.'

(18) *naha nahan ale, deṯ'a deṯ'a pits tsiłahne faʃṯa tsisi tsisikma le.*

   naha   naha=n   ale   deṯ'a deṯ'a pits
   cut/break cut/break=3ABS hearsay well well really/very

   tsi-ałahne   faʃṯa   tsisi tsisi=kma le
   3POSS(KIN)-grandmother belongings burn burn=PERF hearsay

   'He broke and burned all of his grandmother's things.'
   'Ele quebrou e queimou todas as coisas da avó.'

---

[15] As previously mentioned, when Trumai individuals die, their possessions are broken.

[16] There are various Trumai verbs that could be translated into English as 'break', but they have different nuances of meaning: *mapa* 'to break' (in general), *kuʔku* 'to break by hitting many times', *naha* 'cut or break with one single stroke'.

(19) *ina iji ora muketsin ale hen.*

   ina   iji   ora muketsi=n   ale   hen
   DISC.CON PRAG.IN   cry ASP.AUX=3ABS   hearsay   then

   'Then, he kept crying.'
   'Então, continuou a chorar.'[17]

(20) *"hele deke atsedak ha kiwa? adɨ atseda ..."*

   hele   deke   atseda=k   ha kiwa
   why   EMPH   grandmother(VOC)=ERG   1 leave.behind/abandon
   adɨ   atseda
   INTERJ   grandmother(VOC)

   '"Why has grandma left me? Oh poor grandma ..."'
   '"Por que vovó me deixou? Oh coitada da vovó ..."'

(21) *ora muketsin,*

   ora muketsi=n
   cry ASP.AUX=3ABS

   'He kept crying,'
   'Continuou chorando,'

(22) *aj de tsimako faʔtsa mula le de.*

   aj   de   tsi-mako   faʔtsa   mula
   by.then   already   3POSS(KIN)-aunt(mother's.sister) hear   be.indoors
   le   de
   hearsay   already

   'and his aunt heard him.'
   'e a tia dele ouviu.'

(23) *"huk'anik, huta.kaʃ ka a huʔtsa kawa."*

   huk'anik   huta.kaʃ ka   a   huʔtsa kawa
   EXPR   later   1INCL   DU   see   go

   '"Wait, later we are going to see her (i.e., take care of her)."'
   '"Espera, depois a gente vai vê-la (isto é, tomar conta dela)."'

---

[17] Apparently, *muketsi* is an aspectual auxiliary, but its meaning is not totally clear. It seems to indicate persistent action.

(24) "*ka anak t'axet'axer ji hupda hupekawan,*" *kale.*
 ka   ana=k   t'axe-t'axer ji   hupda.hupekawa=n kale
 1INCL DU=ERG RD-poor   PRAG.IN ritual.cry=3ABS like.this

 '"We will cry for her, poor her," his aunt said like this.'
 '"A gente vai chorar para ela, coitada," a tia disse assim.'[18]

---

[18] The morpheme *t'axer* is usually employed with the sense of 'poor' or 'misfortuned', but it can also be used with an offensive tone (wretched, bastard). When used as an adverb, it has a sense of 'poorly' or 'in a modest way'. The pattern that we see in the sentence above is attested in other examples involving this morpheme: it can occur after a noun (as in (i) below), or it can occur without the noun if the verb receives the 3rd person enclitic =*n*/=*e* (as in (ii)).

 (i) *hai=ts kasoro t'axer   hotaka.*
      1=ERG dog   wretched mislead
      'I misled the wretched dog.'

 (ii) *hai=ts t'axer   hotaka=n.*
      1=ERG wretched mislead=3ABS
      'I misled it, the wretched one.'

It might be that *t'axer* is not a modifier, but rather a noun with the sense of 'misfortune, wretched condition' and the noun that comes before it would be its possessor (something like: the wretched condition of the dog = the wretched dog). In the case of example (ii), *t'axer* would be incorporated into the verb, a pattern attested in the language, as in example (iii.b) below:

 (iii) a. *hai=ts Makarea mut'   tuxa?tsi.*
          1=ERG Makarea clothing/wrapping pull
          'I pulled Makarea's shirt.'

       b. *hai=ts mut' tuxa?tsi=n.*
          1=ERG clothing/wrapping pull=3ABS
          'I pulled his shirt (lit: I shirt-pulled him).'

It is possible to propose such an analysis given that other languages exhibit constructions similar to this one. For instance, in Portuguese one can say [*cachorro desgraçado*] or [*a desgraça do cachorro*] with the sense of 'wretched dog'. The literal translation of [*a desgraça do cachorro*] is 'the misfortune of the dog'. Thus, it might be that Trumai has a similar pattern.

(25) *"in ka t̯'axet̯'axer ji ora muketsin."*

    in   ka.in   t̯'axe-t̯'axer ji   ora muketsi=n

    that(place) FOC/TENS RD-poor   PRAG.IN cry ASP.AUX=3ABS

    '"He is there, crying" (his aunt said).'

    '"Ele está lá, chorando" (disse a tia).'[19]

(26) *"hi t̯'axer ji huʔtsa in?!"*

    hi t̯'axer ji   huʔtsa in

    2 poor   PRAG.IN see   FOC

    '"You see, you poor thing?!"'

    '"Tá vendo, seu infeliz?!"'

(27) *"hi ałahneł ka ami ami kawala ke hi t̯'axer ji," kale.*

    hi ałahne=ł   ka.in   ami ami kawala ke

    2 grandmother=DAT FOC/TENS talk talk HABIT DISLOC.ABS

    hi t̯'axer ji   kale

    2 poor   PRAG.IN like.this

    '"You always complain about your grandmother (but now she is gone),"
his aunt said.'

    '"Você fica reclamando da sua avó (mas agora ela se foi)," disse a tia.'

(28) *ina hen tsile ...*

    ina   hen tsile

    DISC.CON then hearsay

    'And then ...'

    'E então...'

(29) *aj de... inis de tsiłahne de wakaʔfɨ lakoktsi de.*

    aj   de   inis   de   tsi-ałahne   de

    by.then already DISC.CON already 3POSS(KIN)-grandmother pitiful

    wa-kaʔfɨ lako=ktsi   de

    MV-walk go.downhill=go.present.place already

    'His grandmother was already coming back home.'

    'A avó dele já estava voltando para casa.'

---

[19] The particle *ka.in* indicates focus, but at the same time also conveys information about the time when the event is taking place (now or in a recent past). In fast speech, it can appear in a reduced form (*ka*), as in the example above. With regard to its internal configuration, cf. Guirardello 1999: 169–178.

(30) *in ka tsinuk inaɬ t̪'axerak tsile sift̪'a ji de etsi lakoktsi ke.*

in	ka.in	tsinuk inaɬ	t̪'axer=a=k	tsile
that(place)	FOC/TENS	then	3ANAPH.FEM poor=EP.VW=ERG	hearsay

sift̪'a	ji	de	etsi	lako=ktsi		ke
firewood	PRAG.IN	already	take	go.downhill=go.present.place		DISLOC.ABS

'There (she was), she was bringing wood.'
'Lá (vinha ela), estava trazendo lenha.'

(31) *ka?fɨ t̪'axer lakoktsin ale hen.*

ka?fɨ	t̪'axer	lako=ktsi=n	ale	hen.
walk	poorly	go.downhill=go.present.place=3ABS	hearsay	then

'She was coming back.'
'Estava voltando.'

(32) *fa?tsan ale hen tsidoxo ji watkan fapt̪'aki de tsile:*

fa?tsa=n	ale	hen	tsi-doxo	ji	watkan
hear=3ABS	hearsay	then	3POSS(KIN)-grandchild	PRAG.IN	weep

fapt̪a=ki	de	tsile
sound=DAT	already	hearsay

'Then she heard her grandson (the Smooth-billed Ani) weeping:'
'Então ela ouviu o neto (o Anu) chorando:'

(33) *"atseda it̪a, atseda it̪a ..."*

atseda	it̪a	atseda	it̪a
grandmother(VOC)	pitiful	grandmother(VOC)	pitiful

'"Poor grandma, poor grandma ..."'
'"Pobre vovó, pobre vovó ..."'[20]

(34) *det̪'a det̪'a pits tsile, oran ale.*

det̪'a det̪'a	pits	tsile	ora=n	ale
well well	really/very	hearsay	cry=3ABS	hearsay

'With great attention, he cried (and by doing so, he invented the crying for mourning someone's death).'

---

[20] The Trumai ritual crying involves the repetition of a vocative (in this case, *atseda*) plus a word that conveys compassion (*it̪a*). Similarly to the adjective *de*, *it̪a* is also used to indicate pity and compassion for the person being mentioned. However, the meaning of *it̪a* is more specific - it is used for a person who is at risk of dying, or for one who has died. The term is employed to express sadness for the situation.

'Bem direitinho, ele chorou (e ao fazer isso, inventou o choro usado para expressar tristeza pela morte de alguém).'

(35) *adis wan oraṭkes inṭ'a nawan kadein,*

    adis   wan ora=ṭke=s   in=ṭ'a   nawan ka.de.in
    Xinguan.Indian PL   cry=DES=TEMP that=PST similar FOC/TENS

'Thus when the Indians of the Upper Xingu want to cry (in a death ritual), it's like that,'

'Por isso, quando os povos do Alto Xingu querem chorar (em um ritual funerário), é assim,'

(36) *niʔde adispa wan ora le de in.*

    niʔde adis-pa   wan ora le   de   in
    DEM Xinguan.Indian-COLLEC PL   cry hearsay already FOC

'all these Indians cry (like that).'

'todos esses índios choram (desse jeito).'

(37) *wan oran, ine oraṭ' ji letsi de wan oran ale.*

    wan ora=n   ine   ora=ṭ'   ji   letsi de
    PL cry=3ABS 3ANAPH.MASC cry=result.of PRAG.IN INS already

    wan ora=n   ale
    PL cry=3ABS hearsay

'They cry using his way of crying.'

'Eles choram usando o choro dele (do Anu).'[21]

(38) *deṭ'a deṭ'a pits hen tsile.*

    deṭ'a deṭ'a pits   hen   tsile
    well well really/very then hearsay

'(He was doing it) very well.'

'(Ele estava fazendo) bem direitinho.'

(39) *kaale hen tsiɬahne de kaʔfɨ lakoktsi le: tɨk!*

    kaale   hen tsi-aɬahne   de   kaʔfɨ
    there(far) then 3POSS(KIN)-grandmother pitiful walk

---

[21] The morpheme =*t'*/=*t'a* is a nominalizer with slightly different meanings, depending on the type of word it modifies. With nouns, it produces the sense of 'past X'. With verbs, the sense is 'the result of an action'.

      lako=ktsi le tɨk
      go.downhill=go.present.place hearsay ID:WALKING

      'His grandmother was already coming: *tɨk*!'
      'A avó dele já estava vindo: *tɨk*!'[22]

(40) "*t̯'axet̯'axer ji lat' mulan apa?*"

      t̯'axe-t̯'axer ji   lat' mula=n apa
      RD-bastard PRAG.IN lie be.indoors PART(I.wonder)

      '"Is this bastard lying?" (she said).'
      '"Esse desgraçado está mentindo?" (disse ela).'

(41) *pookal! t̯'axer kuhmu patan ale.*

      pookal   t̯'axer kuhmu pata=n   ale
      ID:THROWING poor throw arrive=3ABS hearsay

      'She arrived throwing (her wood) on the floor: *pookal*!'
      'Ela chegou jogando (a lenha) no chão: *pookal*!'

(42) *kaale tsiɬahne pumut̯'a, manlopits iji peʃ pit̯an ale.*

      kaale tsi-aɬahne   pumu-t̯'a   manlopits iji
      there 3POSS(KIN)-grandmother enter-result.of at.once   PRAG.IN
      peʃ pit̯a=n   ale.
      run go.out=3ABS hearsay

      'The moment his grandmother entered there (in her house), he immediately left running.'
      'Quando a avó entrou lá (na casa dela), logo ele saiu correndo.'

(43) *endenʃe it̯a iji ora tsuketsin ale.*

      endenʃe it̯a iji   ora tsuketsi=n   ale
      island ALL PRAG.IN cry go.directly=3ABS hearsay

      'Crying, he went straight to an island in the river.'
      'Foi chorando direto para uma ilha no rio.'

(44) "*okaa ... aa ...*"

      '"Okaa ... aa ..." (he stayed there crying).'
      '"Okaa ... aa ..." (ficou lá chorando).'

---

[22] This sentence contains the ideophone used for expressing the action of walking. It is usually repeated several times: *tɨk, tɨk, tɨk*. For further information about Trumai ideophones, cf. Guirardello-Damian 2014.

(45) "ṯ'axeṯ'axer ji lat' muketsin apa?"

ṯ'axe-ṯ'axer ji   lat' muketsi=n   apa?
RD-bastard PRAG.IN lie ASP.AUX=3ABS PART(I.wonder)

'"Will this bastard keep lying?" (his grandmother said).'
'"Esse desgraçado vai ficar mentindo?" (disse a avó).'[23]

(46) ina hen tsiɫahne dek kaʔsa ṯ'axer pupen ale,

ina   hen tsi-aɫahne   de=k   kaʔsa   ṯ'axer
DISC.CON then 3POSS(KIN)-grandmother pitiful=ERG hammock poor

pupe=n   ale
untie=3ABS hearsay

'Then his grandmother untied her poor hammock,'
'Então a avó desamarrou a pobre rede dela,'

(47) inaɫkaṯe sopʃaṯ ṯ'axer paṯa.paṯa le hen.

inaɫ=kaṯe   sopʃaṯ   ṯ'axer paṯa.paṯa le   hen
3ANAPH.FEM=GEN firewood poor   to.place   hearsay then

'(took) the wood out and placed it (on the floor).'
'(tirou) a lenha e colocou-a (no chão).'

(48) ina hen... aj de iji kuʔkuman ale.

ina   hen aj   de   iji   kuʔku=kma=n   ale
DISC.CON then by.then already PRAG.IN break=PERF=3ABS hearsay

'He had broken everything.'
'Ele tinha quebrado tudo.'

(49) ina hen tsiɫahne de huʔtsa paṯa le faʃṯa ṯ'axer mapa mapaṯ'aɫ, aɫaṯ pat ...

ina   hen tsi-aɫahne   de   huʔtsa paṯa le
DISC.CON then 3POSS(KIN)-grandmother pitiful see   arrive hearsay

faʃṯa   ṯ'axer mapa mapa=ṯ'a=ɫ   aɫaṯ   pat
belongings poor   break break=result.of=DAT clay.pan small

'Then his grandmother went and saw the broken pieces of her things, the little clay pans ...'
'Então a avó foi e viu as coisas dela quebradas, as panelinhas de barro...'

---

[23] In another version of this myth obtained by De Vienne (2010: 200), the grandmother tells the Smooth-billed Ani to transform itself into a spirit and stay near the water. And since then, this kind of bird can be heard crying in the low vegetation on the banks of a river.

(50) deṯ'a deṯ'a pits ṯ'axeṯ'axer ji kuʔkukman ale.

deṯ'a deṯ'a pits   ṯ'axe-ṯ'axer ji   kuʔku=kma=n   ale
well well really/very   RD-bastard PRAG.IN   break=PERF=3ABS   hearsay

'The bastard had broken everything.'
'O desgraçado tinha quebrado tudo.'

(51) ina hen tsile hen tsula ṯ'axere ale.

ina   hen tsile   hen tsula ṯ'axer=e   ale
DISC.CON then hearsay then lie   poorly=3ABS hearsay

'Then she lay down, sad (thinking about her things).'
'Então ela ficou deitada, triste (pensando nas coisas dela).'

(52) inande.

inande
PART.DISC

'That's it (the story is over).'
'É isso (fim).'

Acknowledgments

I would like to thank Bruna Franchetto and Kristine Stenzel for their detailed and constructive comments, and Emmanuel de Vienne, who generously shared his field notes with me, providing information about Trumai ritual practices. I would also like to express my sincere thanks and appreciation to the Trumai consultants, in particular Tarukuy, who helped with the transcription, and Kumaru, who was always a very dedicated and patient consultant, kindly receiving me in her home and teaching me her language. She is greatly missed.

5 Trumai

Figure 3: Kumaru, the narrator of the Trumai myth

Figure 4: Kumaru in her village, with relatives

Non-standard abbreviations

ANAPH	anaphoric
ASP.AUX	aspectual auxiliary
COLLEC	collective
DISC.CON	discursive connector
DISLOC.ABS	dislocated absolutive (i.e., the absolutive is not right before the verb)
EMPH	emphatic (i.e., marker of emphatic speech)
EP.VW	epenthetic vowel
EXPR	expression (i.e., fixed expression)
FOC/TENS	focus + tense
HABIT	habitual
INTERJ	interjection
MV	middle voice
PART	particle
3POSS(KIN)	3rd person possessive marker (for kinship terms)
PRAG.IN	pragmatic information marker
RD	reduplication

References

De Vienne, Emmanuel. 2010. *Maladie, chamanisme et rituel chez les Trumai du Haut Xingu, Mato Grosso. Traditions en souffrance*. École des Hautes Études en Sciences Sociales dissertation.

Dourado, Luciana. 2001. *Aspectos morfossintáticos da língua Panará (Jê)*. Linguistics Department, State University of Campinas (Unicamp) dissertation.

Emmerich, Charlotte. 1980. *A fonologia segmental da língua Txikão: Um exercício de análise*. Departamento de Antropologia, Museu Nacional/UFRJ dissertation.

Fargetti, Cristina M. 1992. *Análise fonológica da língua Juruna*. Linguistics Department, State University of Campinas (Unicamp) MA thesis.

Galvão, Eduardo & Mário Simões. 1966. Mudança e sobrevivência no Alto Xingu, Brasil Central. *Revista de Antropologia* 14. 37–52.

Guerreiro Júnior, Antônio. R. 2012. *Ancestrais e suas sombras: Uma etnografia da chefia Kalapalo e seu ritual mortuário*. Anthropology Department, University of Brasília dissertation.

Guirardello, Raquel. 1999. *A reference grammar of Trumai*. Linguistics Department, Rice University dissertation.

Guirardello-Damian, Raquel. 2005. Fonologia, classes de palavras e tipos de predicado em Trumai. *Boletim do Museu Paraense Emílio Goeldi, Série Ciências Humanas* 1(2). 193–306.

Guirardello-Damian, Raquel. 2007. Locative construction and positionals in Trumai. *Linguistics* 45(5/6). 917–954.

Guirardello-Damian, Raquel. 2010. Ergativity in Trumai. In Spike Gildea & Francesc Queixalós (eds.), *Ergativity in Amazonia* (Typological Studies in Language 89), 203–234. Amsterdam & Philadelphia: John Benjamins.

Guirardello-Damian, Raquel. 2012. Um estudo sobre o léxico Trumai: Verbos e auxiliares de movimento. In Cristina M. Fargetti (ed.), *Abordagens sobre o léxico em línguas indígenas*, 171–195. Campinas: Editora Curt Nimuendajú.

Guirardello-Damian, Raquel. 2014. Reduplication and ideophones in Trumai. In Gale Goodwin Gómez & Hein van der Voort (eds.), *Reduplication in indigenous languages of South America*, 217–246. Leiden, Netherlands: Brill.

Heckenberger, Michael J. 2003. The enigma of the great cities: Body and state in Amazonia. *Tipiti: Journal of the Society for the Anthropology of Lowland South America* 1(3).

Kaufman, Terrence. 1994. The native languages of South America. In Christopher Moseley & R. E. Asher (eds.), *Atlas of the world's languages*, 76–96. New York: Routledge.

Monod-Becquelin, Aurore. 1975. *La practique linguistique des indiens Trumai*. Paris: Selaf.

Monod-Becquelin, Aurore & Raquel Guirardello. 2001. Histórias Trumai. In Bruna Franchetto & Michael J. Heckenberger (eds.), *Os povos do Alto Xingu: História e cultura*, 401–443. Rio de Janeiro: Editora da UFRJ.

Murphy, Robert & Buell Quain. 1955. *The Trumai Indians of Central Brazil*. Seattle: University of Washington Press.

Rodrigues, Aryon. 1986. *Línguas brasileiras: Para o conhecimento das línguas indígenas brasileiras*. São Paulo: Edições Loyola.

Seki, Lucy. 2000. *Gramática do Kamayurá, língua Tupi-Guarani do Alto Xingu*. Campinas: Editora da Universidade Estadual de Campinas.

Villas Boas, Orlando & Claudio Villas Boas. 1970. *Xingu: Os índios, seus mitos*. São Paulo: Editora Edibolso.

von den Steinen, Karl. 1940. *Entre os aborígenes do Brasil Central. Separata da Revista do Arquivo Municipal, Vols. XXXIV a lviii*. São Paulo: Departamento de Cultura.

Part II

Beginnings

Chapter 6

Kotiria

Kristine Stenzel
Federal University of Rio de Janeiro, Brazil

Teresinha Marques

José Galvez Trindade

Miguel Wacho Cabral

1 Introduction

This narrative recounts the origin of the sacred cemeteries of the Kotiria people.[1] The Kotiria are one of the sixteen East Tukano groups,[2] living in the upper Rio Negro border region between Brazil and Colombia in northwestern Amazonia and whose total population is approximately twenty-six thousand.[3] There are some 2000 Kotiria, most of whom live in traditional communities located along the Vaupés river, a territory they have occupied for at least seven centuries (Stenzel 2013: 10).

The Sacred Cemeteries narrative was recorded on September 20, 2005, during a community workshop on Kotiria geography and history organized by the *Khumuno Wɨ'ɨ Kotiria* Indigenous School. Participants in this five-day workshop included students, teachers, family members, and elders from several different

---

[1] Although they are also identified as Wanano or Guanano, the traditional, self-determined name Kotiria 'water people' is used here at the request of the speakers.
[2] These are the Kotiria, Bará (Waimajã), Barasana, Desano, Karapana, Kubeo, Makuna, Pisamira, Siriano, Taiwano (Eduuria), Tanimuka (Retuarã), Tatuyo, Tukano, Tuyuka, Wa'ikhana (Piratapuyo), and Yuruti.
[3] According to information from the Instituto Socioambiental (ISA)-PIB online <http://pib.socioambiental.org/en>, and the Colombian 2005 and Brazilian 2010 national censuses.

Kristine Stenzel, Teresinha Marques, José Galvez Trindade & Miguel Wacho Cabral. 2017. Kotiria. In Kristine Stenzel & Bruna Franchetto (eds.), *On this and other worlds: Voices from Amazonia*, 189–275. Berlin: Language Science Press. DOI:10.5281/zenodo.1008783

Kotiria villages, who gathered together in *Koama Phoaye* (Carurú Cachoeira), the largest Kotiria community on the Brazilian side of the Vaupés (see Figure 2). Several non-indigenous outsiders were also present, including the organizer of this chapter, linguist Kristine Stenzel, and two pedagogical consultants, Dr. Marta Maria Azevedo and Lucia Alberta Andrade de Oliveira. At the time, Azevedo was one of the coordinators of the Educational Program of the Instituto Socioambiental, and Andrade had been working as a pedagogical aid on-site with the Kotiria school for many months (for more on the history of the school, see de Oliveira, Trindade & Stenzel (2012)). Workshop activities included map-making, text-writing, research on the history of individual villages, and visits to important regional landmarks. Many of the written materials and illustrations produced during the workshop were later gathered in a book entitled *Phanopɨ, Mipɨ Mahka Bu'erithu* 'Past and Present, Studies of our Origins', from which the illustration at the end of the narrative was taken. There were also a number of talks on different historical topics proffered by invited elders, one of whom was the much-respected author of our narrative, Teresinha Marques.

Figure 1: Teresinha Marques

Teresinha and her family came to the workshop every day from the nearby village of *Bɨhka Khopa* (Matapí, Colombia, see Figure 3), which is the traditional home of one of the highest ranked Kotiria sibs, the *Biari Pho'na* (children/descendants of *Biari*, one of *Dianumia Yairo*'s sons).

The knowledge Teresinha shares was passed down from her own father and was not widely known; indeed, many participants in the workshop were learning about this important episode in Kotiria history for the first time. Teresinha's fifteen-minute narrative was filmed and later integrated into the Kotiria Linguistic and Cultural Archive.[4] Co-author José Galvez Trindade introduces her to the audience at the beginning of the recording and interacts with her at several points

---

[4] All materials in this archive have been deposited at the Endangered Languages Archive, SOAS, University of London https://elar.soas.ac.uk/Collection/MPI132528 and at the PRODOCLIN Archive at the Muséu do Índio/FUNAI, Brazil, with open access granted by the community.

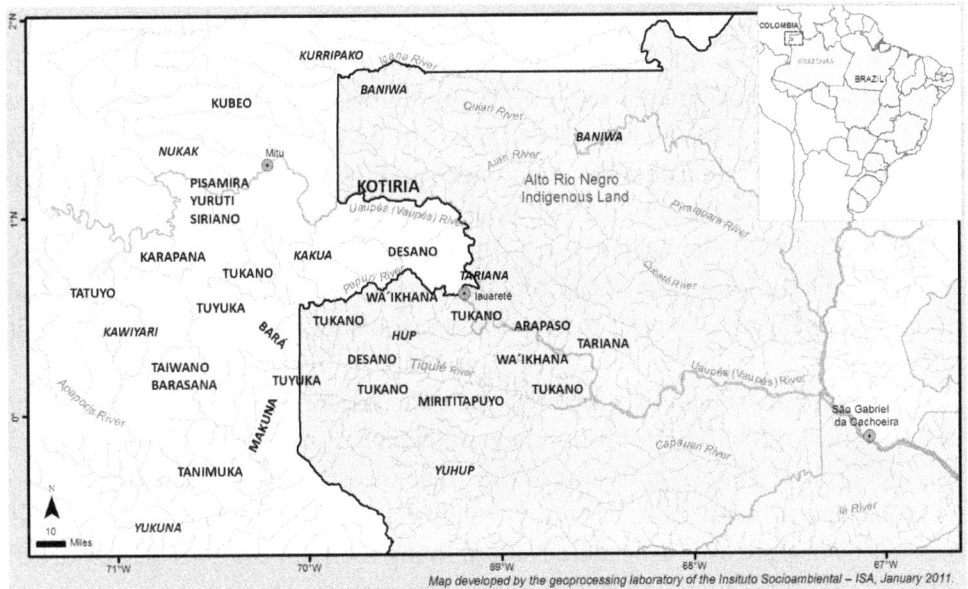

Figure 2: The Upper Rio Negro Region, showing the traditional territory of the Kotiria people on the Vaupés river. (Source: Stenzel 2013: 9)

during the narrative. He was later involved in the initial transcription and translation of the narrative in 2010, and additional detailed analysis was accomplished with the help of co-author Miguel Cabral in 2016.

The series of dramatic and tragic events leading to the origin of the Kotiria sacred cemeteries unfold against a backdrop of significant features of Kotiria cosmology and social organization.[5] Like all Tukanoan groups, the Kotiria have an origin myth in which pre-human beings, still in a state of "transformation", travel underwater upriver in an anaconda canoe from the Milk Lake to their territory on the Vaupés. Stopping at many places along the way ("houses of transformation"), they slowly acquire knowledge, techniques, instruments, encantations or "blessings", dances, and adornments — essential elements that contribute to their transformation into a fully human state.[6] Once reaching the headwaters of the Vaupés, their anaconda canoe turns around, and the mythical ancestors of the different Kotiria kin groups emerge at the places where parts of its body surface.

---

[5] Comprehensive ethnographic analysis of the Kotiria can be found in works by Chernela (1983; 1993; 2004; 2013), among others. For an overview of aspects of shared regional culture, see Epps & Stenzel (2013) and the references cited there.

[6] For similar accounts for other groups, see also Cabalzar (2008: 165) and Andrello (2012).

Those emerging closer to the anaconda's head are considered the higher ranked "older" brothers, those closer to the tail are "younger" brothers. A third, "servant" group, the *Wiroa*, originated separately from birds. Thus, the twenty-five or so Kotiria sibs are organized into three larger groupings with the symbolic roles of "chiefs", "dancers/masters of ceremonies", and "servants/cigar holders" (Chernela 1983, Chernela 1993: 5-15, 51-59; Waltz & Waltz 1997 offers slightly different sib names, numbers and relative rankings). Each individual in Kotiria society inherits a fixed rank in the social hierarchy as a descendant from an ancestral sibling and is highly aware of the roles and responsibilities associated with that rank.

The four main protagonists in Teresinha's Sacred Cemeteries narrative belong to the highest ranked, *Biari* group: they are *Ñahori*, his older brother *Diani*, and younger brother *Yuhpi Diani*, sons of the great ancestor shaman *Dianumia Yairo*. As is the case in many tales of betrayal, vengeance, and bloodshed, this one begins with a dispute over a woman. *Ñahori*, living in *Mukʉ Dʉhpʉri* (see Figure 3) with his own two wives and two children, has promised to capture a new bride for his younger brother *Yuhpi Diani*. However, when *Ñahori* returns with the woman, older brother *Diani* lays claim to her. *Ñahori* goes to *Yuhpi Diani* in *Khãnʉhko* to tell him what has happened, and an indignant *Yuhpi Diani* tries to capture her back, but is unsuccessful. Angered and feeling betrayed, *Yuhpi Diani* prepares an attack on *Ñahori*, who manages to send his wives and children away to safety and bravely resists, but is eventually killed by *Yuhpi Diani*'s men. They set fire to all the houses in *Mukʉ Dʉhpʉri*, and the smoke is seen from afar by *Diani* and the people of *Bʉhka Khopa*. They go downriver to investigate and find the burned homes. Searching for survivors, they eventually entice the terrified wives and children out of hiding and then come across *Ñahori*'s charred body.

Diani returns home and tells *Dianumia Yairo* what has transpired. He ignores *Dianumia Yairo*'s plea for the dispute not to escalate any further, and begins preparations to avenge *Ñahori*'s death. *Dianumia Yairo* reluctantly blesses *Diani* and his warriers, embuing them with valor and violent spirit to ensure their victory in battle. They travel downstream and wage a furious attack on *Yuhpi Diani* and his men in *Khãnʉhko*. *Diani*'s men prevail, forcing *Yuhpi Diani* to escape inland to *Khãphotai*, where he and his men build a fortress with a high lookout platform from which *Yuhpi Diani* hopes to be able to see his attackers approach. In the meantime, *Dianumia Yairo* has come downriver and tries one last time to convince *Diani* to call off the war, but to no avail. In the middle of the night, *Diani*'s men transform themselves into worms and tunnel into the fortress. They trick *Yuhpi Diani* into coming down from the platform, and subsequently capture and dismember him.

6 Kotiria

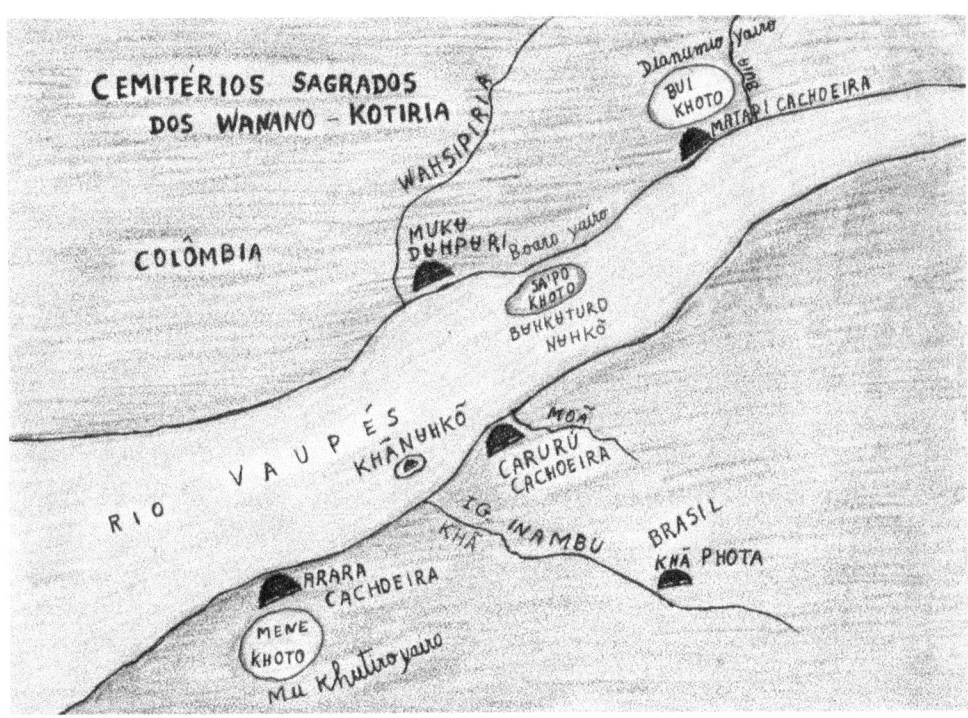

Figure 3: Sites in the Sacred Cemeteries Narrative, by Miguel Cabral Junior.

Diani and his warriors go back to *Bʉhka Khopa* to report their success and celebrate the victory. However, *Dianumia Yairo* is saddened and disheartened by the terrible consequences of his sons' failure to obey social norms — breaking promises and warring against each other — and so announces that he will remove himself to another world, taking with him sacred instruments, adornments, and knowledge. He gathers his sacred objects and together with his two jaguar-dogs, goes up a hill called *Kharẽ Khutu* where he sits and slowly enters the ground alive. After a few days, tremendous thunder announces that he has entered completely, establishing *Bu'i Kho'to*, the burial site for his own *Biari* descendants. Teresinha explains that three other cemeteries were later established for the descendants of the other brothers, each group having its own proper burial place, as divided in death as their ancestors had become in life.

Teresinha's narrative takes us on a journey into Kotiria culture, and at the same time allows us to observe prominent features of Kotiria narrative discourse and grammatical structure.[7] Like all Tukanoan languages, Kotiria is highly synthetic, agglutinative (except in certain verbal inflectional paradigms), and almost exclusively suffixing. It has nominative-accusative syntactic alignment and clear OV word order, with the position of subjects conditioned by discourse-pragmatic considerations. New, topical subjects (often full lexical noun phrases), tend to occur clause-initially, coinciding with the left-edge default focus position. Already known, continuing-topic subjects (commonly in pronominal form), tend to occur clause-finally, but any constituent whose identity is inferable from context can be a null element (Stenzel 2015). Clause-level grammatical relations are established by a combination of fairly rigid OV order, limited subject agreement morphology on verbs, and dependent-marking by means of a small case system. A single 'objective case' suffix –*re* (glossed as -OBJ) occurs on all indirect objects and is differentially marked on direct objects; it is also found on many temporal and locative constituents. Referential status, interacting with distinctions of animacy and definiteness, is the key to understanding 'objective case' marking in this system (Stenzel 2008b). The other case markers are the locative suffixes -*pɨ* or -*i* and the clitic =~*be're*, marking NPs with commitative or instrumental semantic roles.

Kotiria has two basic word classes: nouns and verbs. Both adverbial and adjectival notions are formed from stative "quality" verbs that undergo nominalization in order to function as nominal predicates or as modifiers (Stenzel forthcoming). Kotiria's rich system of noun classification morphology — coding distinctions of countability, animacy, shape, and utility — permeates the grammar, performing a variety of concordial, derivational, and referential functions. Root serialization is extremely productive in verbal words, and is used to express a wide range of adverbial, aspectual, modal, and spatial distinctions (Stenzel 2007a). Verbal morphology includes optional polarity, modal, and aspectual markers, as well as obligatory inflection coding person, aspect, and "clause modality" for different sentential moods. All declarative (realis) statements must be marked by one of five categories of evidentiality: visual, non-visual, inference, assertion, or reported (Stenzel 2008a; Stenzel & Gomez-Imbert 2018).

Prominent characteristics of discourse include several types of linking mechanisms. Generic "summary-head" expressions, such as *āyoa* 'so, then / doing that / because of that' and *āni* 'saying that', respectively mark the close of event and dialog paragraphs, while full tail-head adverbial clause linking strategies create cohesion between sentences. These linking structures interact with a switch-

---

[7]Interesting examples and details of particular structures will be noted throughout the text; see Stenzel 2013 for a comprehensive descriptive grammatical analysis.

reference marking system operating within the resulting complex sentences. Subordinate clauses with the same subject as the main clause are nominalized by cross-referencing noun class markers. If there is a change to a new subject accompanied by a shift in focus, the 'different-subject' suffix *-chʉ* is used (Stenzel 2015; 2016). Teresinha's discourse moreover shows that a specific nominalizer is used for broader "event" or "locational/situational" subordinate clauses.

There are several additional features of Teresinha's discourse that deserve special mention. One of these is how she recreates events and dramatically underscores the fact that they actually occurred *right there*, in the immediate surroundings, through her use of deictic elements (including a distal imperative (see line 110), spatial and motion expressions, onomatopoeia and gestures. It is also interesting to note how Teresinha interacts with her audience, stepping out of the role of narrator at several points to make comments, ask questions, or remind her listeners that they are themselves descendants of the story's protagonists. The result is a mixture of epic narrative and highly personal commentary by a much esteemed and respected Kotiria elder.

Presentation of the narrative gives the Kotiria orthographic representation on the first line, and free translations in English and Portuguese on the final two lines. The second line gives the underlying, segmented representation that includes some important phonological information. Morphemic nasalization is indicated by a tilde [~] preceding an inherently [+nasal] morpheme, and an apostrophe indicates glottalization, which is perceived as a glottal stop and is often accompanied by laryngealization of vowels (see Stenzel 2007b; Stenzel & Demolin 2013). Tone is represented at the word level, with High tone indicated by the acute accent [´] and Low tone left unmarked. Phrase and sentence-level tonal phenomena, including sentence-final downstep patterns, are not represented. The third line gives corresponding glosses, with a list of non-standard abbreviations provided at the end of the text.

Introduction by José Galvez Trindade

(1) *vinte hira, ã yoaro 20 ti khʉ'ma 2005 hichʉ.*

vinte hí-ra   ~a=yóá-ro ti=~khʉ'bá 2005 ~híchʉ
twenty COP-VIS.IPFV.2/3 so=do-SG ANPH=year 2005 TEMP

'It's the twentieth (of September) in the year 2005.'

'É dia vinte (de setembro) do ano 2005.'

(2) *sã a'ríkoro wamañokoro me'ne to durukuare thʉ'o yoana tana niha.*

~sa=a'rí-koro   ~wabáro-koro=~be're
1PL.EXCL.POSS=DEM.PROX-F.RSP father's.sister-F.RSP=COM
to=dú-ruku-a-re   thʉ'ó yoá-~dá tá-~dá ~dí-ha
3SG.POSS=speak-stand-PL-OBJ hear do-PL come-PL PROG-VIS.IPFV.1

'We've come with our aunt[8] (Teresinha) to listen to her stories (about our ancestors).'

'Estamos com nossa tia (Teresinha) para ouvir suas histórias (dos ancestrais).'

(3) *õi Carurui hiha.*

~ó-í   caruru-i   hí-ha
DEIC.PROX-LOC.VIS caruru-LOC.VIS COP-VIS.IPFV.1

'We're here in Carurú Cachoeira.'

'Estamos aqui em Carurú Cachoeira.'

2 Mahsa khõ'akho'topori
'Kotiria sacred cemeteries'
'Cemetérios sagrados dos Kotiria'[9]

(4) *mahsa khõ'akho'topori*

~basá ~kho'á-kho'to-pori
people bone-proper.place-PL.place

'Sacred burial places/cemeteries'

'Cemitérios sagrados'

---

[8] José uses the kinship term specifically for one's father's sister (a paternal aunt, real or classificatory).

[9] Recordings of this story are available from https://zenodo.org/record/997439

(5) *a'rina ñarananumia wi'i, yɨ durukuare thɨ'oduayu'ka.*

a'rí-~da   ~yará-~da-~dubia   wi'í
DEM.PROX-PL white.people-PL-PL.F arrive.CIS
yɨ=dú-ruku-a-re   thɨ'ó-dua-yu'ka
1SG.POSS=speak-stand-PL-OBJ hear-DES-REP.QUOT[10]

'These white ladies have come wanting to hear my stories.' (I was told)

'Chegaram nossas assessoras brancas querendo ouvir minhas histórias.' (me disseram)

(6) *yɨ'ɨ tire michare ya'uko tako niha.*

yɨ'ɨ tí-re   ~bichá-ré ya'ú-ko tá-ko   ~dí-ha
1SG ANPH-OBJ today-OBJ tell-F come-F PROG-VIS.IPFV.1

'(So) today I'm coming to tell (them).'[11]

'(Então) hoje estou vindo contar.'

(7) *yɨ'ɨ hiha wãri khutiro biari pho'nakoro.*

yɨ'ɨ hí-ha   ~wárí khútíró bíári ~pho'dá-kó-ró
1SG COP-VIS.IPFV.1 wãri khutiro biari descendants[12]-F-SG

'I'm a descendant of *wãri khutiro biari*.'

'Sou descendente de *wãri khutiro biari*.'

---

[10] Use of reported evidentials is relatively rare in narratives. Teresinha employs the quotative evidential here, and in line 12, as a polite reported speech strategy indicating, but not directly identifying, the original speaker who had invited her to tell her stories. In fact, the invitation to speak came from José Trindade (Joselito), who was present and introduced her at the beginning of the recording. See lines 20-22, 26, and 173 for additional interesting uses of the reported evidential.

[11] This sentence contains two nominalized verbs, *ya'u* 'tell', as the complement of the purposive construction 'come to X', and *ta* 'come', as the complement of the progressive formed with the auxiliary copula *ni*. This auxiliary copula is cognate to the primary copula found in many Tukanoan languages (Stenzel & Gomez-Imbert 2018), while the primary copula in Kotiria is *hi*, seen in the next line. See lines 25, 289, and 299 for instances of *ni* used with copular semantics, rather than as a component of the progressive construction.

[12] The root *pho'na* literally means 'children' or 'offspring' (e.g. in lines 75, 95, 97, and 117), but is used metaphorically here to refer to the descendants of a specific mythical ancestor, and in lines 52, 58 (and others) to refer to people over whom one has control, such as servants or warriers.

(8) yɨ wama Maria Teresinha Marques.

yɨ=~wabá   Maria Teresinha Marques
1SG.POSS=name Maria Teresinha Marques

'My name (is) Maria Teresinha Marques.'

'Meu nome (é) Maria Teresinha Marques.'

(9) yɨ wama so'toai hira yɨ'ɨre bu'sana phoko wamatiha yɨ'ɨ.

yɨ=~wabá   so'tóá-í   hí-ra   yɨ'ɨ-ré bu'sáná phokó
1SG.POSS=name end-LOC.VIS COP-VIS.IPFV.2/3 1SG-OBJ bu'sana phoko
~wabá-tí-há   yɨ'ɨ
name-VBZ-VIS.IPFV.1 1SG

'(And)[13] this is my last (traditional) name, what I'm called is *bu'sana phoko*.'

'(E) meu sobrenome (nome tradicional), me chamam de *bu'sana phoko*.'

(10) wãri khutiro biaripho'nakoro.

~wári khútíró biári-~pho'da-ko-ro
wãri khutiro biari-descendants-F-SG

'I'm a woman of the *wãri khutiro biari* group.'

'Sou mulher do grupo *wãri khutiro biari*.'

(11) yɨ phɨkɨ yɨ'ɨre hire wĩhoa.

yɨ=phɨkɨ   yɨ'ɨ-ré hí-re   ~wihóá
1SG.POSS=father 1SG-OBJ COP-VIS.PFV.2/3 wĩhoa

'For me, my father was *wĩhoa*.' (I knew him as *wĩhoa*, his traditional name.)

'Para mim, meu pai era *wĩhoa*.' (Eu o conheci como *wĩhoa*, seu nome tradicional.)

(12) tire a'rina thɨ'oduayu'ka.

tí-re   a'rí-~da   thɨ'ó-dua-yu'ka
ANPH-OBJ DEM.PROX-PL hear-DES-REP.QUOT

'These (visitors) want to hear (stories).' (I'm told)

'Esses (visitantes) querem ouvir (histórias).' (Me disseram)

---

[13] There are no overt conjunctions in Kotiria, so these and other elements understood from context are given in parentheses in the translation lines.

(13) ã yoako, yʉ'ʉ tire michadahchore noano me'ne a'rinakinare, yʉ mahsiapokane yʉ thʉ'otuare yʉ'ʉ durukukota.

~a=yóá-kó yʉ'ʉ tí-re   ~bichá-dáchó-ré ~dóá-ro=~be're
so=do-F 1SG ANPH-OBJ today-day-OBJ good-SG=COM
a'rí-~da-~kida-re   yʉ=~basí-a-poka-re
DEM.PROX-PL-PL.RSP-OBJ 1SG.POSS=know-PL-little-OBJ
yʉ=thʉ'ó-tu-a-re   yʉ'ʉ dú-ruku[14]-ko-ta
1SG.POSS=hear-think-PL-OBJ 1SG speak-stand-F-INTENT

'So, today with pleasure I'm going to tell them a little of what I know, what I understand.'

'Por isso vou contar hoje com prazer um pouco do que eu sei, do que entendo.'

(14) a'ri hiri hire wa'manopʉre da'poto.

a'rí   hí-ri   hí-re   ~wa'bá[15]-ro-pʉ-re
DEM.PROX COP-NMLZ COP-VIS.PFV.2/3 young/new-SG-LOC-OBJ
da'pó-tó
origin/roots-NMLZ.LOC/EVNT

(Sigh and moment of silence). 'These are stories about what happened in the origin times.'

(Suspiro e momento de silêncio). 'Essas histórias são sobre o que aconteceu nos tempos de origem.'

(15) pha'muri mahsa õre pha'muyohataa.

~pha'bú-rí   ~basá ~ó-ré
originate-NMLZ people DEIC.PROX-OBJ

---

[14]The serial verb construction *du-ruku* 'speak-stand' means to talk for an extended period of time. It can be used to refer to a single speaker making a speech, bragging (see line 144), or offering a narrative, but can also indicate multiple speakers singing, chanting (see line 236), or having a conversation together. The posture verb *duku* 'stand' (here [ruku], indicating lexicalization) contributes a continuative aspectual reading, and can occur with other verbs, e.g. 'lie-stand' in line 131.

[15]All "adjectival" notions in Kotiria are expressed by stative verbs, e.g. *wa'ma* 'to be young' or 'to be new'. To simplify the glosses, only the qualitative semantics, e.g. young/new/good/evil are given in the gloss line.

~pha'bú-yóhá-tá-á
originate-go.upriver-come-ASSERT.PFV
'The origin beings appeared coming upriver here.'
'Os seres de transformação apareceram subindo pelo rio aqui.'

(16) duhkusʉ yʉ ñʉhchʉsʉmʉa wʉ'ʉsekho'topori khʉaa ōre matapi.
  dukú-~sʉ[16]   yʉ=~yʉchú-~sʉbʉ́á
  stand-arrive.TRNS 1SG.POSS=grandfather-PL:kin
  wʉ'ʉ́-sé(ri)-kho'to-pori   khʉá-a   ~ó-ré
  house-PL:row-proper.place-PL:place have-ASSERT.PFV DEIC.PROX-OBJ
  matapi
  matapi.village
  'Arriving, my ancestors established their houses (their rightful place) here in Matapi.'
  'Chegando, meus antepassados estabeleceram suas casas (seu lugar próprio) aqui em Matapi.'

(17) to hira, bʉhkakhopa wamatira.
  tó   hí-ra   bʉhkákhópá ~wabá-tí-rá
  DEF COP-VIS.IPFV.2/3 bʉhka.khopa name-VBZ-VIS.IPFV.2/3
  'That place is called bʉhkakhopa.'
  'Esse lugar se chama bʉhkakhopa.'

(18) ñarana nia ... matapi nina ti mahkare.
  ~yará-~dá   ~dí-a   matapi   ~dí-ra
  white.people-PL say-ASSERT.PFV matapi.village say-VIS.IPFV.2/3
  ti=~baká-re
  ANPH=village[17]-OBJ
  'White people say ... (they) call that village Matapi.'
  'Os brancos dizem ... chamam essa aldeia de Matapi.'

---

[16] Kotiria has a number of motion verbs with specific deictic semantics, such as two "arrive" verbs: sʉ 'to arrive there (translocative motion)', and wi'i 'to arrive here (cislocative motion)' (some examples are lines 5, 16, and 31, among others). The distinction is indicated in the glosses. When used in serial verb constructions, as we see here, "arrive" verbs indicate the perfectivity or completedness of an event involving motion.

[17] The nominal root *mahka* indicates a 'place of origin or belonging', and when used with human referents, is understood to mean a 'village'. When used with wild plants or animals, it may be understood to indicate the jungle or forest (as in line 66).

(19) *tina a'rina hiphitina, a'rina ñahoriapho'na wa'i khapea ñahoria hia sã ba'ana waro.*

tí-~da   a'rí-~da   híphiti-~da   a'rí-~da   ñáhori-a-~pho'da
ANPH-PL DEM.PROX-PL everyone-PL DEM.PROX-PL ñahori[18]-PL-descendants
wa'í khapea ñáhori-a   hí-a   ~sa=ba'á-~da
wa'i khapea ñahori-PL COP-ASSERT.PFV 1PL.EXCL.POSS=younger.brother-PL
wáró
EMPH

'All of these, descendants (children), *wa'i khapea ñahoria*, are our true younger brothers.'

'Todos esses, descendentes (filhos), *wa'i khapea ñahoria*, são nossos irmãos menores verdadeiros.'

(20) *biari, yabaina, ñahoripho'na hiyu'ka.*

biári yabá-~ida   ñáhori-~pho'da   hí-yu'ka
biari Q:what/how-NMLZ.PL ñahori-descendants COP-REP.QUOT

'(Younger brothers of the) *biari* (Teresinha's group), the *ñahori* descendants are.' (they're saying)

'(Irmãos menores dos) *biari* (grupo da Teresinha), os *ñahori* são.' (estão dizendo)

(21) *tina sã dohka mahkarikurua hiyu'ka a'rina.*

tí-~da   ~sa=doká   ~baká-ri-kuru-a   hí-yu'ka
ANPH-PL 1PL.EXCL.POSS=below origin-PL-group-PL COP-REP.QUOT
a'rí-~da
DEM.PROX-PL

'They are the younger second group.' (they're saying)[19]

'Eles são irmãos menores.' (estão dizendo)

---

[18] To facilitate recognition, the proper names of the main protagonists and places have the same underlying and surface representations, e.g. *ñahori* rather than *~yahori*.

[19] Teresinha's use of the quotative reported evidential in this sequence of sentences is another reported speech strategy, given that throughout the workshop there had been a great deal of discussion about different Kotiria groups. It is also likely a way of softening this series of statements related to group rankings, especially since the audience was mostly composed of people belonging to a group she states to be lower than her own.

(22) tiro õi wʉ'ʉsekho'topori khʉayu'ka, mukʉdʉhpʉri a'rina sã ba'ana.

tí-ró   ~ó-í   wʉ'ʉ-sé(ri)-kho'to-pori
ANPH-SG DEIC.PROX-LOC.VIS house-PL-row-proper.place-PL.place
khʉá-yu'ka   múkʉ.dʉhpʉri a'rí-~da
have-REP.QUOT mukʉ.dʉhpʉri DEM.PROX-PL
~sa=ba'á-~da
1PL.EXCL.POSS=younger.brother-PL

'He (Ñahori) had his houses here in *Mukʉ Dʉhpʉri* (and) these ones here (Carurú villagers are) our younger brothers.' (they're saying).

'Ele (Ñahori) tinha suas casas aqui em *Mukʉ Dʉhpʉri* (e) esses aqui (moradores de Carurú são) nossos irmãos menores.' (estão dizendo)

(23) phʉaro numia, phʉaro numia ti phapʉre namotia tire himarebʉ, tiaro numiapʉ bʉhkʉthurupʉre.

phʉá-ro ~dúbí-á   phʉá-ro ~dúbí-á   ti=phá-pʉ-re
two-SG woman-PL two-SG woman-PL   ANPH=time-LOC-OBJ
~dabó-tí-á   tí-re   hí-~bare-bʉ[20]   tiá-ro
wife-VBZ-ASSERT.PFV ANPH-OBJ COP-REM.IPFV-EPIS three-SG
~dúbí-á-pʉ   bʉkʉ-thúrú-pʉ-ré
woman-PL-LOC ancestor-times-LOC-OBJ

'In those olden times, the custom was to marry two wives, two or even three.'

'Na época antiga, era costume casar com duas mulheres, duas, ou até três.'

---

[20] The expression *himarebʉ* occurs several times in Teresinha's narrative, indicating ways of being or events as specifically related to "origin" times. These may be customs that contrast with current social norms (e.g. having more than one wife), or capabilities that humans nowadays no longer possess, such as the ability to transform themselves into other kinds of beings (see line 197). The expression is clearly formed with the copula *hi*, followed by a morpheme *-ma* or *-mare*, which is analyzed here as 'remote imperfective aspect', but is possibly related to the morpheme *ma* used in conversation to show respect for one's interlocutor. The final morpheme *-bʉ* is cognate to evidential markers in other Tukanoan languages (Stenzel & Gomez-Imbert 2018) but is not regularly found in the Kotiria evidential system. The expression as a whole seems to indicate the speaker's authoritative knowledge about such times and customs, and thus is interpreted as having epistemic value: 'this was how it *was* in those times'. In line 187 it occurs with the initial verb *ni* 'say', indicating 'this was what X was *called* in those times'.

(24) *namoti a'ri, õre matapi wʉ'ʉkho'tori tiro hiyu'ka bʉhkʉro, mari ñʉhchʉ dianumia yairo.*

~dabó-tí a'rí ~ó-ré matapí wʉ'ʉ́-kho'to-ri
wife-VBZ DEM.PROX DEIC.PROX-OBJ matapi.village house-proper.place-PL
tí-ró bʉkʉ́-ró ~bari=~yʉchʉ́ diánúmíá.yáíró
ANPH-SG ancestor-SG 1PL.INCL.POSS=grandfather dianumia.yairo

'The old one, our grandfather (ancestor) *Dianumia Yairo*, was married (and) he had houses there in Matapi.' (they're saying)

'O velho, nosso avô (ancestral) *Dianumia Yairo*, era casado (e) tinha casas alí em Matapi.' (estão dizendo)

(25) *phayʉ mahsa hia niatia.*

phayʉ́ ~basá hí-a ~dí-ati-a
many people COP-PL COP-IPFV-ASSERT.PFV

'There were lots of people living there.'

'Havia muita gente vivendo alí.'

(26) *ã yoa õre hiyu'ka tiro ñahori, a'riro yuhpi dianine:*

~a=yóá ~ó-ré hí-yu'ka tí-ró ñáhórí a'rí-ro
so=do DEIC.PROX-OBJ COP-REP.QUOT ANPH-SG ñahori DEM.PROX-SG
yuhpí.diáni-re
yuhpi.diani-OBJ

'So (they're saying) that *Ñahori* lived just there (in *Mukʉ Dʉhpʉri* and said to) *Yuhpi Diani*:

'Então (estão dizendo que) *Ñahori* vivia logo alí (em *Mukʉ Dʉhpʉri* e disse ao) *Yuhpi Diani*:

(27) *"numia yʉ'ʉ nai wa'ai niha, yʉ buhibo."*

~dúbí-á yʉ'ʉ́ ~dá-i wa'á-i ~dí-ha yʉ=buhíbo
woman-PL 1SG get-M go-M PROG-VIS.IPFV.1 1SG.POSS=sister.in.law

'"I'm going to get women, my sisters-in-law."'

'"Estou indo pegar mulheres, minhas cunhadas."'

(28) nichɨ, tirota sinikaatia:
~dí-chɨ   tí-ró-ta   ~sidí-ka'a-ati-a
say-SW.REF ANPH-SG-EMPH ask.for-do.immediately-IPFV-ASSERT.PFV
'When (Ñahori) said that, (Yuhpi Diani) asked:'
'Quando (Ñahori) falou isso, (Yuhpi Diani) pediu:'

(29) "yɨ'ɨkhɨre kɨkoro natanamoa" niatia a'rina ñahoriapho'na.
yɨ'ɨ-khɨ-ré ~kɨ-kó-ró ~dá-ta-~dabo-a   ~dí-ati-a
1SG-ADD-OBJ one/a-F-SG get-come-wife-PL say-IPFV-ASSERT.PFV
a'rí-~da   ñahóri-a-~pho'da
DEM.PROX-PL ñáhórí-PL-descendants
'"Bring one more wife for me too," (he asked to Ñahori, the father) of all these Ñahoria descendants here.'
'"Traga mais uma para mim também," (pediu ao Ñahori, pai) desses descendentes de Ñahoria aqui.'

(30) ñariro tuakaro kha'mapha, hum … hum.
~yá-rí-ró   túá-ká-ró   ~kha'bá-pha hum…hum
bad-NMLZ-SG strong-INTENS-SG want-SPEC   (laughs)
'I guess the rascal (Yuhpi Diani) really liked/needed (women), hum … hum.' [Teresinha chuckles]
'Parece que o danado (Yuhpi Diani) gostava/precisava mesmo (de mulher), hum … hum.' [risos da Teresinha]

(31) ã yoa tiro nano wa'a, nawi'i, wehse wa'a te õpɨ.
~a=yóá tí-ró   ~dá-ro wa'á ~dá-wi'i   wesé   wa'á té
so=do ANPH-SG get-SG go   get-arrive.CIS garden go until
~ó-pɨ
DEIC.PROX-LOC
'So, he (Ñahori) went to get them, brought (them) back, and went off to the gardens over there (in Mukɨ Dɨhpɨri).'
'Então ele (Ñahori) foi pegar, trouxe de volta (e) foram lá para a roça (em Mukɨ Dɨhpɨri).'

(32) a'rina ñahoria yaro wɨ'ɨkho'to hira õ mukɨ dɨhpɨri.

a'rí-~da   ñáhórí-á   yá-ro   wɨ'ɨ-khó'tó   hí-ra
DEM.PROX-PL ñahori-PL POSS-SG house-proper.place COP-VIS.IPFV.2/3
~ó   múkɨ.dɨhpɨri
DEIC.PROX mukɨ.dɨhpɨri

'Mukɨ Dɨhpɨri is the rightful place of these ñahoria.'

'Mukɨ Dɨhpɨri é o lugar desses ñahoria.'

(33) sekhoa ti yadi'ta te hiro nina to khũre.

(bɨ')sé-khoa   ti=yá-dí'tá   té   hí-ro   ~dí-ra   tó
side-half/part 3PL.POSS=POSS-ground   until COP-SG PROG-VIS.IPFV.2/3   DEF
~khú-re
place-OBJ

'Their place is on the other side of the river, and that place is still theirs.'

'O lugar deles fica no outro lado do rio (e) esse lugar ainda é deles.'

(34) no'o ti tachɨ khũre, noa a'rinare ñahoriapho'nare "do'se yoa ta hihari?"

~do'ó   ti=tá-chɨ   ~khú-re   ~doá   a'rí-~da-re
Q:where[21] 3PL.POSS=come-SW.REF place-OBJ Q:who DEM.PROX-PL-OBJ
ñáhórí-a-~pho'da-re   do'sé yoá ta   hí-hari
ñahori-PL-descendants-OBJ   Q:how do   come COP-Q.IPFV

'If they were to come back there, no one could ask Ñahori's descendants "Why do you come (what are you doing) here?"'

'Se um dia voltassem ao lugar, ninguém podia perguntar aos descendantes de Ñahori "Porque vieram (o que fazem) aqui?"'

(35) ne nito bahsioerara.

~dé ~dí-to   basio-éra-ra
NEG say-NMLZ.LOC/EVNT correct-NEG-VIS.IPFV.2/3

'No one could say that.'

'Ninguem poderia dizer isso.'

---

[21] This sentence contains three different question words glossed with their most common semantics, although most can occur with other morphology to derive other interrogative meanings. For example no'o 'where', can combine with morphemes -pe or -puro, deriving quantity question forms 'how much/many?', do'se 'how' also occurs in the expression do'se hichɨ 'when?' and do'se yoa 'why?' (e.g. in line 273).

(36) *do'poto to hiro hia.*
 do'pó-to   to=hí-ro   hí-a
 origin/roots-NMLZ.LOC/EVNT 3SG.POSS=COP-SG COP-ASSERT.PFV
 'It's his (*Ñahori*'s) origin site.'
 'É o lugar de origem dele (*Ñahori*)'.

(37) *ã yoa mahaa.*
 ~a=yóá ~bahá-a
 so=do go.uphill-ASSERT.PFV
 'So, (*Ñahori* and the woman) came up (towards *Yuhpi Diani*).'
 'Então (eles, *Ñahori* e a mulher) vinham subindo (na direção ao *Yuhpi Diani*).'

(38) "*a'ríkoro yʉ'ʉre numia na, yʉ'ʉ duhtirikoro tire a'rikoro*" *nia tiro.*
 a'rí-kó-ró   yʉ'ʉ́-ré ~dúbí-á   ~dá yʉ'ʉ́ dutí-ri-ko-ro   tí-re
 DEM.PROX-F-SG 1SG-OBJ woman-PL get 1SG order-NMLZ-F-SG ANPH-OBJ
 a'rí-kó-ró   ~dí-a   tí-ró
 DEM.PROX-F-SG say-ASSERT.PFV ANPH-SG
 '"This woman's for me, the one I asked you to get," he (*Yuhpi Diani*) said.'
 '"Essa mulher é minha, a que mandei pegar," dizia ele (*Yuhpi Diani*).'

(39) *a'riro ñahori: "hierare. soropʉ diani yakoro hira" nia.*
 a'rí-ro   ñáhórí hi-éra-re   sóró-pʉ́   diáni
 DEM.PROX-SG ñahori COP-NEG-VIS.PFV.2/3 different.one-LOC diani
 yá-kó-ró hí-ra   ~dí-a
 POSS-F-SG COP-VIS.IPFV.2/3 say-ASSERT.PFV
 '*Ñahori* (speaking): "Not so, this one is promised to *Diani*," he said.'
 'O *Ñahori* (falando): "Não, essa ficou prometida para *Diani*," respondeu.'

(40) "*hierare. yʉ'ʉ duhtii*" *nia.*
 hi-éra-re   yʉ'ʉ́ dutí-i   ~dí-a
 COP-NEG-VIS.PFV.2/3 1SG order-VIS.PFV.1 say-ASSERT.PFV
 '"Not so! I ordered (her)," (*Yuhpi Diani*) said.'
 '"Nada disso! Eu mandei pegar," respondeu (*Yuhpi Diani*).'

(41) *"yɨ'ɨ duhtii. yɨ yakoro hika" nia.*

     yɨ'ɨ dutí-i   yɨ=yá-kó-ró   hí-ka
     1SG order-VIS.PFV.1 1SG.POSS=POSS-F-SG COP-ASSERT.IPFV
     ~dí-a
     say-ASSERT.PFV[22]

     '"I ordered (her). She's mine!" (*Yuhpi Diani*) said.'
     '"Eu mandei (pegar). É minha mulher!" disse (*Yuhpi Diani*).'

(42) *"hierara" nia.*

     hi-éra-ra   ~dí-a
     COP-NEG-VIS.IPFV.2/3 say-ASSERT.PFV

     '"No (she's) not," (*Ñahori*) said.'
     '"Não é," disse (*Ñahori*).'

(43) *ni, wehse wa'a, thuatarikorore ña'atia.*

     ~dí wesé   wa'á thuá-ta-ri-ko-ro-re   ~ya'á-ti-a
     say garden go   return-come-NMLZ-F-SG-OBJ grab-ATTRIB-ASSERT.PFV

     'That said, (she) went to the garden (and) returning, was grabbed.'
     'Ditto isso, (ela) foi para a roça (e) voltando, foi agarrada.'

(44) *"thuaga yɨ'ɨ me'ne" nia.*

     thúá-gá   yɨ'ɨ=~be're ~dí-a
     stay-IMP 1SG=COM   say-ASSERT.PFV

     '"(You) stay with me," said (*Diani*).'
     '"Fica comigo," disse (*Diani*).'

(45) *"hierara. khã'i nire. pakoro nabosaita."*

     hi-éra-ra   ~kha'í   ~dí-re   pá-ko-ro
     COP-NEG-VIS.IPFV.2/3 desire/love PROG-VIS.PFV.2/3 ALT-F-SG
     ~dá-bosa-i-ta
     get-BEN-M-INTENT

     '"(She) isn't (yours). You want (her but) I'll get another one for you," (said *Ñahori*).'

---

[22] The unusual use of the assertive evidential *-a* in this sentence (rather than the expected visual form *-i*, as in the previous line) is quite interesting. It is possible that use of the assertive form gives the statement greater legitimacy, coding it as already internalized "fact" or as collectively recognized knowledge.

'"(Essa) não é (sua). Você quer ficar (com ela mas) vou trazer outra para você," (disse *Ñahori*).'

(46) *"hierara" nia.*

hi-éra-ra   ~dí-a
COP-NEG-VIS.IPFV.2/3 say-ASSERT.PFV

'"No," said (*Diani*).'

'"Não," respondia (*Diani*).'

(47) *ni, tikorore thũkukaa.*

~dí tí-kó-ró-ré   ~thúkuka-a
say ANPH-F-SG-OBJ force-ASSERT.PFV

'Saying that, (*Diani*) grabbed her.'

'Dizendo isso, (*Diani*) segurou a mulher.'

(48) *de tikoro bʉhkoro kʉ̃korotha thuaa.*

dé   tí-kó-ró   bʉkó-ro   ~kʉ́-ko-ro-ta   thúa-a
INTJ:poor.one! ANPH-F-SG ancestor.F-SG alone-F-SG-EMPH stay-ASSERT.PFV

'Poor thing! The old gal was all alone.'

'Coitada da velha, estava sozinha.'

(49) *sʉ to manʉnore yabare, khanʉhkore hiphato tiro Yuhpi Diani:*

~sʉ́   to=~badʉ́-ro-re   yabá-re   khá-~dʉ́kó-ré
arrive.TRNS 3SG.POSS=husband-SG-OBJ Q:what-OBJ hawk-island-OBJ

hí-pha-to   tí-ró   yuhpi.diani
COP-time-NMLZ.LOC/EVNT ANPH-SG yuhpi.diani

'(*Ñahori*) went there to her intended husband in *Kha Nʉhko* (Hawk Island), where *Yuhpi Diani* lived (and said):'

'(*Ñahori*) chegou ao marido pretendido dela em *Kha Nʉhko* (Ilha de Inambú), onde *Yuhpi Diani* morava (e disse):'

(50) *"mʉ namore yoatapʉ mʉ mahsawamino ña'a thũkukare" nia.*

~bʉ=~dabó-re   yoá-tá-pʉ́   ~bʉ=~basá-~wabi-ro   ~ya'á
2SG.POSS=wife-OBJ far-EMPH-LOC 2SG.POSS=people-older.brother-SG grab

~thúkuka-re   ~dí-a
force-VIS.PFV.2/3 say-ASSERT.PFV

'"Your (intended) wife's gone, your older brother's people captured her," said (*Ñahori*).'

'"Sua esposa (prometida) já foi, o povo do seu irmão maior pegou," disse (Ñahori).'

(51) *"kue! do'se yʉ'ʉ tirore ã yoa duhtierai yʉ'ʉ" nia.*
kúé   do'sé   yʉ'ʉ́ tí-ró-ré   ~a=yóá duti-éra-i   yʉ'ʉ́
INTJ:surprise Q:how 1SG ANPH-SG-OBJ so=do order-NEG-VIS.PFV.1 1SG
~dí-a
say-ASSERT.PFV

'"What? How? I forbade him do that!" (*Yuhpi Diani*) said.'
'"O que? Como? Eu o proibi a fazer isso!" (*Yuhpi Diani*) falou.'

(52) *ni to phosapho'nakãre, kʉ̃nʉmʉ ba'aro wa'arokaa, phosa pho'nakã phʉaro.*
~dí to=phosá-~pho'da-~ka-re   ~kʉ́-~dʉ́bʉ́=ba'a-ro
say 3SG.POSS=maku.people-descendants-DIM-OBJ one/a-day=after-SG
wa'á-dóká-á   phosá-~pho'da-~ka   phʉá-ro
go-DIST-ASSERT.PFV maku.people-descendants-DIM two-SG

'Saying that to his servants,[23] the next day two of them went (to check).'
'Falando disso aos seus criados, no dia seguinte, os dois foram (verificar).'

(53) *tikoro kowaro bu'atarikorore pharitaropʉ, tikorore ña'aa tina.*
tí-kó-ró   kówa-ro   bu'á-ta-ri-ko-ro-re
ANPH-F-SG fetch.water-SG go.downhill-come-NMLZ-F-SG-OBJ
pharí-taro-pʉ   tí-kó-ró-ré   ~ya'á-a   tí-~da
form-CLF:lake-LOC ANPH-F-SG-OBJ grab-ASSERT.PFV ANPH-PL

'When the woman came down to fetch water from the pond, they grabbed her.'
'Quando a mulher desceu para pegar água no poço, eles a agarraram.'

(54) *thunua tikorokhʉ, "yʉ'ʉre ñaenatiga! soro mahsawa'mino yakoropʉ hiha" nia.*
~thudú-a   tí-kó-ró-khʉ   yʉ'ʉ́-ré ~ya'a-éra-tiga
resist-ASSERT.PFV ANPH-F-SG-ADD 1SG-OBJ grab-NEG-NEG.IMP

---

[23] The "servants" referred to here are identified as people of one of the Makú ethnic groups, reflecting the unequal social relations between dominant riverine Tukano and Arawak groups and the forest-dwelling peoples, speakers of what are now referred to as languages of the Nadahup and Kákua-Nʉkak families (Epps 2008; Bolaños 2016). Use of the diminutive suffix -~ka highlights their smaller physical stature when compared to the riverine peoples (see lines 58-59), but is also used metaphorically to indicate diminished social status.

  sóro   *~basá-~wa'bi-ro*   *yá-ko-ro-pɨ*   *hí-ha*
different.one people-older.brother-SG POSS-F-SG-LOC COP-VIS.IPFV.1
~dí-a
say-ASSERT.PFV

'She resisted them: "Let me go! I'm reserved for one from the higher clan," she said.'

'Ela resistiu: "Solta-me! Estou prometida para um do clã maior," disse.'

(55) *"mɨ'ɨre phikare khero mɨ manɨ" nima.*
   ~bɨ'ɨ́-ré phí-ka('a)-re   *khé-ro ~bɨ=~badɨ́*
   2SG-OBJ call-do.immediately-VIS.PFV.2/3 fast-SG 2SG.POSS=husband
   ~dí-~ba
   say-FRUS

   '"Your (true) husband is calling you right now," said (the servants, to no avail).'

   '"O seu marido (verdadeiro) está chamando rápido," disseram (em vão, os criados).'

(56) *ne kha'maeraa.*
   ~dé ~kha'ba-éra-a
   NEG want-NEG-ASSERT.PFV

   '[(She) didn't want (to go)!]'[24]

   '[(Ela) não queria (ir)!]'

(57) *kha'maera, thunuwihtika'aa ña'ano.*
   ~kha'ba-éra ~thudú-witi-ka'a-a   *~ya'á-ro*[25]
   want-NEG   resist-escape-do.moving-ASSERT.PFV grab-SG

   '(She) didn't want (to go), resisted (and) escaped (their) embrace.'

   'Não queria ir, resistiu (e) escapou do agarro (deles).'

(58) *to pho'na õ ma'ainakã hia a'rina ñahoria khi'ti.*
   to=~pho'dá   *~ó*   *~ba'á-~ídá-~ká*   *hí-a*
   3SG.POSS=children DEIC.PROX small-NMLZ.PL-DIM COP-ASSERT.PFV

---

[24] [ ] indicates a personal comment or observation by Teresinha or Joselito.
[25] The suffix *-ro* derives a nominal count noun from a verbal root; here, the noun 'embrace' is derived from the verb for 'grab'.

a'rí-~da   ñáhórí-á   khí'ti
DEM.PROX-PL ñahori-PL become

'His (*Yuhpi Diani*'s) servants, [the future *Ñahoria*] were just this tall.'

'Os criados dele (*Yuhpi Diani*) [os *Ñahoria* do futuro] eram deste tamanhinho.'

(59) *phᵾarokã hia.*

phᵾá-ro-~ka   hí-a
two-SG-DIM COP-ASSERT.PFV

'There were two little guys.'

'Eram dois pequenos.'

(60) *mᵾmᵾ mᵾhawa'aa tinakã:*

~bᵾbᵾ ~bᵾhá-wa'a-a   tí-~da-~ka
run   MOV.upward-go-ASSERT.PFV ANPH-PL-DIM

'They ran up (to tell *Yuhpi Diani*):'

'Foram correndo para cima (para avisar ao *Yuhpi Diani*):'

(61) *"de yoatapᵾ mᵾ namore ña'a tu'sᵾre."*

dé   yoá-ta-pᵾ   ~bᵾ=~dabó-re   ~ya'á-tu'sᵾ-re
INTJ:poor.one! far-EMPH-LOC 2SG.POSS=wife-OBJ grab-finish-VIS.PFV.2/3

'"It's too late, your wife's already taken."'

'"Já era, pegaram sua mulher."'

(62) *ti ñari, tiro hi'na ta bᵾea me'ne bᵾepati hi'na.*

tí-~ya-ri   tí-ró   ~hí'da tá   bᵾé-a=~be're   bᵾé-(pa)ti²⁶ ~hí'da
ANPH-bad-NMLZ ANPH-SG EMPH come arrow-PL=COM arrow-VBZ EMPH

'Those servants (and) he (*Yuhpi Diani*) himself came back with arrows and started shooting.'

'Os criados (e) ele (*Yuhpi Diani*) mesmo vieram de volta com flechas e começaram a flechar.'

---

²⁶The verbalizing suffix *-pati* may be an older, longer form of the now more commonly used verbalizer *-ti*, seen in lines 9, 17, 23, 24, and 140, among others.

(63) *mari ñᵾhchᵾsᵾmᵾa bᵾerina phanamana himahana mari.*

~bari=~yᵾchú-~sᵾbᵾá   bᵾé-ri-~da   ~phadába-~da
1PL.INCL.POSS=grandfather-PL.kin arrow.shoot-NMLZ-PL grandchild-PL
hí-~ba-ha-(~hi')da   ~barí²⁷
COP-RSP-VIS.IPFV.1-EMPH 1PL.INCL

'[We're grandchildren (descendants) of grandparents (ancestors) who used arrows.]'

'[Nós somos descendentes dos nossos avôs (ancestrais) que usavam flechas.]'

(64) *bᵾeato õbaroi, to pharokãre sã'aphaato.*

bᵾé-a-to   ~ó-ba'ro-i
arrow.shoot-PL-NMLZ.LOC/EVNT DEIC.PROX-CLF:kind-LOC.VIS
to=phá-ro-~ka²⁸-re   ~sa'á-pha-to
3SG.POSS=stomach-SG-DIM-OBJ MOV.inside-stomach-NMLZ.LOC/EVNT

'(*Diani*'s people) shot (*Yuhpi Diani*'s servant) right here in the stomach.'

'(O pessoal do *Diani*) flecharam (o criado do *Yuhpi Diani*) bem aqui na barriga.'

(65) *tina bᵾathuataa.*

tí-~da   bᵾá-thua-ta-a
ANPH-PL crawl/crouch-return-come-ASSERT.PFV

'They came crawling back.'

'Eles vinham se arrastando.'

(66) *mahkarokahore tirore dᵾhte koaa.*

~baká-dóká²⁹-hó-ré   tí-ró-ré   dᵾté koá-a
forest-DIST-banana-OBJ ANPH-SG-OBJ chop cure-ASSERT.PFV

'(They) found wild bananas (and) chopped (them to extract the liquid) to make a cure for him (the wounded guy).'

---

²⁷Although marked tones reflect word-level patterns, there is tonal downstep on all sentence-final pronouns.

²⁸In this instance and many others, the diminutive suffix *-kã* is used for emphasis.

²⁹The second root in the compound is underlyingly *doka* 'throw', grammaticalized as a marker of "distal" spatial relations: that the object is related to distant place (the case here), that the movement is toward the distance or that the action is occurring at a far off location. See also lines 52, 106, 138, and 153.

'Encontraram banana-do-mato, cortaram (para tirar o líquido e) fizeram curativo para ele (o ferido).'

(67) nathua te ti phʉ'toro yuhpi diani ka'apʉ.
~dá-thúá-a té ti=phʉ'tó-ro yuhpí.diáni ka'á-pʉ
get-return-ASSERT.PFV until 3PL.POSS=master-SG yuhpi.diani beside-LOC
'(They) took (him) right up to their leader *Yuhpi Diani*.'
'Levaram até o chefe deles *Yuhpi Diani*.'

(68) *"mʉ'ʉ sãre ã wa'achʉ yoara"* nia.
~bʉ'ʉ ~sá-re ~a=wa'á-chʉ yoá-ra ~dí-a
2SG 1PL.EXCL-OBJ so=go-SW.REF do-VIS.IPFV.2/3 say-ASSERT.PFV
'"You made this happen to us," they said.'
'"Você fez isso acontecer conosco," disseram.'

(69) *"mʉ'ʉre wãhakãnata"* nia.
~bʉ'ʉ-ré ~wahá-ka'a-~da-ta ~dí-a
2SG-OBJ kill-do.immediately-PL-INTENT say-ASSERT.PFV
'"Now we're going to kill you!" (they) said.'
'"Agora vamos matar você!" disseram.'

(70) *"hierara, yʉ kasero. yʉ'ʉre yoenatiga.*
hi-éra-ra yʉ=kaséro[30] yʉ'ʉ-ré yoa-éra-tiga
COP-NEG-VIS.IPFV.2/3 1SG.POSS=servant 1SG-OBJ do-NEG-NEG.IMP
'"No you won't, my servants. Don't do that to me."'
'"Nada disso, meus criados. Não façam nada a mim."'

(71) *mʉhsa phʉ'toro hiha. yʉ'ʉbahsi mahsita"* nia tiro.
~bʉsa=phʉ'tó-ro hí-ha yʉ'ʉ-basi ~basí[31]-ta
2PL.POSS=master-SG COP-VIS.IPFV.1 1SG-EMPH know-INTENT
~dí-a tí-ró
say-ASSERT.PFV ANPH-SG
'"I'm your leader. I myself can resolve things," he (*Yuhpi Diani*) said.'
'"Sou o chefe. Eu mesmo posso resolver isso," disse ele (*Yuhpi Diani*).'

---

[30] The word *kasero* is a borrowing from Portuguese "caseiro", a housekeeper or servant.
[31] The verb *mahsi* 'know' is also used to indicate ability, to 'know how' to do something.

(72) ni, ñaina hi'na bʉea kha'noari ti(na).

~dí ~yá-~ida ~hí'da bʉé-a ~kha'dó-wa'a-ri tí-~da
say bad-NMLZ.PL EMPH arrow-PL prepare/organize-go-NMLZ ANPH-PL
'Saying that, the servants started making arrows (preparing for war).'
'Falando isso, os criados foram preparar (armas).'

(73) tiro a'rina ñʉhchʉno khi'to hia.

tí-ró a'rí-~da ~yʉchʉ́-ro khí'to hí-a
ANPH-SG DEM.PROX-PL grandfather-SG become COP-ASSERT.PFV
'[He (*Yuhpi Diani* and) the ones who would become (your) grandfathers.]'
'[Ele (*Yuhpi Diani* e) os que seriam os avôs (de vocês).]'

(74) sã ba'ʉ, tiro ñahori kʉirota hia, to namosãnumia, phʉaro numia ...

~sa=ba'ʉ́ tí-ró ñáhórí ~kʉ́-iro-ta
1PL.EXCL.POSS=younger.brother ANPH-SG ñahori alone-NMLZ.SG-EMPH
hí-a to=~dabó-~sadubia phʉá-ro-~dubia
COP-ASSERT.PFV 3SG.POSS=wife-PL.F two-SG-PL.F
'Our younger brother, Ñahori, lived alone with his wives, two women ...'
'Nosso irmão menor, Ñahori, vivia sozinho com as mulheres, duas esposas ...'

(75) to pho'nakã phʉarokã, to phayoa phʉarokã, seista hia tina õre mukʉ dʉhpʉrire.

to=~pho'dá-~ka phʉá-ro-~ka to=phayó-a phʉá-ro-~ka
3SG.POSS=children-DIM two-SG-DIM 3SG.POSS=servant-PL two-SG-DIM
seis[32]=ta hí-a tí-~da ~ó-ré múkʉ.dʉhpʉri-re
six=EMPH COP-ASSERT.PFV ANPH-PL DEIC.PROX-OBJ mukʉ.dʉhpʉri-OBJ
'two children and two servants, they were exactly six here in *Mukʉ Dʉhpʉri.*'
'dois filhos e dois criados, no total eram seis aqui em *Mukʉ Dʉhpʉri.*'

---

[32] Although there are frequently used Kotiria terms for numbers one through five, nowadays it is quite common for both numbers and time expressions, such as *semana* 'week' in line 76, to be borrowed from Portuguese. See also line 264.

(76) *no'oi tiasomana ba'aro, ñariro phiriaka bihsi yohata to kaserua me'ne.*

~do'ó-i   tíá-semana=ba'a-ro   ~yá-ri-ro   phíríá-ká[33]
Q:when-LOC.VIS three-weeks=after-SG bad-NMLZ-SG flute-CLF:round
bisí   yóhá-tá   to=kaséro-a=~be're
sound go.upriver-come 3SG.POSS=servant-PL=COM

'Three weeks later, the warrier (*Yuhpi Diani*) came upstream with his servants, to the sound of *piriaka* flutes.'

'Três semanas depois, o guerreiro (*Yuhpi Diani*) vinha subindo com seus criados, ao som da flauta *piriaka*.'

(77) *ti phapɨre, yarokã tina kha'mawãhaera himarebɨ, tutu ... tutu ... tutuuuuu ...*

tí   phá-pɨ-ré   yá-ró-~ká   tí-~da   ~kha'bá-~waha-éra
ANPH time-LOC-OBJ secret-SG-DIM ANPH-PL bring/do.together[34]-kill-NEG
hí-~bare-bɨ   tutu...tutu...tutuuuuu
COP-REM.IPFV-EPIS ONTP:flute.playing

'In those times, it wasn't the custom to make war silently (but to play flutes) *tutu ... tutu ... tutuuuuu ...*'

'Naqueles tempos, não era costume guerrear em silêncio, (vinham tocando flautas) *tutu ... tutu ... tutuuuuu ...*'

(78) *õ wãhsipiria nɨhkoi wa'asɨ ñaina mahaa. te õi sɨa.*

~ó   ~wahsípíríá ~dɨko-i   wa'á-~sɨ   ~yá-~ida
DEIC.PROX wãhsipiria island-LOC.VIS go-arrive.TRNS bad-NMLZ.PL
~bahá-a   té   ~ó-í   ~sɨ-a
go.uphill-ASSERT.PFV until DEIC.PROX-LOC.VIS arrive.TRNS-ASSERT.PFV

'They arrived here in *Wãhsipiria Nɨhko* (island, and) the warriors came up the path until they arrived (at *Ñahori*'s house).'

'Chegaram aqui em *Wãhsipiria Nɨhko* (ilha, e) os guerreiros foram subindo pelo caminho até chegarem (na casa do *Ñahori*).'

(79) *tiro bi'asãmato tiro. khatarosohpakai duhia tiro bɨhkɨro.*

tí-ró   bi'á-sã'a-~ba-to   tí-ró
ANPH-SG close-MOV.inside-FRUS-NMLZ.LOC/EVNT ANPH-SG

---

[33] *Piriaka* are small wooden flutes held horizontally and played through a single blow hole.
[34] The root *khãbá* 'bring or do X together' (see also Footnote 51), when used in a serialization can indicate reflexive action, as in line 162.

khatá-ró-sópáká-í   duhí-a   tí-ró   bʉkʉ́-ro
flatbread.oven-SG-opening-LOC.VIS sit-ASSERT.PFV ANPH-SG ancestor-SG

'He (*Ñahori*) barred (the entrance, in vain, and), the old guy sat next to the opening to the flatbread oven.'

'Ele (*Ñahori*) se-fechou dentro (em vão, e) o velho ficou sentado na boca do forno.'

(80) *ñahori to wa'masitia me'neta, a'ri wʉhʉnihti, a'ri noano hiphitiro to dohkaa me'ne.*

ñáhórí to=~wa'básítía=~be're³⁵-ta   a'rí   wʉhʉ́~dítí
ñahori 3SG.POSS=adornments=COM-EMPH DEM.PROX ceremonial.perfume
a'rí   ~dóá-ró híphiti-ro   to=doká-a=~be're
DEM.PROX good-SG everything-SG 3SG.POSS=spear-PL=COM

'*Ñahori* with all his adornments, the ceremonial perfume (and) all of his weapons.'

'*Ñahori* com todos os enfeites do corpo, perfume ceremonial (e) com todas as sua armas.'

(81) *tatu'sʉa tina. kʉ̃pho'na mahataa*

tá-thu'sʉ-a   tí-~da   ~kʉ́-~pho'da
come-finish-ASSERT.PFV ANPH-PL one/a-CLF:line
~bahá-ta-a
go.uphill-come-ASSERT.PFV

'They (*Yuhpi Diani* and warriors) arrived. (They) were coming up in a line.'

'Eles (*Yuhpi Diani* e guerreiros) já estavam vindo numa fila.'

(82) *yaba? um ... hum, bo'teapũ, do'se nihari?*

yabá³⁶   hum...hum bo'téa~pu   do'sé   ~dí-hárí
Q:what/how hum...hum embaúba.tree(sp) Q:how say-Q.IPFV

'[What? um, um ... Embaúba tree, [is that what it's called?]]'

'[Como? um, um ... Embaúba, [é assim que chama?]]'

---

³⁵Use of the comitative clitic *me'ne* causes tonal downstep on the tonal element immediately before; the same phenomenon occurs in the second occurrence in this example.

³⁶The question word *yaba* 'what/how' is used as a filler in discourse, when the speaker has a doubt about something or needs a moment to think or reformulate.

(83) *pho'ophĩni peri ti khãtarire khʉaa tinase'e.*

pho'o-~phí-rí   péri   ti=~kháta-ri-re
molongó.tree-CLF:bladelike-PL many 3PL.POSS=cut.separate-NMLZ-OBJ
khʉá-a   tí-~da-se'e
have-ASSERT.PFV ANPH-PL-CONTR

'They had a lot of strips of molongó wood that they had sharpened ...'
'Eles tinham um monte de ripas de molongó que estavam bem afiados ...'

(84) *ti bahtichʉ hipa tinase're.*

tí   batíchʉ hí-pha   tí-~da-se'e-re
ANPH shield COP-SPEC ANPH-PL-CONTR-OBJ

'[That (I suppose) were like a shield for them.]'
'[Que (suponho) era como se fosse escudo para eles.]'

(85) *"tara sõ'o phʉ'toro" nia.*

tá-rá   ~so'ó   phʉ'tó-ró ~dí-a
come-VIS.IPFV.2/3 DEIC.DIST master-SG say-ASSERT.PFV

'"(They're) coming, master!" (Ñahori's servants) said.'
'"(Eles) já vem, chefe!" disseram (os servos do Ñahori).'

(86) *tinakã phʉarokã nia: "to ... to ... tooooooo, ñaina wahpana pho'nañari!"*

tí-~da-~ka   phʉá-ro-~ka ~dí-a   to...to...tooooooo ~yá-~ida
ANPH-PL-DIM two-SG-DIM say-ASSERT.PFV INTJ:taunt   bad-NMLZ.PL
wapá-~da ~pho'dá-~ya-ri
enemy-PL children-bad-PL

'(Ñahori's) two poor servants taunted them: "To ... to ... tooooooo, hated sons of our enemy!"'
'Os dois criados coitados (de Ñahori) gritavam xingando: "To ... to ... tooooooo, malditos filhos do inimigo!"'

(87) *"thʉrekhãnata" nimaati pakhuioina.*

~thʉ́re-~kha-~da-ta   ~dí-~ba-ati   pá-khui-o-~ida
knock.down-chop-PL-INTENT say-FRUS-IPFV ALT-afraid-CAUS-NMLZ.PL

'"We're going to mow you down!" the poor terrified ones yelled.'
'"Vamos derrubar vocês!" gritavam os pobres apavorados.'

(88) *ne bioera, tinase phayɨbia hia.*

~dé bio-éra   tí-~da-se   phayɨ-bia hí-a
NEG defend/resist-NEG ANPH-PL-CONTR many-AUM COP-ASSERT.PFV

'(But) they (Ñahori's servants) were overwhelmed, there were too many of the others.'

'(Mas) não aguentaram (os criados de Ñahori), os outros eram uma multidão.'

(89) *tinakã, a'rí tho'ori khɨamaati pakhuioina, ñahori yainakã ...*

tí-~da-~ka   a'rí   thó'ó-rí   khɨá-~ba-ati
ANPH-PL-DIM DEM.PROX spear-PL have-FRUS-IPFV
pá-khui-o-~ida   ñáhórí yá-~ida-~ka
ALT-afraid-CAUS-NMLZ.PL ñahori POSS-NMLZ.PL-DIM

'Those poor guys who just had spears, were terrified, Ñahori's servants ...'

'Os coitadinhos que só tinham lanças, ficaram com medo, os criados do Ñahori ...'

(90) *duhia tina kho'taphisaa bahtirodita.*

duhí-a tí-~da   kho'tá-phísá[37]-á   batí-ro-dita
sit-PL ANPH-PL wait-be.on-ASSERT.PFV shield-CLF:concave-SOL

'they sat up there waiting with their shields.'

'ficaram em cima sentados só com escudos.'

(91) *bɨemati ne bioera: "phayɨbia hira. sã phɨ'toro, wihaga" nimaa.*

bɨé-~ba-ati   ~dé bio-éra   phayɨ-bia
arrow.shoot-FRUS-IPFV NEG defend/resist-NEG many-AUM
hí-ra   ~sa=phɨ'tó-ro   wihá-ga
COP-VIS.IPFV.2/3 1PL.EXCL.POSS=master-SG MOV.outward-IMP
~dí-~ba-a
say-FRUS-ASSERT.PFV

'Shooting but unable to resist, (the servants) cried (in vain): "There are too many of them, master. Run away!"'

'Flechando mas não resistindo, gritaram (os criados em vão): "São muitos, chefe. Fuja!"'

---

[37] Many verb serializations contain stative positional roots such as *phisa* 'be on', which contribute detailed perspective of the action. Here, we understand that the servants are cowering on higher ground, observing and dreading the arrival of the enemy approaching from below.

(92) *"wa'eraha yʉ'ʉ́se kʉ̃iro pha'ñohita tinare" nia tiro.*
    wa'a-éra-ha   yʉ'ʉ́-se   ~kʉ́-író   ~pha'yó-híta[38]
    go-NEG-VIS.IPFV.1 1SG-CONTR   alone-NMLZ.SG complete-SG.INTENT
    tí-~da-re   ~dí-a   tí-ró
    ANPH-PL-OBJ   say-ASSERT.PFV ANPH-SG
    '"I'm not going! I'm going to defeat them all!" he (Ñahori) said.'
    '"Não vou! Eu mesmo vou acabar com eles," disse ele (Ñahori).'

(93) *"sã phʉ'toro wa'aga, wa'aga, sã phʉ'toro. mʉ'ʉre wãhakãka. sãma'chʉne noano yoahã'ka."*
    ~sa=phʉ'tó-ro   wa'á-gá wa'á-gá ~sa=phʉ'tó-ro
    1PL.EXCL.POSS=master-SG   go-IMP go-IMP 1PL.EXCL.POSS=master-SG
    ~bʉ'ʉ́-ré ~wahá-~ka-ka   ~sá-~ba'chʉ-re   ~dóá-ró yoá-~ha[39]-ka
    2SG-OBJ kill-DIM-PREDICT   1PL.EXCL-ADD-OBJ   good-SG do-COMPL-PREDICT
    '"Master, run away, run away, master! (They) will kill you. (They're) ready to kill us too."'
    '"Chefe, fuja, fuja, chefe! Vão matar você. Nós também, já vão nos matar."'

(94) *"hierara. yʉ'ʉbahsi mahsita," nia.*
    hi-éra-ra   yʉ'ʉ́-basi ~basí-ta   ~dí-a
    COP-NEG-VIS.IPFV.2/3 1SG-EMPH   know-INTENT   say-ASSERT.PFV
    '"No! I myself can (defeat them)," (Ñahori) said.'
    '"Não! Eu mesmo sei (acabar com eles)," disse (Ñahori).'

(95) *ni, tina ñahori pho'nakãre, to namosãnumia "a'rínakãre naaga" nia.*
    ~dí tí-~da   ñáhórí ~pho'dá-~ka-re   to=~dabó-~sadubia
    say ANPH-PL   ñahori children-DIM-OBJ   3SG.POSS=wife-PL.F
    a'rí-~da-~ka-re   ~dá-wa'a-ga ~dí-a
    DEM.PROX-PL-DIM-OBJ   get-go-IMP   say-ASSERT.PFV
    'Saying that, Ñahori ordered his wives: "Take the children away!" he said.'
    'Falando disso, Ñahori mandou as esposas: "Levem as crianças embora!" disse.'

---

[38] The expression *ta hita*, here in reduced form, shows the speaker's intent to do something 'by myself.'

[39] The morpheme *-hã* is analyzed as a shortened form of *phã'yo* (see line 105), which in a serial verb construction adds a 'completive' aspectual reading.

(96) *"hai" ni. tinakãre na, ti yaipiripᵾre naa.*

hai   ~dí tí-~da-~ka-re   ~dá
INTJ:agree say ANPH-PL-DIM-OBJ get

ti=yái-pírí-pᵾ-re   ~dá-a
3PL.POSS=jaguar-teeth-CLF:basket-OBJ get-ASSERT.PFV

'"Yes!" (they) said. They got the children (and) put them in (their basket with) jaguar-teeth necklaces (and other sacred objects).'

'"Sim!" disseram. Pegaram os filhos (e) colocaram no (cesto) de colares de dente-de-onça (e outros objetos sagrados).'

(97) *to namosãnumia pho'nakã phᵾaro.*

to=~dabó-~sadubia ~pho'dá-~ka phᵾá-ro
3SG.POSS=wife-PL.F children-DIM two-SG

'[His wives' two children.]'

'[Os dois filhos das esposas dele.]'

(98) *"toi, sã bioeraka. mᵾ'ᵾbahsi mahsiga sã phᵾ'toro. mᵾ'ᵾre khã'imaha sã," nia.*

tó-i   ~sá   bio-éra-ka   ~bᵾ'ᵾ-basi ~basí-gá
DEF-LOC.VIS 1PL.EXCL defend/resist-NEG-ASSERT.IPFV 2SG-EMPH know-IMP

~sa=phᵾ'tó-ro   ~bᵾ'ᵾ-ré ~kha'í-~ba-ha   ~sá
1PL.EXCL.POSS=master-SG 2SG-OBJ love-RSP-VIS.IPFV.1 1PL.EXCL

~dí-a
say-ASSERT.PFV

'"We can't resist anymore! You take over, master. We love you," (Ñahori's servants) said.'

'"Não aguentamos mais. Você pode resistir, chefe. Nós amamos você," disseram (os criados do Ñahori).'

(99) *tiro tobahsi bᵾawihatamaa bᵾerotaro.*

tí-ró   to-basí   bᵾá-wiha-ta-~ba-a
ANPH-SG DEF-EMPH crawl/crouch-MOV.outward-come-FRUS-ASSERT.PFV

bᵾé-ro-ta-ro
arrow.shoot-SG-come-SG

'He (Ñahori) himself came out crouching down (and) shooting arrows.'

'Ele (Ñahori) mesmo veio saindo agachado (e) flechando.'

(100) *tiata, quatrotari, tirore õ waroi bɨetu'sɨa tina, chɨɨɨɨ! tɨ ... tɨ ..*
.tɨɨɨɨɨɨɨɨɨ, phuhu!

tíá-ta   quátro-ta-ri   tí-ró-ré   ~ó   wáró-i
three-EMPH four-EMPH-PL ANPH-SG-OBJ DEIC.PROX EMPH-LOC.VIS
bɨé-thu'sɨ-a   tí-~da   chɨɨɨɨ!
arrow.shoot-finish-ASSERT.PFV ANPH-PL ONTP:arrows.being.shot
tɨ...tɨ...tɨɨɨɨɨɨɨɨ phuhu!
ONTP:arrows.flying ONTP:falling.on.ground

'After three (or) four rounds, an arrow hit him (Ñahori). *Chɨɨɨɨ! tɨ ... tɨ ... tɨɨɨɨ! phuhu!*' (sounds of arrows flying, striking Ñahori and his falling down.)

'Depois de três (ou) quatro vezes, acertaram nele (Ñahori).*Chɨɨɨɨ! tɨ ... tɨ ... tɨɨɨɨ! phuhu!*' (som das flechas, do acerto nele e Ñahori caindo.)

(101) *thetereka khataro dɨ'tɨka'apɨ.*

thetéré-ká   khatá-ró   dɨ'tɨka'a-pɨ
tremble-ASSERT.IPFV flatbread.oven-CLF:concave edge-LOC

'He collapsed trembling right next to the oven.'

'Caiu tremendo bem do lado do forno.'

(102) *kha'asɨa.*

kha'á-~sɨ-a
fall-arrive.TRNS-ASSERT.PFV

'He fell over.'

'Ficou caido.'

(103) *to kha'asɨchɨ, "noana mari wahpakɨro ñakãre" ni.*

to=kha'á-~sɨ-chɨ   ~dóádá   ~bari=wapá-kɨ-ro
3SG.POSS=fall-arrive.TRNS-SW.REF that's.good 1PL.INCL.POSS=enemy-M-SG
~yá-~ka-re   ~dí
bad-DIM-OBJ say

'After his fall[40] (*Diani*'s warriors cried): "You deserved it, evil enemy!"'

'Depois que caiu, (os guerreiros do *Diani* gritaram): "Bem feito, inimigo malvado!"'

---

[40]These sentences contain a typical "tail-head" linking sequence, in which the finite predicate (or part of it) of one sentence is repeated in the following sentence, usually as an initial subordinate adverbial clause (though the subordinate clauses can occur at the end of the sentence, as in line 195). When the action involves a shift in subject between the subordinate and main clause, the subordinate clause is marked with the switch-reference suffix *-chɨ* (see Stenzel 2016).

(104) doa, ni "hʉʉʉʉ ... bi'oha mari tirore," ni thumaharekũa.

dóa ~dí hʉʉʉʉ bi'ó-há ~barí tí-ró-ré
shout say INTJ:victory.cry successful-VIS.IPFV.1 1PL.INCL ANPH-SG-OBJ
~dí thú-~baha-re-~kua
say push-MOV.upward-OBJ-leave.on.ground

'(They) shouted: "Hʉʉʉʉ! ... We got (killed) him!" (and then) rolled his body over.'

'Gritaram: "Hʉʉʉʉ! ... Nós conseguimos (matar) ele!" (e depois) viraram (o corpo dele) de costas.'

(105) wʉ'ʉ hʉ̃pha'yohã'a.

wʉ'ʉ́ ~hʉ́-pha'yo-~ha-a
house burn-COMPL-COMPL-ASSERT.PFV

'(They) burned down all the houses.'

'(Eles) tocaram fogo em todas as casas.'

(106) ã yoa tina dʉhsetire ñʉrokaa nia.

~a=yóá tí-~da dʉsé-tí[41]-re ~yʉ́-dóká-a ~dí-a
so=do ANPH-PL mouth-ATTRIB-OBJ see/look-DIST-PL PROG-ASSERT.PFV

'So, the others (from Matapi) were watching the confusion from afar.'

'Então, os outros (de Matapi) ficaram observando a confusão de longe.'

(107) a'ri ora hiro hiarĩto?[42]

a'rí hóra hí-ro hí-a-rito
DEM.PROX hour COP-SG COP-go-or.not

'[Was that when it was?]'

'[Era nessa hora ou não?]'

(108) ni ora hiro hiarito to phichanihti mʉhaa tiñʉchʉ.

~dí hóra hí-ro hí-a-rito to=phichá-~dítí
Q:which hour COP-SG COP-go-or.not REM=fire-ash
~bʉhá-a ti=~yʉ́-chʉ́
MOV.upward-ASSERT.PFV 3PL.POSS=see/look-SW.REF

'[Was at this time or not when (the women in Matapi) saw the smoke rising?]'

---

[41] The notion of "confusion" is derived from the root for 'mouth' marked by the attributive suffix -ti, something akin to 'be mouthy'. It can also be used to refer to a discussion.

[42] The expression hiro hiarito is used to express doubt: 'Was that the way it went/was or not?' The verb wa'a 'go' is often shortened to -a when it occurs in serializations (see also line 292).

'[Era essa hora ou não quando (as mulheres de Matapi) viram a fumaça subir?]'

(109) *ã yoa ti manʉsʉmʉare ... sã numia khitiphayʉ nimahana.*
~a=yóá ti=~badʉ́-~sʉbʉa-re   ~sá   ~dubía khití-phayʉ
so=do 3PL.POSS=husband-PL.kin-OBJ 1PL.EXCL women story-many
~dí-~bá-há=~(hi')da
say-FRUS-VIS.IPFV.1=EMPH

'So (they commented to) their husbands ... [we women are such gossips! (story-tellers)]'

'Então (falaram) aos seus maridos ... [como nós mulheres somos fofoqueiras (contadoras de histórias)!]'

(110) *"ñʉhʉ! do'se mari ñahorire wãhahãpha sina."*
~yʉ́-~hʉ[43]   *do'sé ~bari=ñáhórí-ré   ~wahá-~ha-pha*
see/look-IMP.DEIC Q:what 1PL.INCL.POSS=ñahori-OBJ kill-COMPL-SPEC
śi-~da
DEM.DIST-PL

'"Look there! Have those people killed our *Ñahori*?" (they speculated).'

'"Olha lá! Será que aqueles mataram nosso *Ñahori*? (especularam).'

(111) *"yoatapʉ wʉ'ʉma'chʉ hʉ̃mʉhana" nia.*
yoá-tá-pʉ́   wʉ'ʉ́-~ba'chʉ ~hʉ́-~bʉha-ra
long-EMPH-LOC house-ADD   burn-MOV.upward-VIS.IPFV.2/3
~dí-a
say-ASSERT.PFV

'"The smoke from the houses has been rising for a long time!" (they) said.'

'"Faz tempo que sobe fumaça das casas!" disseram.'

(112) *"pa! ã thiharide ni ñʉrokaa.*
pá   ~á thí-hari-de   ~dí ~yʉ-dóká-á
INTJ:neg.surprise so true-Q.IPFV-EMPH say see/look-DIST-ASSERT.PFV

'"Oh no! Is it true?" (they wondered) looking from afar.'

'"Puxa! Será verdade?" (especularam) olhando de longe.'

---

[43]The imperative suffix *-hʉ* has inherent distal deictic semantics.

(113) *"bahsañɨna!"*
 basá-~yɨ-(~hí')da
 EXRT-see/look-EXRT[44]
 '"Let's go see!"'
 '"Vamos ver!"'

(114) *ti phare ma'ari hiatiri himarebɨ taati phaati ... pɨɨɨ ... a'ri mukɨ dɨhpɨripɨ.*
 tí-phá-ré   ~ba'á-ri hí-ati-ri   hí-~bare-bɨ   tá-átí
 ANPH-time-OBJ path-PL COP-IPFV-NMLZ COP-REM.IPFV-EPIS come-IPFV
 phá-ati   pɨ a'rí   múkɨ.dɨhpɨri-pɨ
 time-IPFV LOC DEM.PROX mukɨ.dɨhpɨri-LOC
 '[In those days it seems there were already paths coming all the way to *Mukɨ Dɨhpɨri* (*Ñahori*'s place).]'
 '[Naqueles tempos parece que já existiam as trilhas vindo até ao *Mukɨ Dɨhpɨri* (lugar do *Ñahori*).]'

(115) *de ti wi'ichɨ wɨ'ɨ borawa'aa ... karaa!*
 dé   ti=wi'í-chɨ   wɨ'ɨ
 INTJ:poor.one(s)! 3PL.POSS=arrive.CIS-SW.REF house
 borá-wa'a-a   karaa
 slide/fall-go-ASSERT.PFV ONTP:house.collapsing
 'Poor folks! When they got there, the houses were already collapsing ... *Karaa!*' (sound of houses falling down)
 'Coitados! Quando chegaram, as casas já estavam caindo ... *Karaa!*' (som das casas caindo)

(116) *"kue! do'se wa'aride" ni, phisumahkamaa tina ñahorire.*
 kué   do'sé   wa'á-ri-de[45]   ~dí
 INTJ:surprise Q:what go-NMLZ-NEG.MIR say
 phisú-~báká-~ba-a   tí-~da   ñáhórí-ré
 call-look.for-FRUS-ASSERT.PFV ANPH-PL ñahori-OBJ
 '"What in the world happened?" (they thought) calling out, looking (in vain) for *Ñahori* (and his family).'

---

[44]The exhortative is composed of elements bracketing the verb: initial *(ba)sa* and final *(hí')na*, both of which are frequently shortened as indicated.

[45]The morpheme *-de* seems to be a negative mirative, indicating both unexpected information and fear.

'"O que será que aconteceu?" (pensaram) chamando e procurando (em vão) *Ñahori* (e a familia).'

(117) *"ñahoriiii, ñahori pho'nakããããã, mʉhsare wãhapha'ñonohkaka," nia tina biarise.*

ñáhórí ñáhórí ~pho'dá-~ká ~bʉsá-re ~wahá-~pha'yo-~doka-ka
ñahori ñahori children-DIM 2PL-OBJ kill-complete-together-ASSERT.IPFV
~dí-a tí-~da bíári-se
say-ASSERT.PFV ANPH-PL biari-CONTR

'"*Ñahori* ... *Ñahori* children ... (they've) killed all of you together!" the *Biari* cried.'

'"*Ñahori* ... *Ñahori* filhos ... mataram todos vocês juntos!" gritaram eles, os *Biari*.'

(118) *yʉ'tiera tina, yo'o khuinohkaa.*

yʉ'ti-éra tí-~da yo'ó khuí-~doka-a
answer-NEG ANPH-PL slaughter afraid-together-ASSERT.PFV

'They (the ones who had escaped) didn't answer, fearful of being slaughtered.'

'Não respondiam (os que tinham escapado), com pavor de serem mortos.'

(119) *"marire pharituri wãhataa nina" nia.*

~barí-re pharí-thu(a)-ri ~wahá-ta-a ~dí-ra
1PL.INCL-OBJ time-return-NMLZ kill-come-PL PROG-VIS.IPFV.2/3
~dí-a
say-ASSERT.PFV

'"(They're) coming back to kill us!" (they) thought.'

'"Vão vir de novo para nos matar!" pensaram.'

(120) *ba'aro, "no'oi wa'ari mʉhsa ñahori pho'nakã" nia.*

ba'á-ró[46] ~do'ó-i wa'á-ri ~bʉsá ñáhórí ~pho'dá-~ká
after-SG Q:where-LOC.VIS go-Q.PFV 2PL ñahori children-DIM
~dí-a
say-ASSERT.PFV

'Later, (the *Biari*) cried out, "Where have you gone, *Ñahori* children?"'

'Mais tarde, (os *Biari*) gritaram, "Onde foram vocês, filhos do *Ñahori*?"'

---

[46] Relative temporal reference is accomplished by stative roots 'do/be after' (also in line 76) or 'do/be before' (as in line 282), glossed with their basic semantics.

(121) *"mʉhsare wãhapha'ñoboari chẽ" nia.*
~bʉsá-re ~wahá-~pha'yo-bo-a-ri   ~ché   ~dí-a
2PL-OBJ kill-complete-DUB-AFFECT-Q.PFV INTJ:doubt say-ASSERT.PFV
'"Could they have killed all of you?"'
'"Será que mataram todos vocês?"'

(122) *tina a'rina yuhpi diani tinakãre wãhapha'ñochʉre, a'rina ne ñahoria maniaboka.*
tí-~da   a'rí-~da   yuhpi.diání tí-~da-~ka-re
ANPH-PL DEM.PROX-PL yuhpi.diani ANPH-PL-DIM-OBJ
~wahá-~pha'yo-chʉ-re   a'rí-~da   ~dé ~yáhórí-á
kill-complete-SW.REF-OBJ DEM.PROX-PL NEG ñahori-PL
~badía-bo-ka
not.exist-DUB-ASSERT.IPFV
'[If *Yuhpi Diani* had killed off the little ones, there wouldn't be all these *Ñahoria*.]' (referring to the audience)
'[Se *Yuhpi Diani* tivesse matado os pequenos, não existiriam esses *Ñahoria*.]' (falando da plateia assistindo)

(123) *tinakã phʉaro mʉakã hia.*
tí-~da-~ka   phʉá-ro ~bʉ́-a-~ka   hí-a
ANPH-PL-DIM two-SG man/person-PL-DIM COP-ASSERT.PFV
'There were two little boys.'
'Havia dois meninos.'

(124) *ã yoa mahkaphome yʉ'tia. "ʉʉʉʉʉʉʉʉ" nia.*
~a=yóá ~baká-~phóbé   yʉ'tí-a   ʉʉʉʉʉʉʉʉ ~dí-a
so=do look.for-give.up answer-ASSERT.PFV INTJ:here! say-ASSERT.PFV
'When (the *Biari*) were about to give up looking, (the boys) answered: "ʉʉʉʉʉʉ." (We're here!)'
'Então quando (os *Biari*) já estavam cansandos de procurar, (os meninos) responderam: "ʉʉʉʉʉʉ." (Estamos aqui!)'

(125) *"phi'atakɨ mɨhsare, mahkaha" nia.*

phi'á-tá-kɨ ~bɨsá-re ~baká-há ~dí-a
MOV.out-come-M 2PL-OBJ look.for-VIS.IPFV.1 say-ASSERT.PFV

'"Come on out! We're looking for you," (the *Biari*) cried.'

'"Venham! Estamos procurando vocês," (os *Biari*) gritaram.'

(126) *de tinakã to namosãnumia ti wi'iphi'tichɨ, tinakãre "ne do'se wa'ari mɨhsa?" nia.*

dé   tí-~da-~ka   to=~dabó-~sadubia
INTJ:poor.one(s)! ANPH-PL-DIM 3SG.POSS=wife-PL.F
ti=wi'í-phi'ti-chɨ   tí-~da-~ka-re   ~dé do'sé wa'á-ri
3PL.POSS=arrive.CIS-end-SW.REF ANPH-PL-DIM-OBJ NEG Q:what go-Q.PFV
~bɨsá ~dí-a
2PL say-ASSERT.PFV

'When the poor little ones and *Ñahori*'s wives arrived, (they asked) them: "What happened to you?"'

'Quando os pequenos coitados (e) as esposas (do *Ñahori*) chegaram, perguntaram a eles: "O que aconteceu com vocês?"'

(127) *"yoatapɨ sã manɨre wãhanohkare" nia.*

yoá-tá-pɨ   ~sa=~badú-ré   ~wahá-~doka-re
do-come-LOC 1PL.EXCL.POSS=husband-OBJ kill-together-VIS.PFV.2/3
~dí-a
say-ASSERT.PFV

'"(They) all came to kill our husband," (the women) said.'

'"Vieram matar nosso marido," disseram (as mulheres).'

(128) *"sãwaro a'rinakãre sã nai."*

~sá-waro   a'rí-~da-~ka-re   ~sá   ~dá-i
1PL.EXCL-EMPH DEM.PROX-PL-DIM-OBJ 1PL.EXCL get-VIS.PFV.1

'"It was us, we took the little ones away."'

'"Nós mesmo, nós levamos esses pequenos."'

(129) *"noana" nia.*

~dóádá   ~dí-a
that's.good say-ASSERT.PFV

'"Good thing!" (the *Biari*) answered.'

'"Que bom!" responderam (os *Biari*).'

(130) *"a'rinakã phɨaro a'ri yaipiripɨre tuaro sã khã'i" nia a'rina to mahsawamisɨmɨabɨ'se.*

a'rí-~da-~ka   phɨá-ro a'rí   yaí-pírí-pɨ-re
DEM.PROX-PL-DIM two-SG DEM.PROX jaguar-teeth-CLF:basket-OBJ
túá-ró   ~sá   ~khã'í   ~dí-a   a'rí-~da
strong-SG 1PL.EXCL care.for say-ASSERT.PFV DEM.PROX-PL
to=~basa-~wabi-~sɨbɨa-bɨ'se⁴⁷
3SG.POSS=people-older.brother-PL.kin-side

'"We will care for the two little ones (and) the jaguar-teeth basket (and) other sacred objects)," his older brothers (the *Biari*) said.'

'"Nós cuidamos desses dois pequenos (e) o cesto de dentes-de-onça (e outros objetos sagrados)," diziam os irmão maiores dele (os *Biari*).'

(131) *tinakãre nawa'a te ti ñɨwa'aka'aa no'oi hɨphi'ti, de khataro dɨ'tɨka'ai, ti yiriwɨrɨ khõaduhkua.*

tí-~da-~ka-re   ~dá-wa'a té   tí(~da)
ANPH-PL-DIM-OBJ get-go until ANPH
~yɨ-wa'a-ka'a-a   ~do'ó-i   ~hɨ-phi'ti
see/look-go-do.moving-ASSERT.PFV Q:where-LOC.VIS burn-end
dé   khatá-ró-dɨ'tɨka'a-i
INTJ:poor.one! flatbread.oven-CLF:concave-edge-LOC.VIS
ti=yírí-wɨ'rɨ   ~khoá-duku⁴⁸-a
3PL.POSS=skull-AUG lie-stand-ASSERT.PFV

'Taking the little ones (they) went looking around where the fire was going out, (and saw) the poor guy fallen at the edge of the oven, his big skull lying on the ground.'

---

⁴⁷Teresinha's use of the noun *bɨ'se* 'side' here indicates this as a possible lexical origin of the contrastive marker *-se('e)* (see lines 84, 165, 273, 275, among others), a grammaticalization path from 'side' to 'contrastive other'.

⁴⁸Note the serialization of two posture verbs, in which the second root *-duku* 'stand' indicates durative aspect. In this case, it emphasizes the complete immobility of the burned corpse lying there.

'Levando os pequenos, indo olhando onde o fogo estava acabando, (viram) o pobre corpo queimado do lado do forno, a caveira grande deitada no chão.'

(132) ñahorikiro hṳ khõano.
 ñáhórí-kíró ~hṳ ~khoá-ro
 ñahori-M.RSP burn lie-SG
 'It was Ñahori lying there all burned up.'
 'Era Ñahori deitado queimado.'

(133) sua yʉ'dʉa mʉawa'a ñaina.
 súá yʉ'dʉ́-á ~bʉ́-a-wa'a ~yá-~ida
 angry INTENS-ASSERT.PFV man/person-PL-go bad-NMLZ.PL
 'They became furious.'
 'Ficaram enfurecidos.'

(134) "noana, sã ba'ʉre yoaka" nia.
 ~dóádá ~sa=ba'ʉ́-re yoá-ka[49]
 very.well 1PL.EXCL.POSS=younger.brother-OBJ do-ASSERT.IPFV
 ~dí-a
 say-ASSERT.PFV
 '"Very well, (they've) done this to our younger brother (killed him)," (the Biari) said.'
 '"Tudo bem, já fizeram isso (mataram) nosso irmão," disseram (os Biari).'

(135) thua wa'aa.
 thúa-wa'a-a
 return-go-ASSERT.PFV
 'They returned home.'
 'Voltaram.'

(136) hia ti phʉkʉro a'riro dianumia, mari ñʉhchʉ.
 hí-a ti=phʉkʉ́-ró a'rí-ro diánúmíá
 COP-ASSERT.PFV 3PL.POSS=father-SG DEM.PROX-SG dianumia

---

[49] Use of the imperfective assertion marker –ka (rather than the perfective –a) suggests a shared conclusion based on evidence they can all see.

~bari=~yɨchɨ
1PL.INCL.POSS=grandfather
'Their father, *Dianumia (Yairo)*, our grandfather was there.'
'Lá estava o pai deles, *Dianumia (Yairo)*, nosso avô.'

(137) *"ne do'se wa'ari, pho'na."*
~dé   do'sé   wa'á-ri   ~pho'dá
INTJ:well Q:what go-Q.PFV children
'"Well, what happened, sons?" (*Dianumia Yairo* asked).'
'"Então, o que aconteceu, filhos?" (*Dianumia Yairo* perguntou).'

(138) *"yoatapɨ sã ba'ɨre hɨkhõarokare. wãhahare" nia.*
yoá-tá-pɨ   ~sa=ba'ɨ-ré
do-EMPH-LOC 1PL.EXCL.POSS=younger.brother-OBJ
~hɨ-~khoa-doka-re   ~wahá-~ha-re   ~dí-a
burn-lie-DIST-VIS.PFV.2/3 kill-COMPL-VIS.PFV.2/3 say-ASSERT.PFV
'"Over there they burned our younger brother. (They) killed (him)!" (they) said.'
'"Lá longe queimaram nosso irmão. Mataram!" relataram.'

(139) *"noanoka yɨ pho'na, topuruta hiro, to yabu'iri hika."*
~dóároka yɨ=~pho'dá   tópuru-ta   hí-ro
enough!   1SG.POSS=children that's.all-EMPH COP-SG
to=yá-bu'i-ri   hí-ka
3SG.POSS=POSS-cause-NMLZ   COP-ASSERT.IPFV
'"Enough, my sons, it's over, it was his own fault."'
"Basta, meus filhos, já chega, foi culpa dele mesmo."'

(140) *"ya'uchɨ, thɨ'o wamatierare" tiro nia tota ti phɨkɨrose dianumiase.*
ya'ú-chɨ   thɨ'ó ~waba-ti-éra-re   tí-ró   ~dí-a
warn-SW.REF   hear   word-VBZ-NEG-VIS.PFV.2/3   ANPH-SG   say-ASSERT.PFV
to-ta[50]   ti=phɨkú-ro-se   diánúmíá-sé
ANPH(3SG)-EMPH   3PL.POSS=father-SG-CONTR   dianumia-CONTR
'"I warned him, but he ignored (it)," he (*Dianumia Yairo*) retorted [disgusted].'

---

[50] Teresinha uses the expression *tota* (a short form of *tiro-ta* 'he there') for emphasis; indicating that *Dianumia Yairo* was expecting this to happen and is angered and disgusted by the situation. See the plural form of the expression, *tita* shortened from *tina-ta* in line 142.

"'Eu aconselhei, mas ele ignorou," ele (*Dianumia Yairo*) respondeu [desapontado]."

(141) *"hierara, kha'maeraha, sã phᵾkᵾ, (wāha)kha'makasininatha tirore."*

hi-éra-ra ~kha'ba-éra-ha ~sa=phᵾkᵾ́
COP-NEG-VIS.IPFV.2/3 want-NEG-VIS.IPFV.1 1PL.EXCL.POSS=father
(~waha)~kha'báka[51]-~sidi-~da-ta tí-ró-ré
(kill)RECP-do.still-PL-INTENT ANPH-SG-OBJ

"'No, we won't leave it at that, father. We're still going to avenge him.'"

"'Não queremos deixar por isso mesmo, pai. Vamos ainda vingar ele).'"

(142) *"bu'irimaniano tiro buhtibokari" nia tita tikhᵾre.*

bu'í-rí-~badia-ro tí-ró butí-bo-kari ~dí-a
cause-NMLZ-not.exist-SG ANPH-SG disappear-DUB-Q.SPEC say-ASSERT.PFV
tí-ta tí-khᵾ-re
ANPH(3PL)-EMPH ANPH-ADD-OBJ

'"How could he just disappear without being avenged?" (they) added that too.'

'"Como ele podia sumir sem ser vingado?" disseram bem assim também.'

(143) *ã hi'na mᵾhsa mᵾa ã nika patere.*

~a=~hí'da ~bᵾsá ~bᵾ́-a ~a=~dí-ka pá-tere
SO=EMPH 2PL man/person-PL SO=say-ASSERT.IPFV ALT-time

'[Yes, you men sometimes like to say things like that.]'

'[Sim, vocês homens às vezes gostam de falar essas coisas.]'

(144) *sã wāhahachᵾ, sã ba'ᵾre õse yoari hire nika, pairo duruku tuariro thᵾ'omahsiriro.*

~sá ~wahá-~ha-chᵾ ~sa=ba'ᵾ́-re ~óse
1PL.EXCL kill-COMPL-SW.REF 1PL.EXCL.POSS=younger.brother-OBJ like.this
yóá-rí hí-re ~dí-ka pá-író dú-rúkú
do-NMLZ COP-OBJ say-ASSERT.IPFV ALT-NMLZ.SG speak-stand
tuá-ri-ro thᵾ'ó-~basi-ri-ro
strong-NMLZ-SG hear-know-NMLZ-SG

'[When one of us is killed, (you) tell our brother to do that (fight, seek revenge), (or) some other one who talks big, is a braggart.]'

---

[51] The form *kha'maka* is a shortened form of *wāhakha'maka* 'kill together', meaning 'to avenge' (also in line 192).

'[Quando um de nós é morto, (vocês) falam ao nosso irmão assim mesmo (para brigar, vingar), (ou) algum outro que fala muito, que se acha valente.]'

(145) "*hai, ya'umai, ya'ukɨse, noana.*"
hái   ya'ú-~ba-i   ya'ú-kɨ-se   ~dóádá
INTJ:agree warn-FRUS-VIS.PFV.1 tell-M-CONTR very.well
'"Well then, I warned (you, in vain), I told (you) otherwise, (but) so be it."' (*Dianumia Yairo* speaking)
'"Então tá, eu avisei (em vão), aconselhei diferente, (mas) que seja assim."' (*Dianumia Yairo* falando)

(146) "*mɨhsabahsi mahsia, yɨ pho'na.*"
~bɨsá-bási ~basí-á   yɨ=~pho'dá
2PL-EMPH know-ASSERT.PFV 1SG.POSS=children
'"You take care of it yourselves, my sons."'
'"Vocês mesmo resolvem, meus filhos."'

(147) "*mɨhsa padahchopɨ mɨhsa õse ya'uchɨ, thɨ'oduerana nina.*"
~bɨsá pá-dacho-pɨ ~bɨsá ~óse   ya'ú-chɨ   thɨ'ó-dua-era-~da
2PL   ALT-day-LOC 2PL   like.this warn-SW.REF hear-DES-NEG-PL
~dí-ra
PROG-VIS.IPFV.2/3
'"(I'm) warning you like this, (you) of this next (younger) generation, (but you) aren't listening."'
'"Eu estou aconselhando vocês assim, (vocês) dessa outra geração (mais nova), (mas vocês) não estão querendo ouvir."'

(148) *nisua, bu'sa wã'koa.*
~dí-súá   bu'sá   ~wa'kó-a
say-angry adornment prepare-ASSERT.PFV
'Saying that angrily, (*Dianumia Yairo*) prepared adornments.'
'Dizendo assim chateado, (*Dianumia Yairo*) preparou enfeites.'

(149) *tiro bɨhkɨro, mɨ'nokɨ phɨadɨ noano ñariro phutisu'aa.*
tí-ró   bɨkú-ro   ~bɨ'dó-kɨ   phɨá-dɨ
ANPH-SG ancestor-SG tobacco-CLF:cylindrical two-CLF:cylindrical

~dóá-ró ~yá-ri-ro   phutí-su'a-a
good-SG bad-NMLZ-SG blow-penetrate-ASSERT.PFV

'The old guy made two cigars, blowing smoke on them (to bless, or imbue them with violence for success in battle).'

'O velho fez dois bons cigarros e soprou neles (fez benzimento de força e violência para vencer na guerra).'

(150) tina, ã yoata ni, wamoare kha'notu'sʉa.

tí-~da   ~a=yóá-ta   ~dí ~wabóá-rí
ANPH-PL SO=do-EMPH say weapons-PL

~kha'dó-tu'sʉ-a
prepare/organize-finish-ASSERT.PFV

'They (the *Biari*), as soon as he said that, set straight away to preparing their weapons.'

'Eles (os *Biari*), assim que ele (*Dianumia Yairo*) falou isso, já começaram a preparar as armas.'

(151) sõ'o sã mipʉ hirore, bʉeakhanʉ peri hiatimare, bʉea, bʉeakhanʉ õmahadohtori waro.

~so'ó   ~sa=~bí-pʉ   hí-ro-re   bʉé-a-~khadʉ péri
DEIC.DIST 1PL.EXCL.POSS=now-LOC COP-SG-OBJ arrow-PL-cane many

hí-ati-~bare   bʉé-a   bʉé-a-~khadʉ
COP-IPFV-REM.IPFV arrow-PL arrow-PL-cane

~ó-~báhá-dótó-rí   wáró
DEIC.PROX-MOV.upward-bundle-PL EMPH

'[There, in the place we live now (Matapi), there used to be a lot of arrow-cane, arrows, arrow-cane, big bundles this tall.]'

'[Ali, no lugar onde moramos agora (Matapi), havia muita cana-de-flecha, flechas, cana-de-flecha, montes de feixes altos assim.]'

(152) seis dohtori noano yoaa.

seis dotó-rí   ~dóá-ró yoá-a
six bundle-PL good-SG do-ASSERT.PFV

'(Each warrier) made six good bundles (of arrows).'

'(Cada guerreiro fez seis feixes (de flechas).'

(153) *"kho'taharo sãre sã ba'ʉ yuhpi diani," nirokaata.*

kho'tá-ha-ro ~sá-re ~sa=ba'ʉ yuhpí.diáni
wait-COMPL-SG 1PL.EXCL-OBJ 1PL.EXCL.POSS=younger.brother yuhpi.diani
~dí-dóká-á-tá
say-DIST-ASSERT.PFV-EMPH

'"Tell our younger brother *Yuhpi Diani* to be expecting us," they sent off a message.'

'"Avisa ao nosso irmão menor *Yuhpi Diani* que vamos chegar," mandaram recado.'

(154) *mʉ'ʉ hii di'tamaniano wãhaboakʉ.*

~bʉ'ʉ hí-i di'tá-~badia[52]-ro ~wahá-bo-a-kʉ
2SG COP-M dirt-not.exist-SG kill-DUB-AFFECT-M

'[(But) if it were you, better to attack without letting them know!]' (Teresinha jokes with Joselito)

'[(Mas) se fosse você, melhor atacar sem avisar!]' (Teresinha brinca com Joselito)

(155) *ñaina bʉrʉta õna ma'apʉ taa te wãhsipiria tũhkui.*

~yá-~ida bʉrú-ta ~ó-(~hí')da ~ba'á-pʉ
bad-NMLZ.PL go.downriver-come DEIC.PROX-EMPH path-LOC
tá-á té wãhsipiria ~túkú-í
come-ASSERT.PFV until wãhsipiria pond-LOC.VIS

'The warriors came down right over here, on the river, coming right up to the *Wãhsipiria* pond (river port).'

'Os guerreiros vinham descendo bem aqui, no caminho (pelo rio), vindo até o poço de *Wãhsipiria* (porto no rio).'

(156) *ti bʉhsoka hia phiriaka'saribʉhsoka.*

ti=bʉsó-ka hí-a
3PL.POSS=canoe-CLF:round COP-ASSERT.PFV
phí-ria-ka'sa-ri-bʉso-ka
big-CLF:round-bark-NMLZ-canoe-CLF:round

'Their canoes were huge bark canoes.'

'Suas canoas enormes eram feitas com casca de árvores.'

---

[52] The expression *di'tamania* 'no dirt' means to 'do something in silence'.

(157) *do'se ka'saribʉhsokare yoari hi'na ñaina.*

    do'sé   ka'sá-rí-bʉsó-ká-ré   yoá⁵³-ri   ~hí'da

    Q:how bark-NMLZ-canoe-CLF:round-OBJ do/make-Q.PFV EMPH

    ~yá-~ida

    bad-NMLZ.PL

    '[How did the warriors make those bark canoes?]'

    '[Como os guerreiros faziam essas canoas de casca?]'

(158) *õna bʉrʉtaa.*

    ~ó-(~hi')da   bʉrú-ta-a

    DEIC.PROX-EMPH go.downriver-come-ASSERT.PFV

    'Right down here (they) came.'

    'Desceram bem para cá.'

(159) *õre wa'aa, õre yʉ'dopo'o.*

    ~ó-ré   wa'á-a   ~ó-ré   yʉ'dó-po'o

    DEIC.PROX-OBJ go-ASSERT.PFV DEIC.PROX-OBJ drag.canoe-place.floating

    'They went (through the rapids), dragging the canoes (on the rocks) over here.'⁵⁴

    'Passaram (a cachoeira), arrastando as canoas (pelas pedras) aqui.'

(160) *ñaina phiriaka bihsibʉrʉaduhkua noano me'neta pu … pu .. .puuuuuuu,*

    ~yá-~ida   phíríá-ká   bisí-bʉrú-á-dúkú-a

    bad-NMLZ.PL flute-CLF:round sound-go.downriver-go-stand-ASSERT.PFV

    ~dóá-ró=~be're-ta   pu…pu…puuuuuuu

    good-SG=COM-EMPH ONTP:flute.playing

    'The warriors came down to the constant sound of *phiriaka* flutes: *pu … pu … puuuuuuu!*'

    'Os guerreiros vinham descendo sempre ao som das flautas *phiriaka: pu … pu … puuuuuuu!*'

---

⁵³ The root *yoa* means 'do' or 'make', and is glossed with the meaning appropriate to the context.

⁵⁴ Teresinha gestures to the locations she is referring to, all near the village where the narrative was recorded.

(161) kho'tathu'sʉmaa, tinakãkhʉ. sʉ̃pa tina bʉeri himarepha tinare.
kho'tá-thu'sʉ-~ba-a   tí-~da-~ka-khʉ
wait-finish-ready-ASSERT.PFV ANPH-PL-DIM-ADD
~sʉ́-pa   tí-~da   bʉé-rí   hí-~bare-pha
arrive.TRNS-bring.to.shore ANPH-PL arrow.shoot-PL COP-REM.IPFV-time
tí-~da-re
ANPH-PL-OBJ

'(*Yuhpi Diani*'s men) were already there ready waiting, (and) when (the *Biari*) landed, they starting right in firing arrows at them.'

'Os (guerreiros de *Yuhpi Diani*) também já estavam esperando de prontidão (e) quando (os *Biari*) encostaram, já começaram a flechá-los.'

(162) tinakãkhʉ yoakha'ma, wãhañoeraa ñaina.
tí-~da-~ka-khʉ   yoá-~kha'ba ~waha-~yo-éra-a
ANPH-PL-DIM-ADD do-RECP kill-do.immediately-NEG-ASSERT.PFV
~yá-~ida
bad-NMLZ.PL

'They too (*Yuhpi Diani*'s men) returned fire, (but the *Biari*) weren't hit.'

'Os (guerreiros do *Yuhpi Diani*) também começaram a flechar de volta, (mas os *Biari*) não morriam.'

(163) de to kaseroakã ...
dé   to=kaséro-a-~ka
INTJ:poor.one(s)! 3SG.POSS=servant-PL-DIM

'Poor guys, his (*Yuhpi Diani*'s) servants ...'

'Coitados, os criados (do *Yuhpi Diani*) ...'

(164) tiata noano wi'ichʉ, de õita tiro du'tihã hi'na, bʉea tinare phi'tiawa'aa.
tíá-ta   ~dóá-ró wi'í-chʉ   dé
three-EMPH good-SG arrive.CIS-SW.REF INTJ:poor.one!
~ó-i-ta   tí-ró   du'tí-~ha   ~hí'da bʉé-a
DEIC.PROX-LOC.VIS-EMPH ANPH-SG escape-COMPL EMPH arrow-PL
tí-~da-re[55]   phi'tí-a-wa'a-a
ANPH-PL-OBJ end-AFFECT-go-ASSERT.PFV

'After three rounds (of arrows) had arrived, with the next round, the poor guy (*Yuhpi Diani*) ran off, the arrows running out on them.'

---

[55] Use of the objective case suffix -*re* on the pronoun *tina* and the marker -*a* on the verb emphasize how the subject is being negatively affected by the situation.

'Depois de chegarem três levas (de flechas), na outra o coitado (*Yuhpi Diani*) acabou fugindo, as flechas deles acabando.'

(165) *siesere ã yoa duhkuhãa nia painase.*
sié-(bʉ')se-re ~a=yóá dukú-~ha-a ~dí-a
front-side-OBJ so=do stand-COMPL-PL PROG-ASSERT.PFV
pá-~ida-se
ALT-NMLZ.PL-CONTR

'(While) from the opposite side the others (*Biari*) continued on (shooting).'

'(Enquanto) do outro lado os outros (os *Biari*) continuavam (a flechar).'

(166) *phome, ba'aro utimu, ti sʉchʉ, tinare tãa dohkare.*
~phobé ba'á-ró utimu ti=~sʉ́-chʉ́   tí-~da-re
give.up after-SG last.one 3PL.POSS=arrive.TRNS-SW.REF ANPH-PL-OBJ
~tá-a   doká-re
rock-PL throw-VIS.PFV.2/3

'Already exhausted, after their (the *Biari*'s) last (arrow) arrived, (*Yuhpi Diani*'s servants) threw rocks (at the *Biari*).'

'Já cansados, depois que chegou a última (flecha dos *Biari*), (os criados de *Yuhpi Diani*) jogaram pedras (nos *Biari*).'

(167) *toi ni ã yoari himarebʉ sõ'o khã nʉhkore ...*
tó-i   ~dí ~a=yóá-rí hí-~bare-bʉ   ~so'ó
REM-LOC.VIS say so=do-NMLZ COP-REM.IPFV-EPIS DEIC.DIST
~khá-~dʉko-re
hawk-island-OBJ

'There, it's said (that), in the old times, there in *Khã Nʉhko* ...'

'Lá, dizem então, que lá nos tempos antigos, em *Khã Nʉhko* ...'

(168) *thu'sʉ, pitiasama sa'ari himarebʉta.*
thu'sʉ pítia~saba sa'á-ri hí-~bare-bʉ-ta
finish war.trench dig-NMLZ COP-REM.IPFV-EPIS-EMPH

'in the end, (*Yuhpi Diani*'s men) dug trenches, it seems that's just how it was.'

'no final (os criados de *Yuhpi Diani*) cavaram trincheiras, parece que foi assim mesmo.'

(169) "ã hiro to pitiasama to di khõarinɨhko hira, yɨ mahko."

~a=hí-ro   to=pítia~saba   to=dií   ~khoá-ri-~dɨko
so=COP-SG 3SG.POSS=war.trench 3SG.POSS=blood lie-NMLZ-island
hí-ra   yɨ=~bakó
COP-VIS.IPFV.2/3 1SG.POSS=daughter

'["That why it's an island (that has) trenches with their spilled blood, my daughter," (my father said).⁵⁶]'

'["Por isso, é uma ilha (que tem) buracos com sangue deles derramado, minha filha," (dizia meu pai).]'

(170) "patere bɨhkɨthuru so'toapɨre kha'mawãha buhtiaka a'ri nɨhkore."

pátere   bɨkɨ́-thúrú   so'tóa-pɨ-re   ~kha'bá-~waha
maybe   old-times   end-LOC-OBJ   do/bring.together-kill
butí-a-ka   a'rí   ~dɨkó-re
disappear-PL-PREDICT DEM.PROX island-OBJ

'["Maybe, in the future they're all going to kill each other and disappear from the island."]'

'["Talvez, no futuro vão se-matar e sumir todos dessa ilha."]'

(171) niatire mai, yɨ ñɨhchɨmɨnano.

~dí-átí-ré   ~baí   yɨ=~yɨchɨ́-~bɨ́dá-ró
say-IPFV-VIS.PFV.2/3 father 1SG.POSS=grandfather-deceased-SG

'[My dad (and) my late grandfather used to say that.]'

'[Assim papai (e) meu avô finado contavam.]'

(172) yɨ phɨkɨ niya'ure, niya'utire.

yɨ=phɨkɨ́   ~dí-yá'ú-ré   ~dí-yá'ú-átí-ré
1SG.POSS=father say-tell-VIS.PFV.2/3 say-tell-IPFV-VIS.PFV.2/3

'[My father told (me), used to tell (me).]'

'[Meu pai contou, contava.]'

---

⁵⁶Teresinha explicitly attributes this negative assessment of the neighboring island and its inhabitants to her father, perhaps as a way to sidestep responsibility for it. Her use of the epistemic expression *himarebɨta* just two lines earlier may also signal that she is aware she is entering into delicate politico-narrative territory.

(173) ã to dikhõano hiro niyu'ka to. ã hia tina kha'machɨa phayɨ nika tore.

~a=tó   dií-~khoa-ro hí-ro   ~dí-yu'ka[57]   tó   ~a=hí-a
SO=REM blood-lie-SG COP-SG say-REP.QUOT REM SO=COP-ASSERT.PFV
tí-~da   ~kha'báchɨ-a phayɨ ~dí-ka   tó-re
ANPH-PL fight-PL   many PROG-ASSERT.IPFV REM-OBJ

'[So they say it's a place that has spilled bood. That's why they're always fighting there.]'

'[Dizem que é um lugar de sangue derramado. É por isso que estão sempre brigando lá.]'

(174) ti(na) pimɨ'nonore bahsama'noeina, õse ti(na) bihsiawe boowema'noeno.

tí   pí-~bɨ'do-ro-re   basá[58]-~ba'doé-~ida   ~óse
ANPH war-tobacco-SG-OBJ bless-not.do-NMLZ.PL like.this
ti=bisí-a-we
3PL.POSS=sweet-AFFECT-MOV.through
bó-o-we-~ba'doé-ro
descend-CAUS-MOV.through-not.do-SG

'[They're ones who never received the (anti-)war blessing, to make them sweet (calm, non-violent).]'

'[Eles que são não benzidos (contra) guerra, que os tornariam doces (calmos, não-violentos).]'

(175) bahsama'noeri nɨhko hikano nika, yo'o ti nɨhko.

basá-~ba'doé-ri   ~dɨkó hí-ka-ro   ~dí-ka   yo'ó
bless-not.do-NMLZ island COP-PREDICT-SG PROG-ASSERT.IPFV slaughter
tí   ~dɨkó
ANPH island

'[It will always be an unblessed island, a violent island.]'

'[Será sempre uma ilha que não foi benzida, uma ilha de violência.]'

---

[57] Use of the quotative evidential in these statements is another strategy by which Teresinha can attribute a negative opinion to others.

[58] The root *bahsa* is used with a range of meanings, including 'dance/sing' (see lines 235, 237 and 'bless'.

(176) õse wamoa ti da'rasuariro.
 ~óse   ~wabóá tí   da'rá-sua⁵⁹-ri-ro
 like.this violence ANPH work-angry-NMLZ-SG
 '[So everyone is violent.]'
 '[Assim todos são violentos.]'

(177) ã yoa phomea.
 ~a=yóá ~phobé-a
 so=do   give.up-ASSERT.PFV
 'So, (they, Yuhpi Diani's servants) gave up.'
 'Então, (eles, os criados de Yuhpi Diani) desistiram.'

(178) "marire phi'tiera a'ri marire" ni tinakã du'tika'aa te khã pho'tai.
 ~barí-re   phi'ti-éra a'rí   ~barí-re   ~dí tí-~da-~ka
 1PL.INCL-OBJ end-NEG DEM.PROX 1PL.INCL-OBJ say ANPH-PL-DIM
 du'tí-ka'a-a   té   ~khá-pho'ta-i   )
 escape-do.moving-ASSERT.PFV until hawk-headwater-LOC.VIS
 '"This (attack) against us never ends!" (they) said (and escaped off to the headwaters of the Inambú stream (Khã Pho'tai).'
 '"Esse (ataque) não acaba!" disseram (e) fugiram até a cabeceira do igarapé Inambú (Khã Pho'tai).'

(179) no'oi hiharita baraphoa? no'oi hikarita ti phoayeri?
 ~do'ó-i   hí-hari-ta   bará-phoa
 Q:where-LOC.VIS COP-Q.IPFV-EMPH potato.sp-falls/rapids
 ~do'ó-i   hí-kari-ta   tí   phoá-yeri
 Q:where-LOC.VIS COP-Q.SPEC-EMPH ANPH falls/rapids-PL
 '[Where are those 'potato' rapids?⁶⁰ I wonder where those rapids are.]'
 '[Onde fica essa cachoeira de 'batata'? Não sei onde fica essa cachoeira.]'

---

[59] The expression *da'ra-sua* indicates it's as if they always had weapons in their hands (instead of tools or other normal work instruments), see line 150.

[60] Teresinha uses the name by which the rapids are currently known.

(180)   *kha pho'tai, toi hia.*

       khá-pho'ta-i   *tó-i*   *hí-a*
       hawk-headwater-LOC.VIS REM-LOC.VIS COP-ASSERT.PFV
       (Joselito responds) '[The Inambú (hawk) headwaters are over there.]'
       (Joselito responde) '[A cabeçeira do Inambú (gavião) é para lá.]'

(181)   *"ne," nimato, de ne mania.*

       ~dé   *~dí-~ba-to*   *dé*   *~dé ~badía*
       INTJ:hello say-FRUS-NMLZ.LOC/EVNT INTJ:poor.one(s)! NEG not.exist
       '"Hello?" (*Diani*'s warriors, the *Biari*) called out (in vain), but poor guys, there was no one.'
       '"Alô?" (os guerreiros do Diani, os *Biari*) chamaram (em vão), mas coitados, não havia ninguém.'

(182)   *mahka tini manieno: "no'oi wa'ari" ni.*

       ~baká-~tidi   *~badié-ro*   *~do'ó-i*   *wa'á-ri*   *~dí*
       look.for-wander.around not.have-SG Q:where-LOC.VIS go-Q.PFV say
       'Looking all over (the island): "Where have they gone?" (they) wondered.'
       'Procurando por toda parte (da ilha): "Onde foram?" se perguntaram.'

(183)   *tia nɨmɨ hi, panɨmɨ ñami bɨrɨta ñaina.*

       tíá   *~dɨbú hí*   *pá-~dɨbɨ ~yabí bɨrú-ta*   *~yá-~ida*
       three day COP ALT-day night go.downriver-come bad-NMLZ.PL
       'Three days passed (and) the next night (*Dianumia Yairo* and his warriors from Matapi) came downriver.'
       'Passaram três dias (e) no dia seguinte de noite (*Dianumia Yairo* e os guerreiros de Matapi) vinham descendo.'

(184)   *de thɨ'oboropɨ tho! tho! tho!*

       dé   *thɨ'ó-boro-pɨ*   *tho!...tho!...tho!*
       INTJ:poor.one(s)! hear-separate.into.pieces-LOC ONTP:chopping
       'Poor guys (*Yuhpi Diani*'s servants). (The *Biari*) could hear from afar the sound of chopping: *Tho! Tho! Tho!*'
       'Coitados (os criados de *Yuhpi Diani*). (Os *Biari*) ouviram de longe o som de batidas: *Tho! Tho! Tho!*'

(185) *yoati pakhuoina, a'ri wʉ'ʉ thu'sʉpha'yoa thu'sʉa.*
 yoá-ati pá-khui-o⁶¹-~ida   a'rí   wʉ'ʉ
 do-IPFV ALT-afraid-CAUS-NMLZ.PL DEM.PROX house
 thu'sʉ́-phá'yó-á   thu'sʉ́-a
 finish-complete-AFFECT finish-ASSERT.PFV
 'The other frightened ones (*Yuhpi Diani*'s servants) were finishing up (the construction) of a barricade.'
 'Os outros apavorados (os criados de *Yuhpi Diani*) estavam acabando (de construir) uma barricada.'

(186) *a'ri cerca thu'sʉa to mʉhapisaato.*
 a'rí   cerca⁶² thu'sʉ́-a
 DEM.PROX fence   finish-ASSERT.PFV
 to=~bʉhá-phísá-tó
 3SG.POSS=MOV.upward-be.on-NMLZ.LOC/EVNT
 'They finished the barricade, where they could be up high (on a platform).'
 'Acabaram a barricada, onde subiam bem no alto (numa plataforma).'

(187) '*khakhasario' nimarebʉ tokhʉre, khakhasario ti yoario.*
 khá-khásá-ríó   ~dí-~bare-bʉ   tó-khʉ-re
 hawk-platform-CLF:flat say-REM.IPFV-EPIS DEF-ADD-OBJ
 khá-khásá-ríó   ti=yoá-rio
 hawk-platform-CLF:flat 3PL.POSS=do-CLF:flat
 'It was called then *khakhasario*, it was a "hawk's nest" that they built.'
 'Era chamada naquele tempo de *khakhasario*, foi "ninho de gavião" que fizeram.'

(188) *tiñami toi koatare nia, "ne hiharo khatiduaro" nika tiro.*
 tí-~yábí   tó-i   koá-ta-re   ~dí-a   ~dé
 ANPH-night REM-LOC.VIS make.noise-come-OBJ say-ASSERT.PFV NEG

---

[61] Some verbs in Kotiria have causative forms derived from the root+causative suffix *-o*, as we see here in the nominalized form *pakhuoina* 'other frightened/terrified ones'.

[62] Here Teresinha uses a borrowed word from Portuguese *cerca* 'fence' to refer to the barricade.

hí-haro[63] khatí-dúa-ró ~dí-ka   tí-ró
COP-IMP.3 live-DES-SG   say-ASSERT.IPFV ANPH-SG

'That night, hearing the noise from up there (*Dianumia Yairo*) said: "Don't (attack), let (*Yuhpi Diani*) survive."'

'Naquela noite, ouvindo o som vindo de lá (*Dianumia Yairo*) disse: "Não (ataca), deixa (*Yuhpi Diani*) sobreviver."'

(189) *"to yabu'iri, mɨhsa koiro thɨ'oerare."*

to=yá-bu'i-ri   ~bɨsa=kó-iro
3SG.POSS=POSS-cause-NMLZ   2PL.POSS=relative-NMLZ.SG

thɨ'o-éra-re
hear-NEG-VIS.PFV.2/3

'"He's at fault, your brother wouldn't listen."'

'"Ele é culpado, seu irmão não ouvia (meus conselhos)."'

(190) *"hira to pho'nakã ñahoriakã, tina mahsaphutiaka" nimaati.*

hí-ra   to=~pho'dá-~ka   ñáhórí-á-~ká tí-~da
COP-VIS.IPFV.2/3 3SG.POSS=children-DIM   ñahori-PL-DIM ANPH-PL

~basá-phú-tí-á-ká   ~dí-~ba-ati
people-expand-VBZ-PL-PREDICT   say-FRUS-IPFV

'"(But) there are two *Ñahori* children, they will multiply (reproduce)," (*Yuhpi Diani*) said (in vain, still trying to convince them).'

'"(Mas) há dois pequenos filhos do *Ñahori*, eles se multiplicarão," disse (*Yuhpi Diani* em vão, tentando convencê-los).'

(191) *"kha'maeraha, kha'maeraha, kha'maeraha, kha'maerakãha" nia.*

~kha'ba-éra-ha   ~kha'ba-éra-ha   ~kha'ba-éra-ha
want-NEG-VIS.IPFV.1 want-NEG-VIS.IPFV.1 want-NEG-VIS.IPFV.1

~kha'ba-éra-~ka-ha   ~dí-a
want-NEG-dim-VIS.IPFV.1   say-ASSERT.PFV

'"We refuse! We refuse! We refuse! We absolutely refuse!" (they) insisted.'

'"Não queremos! Não queremos! Não queremos! Não queremos mesmo!" insistiram.'

---

[63] The suffix *-haro* is a third-person imperative 'allow him to be one who lives'. See another instance of the same morpheme in line 234.

(192) *"(wãha)kha'makasininatha ñatiaro yoari hire,"* niatia.
   (~waha)~kha'báka-~sidi-~da-ta⁶⁴   ~yá-ti-a-ro
   (kill)RECP-do.still-PL-EMPH   bad-ATTRIB-AFFECT-SG
   yoá-ri   hí-re   ~dí-ati-a
   do-NMLZ(INFER) COP-VIS.PFV.2/3 say-IPFV-ASSERT.PFV
   '"We're still going to avenge (our brother) for the evil done to him," they kept saying.'
   "Ainda vamos vingá-lo (nosso irmão) pelo mal feito a ele," ficavam dizendo.'

(193) *"hai"* ni.
   hái   ~dí
   INTJ:agree say
   '"All right" (Dianumia Yairo) said.'
   '"Está bom," falou (Dianumia Yairo).'

(194) *thʉ'oa, ñami no'opeina taa nia ñaina, quatro ou seis hiari ti(na)?*
   thʉ'ó-a ~yabí ~do'ó-pe-~ida   tá-a   ~dí-a
   hear-PL night Q-QUANT.C-NMLZ.PL come-PL PROG-ASSERT.PFV
   ~yá-~ida   quatro ou seis hí-a-ri   tí(~da)
   bad-NMLZ.PL   four   or six COP-PL-Q.PFV ANPH
   'Hearing (the sounds from the barracade), at night ... [how many warriors were there – four or six of them maybe?]'
   'Ouvindo (os barulhos da barricada), de noite ... [quantos guerreiros eram – quatro ou seis talvez?]'

(195) *wa'awa'atha ñamitha pʉ cerca.*
   wa'á-wa'a-a-ta   ~yabí-ta   pʉ́   cerca
   go-go-ASSERT.PFV-EMPH night-EMPH DIST fence
   '(They) went right up to the barricade.'
   'Foram indo até perto da barricada.'

---

⁶⁴Here we see an example of the suffixes *-na-ta* marking 1PL intent (see also lines 69 and 87) in contrast to 1SG intent (in lines 13, 45, and others). We also find a good example of inference evidential marking, used because the speakers only saw the result of what was done to their brother, but not the actual actions. The expression *(wãha)kha'maka* is understood to mean 'kill as was done to them', in other words, to avenge.

(196) *noano õsekã yoamaati tinakã, cerca ne suhsueraro.*

~dóá-ró ~óse-~ka yoá-~ba-ati tí-~da-~ka cerca ~dé
good-SG like.this-DIM do-FRUS-IPFV ANPH-PL-DIM fence NEG
susu-éra-ro
have.holes-NEG-SG

'They (*Yuhpi Diani*'s servants) were making a good barricade, like this with no open spaces (to get through).'

'Eles (os criados do *Yuhpi Diani*) estavam fazendo a barricada bem feita assim, sem frestas (para alguem passar).'

(197) *ñariro hũiro dohomʉaa.*

~yá-ri-ro ~hú-iro dohó-~bʉ[65]-(wa')a-a
bad-NMLZ-SG worm-NMLZ.SG transform-run-go-ASSERT.PFV

'*Dianumia Yairo* (and his men) quickly transformed into worms.'

'*Dianumia Yairo* (e os guerreiros) rapidamente se transformaram em minhocas.'

(198) *bʉhkʉthurupʉ hiri himarero, doho sã'a phitiawa'aa.*

bʉkú-thúrú-pʉ   hí-ri   hí-~bare-ro   dohó   ~sa'á
ancestor-times-LOC COP-NMLZ COP-REM.IPFV-SG transform MOV.inside
phíti-a-wa'a-a
accompany-PL-go-ASSERT.PFV

'[That's the way it was in ancient times, (they) transformed (and) all of them went (into the ground).]'

'[Era assim nos tempos antigos, se transformavam (e) entraram todos (na terra).]'

(199) *ti sãsʉruka'achʉwaro, nia to kaseroa:*

ti=~sá('a)-sʉrʉ-ka'a-chʉ-waro   ~dí-a
3PL.POSS=MOV.inside-pause-beside-SW.REF-EMPH say-ASSERT.PFV
to=kaséro-a
3SG.POSS=servant-PL

'When they came out right beside (*Yuhpi Diani*'s) servants, they cried out:'

'Quando eles sairam bem perto dos criados (do *Yuhpi Diani*), eles gritaram:'

---

[65] When the root *mʉ* 'run' occurs in a serial verb construction it adds the adverbial notion to 'do X quickly'.

(200) *"sã phɨ'toro duhitaga mɨ'ɨ."*

~sa=phɨ'tó-ro   duhí-ta-ga   ~bɨ'ɨ
1PL.EXCL.POSS=master-SG descend-come-IMP 2SG

'"Come down, master!"'

'"Desça, chefe!"'

(201) *"mɨ'ɨ 'dɨhkaboha nimeheta', mɨ'ɨ sãre tire wã'kore."*

~bɨ'ɨ duka-bo-ha   ~dí-~beheta   ~bɨ'ɨ ~sá-re
2SG   begin-DUB-VIS.IPFV.1 say-NEG.INTENS 2SG 1PL.EXCL-OBJ
tí-re   ~wa'kó-re
ANPH-OBJ cause.to.happen-VIS.PFV.2/3

'"You (decided) 'I'm going to start (this war)', it's your fault this is happening to us!"'

'"Você (resolveu) 'Eu vou começar (essa guerra)', é sua culpa o que está acontecendo conosco!"'

(202) *taga mɨ'ɨkhɨ sã da'rana yoakha'maha sã," nia.*

tá-gá   ~bɨ'ɨ-khɨ ~sa=da'rá-~da   yoá-~kha'ba-ha   ~sá
come-IMP 2SG-ADD   1PL.EXCL.POSS=work-PL do-RECP-VIS.IPFV.1 1PL.EXCL
~dí-a
say-ASSERT.PFV

'"You come too, to help with our work," (the servants) said.'

'"Venha você também ajudar o nosso trabalho," falaram.'

(203) *"hai" ni.*

hái   ~dí
INTJ:agree say

'"All right," said (*Yuhpi Diani*).'

'"Está bom," disse (*Yuhpi Diani*).'

(204) *ñaina dohamɨaa ti(na)tha tirore.*

~yá-~ida   dohá-~bɨa-a   tí-ta   tí-ró-ré
bad-NMLZ.PL neg.curse-high-ASSERT.PFV ANPH-EMPH ANPH-SG-OBJ

'(The servants) sent up a curse on him (*Yuhpi Diani*).'

'(Os criados) amaldiçoaram o (*Yuhpi Diani*).'

(205) *"hai" ni tirore sĩ'ariphĩ sĩ'a.*

   hái   ~dí tí-ró-ré   ~si'á-ri-~phi
   INTJ:agree say ANPH-SG-OBJ set.fire.to-NMLZ-CLF:bladelike
   ~si'á-a
   set.fire.to-ASSERT.PFV

   '"All right," he said (and they) lit up a torch (to light the way) for him.'

   '"Está bom," ele disse (e) acenderam uma tocha para (clarear o caminho) para ele.'

(206) *sĩ'a duhiato pakhuoriro ...*

   ~si'á   duhí-(wa')a-to   pá-khui-o-ri-ro
   set.fire.to descend-go-NMLZ.LOC/EVNT ALT-afraid-CAUS-NMLZ-SG

   'With the light, the poor terrified guy (*Yuhpi Diani*) started down ...'

   'Com a luz, o coitadinho assustado foi descendo ...'

(207) *pɨ! "mɨ'ɨ ... yabari ... dahchomahkamahkari tañore dɨhte taga mɨ'ɨbahsi" nia.*

   pɨ́   ~bɨ'ɨ́ yabá-rí   dachó~baka-~baka-ri   ~tayó-re
   DIST 2SG Q:what/how-Q.PFV middle/center-origin-NMLZ beam-OBJ
   dɨte-ta-ga   ~bɨ'ɨ́-básí ~dí-a
   chop-come-IMP 2SG-EMPH say-ASSERT.PFV

   'Coming way down! "You [how was it?] you yourself cut the central beam (of the barricade)," (the servants) said.'

   'Descendo tudo! "Você [como foi?] você mesmo venha cortar o travessão do meio (da barricada)," disseram (os criados).'

(208) *"hai" ni. sĩ'aborataa.*

   hái   ~dí ~si'á-bora-ta-a
   INTJ:agree say set.fire.to-slide/fall-come-ASSERT.PFV

   '"OK" (*Yuhpi Diani*) said (and) came sliding down.'

   '"Está bom," respondeu (*Yuhpi Diani*), e veio descendo escorregando.'

(209) *to sĩ'aphĩri sĩ'a, yoariphĩ ña'a, to dɨhteka'achɨwaro, ñaina ña'atu'sɨa tirore.*

   to=~si'á-~phi-ri   ~si'á   yoá-rí-~phí
   3SG.POSS=set.fire.to-CLF:bladelike-PL set.fire.to long-NMLZ-CLF:bladelike

~ya'á to=dɨté-ká'á-chɨ-wáró   ~yá-~ida
grab 3SG.POSS=chop-do.moving-SW.REF-EMPH bad-NMLZ.PL
~ya'á-thu'sɨ-a   tí-ró-ré
grab-finish-ASSERT.PFV ANPH-SG-OBJ

'With his torch burning, he grabbed his machete (and) when he started to chop (the beam), the warriors (*Biari*) captured him.'

'Com a tocha acesa, pegou o terçado (e) quando começou a cortar (o travessão), os guerreiros (*Biari*) o capturaram.'

(210) *"kueeeee! yɨ kha'makã, yɨ'ɨre ña'atu'sɨra ñaina."*

kueeeee! yɨ=~kha'bá-~ka   yɨ'ɨ-ré ~ya'á-thu'sɨ-ra
INTJ:No! 1SG.POSS=bring.together-DIM 1SG-OBJ grab-finish-VIS.IPFV.2/3
~yá-~ida
bad-NMLZ.PL

'"No! Servants, the warriors have captured me!"'

'"Não! Criados, os guerreiros me pegaram!"'

(211) *"khero, mɨhsakhɨ bɨea nataga" nia.*

khé-ro ~bɨsá-khɨ bɨé-a   ~dá-ta-ga   ~dí-a
fast-SG 2PL-ADD arrow-PL get-come-IMP say-ASSERT.PFV

'"Quickly, you get your arrows too!" (*Yuhpi Diani*) cried.'

'"Rápido, vocês pegam as flechas também!" disse (*Yuhpi Diani*).'

(212) *tina, ñamire, yo'o da'ramahkatinikaa.*

tí-~da   ~yabí-ré   yo'ó
ANPH-PL night-OBJ in.contrast
da'rá-~baka-~tidi-ka('a)-a
work-look.for-wander.around-do.moving-ASSERT.PFV

'(But) in the dark, they just ran around like this looking for (things).'

'(Mas), no escuro, eles só andaram assim para lá e para cá procurando.'

(213) *tirore ña'atu'sɨrasi, ña'adi'okãhãa.*

tí-ró-ré   ~ya'á-thu'sɨra-~si(di)
ANPH-SG-OBJ grab-finish-do.now
~ya'á-di'o-~ka-~ha-a
grab-restrain-DIM-COMPL-ASSERT.PFV

'(The warriors) had already captured him (*Yuhpi Diani*), (and he) couldn't move.'

'(Os guerreiros) já tinham capturado *Yuhpi Diani*, (e ele) não conseguia se mexer.'

(214) *ña'amahare kãku õi su'su.*

~ya'á-~báhá-ré ~kákú ~ó-i
grab-MOV.upward-VIS.PFV.2/3 throw.on.ground DEIC.PROX-LOC.VIS
su'sú
embrace

'(They) threw him down on the ground, holding him here.'

'Derrubaram jogando no chão, segurando aqui assim.'

(215) *ti(na) to a'ri tañobaro topɨta du'upayoa to dɨhsore.*

tí to a'rí ~tayó=ba'ro tó-pɨ-ta
ANPH DEF DEM.PROX beam=CLF:kind DEF-LOC-EMPH
du'ú-páyó-á to=dɨsó-re
leave-put.on.top-ASSERT.PFV 3SG.POSS=thigh-OBJ

'On a beam just like this one here, they (*Diani*'s warriors) left his (*Yuhpi Diani*'s) leg.'

'Eles (os guerreiros do *Diani*), num travessão tipo esse mesmo, deixaram a coxa dele (do *Yuhpi Diani*) bem em cima.'

(216) *yo'o tinapɨ (hi')na khomakhɨ, yaba hiri himarero?*

yo'ó tí-~da-pɨ ~(hi')da ~khobá-khɨ yabá hí-ri
in.contrast ANPH-PL-LOC EMPH ax-ADD Q:what/how COP-NMLZ
hi-~bare-ro
COP-IPFV.EPIS-SG

'[But those guys then had axes too — what were they?]'

'[Mas naquela época eles também tinham machado — como é que era?]'

(217) *bookhoma! ɨ̃hɨ, ti khoma sioripha tinapɨre?*

bóó-~khómá ɨ̃hɨ tí ~khóbá sió-ri-pha tí-~da-pɨ-re
stone-axe INTJ:yes ANPH ax sharp-NMLZ-SPEC ANPH-PL-LOC-OBJ

'[*Bookhoma*! Yes ... do you suppose to them that (kind of) axe[66] was sharp?]'

---

[66] Teresinha is referring to axes with stone heads, still used in the region in the early twentieth century (Koch-Grünberg 1995 [1909]: 171-172).

'[*Bookhoma*! Sim ... será que para eles aquele (tipo de) machado era afiado?]'

(218) *mari (hi')na khoma hieramarero, tãphĩ, tã hia nimarero.*
~barí   ~(hi')da ~khobá hi-éra-~bare-ro   ~tá-~phi   ~tá
1PL.INCL EMPH   ax   COP-NEG-REM.IPFV-SG   rock-CLF.bladelike   rock
hí-a   ~dí-~bare-ro
COP-ASSERT.PFV   COP-REM.IPFV-SG

'[(For) us (that old kind) aren't axes, (just) rocks, they were rocks.]'

'[(Para) nós mesmo (aquele tipo) não seria machado, (só) pedra, era pedra.]'

(219) *ũhʉ.*
ũhʉ
INTJ:yes
(Joselito) '[Yes.]'
(Joselito) '[Sim.]'

(220) *dʉhtetaroka, dohkapayoa te to ka'apʉ khakhasario ti ninopʉ.*
dʉté-tá-dóká   doká-payo-a   té   to   ka'á-pʉ
chop-separate-DIST throw-put.on.top-ASSERT.PFV   until REM beside-LOC
khá-khásá-río   ti=~dí-ro-pʉ
hawk-platform-CLF:flat 3PL.POSS=say-SG-LOC

'(They) chopped off (his leg and) threw it all the way up near that (thing) they call the hawk's nest platform.'

'Cortaram fora (a perna) e jogaram lá em cima perto (daquilo) que chamavam de ninho de gavião.'

(221) *dohkapayoroka, "maa! bi'oha hi'na ʉʉʉʉʉʉ ... wiiiii!"*
doká-payo-doka⁶⁷   ~báa   bi'ó-há   ~hí'da
throw-put.on.top-DIST INTJ:done/ready! successful-VIS.IPFV.1 EMPH
"*ʉʉʉʉʉʉ...wiiiii!*"
ONTP:cries...whistles

'Throwing his leg way up there (they cried) "There! We've done it! *ʉʉʉʉʉ ... wiiiiii*"' (cries and whistles)

---

⁶⁷Note the two instances of the root *doka* 'throw', the first meaning literally 'to throw', and the second indicating "distal" motion.

'Jogando lá em cima (gritaram) "Acabou! Conseguimos mesmo! ʉʉʉʉʉ ... wiiiiii"' (gritos e assobios)

(222) *"wahpʉro, mahkʉnoñakãre, tirobahsitha, sã ba'ʉre to ã yoari bu'iri!"*
wapʉ́-ro ~bakʉ́-ro-~ya-~ka-re tí-ró-basi-ta
enemy-SG son-SG-bad-DIM-OBJ ANPH-SG-EMPH-EMPH
~sa=ba'ʉ́-re   to=~a=yóá-rí   bu'í-ri
1PL.EXCL.POSS=younger.brother-OBJ 3SG.POSS=so-do-NMLZ cause-NMLZ
'"Enemy, evil son, (we got) him for what he himself did to our brother!"'
'"Inimigo, filho malvado, (pegamos) ele mesmo pelo o que fez ao nosso irmão!"'

(223) *"bu'iriti wãhanona mʉ'ʉ ñaka si'ro."*
bu'í-rí-tí   ~wahá-ro-(~hi')da ~bʉ'ʉ́ ~yá-ká   sí'ro
cause-NMLZ-ATTRIB kill-SG-EMPH   2SG   bad-ASSERT.IPFV bastard
'"Guilty one! Murderer! You evil bastard!"'
'"Culpado! Assassino! Você malvado!"'

(224) *samu te yohaa te õpʉ mahasʉ̃, sʉ̃a.*
~sabú   té   yohá-a   té   ~ó-pʉ́
embark.in.canoe until go.upriver-ASSERT.PFV until DEIC.PROX-LOC
~bahá-~sʉ   ~sʉ́-a
go.uphill-arrive.TRNS arrive.TRNS-ASSERT.PFV
'(They) got into their canoes (and) came upriver here, went up (the hill and) arrived home.'
'Embarcaram nas canoas (e) subiram para cá, subiram até em cima (e) chegaram em casa.'

(225) *"ne, yʉ pho'na bi'ori."*
~dé yʉ=~pho'dá   bi'ó-ri
so 1SG.POSS=children be.successful-Q.PFV
'(Their father *Dianumia Yairo* asked): "Were you successful, sons?"'
'(O pai deles *Dianumia Yairo* perguntou): "Conseguiram, meus filhos?"'

(226) *"bi'oi yʉ phʉkʉ,"* nia.
      bi'ó-i   yʉ=phʉkʉ   ~dí-a
      successful-VIS.PFV.1 1SG.POSS=father say-ASSERT.PFV
      '"We were, father," (*Diani*) responded.'
      '"Conseguimos, pai," falou (*Diani*).'

(227) *"bi'oi, to yabu'iri sã koirore to ñano yoari bu'iri,"* nia.
      bi'ó-i   to=yá=bu'i-ri
      successful-VIS.PFV.1 3SG.POSS=POSS=cause-NMLZ
      ~sa=ko-iro-re   to=~yá-ró   yoá-rí
      1PL.EXCL.POSS=relative-NMLZ.SG-OBJ 3SG.POSS=bad-SG do-NMLZ
      bu'í-ri   ~dí-a
      cause-NMLZ say-ASSERT.PFV
      '"We did it, (killed) the one responsible for the evil he did to our relative," (*Diani*) said.'
      '"Conseguimos (matar) o culpado, aquele que fez tanto mal ao nosso parente," disse (*Diani*).'

(228) *"tina ti ñano sã koirore yoare."*
      tí-~da   ti=~yá-ró   ~sa=kó-iro-re
      ANPH-PL ANPH=bad-SG 1PL.EXCL.POSS=relative-NMLZ.SG-OBJ
      yoá-re
      do-VIS.PFV.2/3
      '"Those evil ones who did that to our brother."'
      '"Aqueles malvados que fizeram mal ao nosso irmão."'

(229) *"tiro yoerarirota noano yʉ'dʉbohkari,"* nia.
      tí-ró   yoa-éra-ri-ro-ta   ~dóá-ró yʉ'dʉ-boka-ri
      ANPH-SG do-NEG-NMLZ-SG-EMPH good-SG INTENS-find-NMLZ
      ~dí-a
      say-ASSERT.PFV
      '"He couldn't expect anything good to happen," (*Diani*) said.'
      '"Ele não podia esperar coisa boa," disse (*Diani*).'

(230) *"noana, yʉ pho'na mʉhsa yʉ'ʉ ba'arore, mʉhsa ne thʉ'oduerara," nia.*

~dóádá   yʉ=~pho'dá   ~bʉsá yʉ'ʉ ba'á-ró-ré   ~bʉsá ~dé
very.well 1SG.POSS=children 2PL   1SG after-SG-OBJ 2PL   NEG
thʉ'o-dua-éra-ra   ~dí-a
hear-DES-NEG-VIS.IPFV.2/3 say-ASSERT.PFV

'"Very well, you, my children who come after me (of the next generation) just won't listen/obey," (Dianumia Yairo) said.'

'"Bem, vocês, meus filhos que vem depois de mim (da outra geração) não querem mais ouvir/obedecer," disse (Dianumia Yairo).'

(231) *"õse yoanakã nichʉ, mʉhsa thʉ'otina hierara," nia.*

~óse   yoá-~da-~ka ~dí-chʉ   ~bʉsá thʉ'ó-ti-~da
like.this do-PL-DIM   say-SW.REF 2PL   hear-ATTRIB-PL
hi-éra-ra   ~dí-a
COP-NEG-VIS.IPFV.2/3 say-ASSERT.PFV

'"Just like now, you ignore (me, you aren't ones who listen)," said (Dianumia Yairo).'

'"Como agora, vocês ignoram (não são gente que escuta)," disse (Dianumia Yairo).'

(232) *"noanokã" ni, to suabu'sa to doharire tinare phãawe.*

~dóá-ró-~ká ~dí to=súá-bú'sá
good-SG-DIM say 3SG.POSS=angry-adornment
to=dohá-ri-re   tí-~da-re
3SG.POSS=neg.curse-NMLZ-OBJ ANPH-PL-OBJ
~phaá-wé
remove.curse/blessing-MOV.through

'"So be it," he said (and) took back his war adornments (and) his blessing for courage.'

'"Bem," disse (e) tirou deles os adornos de bravura e benzimento de coragem.'

(233) *tinare mʉ'nophuti, tina mipʉse thʉ'otua, tina ne thʉ'omahsieraphati.*
   tí-~da-re   ~bʉ'dó-phútí   tí-~da   ~bí-pʉ-se
   ANPH-PL-OBJ tobacco-blow ANPH-PL now-LOC-CLF:similar
   thʉ'ó-thu-a   tí-~da   ~dé thʉ'ó-~basi-era-pha-ati[68]
   hear-think-ASSERT.PFV ANPH-PL NEG hear-know-NEG-TIME-IPFV

   'Blowing smoke on them, they became the way they are now (peaceful), no longer in that violent state.'

   'Soprando fumaça neles, se tornaram como hoje (calmos), não mais naquele estado de violência.'

(234) *"ã yoa ñamichakã bo'rearoi, khʉ naharo, mʉhsa namosãnumia" nia.*
   ~a=yóá   ~yabíchá-~ká   bo'ré-(wa')a-ro-i   khʉ́[69]   *~dá-haro*
   so=do tomorrow-DIM lighten-go-SG-LOC.VIS manioc get-IMP.3
   ~bʉsa=~dabó-~sadubia ~dí-a
   2PL.POSS=wife-PL.F say-ASSERT.PFV

   '"So, the day after tomorrow, send your wives to get manioc," he ordered.'

   '"Então, depois de amanhã, mande as suas esposas tirarem maniva," ele disse.'

(235) *tina bahsabahtoa taro tina khʉna, da're.*
   tí-~da   basá-bátóá-ró   tá-ro   tí-~da   khʉ́-~da   da'ré
   ANPH-PL sing/dance-last-SG come-SG ANPH-PL manioc.root-get prepare

   'For the last ceremony (celebrating their victory in war), they got manioc (and) prepared (caxiri).'[70]

   'Para a última cerimonia (festejando a vitória na guerra), eles foram pegar maniva e prepararam (caxiri).'

---

[68] The construction *thʉ'ómahsieraphaati* indicates a 'state of violence'.

[69] Here we see an example of an unmarked object, *khʉ* 'maniva/manioc root', that is nonreferential and therefore does not require use of the objective case marker *-re*. In the following sentence, the same unmarked object is phonologically incorporated with the verb *na* 'get/pick'. A rare example of an unmarked pronominal object occurs in line 144, where the pronoun *sã* '1PL.EXCL' is nonreferential and thus is also unmarked by *-re*.

[70] "Caxiri" (also referred to as "chicha" in some of the chapters in this volume) is a type of drink, usually made from toasted manioc flatbread diluted in water and left to ferment for a couple of days.

(236) *pharinʉmʉ tina bagapo durukua, nahubahsapore.*

    pha-rí-~dʉbʉ   tí-~da   bagápó
    time-NMLZ-day ANPH-PL cerimonial.dance/chant
    dú-rúkú-á   ~dahú-básápó-ré
    speak-stand-ASSERT.PFV flatbread-dance-OBJ

    '[On those celebration days, they chanted ceremonial dances (like) the flatbread dance.]'

    '[Nesses dias de festa, eles cantavam as danças (como) a dança do beijú.]'

(237) *ti hika bahsabʉhkʉ nahubahsa, sa'waroa, [yaba] miniawahkʉ, wamo thi'biri.*

    tí   hí-ka   basá-bʉkʉ   ~dahú-básá
    ANPH COP-ASSERT.IPFV sing/dance-ancestor flatbread-sing/dance
    sa'wáró-á   yabá   ~bidíawakʉ ~wabó-thí'bi-ri
    brown.lizard-PL Q:what/how fruit.dance arm/hand-intertwine-NMLZ

    '[These are traditional (origin) dances: flatbread dance, lizard dance — what else? — fruit dance, peace (holding hands) dance.]'

    '[As danças originais são a dança do beijú, dança do calango marrom — que mais? — dança dos frutos, dança da paz (mãos dadas).]'

(238) *tina bahsañopha'ño phʉanʉmʉtha, hi('na):*

    tí-~da   basá-~yo-~pha'yo   phʉá-~dʉbʉ-ta ~hí('da)
    ANPH-PL sing/dance-show-complete two-day-EMPH EMPH

    'They performed all the dances for two days (and then *Dianumia Yairo* said):'

    'Eles apresentaram todas as danças durante dois dias (e então *Dianumia Yairo* disse):'

(239) *"yʉ'ʉ wa'awa'aika hi'na" nia, mipʉ to duhitore.*

    yʉ'ʉ   wa'á-wa'a-i-ka   ~hí'da ~dí-a   ~bí-pʉ
    1SG go-go-M-PREDICT EMPH say-ASSERT.PFV now-LOC
    to=duhí[71]-a-to-re
    3SG.POSS=sit-PL-NMLZ.LOC/EVNT-OBJ

    '"I'm going away now." [To the place he still is sitting.]'

    '"Agora eu vou indo." [Ao lugar onde ele ainda está sentado.]'

---

[71] The verb *duhi* 'sit' is used in the sense of 'being'. This root is analyzed as a possible lexical origin of the Kotiria copula verb *hi* in Stenzel (forthcoming).

(240) *"wa'aika yʉ'ʉ, yʉ pho'na, mʉhsare ne khũsi" nia.*

wa'á-i-ka   yʉ'ʉ́ yʉ=~pho'dá   ~bʉsá-ré ~dé ~khú-sí
go-M-PREDICT 1SG   1SG.POSS=children 2PL-OBJ NEG leave/place-NEG.IRR
~dí-a
say-ASSERT.PFV

'"I'm going (and) I'm not leaving you anything, my children," *Dianumia Yairo*) said.'

'"Vou mesmo (e) não vou deixar nada para vocês, meus filhos," disse (*Dianumia Yairo*).'

(241) *"ne a'ri wĩho yaichʉawĩho, warimahsawĩho, khʉ'mawĩho, hʉka phiri ne mʉhsare khũsi" nia.*

~dé   a'rí   ~wihó⁷²   yaí-chʉ́-á-~wíhó
NEG DEM.PROX halluc.powder jaguar-eat-PL-halluc.powder
wári-~basa-~wiho   ~khʉ'bá-~wiho   hʉ́ká   phí-ri
kidnap-people-halluc.powder summer-halluc.powder hungry big-NMLZ
~dé   ~bʉsá-ré ~khú-sí   ~dí-a
NEG 2PL-OBJ leave/place-NEG.IRR say-ASSERT.PFV

'"Not my hallucinogenic powder, nor the one that can transform you into jaguars to eat people, nor the one to kidnap people (to become invisible), nor the one that brings on summer, nor will I leave the one that causes hunger," (*Dianumia Yairo*) said.'

'"Nem meu paricá, meu paricá de virar onça e comer gente, paricá de roubar gente (de ficar invisível), paricá de verão, nem vou deixar o de causar fome," dizia (*Dianumia Yairo*).'

(242) *"hiphiti a'ri phinitare naita yʉ'ʉ" nia.*

híphiti   a'rí   ~phídi-ta-re   ~dá-i-ta   yʉ'ʉ́
everything DEM.PROX right.here-EMPH-OBJ get-M-INTENT 1SG
~dí-a
say-ASSERT.PFV

'"All of these things here I'm taking away," (*Dianumia Yairo*) said.'

'"Vou levar todas essas coisas aqui," disse (*Dianumia Yairo*).'

---

⁷²Note the various tones on the nominal root *wiho* 'hallucinogenic powder'. As an independent root, it has a LH melody, but when incorporated into compound words, it receives the final tone of the root to its left through processes of tonal spread.

(243) *"mɨsa thɨ'omasiduerara pa thurupɨre."*
~busá thɨ'ó-~basi-dua-era-ra   pá-thuru-pɨ-re
2PL hear-know-DES-NEG-VIS.IPFV.2/3 ALT-times-LOC-OBJ
"'In the future, you won't want (you won't know *how*) to use them appropriately.'"
"'Vocês no futuro não vão querer (não vão saber *como*) usar bem.'"

(244) *"do'se mɨhsa yoaro, yoakãduara."*
do'sé   ~busá yoá-ro yoá-~ka-dua-ra
Q:how 2PL do-SG do-DIM-DES-VIS.IPFV.2/3
"'(Because) you will always just do what you want.'"
"'(Porque) vocês sempre fazem como querem.'"

(245) *mari suamɨa, wĩhõ wĩhi marire khãrirore ɨɨɨ ... yaichɨ khoakana.*
~barí   súa-~bɨ-á   ~wihó   ~wihí ~barí-re
1PL.INCL angry-man/person-PL halluc.powder sniff 1PL.INCL-OBJ
~khári-ro-re   ɨɨɨ   yaí-chɨ   khoá-ka-~(hi')da
offend-SG-OBJ ONTP:hurting jaguar-eat finish-ASSERT.IPFV-EMPH
'[When we get angry, we sniff powder to turn into a jaguar and devour (fight with, or kill) the one who has offended us.]'
'[Quando ficamos com raiva, cheiramos paricá para nós nos transformar em onça e devorar (brigar, ser capaz de matar) aquele que nos ofendeu.]'

(246) *ã hia hima mari wĩhõ, kotiria wĩho.*
~a=hí-a   hí-~ba   ~bari=~wiho   kótiria
SO=COP-ASSERT.PFV COP-REM.IPFV 1PL.INCL.POSS=halluc.powder Kotiria
~wihó
halluc.powder
'[That's how our powder used to be, Kotiria powder.]'
'[Assim era o nosso paricá, dos Kotiria.]'

(247) *yo'omeheta wĩhi wahpɨatia hieraa a'ri.*
yo'ó-~beheta   ~wihí wapɨ́-ati-a
in.contrast-NEG.INTENS sniff do.for.long.time-IPFV-PL

hi-éra-a   a'rí
COP-NEG-ASSERT.PFV DEM.PROX

'[But people weren't supposed to keep sniffing it all the time.]'

'[Mas não era para ficar cheirando muito isso.]'

(248) *a'ri do'beba'roñoa.*

a'rí   do'bé-ba'ro-~yo-a
DEM.PROX paint.with.finger-CLF:kind-show-ASSERT.PFV

'[It was just the kind for face-painting (which already has an effect).]'

'[Era só para usar pintando (que já fazia efeito).]'

(249) *tiro pharipʉta, tipʉre khʉaa.*

tí-ró   pharí-pʉ-ta   tí-pʉ-re   khʉá-a
ANPH-SG form-CLF:basket-EMPH ANPH-CLF:basket-OBJ have-ASSERT.PFV

'The whole basket (with all the materials), (he) had that basket.'

'O aturá inteiro (com todo o material), (ele) tinha aquele cesto.'

(250) *to yaichʉre thuaka'a, to bahtichʉre sĩosuahã.*

to=yaíchʉ-re   thuá-ka'a-a
3SG.POSS=shaman.staff-OBJ lean.on-do.moving-ASSERT.PFV
to=batíchʉ-re   ~siósua-~ha
3SG.POSS=shield-OBJ place.around.arm-COMPL

'(He) took up his staff (and) put his shield on his arm.'

'Segurou no bastão (e) enfiou o escudo no braço.'

(251) *to diero mʉta, toi hia to diero.*

to=dié-ró   ~bʉtá   tó-i   hí-a   to=dié-ró
3SG.POSS=dog-SG advance REM-LOC.VIS COP-ASSERT.PFV 3SG.POSS=dog-SG

'His dog went up ahead, up there.'

'O cachorrro ia lá, na frente.'

(252) *tina hia yaiya wʉ'ʉ.*

tí-~da   hí-a   yaí-yá   wʉ'ʉ
ANPH-PL COP-ASSERT.PFV jaguar-PL casa

'[They were the house jaguars (guards).]'

'[Eles eram as onças da casa (guardiões).]'

(253) *tina hira mipᵾre tore khuaina, sã hiromahanone.*
       tí-~da   hí-ra   ~bí-pᵾ́-ré   tó-re   khuá-~ida
       ANPH-PL COP-VIS.IPFV.2/3 now-LOC-OBJ REM-OBJ dangerous-NMLZ.PL
       ~sa=hí-ro-~baha-ro-re
       1PL.EXCL.POSS=COP-SG-go.uphill-SG-OBJ

   '[They're the ones (jaguars) that nowadays are a danger to us, there where we live (in Matapi).]'

   '[São esses (as onças) que hoje são perigosos, perto de onde nós moramos (em Matapi).]'

(254) *wa'ato pᵾᵾᵾᵾ, to namonokoro nᵾnᵾti.*
      wa'á-to   pᵾ́   to=~dabó-ro-koro   ~dᵾdᵾ́-atí
      go-NMLZ.LOC/EVNT DIST 3SG.POSS=wife-SG-F.RSP follow-IPFV

   'He went way off (to the place he had selected), and his wife was following behind.'

   'Foi longe (até o lugar escolhido por ele), e a mulher foi indo atrás dele.'

(255) *sã hiromahanota himanaro to dᵾruwero.*
      ~sa=hí-ro-~baha-ro-ta   hí-~ba-~da-ro   tó
      1PL.EXCL.POSS=COP-SG-go.uphill-SG-EMPH COP-REM.IPFV-PL-SG DEF
      dᵾrú-we-ro
      thunder-MOV.through-SG

   'It was our place up there where it thunders, the sacred place (called) *Dᵾrᵾwero*.'[73]

   'É nosso lugar bem lá em cima, lugar sagrado (chamado de) *Dᵾrᵾwero*.'

(256) *toi tikorokoro tᵾkuñᵾa õse thᵾ! thᵾ! thᵾ!*
      tó-i   tí-kó-ró-kóró   ~tᵾ́ku-~yᵾ-a   ~óse
      REM-LOC.VIS ANPH-F-SG-F.RSP stomp-try-ASSERT.PFV like.this
      thᵾ!...thᵾ!...thᵾ!
      ONTP:thundering

   'There she stomped on the ground like this: *Thᵾ! Thᵾ! Thᵾ!*' (making a thundering sound)

   'Alí ela bateu com o pé assim: *Thᵾ! Thᵾ! Thᵾ!*' (fazendo ruido de trovão)

---

[73] The placename *Dᵾrᵾwero* means 'where you can feel the thunder'.

(257) *"yaba hihari" ni ... mahareñʉ thuatera.*

yabá hí-hari ~dí ~baháré⁷⁴-~yʉ
Q:what/how COP-Q.IPFV say turn.around-see/look
thuá-te-ra
return-NEG-VIS.IPFV.2/3

'"What's that?" she wondered (but *Dianumia Yairo*) didn't even turn around.'

"O que é isso?" ficou pensando (mas *Dianumia Yairo*) nem olhou para trás.'

(258) *do'se chõa mari buhtito warore yoarota niri hireto tiro bʉhkʉro ... ne mahare ñʉeraa, wa'awa'aa.*

do'sé ~chóa ~bari=butí-to waro-re
Q:how nephew 1PL.INCL.POSS=disappear-NMLZ.LOC/EVNT EMPH-OBJ
yoá-ro-ta ~dí-ri hí-re-to tí-ró
far-SG-EMPH COP-NMLZ COP-CLF:gen-NMLZ.LOC/EVNT ANPH-SG
bʉkʉ-ro ~dé ~baháré ~yʉ-éra-a wa'á-wa'a-a
ancestor-SG NEG turn.around look-NEG-ASSERT.PFV go-go-ASSERT.PFV

(addressing Joselito) '[Because, nephew, (for him) it was just as it will be for us in the future (our disappearance, death, burial) — the old ancestor ... didn't even look back, off he went.]'

(falando com Joselito) '[Porque, sobrinho, (para ele) era como vai ser para nós no futuro (nosso sumiço, morte, enterro) — o velho ... nem olhou para trás, foi embora.]'

(259) *te mipʉ to khã're khu'tu to nino nuhusʉa.*

té ~bí-pʉ to ~kha'ŕe khu'tú to=~dí-ro
until now-LOC DEF abiú/cucura.fruit cemetery 3SG.POSS=say-SG
~duhú-~sʉ-a
accomodate.oneself-arrive.TRNS-ASSERT.PFV

'Until he (got to the place) now called *Khãre Khu'tu* (and) made himself comfortable.'

'Até chegar (no lugar) que hoje chamam de *Khãre Khu'tu* (e) se acomodou.'

---

⁷⁴The form *maháré* is used for the actions of 'turning around' or 'going back and forth/going and returning', as in line 288.

(260) *to phosapho'nakã phʉarokã hia.*
 to=phosá-~pho'da-~ka   phʉá-ro-~ka hí-a
 3SG.POSS=maku.people-children-DIM two-SG-DIM COP-ASSERT.PFV
 'He had his two servants.'
 'Havia os seus dois criados.'

(261) *khumuno naa, to muyaichʉ to bahtichʉ.*
 ~khubú-ro ~dá-a   to=~búyaichʉ   to=batíchʉ
 bench-SG get-ASSERT.PFV 3SG.POSS=shaman.staff 3SG.POSS=shield
 '(They) carried his bench, his shaman staff (and) shield.'
 '(Eles) carregaram seu banco do pajé, seu bastão de pajé (e) escudo.'

(262) *a'riase to diero, ba'arose to diero, sieseñʉroka yoaa.*
 a'ría-(bʉ')se   to=dié-ro   ba'á-ro-(bʉ')se to=dié-ro
 DEM.PROX-side 3SG.POSS=dog-SG after-SG-side 3SG.POSS=dog-SG
 sié-(bʉ')sé-~yʉ-dóká   yoá-a
 front-side-see/look-DIST far-ASSERT.PFV
 'Here (in front was) his dog/jaguar and behind his (other) dog/jaguar (and he sat) looking off straight ahead into the distance.'
 'Aqui (na frente ficou) um cachorro/onça e atrás seu (outro) cachorro/onça (e ele sentou) olhando para frente bem longe.'

(263) *duhia phʉanʉmʉ, tia nʉmʉ, õpʉ hitu'sʉa.*
 duhí-a   phʉá-~dʉbʉ tiá-~dʉbʉ ~ó-pʉ
 sit-ASSERT.PFV two-day   three-day DEIC.PROX-LOC
 hí-thu'sʉ-a
 COP-finish-ASSERT.PFV
 '(He) sat for two days (and) on the third day, it was already up to here (his body entering into the ground).'
 'Sentou dois dias e no terceiro dia já estava até aqui (o corpo entrando dentro da terra).'

(264) *"quatro, cinco, kʉ somana ba'aro taga," nia.*
 quatro cinco ~kʉ-sómáná=ba'a-ro   tá-gá   ~dí-a
 four   five one/a-semana=after-SG come-IMP say-ASSERT.PFV
 '"Come back in four, five (days), a week," (Dianumia Yairo) said.'
 '"Daqui a quatro, cinco (dias), uma semana, venham," (Dianumia Yairo) disse.'

(265) *"yʉ'ʉ, mʉhsa phʉkʉ, yʉ ñʉto bahsioro, ñamidahchomahka waroi sãika."*

yʉ'ʉ́ ~bʉsa=phʉkʉ́   yʉ=~yʉ́-tó   bahsí-o-ro
1SG 2PL.poss=father 1SG.POSS=try-NMLZ.LOC/EVNT true-CAUS-SG
~yabí-dáchó~báká   wáró-í   ~sá-i-ka
night-middle/center EMPH-LOC.VIS inside-M-PREDICT

"'I, your father, will truly be going (to another world), right in the middle of the night.'"

"'Eu, o pai de vocês, estarei indo de verdade (ao outro mundo), bem no meio da noite.'"

(266) *"yʉ'ʉre bihsiroka, yʉ'ʉre thʉ'onaka mʉhsa yʉ pho'na" nia.*

yʉ'ʉ́-re bisí-doka   yʉ'ʉ́-ré thʉ'ó-~da-ka   ~bʉsá yʉ=~pho'dá
1SG-OBJ sound-DIST 1SG-OBJ hear-PL-PREDICT 2PL 1SG.POSS=children
~dí-a
say-ASSERT.PFV

"'I'll be going in (to the ground and) there will be a thunderous sound for me (and) you, my children will hear,' (*Dianumia Yairo*) said.'

"'Entrarei (na terra e) fará trovão bem forte para mim (e) todos vocês, meus filhos, vão ouvir,' disse (*Dianumia Yairo*).'

(267) *"hai" nia, dee ... topuro to niriba'ro bihsia thʉʉʉʉʉ ...*

hái   ~dí-a   dé   tó-puro
INTJ:agree say-ASSERT.PFV INTJ:poor.one! DEF-QUANT.MS
to=~dí-rí-ba'ro   bisí-a   tʉʉʉʉʉ
3SG.POSS=say-NMLZ-CLF:kind sound-go ONTP:thunder

"'All right,' (they) answered (and) poor guy ... just at the time he indicated, there was a sound: *Thʉʉʉʉʉ ...*' (thunder)"

"'Está bom,' responderam (e) coitado... bem na hora que ele indicou, deu ruído: *Thʉʉʉʉʉ ...*' (trovoada)

(268) *"de mari phʉkʉ wa'awa'aka" nia.*

dé   ~bari=phʉkʉ́   wa'á-wa'a-ka   ~dí-a
INTJ:poor.one! 1PL.INCL.POSS=father go-go-ASSERT.IPFV say-ASSERT.PFV

"'Poor guy! Our father's gone,' (they) said.'

"'Coitado! Nosso pai foi embora,' falaram.'

(269) *"ñʉna wa'ahʉta" nia. ne mania.*

~yʉ́-~dá wa'á-~hʉ-ta ~dí-a ~dé ~badía
see/look-PL go-IMP.DEIC-EMPH say-ASSERT.PFV NEG not.exist

'"Go there and see," (they) said. (But) there was nothing there.'

'"Vão lá ver," disseram. (Mas) lá não havia nada.'

(270) *ãta buhti sãwa'aa.*

~áta butí ~sa'á-wa'a-a
because disappear MOV.inside-go-ASSERT.PFV

'Because (*Dianumia Yairo*) had disappeared into (the ground, alive).'

'Porque (*Dianumia Yairo*) havia sumiu entrando (na terra, vivo).'

(271) *ã yoaroto, numia bu'iri, bu'iri nia tore, bu'ikho'to hiphakato.*

~a=yóá-ró-tó ~dubía bu'í-ri bu'í-ri
so=do-SG-NMLZ.LOC/EVNT women cause-NMLZ cause-NMLZ

~dí-a tó-ré bu'í-kho'to hí-phaka-to
say-ASSERT.PFV DEF-OBJ cause-proper.place COP-SPEC-NMLZ.LOC/EVNT

'That's why, because of women, (that cemetery) is called *Bu'i Kho'to* (place of guilt/problem), it seems so.'

'Por isso, por causa de mulher, que (o cemetério) lá é chamado de *Bu'i Kho'to* (lugar de culpa/problema), parece que é.'

(272) *numia bu'iri õse yoa, sua to sãnuhʉriro ti khu'tu, mahsa yarikhu'tu.*

~dubía bu'í-ri ~óse yoá súá
women cause-NMLZ like.this do angry

to=~sa'á-~duhʉ-ri-ro tí-khu'tu[75] ~basá
3SG.POSS=MOV.inside-remain-NMLZ-SG ANPH-cemetery people

yá-ri-khu'tu
POSS-NMLZ-cemetery

'It was because of women that he angrily went into that ground, the cemetery for our own bodies.'

---

[75] From this point on in the narrative, Teresinha switches to the form *khu'tu*, which literally means 'clearing', to refer to actual cemeteries. This term is phonologically similar to *kho'to*, 'proper place' (see lines 16, 22, and 24), which is also used in the narrative in the names of specific cemeteries (e.g. line 271) and to refer to these as the 'proper places' for burial, as in the title (line 4). It is likely the terms are etymologically related.

'Foi por causa das mulheres que ele foi com raiva dentro da terra, no cemetério para nossos corpos.'

(273) bu'ikho'to hia. to se'reta sãse' bohkaerati, "do'se yoa bu'ikho'to niari" ni wãhkui.

bu'í-kho'to   hí-a   tó=se'e-re-ta
cause-proper.place COP-ASSERT.PFV DEF=CONTR-OBJ-EMPH
~sá-se'e   boka-éra-ti   do'sé yoá bu'í-kho'to
1PL.EXCL-CONTR find-NEG-ATTRIB Q:how do   cause-proper.place
~dí-á-rí   ~dí ~wakú-i
say-PL-NMLZ say wonder-VIS.PFV.1

(Joselito speaking) '[(Yes) it's *Bu'i Kho'to*. So that's it ... we didn't know why (people) called it that ...'

(Joselito falando) '[(Sim) é *Bu'i Kho'to*. Então, é por isso ... não sabíamos por que (as pessoas) chamavam assim ...'

(274) ãni ya'uatire maikiro.

~a=~dí ya'ú-átí-ré   ~baí-kíró
so-say tell-IPFV-VIS.PFV.2/3 father-M.RSP

(Teresinha responding) '[That's the way my father used to tell it.]'

(Teresinha respondendo) ' [Assim contava meu pai.]'

(275) yʉ'ʉ ninose'ta mʉno hiko, noano sinitu thʉ'otuboa.

yʉ'ʉ ~dí-ro-se'e-ta   ~bʉ́-ro hí-ko ~dóá-ró sinítu
1SG say-SG-CONTR-EMPH man-SG COP-F good-SG ask
thʉ'ó-tu-bo-a
hear-think-DUB-ASSERT.PFV

'[Like I said, if I were a man, I would have asked (and) understood more.[76]]'

'[Como disse, se fosse homem, teria perguntado (e) entendido mais.]'

(276) õse ni to ya'uakãre thʉ'oatikʉrʉ, mahsihari?

~óse   ~dí to=ya'ú-a-~ka-re   thʉ'ó-ati-kʉrʉ   ~basí-hárí
like.this say 3SG.POSS=tell-PL-DIM-OBJ hear-IPFV-ADVERS know-Q.IPFV

'[(But) I unfortunately wasn't paying enough attention to what little he said, you know?]'

---

[76] The composition of the conditional sentence is worth noting: the protasis is a nominalization with person marking *-ko* 'feminine', and the apodosis contains the dubitative marker *-bo*, showing that the result was not forthcoming.

'[(Mas) eu infelizmente não prestava atenção ao pouco que ele contava, sabe?]'

(277) õse hiatia mahko," niatire.

~óse   hí-ati-a   ~bakó   ~dí-ati-re
like.this COP-IPFV-ASSERT.PFV daughter say-IPFV-VIS.PFV.2/3

'"That's what happened, daughter," (father) used to say.'

'"Era assim, filha" contava (meu pai).'

(278) "ãhia mahsapekururi yaaka" nia.

~a=hí-a   ~basá-pé-kúrú-rí   yá-a-ka
so=COP-PL people-QUANT.C-group-NMLZ bury-PL-PREDICT
~dí-a
say-ASSERT.PFV

'"So that all the (Kotiria) groups would have (a place) to be buried."'

'"Para que todos os grupos kotiria tivessem (o seu lugar) de ser enterrado."'

(279) "a'ría nari siria, nari ya'saria, nari ñiria, nari ye'seria khõaroka" nia.

a'rí-á   ~dá-rí   sí-ria   ~dá-rí
DEM.PROX-PL small.stone-PL shiny-CLF:round small.stone-PL
ya'sá-ria   ~dá-rí   ~yí-ria   ~dá-rí
green/blue-CLF:round small.stone-PL black-CLF:round small.stone-PL
ye'sé-ria   ~khoá-ro-ka   ~dí-a
white-CLF:round lie-SG-PREDICT say-ASSERT.PFV

'"There will be the place of Shiny Stones, the place of Green Stones, the place of Black Stones (and) the place of White Stones," (father) said.'

'"O lugar de Pedra Luminosa, lugar de Pedra Verde, lugar de Pedra Preta (e) lugar de Pedra Branca, esses vão ficar," dizia (papai).'

(280) mari mipɨ hi ti kururire, õse nahu tha'rose.

~barí   ~bí-pɨ́   hí   ti=kurú-ri-re   ~óse   ~dahú
1PL.INCL now-LOC COP ANPH=group-NMLZ-OBJ like.this flatbread
tha'ró-sé
cut.in.quarters-CLF:similar

'(And) now we're divided into groups, like a flatbread cut into fourths.'

'(E) nós agora ficamos divididos em grupos, como beijú cortado em quatro.'

(281) ã hiro õba'roi wa'masɨrore nari phichasiria khõaa, sã yakhu'tu.

~a=hí-ro   ~ó=ba'ro-i   ~wa'básɨ-ro-re ~dá-rí
so=COP-SG DEIC.PROX=CLF:kind-LOC.VIS entrance-SG-OBJ small.stone-PL
phichá-sí-ríá   ~khoá ~sa=yá-khu'tu
fire-shiny-CLF:round lie   1PL.EXCL.POSS=POSS-cemetery

'So, the entrance (first part) is for Shiny Stone burials, our grounds (for the highest clan).'

'Então na primeira parte (na entrada), é lugar para Pedra Luminosa se enterrar, nosso lugar (do clã maior).'

(282) ã hiro mahsawa'mino yariato, phano ñamidahchomahka bihsipakato nariwɨ'ɨ.

~a=hí-ro   ~basá-~wa'bi-ro   yaríá-tó   ~phádó
so=COP-SG people-older.brother-SG die-NMLZ.LOC/EVNT before
~yabí-dáchó~báká   bisí-pá-ká-tó
night-middle/center sound-ALT-do.moving-NMLZ.LOC/EVNT
~dá-ri-wɨ'ɨ
get-NMLZ-house

'That's why, before an older brother dies, in the middle of the night, a loud noise comes from the house/cemetery (where the person will be) taken.'

'Por isso, antes de morrer um irmão maior, no meio da noite soa da casa/cemetério (para onde a pessoa vai ser) levada.'

(283) thɨɨɨɨɨɨ! patere khaaaa! bihsimarero.

tɨɨɨɨɨɨ   pá-tere   khaaaa   bisí-~bare-ro
ONTP:thunder ALT-time ONTP:thunder sound-REM.IPFV-SG

'Thɨɨɨɨ! (or) sometimes Khaaaa! is always the sound.'

'Thɨɨɨɨ! (ou) às vezes Khaaaa! sempre soa assim.'

(284) a'riase khɨre ãta mɨhsa yakhu'tu a'riase nari ye'seria, ñahori yaro ya'saria.

a'rí-a-se   khɨ́-ré   ~átá ~bɨsá yá-khu'tu
DEM.PROX-PL-CLF:similar ADD-OBJ also 2PL POSS-cemetery
a'rí-a-se   ~dá-rí ye'sé-ria   ñáhórí yá-ró
DEM.PROX-PL-CLF:similar get-NMLZ white-CLF:round ñahori POSS-SG

ya'sá-ria
green/blue-CLF:round

'It's the same in other places, your place, White Stones (for the *Diani* and) for the *Ñahori*, Green Stones.'

'É assim no outro lado também, o lugar de vocês, Pedra Branca (dos *Diani* e), o lugar dos *Ñahori*, Pedra Verde.'

(285) sõ'o ñahoripho'na yaro ñiria khõaa.

~so'ó   ñáhórí-~pho'da   yá-ró   ~yí-ria   ~khoá-a
DEIC.DIST ñahori-descendants POSS-SG black-CLF:round lie-ASSERT.PFV

'Over there in Black Stones is where *Ñahori* children lie.'

'Lá na Pedra Preta enterra-se os filhos de *Ñahori*.'

(286) "ã hiro nahu tha'rose hira" niatire.

~a=hí-ró   ~dahú   tha'ró-se   hí-ra
so=COP-SG flatbread cut.in.quarters-CLF:similar COP-VIS.IPFV.2/3
~dí-ati-re
say-IPFV-VIS.PFV.2/3

'"So, it's like a flatbread divided in fourths," (my father) used to say.'

'"Assim são como beijú dividido em quatro partes," (meu pai) contava.'

(287) mahsape, tina yabaina puertu paloma, yabaro hihari?

~basá-pé   tí-~da   yabá-~ida   puertu paloma,
people-QUANT.C ANPH-PL Q:what/how-NMLZ.PL puerto paloma,
yabá-ro   hí-hari
Q:what/how-SG COP-Q.IPFV

'Everyone, those ones from Puerto Paloma (the last Kotiria village) — how's it called?'

'Todo mundo, aqueles de Puerto Paloma (última comunidade Kotiria) — como se chama?'

(288) ye'pua phitomahkainapɨ mahsa ya mahareatia, "kue," nia niha.

ye'pú-á   phíto-~baka-~ida-pɨ   ~basá yá
cucura.fruit-PL mouth.of.stream-village-NMLZ.PL-LOC people bury
~baháré-átí-á   kué   ~dí-a ~dí-ha
go.and.return-IPFV-ASSERT.PFV INTJ:surprise say-PL PROG-VIS.IPFV.1

'Ye'pua Phito (mouth of the cucura stream) villagers went back and forth to bury people, always saying "It's so far!"'

'Moradores de Ye'pua Phito (boca do igarapé cucura) vinham para cá e voltavam para enterrar gente, sempre dizendo "Como é longe!"'

(289) paina ɨrinapɨre namɨha, ti ma'a bɨhkɨma'a hiro nimanaro, to bu'iare ti ma'a.

pá-~ida   ~ɨrí-~da-pɨ-re   ~dá-~bɨha   tí-~ba'a
ALT-NMLZ.PL smelly-PL-LOC-OBJ carry-MOV.upward ANPH-path
bɨkɨ́-~ba'a hí-ro   ~dí-~ba-~da-ro   to=bu'ía-re
old-path   COP-SG COP-REM.IPFV-PL-SG DEF=bu'ia.stream-OBJ
tí-~ba'a
ANPH-path

'They carried other rotting bodies up that old path that's always been there, the path from the Bu'ia stream (leading to the cemetery).'

'Carregavam outros corpos podres no caminho antigo, que sempre esteve ali, o caminho do igarapé Bu'ia.'

(290) ti ma'aita mahareatii sã.

tí-~ba'a-i-ta   ~baháré-átí-í   ~sá
ANPH-path-LOC.VIS-EMPH go.and.return-IPFV-VIS.PFV.1 1PL.EXCL

'It's the same path we always use to go back and forth (to our gardens).'

'Nesse mesmo caminho nós sempre vamos e voltamos (da roça).'

(291) tina te ɨrinapɨre ti khã'rekho'toi nawi'ika.

tí-~da   té   ~ɨrí-~da-pɨ-re
ANPH-PL until smelly-PL-EMPATH-OBJ
ti=~kha'ré-khu'tu-i   ~dá-wi'i-ka
ANPH=abiú/cucura.fruit-cemetery-LOC.VIS get-arrive.CIS-ASSERT.IPFV

'They brought the poor decomposing bodies (on that path) to Khãre Kho'to.'

'Traziam os pobres fedendos (nesse caminho) até Khãre Kho'to.'

(292) tina tia, tia, tara: "sã ñɨhchɨ, mɨ'ɨ kha'mana mahsane nana sã khã'inare."

tí-~da   tí-a   tí-a   tá-rá   ~sa=~yɨchɨ́
ANPH-PL cry-go cry-go come-VIS.IPFV.2/3 1PL.EXCL.POSS=grandfather

~~bʉ'ʉ~ ~kha'bá-rá   ~basá-re   ~dá-~da
2SG want-VIS.IPFV.2/3 people-OBJ get-PL
~sa=~kha'i-~ida-re
1PL.EXCL.POSS=love-NMLZ.PL-OBJ

'They come weeping, weeping (saying): "You, our grandfather, want it, so we give you the body of the ones we love."'

'Vêm chorando, chorando (dizendo): "A você nosso avô, que quer, estamos entregando o corpo das pessoas que amamos."'

(293) "mipʉre wi'boga hi'na" ni, phayʉ nikhʉ kha'machʉ tia.
~bí-pʉ́-ré   wi'bó-gá   ~hí'da ~dí phayʉ́ ~dí-khʉ
now-LOC-OBJ take.care-IMP EMPH say many say-ADD
~kha'bá-chʉ   tí-a
do.together-SW.REF cry-ASSERT.PFV

'"Now take good care (of this body)," (they said), and said many other things, weeping together.'

'"Agora guarda bem (o corpo)," diziam, e falavam muitas outras coisas, chorando juntos.'

(294) yo'omeheta nu'miriinadita, ti mahkari phaakãmahkanumiadita wa'aina topʉre.
yo'ó-~beheta   ~du'bí-ri-~ida-dita   tí-~baka-ri
in.contrast-NEG.intens body.paint-PL-NMLZ.PL-SOL ANPH-village-NMLZ
phaá-~ka-~baka-~dubia-dita   wa'a-~ida to-pʉ-re
clan.members-DIM-village-PL.F-SOL go-NMLZ.PL DEF-LOC-OBJ

'But (they) would only go painted, and only the women of that clan (family of that specific community) could go along.'

'Mas iam só pintados, e só podiam ir as mulheres que faziam parte daquela clã (família da comunidade).'

(295) mahkari phaakãmahkono hieraro ti khu'tuita thuaa.
~baká-ri   phaá-~ka-~bako-ro   hi-éra-ro
origin-NMLZ clan.members-DIM-daughter-SG COP-NEG-SG
tí-khu'tu-i-ta   thúa-a
ANPH-cemetery-LOC.VIS-EMPH return-ASSERT.PFV

'A woman who wasn't part of the clan had to return before getting to the cemetery.'

'A mulher que não fazia parte do clã tinha que retornar antes de chegar no cemetério.'

(296) wi'i, thuawi'i ko toawe, ku'sʉwe, khõ'aroka, mahkachʉ ...
wi'í   thúa-wi'i   kó   toá-we
arrive.CIS return-arrive.CIS medicine vomit-MOV.through
ku'sʉ́-we   ~kho'a-doka ~baká-chʉ
bathe-MOV.through   throw-DIST   look.for-eat

'Arriving home, (they cleansed themselves with) vomit medicine, bathed to throw off (the effect of the burial), then had something to eat ...'

'Quando chegavam (do enterro) faziam limpeza de estômago (vomitando), tomavam banho para jogar fora (o efeito do enterro), depois se alimentavam ...'

(297) "yoaro hiro nira," niatire maimʉnano ti khu'ture.
yoá-ró hí-ro   ~dí-ra[77]   ~dí-átí-ré   ~baí-~bʉda-ro
do-SG COP-SG PROG-VIS.IPFV.2/3 say-IPFV-VIS.PFV.2/3 father-deceased-SG
tí-khu'tu-re
ANPH-cemetery-OBJ

'"This is how it's (always) done," my late father used to tell (me) about the cemetery.'

'"Assim é que se faz (sempre)," contava meu pai finado sobre o cemetério.'

(298) ã yoa mahariro tiro bʉhkʉro toi duhika.
~a=yóá ~bahá-ri-ro   tí-ró   bʉkʉ́-ro   tó-i
so=do   go.uphill-NMLZ-SG   ANPH-SG   ancestor-SG   REM-LOC.VIS
duhí-ka
sit-ASSERT.IPFV

'Because our old ancestor (*Dianumia Yairo*) who went up there is still sitting there (still exists, lives there).'

'Porque o velho nosso avô (*Dianumia Yairo*) que subiu ainda está sentado alí (ainda existe, vive alí).'

---

[77]This sentence is a good example of how the visual imperfective suffix used on the copula is understood as a statement of fact, rather than having any type of specific temporal reference (see Stenzel 2013: 281).

(299) *a'ri phakɨi hirota nira.*

a'rí   phákɨ-i   hí-ro-ta   ~dí-ra
DEM.PROX body-LOC.VIS COP-SG-EMPH COP-VIS.IPFV.2/3

'That body is there.'

'O corpo está lá.'

(300) *tiro yariariro hierare. himarero tiro, a'ri phakɨi tiro.*

tí-ró   yariá-rí-ró   hi-éra-re   hí-~bare-ro   tí-ró
ANPH-SG die-NMLZ-SG COP-NEG-VIS.PFV.2/3 COP-REM.IPFV-SG ANPH-SG

a'rí   phákɨ-i   tí-ró
DEM.PROX body-LOC.VIS ANPH-SG

'He isn't dead, he's there (alive), his body.'

'Ele não está morto, está (vivo), o corpo dele.'

(301) *"do'se tiro thíkari khõ'amahkɨ" ni dohoatiti patena.*

do'sé   tí-ró   thí-kari   ~khoabakɨ ~dí dohó-ati-ti   páte~da
Q:how ANPH-SG true-Q.SPEC god   say ask-IPFV-REFL sometimes

'[Sometimes I ask myself: "Could he be God?"]'

'[Às vezes me pergunto: "Será que é ele Deus?"]'

(302) *tiro hira a'ri dahchore khɨariro.*

tí-ró   hí-ra   a'rí   dachó-ré khɨá-ri-ro
ANPH-SG COP-VIS.IPFV.2/3 DEM.PROX day-OBJ have-NMLZ-SG

'He's the one who has/controls time.'

'Ele é quem é o dono do tempo.'

(303) *ni maimɨnano ya'uatire ti khu'ture, ãhia wa'manopɨre.*

~dí ~baí-~bɨda-ro   ya'ú-áti-ré   tí-khu'tu-re
say father-deceased-SG tell-IPFV-VIS.PFV.2/3 ANPH-cemetery-OBJ

~a=hí-a   ~wa'bá-ro-pɨ-re
so=COP-PL young/new-SG-LOC-OBJ

'That's what my late father told (me) about this cemetery, about how things were back then.'

'Assim contava meu pai a respeito desse cemetério, assim como era antigamente.'

Figure 4: *Bu'i Kho'to*. Illustration by Moisés Galvez Trindade and Auxiliadora Figueiredo

Acknowledgments

I am deeply grateful to the Kotiria people who have welcomed me so warmly into their communities over our many years of work together.

Figure 5: Kris and Teresinha in 2017

Special thanks are due to the wise and witty Teresinha Marques for offering this epic narrative and to José Galvez Trindade for his recognition of its importance and for his dedicated work on the initial transcription. This analysis also owes a great deal to Miguel Cabral and his vast knowledge of Kotiria culture and language. Finally, my thanks to Bruna Franchetto for her careful reading and help with the Portuguese translations.

My research on Kotiria and other East Tukano languages has received financial support from the National Science Foundation Linguistics Program (dissertation grant 0211206), the NSF/NEH Documenting Endangered Languages Program (FA-52150-05; BCS-1664348), ELDP/SOAS (MDP-0155), the Brazilian National Council for Scientific and Technological Development (CNPq, post-doctoral grant 2005-2007), the Brazilian Ministry of Education's Program for Continuing Academic Development (CAPES, post-doctoral 'Estágio Senior' grant, 2014-2015), and the Federal University of Rio de Janeiro. Renata Alves of the Instituto Socioambiental is gratefully acknowledged for her design of Figure 2, as is Miguel Cabral Junior for his rendition of Figure 3.

Non-standard abbreviations

ADD	additive	INTENT	intention
AFF	affected	INTENS	intensifier
ALT	alternate	MIR	mirative
ANPH	anaphoric	PREDICT	prediction
ASSERT	assertion	QUANT.C	quantitative for count noun
ATTRIB	attributive		
AUM	augmentative	QUANT.MS	quantitative for mass noun
CIS	cislocative		
CONTR	contrastive	REFL	reflexive
DEIC	deictic	REM	remote
DES	desiderative	REP	reported
DIM	diminutive	RSP	respect
EMPATH	empathetic	SPEC	speculative
EMPH	emphasis	SOL	solitary
EPIS	epistemic	SW.REF	switch reference
EVNT	event	TEMP	temporal
EXRT	exhortative	TRNS	translocative
FRUS	frustrative	VBZ	verbalizer
INFER	inference	VIS	visual

References

Andrello, Geraldo (ed.). 2012. *Rotas de criação e transformação: Narrativas de origem dos povos indígenas do rio Negro.* São Paulo/São Gabriel da Cachoeira: Instituto Socioambiental/Federação das Organizações Indígenas do Rio Negro.

Bolaños, Katherine. 2016. *A grammar of Kakua.* University of Amsterdam: LOT Publications 433.

Cabalzar, Aloisio. 2008. *Filhos da cobra de pedra: Organização social e trajetórias tuyuka no rio Tiquié (noroeste amazônico).* São Paulo: Editora UNESP.

Chernela, Janet. 1983. *Hierarchy and economy of the Uanano (Kotiria) speaking peoples of the middle Uaupes basin.* New York, NY: Columbia University dissertation.

Chernela, Janet. 1993. *The Wanano Indians of the Brazilian Amazon: A sense of space.* Austin: University of Texas Press.

Chernela, Janet. 2004. The politics of language acquisition: Language learning as social modeling in the northwest Amazon. *Women and Language* 27. 13–21.

Chernela, Janet. 2013. Toward an East Tukano ethnolinguistics: Metadiscursive practices, identity, and sustained linguistic diversity in the Vaupés basin of Brazil and Colombia. In Patience Epps & Kristine Stenzel (eds.), *Upper Rio Negro: Cultural and linguistic interaction in northwestern Amazonia,* 197–244. Rio de Janeiro: Museu Nacional, Museu do Índio-FUNAI.

de Oliveira, Lucia Alberta Andrade, José Galvez Trindade & Kristine Stenzel. 2012. Escola Indígena Kotiria Khumuno Wʉ'ʉ. In Flora Dias Cabalzar (ed.), *Educação escolar indígena do rio Negro, 1998-2011: Relatos de experiências e lições aprendidas,* 286–305. São Paulo/São Gabriel da Cachoeira: Instituto Socioambiental/Federação das Organizações Indígenas do Rio Negro.

Epps, Patience. 2008. *A grammar of Hup* (Mouton Grammar Library 43). Berlin: Mouton de Gruyter.

Epps, Patience & Kristine Stenzel. 2013. Introduction. In Patience Epps & Kristine Stenzel (eds.), *Upper Rio Negro: Cultural and linguistic interaction in northwestern Amazonia,* 197–244. Rio de Janeiro: Museu do Índio-FUNAI.

Koch-Grünberg, Theodor. 1995 [1909]. *Dos años entre los indios: Viajes por el noroeste brasileño (1903–1905).* Vol. 1. German original published in 1909-10. Bogotá: Editorial Universidad Nacional.

Stenzel, Kristine. 2007a. The semantics of serial verb constructions in Wanano and Wa'ikhana (Eastern Tukanoan). In Amy Rose Deal (ed.), *Proceedings of the 4th conference on the semantics of under-represented languages in the Americas (University of Massachusetts Occasional Papers 35),* 275–290. Amherst: GLSA.

Stenzel, Kristine. 2007b. Glottalization and other suprasegmental features in Wanano. *International Journal of American Linguistics* 73(3). 331–66.

Stenzel, Kristine. 2008a. Evidentials and clause modality in Wanano. *Studies in Language* 32. 405–445.

Stenzel, Kristine. 2008b. Kotiria 'differential object marking' in cross-lingustic perspective. *Amerindia* 32. 154–181.

Stenzel, Kristine. 2013. Contact and innovation in Vaupés possession-marking strategies. In Patience Epps & Kristine Stenzel (eds.), *Upper Rio Negro: Cultural and linguistic interaction in northwestern Amazonia*, 353–402. Rio de Janeiro: Museu Nacional, Museu do Índio-FUNAI.

Stenzel, Kristine. 2015. Considerações sobre ordem de palavras, tópico e o 'efeito foco' em Kotiria. *ReVEL, edição especial n* 10. [www.revel.inf.br], 223–246.

Stenzel, Kristine. 2016. More on switch-reference in Kotiria (Wanano, East Tukano). In Rik van Gijn & Jeremy Hammond (eds.), *Switch-Reference 2.0*, 425–452. [Typological Studies in Language 114] Amsterdam/Philadelphia: John Benjamins.

Stenzel, Kristine. Forthcoming. To *hi* or not to *hi*? Nonverbal predication in Kotiria and Wa'ikhana (East Tukano). In Simon Overall, Rosa Vallejos & Spike Gildea (eds.), *Nonverbal predication in Amazonian languages* (Typological Studies in Language). Amsterdam/Philadelphia: John Benjamins.

Stenzel, Kristine & Didier Demolin. 2013. Traços laringais em Kotiria e Wa'ikhana (Tukano Oriental). In Leda Besol & Giselle Collischonn (eds.), *Fonologia: Teorias e perspectivas*, 77–100. Porto Alegre: EdiPUCRS.

Stenzel, Kristine & Elsa Gomez-Imbert. 2018. Evidentiality in Tukanoan languages. In Alexandra Y. Aikhenvald (ed.), *Oxford handbook of evidentiality*, 257–387. Oxford: Oxford University Press.

Waltz, Nathan E. & Carolyn Waltz. 1997. *El agua, la roca y el humo: Estudios sobre la cultura wanana del Vaupés*. Bogotá: Instituto Lingüístico de Verano.

Chapter 7

Hup

Patience Epps
University of Texas Austin, USA

Isabel Salustiano

Jovino Monteiro

Pedro Pires Dias

1 Introduction

This narrative tells the story of a liaison between a deer spirit and a woman, and the troubles that came of it. The tale is one of many stories told by the Hupd'äh, who live in the Vaupés region, straddling the border of Brazil and Colombia (Figure 1). Hup, the language of the Hupd'äh (lit. 'person-PL') belongs to the small Naduhup family (formerly known as Makú; see Epps & Bolaños 2017); the speakers of the four Naduhup languages inhabit the interfluvial zones south of the Vaupés River and the middle Rio Negro. The approximately 2000 Hupd'äh live in communities ranging from a few families to several hundred people, located between the Vaupés and the Tiquié Rivers.

The version of the Deer Story narrative presented here was recorded in November 2001 in the Hup community of Taracua Igarapé, known in Hup as *Tát Dëh*, or 'Ant (sp.) Creek' (Figure 2). Taracua Igarapé is located along the large creek that bears the same name, at about an hour's walk into the forest from the banks of the Tiquié River, and is home to about 150 people. While the residents of Taracua Igarapé belong to a number of clans, the community is understood to be in the principal territory of the *Sokw'ät Nok'öd Tëhd'äh*, the 'Descendents of the Toucan's Beak', and is itself the most recent of a series of communities associated with the Toucan's Beak clan, which over the past six to eight generations

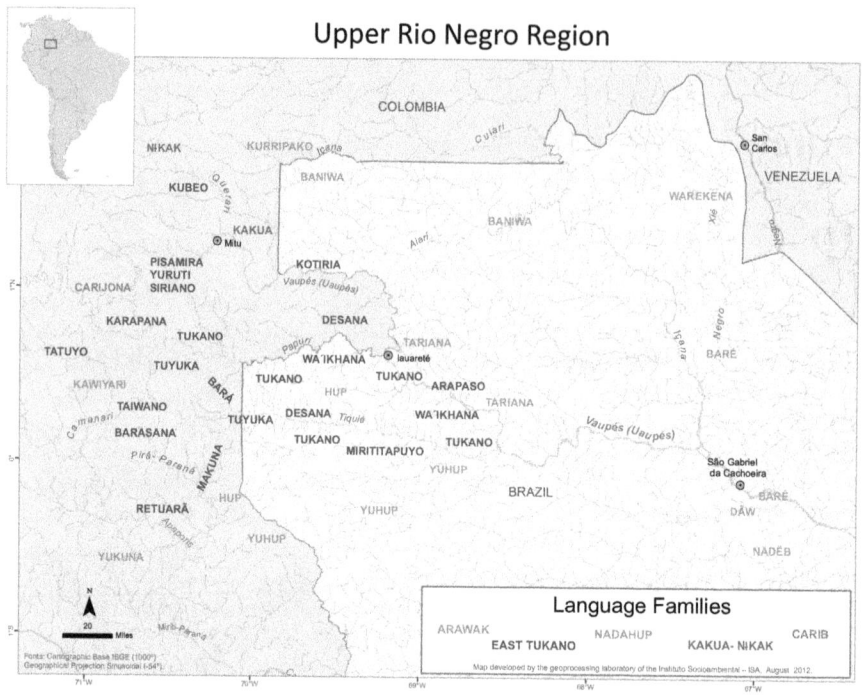

Figure 1: Map of the Upper Rio Negro Region (Epps & Stenzel 2013b)

Figure 2: Taracua Igarapé community

have relocated incrementally from the more remote interfluvial zones toward the Tiquié River.

The Deer Story was performed by Isabel Salustiano, a talented storyteller with a vast repertoire of traditional stories and a masterful delivery. She is originally from the nearby community of Cabari do Japu (*Pìj Dëh*), and is married to Américo Monteiro Socot, who is himself a Toucan's Beak clansman and an influential figure in the community. The story was recorded outdoors in the community, in a central area near a cluster of houses, and in the presence of several of her children and other community members. The text was subsequently transcribed and checked over by Patience Epps, Jovino Monteiro Socot, and Pedro Pires Dias (of Barreira Alta). It appears in the book of Hup stories that was produced for the Middle Tiquié River Hup communities (ed. by Epps, 2005/2016), with illustrations drawn by Estevão Socot (Jovino's son). Several of these illustrations are included here.

As the story begins, a widow, struggling to feed herself and her children, is following a forest stream, collecting tiny freshwater shrimp. This is poor fare, but the most she can manage without a husband to hunt and fish for her. As she moves upstream, she begins to find fish, freshly caught and set out on the bank (Figures 3–4). In her desperation, she takes the fish, although she knows that by doing so she is entering into a relationship with an unknown and potentially

Figure 3: Forest creek in the region of Taracua Igarapé

Figure 4: The woman finding fish set out for her (Estevão Socot)

dangerous other. Soon after, she hears a whistle, and looks up to see a deer spirit in man's form, brilliant with red body paint, looking down at her from the bank. He tells her that he will come that evening to see her, and she agrees. The woman then returns home, feeds her children and puts them to bed, and waits for the deer spirit. He arrives, laden with game, and the two of them spend the evening eating, leaving none for the children. The deer spirit then sleeps with her, together in one hammock, and leaves just before dawn.

The deer spirit continues to visit the woman nightly, always bringing large quantities of game, which they eat together without saving any for the children. During the day, the woman prepares special *manicuera*, a drink made from boiled manioc juice mixed with tasty fruits, to offer her deer husband at night, while she gives only old sour manicuera to the children. Eventually the oldest boy, wondering why his mother always sends them to bed at night with such haste, resolves to stay up and watch. He hides in his hammock and peeks through the holes in the loosely woven palm-fiber mesh, and sees the deer spirit and his mother feasting on the game the spirit has brought (Figure 5). Furious with this revelation, the boy tells his siblings their mother's secret. Together they dig fish-poison root (*Lonchocarpus* sp.), beat it to extract the poison, and squeeze it into the special manicuera that their mother had prepared for her husband.

That night, the boy lies watching again as the deer spirit and his mother feast and go to sleep. In the morning, the mother frantically shakes her husband to

Figure 5: The boy watching his mother and the deer spirit (Estevão Socot)

waken him, but finds him dead. Sending the children out of the house to bathe, she breaks up her husband's body and squeezes it into a large burden-basket, which she carries into the sky for burial (Figure 6). The spot where she leaves him becomes a formation known as the Deer's Tomb, visible in the night sky.

Figure 6: The woman carrying the body of the deer spirit (Estevão Socot)

This formation is also recognized by the Tukano people, who call it by the same name in their own language, but its location has not yet been identified in the ethnoastronomical work carried out in the region (see Cardoso 2007; Oliveira 2010); it is probably one of the "constellations" that peoples of this region visualize in the dark spaces between clusters of stars, rather than in the stars themselves.

The mother returns, and before long she gives birth to the deer spirit's child. She conceals the infant from her children by hanging it up in a bag of charcoal from the rafters of the house, and only takes it down twice a day to nurse it. However, her actions do not go unnoticed by her children, who become curious about the contents of the bag, and climb up one day to have a look while their mother is out in her manioc garden. They discover the baby with delight, and take it out with them into the overgrown swidden (garden areas that have been abandoned in the cycle of slash-and-burn farming) to play with it. There they feed it manioc leaves, potato leaves – all the garden plants to which deer help themselves today – and proceed to play with it by pushing it back and forth among them. As they do so, the baby deer rapidly gains strength, and suddenly it gives a snort, leaps over the children's heads, and disappears into the forest.

The loss of the baby deer is the final step in severing the children's relationship with their mother. Fearful of her anger, they have already begun a transformation into curassow birds (*Nothocrax urumutum*, Figure 7) by the time she discovers the missing baby. Other birds have filled the children's skin with feathers and drawn circles around their eyes, and the children have dug holes in the ground

Figure 7: Nocturnal Curassow *Nothocrax urumutum* (Photo: Jelle Oostrom) http://www.flickr.com/photos/jelle82/4823615464/;CC-BY-SA 2.0 http://creativecommons.org/licenses/by-sa/2.0)

like those of curassows. When their mother rushes into the house to beat them, the children scatter, flying off to hide in their holes. The mother tries in vain to catch one little girl by putting a basket over her hole, but the bird-child only tunnels away, comes up in another place, and flies off. The poor mother wanders crying after her children, and thus transforms herself into a *bëbë* bird – a small brown bird, probably a type of antthrush (family *Formicariidae*), that walks on the forest floor and whose call is reminiscent of crying.

A major theme of the Deer Story is one of transformation, carried out in the context of liminality of behavior and existence. Through their actions, the figures in the story occupy the zones between the human, animal, and spirit "worlds", and their engagement with the occupants of these other worlds ultimately propels them wholly into their domains. This theme is a familiar one in verbal art and cultural practice throughout the Amazon basin: humans, animals, and spirits are understood to share a similar conception of their worlds, but with a fundamental disconnect such that, for example, what a vulture sees as grilled fish appears to a person as maggots in rotting meat (Viveiros de Castro 1998, *inter alia*). One must maintain one's own position as the inhabitant of a particular subjective world by means of appropriate actions – in particular, appropriate social actions – while direct engagement with entities outside this domain is inherently perilous (see, e.g. Santos-Granero 2006; Londoño Sulkin 2005; Uzendoski 2005; Vilaça 2000). It is through this engagement that one may lose one's own subjectivity and enter that of one's interlocutor. Thus the widow, by accepting the fish presented by the deer spirit, opens herself to his "world", and in so doing takes a step out of her own. Her deepening relationship with the spirit and ongoing mistreatment of her own children represent this liminal space that she has entered. Similarly, the children's withdrawal from their mother ultimately propels them into the domain of the curassows. Finally, the mother's own liminality leads her to abandon her human speech and resort only to crying, such that she transforms into the ever-crying *bëbë* bird.

The Deer Story is also representative of the multilingual Vaupés region. The Hupd'äh, like the other peoples of the area, are participants in the regional melting pot of culture, discourse, and language, which has led to striking parallels in verbal art and other practices across many of the Upper Rio Negro peoples (see e.g. Epps & Stenzel 2013a). The Deer Story, like many others, is told widely in the region, and (as noted above) the Deer's Tomb constellation is recognized among other groups as well. Like many other peoples in the region, the Hupd'äh are multilingual, but avoid overt mixing of languages; code-switching is therefore tightly constrained, but is acceptable and even preferred for certain functions –

in particular, marking the speech of entities who are treated as social "others" in narrative. Isabel's telling of the Deer Story makes expert use of this device: when the deer spirit first comes to the woman, he inquires about the children in Tukano, the principal second language of the middle Tiquié River Hupd'äh. Here Isabel departs from her narrative momentarily to comment (perhaps for the benefit of the recording?) that the spirit apparently spoke in "River-Indian language" (Tukano). Later on, when the spirit makes the same inquiry, Isabel comments that he still is speaking in Tukano, but provides his quoted speech in Hup. Finally, at the end of the story, Isabel quotes the woman's crying "my children! my children" – but notably this quote is given in a *mix* of Hup and Tukano (*nɨ põ'ra!* 'my[Hup] children[Tukano]'). Her representation of this mixed-language cry appears to index its semi-human, transformative quality, i.e. a metaphorical use of code-switching. Moreover, the compound (serial) verb construction – which presents components of an event as a conceptually linked package – that Isabel uses to describe the event itself highlights that the transformation comes about *through* this act of speaking: *ʔɨd-ham-döhö-* [speak-go-transform-] 'went saying and transformed'.

In Isabel's telling of the Deer Story, she inserts a number of comments in the narrative; some of these are directly relevant to the story, while others reflect on her own narration. She observes at several points that the events she describes – which are understood to have taken place in a distant, mythic past – set a sort of precedent that shaped the world as we currently know it; for example, that women who remarry sometimes do not treat the children of their first marriage well, and that the leaves fed to the baby deer were exactly those that deer now eat from gardens, thus damaging the crop. Among her more self-reflective comments, she stumbles slightly over the first Tukano utterance of the spirit, and laughs that she did not deliver it so well; later on she hesitates momentarily and comments that she is trying to remember the story line. I have moved this second type of comments out of the main text and into the footnotes, so as not to distract from the flow of the story.

The text also makes use of a number of notable grammatical and discursive features that are characteristic of the Hup narrative genre more generally. The reported evidential (*mah*) is heavily used throughout, normally at least once per main clause, while the inferred evidential marker (*sud*) is mostly limited to quoted speech (such as, for example, the children are speculating about their mother's actions). The nonvisual evidential (*hõ*) occurs only in one of Isabel's asides, where she is commenting on her memory of the story; her asides also include a number of instances of the inferred evidential. Hup's second inferred or assumed evidential (*ni*), which is restricted to past tense and is less dependent on tangible evidence, also occurs occasionally in the text. The distant past contrast marker (*s'ǎh*) only appears sporadically, in keeping with its generally infrequent use in Hup discourse, although some speakers use it more regularly in traditional narrative to index the distant time of the events and/or of when they themselves learned the stories (both considerations seem to be relevant). Other discursively important grammatical resources include the compound (serial) verb constructions, which offer a neat conceptual packaging of associated events or sub-events, as in the example of speaking and transforming given above. Finally, the text provides ample illustration of the head-tail linkage strategy that is common in Hup narrative, such that preceding clauses are often briefly summarized in the first part of the following sentence, marked with the sequential suffix –*yǒʔ* (i.e., 'having done [verb], ...'). These characteristics of Hup grammar and discourse are generally in keeping with those found in other Vaupés languages, while also exhibiting certain differences – for example, the very sporadic use of past-tense marking contrasts with its ubiquitous use in Tukanoan languages, and Stenzel (this volume) notes that Kotiria narrative makes much lighter use of reported evidential marking. Otherwise, closely similar evidential categories, compound/serial verb constructions, and head-tail linkage strategies are widely represented in the area, and Hup's fairly rigid verb-final constituent order, sensitivity of object (non-subject) case marking to animacy and definiteness, use of nominal classifiers, and range of aspectual categories are likewise generally consistent with a wider Vaupés linguistic profile (e.g. Gomez-Imbert 1996; Aikhenvald 2002; Epps 2007; Stenzel 2013; see also Stenzel, this volume). More information on these and many other aspects of Hup grammar can be found in Epps (2008).

The transcription conventions followed here make use of the Hup practical orthography, which has been adopted by Hup teachers in the local schools (see Ramirez 2006). The majority of symbols correspond to those found in the International Phonetic Alphabet, with the following exceptions. For vowels, orthographic <ë> = IPA /e/, <ä> = /ə/, <ö> = /o/, <e> = /æ/, and <o> = /ɔ/. For consonants, <s> = /c/ (palatal voiceless stop), with a word-initial allophone [ʃ], < ' > = /ʔ/, <j> = /ɟ/, and <y> = /j/. Hup's phonological inventory contains voiced, voiceless, and glottalized consonants; while glottalized consonants do not contrast underlyingly for voicing, the practical orthography distinguishes the allophones <s'/j'> and <k'/g'>, respectively (as realized in syllable onset and coda positions). Nasalization is a morpheme-level prosody in Hup, as is the case in other Vaupés languages, but nasal and oral allophones of voiced obstruents (<m/b> and <n/d>) are distinguished depending on whether the context is oral or nasal; otherwise, a tilde on the vowel indicates that the entire syllable (in most cases, morpheme) is nasalized. Vowel-copying suffixes take their nasal/oral quality from the final element in the stem they attach to. Hup has two contrastive tones, which occur only on stressed syllables; these are marked via a diacritic on the vowel of the relevant syllable (v́ = high tone [of which a falling contour is an allophone], v̌ = rising tone).

The first line of transcribed text follows the full set of conventions of word segmentation and phonemic representation current in the practical orthography. The second transcription line deviates from these conventions in several respects: it provides a morphological breakdown, and in so doing it indicates morpheme/clitic boundaries within the phonological word (via - and =, respectively), in keeping with the morphological analysis provided in Epps (2008), including where these are represented by spaces between etyma in the practical orthography. The second transcription line also includes morpheme-initial glottal stops (which are phonemic but are omitted in the practical orthography), since these help to clarify the distinction between consonant- and vowel-initial suffixes within phonological words; it also uses the IPA symbol <ʔ> for the glottal stop consonant in order to differentiate this phoneme from the glottalized consonants (represented as <C'>). The third line provides a morpheme-by-morpheme gloss, with a list of non-standard abbreviations provided at the end of the text.

The line-by-line translations attempt to maintain a relatively literal reading that closely mirrors the discourse norms of the original, while balancing this goal with readability in English. In general, I have leaned toward transparency in the morpheme-by-morpheme glosses that correspond to relatively lexicalized multimorphemic constructions, while the meaning of the collocation as a whole is given in the translation line; e.g. *s'äb-te-yɨ'* (night-still-ADV) 'morning'.

2 Mohə̌y wäd nìh pinìg

'Story of the Deer Spirit'

'História do Espírito Veado'[1]

(1) Sằ' ségep mah tɨh hámáh.
sằʔ ség-ep=mah tɨh hám-áh
shrimp net-DEP=REP 3SG go-DECL

'She went netting shrimp, it's said.'

'Ela foi pegando camarão, dizem.'

(2) Hɨn'ɨ̀h pằãp mah, tẽhíp pằãp mah tɨh hámáh.
hɨn'ɨ̀h pằ-ãp=mah, tẽh=ʔíp pằ-ãp=mah tɨh hám-áh
what NEG.EX-DEP=REP child=father NEG.EX-DEP=REP 3SG go-DECL

'With nothing, it's said, with no husband, it's said, she went.'

'Sem nada, dizem, sem marido, dizem, ela foi.'

(3) Ham yə̋ʔ, dëh-míit sắʔ mah tɨh ségéh.
ham-yə̋ʔ, dëh=mí-it sắʔ=mah tɨh ség-éh
go-SEQ water=course-OBL shrimp=REP 3SG net-DECL

'Having gone, it's said, she was netting shrimp in the stream.'

'Tendo ido, dizem, ela estava pegando camarão no igaparé.'

(4) Yúp mah tɨh seg péét mah, d'ə̀bn'àn tɨh käk w'öb pe níh, húpup ĩhíh.
yúp=mah tɨh seg-pé-ét=mah, d'ə̀b=n'àn tɨh
that=REP 3SG net-go.upstream-OBL=REP acará=PL.OBJ 3SG
käk-w'öb-pe-ní-h húp-up-ʔɨh-íh
pull-set-go.upstream-INFR2-DECL person-DEP=MSC-DECL

'So, it's said, as she went upstream netting, it's said, he was (also) going upstream, fishing acará (*Pterophyllum* sp.) and setting them out (for her), a man.'

'Aí, dizem, enquanto ela ia rio acima pegando camarão, dizem, ele (também) estava indo rio acima, pescando acará e deixando lá (para ela), um homem.'

---

[1] Recordings of this story are available from https://zenodo.org/record/999238

(5) *Tḗ käk w'öb pe yő', tḗ tɨh-k'etd'őhanay mah, tiyì' b'ay këy d'öb k'ët níayáh, mohòyóh.*

tḗ   käk-w'öb-pe-yő?,   tḗ   tɨh=k'etd'őh-an-ay=mah, tiyì?=b'ay
until pull-set-go.upstream-SEQ until 3SG=end-DIR-INCH=REP man=again
këy-d'öb-k'ët-ní-ay-áh,   mohòy-óh.
see-descend-stand-be-INCH-DECL deer-DECL

'Until, having gone upstream fishing and setting out (the fish), all the way to the headwaters (of the stream), it's said, the man was standing (on the bank) looking down (at her), a deer.'

'Até, tendo indo rio acima pescando e deixando (o peixe), até a cabeceira (do igarapé), dizem, o homem ficou (na beira) olhando para baixo para ela.'

(6) *Yúp mah, "Ùy sap ừh àn hồp käk w'öb pée' páh?" tɨh nóop b'ay.*

yúp=mah, ʔùy sap ʔừh ʔàn hồp käk-w'öb-pé-e'   páh?
that=REP who INTS EPIST 1SG.OBJ fish pull-set-go.upstream-Q PROX.CNTR
tɨh   nó-op=b'ay.
3SG say-DEP=again

'So, it's said, "Who can it be, who has been going upstream fishing and setting out (fish) for me?" she said.'

'Aí, dizem, "Quem pode ser, que estava rio acima para a cima e deixando (peixe) para mim?" ela falou.'

(7) *Yɨnɨh yő' mah, hồp wed túup k'őhőy nih, tẽhíp pằap k'őhőy nih, hí tɨh d'ö' pe yíʔɨh.*

yɨ-nɨh-yő?=mah,   hồp wed-tú-up   k'őh-őy=nih,
DEM.ITG-be.like-SEQ=REP fish eat-want-DEP be-DYNM=EMPH.CO
tẽh=ʔíp   pằ-ãp   k'őh-őy=nih,   hí tɨh
child=father NEG.EX-DEP be-DYNM=EMPH.CO only 3SG
d'öʔ-pe-yíʔ-ɨh.
take-go.upstream-TEL-DYNM

'So, it's said, wanting to eat fish, being without a husband, she just went upstream taking the fish.'[2]

'Aí, dizem, querendo comer peixe, sem marido, ela ia para rio acima pegando o peixe.'

---

[2] Isabel uses the verb *k'őh-* 'be' throughout this text; this verb is a salient feature of the Japu dialect (whereas the middle Tiquié dialects use only the form *ni-*), and is often a source of comment among speakers regarding dialectal differences.

7 Hup

(8) *D'ö' pe yő' mah, "Ya'àp yɨ' ãh wed tếh, níiy," no yő' mah, tɨh hup käd b'ay yɨ' kamí mah, tɨ̀hàn tɨh wíçíy.*
d'ö'-pe-yő?=mah, ya'àp=yɨ? ʔãh wed-té-h, ní-íy,
take-go.upstream-SEQ=REP all.gone=ADV 1SG eat-FUT-DECL be-DYNM
no-yő?=mah, tɨh hup-käd-b'ay-yɨ?-kamí=mah, tɨ̀h-àn tɨh
say-SEQ=REP 3SG REFL-pass-return-TEL-moment.of=REP 3SG-OBJ 3SG
wíç-íy.
whistle-DYNM

'Taking (the fish) as she went upstream, it's said, saying, "Just this I'll (take to) eat," it's said, just as she turned around to go back, he whistled to her.'

'Pegando (o peixe), rio acima, dizem, falando, "Só isso vou (levar para) comer," no momento em que ela virou para voltar, ele assobiou para ela.'

(9) *Tɨ̀hàn tɨh wíçíy këyő' mah, "Ùy sap ùh, àn tiyɨ' pằãt, àn wiç k'ët k'ő'ö' páh?"³ no yő' mah.*
tɨ̀hàn tɨh wíç-íy këyő?=mah, ʔùy sap ʔùh, ʔàn tiyɨ?
3SG.OBJ 3SG whistle-DYNM because=REP who INTS EPIST 1SG.OBJ man
pà̃-ãt, ʔàn wiç-k'ët-k'ő?-ö? páh? no-yő?=mah.
NEG.EX-OBL 1SG.OBJ whistle-stand-go.around-Q PROX.CNTR say-SEQ=REP

'As he whistled, it's said, "Who could it be, (I being) without a husband, who could be going around whistling for me?" she said, it's said.'

'Como ele assobiou, dizem, "Quem pode ser, (eu) sem marido, quem está por aí assobiando para mim?" ela falou, dizem.'

(10) *Tɨh këy sop k'ếtếh, tɨh këy sop k'ếtết mah, tɨh mè' sój d'öb k'ët pő ayáh.*
tɨh këy-sop-k'ët-éh, tɨh këy-sop-k'ët-ét=mah, tɨh m'è?
3SG see-ascend-stand-DECL 3SG see-go.up-stand-OBL=REP 3SG carajuru
sój d'öb-k'ët-pő-ay-áh.
brilliant descend-stand-EMPH1-INCH-DECL

'She stood looking up (toward the bank), as she stood looking up, it's said, he stood looking down, brilliant with *carajuru*.[4]'

'Ela ficou olhando para cima (na beira), e enquanto ficava olhando, dizem, ele olhava para baixo, brilhante com carajuru.'

---

[3] The particle *páh* marks recent past, but is used primarily in a contrastive sense; it is the counterpart of the distant past contrast marker mentioned above in the Introduction.

[4] *Carajuru* is the regional term for the *Arrabidaea chica* plant and the red body paint made from its leaves.

(11) *Yup m'é' sój d'öb k'ët yő' mah, tíhàn tih ídíh.*
yup m'éʔ   sój   d'öb-k'ët-yőʔ=mah,   tíh-àn   tih   ʔíd-íh.
that carajuru brilliant descend-stand-SEQ=REP 3SG-OBJ 3SG speak-DECL

'Standing there looking down, brilliant with *carajuru*, it's said, he spoke to her.'

'Ficando lá olhando para ela, brilhante com carajuru, dizem, ele falou para ela.'

(12) *Yít páh, "Hȍp ámàn ãh käk w'öb péét, d'ő'őy ám páh?" nóóy mah.*
yít   páh,   hȍp ʔám-àn ʔãh käk-w'öb-pé-ét,   d'őʔ-őy
thus PROX.CNTR fish 2SG-OBL 1SG pull-set-go.upstream-DECL take-DYNM
ʔám páh?   nó-óy=mah.
2SG PROX.CNTR say-DYNM=REP

'And then, "Where I went upstream catching fish and setting them out for you; have you taken them?" he said, it's said.'

'Aí, "Lá onde fui rio acima, pescando e deixando peixe, você pegou?" ele falou, dizem.'

(13) *"D'ő'őy páh ȁhȁh," nóóy mah tíhíh.*
d'őʔ-őy   páh   ʔȁh-ȁh,   nó-óy=mah   tíh-íh.
take-DYNM PROX.CNTR 1SG-DECL say-DYNM=REP 3SG-DECL

'"I have taken them," she said, it's said.'

'"Eu peguei," ela falou, dizem.'

(14) *"D'ö' wéd, am máhan wed ay yő' páh ámàn käk w'öb pe nííy mah.*
D'ö'-wéd,   ʔam máh-an wed-ʔay-yőʔ   páh   ʔám-àn
take-eat.IMP 2SG near-DIR eat-VENT-SEQ PROX.CNTR 2SG-OBJ
käk-w'öb-pe-ní-íy=mah
pull-set-go.upstream-be-DYNM=REP

'"Take and eat them; having gone and eaten at your place I (will) be setting out fish for you," it's said.'

'"Leve-os para comer; depois de você ir e comer em casa, estarei deixando peixe para você", dizem.'

(15) "Tán, am máhan, d'ú' ãh yë tḗh," nóóy mah.
 tán, ʔam máh-an, d'úʔ   ʔãh yë-tḗ-h,   nó-óy=mah.
 later 2SG near-DIR evening 1SG enter-FUT-DECL say-DYNM=REP
 '"Later, in the evening I will come to you," he said, it's said.'
 '"Depois, no final do dia, chegarei até você," ele falou, dizem.'

(16) "Hàˀ," nóóy mah tɨhɨh.
 hàʔ, nó-óy=mah   tɨh-ɨh.
 yes say-DYNM=REP 3SG-DECL
 '"All right," she said, it's said.'
 '"Tá bom," ela falou, dizem.'

(17) Yɨ́ no yőˀ mah tɨh b'ay yɨ'ayáh.
 yɨ́-no-yőʔ=mah   tɨh b'ay-yɨ́ʔ-ay-áh.
 DEM.ITG-say-SEQ=REP 3SG return-TEL-INCH-DECL
 'Having said that, it's said, she went back.'
 'Tendo dito isso, dizem, ela voltou.'

(18) B'ay yőˀ, tḗ wɨdb'ay yɨ' nííy ni yőˀ mah, tɨh tḗhn'àn.
 b'ay-yőʔ, tḗ   wɨd-b'ay-yɨʔ   ní-íy   ni-yőʔ=mah, tɨh
 return-SEQ until arrive-return-TEL be-DYNM be-SEQ=REP 3SG
 tḗh=n'àn.
 offspring=PL.OBJ
 'She went back, until she had arrived to where her children were.'
 'Ela voltou, até chegar onde estavam as suas crianças.'

(19) Yúp sắˀ mehn'àn tɨh k'ët hipud yőˀ mah, tɨh k'ët wed yőˀ mah, tɨh k'ët õh yɨ'ɨh.
 yúp   sắʔ=meh=n'àn   tɨh k'ët-hipud-yőʔ=mah,   tɨh
 DEM.ITG shrimp=DIM=PL.OBJ 3SG stand-mix.broth-SEQ=REP 3SG
 k'ët-wed-yőʔ=mah, tɨh k'ët-ʔõh-yɨ́ʔ-ɨh.
 stand-eat-SEQ=REP 3SG stand-sleep-TEL-DECL
 'Then, having made *mojica*[5] for them from the little shrimp, it's said, having fed them, she put them to sleep.'
 'Aí, depois de fazer uma mojica de pequenos camarões para elas, dizem depois de tê-las alimentado, as colocou para dormir.'

---

[5] *Mojica* is a stew, usually made with fish, flavored with hot pepper, and thickened with tapioca.

(20) *Yúp k'ët õh yő' mah yúp, "Nɨg õháy, hḗgyɨ' nɨg õh hḗgyɨ' áy, kayak dèh äg tu yő' nɨg õh hḗgyɨ' áy!" tɨh nóóh.*
yúp   k'ët-ʔõh-yőʔ=mah   yúp,   "nɨg ʔõh-áy,   hḗg-yɨʔ   nɨg
DEM.ITG stand-sleep-SEQ=REP DEM.ITG 2PL sleep-INCH.IMP quick-ADV 2PL
ʔõh-hḗg-yɨʔ-ʔáy,   kayak=dèh   ʔäg-tu-yőʔ   nɨg
sleep-quick-TEL-VENT.IMP manioc=liquid drink-immerse-SEQ 2PL
ʔõh-hḗg-yɨʔ-ʔáy!   tɨh nó-óh.
sleep-quick-TEL-VENT.IMP 3SG say-DECL

'Putting them to sleep, "Quick, you all go to sleep quickly, having drunk up your *manicuera*,⁶ you all go to sleep quickly!" she said.'

'Mandando eles dormir, "Rápido, durmam rápido, depois de beber toda a manicuera de vocês, durmam logo!" ela falou.'

(21) *Yĩ nóóy këyőʔ mah yúp, yɨd'àh mèhd'äh, tɨh-dö' mèhd'äh mah, íp pà mèhd'äh, hɨd õh yɨ'ɨh.*
yĩ   nó-óy   këyőʔ=mah   yúp,   yɨ-d'àh   mèh=d'äh,
DEM.ITG say-DYNM because=REP DEM.ITG DEM.ITG-PL DIM=PL
tɨh=döʔ=mèh=d'äh=mah, ʔíp   pà   mèh=d'äh, hɨd ʔõh-yɨʔ-ɨh.
3SG=child=DIM=PL=REP father NEG.EX DIM=PL 3PL sleep-TEL-DECL

'Upon her saying this, it's said, those little ones, those little fatherless ones, they went to sleep.'

'Com ela falando isso, dizem, esses pequenos, esses pequenos sem pai, eles dormiram.'

(22) *Yúp mah bɨ́g nonɨ́h mah tɨh yë yɨ'ayáh.*
yúp=mah bɨ́g no-nɨ́h=mah tɨh yë-yɨʔ-ay-áh.
that=REP HAB say-NEG=REP 3SG enter-TEL-DYNM-DECL

'Then, it's said, it was not long before he came in.'

'Aí, dizem, não foi muito antes dele chegar.'

---

⁶ As noted above, *manicuera* is a drink made from boiled manioc juice, often flavored with fruits.

(23) Tɨh kètd'öh s�ő'őy őy', hɨ̀ytu s�ő'őy őy', hakténéyd'äh őy'.
tɨh kètd'öh sőʔ-őy ʔőy', hɨ̀ytu sőʔ-őy ʔőy', haktén-éy=d'äh
3SG end   LOC-DYNM bunch behind LOC-DYNM bunch side-DYNM-PL
ʔőy'.
bunch

'With a bunch of game at the end (of a pole) in front, a bunch of game in back, bunches of game on either side.'

'Com umas caças no extremo (de um pau) na frente, umas caças atrás, caças dos dois lados.'

(24) Mòh őy'd'äh k'őh maháh. Hisɨhnɨ́h mah yɨd'àháh. Hȍpd'ähä́t yɨʔ, mòhd'ähä́t yɨʔ mah tɨh k'õhnɨ́h.
mòh   ʔőyʔ=d'äh k'őh-mah-áh. hisɨhnɨ́h=mah yɨ-d'àh-áh.
tinamou bunch=PL be-REP-DECL many=REP   DEM.ITG-PL-DECL
hȍp=d'äh-ä́t=yɨʔ, mòh=d'äh-ä́t=yɨʔ=mah tɨh k'õh-nɨ́-h.
fish=PL-OBL=ADV tinamou=PL-OBL=ADV=REP 3SG be-INFR2-DECL

'They were bunches of tinamous.[7] Lots of them. With fish, with tinamous he was thus (laden).'

'Tinham inambus. Muitos. Com peixes, com inambus, ele estava (carregado).'

---

[7] These birds of the family *Tinamidae* are a preferred type of game.

(25) Yɨnɨh yő' mah yúp, "Marĩ põ'ra, marĩ põ'ra karĩrã?" nóóy mah.
yɨ-nɨh-yő?=mah   yúp,   marĩ põ'ra, marĩ põ'ra   karĩ-rã?
DEM.ITG-be.like-SEQ=REP DEM.ITG [1PL children 1PL children sleep-PL]
nó-óy=mah
say-DYNM=REP

'Thus, it's said, [in Tukano] "Are our children, our children asleep?" he said, it's said.'[8]

'Aí, dizem, [em Tukano] "Os nossos filhos, nossos filhos estão dormindo?" ele falou, dizem.'

(26) Wòh ĩh sud ũhnɨ́y. "Marĩ põ'ra karĩrã?" nóóy mah.
wòh=ʔĩh=sud   ʔũhnɨ́y. Marĩ põ'ra   karĩ-rã? nó-óy=mah.
river.indian=MSC=INFR1 maybe [1PL children sleep-PL] say-DYNM=REP

'He was apparently a River Indian, perhaps.[9] [In Tukano] "Are our children asleep?" he said.'

'Era um indio do rio, parece. [em Tukano] "Nossos filhos estão dormindo?" ele falou.'

---

[8]Isabel stumbled a little over the Tukano phrase, and added a further comment:

(i) Yúp āh d'äh d'äh ham nɨ́h dɨ' kodé, wòh ɨd mɨ̀' sud ũhnɨy yéh yúwúh.
Yúp   ʔāh d'äh-d'äh-ham-nɨ́h dɨʔ-kodé, wòh   ʔɨd   mɨ̀ʔ sud-ʔũhnɨy
DEM.ITG 1SG send-send-go-NEG remain-VDIM river.indian speech UNDER INFR-maybe
yéh   yúw-úh.
FRUST DEM.ITG-DECL

'I didn't say that very well, even though it was supposed to be Tukano.'

'Não falei muito bem, mesmo que deveria ter sido em Tucano.'

[9]As discussed in the Introduction, the use of Tukano marks the deer spirit as an "Other". Here Isabel's meta-comment regarding his choice of language may have been motivated by the fact that her story was being recorded.

(27) *Yúp mah, yɨno yő' mah yúp, yúp hǒp tɨh k'ët wédéh, hǒp tɨh k'ët wèd, mòh tɨh k'ët wèd, nííy mah.*
yúp=mah,   yɨ-no-yő?=mah   yúp,   yúp   hǒp tɨh
DEM.ITG=REP DEM.ITG-say-SEQ=REP DEM.ITG DEM.ITG fish 3SG
k'ët-wéd-éh,[10] hǒp tɨh k'ët-wèd, mòh   tɨh k'ët-wèd, ní-íy=mah.
stand-eat-DECL fish 3SG stand-eat tinamou 3SG stand-eat be-DYNM=REP

'Having said that, it's said, he gave her fish to eat; he went on giving her fish to eat, to give her tinamous to eat, it's said.'

'Tendo falado assim, dizem, ele deu peixe para ela comer; ele continuou dando peixe, inambu, dizem.'

(28) *Yɨ́t tɨh nɨhít yɨ' tɨh k'ët hiwag yɨ'ɨ́h.*
yɨ́t   tɨh nɨh-ít=yɨ?   tɨh k'ët-hi-wag-yɨ?-ɨ́h.
thus 3SG be.like-OBL=ADV 3SG stand-FACT-day-TEL-DECL

'Doing thus, he accompanied her until dawn.'

'Assim, ele a acompanhou até amanhecer.'

(29) *Të sadakà' õh säwä' tég kót'ah meh mah, tɨh tẽh-ɨnít tɨh säk te' sak k'ã' yɨ'ayáh.*
të   sadakà? ?õh-säwä?-tég   kót'ah=meh=mah, tɨh tẽh=?ɨn-ɨ́t
until chicken sleep-wake-FUT before=DIM=REP   3SG child=mother-OBL
tɨh säk   te?-sak-k'ã?-yɨ?-ay-áh.
3SG buttocks join.with-go.up-hang-TEL-INCH-DECL

'Until just before the time that the rooster wakes and crows, he lay together with his wife in the hammock.'

'Até pouco antes do tempo do galo acordar e cantar, ele ficava deitado na rede com a mulher dele.'

---

[10] Hup derives causative constructions by means of compounded verb roots. The verb *d'ö?-* 'take' is used for direct causation; *d'äh-* for less direct causation, and *k'ët-* 'stand' for indirect or 'sociative' causation, as in this example.

(30) *Yɨnɨh yő' mah yúp sadakà' õh säwä' kamí pɨd mah tɨh way yɨ'ay pɨdɨp b'ay.*
    yɨ-nɨh-yő?=mah   yúp sadakà? ʔõh-säwä?-kamí   pɨd=mah
    DEM.ITG-be.like-SEQ=REP that chicken sleep-wake-moment.of DIST=REP
    tɨh way-yɨ?-ay   pɨd-ɨp=b'ay.
    3SG go.out-TEL-INCH DISTR-DEP=again

    'Thus, it's said, at the time when the rooster awakes and crows, it's said, he went out again.'

    'Assim, dizem, no momento em que o galo acorda e canta, dizem, ele foi embora de novo.'

(31) *Tế way yő' mah tɨh s'ùg kakáh ham yɨ' ni pɨdɨh, yup tiyɨ'íh.*
    tế   way-yő?=mah   tɨh s'ùg kakáh ham-yɨ?-ni-pɨd-ɨh,   yup
    until go.out-SEQ=REP 3SG forest among go-TEL-be-DISTR-DECL that
    tiyɨ?-íh.
    man-DECL

    'On going out, it's said, he went off into the forest, that man.'

    'Saindo, dizem, ele foi embora no mato, esse homem.'

(32) *Yɨnɨh mɨ' mah tɨh, "Nɨg s'om áyáy, tếh!" no d'äh d'öb yɨ' pɨdɨh.*
    yɨ-nɨh   mɨ?=mah   tɨh, "Nɨg s'om-ʔáy-áy,   tếh!"
    DEM.ITG-be.like UNDER=REP 3SG 2PL bathe-VENT-INCH.IMP offspring
    no-d'äh-d'öb-yɨ?-pɨd-ɨh.
    say-send-descend-TEL-DISTR-DECL

    'With that, it's said, "You all go bathe, children!" she said, sending them down to the water.'

    'Assim, dizem, "Vão tomar banho, filhos!" ela falou, mandando eles para o igarapé.'

(33) *Yɨnɨh yő', s'äbtéyɨ' b'òt ham yő' mah, kayak dèh tɨh bɨ'íh.*
    yɨ-nɨh-yő?,   s'äb-té-yɨ? b'òt   ham-yő?=mah, kayak
    DEM.ITG-be.like-SEQ night-still-ADV swidden go-SEQ=REP   manioc
    dèh   tɨh bɨ?-íh.
    liquid 3SG make-DECL

    'Having done thus, having gone early in the morning to her garden, it's said, she prepared *manicuera*.'

    'Tendo feito assim, tendo ido de manhã cedo para a roça, dizem, ela preparou a manicuera.'

(34) *Kayak dèh bɨ' yő' mah yúp, dɨ' téyɨ' pɨ́d mah, tɨh-dëhwàh mah tɨh tȅhn'àn tɨh b'äh k'ët űhűh.*
 kayak dèh   bɨʔ-yőʔ=mah   yúp, diʔ   té-yɨʔ   pɨ́d=mah,
 manioc liquid make-SEQ=REP that remain still-ADV DISTR=REP
 tɨh=dëh-wàh=mah   tɨh tȅh=n'àn   tɨh b'äh-k'ët-ʔűh-űh.
 3SG=liquid-old.food=REP 3SG offspring=PL.OBJ 3SG pour-stand-APPL-DECL

 'Having prepared *manicuera*, it's said, she would take a little that was left over, it's said, the part that isn't tasty, it's said, and she would pour that out for her children.'

 'Tendo preparado a manicuera, dizem, ela tirou um pouco que sobrou, a parte sem gosto, e a despejou para os seus filhos'

(35) *Yɨnɨh mɨ̀' mah yúp tɨh tȅhípàn b'ay tɨh-dèh húp b'ay, tɨh k'ắh náw, sanàát hitú'úp náw, hipud y'et yɨ́'ɨh.*
 yɨ-nɨh   mɨ̀ʔ=mah yúp tɨh tȅh=íp-àn=b'ay   tɨh=dèh
 DEM.ITG-be.like UNDER=REP that 3SG child=father-OBJ=again 3SG=liquid
 húp=b'ay,   tɨh=k'ắh náw, sanà-át   hi-túʔ-úp   náw,
 beautiful=again 3SG-sweet good pineapple-OBL FACT-immerse-DEP good
 hipud-y'et-yɨ́ʔ-ɨh.
 mix.broth-lay-TEL-DECL

 'But, it's said, for her husband, she would mix up good *manicuera*, sweet, mixed nicely with pineapple.'

 'Mas, dizem, para o marido dela ela misturava a manicuera gostosa, doce, bem mixturada com abacaxí.'

(36) *Pȅdét tɨh-kúút tɨh hipúdup, náw mah.*
 pȅd-ét   tɨh=kú-út   tɨh hipúd-up,   náw=mah.
 cunuri-OBL 3SG-age.bury-OBL 3SG mix.broth-DEP good=REP

 'She mixed it with aged *cunuri*;[11] it was good, it's said.'

 'Ela misturou com cunuri enterrado, era muito boa, dizem.'

---

[11] The nuts of the *cunuri* tree (*Cunuria spruceana*) are prepared via a technique of burying them in the ground and leaving them for some time to ferment.

(37) *Tɨh bɨ' y'et yɨ' pídíh, yúp tɨh tẽhípànáh, mohòy wädànáh.*[12]
 tɨh bɨʔ-y'et-yɨʔ-píd-íh,   yúp tɨh tẽh=ʔíp-àn-áh,
 3SG make-lay-TEL-DIST-DECL that 3SG child=father-OBJ-DECL
 mohòy=wäd-àn-áh.
 deer=RESP-OBJ-DECL

 'She would make it and set it down, for her husband, the deer.'

 'Ela fazia e colocava, dizem, para o marido dela, o veado.'

(38) *Yúp mah yúp tɨhpày mah yúp tɨh tȅhn'àn tɨh bɨ' nó'op b'ay.*
 yúp=mah yúp tɨh=pày=mah yúp tɨh tȅh=n'àn   tɨh
 that=REP that 3SG=bad=REP that 3SG offspring=PL.OBJ 3SG
 bɨʔ-nóʔ-op=b'ay.
 make-give-DEP=again

 'Thus, it's said, she did badly for her children.'

 'Assim, dizem, ela fez mal para seus filhos.'

(39) *Nutèn ã̌yd'äh, ɨn tȅhn'àn hitama' níh, ɨn ní-tëg yɨ' tɨh níhɨp mah yúp hiníp.*
 nutèn ʔã̌y=d'äh, ʔɨn tȅh=n'àn   hitamaʔ-níh, ʔɨn
 today woman=PL 1PL offspring-OBJ.PL do.well.by-NEG 1PL
 ní-tëg=yɨʔ   tɨh níh-ɨp=mah   yúp=hin-íp
 be-CLF:THING=ADV 3SG be.like-DEP=REP that=also-DEP

 'Women of today, (when) we (who remarry) don't treat our children well, our way is as she did, it's said, likewise.'

 'As mulheres de hoje, (quando casam de novo e) não tratam bem nossos filhos, esse jeito é como o jeito dela, dizem, assim mesmo.'

(40) *Yúwàn ùy d'äh këy d'äh hám b'ayáh, yúpyɨ' tɨh bɨ' ni nɨh níh.*
 yúw-àn=ʔùy=d'äh këy-d'äh-hám-b'ay-áh,   yúp-yɨʔ tɨh
 that-OBJ=who=PL see-send-go=again-DEP-DECL that-ADV 3SG
 bɨʔ-ni-nɨh-ní-h.
 make-be-be.like-INFR2-DECL

 'Because that's how it is for those people, thus in this way she behaved.'

 'Por que é assim mesmo para essas pessoas, assim desse jeito ela fez.'

---

[12] The 'respected' marker *wäd* is an honorific device used for male referents, derived from *wähäd* 'old (male)' (compare *wa*, for old/respected female referents).

(41) *Hitama'nɨ́h nutèn ǎyd'äh ɨn hinɨ́h tíh.*
 hitamaʔ-nɨ́h   nutèn ʔǎy=d'äh   ʔɨn=hin-ɨ́h   tíh.
 do.well.by-NEG today woman=PL 1PL=also-DECL EMPH2

 'We (women who remarry) of today likewise do not treat (our children) well.'

 'Nós (mulheres que casam outra vez) hoje em dia também não tratamos bem nossos filhos.'

(42) *Yɨnɨhɨ́y mah yup d'ú' nénéy, nɨhɨ́y pɨ́d mah, "ɨn tě̌h=d'äh õh yɨ' sɨ̌wɨ́y hɨ́dʔ" tɨh no wɨdyë pɨ́dɨ́h, yup wòh ɨ́dɨtɨ́h.*
 yɨ-nɨ́h-ɨ́y=mah   yup d'úʔ   nén-éy,   nɨ́h-ɨ́y
 DEM.ITG-be.like-DYNM=REP that evening come-DYNM be.like-DYNM
 pɨ́d=mah,   ʔɨn tě̌h=d'äh   ʔõh-yɨʔ-sɨ́w-ɨ́y   hɨ́dʔ tɨh
 DISTR=REP 1PL offpring=PL sleep-TEL-COMPL-DYNM 3PL 3SG
 no-wɨdyë-pɨ́d-ɨ́h,   yup wòh   ʔɨ́d-ɨt-ɨ́h.
 say-arrive.enter-DISTR-DECL that river.indian language-OBL-DECL

 'Then like that, it's said, the evening would arrive, it would go like this, it's said: "Are our children already asleep?" he would say as he entered, he would speak in River Indian language.'[13]

 'Assim, dizem, no final do dia, era sempre assim, dizem: "Nossos filhos já estão dormindo?" ele dizia, entrando, dizia na língua dos indios do rio.'

(43) *Yɨnɨh yǒ' pɨ́d mah yúp, dɨ' téyɨ' pɨ́d, "nig õh yɨ', hě̌gay!" tɨh no pɨ́dɨ́h.*
 yɨ-nɨ́h-yǒʔ   pɨ́d=mah yúp, dɨʔ   té=yɨʔ   pɨ́d,   nig
 DEM.ITG-be.like-SEQ DISTR=REP that remain still=ADV DISTR 2PL
 ʔõh-yɨʔ,   hě̌g-ay!   tɨh no-pɨ́d-ɨ́h.
 sleep-TEL.IMP quick-INCH 3SG say-DISTR-DECL

 'Thus, it's said, just before (he would come), "You all go to sleep, quickly!" she would say.'

 'Aí, dizem, pouco antes (dele chegar), "Vocês durmam logo!" ela falava."

---

[13] Here Isabel provides the Deer Spirit's quoted speech in Hup, but comments that he actually would have spoken in Tukano.

(44) *Yúp mah yúp, ya'ápyɨ' pɨ́d mah yup tɨh d'ö' níh, tɨh kètd'öh ső'őy mòh ò̰y',*
hṵ̈ytu ső'őy mòh ò̰y', háktenéyd'äh hṹ sáp ni bahadníh pɨ́d mah tɨh yéẽh.
yúp=mah yúp, yaʔáp=yɨʔ   pɨ́d=mah yup tɨh d'öʔ-ní-h,   tɨh
that=REP that all.that=ADV DISTR=REP that 3SG take-INFR2-DECL 3SG
kètd'öh sőʔ-őy   mòh   ʔò̰y',   hṵ̈ytu sőʔ-őy   mòh   ʔò̰y',
end   LOC-DYNM tinamou bunch behind LOC-DYNM tinamou bunch
hákten-éy=d'äh hṹ   sáp ni-bahad-níh   pɨ́d=mah tɨh yé-ẽh.
side-DYNM=PL   animal INTS be-appear-NEG DISTR=REP 3SG enter-DECL
'So, it's said, he would take all that, it's said, a bunch of tinamou at the end (of the pole), a bunch of tinamou behind, (with so much game) on either side that he could hardly be seen, he would come in.'

'Aí, dizem, ele sempre levava tudo isso, dizem, um monte de inambu no final (de um pau), uns inambus atrás, (com tanta caça) nos dois lados que o corpo dele quase não aparecia, ele entrava.'

(45) *Yɨ̃nɨ́hɨ́y pɨ́d mah yup d'ṹ' tɨh k'ët wed wɨdyéẽ́p, tế hiwag noh yet yɨ' pɨ́dɨ́h,*
tế sadakà' õh säwä' tég̃ kót'ah mah pɨ́d, hɨd yāhá̰'áh, hɨd wédep.
yɨ-nɨ́h-ɨ́y   pɨ́d=mah yup d'ṹʔ tɨh
DEM.ITG-be.like-DYNM DISTR=REP that evening 3SG
k'ët-wed-wɨdyé-ëp,   tế   hi-wag-noh-yet-yɨʔ-pɨ́d-ɨ́h,   tế
stand-eat-arrive.enter-DEP until FACT-day-fall-lie-TEL-DISTR-DECL until
sadakàʔ ʔõh-säwäʔ-tég̃ kót'ah=mah pɨ́d, hɨd yāhá̰ʔ-áh, hɨd wéd-ep.
chicken sleep-wake-FUT before=REP DISTR 3PL stop-DECL 3PL eat-DEP
'Thus, it's said, he would arrive in the evening with food for her, and they would eat, stopping only when day was breaking, just before the rooster crows, it's said.'

'Assim, dizem, ele chegava no final do dia com comida para ela, e eles comiam até amanhecer, parando só pouco antes de o galo cantar, dizem.'

(46) *Yɨnɨh yő' pɨ́d mah tɨh tẽ́hn'àn wèd dɨ'níh tɨh ni yɨ' pɨ́dɨ́h.*
yɨ-nɨh-yőʔ   pɨ́d=mah tɨh tẽ́h=n'àn   wèd dɨʔ-nɨ́h
DEM.ITG-be.like-SEQ DISTR=REP 3SG offspring=PL.OBJ food remain-NEG
tɨh ni-yɨʔ-pɨ́d-ɨ́h.
3SG be-TEL-DISTR-DECL
'Always thus, it's said, she/they would leave nothing for her children.'

'Sempre era assim, dizem, não deixavam nada para os filhos.'

(47) *Tɨh téhn'àn wèd dɨ'nɨh ni yő' pɨ́d, tɨh tēhɨ́n máh tɨh sak k'ã' yő' pɨ́d, hɨd këynɨ́h yɨ' pɨ́d, tɨh way yɨ'ɨ́h.*
tɨh téh=n'àn   wèd dɨʔ-nɨh   ni-yő? pɨ́d, tɨh tēh=ʔín
3SG offspring=PL.OBJ food remain-NEG be-SEQ DISTR 3SG child=mother
máh tɨh sak-k'ãʔ-yő?   pɨ́d, hɨd këy-nɨ́h=yɨʔ pɨ́d, tɨh
near 3SG climb-hang-SEQ DISTR 3PL see-NEG=ADV DISTR 3SG
way-yɨʔ-ɨ́h.
go.out-TEL-DECL

'Always leaving no food for her children, he would climb into the hammock with his wife, (and later) while they (the children) did not see, he would go out.'

'Sem deixar nada para os filhos, ele sempre subia na rede com a mulher dele, e (depois), sem as crianças ver, ele sempre saía.'

(48) *Téh bɨ' yő' pɨ́d mah yɨ́t tɨh way yɨ' ni pɨ́dɨh.*
téh   bɨʔ-yő?   pɨ́d=mah   yɨ́t tɨh way-yɨʔ-ni-pɨ́d-ɨ́h.
offspring make-SEQ DISTR=REP thus 3SG go.out-TEL-be-DISTR-DECL

'After producing a child,[14] it's said, he would go out.'

'Depois de fazer um filho, dizem, ele sempre saiu.'

(49) *Të bɨ́gay mah yúp, "Hɨn'ɨ̌h yő' sáp ɨn ín, ɨ̌nàn yɨ̃ no bɨ́áh tì, yã̀' ɨ̌nàn yɨ̃ no bɨ́áh?" no yő' mah, hɨd pɨb sákáy nih sud ũhnɨ́y, hɨ́dɨh.*
të   bɨ́g-ay=mah   yúp, hɨn'ɨ̌h-yő? sáp ʔɨn ʔín,   ʔɨ̌n-àn
until long.time-INCH=REP that what-SEQ INTS 1PL mother 1PL-OBJ
yɨ̃-no-bɨ-áh   tì,   yã̀? ʔɨ̌n-àn   yɨ̃-no-bɨ-áh?
DEM.ITG-say-HAB-FOC Q.EMPH mom 1PL-OBJ DEM.ITG-say-HAB-FOC
no-yő?=mah, hɨd pɨb sák-áy=nih=sud   ʔũhnɨ́y, hɨ́d-ɨ́h.
say-SEQ=REP 3PL strong go.up-DYNM=EMPH.CO=INFR maybe 3PL-DECL

'Until, after a long time, it's said, (the children) said, "Why in the world does our mother always say this to us, does Mama always say this to us?" They were growing up, perhaps, those (children).'

'Até, depois de muito tempo, "Por que será que a nossa mãe sempre fala assim para nós, Mamãe sempre nos fala assim?" Eles estavam crescendo, parece, essas (crianças).'

---

[14] That is, they would make love, such that after a time his wife became pregnant. The wording here may refer to the model of conception in which repeated love-making events are understood to produce a child.

(50) Yɨnɨ́hɨ́y mah yúp ayùp ɨ̃h, tɨh-wàh díyɨ', këy k'ã́'ayáh.
 yɨ-nɨ́h-ɨ́y=mah yúp ʔayùp=ɨ̃h, tɨh=wàh díyɨʔ,
 DEM.ITG-be.like-DYNM=REP that one=MSC 3SG=mature CPM
 këy-k'ã́ʔ-ay-áh.
 see-hang-INCH-DECL

'So, it's said, one boy, the oldest one, (stayed awake) watching from his hammock.'

'Aí, dizem, um rapaz, o mais velho, (ficou acordado) olhando da rede dele.'

(51) Këy k'ã́' yő' mah yúp, "Hɨn'ɨ̀h pöy sáp bɨ́g yë́h tɨ́hah?! D'ú' ɨ̀nàn 'hḛ̀gyɨ' nɨg õhyɨ' áy tḛ́h, nɨg ápyɨ' nɨg õh hḛ̀gyɨ' áy!' ɨ̀nàn tɨh no bɨ́ɨ' s'ã́h?" no yő' mah,
 këy-k'ã́ʔ-yő?=mah yúp, hɨn'ɨ̀h pö-y sáp bɨ́g yë́h tɨ́h-ah?!
 see-hang-SEQ=REP that what EMPH-DYNM INTS HAB FRUST 3SG-FOC
 d'ú? ʔɨ̀n-àn hḛ̀g-yɨʔ nɨg ʔõh-yɨʔ-ʔáy tḛ́h, nɨg ʔápyɨʔ
 evening 1PL-OBJ quick-ADV 2PL sleep-TEL-VENT.IMP offspring 2PL all
 nɨg ʔõh-hḛ̀g-yɨʔ-ʔáy! ʔɨ̀n-àn tɨh no-bɨ́-ɨʔ s'ã́h?
 2PL sleep-quick-TEL-VENT.IMP 1PL-OBJ 3SG say-HAB-Q DST.CNTR[15]
 no-yő?=mah,
 say-SEQ=REP

'Watching from the hammock, saying, "What in the world is she always doing?! Why does she always say, in the evening, 'Go quickly to sleep, children, all of you go quickly to sleep!'?"'

'Olhando da rede dele, dizendo, "O que é que ela pode estar fazendo?! Porque ela sempre fala, no final do dia, 'Vão dormir logo, filhos, vocês todos durmam logo!'?"'

(52) yúp tɨh wãg yäd k'ã́'ayáh, yág seseg ë' ní-íy mah, s'ámyɨ' hä';
 yúp tɨh wãg-yäd-k'ã́ʔ-ay-áh, yág seseg-ʔë̃ʔ-ní=mah,
 that 3SG spy-hide-hang-INCH-DECL hammock perforated-PFV-INFR2=REP
 s'ám=yɨʔ hä?;
 DST.CNTR=ADV TAG2

'He hung spying, hidden; it was a net-woven hammock, it's said, (the kind from) the old days;'

'Ele ficou lá espiando, escondido; era uma rede tecida (de fibra), dizem, de antigamente;'

---

[15] The 'distant past contrast' marker (DST.CNTR) s'ã́h in this context clarifies that the situation has been going on for a long time.

(53) s'àk s'ó yág ë' ní mah, s'ámyɨ'ɨy yagáh.
    s'àk   s'ó   yág-ʔëʔ-ní=mah,   s'ám=yɨʔ-ɨy
    buriti flower hammock-PFV-INFR2=REP DST.CNTR=ADV-DYNM
    yág-áh.
    hammock-DECL

'in the old days they were buriti-fiber hammocks, those hammocks in the old days.'[16]

'antigamente tinham redes de fibra de buriti, essas redes antigas.'

(54) Nutènep tëghǒd'äh nɨh yágay, nutènep, yág húpútay nɨg k'ǎ'ãhǎ'; páy mah ɨn pem k'ö' ëh, s'ámyɨ'ɨh.
    nutèn-ep   tëghǒ=d'äh   nɨh   yág-ay,   nutèn-ep,   yág
    today-DEP non.indian=PL POSS hammock-INCH today-DEP hammock
    húp-út-ay   nɨg k'ǎʔ-ãhǎʔ;   páy=mah   ʔɨn pem-k'ö'-ʔëh,
    beautiful-OBL-INCH 2PL hang-TAG2 bad=REP 1PL sit-go.around-PFV
    s'ám=yɨʔ-ɨh.
    DST.CNTR=ADV-DECL

'Nowadays you all lie in the non-Indian people's nice hammocks; we went badly in the old days, it's said.'

'Hoje em dia vocês deitam nas redes bonitas dos brancos; foi mal para nós antigamente.'

(55) Yɨn'ɨh yág hitǎ'äp mah yúp tɨh wãg yäd k'ǎ'ǎh, yup tiyɨ' mehéh.
    yɨ-n'ɨh   yág   hitǎʔ-äp=mah   yúp tɨh   wãg-yäd-k'ǎʔ-ǎh,
    DEM.ITG-NMLZ hammock covered-DEP=REP that 3SG spy-hide-hang-DECL
    yup tiyɨʔ=meh-éh.
    that man=DIM-DECL

'So, covered by that hammock, it's said, he hung spying, hidden, that boy.'

'Assim, coberto pela rede, dizem, ele ficou lá espiando, escondido, aquele rapazinho.'

---

[16] Here Isabel offers an explanatory comment; today most indigenous people of the region use manufactured cotton hammocks bought or traded for from local merchants. Buriti is the regional name for the palm *Mauritius flexuosa*.

(56) *Yúp yɨnɨh yő' mah yúp, "hɨn'ɨ̃h tḗg ɨn yà?! ɨ́nàn yɨnɨ́hɨ́y sud ɨn ɨ́níh, páy bɨ́'ɨ́y sud ɨ́n ɨ́n ɨ́nànáh!*[17]
yúp yɨ-nɨh-yő?=mah   yúp, hɨn'ɨ̃h-tḗg ʔɨn yà?! ʔɨ́n-àn
that DEM.ITG-be.like-SEQ=REP that what-FUT 1PL TAG1 1PL-OBJ
yɨ-nɨ́h-ɨ́y=sud   ʔɨn ʔɨ́n-íh,   páy bɨ́ʔ-ɨ́y=sud   ʔɨn
DEM.ITG-be.like-DYNM=INFR 1PL mother-DECL bad work-DYNM=INFR 1PL
ʔɨ́n   ʔɨ́n-àn-áh!
mother 1PL-OBJ-DECL

'So, it's said, "What can we do?! Our mother has been doing thus to us, it seems, our mother has been doing badly by us, it seems!'

'Aí, dizem, "O que podemos fazer?! Parece que a nossa mãe está nos tratando assim, parece que a nossa mãe está nos fazendo mal!'

(57) *"Ya'áp s'ä̃h hɨd wed bɨg súdúh! Kḗyḗy s'ä̃h ä̃hä̃h, méh!" tɨh nóayáh.*[18]
yaʔáp s'ä̃h   hɨd wed-bɨg-súd-úh! kḗy-ḗy   s'ä̃h   ʔä̃h-ä̃h,
all.that DST.CNTR 3PL eat-HAB-INFR-DECL see-DYNM DST.CNTR 1SG-DECL
méh!   tɨh nó-ay-áh.
younger.sister 3SG say-INCH-DECL

'"They've been eating so much all this time, apparently! I've seen it, younger sister!" he said.'

'Faz tempo que eles estão comendo tanto, parece! Eu vi, minha irmã menor!" ele falou.'

---

[17] The boy's comment makes use of the inferential evidential, in contrast to the reported evidential that is used more heavily throughout the narrative text.

[18] In this utterance, the distant past contrast marker (together with the inferential evidential) clarifies that the event must have been going on for a long time.

(58) Yɨnɨh yő' mah yúp, s'äbtéyɨ' s'om d'ǒb d'äh mah hɨd ūh ɨ́dɨ́h.[19]
yɨ-nɨh-yóʔ=mah   yúp, s'äb-té=yɨʔ   s'om-d'ǒb=d'äh=mah   hɨd
DEM.ITG-be.like-SEQ=REP that night-still=ADV bathe-descend=PL=REP 3PL
ʔūh=ʔɨ́d-ɨ́h.
RECP=speak-DECL

'So, it's said, in the morning as they were going to bathe they spoke together.'

'Aí, dizem, de manhã, quando estavam indo para tomar banho, eles falavam entre eles.'

(59) Yúp ësáp b'ay mah tɨh b'òt ham yɨ'ɨp b'ay.
yúp ʔësáp=b'ay=mah   tɨh b'òt   ham-yɨʔ-ɨp=b'ay.
that tomorrow=again=REP 3SG swidden go-TEL-DEP=again

'So the next day, it's said, she (their mother) went to her swidden garden.'

'O dia depois, dizem, ela (a mãe) foi para a roça.'

(60) Yúp tɨh b'òt hámap, yɨ́tyɨ' pɨ́d, tɨh-dëhwàh yɨ' pɨ́d mah hɨ́dàn tɨh b'äh k'et käsät ǚhǔh.
yúp tɨh b'òt   hám-ap, yɨ́t=yɨʔ   pɨ́d,
that 3SG swidden go-DEP   thus=ADV DISTR
tɨh=dëh-wàh=yɨʔ   pɨ́d=mah   hɨ́d-àn   tɨh
3SG=water-old.food=CNTR.EMPH DISTR=REP 3PL-OBJ   3SG
b'äh-k'et-käsät-ʔǚh-ǔh.
pour-stand-be.first-APPL-DECL

'As she was going to the garden, as always, she poured out old tasteless *manicuera* for (the children), it's said.'

'Saindo para a roça, como sempre, ela deixou a manicuera ruim para (as crianças), dizem.'

---

[19]This utterance illustrates the use of the reciprocal prefix -ʔǔh, which is formally identical to several other morphemes in Hup (as evident in this text), including the applicative suffix and the epistemic modal particle. See Epps (2010) for discussion of the historical connection among these forms.

(61) *Yúp b'ay mah, tɨh tēhípàn tɨh-dëh húp yɨ' píd, sanàát tɨh hitú'up náw píd, tɨh hipud y'et yɨ'ɨh, pèdə́t hitú'up.*
yúp=b'ay=mah, tɨh tēh=ʔíp-àn tɨh=dëh húp=yɨʔ
that=again=REP 3SG child=father-OBJ 3SG=liquid beautiful=CNTR.EMPH
píd, sanà-át tɨh hitúʔ-up náw píd, tɨh
DISTR pineapple-OBL 3SG mix-DEP good DISTR 3SG
hipud-y'et-yɨʔ-ɨh, pèd-ə́t hitúʔ-up.
mix.broth-lay-TEL-DECL cunuri-OBL mix-DEP

'And again, it's said, for her husband it was good *manicuera*, nicely mixed with pineapple, that she mixed and set out, mixed with *cunuri*.'

'E como sempre, dizem, para o marido dela ela misturou e colocou a manicuera boa, bem misturada com abacaxí, misturada com cunuri.'

(62) *Yɨnɨh yő' mah yúp, "hɨn'ɨh tég ɨ́n, ɨ́nàn yúpyɨ' bɨ' nɨ́hɨ́y sud yúwúh?!" no yő' mah, hɨd tɨh-dő'd'äh hɨd hámayáh.*
yɨ-nɨh-yő́ʔ=mah yúp, hɨn'ɨh-tég ʔɨ́n, ʔɨ́n-àn yúp=yɨʔ
DEM.ITG-be.like-SEQ=REP that what-FUT 1PL 1PL-OBJ thus=ADV
bɨʔ-nɨ́h-ɨ́y=sud yúw-úh?! no-yőʔ=mah, hɨd tɨh=dőʔ=d'äh
make-be.like-DYNM=INFR DEM.ITG-DECL say-SEQ=REP 3PL 3SG=child=PL
hɨd hám-ay-áh.
3PL go-INCH-DECL

'So then, it's said, saying, "What will we do, (since) she's apparently treating us this way?!" it's said, the children went off.'

'Assim, dizem, falando "O que vamos fazer, com ela nos tratando assim?!" dizem, as crianças foram embora.'

(63) *Ham yő' mah, d'ùç hɨd hátáh.*
ham-yő́ʔ=mah, d'ùç hɨd hát-áh.
go-SEQ=REP timbó 3PL dig-DECL

'Having gone, it's said, they dug up fish-poison (root/vine).'[20]

'Foram, dizem, e desenterravam timbó.'

---

[20] Fish-poison (regional name "timbó"; *Lonchocarpus* sp.) is used to poison sections of streams in order to kill fish, but can also be used as a means of poisoning people. The root is beaten in water to release the poison.

(64) *D'ùç hat yő' mah, s'ómop tɨh kädd'öb mɨ̀' mah, d'ùç hɨd tätäd d'ő'ayáh.*
 d'ùç hat-yő?=mah, s'óm-op tɨh kädd'öb-mɨ̀?=mah, d'ùç hɨd
 timbó dig-SEQ=REP bathe-DEP 3SG pass.descend-UNDER=REP timbó 3PL
 tätäd-d'ő?-ay-áh.
 beat.timbó-take-INCH-DECL

 'Having dug fish-poison, as she (their mother) was on her way down (to the stream) to bathe, they beat the fish-poison (to release the poison).'

 'Depois de desenterrar o timbó, enquanto (a mãe) estava indo para tomar banho, eles baterem o timbó (para fazer o veneno sair).'

(65) *Tätäd d'ö' yő', yúp tɨh-dëh húpút, tɨh hipud y'et yɨ́'ɨwɨ́t hɨd köw'öw' tu' y'et yɨ́'ayáh.*
 tätäd-d'ö?-yő?, yúp tɨh=dëh húp-út, tɨh
 beat.timbó-take-SEQ that 3SG=liquid beautiful-OBL 3SG
 hipud-y'et-yɨ́?-ɨw-ɨ́t hɨd köw'öw'-tu?-y'et-yɨ́?-ay-áh.
 mix.broth-lay-TEL-FLR-OBL 3PL squeeze-immerse-lay-TEL-INCH-DECL

 'Having beaten the fish-poison, they squeezed (the juice) into the tasty *manicuera*, into the *manicuera* that (their mother) had set out (for her husband).'

 'Depois de bater timbó, eles espremiam (o líquido) na manicuera boa, na manicuera que (a mãe) tinha colocado (para o marido).'

(66) *Köw'öw' tu' y'et yɨ' yő' mah, hɨd yɨn'ɨ̀h nonɨ́h õh yɨ́'ayáh.*
 köw'öw'-tu?-y'et-yɨ?-yő?=mah, hɨd yɨ-n'ɨ̀h no-nɨ́h
 squeeze-immerse-lay-TEL-SEQ=REP 3PL DEM.ITG-COMPL say-NEG
 ʔõh-yɨ́?-ay-áh.
 sleep-TEL-INCH-DECL

 'Having squeezed the juice into (it), it's said, they went to sleep, saying nothing about it.'

 'Depois de espremer o líquido (na manicuera), dizem, eles dormiram, sem dizer nada.'

(67) Yúp mah ayùp ĩh, këy k'ã' bɨ́gɨp ĩh yɨ' pɨ́d, këy k'ã̌' b'ayáh.
yúp=mah ʔayùp=ʔĩh, këy-k'ã́ʔ-bɨ́g-ɨp=ʔĩh=yɨʔ pɨ́d,
DEM.ITG=REP one=MSC see-hang-HAB-DEP=MSC=CNTR.EMPH DISTR
këy-k'ã̌ʔ-b'ay-áh.
see-hang-again-DECL

'So, it's said, one boy, the one who had been watching from his hammock, watched from his hammock again.'

'Aí, dizem, um rapaz, aquele que estava olhando da rede, ficou olhando da rede de novo.'

(68) Yúp mah tɨh wɨdyë yɨ́'ay b'ayáh.
yúp=mah tɨh wɨdyë-yɨ́ʔ-ay=b'ay-áh.
that=REP 3SG arrive.enter-TEL-INCH=again-DECL

'Then, it's said, he (the deer) came in.'

'Aí, dizem, o veado entrou.'

(69) "Õh yɨ' sɨ̌wɨ̌y hɨ́d, ɨ́n téhd'äh?" no wɨdyéëy b'ay mah.
ʔõh-yɨʔ-sɨ̌w-ɨ̌y hɨ́d, ʔɨ́n téh=d'äh?
sleep-TEL-COMPL-DYNM 3PL 1PL offspring=PL
no-wɨdyë́-ë́y=b'ay=mah.
say-arrive.enter-DYNM=AGAIN=REP

'"Are our children asleep?" he said, entering, it's said.'

'"Nossos filhos estão dormindo?" ele falou entrando, dizem.'

(70) "Õh yɨ' sɨ̌wɨ̌y yɨd'àhä́h, páhyɨ' hɨd õh yɨ'ɨ́h," nóóy mah yúp, tɨh tēhín waáh.
ʔõh-yɨʔ-sɨ̌w-ɨ̌y yɨ-d'àh-ä́h, páh=yɨʔ hɨd
sleep-TEL-COMPL-DYNM DEM.ITG-PL-DECL PROX.CNTR=ADV 3PL
ʔõh-yɨʔ-ɨ́h, nó-óy=mah yúp, tɨh tēh=ʔɨ́n=wa-áh.
sleep-TEL-DECL say-DYNM=REP that 3SG offspring=mother=RESP-DECL

'"They're already asleep, they went to sleep a short while ago," she said, his wife.'

'"Já dormiram, dormiram há pouco tempo," ela falou, a mulher dele.'

(71) Yɨ̃ no yő' mah yúp, tɨh ǎgayáh, yúwädǎh, wed hupsip̀, yup hɨd kö'wöw' tu' y'et yɨ' pög ẽ̀wànáh.
yɨ-no-yő?=mah   yúp,   tɨh ʔǎg-ay-áh,   yú-wäd-ǎh,
DEM.ITG-say-SEQ=REP DEM.ITG 3SG drink-INCH-DECL DEM.ITG-RESP-DECL
wed-hup-sip̀,   yup hɨd
eat-REFL-COMPL that 3PL
kö'wöw'-tuʔ-y'et-yɨʔ-pög-ʔḛ̀-w-àn-áh.
squeeze-immerse-lay-TEL-AUG-PFV-FLR-OBJ-DECL

'Having said that, it's said, he drank it, that respected one, after eating, that which they had squeezed (poison) into and left there.'

'Falando isso, dizem, ele tomou (a manicuera), esse (veado), depois de comer, aquela que eles tinham deixado com (o veneno) espremido.'

(72) Yúp äg yő' mah tɨh sak k'ã' yɨ'ayáh, hɨd ka'àpd'äh.
yúp   ʔäg-yőʔ=mah   tɨh sak-k'ã?-yɨʔ-ay-áh,   hɨd kaʔàp=d'äh.
DEM.ITG drink-SEQ=REP 3SG climb-hang-TEL-INCH-DECL 3PL two=PL

'Having drunk, it's said, he climbed into the hammock, the two of them (together).'[21]

'Depois de tomar, ele subiu na rede, os dois juntos.'

---

[21]Here Isabel briefly lost her train of thought and commented:

(i) Hɨ̃ no pő́y ũh mah s'ǎh yúw? Ãh hipãhnɨ́h yúwàn, ǎháh, yúp, hằy, hɨ̃ no pő́y mah s'ǎh yúw? Yúwàn ãh hipãhnɨ́h hõ.
Hɨ̃   no-pő́-y   ʔũh=mah s'ǎh   yúw?   ʔÃh hipãh-nɨ́h yúw-àn,
what say-EMPH1-DYNM EPIST=REP DST.CNTR DEM.ITG 1SG know-NEG DEM.ITG-OBJ
ʔǎh-ǎh,   yúp,   hằy, hɨ̃   no-pő́-y=mah   s'ǎh   yúw? Yúw-àn   ʔǎh
1SG-DECL DEM.ITG um what say-EMPH1-DYNM=REP DST.CNTR DEM.ITG DEM.ITG-OBJ 1SG
hipãh-nɨ́h=hõ.
know-NEG=NONVIS

'Now how does it (the story) go? I don't remember this part, um, how does it go? I don't remember this part.'

'Então, como é essa parte (da história)? Não lembro essa parte, eh, como é? Não lembro essa parte.'

(73) Tɨh äg yő' tɨh na' sak k'ã́'awayáh.
Tɨh ʔäg-yőʔ   tɨh naʔ-sak-k'ãʔ-aw-ay-áh.
3SG drink-SEQ 3SG lose.consciousness-climb-hang-FLR-INCH-DECL
'Having drunk, he climbed up drunkenly into the hammock.'
'Depois de tomar, ele subiu, bêbado, na rede.'

(74) Yúp sak k'ã' yő' mah yúp tɨh äg ná'awɨt yɨ' mah, tɨh õh kädham yɨ' níayáh.
yúp   sak-k'ãʔ-yőʔ=mah   yúp   tɨh
DEM.ITG climb-hang-SEQ=REP DEM.ITG 3SG
äg-náʔ-aw-ɨt=yɨʔ=mah,   tɨh
drink-lose.consciousness-FLR-OBL=ADV=REP 3SG
ʔõh-kädham-yɨʔ-ní-ay-áh.
sleep-pass.go-TEL-be-INCH-DECL
'Having climbed into the hammock, it's said, in his drunken(-like) state, he went directly to sleep.'
'Tendo subido na rede, dizem, bêbado, ele dormiu direto.'

(75) Yɨ́t mah tɨh na' yɨ' níayáh tɨh tẽhín hupáh máh, tɨh tawak k'ã' pög níayáh.
yɨ́t=mah tɨh naʔ-yɨʔ-ní-ay-áh   tɨh tẽh=ʔín
thus=REP 3SG lose.consciousness-TEL-be-INCH-DECL 3SG child=mother
hupáh máh, tɨh tawak-k'ãʔ-pög-ní-ay-áh.
back near 3SG stiff-hang-AUG-be-INCH-DECL
'Thus, it's said, he died there against his wife's back, he lay there stiff.'
'Assim, dizem, ele morreu lá contra as costas da mulher dele, ele ficou lá rígido.'

(76) Yúp mah yúp, "ɨn tẽ́hd'äh säwắ'ayáh!" noyő' mah, tɨh yũy' yẽ́hayáh, tɨh yũy' yẽ́hayáh, säwä'níhay mah,
yúp=mah   yúp,   ʔɨn tẽ́h=d'äh   säwắʔ-ay-áh!   no-yőʔ=mah,
DEM.ITG=REP DEM.ITG 1PL offspring=PL awake-INCH-DECL say-SEQ=REP
tɨh yũy'-yẽ́h-ay-áh,   tɨh yũy'-yẽ́h-ay-áh,
3SG shake-FRUST-INCH-DECL 3SG shake-FRUST-INCH-DECL
säwäʔ-nɨ́h-ay=mah,
awake-NEG-INCH=REP
'So, it's said, saying "Our children are waking up!" she shook him and shook him in vain; he did not wake up.'
'Aí, dizem, falando, "Nossos filhos estão acordando!" dizem, ela o sacudiu, o sacudiu, para nada; ele não acordou.'

(77) *Säwä' huphipāhnɨh, tawak d'ak pṍay mah, tɨh hupáh, tɨh tēhín hupáh, mohòyṍh.*
säwä?-hup-hipāh-nɨh, tawak-d'ak-pṍ-ay=mah,   tɨh hupáh, tɨh
awake-REFL-know-NEG stiff-be.against-AUG-INCH=REP 3SG back   3SG
tēh=?ín   hupáh, mohòy-ṍh.
offspring=mother back   deer-DECL

'He did not awake to consciousness, he lay there stiff against his wife's back, it's said, the deer.'

'Ele não acordou, ficou lá rígido contra as costas da mulher dele, dizem, o veado.'

(78) *"Nɨ́g s'õm áy ham áy tḗh! Hɨn'ɨ̀h nɨg k'ǎ́'ǎ́y nɨ́g?" no ẽ̀y mah yúp, hɨd ín waáh.*
nɨ́g s'õm-?áy   ham-?áy   tḗh!   hɨn'ɨ̀h nɨg k'ǎ́?-ǎ́y   nɨ́g?
2PL bathe-VENT.IMP go-VENT.IMP offspring what 2PL hang-DYNM   2PL
no-?ḕ-y=mah   yúp,   hɨd ?ín=wa-áh.
say-PFV-DYNM=REP DEM.ITG 3PL mother=RESP-DECL

'"You all go bathe, children! What are you doing still in your hammocks?" she said, it's said, their mother.'

'"Vão embora tomar banho, filhos! Por que vocês ficam ainda nas redes?" ela falou, dizem, a mãe deles.'

(79) *Yɨnɨ́hɨ́y këyṍ? sud'ɨ̀h hɨd d'öb yɨ́'ay ɨ̃h.*
yɨ-nɨh-ɨ́y   këyṍ?   sud?ɨ̀h   hɨd d'öb-yɨ́?-ay=?ɨ̃h.
DEM.ITG-be.like-DYNM because INFR.EPIST 3PL descend-TEL-INCH=MSC

'So with that, apparently, they went down to the water.'

'Assim, parece, eles foram para o igarapé.'

(80) *Yúp mah tɨh mɨ̀' sud'ɨ̀h tȅg b'ók pȍg bug' k'ët d'ö'ö'ɨ̃h.*
yúp=mah   tɨh mɨ̀'   sud'ɨ̀h   tȅg=b'ók   pȍg bug'-k'ët-dö?-ö?ɨ̃h.
DEM.ITG=REP 3SG UNDER INFR.EPIST tree=bark big bundle-stand-take-MSC

'So, it's said, while (they were out), apparently, she gathered up a big bundle of bark.'

'Aí, dizem, enquanto (eles estavam fora), parece, ela juntou um feixe grande de casca de árvore.'

(81) *Yɨ́t mah yúp tɨh päd hiyet yɨ' pŏ́ayáh, tɨh tẽhíp pögàn, mohòy wädàn.*
 yɨ́t=mah yúp tɨh päd-hi-yet-yɨʔ-pŏ́-ay-áh, tɨh
 thus=REP DEM.ITG 3SG encircle-FACT-lie-TEL-AUG-INCH-DECL 3SG
 tẽh=ʔíp=pög-àn, mohòy=wäd-àn.
 offspring=father=AUG-OBJ deer=RESP-OBJ

 'So, it's said, she laid (his body) encircled (in the bark), her husband, the deer.'

 'Aí, dizem, ela envolveu (o corpo dele na casca), o marido dela, o veado.'

(82) *Yúp päd hiyet yɨ' yŏ́' mah yúp tëg b'ók pögŏ́t yɨ́t tɨh m'am'an' d'ö' kädway yɨ́'ayáh,*
 yúp päd-hi-yet-yɨʔ-yŏ́ʔ=mah yúp tëg=b'ók pög-ŏ́t yɨ́t
 DEM.ITG encircle-fact-lie-TEL-SEQ=REP DEM.ITG tree=bark big-OBL thus
 tɨh m'am'an'-d'öʔ-kädway-yɨ́ʔ-ay-áh,
 3SG roll.up-take-pass.go.out-TEL-INCH-DECL

 'Having laid out (his body) out encircled, it's said, she rolled (it) up in the bark and took it quickly out (of the house),'

 'Depois de envolver (o corpo dele), dizem, ela o enrolou na casca e levou fora da casa.'

(83) *täh sud d'ö' kädway yɨ́'ayáh, tɨnɨ̀h máj pöŏ́t.*
 täh-sud-d'öʔ-kädway-yɨ́ʔ-ay-áh, tɨnɨ̀h
 break-be.inside-take-pass.go.out-TEL-INCH-DECL 3SG.POSS
 máj=pö-ŏ́t.
 basket=AUG-OBL

 'She broke up (his body, to fit) inside (the basket) and took it quickly out, in her basket.'

 'Ela quebrou (o corpo para fazer entrar) dentro (de uma cesta), e levou rapidamente fora, no aturá dela.'

(84) Täh sud d'ö' kädway yő' mah, tɨh kế'ay mah s'a̋h tí, pőhőy mòyan.
täh-sud-d'ö?-kädway-yő?=mah,   tɨh kế?-ay=mah   s'a̋h
break-be.inside-take-pass.go.out-SEQ=REP 3SG bury-INCH=REP DST.CNTR
tí,   pőh-őy   mòy-an.
EMPH.DEP high-DYNM house-DIR

'Having broken it up inside and gone out quickly, it's said, she buried him, it's said, in a place high up (in the sky).'

'Depois de quebrâ-lo dentro e sair rápido, dizem, ela enterrou ele, dizem, num lugar alto (no céu).'

(85) Pőhőy mòyan s'a̋h, yɨd'äha̋h, nusá'áh yɨd'äha̋h, mohòy höd nóop bahad bɨɨtíh, pőhőy sa'ah sö'ötíh, mohòy höd hɨd nóowóh.
pőh-őy   mòy-an s'a̋h,   yɨ-d'äh-a̋h,   nu-sá?áh
high-DYNM house-DIR DST.CNTR DEM.ITG-PL-DECL here-side
yɨ-d'äh-a̋h,   mohòy höd nó-op bahad-bɨ-ɨtíh, pőh-őy
DEM.ITG-PL-DECL deer hole say-DEP appear-HAB-EMPH2 high-DYNM
sa?ah sö?-ötíh   mohòy höd hɨd nó-ow-óh.
side   LOC-EMPH2 deer hole 3PL say-FLR-DECL

'In a place high up (in the sky), over here, people from here (say), that which they call the Deer's Tomb always appears, up high (in the sky), they call (it) the Deer's Tomb.'[22]

'Num lugar alto (no céu); sempre aparece para cá, gente daqui (dizem), aquele que chamam de Túmulo do Veado, bem alto, o que chamam de Túmulo do Veado.'

(86) Yúp mah yúwúh, mohòy höd hɨd nóowóh.
yúp=mah   yúw-úh,   mohòy höd hɨd nó-ow-óh.
DEM.ITG=REP DEM.ITG-DECL deer hole 3PL say-FLR-DECL

'That's it, it's said, they call it the Deer's Tomb.'

'É isso, dizem, que chamam de Túmulo do Veado.'

---

[22] As noted in the Introduction, the location of this formation is uncertain, but it appears to be one of the "constellations" represented by a gap among stars.

(87) *Yɨnɨhyṍ' mah yúp tɨh wɨdyë ni yɨ'ɨp b'ay, konnɨ́h ni yɨ́'ɨ̨y mah, tɨh-tḗhn'àn.*
yɨ-nɨh-yó?=mah   yúp   tɨh wɨdyë-ni-yɨ́?-ɨp=b'ay,
DEM.ITG-be.like-SEQ=REP DEM.ITG 3SG arrive.enter-be-TEL-DEP=again
kon-nɨ́h ni-yɨ́?-ɨ̨y=mah,   tɨh tḗh=n'àn.
like-NEG be-TEL-DYNM=REP 3SG offspring=PL.OBJ

'After that she came back, and there she stayed with dislike (unhappiness) towards her children.'

'Depois disso ela voltou, e ficou lá infeliz com os filhos dela.'

(88) *Yúp konnɨ́h tɨh ni yɨ́'ɨ̨y këyṍ' mah yúp, hɨ́d b'ay hipãh yɨ' sɨ̋wɨ̋y b'ay.*
yúp   kon-nɨ́h tɨh ni-yɨ́?-ɨ̨y   këyó?=mah yúp,   hɨ́d=b'ay
DEM.ITG like-NEG 3SG be-TEL-DYNM because=REP DEM.ITG 3PL=again
hipãh-yɨ?-sɨ̋w-ɨ̋y=b'ay.
know-TEL-COMPL-DYNM=again

'As she stayed there unhappy with them, they became aware of it.'

'Como ela ficou lá infeliz com eles, eles já perceberam.'

(89) *"Hɨ̃n'ɨh tḗg ũ̀h ɨn ín ɨ̀nàn páh?" nóóy mah hɨ́dɨ́h.*
hɨ̃n'ɨh=tḗg ?ũ̀h ?ɨn ?ín   ?ɨ́n-àn páh?"   nó-óy=mah   hɨ́d-ɨ́h.
what=FUT EPIST 1PL mother 1PL-OBJ PROX.CNTR say-DYNM=REP 3PL-DECL

'"What will our mother do to us?" they said, it's said.'

'"O que é que a nossa mãe vai nos fazer?" eles falaram, dizem.'

(90) *Yɨnɨh yṍ' mah, tɨh b'òtan ham yɨ́'ɨ̨y b'ay.*
yɨ-nɨh-yó?=mah,   tɨh b'òt-an   ham-yɨ́?-ɨ̨y=b'ay.
DEM.ITG-be.like-SEQ=REP 3SG swidden-DIR go-TEL-DYNM=again

'(One day) after that, she went to her swidden garden.'

'Aí, (un dia) ela foi para a roça.'

(91) *Yúp tɨnɨh heyó kakah yɨ́' b'ay mah tɨh-dṍ'àn tɨh su' ní b'ayáh, mohòy tḗhànáh.*
yúp   tɨnɨh   heyó   kakah=yɨ́?=b'ay=mah tɨh=dṍ?-àn   tɨh
DEM.ITG 3SG.POSS middle among=ADV=again=REP 3SG=child-OBJ 3SG
su?-ní-b'ay-áh,   mohòy tḗh-àn-áh.
catch-be-again-DECL   deer offspring-OBJ-DECL

'There in the middle (of the swidden) she had a child, the deer's child.'

'Lá no meio (da roça) ela teve filho, o filho do veado.'

(92) *Yúp mohòy téhàn sú'up mah yúp, pŏh, máját, sákuút tíhàn tɨh yö k'ã' ni b'ayáh, yúp tɨh téh mehànáh*
yúp   mohòy téh-àn   sú?-up=mah   yúp,   pŏh,   máj-át,
DEM.ITG deer   offspring-OBJ catch-SEQ=REP DEM.ITG high   basket-OBL
sáku-út   tɨh-àn   tɨh   yö-k'ã?-ni-b'ay-áh,   yúp   tɨh
bag-OBL 3SG-OBJ 3SG   dangle-hang-be-again-DECL DEM.ITG 3SG
téh=meh-àn-áh.
offspring=DIM-OBJ-DECL

'Having given birth to the deer's child, she put it into a basket, a sack, and she hung it up high (in the house), her little child.'

'Depois de ter o filho do veado, ela colocou (o nenê) em um aturá, em um saco, e pendurou no alto (da casa), o filhinho dela.'

(93) *Tëg-sàhát mone yő' mah, tɨh d'ö' sud k'ã' yɨ' níh.*
tëg=sàh-át   mone-yő?=mah,   tɨh
wood=charcoal-OBL   mix-SEQ=REP   3SG
d'ö?-sud-k'ã?-yɨ?-ní-h.
take-be.inside-hang-TEL-INFR2-DYNM

'Having mixed in charcoal (in order to conceal the child in the basket), she put it in (the basket) and hung it up.'

'Misturando com carvão (para esconder o nenê), ela colocou (no aturá) e pendurou no alto.'

(94) *S'äbtéyɨ' tɨh no' púdup, b'òt wɨdyéép tɨh no' púdup, ya'àp yɨ' mah tɨh no' pud pɨdíh.*
s'äbtéyɨ? tɨh   no?-púd-up,   b'òt   wɨdyé-ép   tɨh
morning 3SG give-nurse-DEP   swidden arrive.enter-DEP 3SG
no?-púd-up,   ya?àp=yɨ?=mah   tɨh   no?-pud-pɨd-íh.
give-nurse-DEP   all.that=ADV=REP   3SG   give-nurse-DISTR-DECL

'She would nurse it in the early morning, she would nurse it when she came back from her swidden garden, those were the only (times) she would nurse it.'

'De manhã, ela dava peito, chegando da roça ela dava peito, só nessas (vezes), dizem, ela dava peito (para ele).'

(95) *"Hɨn'ɨh bɨ́g yéh, yà̰' b'òt wɨdyéëp yɨkán käkäynɨ́h yɨ' kädsak wög bɨg yéhẽ' yà?" no yő' mah, hɨd sákayáh, dő'd'ähä́h.*
hɨn'ɨh bɨ́g yéh, yà̰? b'òt wɨdyḛ́-ëp yɨkán käkäy-nɨ́h=yɨ?
what HAB FRUST mama swidden arrive.enter-DEP there gap-NEG=ADV
kädsak-wög-bɨg-yéh-ē? yà? no-yő?=mah, hɨd sák-ay-áh,
pass.climb-AUG-HAB-FRUST-Q QTAG say-SEQ=REP 3PL climb-DYNM-DECL
dő?=d'äh-ä́h.
child=PL-DECL

'"What could it be, why does Mama always climb up there when she comes back from the swidden garden?" Saying this, it's said, they climbed up (to see), the children.'

'"O que será? Por que mamãe sempre sobe lá quando ela volta da roça?" Falando assim, dizem, eles subiram para ver, as crianças.'

(96) *Huphipãhnɨ́h yéháh dő'd'ähätíh, nutènéyd'äh hɨ́nitíh!*
hup-hipãh-nɨ́h yéh-áh dő?=d'äh-ätíh, nutènéy=d'äh=hɨ́n-itíh
REFL-know-NEG FRUST-FOC child=PL-EMPH2 today=PL=also-EMPH2

'Those children did not know better,[23] just like children of today!'

'Essas crianças não entenderam, como as crianças de hoje em dia.'

(97) *Sak yő' mah hɨd kḗyayáh, pɨb dɨ́'ay níɨ́y sud mah.*
sak-yő?=mah hɨd kḗy-ay-áh, pɨb dɨ́?-ay
climb-SEQ=REP 3PL see-INCH-DECL strong remain-INCH
nɨ́-ɨ́y=sud=mah.
be-DYNM=INFR2=REP

'Climbing up they saw it, it apparently was already growing strong, it's said.'

'Subindo, eles viram, já estava crescendo forte, dizem.'

---

[23] That is, they lacked a sense of what is right and/or socially acceptable (*hup-hipãh-nɨ́h* [REFL-know-NEG] lit. 'did not know themselves').

(98) Yɨt mah "Apá! ɨn ín-tẽ́h sud yúwúh, ä́y!" hɨd ũh nóayáh, "méh!" hɨd ũh
nóayáh.
yɨt=mah ʔapá! ʔɨn ʔín=tẽ́h=sud yúw-úh, ʔä́y!"
thus=REP INTERJ 1PL mother=offspring=INFR2 DEM.ITG-DECL old.sister
hɨd ʔũh-nó-ay-áh, "méh!" hɨd ʔũh=nó-ay-áh.
3PL RECP=say-INCH-DECL younger.sister 3PL RECP=say-INCH-DECL

'So, it's said, "Ah, this must be our sibling, older sister!" they said to each other, "younger sister!" they said to each other.'[24]

'Aí, dizem, "Ô, deve ser o filho de nossa mãe, irmã maior!" eles se falavam, "irmã menor!" eles se falavam.'

(99) Yɨno yő' mah yúp, tɨ́hàn hɨd dö' híayáh.
yɨ-no-yő́ʔ=mah yúp, tɨ́h-àn hɨd döʔ-hí-ay-áh.
DEM.ITG-say-SEQ=REP DEM.ITG 3SG-OBJ 3PL take-descend-INCH-DECL

'Saying thus, it's said, they took (the baby deer) down.'

'Falando assim, dizem, eles trouxeram (o nenê veado) para baixo.'

(100) D'ö' hi yő' mah, "Máy! n'ikán, kayak tɨg k'et, pí' k'et ɨn no' k'ő́'ayáh,
yɨ́'an!" no yő' mah,
d'öʔ-hi-yő́ʔ=mah, máy! n'ikán, kayak=tɨg=k'et, píʔ=k'et
take-descend-SEQ=REP let's.go over.there manioc=stem=leaf potato=leaf
ʔɨn noʔ-k'ő́ʔ-ay-áh, yɨ́ʔ-an!" no-yő́ʔ=mah,
1PL give-go.about-INCH-DECL capoeira-DIR say-SEQ=REP

'Taking (it) down, saying, "Come on! Let's go give it manioc and potato leaves out there in the *capoeira* (overgrown swidden)!" it's said,'

'Depois de baixâ-lo, falando, "Bora! Vamos lá na capoeira para dar folhas de mandioca, folhas de batata para ele!" dizem,'

(101) hɨd ton hámayáh, hɨd ín b'òtan ham yɨ' mɨ̀', "ɨn ín-tẽ́h sud yúwúh!" no yő'.
hɨd ton-hám-ay-áh, hɨd ʔín b'òt-an ham-yɨ́ʔ-mɨ̀ʔ, ʔɨn
3PL hold-go-INCH-DECL 3PL mother swidden-DIR go-TEL-UNDER 1PL
ʔín=tẽ́h=sud yúw-úh! no-yő́ʔ.
mother=offspring=INFR DEM.ITG-DECL say-SEQ

'they took (it) off, while their mother was away in the garden, saying, "It must be our sibling!"'

'eles levaram (o nenê), enquanto que a mãe deles estava na roça, dizendo, "Deve ser o filho de nossa mãe!"'

---

[24]The children are using these terms of address to each other, as is common in Hup discourse.

(102) *Yɨkán mah kayak tìg k'et hɨd nó'óh, pí' k'et mah hɨd nó'óh,*
yɨkán=mah kayak=tìg=k'et hɨd nóʔ-óh, píʔ=k'et=mah hɨd
out.there=REP manioc=stem=leaf 3PL give-DECL potato=leaf=REP 3PL
nóʔ-óh,
give-DECL

'Out there, it's said, they gave it manioc leaves, they gave it potato leaves, it's said,'

'Lá, dizem, eles deram folhas de mandioca, folhas de batata, dizem,'

(103) *hɨd no' ë' ȧpyɨ' mah, nutèn hin tɨh wéd b'ayáh, mohòyóh.*
hɨd noʔ-ʔëʔ ʔȧpyɨʔ=mah, nutèn=hin tɨh wéd-b'ay-áh, mohòy-óh.
3PL give-PFV all=REP today=also 3SG eat-again-DECL deer-DECL

'they gave it everything, it's said, that the deer eats today.'

'deram tudo, dizem, que o veado come hoje em dia.'

(104) *Yúp mah hɨd nó'óh, hɨd kakàh d'ö' k'ët yő' mah, "ɨn ín-téh sud yúwúh!" no yő' pɨd,*
yúp=mah hɨd nóʔ-óh, hɨd kakàh d'öʔ-k'ët-yőʔ=mah, "ʔɨn
DEM.ITG=REP 3PL give-DECL 3PL middle take-stand-SEQ=REP 1PL
ʔín=téh=sud yúw-úh!" no-yőʔ pɨd,
mother=offspring=INFR DEM.ITG-DECL say-SEQ DISTR

'So they gave it (food), it's said, (the children) put (the baby deer) in the middle (of the circle they formed), saying "It must be our sibling!"'

'Aí (as crianças) deram (comida), dizem, e colocaram (o nenê veado) no meio deles, dizendo "Deve ser o filho de nossa mãe!"'

(105) *sá'äh mah pɨd mah hɨd tɨy d'äh ham muhú'úh.*
sáʔäh=mah pɨd=mah hɨd tɨy-d'äh-ham-muhúʔ-úh.
other.side=REP DISTR=REP 3PL push-send-go-play-DECL

'they playfully pushed it back and forth.'

'eles brincaram empurrando-o de um lado a outro.'

(106) *Yɨ́t hɨd nɨ́hɨ́t yɨ', yɨ́t hɨd nɨ́hɨ́t yɨ', tɨh m'em'em' k'ët k'ö̃'ö́t mah yúp, tɨh pɨb yɨ'ɨ́h.*
yɨ́t   hɨd   nɨ́h-ɨ́t=yɨʔ,   yɨ́t   hɨd   nɨ́h-ɨ́t=yɨʔ,   tɨh
thus 3PL be.like-OBL=ADV thus 3PL be.like-OBL=ADV 3SG
m'em'em'-k'ët-k'ö̃ʔ-ö́t=mah   yúp,   tɨh   pɨb-yɨʔ-ɨ́h.
weak-stand-go.about-OBL=REP DEM.ITG 3SG strong-TEL-DECL

'As they did thus, as they did thus, as it went wobbling about, it's said, it grew strong.'

'Enquanto eles foram assim, foram assim,(o nenê), balançando aqui e lá, dizem, cresceu forte.'

(107) *Yɨ̃ nɨhɨy mah yúp, tɨh kädham yɨ'ayáh, tɨh s'äk kädham yɨ'ayáh,*
yɨ̃-nɨh-ɨy=mah   yúp,   tɨh   kädham-yɨʔ-ay-áh,   tɨh
DEM.ITG-be.like-DYNM=REP DEM.ITG 3SG pass.go-TEL-INCH-DECL 3SG
s'äk-kädham-yɨʔ-ay-áh,
jump-pass.go-TEL-INCH-DECL

'As they (playfully pushed the deer) thus, it's said, it took off, it leapt (over them) and took off;'

'Fazendo assim (brincando com o veado), dizem, ele foi embora, pulou (por cima deles) e foi embora,'

(108) *hɨd kakàh yɨ' mah yúp, s'ɛ̃́ç no kädham yɨ'ay mah.*
hɨd kakàh=yɨʔ=mah   yúp,   s'ɛ̃́ç   no-kädham-yɨʔ-ay=mah.
3PL middle=ADV=REP DEM.ITG deer.snort say-pass.go-TEL-INCH=REP

'it leapt out of the middle (of the circle of children) and took off, it gave a snort *sɛ̃́ç!* and took off, it's said.'

'ele pulou do meio (das crianças) e foi embora, bufou *sɛ̃́ç!* e foi embora, dizem.'

(109) *Yɨ̃nóóy yɛ́h tɨ́h-ɨ̃hɨ̃tɨ́h, sɛ̃́ç! no kädham yɨ'ay mah.*
yɨ̃-nó-óy   yɛ́h   tɨ́h=ɨ̃h-ɨ̃tɨ́h,   sɛ̃́ç!
DEM.ITG-say-DYNM FRUST 3SG=MSC-EMPH2 deer.snort
no-kädham-yɨʔ-ay=mah.
say-pass.go-TEL-INCH=REP

'That's what it said: *sɛ̃́ç!* and it took off, it's said.'

'Assim que ele falou: *sɛ̃́ç!* e foi embora, dizem.'

(110) *Yɨnɨh yő' mah yɨ́tyɨ', bahadnɨ́h tɨh níayáh, yúp hɨd ín-tĕ́hayáh.*
 yɨ-nɨh-yő?=mah   yɨ́t=yɨ?,   bahad-nɨ́h   tɨh   ní-ay-áh,
 DEM.ITG-be.like-SEQ=REP thus=ADV appear-NEG 3SG be-INCH-DECL
 yúp   hɨd ín=tĕ́h-ay-áh.
 DEM.ITG 3PL mother=offspring-INCH-DECL
 'So with that, it's said, it disappeared, their sibling.'
 'Assim, dizem, ele desapareceu, o filho da mãe deles.'

(111) *Yúp won d'ak k'ö' këy ĕ́y yéh mah yɨd'ähắh, won d'ak k'ö' këy ĕ́y mah.*
 yúp   won-d'ak-k'ö?-këy-?ĕ́-y   yĕ́h=mah
 DEM.ITG follow-be.against-go.about-see-PFV-DYNM FRUST=REP
 yɨ-d'äh-ắh,   won-d'ak-k'ö?-këy-?ĕ́-y=mah.
 DEM.ITG-PL-DECL follow-be.against-go.about-see-PFV-DYNM=REP
 'They went wandering around looking for it in vain, it's said, those (children), wandering around looking for it in vain, it's said.'
 'Eles andavam procurando-o em vão, dizem, essas (crianças), andavam procurando-o em vão, dizem.'

(112) *Hɨd yë yɨ'ayáh, "Hɨn'ɨh tëg ɨ́n?! ɨ́n ɨ́n ɨ́nàn meh tḗg ɨ́nànáh!" no yő' mah,*
 hɨd yë-yɨ́?-ay-áh,   "Hɨn'ɨh-tëg ?ɨ́n?! ?ɨ́n ?ɨ́n   ?ɨ́n-àn   meh-tḗg
 3PL enter-TEL-INCH-DECL what-FUT 1PL 1PL mother 1PL-OBJ beat-FUT
 ?ɨ́n-àn-áh!"   no-yő?=mah,
 1PL-OBJ-DECL say-SEQ=REP
 'They returned home, it's said, saying, "What shall we do?! Our mother will beat us!"'
 'Eles voltarem, dizem, falando, "Como vamos fazer?! Nossa mãe vai nos bater!"'

(113) *tëg sàh b'ɨ́yɨ' mah hɨd mug sud hitab k'ã' yɨ'ayáh, yúp sákuan b'ay.*
 tëg=sàh   b'ɨ́yɨ?=mah hɨd
 wood=charcoal only=REP 3PL
 mug-sud-hitab-k'ã?-yɨ?-ay-áh,   yúp
 scoop.by.hand-be.inside-fill-hang-TEL-INCH-DECL DEM.ITG
 sáku-an-b'ay.
 bag-DIR-again
 'They filled that sack up with charcoal and hung it up again.'
 'Eles encherem o saco com carvão e penduraram de novo.'

(114) *Yɨnɨ́hɨ́y mah hid s'omd'äh tu' k'ö' yɨ́'ɨh, hid yɨnɨh mɨ̀', mòy hat hupsɨ̌p yɨ' sɨ̌wɨ́y sud mah, hídɨwɨ́h.*
yɨ-nɨ́h-ɨ́y=mah   hid s'om=d'äh tuʔ-k'öʔ-yɨ́ʔ-ɨh,
DEM.ITG-be.like-DYNM=REP 3PL bathe=PL immerse-go.about-TEL-DECL
hid yɨ-nɨh   mɨ̀ʔ,   mòy
3PL DEM.ITG-be.like UNDER dwelling.hole
hat-hupsɨ̌p-yɨʔ-sɨ̌w-ɨ́y=sud=mah,   hid-ɨw-ɨ́h.
dig-finish-TEL-COMPL-DYNM=INFR=REP 3PL-FLR-DECL

'Thus, it's said, while they were going about bathing, they had apparently already dug (dwelling-)holes, it's said.'

'Aí, dizem, enquanto estavam indo tomar banho, eles já tinham cavado os buracos deles, dizem.'

(115) *Yɨkán mah yúp, moytùd mòy hid nóowóh.*
yɨkán=mah yúp,   moytùd   mòy   hid nó-ow-óh.
there=REP DEM.ITG curassow dwelling.hole 3PL say-FLR-DECL

'Out there, it's said, curassow (*Nothocrax urumutum*) holes, they call them.'

'Para lá, dizem, buracos de urumutum, como chamam.'

(116) *Yɨkán ũhnɨ́y yúp mòyóh.*
yɨkán ʔũhnɨ́y yúp   mòy-óh.
there maybe DEM.ITG dwelling.hole-DECL

'Those holes were out there, maybe [pointing].'

'Esses buracos estavam para lá, talvez [apontando].'

(117) *Yɨnɨ́hɨ́y mah, wɨdyë yɨ' nɨ́ɨ́y ni yő', "huphipãh nɨ́h nɨg nɨnɨ́h!" no yő' mah,*
yɨ-nɨ́h-ɨ́y=mah,   wɨdyë-yɨʔ   nɨ́-ɨ́y   ni-yőʔ,
DEM.ITG-be.like-DYNM=REP arrive.enter-TEL be-DYNM be-SEQ
"hup-hipãh-nɨ́h nɨg ni-nɨ́-h!"   no-yőʔ=mah,
REFL-know-NEG 2PL be-INFR-DECL say-SEQ=REP

'So, it's said, (their mother) having come home, saying, "You all don't know what's right (acted irresponsibly)!"'

'Aí, dizem, (a mãe), tendo voltado para a casa, ficou dizendo, "Vocês não têm inteligência!"'

(118) *hídàn tɨh sɨwɨp sij d'äh way yɨ́'ɨ́h, hídàn tɨh méhéway, tɨh in, hɨd ínay.*
hɨ́d-àn tɨh sɨwɨp-sij-d'äh-way-yɨ́ʔ-ɨ́h, hɨ́d-àn tɨh
3PL-OBJ 3SG whip-scatter-send-go.out-TEL-DECL 3PL-OBJ 3SG
méh-éw-ay, tɨh in, hɨd ʔín-ay.
beat-FLR-INCH 3SG mother 3PL mother-INCH

'She whipped them until they (fled) scattering, she beat them, their mother.'

'Ela os bateu até que eles voaram, espalhando-se, ela os bateu, a mãe.'

(119) *Méhéy këyő' mah yúp, moytùdd'äh, hɨd hidöhö ham yɨ́'ayáh, hɨd b'ayáh, tɨh téhd'äh k'õh è̩'d'äh b'ayáh.*
méh-éy këyő́ʔ=mah yúp, moytùd=d'äh, hɨd
beat-DYNM CAUSE=REP DEM.ITG curassow=PL 3PL
hidöhö-ham-yɨ́ʔ-ay-áh, hɨ́d=b'ay-áh, tɨh téh=d'äh
transform-go-TEL-INCH-DECL 3PL=again-DECL 3SG offspring=PL
k'õh-ʔè̩ʔ=d'äh=b'ay-áh.
be-PFV=PL=again-DECL

'Because she beat them, they transformed into curassows, they did, those who had been her children.'

'Porque ela os bateu, eles se transformaram em urumutuns, eles, os que eram os filhos dela.'

(120) *Hídàn tɨh-kḗ sĩy' hũ' sɨ̃wɨ̃y sud mah hɨd hiníh.*
hɨ́d-àn tɨh=kḗ sĩy'-hũʔ-sɨ̃w-ɨ̃y=sud=mah hɨ́d=hin-íh.
3PL-OBJ 3SG=wing poke.in-finish-COMPL=INFR=REP 3PL=also-DECL

'They (other birds) had already filled their wings (with feathers), apparently, it's said.'

'Eles (outros pássaros) já tinham enchido as asas deles (com penas), parece, dizem.'

(121) *Hũtéhd'äh nihṹ' mah hídàn kḗ hɨd sĩy'níh.*
hũtéh=d'äh ni-hṹʔ=mah hɨ́d-àn kḗ hɨd sĩy'-ní-h.
bird=PL be-finish=REP 3PL-OBJ wing 3PL poke.in-INFR2-DECL

'All the birds, it's said, filled their wings (with feathers).'

'Todos os pássaros, dizem, encheram as asas deles (com penas).'

(122) Yúp tɨh kɛ̌ sĩy' hũ' yɨ́'ɨway k'ǒhǒy nih mah yúp,
yúp tɨh kɛ̌ sĩy'-hũʔ-yɨʔ-ɨw-ay k'ǒh-ǒy=nih=mah
DEM.ITG 3SG wing poke.in-finish-TEL-FLR-INCH be-DYNM=EMPH.CO=REP
yúp,
DEM.ITG

'Thus with their wings already filled up (with feathers),'

'Assim com as asas já preenchidas (com penas),'

(123) hɨd hin b'ay do'kɛ́y, hɨd ín hɨdàn meh wɨdyɛ́ɛ́t, hɨd do'kɛ́y, hɨd waydö' kädway yɨ́'ayáh.
hɨd=hin=b'ay do'kɛ́y, hɨd ʔín hɨd-àn meh-wɨdyɛ̌-ɛ́t, hɨd
3PL=ALSO=again correct 3PL mother 3PL-OBJ beat-arrive.enter-OBL 3PL
do'kɛ́y, hɨd waydöʔ-kädway-yɨʔ-ay-áh.
correct 3PL fly-pass.go.out-TEL-INCH-DECL

'straightaway, when their mother entered to beat them, straightaway they flew out (of the house).'

'direto, quando a mãe deles entrou para bater neles, eles saíram voando direto (da casa).'

(124) Hɨdnɨ̀h käwàgát pɨ́d mah hɨd hɨ́' popot nihíh.
hɨdnɨ̀h käwàg-át pɨ́d=mah hɨd hɨʔ-popot=nih-íh.
3PL.POSS eye-OBL DISTR=REP 3PL draw-encircle=EMPH.CO-DECL

'They (the birds) had also drawn circles around their eyes (as curassows have).'[25]

'Eles (os pássaros) também tinham desenhado círculos ao redor de seus olhos (como têm os urumutuns).'

(125) Yɨnɨ́hɨ́y mah yup do'kɛ́y hɨd moytùd hɨd hɨdöhö kädsak yɨ́'ayáh.
yɨ-nɨ́h-ɨ́y=mah yúp do'kɛ́y hɨd moytùd hɨd
DEM.ITG-be.like-DYNM=REP DEM.ITG correct 3PL curassow 3PL
hɨdöhö-kädsak-yɨʔ-ay-áh.
transform-pass.climb-TEL-INCH-DECL

'Thus, it's said, straightaway they transformed into curassows and (flew) quickly up.'

'Assim, dizem, transformaram-se imediatamente em urumutuns e subiram (voando).'

---

[25] The other birds assisted them in their transformation by filling their new wings with feathers and drawing circles around their eyes.

(126) Opíd hɨd mòy hat ë́yay k'ṍhṍy nihíh.
opíd   hɨd mòy   hat-ʔë́y-ay   k'ṍh-ṍy=nih-íh.
right.away 3PL dwelling.hole dig-PFV-INCH   be-DYNM=EMPH.CO-DECL

'They had already dug their dwelling-holes.'

'Eles já tinham cavado os buracos deles.'

(127) Yɨnɨhɨ́y mah yúp hɨd ham sij yɨ́'ayáh, waydö' ham sij yɨ́'ay mah.
yɨ-nɨ́h-ɨ́y=mah   yúp   hɨd ham-sij-yɨ́ʔ-ay-áh,
DEM.ITG-be.like-DYNM=REP DEM.ITG 3PL go-scatter-TEL-INCH-DECL
waydö́ʔ-ham-sij-yɨ́ʔ-ay=mah.
fly-go-scatter-TEL-INCH=REP

'So like that, it's said, they went scattering off, flew scattering off, it's said.'

'Assim, dizem, eles foram espalhando-se, voaram dispersando-se, dizem.'

(128) Tã'ã́y mehàn mah tɨh woy ë̀' yë́hë́h, tã'ã́yàn mah tɨh hituk hiyet ë̀' yë́hë́h.
tãʔã́y=meh-àn=mah   tɨh   woy-ʔë̀ʔ-yéh-ë́h,   tãʔã́y-àn=mah
woman=DIM-OBJ=REP 3SG be.stingy-PFV-FRUST-DECL woman-OBJ=REP
tɨh hi-tuk-hi-yet-ʔë̀ʔ-yéh-ë́h.
3SG FACT-face.down-FACT-lie-PFV-FRUST-DECL

'But she (the mother) tried in vain to keep one little girl, she overturned (a basket on the hole to catch) the girl, in vain.'

'Mas ela (a mãe) tentou em vão segurar uma menina, ela virou (um aturá sobre o buraco para pegar) a menina, em vão.'

(129) Yɨnɨ́h mɨ̀' mah, mɨ̀'ay, s'áh k'öd sṍ', tɨh hupkäd kädhi níɨ́y yúwúh,
yɨ-nɨ́h   mɨ̀ʔ=mah,   mɨ̀ʔ-ay,   s'áh k'öd=sṍʔ,   tɨh
DEM.ITG-be.like UNDER=REP UNDER-INCH earth inside=LOC 3SG
hupkäd-kädhi-ní-ɨ́y   yúw-úh,
turn.around-pass.descend-be-DYNM DEM.ITG-DECL

'As she did this, it's said, underneath, inside the hole, she (the child) turned around and quickly descended (digging deeper);'

'Assim, ela fez, dizem, para baixo, dentro do buraco, ela (a menina) virou e desceu rapidamente (cavando mais ainda);'

(130) tã'ǎy b'ay, yɨnɨhɨy mah nusǒ' b'ay tɨh bahad kädway yɨ'ayáh.
tãʔǎy=b'ay,   yɨ-nɨ́h-ɨ́y=mah   nu-sǒʔ=b'ay   tɨh
woman=again DEM.ITG-be.like-DYNM=REP this-LOC=again 3SG
bahad-kädway-yɨ́ʔ-ay-áh.
appear-pass.go.out-TEL-INCH-DYNM
'then like this, it's said, the girl appeared over here (dug up to the surface in a different spot), and quickly went out (and flew away).'
'e assim a menina, dizem, apareceu para cá (cavando para cima até a superfície em outro lugar) e saiu (voando).'

(131) Huphipö' nɨhay nɨ́ɨ́y mah yɨd'ähä́h.
hup-hipöʔ-nɨh-ay   ní-ɨ́y=mah   yɨ-d'äh-ä́h.
REFL-FACT.cover-NEG-INCH be-DYNM=REP DEM.ITG-PL-DECL
'They would not be caught, it's said.'
'Eles não deixaram que fossem pegos, dizem.'

(132) Yɨn'ɨh hɨd hɨdöhö́öway k'ǒhǒy nih.
yɨ-n'ɨh   hɨd   hɨdöhǒ-öw-ay   k'ǒh-ǒy=nih.
DEM.ITG-NMLZ 3PL FACT.transform-FLR-INCH be-DYNM=EMPH.CO
'They had transformed into those (curassows).'
'Eles tinham se transformado nesses (urumutuns).'

(133) Yɨnɨhɨy mah yúp hɨd ham yɨ'ayáh.
yɨ-nɨ́h-ɨ́y=mah   yúp   hɨd ham-yɨ́ʔ-ay-áh.
DEM.ITG-be.like-DYNM=REP DEM.ITG 3PL go-TEL-INCH-DECL
'Thus, it's said, they went away.'
'Assim, dizem, eles foram embora.'

(134)   *Yúp mah yúp hɨd ín b'ay ot d'ak k'ǒ'öp b'ayáh, bëbë́ ɨn notég̊ ́eh, bëbë́ ɨn notég̊ ́eh.*
yúp=mah   yúp   hɨd ʔín=b'ay
DEM.ITG=REP DEM.ITG 3PL mother=again
ʔot-d'ak-k'ǒʔ-öp=b'ay-áh,   bëbë́   ʔɨn no-tég-ę́h,
cry-be.against-go.about-DEP=again-DECL bird.sp 1PL sayFUT-DECL
bëbë́   ʔɨn no-tég-ę́h.
bird.sp 1PL sayFUT-DECL

'Then, it's said, their mother went following after them crying, like what we call a *bëbë* bird'.

'Aí, dizem, a mãe deles andava atrás, chorando, como o que chamamos de pássaro *bëbë*.'

(135)   *Yúp mah yúp tɨh těhn'àn tɨh ótayáh.*
yúp=mah   yúp   tɨh těh=n'àn   tɨh ʔót-ay-áh.
DEM.ITG=REP DEM.ITG 3SG offspring=PL.OBJ 3SG cry-INCH-DECL

'So it's said, she (went) crying for her children.'

'Aí, dizem, ela foi chorando por causa dos filhos dela.'

(136)   *Tɨh těhn'àn tɨh ot ę̌' yɨ̨', "nɨ̨ põ'ra, nɨ̨ põ'ra!" tɨh no ę̌' yɨ̨' mah, yúp ɨd ham döhö yɨ̨'ayáh.*
tɨh těh=n'àn   tɨh ʔot-ʔę̌ʔ=yɨ̨ʔ,   "nɨ̨   põ'ra,   nɨ̨
3SG offspring=PL.OBJ 3SG cry-PFV=ADV 1SG.POSS [offspring.PL] 1SG.POSS
põ'ra!"   tɨh no-ʔę̌ʔ=yɨ̨ʔ=mah,   yúp
[offspring.PL] 3SG say-PFV=ADV=REP DEM.ITG
ʔɨd-ham-döhö-yɨ̨ʔ-ay-áh.
say-go-transform-TEL-INCH-DECL

'Crying for her children, saying, "My children, my children!" so saying, she transformed (into a *bëbë* bird).'[26]

'Chorando pelos filhos, dizendo, "Meus filhos! meus filhos!" falando assim, ela se transformou (em pássaro *bëbë*).'

---

[26]This quoted speech combines two languages: the first word ('my') is in Hup, while the second word ('children') is in Tukano. As noted above, this multilingual quotation, together with the compound verb 'say-do-transform' indexes the mother's transformation via the act of crying, i.e. speaking the "language" of the *bëbë* bird.

(137) Ya'àpay nih s'ə̌h yúp ídɨwɨ́h.
 yaʔə̀p-ay=nih   s'ə̌h   yúp   ʔɨ́d-ɨw-ɨ́h.
 that.much-INCH=EMPH.CO DST.CNTR DEM.ITG speech-FLR-DECL
 'That's all there is to this tale.'
 'Tem só isso nessa fala.'

Acknowledgments

Epps expresses her gratitude to the Hup people of Taracua Igarapé and other communities of the Tiquié River for welcoming her into their homes and villages, and for their ongoing friendship and collaboration. This work was supported by funding from Fulbright-Hayes, National Science Foundation, and the Max Planck Institute for Evolutionary Anthropology. Epps also thanks CNPq and FUNAI for the permission to work in the Upper Rio Negro Region, and the Museo Paraense Emilio Goeldi, the Instituto Socioambiental, and FOIRN for practical support in Brazil. Thanks to Tony Woodbury for comments on the text, and to Kristine Stenzel and Bruna Franchetto for the invitation to participate in this volume.

Non-standard abbreviations

Several abbreviations in this list (EMPH, INFR, TAG) correspond to more than one morpheme; these cases are distinguished by numbers in the gloss lines (e.g. EMPH1, EMPH2)

AUG	augmentative	FRUS	frustrative
CNTR	contrast	HAB	habitual
CO	coordinator	INCH	inchoative
CPM	comparative	INFR	inferential evidential
DEP	dependent	INTERJ	interjection
DIM	diminutive	INTS	intensifier
DIR	directional	ITG	intangible
DST	distant (past)	NONVIS	nonvisual evidential
DYNM	dynamic	QTAG	question tag
EMPH	emphasis	REF	reflexive
EPIST	epistemic	REM	remote
EX	existential	REP	reported evidential
FACT	factitive	RESP	respect marker
FLR	filler	SEQ	sequential

TAG	discourse tag	VDIM	verbal diminutive
TEL	telic	VENT	venitive
UNDER	simultaneous/under		

References

Aikhenvald, Alexandra Y. 2002. *Language contact in Amazonia*. Oxford: Oxford University Press.

Cardoso, Walmir Thomazi. 2007. *O céu dos Tukano na Escola Yupuri: Construindo um calendário dinâmico*. PUC-SP dissertation.

Chernela, Janet. 1993. *The Wanano Indians of the Brazilian Amazon: A sense of space*. Austin: University of Texas Press.

Epps, Patience (ed.). 2005/2016. *Hupd'äh nɨh pinigd'äh: Stories of the Hupd'äh*. CreateSpace self-publishing.

Epps, Patience. 2007. The Vaupés melting pot: Tukanoan influence on Hup. In Alexandra Y. Aikhenvald & R. M. W. Dixon (eds.), *Grammars in contact: A cross-linguistic typology* (Explorations in linguistic typology 4), 267–289. Oxford: Oxford University Press.

Epps, Patience. 2008. *A grammar of Hup* (Mouton Grammar Library 43). Berlin: Mouton de Gruyter.

Epps, Patience. 2010. Linking valence change and modality: Diachronic evidence from Hup. *Diachronica* 76. 334–356.

Epps, Patience & Katherine Bolaños. 2017. Reconsidering the 'Makú' family of northwest Amazonia. *International Journal of American Linguistics* 83(3). 467–507.

Epps, Patience & Kristine Stenzel. 2013a. Introduction. In Patience Epps & Kristine Stenzel (eds.), *Upper Rio Negro: Cultural and linguistic interaction in northwestern Amazonia*, 13–50. Rio de Janeiro: Museu Nacional, Museu do Índio-FUNAI.

Epps, Patience & Kristine Stenzel (eds.). 2013b. *Upper Rio Negro. Cultural and linguistic interaction in northwestern Amazonia*. Rio de Janeiro: Museu do Índio/FUNAI. http://etnolinguistica.wdfiles.com/local--files/biblio%3Aepps-stenzel-2013/epps_stenzel_2013_upper_rio_negro.pdf.

Gomez-Imbert, Elsa. 1996. When animals become 'rounded' and 'feminine': Conceptual categories and linguistic classification in a multilingual setting. In John Gumperz & Stephen Levinson (eds.), *Rethinking linguistic relativity*, 438–469. Cambridge: Cambridge University Press.

Londoño Sulkin, Carlos D. 2005. Inhuman beings: Morality and perspectivism among Muinane people (Colombian Amazon). *Ethnos* 70. 7–30.

Oliveira, Melissa. 2010. *Astronomia Tukano.* Instituto Socioambiental (ed.). http://pib.socioambiental.org/pt/c/nobrasil-atual/modos-de-vida/astronomia-tukano.

Ramirez, Henri. 2006. *A língua dos Hupd'äh do alto Rio Negro: Dicionário e guia de conversação.* São Paulo: Associação Saúde Sem Limites.

Santos-Granero, Fernando. 2006. Vitalidades sensuais: Modos não corpóreos de sentir e conhecer na Amazônia indígena. *Revista de Antropología, São Paulo, USP* 49. 93–131.

Stenzel, Kristine. 2013. Contact and innovation in Vaupés possession-marking strategies. In Patience Epps & Kristine Stenzel (eds.), *Upper Rio Negro: Cultural and linguistic interaction in northwestern Amazonia,* 353–402. Rio de Janeiro: Museu Nacional, Museu do Índio-FUNAI.

Uzendoski, Michael. 2005. *The Napo Runa of Amazonian Ecuador.* Urbana: University of Illinois Press.

Vilaça, Aparecida. 2000. O que significa tornar-se outro? Xamanismo e contato interétnico na Amazônia. *Revista Brasileira de Ciencias Sociais* 15. 56–72.

Viveiros de Castro, Eduardo. 1998. Cosmological deixis and Amerindian perspectivism. Trans. by Elizabeth Ewart. *Journal of the Royal Anthropological Institute* 4. 469–488.

Chapter 8

Sakurabiat

Ana Vilacy Galucio
Museu Paraense Emílio Goeldi

Mercedes Guaratira Sakyrabiar

Manoel Ferreira Sakyrabiar

Rosalina Guaratira Sakyrabiar

Olimpio Ferreira Sakyrabiar

1 Introduction

This short narrative is a fragment of a mythological tale that describes the origin of maize and other crops, such as beans and manioc (yucca), among the Sakurabiat people. Sakurabiat is pronounced [sa'kɨrabiat]. In the orthographic convention for the language the grapheme <u> represents the hight central vowel [ɨ]. The Sakurabiat are very reduced in number. In the last survey done in 2016, there were only 65 people living in the Rio Mekens Indigenous Land.

The *Kõtkõra asisi* story is told by Mercedes Guaratira Sakyrabiar, one of the oldest speakers of Sakurabiat at the time of the recording. Sadly, she passed away in December of 2015. Mercedes's age was not known for certain, but she was believed to be more than 75 years old when she told this story in 2006. The story was recorded in audio as part of a long term project for the documentation and study of the Sakurabiat (Mekens) language, which had partial support from the Endangered Language Documentation Program, funded by the School of Oriental and African Studies (SOAS).

Transcription and analysis was done by Galucio with the assistance of Rosalina Guaratira Sakyrabiar, Mercedes's daughter, and the two brothers who have

been Galucio's main collaborators in the study of the Sakurabiat language: Manoel Ferreira Sakyrabiar, a very talented man and an enthusiast of the study of his language, who was brutally murdered in 2016, and his younger brother Olimpio Ferreira Sakyrabiar. All three are bilingual speakers of Sakurabiat and Portuguese.

This text is one of the 25 mythological tales, recounted by some of the most distinguished Sakurabiat elders, that appear in the book *Narrativas Tradicionais SAKURABIAT mayãp ebõ* (organized by Galucio 2006). Some of the illustrations used in that book, which were drawn by two Sakurabiat children at the time of publication, Lidia Sakyrabiar and Ozelio Sakyrabiar, are included here.

According to the account given in the narrative, the Sakurabiat were unfamiliar with maize and other edible crops until one day *Arik^{w}ajõ* discovered that *Kõtkõra*, a shaman from a neighboring group, had maize. *Arik^{w}ajõ* then went to visit that shaman and stole the seeds.

Figure 1: *Arik^{w}ajõ* following the black-fronted piping guan bird. Illustration by Lidia Sakyrabiar and Ozélio Sakyrabiar

Arik^{w}ajõ is the great mythological figure in Sakurabiat traditional stories. He is considered to be the great shaman with vast powers and wisdom. In the mythological narratives, he appears as the creator of many aspects of nature. For instance, he created the mountains and the valleys, and he had water and fire when no one else had them. He is also portrayed as the father of the sun, named *Kiakop* 'our warmth', and the moon, named *Pakori*, and the one responsible for sending them both away from earth as punishment for inappropriate social behavior. *Kiakop*, the sun, had set his sisters on fire, and *Pakori*, the moon, had tricked his sister into having an incestuous sexual relationship with him. In the present narrative *Arik^{w}ajõ* is married to his second wife, *Pãrãrẽkosa*.

The other main character in the narrative, *Kõtkõra*, which means 'cicada', is another mythological shaman, apparently from a distinct ethnic mythological group. *Kõtkõra*'s group had edible crops that *Arɨkʷajõ*'s people, the Sakurabiat, did not have.

The fragment of the story analyzed here focuses on how, after noticing that a black-fronted piping guan bird was defecating corn, *Arɨkʷajõ* followed the bird to find out where it was eating corn. When he discovered that it was at *Kõtkõra*'s village, he visited the other shaman's house with the intent to get corn for himself and his family. Thus, despite being well received by *Kõtkõra*, *Arɨkʷajõ* used his special powers to steal the seeds from *Kõtkõra*'s house. After bringing the crops to his village, and starting to make his food from maize and yucca, he changed his children's teeth, adapting them to their new condition of eating crops rather than stones. That is, since they no longer had to eat stones and wild seeds, they could have softer teeth, teeth that would fall out, eventually. The complete narrative recalls the first meeting of these two shamans and how both ended up having crops to eat. After *Arɨkʷajõ* was received in *Kõtkõra*'s house, he took seeds for his village, but did not destroy *Kõtkõra*'s fields. Thus, it is a mythological tale that touches upon relationships of hospitality and rivalry among neighbors.

Figure 2: The arrival at *Kõtkõra*'s house. Illustration by Lidia Sakyrabiar and Ozélio Sakyrabiar

The language of the Sakurabiat people has been traditionally referred to in the literature as "Mekens". In more recent years, it has also been referred to as Sakurabiat in an attempt to acknowledge the self denomination of the group, and we adopt this name in this work, to refer to the language, one of the five surviving languages of the Tuparian branch of the large Tupian family.

The Tupian family is composed of ten subfamilies (Rodrigues 1985), which include about 40-45 languages that are spread throughout the Amazon (Moore, Galucio & Gabas Júnior 2008). Alongside Sakurabiat, the other four languages of the Tuparian branch are: Akuntsú, Makurap, Tupari, and Wayoro. All five languages are spoken in the state of Rondônia, in the northwestern part of Brazil, near the Brazil-Bolivia border, and they are all highly endangered due to the greatly reduced number of speakers. According to information collected in 2016, from Galucio's field work and from colleagues working with these specific languages, Tupari has about 300 speakers, Makurap has about 55-60 speakers, Akuntsú only 4, and Wayoro just 3 speakers. Sakurabiat has about 16 speakers, and they are all adults.

Figure 3: The Rio Mekens Indigenous Land, where the Sakurabiat live in the Brazilian state of Rondônia, is shown in yellow.

It is noteworthy that the current state of Rondônia houses representatives of six of the ten Tupian subfamilies, including five that are spoken exclusively there: Arikém, Puruborá, Mondé, Ramarama, and Tupari. The other five subfamilies are Juruna, Munduruku, Mawé, Aweti, and Tupi-Guarani, which is the largest and most widespread of the Tupian subfamilies.

Sakurabiat is a typical Tupian language. It is a primarily suffixing language, but it also has a few prefixes, such as the pronominal person markers and valence changing morphemes (causative and intransitivizer). The language shows a head-marking profile, with locus of morphosyntactic marking on the head of the phrase. In clauses, the syntactic functions of subject and object are marked on the verb rather than on the nominal arguments. In simple transitive clauses with nominal arguments, both noun phrases tend to precede the verb, following basic SOV order. There are three types of lexical verbs: intransitive, transitive, and uninflectible or particle verbs. Transitive and intransitive verbs take person agreement and TAM inflectional markers. Only one argument is indexed on the verb by means of person prefixes. The intransitive verb indexes the subject and the transitive verb indexes the object. The particle verbs do not inflect in that way. In order to take person and TAM inflection, they undergo derivation via the verb formatives (-*ka*, -*kwa*, *e*-), which give as output transitive or intransitive verb stems.

Based on the distribution of the person markers, the morphosyntactic alignment can be described as nominative-absolutive in simple main clauses, as proposed for some Cariban and Northern Jê languages by Gildea & de Castro Alves (2010). The set of prefixes marks the absolutive argument (S/P), while the set of free pronouns expresses the nominative (A/S). In the case of transitive verbs, pronominal subjects obligatorily occur as free pronouns, except for third person, which can be left unmarked. With intransitive verbs, on the other hand, free pronouns are optionally used, co-occurring with the subject verb agreement markers. For its part, the O argument is never expressed by a free pronoun. For an overall description of Sakurabiat verb agreement and argument structure, see Galucio (2014).

Auxiliaries also show person agreement and TAM inflections. Person indexation on auxiliaries follows a nominative pattern, always indexing the clause subject (A or S). Auxiliaries and demonstratives are positional roots that indicate the body posture of the subject, in the case of auxiliaries, and of the referent, in the case of demonstratives. In addition to the positional demonstratives, there is a series of discourse anaphoric demonstratives or proforms that are used to replace a syntactic unit: they can replace a syntactic phrase, an entire clause, or even larger stretches of discourse.

Nominalization is the main strategy used to form adverbial (temporal, conditional, causal, and final) clauses in Sakurabiat (Galucio 2011). The adverbial modification is encoded by a nominalized verb form (with the nominalizer *-ap* 'instrumental; circumstantial') or one of the demonstrative proforms followed by a postposition. The ablative postposition *eri* is used for causal clauses, and the locative postposition *ese* for temporal/conditional and also some causal clauses.

Three dialects have been identified for Sakurabiat: Guaratira, which is the one spoken by the narrator of this story, Siokweriat, and Sakurabiat/Guarategayat. The major differences among them are phonological and lexical.

The *Kõtkõra asisi* story is transcribed phonetically in the first line, and segmented phonologically and morphologically in the second line. There is nasal harmony inside the word in Sakurabiat. Nasality spreads rightwards from a nasal consonant or vowel, and is blocked only by an obstruent in onset position. Thus, in the second line, only the underlying nasal element is indicated as being nasal. The third line gives a morpheme-by-morpheme gloss. English and Portuguese free translations are given in the fourth and fifth lines. The Portuguese translation attempts to maintain in as much as possible the structure of the original Sakurabiat narrative.

2 Kõtkõra asisi

'*Kõtkõra*'s corn' or 'The origin of maize and other crops among the Sakurabiat people'

'O milho do *Kõtkõra*' ou 'A origem do milho e outras plantas entre o povo Sakurabiat'[1]

(1) *Arɨkʷajõ asisi aapi ara sekoa kõnkõrã tegeri.*
    arɨkʷajõ asisi aapi   at-a   se-ko-a   kõtkõra tek=eri
    Arɨkʷajõ corn crop.seed get-THV 3COR-AUX.MOV-THV cicada house=ABL
    '*Arɨkʷajõ* got corn seed from *Kõtkõrã*'s house.'
    '*Arɨkʷajõ* arrumou semente de milho na casa da Cigarra.'

---

[1]Recordings of this story are available from https://zenodo.org/record/997447

(2) Kʷako sejẽrora ek piitse.

    kʷako   se-jẽt   ot-a   ek   pi=ese
    black-fronted.piping.guan 3COR-feces leave-THV house inside=LOC

    'The black-fronted piping guan bird[2] (that was around) defecated inside the house.'

    'Jacutinga (filhote de jacutinga que estava andando por lá) defecou dentro da casa.'

(3) Pɨ ke itoa[3] enɨɨtse.

    pɨ   ke   i-to-a   eni=ese
    lying DEM 3SG-AUX.LIE-THV hammock=LOC

    'He (Arɨkʷajõ) was there just lying in the hammock.'

    'E ele (Arɨkʷajõ) estava lá deitado na rede.'

(4) Sete itsoa ajẽẽri te kẽrã atsitsi ko?

    sete i-so-a   a-jẽ=eri   te   kẽrã   asisi ko
    3SG 3SG-see-THV Q-DEM.PROX=ABL FOC NASSERT corn ingest

    '(Then) he looked, (and thought): "Where does he (the bird) eat corn?"'

    'Aí ele olhou (e pensou): "Aonde será que ele come milho?"'

(5) Sitõm[4] nẽ pa õt, otagiat.

    s-itõp   ne   pa   õt   o-tag-iat
    3SG-follower COP FUT 1SG 1SG-daughter-COL

    'Then (he said to this daughters): "I will follow him, my daughters."'

    'Aí (falou pras filharadas): "Eu vou atrás dele, minhas filhas."'

---

[2] The black-fronted piping guan bird (*Aburria jacutinga*) is a large bird that is easily identified, since in almost all its area of occurrence it is the only cracid with a white spot on the wing. Its scientific name comes from *burria, aburri, aburria* = Colombian Amerindian onomatopoeic name for birds generally called *jacu*; and from Old Tupi *jacú* = Jacu, and *tinga* = white, in reference to the head, nape and wings of this bird that has feathers with white coloration (http://www.wikiaves.com.br/jacutinga).

[3] The third person singular prefix has two allomorphs: *i-* before consonant-initial stems; and *s-* before vowel-initial stems.

[4] *-itõp* is an adjective root that is reported by Sakurabiat speakers to mean something like 'the follower, the one that follows someone or something, the one that accompanies someone'.

(6) *Soa kot kaap⁵ te pekaat soa kot.*

    so-a   kot   kaap te pe=kaat so-a   kot
    see-THV IM.FUT QUOT FOC OBL=DEM see-THV IM.FUT

    '"I will look to see, I will look at that."'

    '"Eu vou atrás pra ver."'

(7) *Pia⁶ setoa õẽm te kʷako setset nẽãrã.*

    pia se-to-a   õẽp   te   kʷako
    wait 3COR-AUX.LIE-THV already FOC black-fronted.piping.guan
    se-set   neara
    3COR-leave again

    'He (*Arɨkʷajõ*) stayed there waiting for the black-fronted piping guan bird to come back.'

    'Ele (*Arɨkʷajõ*) ficou esperando esse jacu para poder ver a hora que ele ia de novo lá (comer).'

(8) *Atɨ⁷ sete sitõmnã tõpnã sekoa pɨbot Kõnkõrã taap.⁸*

    atɨ   sete s-itõp=na   tõp=na   se-ko-a   pɨbot
    INTJ 3SG 3SG-follower=VBLZ follower=VBLZ 3COR-AUX.MOV-THV arrive
    kõtkõra taap
    cicada   village

    'Poor guy, he followed him all the way until he arrived at *Kõtkõrã*'s (Cicada's) village.' (*Arɨkʷajõ* followed the bird all the way to *Kõtkõra*'s house)

    'Aí ele coitado acompanhou (o jacu), acompanhou, acompanhou até que chegou na casa da Cigarra.'

---

⁵There are two third person quotative forms: *kaap* and *kaat*. The quotative in combination with the immediate future morpheme *kot* derives a desiderative clause. Desideratives are grammaticalizing as future. The quotative form *kaat* is also homophonous to the demonstrative *kaat*, a proform that is used anaphorically to replace a stretch of discourse.

⁶*pia* 'wait' is the form in the Guaratira and Siokweriat dialects. It corresponds to *pisa* in the Sakurabiat dialect.

⁷*atɨ* is an interjection used as a negative exclamation expressing an emotional reaction, such as negative astonishment or bewilderment. It does not form a syntactic constituent to the rest of the sentence. It can be translated sometimes as 'pitied guy' or 'pitied thing'. It is used to cast doubt about the proposition that one considers to be unlikely or absurd. For instance, if someone says to you *osera kot ameko miapna* 'I'm going over there to kill a jaguar', you can respond with *atɨ nop* 'Poor you, no (you won't).'

⁸*taap* is a word that has several meanings, it could be translated as either 'village' or 'house', but it contrasts with the regular word for house, which is *ek*.

(9) *Kerep itegõ⁹ kõjẽ siko õpinã.*

    kerep i-tek=õ   kõjẽ s-iko   õp-pit=na
    enter 3SG-house=DAT sit   3SG-food give-NMLZ=VBLZ

    'He (Arik*ʷ*ajõ) entered the house, sat himself down, and was given food.'

    '(Arik*ʷ*ajõ) entrou na casa, sentou, aí começaram dar comida pra ele comer.'

(10) *Kõjẽ poget kop.*

    kõjẽ poget   kop
    sit standing AUX.MOV

    'He sat down, then got up, and stayed around there.'

    'Ele sentou, depois levantou, ficou por ali.'

(11) *Ma te kẽrã eke aose setserara, ke te Kõnkõrã tagiat.*

    ma   te   kẽra   eke   aose se-set-a-ra   ke   te   Kõtkõra
    when FOC NASSERT DEM.N man 3COR-leave-THV-REP DEM FOC cicada
    tak-iat
    daughter-COL

    '"When is that man leaving?" said Kõtkõrã's daughters.'

    '"É esse homem não vai não embora, não, será?" Assim que a filharada do Kõtkõra falou.'

(12) *Teeri ka aotse atsitsi 'ara nããn kop.*

    te-eri   ka   aose asisi 'at-a   naat kop
    3SG=ABL move man corn get-THV COP AUX.MOV

    'Through his mind, the man is carrying off the corn.' (Lit. 'It comes from him, the man is taking the corn.')

    'Ele no pensamento dele tá carregando milho.'

---

⁹The dative postposition has two allomorphs: õ after consonant-final stems; and bõ after vowel-final stems. This postposition has a meaning that is broader than the usual datives. It can express the indirect object, but also the instrumental, the general locative, and the temporal locative.

(13) *Tapsɨrõ i'ara atsitsibõ i'ara arakʷibõ i'ara komatabõ i'ara kaat naat kop aose.*

tapsɨt=bõ   i-'at-a   asisi=bõ   i-'at-a   arakʷi=bõ   i-'at-a
yucca=DAT 3SG-get-THV corn=DAT 3SG-get-THV peanut=DAT 3SG-get-THV
komata=bõ i-'at-a   kaat naat kop   aose
beans=DAT 3SG-get-THV DEM COP AUX.MOV man

'He got manioc, corn, peanuts, beans, he stayed there doing that (taking everything), the man (i.e., Arɨkʷajõ).'

'Levou mandioca, milho, amendoim, feijão, ficou carregando tudo, o homem.'

(14) *Poret õẽm 'arabetse set nẽãrã.*

poret õẽp   'ar-ap=ese   set   neara
now already get-NMLZ=LOC leave again

'Then, when he had already got it all, he left again.'

'Aí quando já tinha carregado tudo, ele foi embora de novo.'

(15) *Pɨbot nẽãrã setoabõ.*[10]

pɨbot neara se-top-ap=õ
arrive again 3COR-lying.down-NMLZ=DAT

'He arrived again at his own hammock.'

'E chegou na sua rede (na casa dele) novamente.'

(16) *Tamõ'ẽm porẽtsopega*[11] *petsetagiat:*

ta=bõ='ẽp   porẽsopeg-a pe=se-tak-iat
DEM.STAND=DAT=EMPH ask-THV   OBL=3COR-daughter-COL

'He just got there and asked his daughters:'

'Entrou, foi direto perguntar pra filharada dele:'

---

[10] The word *toap* 'hammock' is a derived noun, formed by the auxiliary root *top* 'AUX.LIE' plus the circumstantial nominalizer *-ap*; the final *-p* is deleted before the vowel *-a*: *top+ap* → *toap*.

[11] We have not been able to do a morphological analysis of the word *porẽsopega* 'ask', but it is clearly a complex word, where it is possible to identify the root *pek* 'call'. Monomorphemic words in Sakurabiat are usually shorter than four syllables.

(17) *Aeke te ejatsi?*

    a-eke   te   ejat-si
    Q-DEM.N FOC 2PL-mother

    '"Where is your mother?"'

    '"Para onde foi a mãe de vocês?"'

(18) *Osesi jãõmõ ka te ikãw taaga kɨt ara naat te kɨjkona taaga kɨt ara.*

    ose-si   jãõ=bõ   ka   te   ikão   taaga   kɨt
    1PL.EXCL-mother DEM.DIST=DAT move FOC DEM.TIME walking.palm seed
    at-a   naat te   kɨ-iko=na   taaga   kɨt   at-a
    get-THV COP FOC 1PL.INCL-food=VBLZ walking.palm seed get-THV

    '"Our mother went over there at that time to get walking palm's seed for us to eat, get walking palm's seed," (they replied).'[12]

    '"Nossa mãe foi por ali, buscar caroço de paxiúba pra nós comermos."'

(19) *Poret ejarora*[13] *ipegara taaga kɨt aratkʷa nõm pegat.*[14]

    poret ejat-ot-a   i-pek-a-ra   taaga   kɨt
    now 2PL-leave-THV 3SG-call--THV-REP walking.palm seed
    at-a-t-kʷa   nop pegat
    get-THV-PST-PL.EV NEG IRR.FUT

    '"Then, go call her, it is no longer necessary to bring walking palm seed" (Arɨkʷajõ told his daughters).'

    'Aí (Arɨkʷajõ disse:) "Vão chamar ela, não era pra trazer mais semente de paxiúba, não."'

(20) *Kiopap ta eba jẽ ẽma kaareri imãã ke te kɨape, kieba mõtkʷa ke te sɨraamnã.*[15]

    kɨ-opap   ta   eba jẽ   eba kaat=eri i-ma-a
    1PL.INCL-corn DEM.STAND EVID DEM.SIT EVID DEM=ABL 3SG-make-THV

---

[12] The walking palm tree (*Socratea exorrhiza*) is known as *paxiúba* in Brazil. Its seeds are not edible.

[13] Sakurabiat has two types of hortative constructions. The first type uses the special hortative verb *soga* following the lexical verb. The other type of hortative construction, illustrated in this example, uses the verb *ot* 'leave, go' prefixed by either first person plural or second person (plural) subject agreement, followed by the lexical verb.

[14] The irrealis future morpheme *pegat* seems to be a complex form that contains the morpheme *pek* 'FUT' plus an allomorph of the past tense morpheme -(*a*)*t*.

> ke   te   ki-ɨape   kieba mot-kʷa   ke   te   sɨraap=na
> DEM FOC 1PL.INCL-our.beverage tuber make-PL.EV   DEM FOC   massaco=VBLZ
>
> '"Our corn is here, make our beverage from it, and prepare the manioc to make (our) *massaco*."'[16]
>
> '"Nosso milho tá aqui pra fazer nossa chicha, e amassar macaxeira pra fazer massaco."'

(21) *Ikʷaksoa te itagiat sɨrɨk=nẽ'ẽp pɨbot.*

> i-kʷak-so-a   te   i-tak-iat   sɨrɨk=ne='ẽp   pɨbot
> 3SG-sound-see-THV   FOC 3SG-daughter-COL   go.PL.SBJ=?=EMPH   arrive
>
> 'They heard him, the daughters, then they left, went straight there and arrived (where their mother was).'
>
> 'Escutaram o que ele falou, as filhas. Aí saíram foram até lá (onde a mãe estava).'

(22) *Akʷa kɨp perek piora nããn kop.*

> akʷa   kɨp   perek piora   naat   kop
> cará[17] stick long   dig   COP   AUX.MOV
>
> 'She was digging for wild *cará* tubers.'[18]
>
> 'Ela estava cavando cará do mato.'

(23) *Abitop[19] epegarat, osi.*

> abi-top   e-pek-a-ra-t   o-si
> father-father   2SG-call-THV-REP-PST   1SG-mother
>
> '"Our father called you, mother."'
>
> '"Nosso pai te chamou, mamãe."'

---

[15] Two pieces of information are necessary here. First, the words *ma* and *mot(kwa)* are synonymous, both translate as 'make, prepare, build'. The root *mot* is generally used with the verb formative suffix *-kwa* that is also a marker of event plurality. Secondly, the noun *kieba* is a general word that can refer to any type of edible tuber, either manioc (yucca), sweet potato, *cará*, etc.

[16] *Massaco* is a Portuguese word used to describe a dish that is made with cooked banana or yucca, pounded with a pestle. This dish is very popular among the Sakurabiat.

[17] *akwa 'cará'* is a cultivated type of tuber. The wild, uncultivated *cará* is called *akwa kup perek* because is elongated (stick-like), unlike the cultivated one, which is more round.

[18] This sentence is translated in the past tense, to agree with the rest of the text. However, the auxiliary form *kop* is the present tense form; the past tense form would be *koa*.

[19] This form is the special vocative for father for female egos. It combines the vocative *abi* 'my father' for male egos, and the referential stem *-top* 'father'.

(24) *Kɨape mã ke te kiopaberi ita kaat ikãw.*

    ki-ɨape   ma   ke   te   ki-opap=eri   i-ta
    1PL.INCL-beverage make DEM FOC 1PL.INCL-corn=ABL 3SG-AUX.STAND
    kaat ikão
    QUOT DEM.TIME

    '"(Call her) to make our *chicha*[20] from our corn here, that (is what he) said at that time."'

    '"(Chama ela) pra fazer chicha pra nós, do nosso milho que tá aqui." Assim (ele disse) àquela hora.'

(25) *Kieba mõtkʷa sɨraapnã kaat ikãw.*

    kieba mot-kʷa   sɨraap=na   kaat ikão
    tuber make-PL.EV *massaco*=VBLZ QUOT DEM.TIME

    '"To prepare manioc to make *massaco*," that (is what he) said at that time.'

    '"Pra amassar macaxeira pra fazer massaco." Assim ele disse àquela hora.'

(26) *Erek tɨɨnã sitoabip etoabip tõen, ejattaɨbiat sara, aose igorerõp sete.*

    erek tɨɨ=na   s-itoabip   e-toabip   tõet ejat-taɨp-iat
    speak INTJ=COP 3SG-cultivated.field 2SG-cultivated.field DUB 2PL-son-COL
    sara   aose igot-e-rõp   sete
    pitied man possessor-?-NEG 3SG

    'She said: "Poor bastard, I doubt he has a crop. You poor children, he is a man who has nothing."' (Lit. 'She said: "Pitied one, I doubt his crop (exists). Poor people of your children, this man has nothing."')

    'Aí ela falou: "Esse coitado aí, plantação dele! Plantou nada! Coitados dos filhos de vocês, esse aí é homem que não tem nada."'

(27) *Arẽm sɨrɨk nẽãrã te itagiat.*

    arẽp sɨrɨk   neara te   i-tak-iat
    then go.PL.SBJ again FOC 3SG-daughter-COL

    'They went again, his daughters.'

    'Foram embora de novo, as filhas dele.'

---

[20] *Chicha* is a regional word in Brazilian Portuguese to refer to a fermented beverage. This beverage, which is very popular among several indigenous groups in Amazonia, can be made out of corn, yucca or any other kind of tuber.

(28) *Kaap tẽẽn te otsetsi.*

kaap tẽet te ose-si
DEM only FOC 1PL.EXCL-mother

'"Mom said just that." (And, thus, the daughters told their father what their mother had said.)'

'"Mamãe disse assim." (Assim as filhas contaram pro pai o que a mãe falara.)'

(29) *Ke ebõ te setaɨpkʷa paat te.*

ke ebõ te se-taɨp-kʷa paat te
DEM really FOC 3COR-get.calm-VBLZ FUT.3 FOC

'"It is like that now (she is angry at me), but she'll calm down."'

'"Só agorinha que tá assim (brava comigo), vai se amansar."'

(30) *Setoorekʷa mãjã ikoop sete.*

se-toorekʷa maj-a i-koop sete
3COR-laugh tell-THV 3SG-AUX.MOV 3SG

'"She is still going to laugh," he (said).' (That is what *Arɨkʷajõ* thought about his wife.)

'"Ela ainda vai dar risada." Ele disse.'

(31) *Pia setoa arẽm te aramĩrã 'ibat nẽãrã.*

pia se-to-a arẽp te aramira 'ip-a-t neara
wait 3COR-AUX.LIE-THV then FOC woman come-THV-PST again

'He stayed there waiting, then the woman came back again.'

'Ele ficou esperando, aí a mulher chegou de novo.'

(32) *Taibap sekẽrẽkʷa saraka te Pãrãrẽkotsa.*

taib-ap se-e-kẽrẽ-kʷa sara-ka te Pãrarekosa
gentle-NEG 3COR-INTRVZ-angry-VBLZ pitied-VBLZ FOC Pãrarekosa

'She was angry, poor *Pãrarekosa*.'

'Estava brava, coitada dela, a *Pãrarekosa*.'

(33) *Poget kop peropka pe akʷa kɨp perek*

poget   kop   perop-ka   pe=akʷa kɨp perek
standing AUX.MOV cooked-VBLZ OBL=*cará* stick long

'She stayed there, and then went to cook wild *cará* tubers.'

'Ficou por aí, e foi cozinhar cará do mato.'

(34) *Kaa kaat ebõ nã sekoa ɨmẽ.*

ko-a   kaat ebõ=na   se-ko-a   'ɨme
ingest-THV DEM really=VBLZ 3COR-AUX.MOV-THV dark

'She ate, and stayed there the way she was (angry), until it got dark.'

'Comeu, ficou por ali assim (brava mesmo), até que escureceu.'

(35) *Era kʷirik poret.*

et-a   kʷirik poret
sleep-THV clear now

'Then it dawned.'[21]

'Aí amanheceu.'

(36) *Ejarɨape kaabõpkʷa[22] kot.*

ejat-ɨape   kaabõp-kʷa   kot
2PL-beverage bless;heal-PL.EV IM.FUT

'(After that *Arɨkʷajõ* came and said to his children:) "I will cure your beverage."'

'(Aí *Arɨkʷajõ* veio e disse:) "Vou curar a chicha de vocês."'

(37) *Ko soga!*

ko   soga
ingest HORT

'"You can drink! Drink!"'

'"Pode beber! Bebe!"'

---

[21] *era kʷirik*, which literally means 'sleep and clear' is the expression used to announce that the day dawned, and also to count how many nights/days have passed, in an iterative way. Thus, to say something like 'two days after' one would say *era kʷirik era kʷirik*.

[22] The consultant that was helping with translation and morphemic analysis explained that the verb form should be *kaabõa*, not *kaabõp*, but he could not explain why. We chose to keep the form that was given by the narrator.

(38) *Ejatjãj sɨgɨka kotke²³ õn.*

ejat-jãj   sɨgɨ-ka   kot=ke=õt
2PL-tooth drop-VBLZ IM.FUT=QUOT=1SG

"'I am going to make your teeth fall out.'"

"'Eu vou fazer o dente de vocês cair tudo.'"

(39) *Kaabõ'ĕm sɨgɨ tejatjãj.*

kaap õ'ĕp   sɨgɨ   te-jat-jãj
DEM already drop 3SG-COL-tooth

'It happened really that way, their teeth fell out.'

'Fez mesmo, caiu todos os dentes delas.'

(40) *Pĕrãm te otagiat ejariko pek.*

pĕt-ap   te   o-tak-iat   e-jat-iko   pek
hard-NMLZ FOC 1SG-daughter-COL 2SG-COL-food FUT

"'It won't be hard, your food, my daughters.'" (This sentence continues the speech of *Arɨkʷajõ* to his children.)

"'Não vai ser duro, minhas filhas, a comida de vocês.'"

(41) *Kaanã'ĕp poret kap kapnã te kijãj pogeri poret.*

kaat=na='ĕp   poret ko-ap   ko-ap=na   te
DEM=VBLZ=EMPH now ingest-NMLZ ingest-NMLZ=VBLZ FOC
ki-jãj   poget=i   poret
1PL.INCL-tooth standing=AUX.PL now

'They stayed that way, our teeth, in order for us to eat.' (Lit. 'They became that way in order to be (our) eating instrument, our teeth stayed that way.')

'Ficou assim mesmo pra ser aquilo com que se come, os nossos dentes ficaram assim.'

---

[23] The first and second person desiderative construction is formed with a combination of the immediate future morpheme plus the quotative morpheme for first and second persons (*kot+ke* 'IM.FUT + QUOT'= DESIDERATIVE).

(42) *Kaannã²⁴ te te kijãj ipẽnnã kenõm.*

    kaat=na te te ki-jãj   i-pẽt=na   ke   nop
    DEM=VBLZ really FOC 1PL.INCL-tooth 3SG-hard=VBLZ DEM NEG

    'That's why our teeth are not hard,' (Lit. 'In being that way really, our teeth are not hard.')

    'Por isso que o nosso dente (de hoje em dia) nao é duro.'

(43) *Sesɨgɨka kʷaap tẽẽn.*

    se-sɨgɨ-ka   kʷaap tẽet
    3COR-drop-VBLZ HAB   only

    'They just drop out (and grow again).'

    'Só cai (e nasce de novo).'

(44) *Kɨrɨt sĩit jãj etsɨgɨka.*

    kɨrɨt sĩit jãj   e-sɨgɨ-ka
    child DIM tooth INTRVZ-drop-VBLZ

    '(That's why) kids' teeth drop out.'

    '(Por isso que agora) dente de criança cai tudo.'

(45) *Kekʷaap nããm²⁵ tẽẽn.*

    Ke   kʷaap=na-ap   tẽet
    DEM HAB=VBLZ-NMLZ only

    'It is always just that way.' ('The cycle keeps repeating itself, it is always like that.')

    'É todo tempo só assim.'

(46) *ke te kijãj.*

    ke   te   ki-jãj
    DEM FOC 1PL.INCL-tooth

    'That's how our teeth are.'

    'É assim nosso dente.'

---

[24] One of the morphosyntactic strategies to express causal adverbial clauses in Sakurabiat is to use a derived verb phrase formed by the anaphoric demonstrative *kaat* with the verbalizer *nã* (see Galucio (2011), for a thorough discussion of adverbial clauses in Sakurabiat.)

[25] It is possible to delete the nominalizer morpheme *-ap*, with no apparent change in meaning. The consultant said that another way of saying the same thing was *kekwaapnã tẽet*.

(47) Kaabese nããn aapi õtsop te atsitsi.

kaap=ese naat aapi õ-sop te asisi
DEM=LOC COP crop.seed CAUS-see FOC corn

'That is how (they) found corn seed.'

'Foi assim que acharam semente de milho.'

(48) Kʷeet piro kiiko pek kĩrẽp.

kʷeet piro ki-i-ko pek kĩrep
thing exist 1PL.INCL-OBJ.NMLZ-ingest FUT now

'And that's how it appeared the things that we eat.'

'Assim que apareceram as coisas de comer.'

(49) Kaap te eba nããriat.

kaap te eba naat=iat
DEM FOC EVID COP=REM.PST

'(But) that's how it was at those times.'

'Mas era assim antigamente.'

(50) Kõnkõrãrõpnã arobõ te atsitsi nããn eteet.

kõtkõra-rop=na arop-õ te asisi naat eteet
cicada-NEG=VBLZ thing-NEG FOC corn COP HYP

'If it were not for *Kõtkõra*, there would be nothing, no corn. (All edible things were first planted by *Kõtkõra*, who was also a shaman).'

'Se não fosse *Kõtkõra*, não tinha nada, não tinha milho, não. (Tudo foi *Kõtkõra* quem plantou, ele era *kwamoa* ('pajé') também.)'

(51) Asisirõp.

asisi-rõp
corn-NEG

'(There would be) no corn.'

'Não tinha milho.'

(52) Arobõ te piro tapsɨt akʷa kʷaako piroap.

arop-õ te piro tapsɨt akʷa kʷaako piro-ap
thing-NEG FOC exist yucca cará sweet.potato exist-NEG

'There wouldn't be anything, no yucca, no *cará* tuber, no sweet potato.'

'Não tinha nada, nem mandioca, nem cará, nem batata, não tinha nada.'

(53) Arɨkʷajõ ekap sigot nẽnõã.

arɨkʷajõ ekap s-igot ne=no-a
Arɨkʷajõ SBJV 3SG-possessor COP=NEG-THV

'If it were up to Arɨkʷajõ, he wouldn't own anything.'

'Arɨkʷajõ não tinha nada.'

(54) Sigot tɨɨɨ nẽnõã.

s-igot tɨɨ ne=no-a
3SG-possessor INTJ COP=NEG-THV

'He possessed nothing.'

'Ele não tinha nada, não.'

(55) Kʷai mariko kɨpkɨba 'a mariko[26] sete.

kʷai mat i-ko kɨpkɨba 'a mat i-ko sete
stone ? OBJ.NMLZ-ingest tree fruit ? OBJ.NMLZ-ingest 3SG

'He only eats stone and fruit (as if he were not human).' (Lit. 'Stone is what he eats, and fruit is what he eats.')

'Comida dele é pedra, é fruta de pau (como se não fosse gente).'

(56) Aose eteet.

aose eteet
man HYP

'If it were not for this man (Kõtkõrã), (there would be nothing.)'

'Se não fosse esse homem (Kõtkõra), (não teria nada mesmo, não.)'

(57) Õẽm.

õẽp
already

'It's finished.'

'Acabei.'

---

[26] The expression N mariko is used when you want to refer to something that is someone's preferred choice of food. For instance, Kwe mariko õrõn. 'I only like to eat game meat.'/ 'I only eat game meat.' (kwe 'game meat' – mat (?) – i-ko 'OBJ.NMLZ-ingest' – õr-õn 1SG-EMPH).

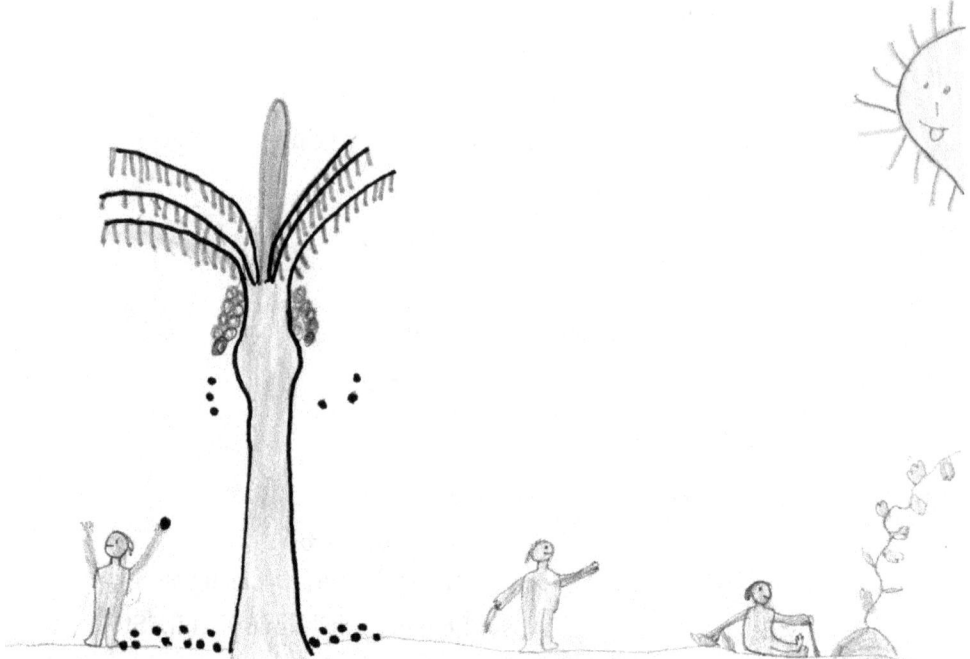

Figure 4: The old and the newly acquired crops. Illustration by Lidia Sakyrabiar and Ozélio Sakyrabiar

Acknowledgments

Galucio would like to acknowledge the continued support of the Sakurabiat people, especially the elders who shared the wonders of their traditional narratives, and her collaborators in this article. A special token of gratitude goes to the late Mercedes Guaratira Sakyrabiar and Manoel Ferreira Sakyrabiar, *in memoriam*. Manoel was a very good friend, and an enthusiast and great supporter of the study of Sakurabiat. Dona Mercedes was not only a supporter but also a grandmother figure in all the visits to the Sakurabiat village. They are both greatly missed. We thank Ana Carolina Alves for helping with the audio files, Ellison Santos for helping with the figures, and Hein van der Voort for facilitating permission of the map. The present work was carried out with the support of CNPq, the National Council of Scientific and Technological Development, Brazil (Process number 308286/2016-2).

Non-standard abbreviations

COL	collective	IM	immediate
COR	co-referential	INTRVZ	intransitivizer
DUB	dubitative	LIE	lying
DEM.TIME	temporal demonstrative	MOV	moving
EMPH	emphatic	NASSERT	non-assertive
EV	event	REP	repetitive
EVID	evidential	SIT	sitting
HAB	habitual	STAND	standing
HORT	hortative	THV	thematic vowel
HYP	hypothetical	VBZL	verbalizer

References

Galucio, Ana Vilacy. 2011. Subordinate adverbial constructions in Mekens. In Rik van Gijn, Katharina Haude & Pieter Muysken (eds.), *Subordination in native South American languages*, 25–44. Amsterdam/Philadephia: John Benjamins Publishing Company.

Galucio, Ana Vilacy. 2014. Estrutura argumental e alinhamento gramatical em Mekens. In Luciana Storto, Bruna Franchetto & Suzi Oliveira de Lima (eds.), *Sintaxe e semântica do verbo em línguas indígenas no Brasil*, 167–196. Campinas: Mercado de Letras.

Gildea, Spike & Flávia de Castro Alves. 2010. Nominative-absolutive: Counter-universal split ergativity in Jê and Cariban. In Spike Gildea & Francesc Queixalós (eds.), *Ergativity in Amazonia* (Typological Studies in Language 89), 159–200. Amsterdam: John Benjamins.

Moore, Denny, Ana Vilacy Galucio & Nílson Gabas Júnior. 2008. O desafio de documentar e preservar as línguas amazônicas. *Scientific American (Brasil)* 3. 36–43.

Rodrigues, Aryon Dall'lgna. 1985. Relações internas na família lingüística Tupi-Guarani. *Revista de Antropologia* 27/28. 33–53.

Part III

Ancestors and tricksters

Chapter 9

Kĩsêdjê

Rafael Nonato
UMass Amherst, USA

Kujusi Suyá

Jamthô Suyá

Kawiri Suyá

1 Introduction

In this narrative, an ancestor of the Kĩsêdjê goes hunting and kills a monkey up in a tree. He climbs up the tree to fetch it and when he comes down, the monster *Khátpy* is already waiting for him. *Khátpy* hits him unconscious and puts him in a basket to carry home and feed to his hungry children. Stopping mid-way to open a trail in the forest, *Khátpy* leaves the basket on the ground unattended. When he finishes cutting part of the trail open, he comes back, fetches the basket and carries it up to the end of the trail. He repeats this process a few times until the Kĩsêdjê ancestor wakes up and realizes what is happening. The ancestor quietly waits for the monster to leave the basket unattended again and counts the time it takes for the monster to come back. *Khátpy* comes back, fetches the basket and carries it up to the end of the trail. He then leaves the basked unattended once more to continue opening the trail. The ancestor then comes out of the basket but, before running away, he fills it with rocks so the monster won't realize he has escaped. Though *Khátpy* feels that the basket has become heavier, he still carries it home without checking its contents. When he arrives home, his wives tell him there are only rocks and a few monkeys in the basket, but none of the big prey *Khátpy* claims he's killed. Enraged, *Khátpy* fetches his club and goes back into the forest after the Kĩsêdjê ancestor. That is when the story ends, with the narrator excusing himself for only knowing what happened up to that point. That is how his father told him this story, how his people tell it. The title of the story, the expression the Kĩsêdjê use to refer to it, is basically a summary of how it begins, turned into a headless relative clause:

(1) Khátpy re wapãmjê thõ thurun tho thẽm nda
  [Khátpy=re wa-pãm-jê=thõ   thu-ru=n   t⟨h⟩o
   K.=ERG   1INCL-father-PL=one load.on.back-NMLZ=&.SS ⟨3⟩with
   ∅-thẽ-m]=nda
   3-go-NMLZ =DEF

'The one (story) in which the Khátpy monster loads a forefather of ours onto his back and carries him away'

1.1 The circumstances of the narration

This story was narrated by Kuiussi Suyá, the chief of the Kĩsêdjê. He is recognized in the community as a great storyteller and knower of their traditions. He told it from his hammock, in his house at the *Ngôjhwêrê* village, on December 5th 2009. It was recorded by Rafael Nonato as part of PRODOCLIN–Kĩsêdjê,[1] a documentation project for the Kĩsêdjê language sponsored by the Museu do Índio.[2] This narrative was transcribed and translated by Jamthô Suyá, and was interlinearized by Rafael Nonato with assistance from Jamthô Suyá and Kawiri Suyá. It had also been previously adapted into a short film.[3]

1.2 The Kĩsêdjê people

The Kĩsêdjê are roughly 450 people, most of whom live in the Wawi Indigenous Land, in the State of Mato Grosso, Brazil. The largest Kĩsêdjê village, named *Ngôjhwêrê*, 'the origin of the water', is located near the southern borders of this land at 11°51′53″ S; 52°54′02″ W.[4] The Wawi Indigenous Land is situated in the southern fringes of the Amazon forest, encompassing most of the basin of the Suyá river, a western tributary of the Xingu river, itself a southeast tributary of the Amazon.

---

[1] http://prodoclin.museudoindio.gov.br/index.php/etnias/kisedje
[2] The "Museum of Indigenous Peoples", located in Rio de Janeiro is an organ of FUNAI, the Brazilian Bureau of Indigenous Affairs.
[3] At the time of writing, the short could be accessed at https://www.youtube.com/watch?v=wmtwNxYCUvo.

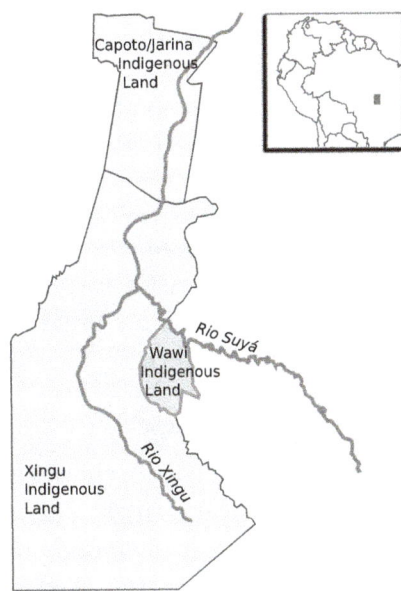

Figure 1: The Wawi Indigenous Land.

The Wawi Indigenous Land is contiguous to and located to the east of the Xingu Indigenous Park, where the Kĩsêdjê used to live until the recent official recognition of their own land. They arrived in the region of the Xingu basin in the latter part of the 19th century and have since forged an intricate history of alliances, wars, and exchanges of technology with the peoples that inhabited the region prior to their arrival.

The Kĩsêdjê used to be known by the exonym "Suyá", after the river whose basin they inhabit. This name was given to the river by another people, possibly the Trumai, and the Kĩsêdjê dislike the term, and ask the researchers that work with them to avoid using it. Their autodenomination, "Kĩsêdjê" (2), makes reference to the traditional technique they employ to create village sites, namely, burning a patch of forest into a circular clearing, on the rims of which they then proceed to build their houses.

(2) Kĩsêdjê

 kĩ sêt-∅ jê
 village burn-NMLZ PL
 'The ones who burn villages'

---

[4]https://goo.gl/maps/i7kyoGZAb6L2

1.3 The Kĩsêdjê language

The Kĩsêdjê speak a Northern Jê language (Jê family, Macro-Jê stock). Similar to other Northern Jê languages, Kĩsêdjê is strictly head-final, with the exception of a single head, to be mentioned below.

The main verb is always clause-final. In the neutral order, verbs are immediately preceded by their direct argument, whether it be a noun phrase or a verb phrase. Any postpositional phrase that is also argumental must come immediately before the direct argument, and these are preceded by any adjunct postpositional phrases and/or adverbs.[5] The subject comes before all the constituents mentioned above.[6]

The only exception to the pervasive head-final character of the language are the TAM particles. They are obligatory in main clauses and ungrammatical in embedded clauses. Main clauses must bear a single TAM particle, either in initial[7] or in second position. When they appear in second position, the TAM particles must be preceded by a dislocated constituent marked for topic or focus interpretation.[8]

(3) *Word-order in the clausal domain*

   (Foc/Top) [Mood/Tense [S (Adjuncts) (PP Args) [(DO) V]]]

Note that when they are in initial position, the *factual future* and the *factual non-future* TAM particles can be deleted. The contexts for their deletion are in almost perfect complementary distribution, though, and for that reason their meaning can usually be recovered. The factual future particle can be deleted when it precedes a nominative participant pronoun, whereas the factual non-future particle cannot be deleted precisely when it precedes a nominative participant pronoun. Both can be deleted when the subject is phrasal, though. In narrative style, deletion of the factual non-future particle is very pervasive, as we can notice in the narrative to be presented below.

Consistent with Kĩsêdjê's head-finality, postpositions follow their arguments, possessed nouns follow their possessors and nominal determiners follow the nouns they modify.[9] There are no nominal categories that express amount (nu-

---

[5] (11) exemplifies the order *adjunct PP + direct object + verb*. (26) exemplifies the order *adjunct PP + argument PP + verb*. The text doesn't contain any sentences that exemplify the order *adjunct PP + argument PP + direct object + verb*.
[6] (37) exemplifies the order *subject + adjunct PP + direct argument*.
[7] (81) and (94) exemplify TAM particles in initial position.
[8] (93) and (110) exemplify TAM particles in second position.
[9] (9) exemplifies the order *noun + determiner*.

merals) or quality (adjectives). The amount and quality of a noun are expressed verbally,[10] often through relative clauses, which in Kĩsêdjê are internally headed.[11]

(4) *Word-order in the sub-clausal domain*
    [[(Possessor) Noun] (Det)] (P)

Kĩsêdjê is a strictly dependent-marking language, with a single phenomenon reminiscent of agreement: when a direct argument is dislocated (either to the first position, for topic/focus purposes, or to a position preceding the adjuncts it normally follows, for less clear discourse reasons), a resumptive pronoun obligatory marks its base position.[12] A nominative-accusative frame is found in main clauses and an ergative-absolutive frame in embedded clauses.[13] Most verbs show two distinct forms: a morphologically simpler one used in main clauses and a derived (nominalized) one used in embedded clauses.[14] Case on noun phrases is marked by phrasal enclitics, with distinct ergative and nominative forms. Noun phrases in the absolutive and accusative cases are unmarked. As for the pronouns, their ergative forms are free accented words, their nominative forms are phonological clitics and their accusative and absolutive forms are prefixes. Only 3rd person pronouns have distinct accusative and absolutive forms, and only in certain restricted environments. Santos (1997) and Nonato (2014) give more detailed descriptions of the language.

---

[10] (64) exemplifies the order *noun + determiner + amount-denoting verb*.
[11] (40) and (90) exemplify internally headed relative clauses. The head of the former is *hry* 'trail' and the head of the latter is *khukwâj* 'monkey'.
[12] (64) and (110) exemplify this phenomenon.
[13] (16) exemplifies an intransitive main verb with nominative subject and (38) exemplifies a transitive main verb with nominative subject and accusative object. (29) exemplifies a transitive embedded verb with ergative subject and (99) exemplifies intransitive embedded verbs with absolutive subjects, as well as the use of ergative pronouns to double the subject of intransitive embedded verbs.
[14] (99) exemplifies many different nominalizing suffixes.

2 Khátpy re wapãmjê thõ thurun tho thẽm nda

'When the *Khátpy* monster loaded our forefather onto his back and carried him away'

'Quando o monstro *Khátpy* botou nosso ancestral nas costas e levou embora'[15]

(5) *Ne nhy ne.*
   ne=nhy   ne
   be.so[16]=&.DS[17] be.so
   'Then it was like this.'
   'Aí foi assim.'

(6) *Ajipãmjê thõ ra, ajipãmjê ra,*
   aj-i-pãm-jê=thõ=ra   aj-i-pãm-jê=ra
   PL[18]-1-father-PL=one=NOM PL-1-father-PL=NOM
   'A forefather of ours, our forefathers,'
   'Um dos nossos antepassados, nossos antepassados,'

(7) *khajkhwa khrat mã, khajkhwa khrat mã...*
   khajkhwa khrat=mã   khajkhwa khrat=mã
   sky   beginning=to sky   beginning=to
   'towards the east, towards the east ...'
   'na direção do leste, na direção do leste ...'

---

[15] Recordings of this story are available from https://zenodo.org/record/997437

[16] The verb *ne* can be translated as 'to do so' or as 'to be so'. Each occurrence will be glossed in the most appropriate way.

[17] The form of the Kĩsêdjê coordinating conjunction marks a number of distinctions. The most salient is the distinction, labeled "switch-reference marking" by Jacobsen (1967), between the coordination of clauses with the same subject (SS) and that of clauses with different subjects (DS). Moreover, in certain syntactic contexts, the DS conjunction has distinct forms indicating agreement with the subject of the next clause. If that subject is of the third person, the DS conjunction also marks tense.

[18] Though Kĩsêdjê makes a distinction between inclusive and exclusive first person plural, there is no specialized first person exclusive morphology. There is specialized morphology used to mark first person plural *inclusive* (as in (19)), while the simple pluralization of first person results in the exclusive interpretation. The latter is the form employed in this sentence, since the narrator is telling this story to a non-Kĩsêdjê person.

(8) *tê, khajkhwajndo mã khátpy ra khatxi kumẽn nhy ajipãmjê ra sarẽn ndo pa.*

    tê   khajkhwa=jndo=mã kátpy=ra   khatxi   kumẽn=nhy
    oops sky=end=to   monster=NOM be.numerous be.intense=&.DS
    aj-i-pãm-jê=ra   s-arẽ-n=ndo   pa
    PL-1-father-PL=NOM 3-talk.about-NMLZ=with stay.PL

'I mean, towards the west there were many *khátpy* monsters and our forefathers always told us so.'

'Quero dizer, na direção do oeste tinha muitos monstros *khátpy* e nossos antepassados sempre contavam isso.'

(9) *Nenhy ajipãmjê thõ ra pá khôt thẽ.*

    ne=nhy   aj-i-pãm-jê=thõ=ra   pá   khôt   thẽ
    be.so=&.DS PL-1-father-PL=one=NOM forest along go.SG

'And so one of our forefathers went hunting in the forest.'

'E então um dos nossos antepassados foi caçar na floresta.'

(10) *Pá khôt thẽ... pá khôt thẽn jowi,*

    pá=khôt   thẽ-...[19]   pá=khôt   thẽ=n   jowi
    forest=along go.SG-INTS forest=along go.SG=&.SS as.they.say

'He was in the forest for a while, he was in the forest and then, as they say,'

'Ele ficou na floresta bastante tempo, ele estava na floresta e dizem que,'

(11) *khyj wê khukwâj sak nhy jêt.*

    khyj=wê   khukwâj sak=nhy   jêt
    above=from monkey pierce=&.DS hang.SG

'he shot a monkey with an arrow and the monkey got stuck up there.'

'ele flexou um macaco e o macaco ficou preso lá em cima.'

(12) *Khukwâj sak nhy jêt nhy*

    khukwâj sak=nhy   jêt=nhy
    monkey pierce=&.DS hang.SG=&.DS

'He shot the monkey with an arrow, it got stuck and'

'Ele flexou o macaco, ele ficou preso e'

---

[19] Suspension points are used thorough the text to indicate phonological lengthening. In English or Portuguese, lengthening doesn't always serve the same function as it does in Kĩsêdjê. In particular, in Kĩsêdjê, verb lengthening can indicate an intensification or prolongation of the action depicted by the verb. Whenever that is the case, I add an appropriate adverbial to the free translation.

(13) swârâ apin, swârâ apin kukwâj me nhy thẽn "ty"... ne nhy

Ø-swârâ   api=n   Ø-swârâ   api=n   kukwâj
3-towards climb.up=&.ss 3-towards climb.up=&.ss   monkey
me=nhy   thẽ=n   ty   ne=nhy
throw.SG[20]=&.DS go.SG=&.SS ONTP:falling be.so=&.DS

'he climbed up after the monkey, pushed it, and then the monkey went and "ty"... and then'

'ele subiu atrás do macaco, empurrou e aí o macaco foi e "ty"... e aí'

(14) arâ kátpy ra jáwi arâ sahwan tho ta.

arâ   kátpy=ra   jáwi   arâ   s-ahwa=n   t<h>o   ta
already monster=NOM as.they.say   already 3-wait=&.ss <3>[21]at stand.SG

'as they say, the khátpy monster was already waiting for him, was standing underneath him.'

'como dizem, o monstro khátpy já estava esperando por ele, estava esperando embaixo dele.'

(15) Sahwan tho ta nhy

s-ahwa=n   t<h>o ta=nhy
3-wait=&.ss <3>at stand.SG=&.DS

'He was waiting for him, was underneath him and then'

'Ele estava esperando ele, estava debaixo dele e aí'

(16) khukwâj me ne nen, akwyn rwâk mã thẽ, tên... khátpy ra arâ hwaj wê ta.

khukwâj me=ne   ne=n   akwyn rwâ-k=mã   thẽ
monkey throw.SG=&.ss   do.so=&.ss back climb.down-NMLZ=to   go.SG
tên   khátpy=ra   arâ   Ø-hwaj=wê   ta
unexpectedly   monster=NOM already 3-feet=from   stand.SG

'he (the forefather) had thrown the monkey and so was climbing back down, but to his surprise the khátpy monster was already standing under him.'

---

[20] Verbal number in Kĩsêdjê is indicated by suppletive forms. Not all verbs distinguish between a singular and a plural form, but many of the high-frequency verbs do. The plural form indicates either that the absolutive argument (intransitive subject or transitive object) is numerous (usually 3 or more) or that the event depicted by the verb is somehow extended.

[21] Many heads that begin with an unaspirated 't' or 'k' mark agreement with third person through aspiration of their initial consonant.

'ele (o antepassado) tinha jogado o macaco e estava descendo de volta, mas para a sua surpresa o monstro *khátpy* já estava esperando embaixo dele.'

(17) *"Tuu... wâtân tã khupẽ kasák, khupẽ kasák ta ikhôt thẽ?"*

tuu   wâtâ=n   tã   khupẽ   kasák   khupẽ   kasák=ta   i-khôt
damn what=NFUT though foreigner be.evil foreigner be.evil=NOM 1-along
thẽ
go.SG

"'Damn! Why did the evil foreigner follow me, though?'"
"'Droga! Mas então por que o estrangeiro malvado me seguiu?'"

(18) *Pá txi, pá txi, wet khôt athẽm wa itôra nhimbry jawê ithẽm na thã!*

pá   txi   pá   txi   [22 wet   khôt   a-thẽ-m=wa
forest be.big forest be.big   other along 2-go.SG-NMLZ=&.DS.1
i-tôra   nhimbry j-awê   i-thẽ-m   ]=na thã
1-differently game   E-after 1-go.SG-NMLZ =NFUT INTJ:surprise

"'The forest is big, the forest is big, you should have gone to a part of it and I should have gone to a different part after my game!'"
"'A floresta é grande, a floresta é grande, você devia ter ido para uma parte dela e eu devia ter ido para uma outra parte atrás da minha caça!'"

(19) *Wapãmjê thõ ra swârâ rwâk mã thẽ.*

wa-pãm-jê=thõ=ra   Ø-swârâ   rwâ-k=mã   thẽ
1INCL²³-father-PL=one=NOM 3-towards climb.down-NMLZ=to go.SG

'Our forefather came climbing down.'
'Nosso antepassado veio descendo.'

(20) *Swârâ rwâk mã thẽn... thât rwâk mã thẽ nhy khuthã khura.*

Ø-swârâ   rwâ-k=mã   thẽ=n   thât   rwâ-k=mã
3-towards climb.down-NMLZ=to go.SG=&.SS though climb.down-NMLZ=to

---

[22] When I consider it relevant for understanding the structure of the sentence, I indicate the boundaries of an embedded clause with square brackets.

[23] The narrator seems to have slipped into first inclusive forms, in spite of the fact that he's narrating this story to a non-Kĩsêdjê person. Since he usually tells this narrative to other Kĩsêdjê people, these are probably the forms he's used to employing, and doing otherwise may require conscious effort.

thẽ=nhy   k<h>uthã   k<h>ura
go.SG=&.DS <3>before <3>hit

'Came climbing down towards him... He was going to finish coming down, but he (the *khátpy* monster) hit him before he did so.'
'Veio descendo para perto dele... Ele ia terminar de descer, mas ele (o monstro *khátpy*) bateu nele antes dele acabar.'

(21) *Khuthã khura nhy thẽn "ty" nen thãm ne no.*

k<h>uthã   k<h>ura=nhy   thẽ=n   ty   ne=n
<3>before   <3>hit=&.DS   go.SG=&.SS ONTP:falling do.so=&.SS
thãm=ne   no
fall.down.SG=&.SS   lie.down.SG

'He (the *khátpy* monster) hit him before he did so, he (the forefather) went and "*ty*", and so he fell and lay there.'
'Ele (o monstro *khátpy*) bateu nele antes dele acabar (de descer), ele (o antepassado) foi e "*ty*", e assim foi que ele caiu e ficou deitado.'

(22) *Thẽn thãm nhy:*

thẽ=n   thãm=nhy
go.SG=&.SS   fall.down.SG=&.DS

'He went and fell, and he (the *khátpy* monster):'
'Ele foi e caiu, e ele (o monstro *khátpy*):'

(23) *"Haha... hahaa hwararo ikhrajê re samdep khãm sãm ndo sambak nhy ire ngrytxi pĩrĩ wyrák thã."*

haha   hahaa   [hwararo   i-khra-jê=re
INTJ:satisfaction INTJ:satisfaction yesterday   1-child-PL=ERG
s-amdep-Ø   khãm   s-ã-m=ndo
3-be.hungry-NMLZ   in   3-be.standing.SG-NMLZ=with
s-amba-k=nhy   ire   ngry-txi   pĩ-rĩ   ] wyrák thã
3-mind-NMLZ=&.DS   1.ERG beast-big   kill.SG[24]-NMLZ happen.indeed

'"That's good, that's good. Yesterday my children were hungry all day long and today I have killed a big beast indeed."'
'"Isso é bom, isso é bom. Ontem minhas crianças ficaram com fome o dia inteiro e hoje eu matei um animal grande mesmo."'

---

[24] The verb *pĩ* actually means 'to wound unconscious'. For simplicity, I gloss it as 'kill'.

(24) *Nen khatyp khôsátxi nhihwêt ne thore khãm sarõn ne khutá.*

ne=n   Ø-khatyp khôsátxi nh-ihwêt=ne thore Ø-khãm s-arõn=ne
do.so=&.ss 3-for   basket   E-make=&.ss then 3-in   3-fold=&.ss
khu-tá
3-put.inside.SG

'He did (said) so, made a basket for him (the ancestor), and then he (the monster) folded him and put him inside.'
'Ele fez (disse) assim, fez um cesto para ele (o ancestral), e então ele (o monstro) dobrou e colocou ele dentro.'

(25) *Thore sĩpy khukwâj ngrên hwan nen arêkmã khuthun tho mo.*

thore s-ĩpy   khukwâj ngrê-n   hwa=n   ne=n
then 3-on.top monkey put.inside.PL-NMLZ finish=&.ss be.so=&.ss
arêkmã khu-thu=n   t<h>o   mo
soon   3-load.on.back=&.ss <3>with go.PL

'Then he finished putting the monkeys inside on top of him, and this way he loaded it onto his back and carried it far away.'
'Então ele acobu de botar os macacos em cima dele, e dessa forma ele botou nas costas e foi carregando lá para longe.'

(26) *Khwã hry ro thẽn... sĩthep ne, khwã hry ro thẽn sĩthep ne,*

kh-wã hry ro   thẽ=n-...   s-ĩthep=ne kh-wã hry ro   thẽ=n
3-to   trail with go.SG=&.ss-INTS 3-stop=&.ss 3-to   trail with go.SG=&.ss
s-ĩthep=ne
3-stop=&.ss

'He would be opening the trail for a while and then stop, would be opening the trail and then stop,'
'Ele ia abrindo a trilha por um tempo e então parava, ia abrindo a trilha e então parava,'

(27) *khwã hwĩ khrakhrak to thẽn khwã hry ro thẽn hwĩ khrakhrak to thẽn sĩthep ne,*

kh-wã hwĩ   khrakhrak to   thẽ=n   kh-wã hry ro   thẽ=n
3-to   branch break   with go.SG=&.ss 3-to   trail with go.SG=&.ss
hwĩ   khrakhrak to   thẽ=n   s-ĩthep=ne
branch break   with go.SG=&.ss 3-stop=&.ss

'he was breaking branches, opening a trail, breaking branches and then he stopped,'

'ele estava quebrando galhos, abrindo uma trilha, quebrando galhos então ele parou,'

(28) *akwyn thẽn khuthun, khuthun tho mo.*

akwyn thẽ=n   khu-thu=n   khu-thu=n   t<h>o
back   go.SG=&.SS 3-load.on.back=&.SS 3-load.on.back=&.SS <3>with
mo
go.PL

'came back and loaded it onto his back, loaded it onto his back and carried it far away.'
'voltou e botou nas costas, botou nas costas e carregou para longe.'

(29) *Tho mon... kôre hwĩ khrakhrak ne hry nhithep khãm khutan,*

t<h>o   mo=n-...   [kôre   hwĩ   khrakhrak-∅=ne hry nh-ithep]
<3>with go.PL=&.SS-INTS 3.ERG branch break-NMLZ=&.SS trail E-stop
khãm khu-ta=n
in   3-put.standing.SG=&.SS

'He carried it for a long time and placed it where he had stopped breaking branches, at the end of the trail, and'
'Ele carregou muito tempo e colocou no lugar onde ele parou de quebrar galho, no fim da trilha, e'

(30) *amu nen khwã hwĩ khrakhrak to thẽn,*

amu   ne=n   kh-wã hwĩ   khrakhrak-∅ to   thẽ=n
farther do.so=&.SS 3-to branch break-NMLZ with go.SG=&.SS

'continued breaking branches,'
'continuou quebrando galhos,'

(31) *hwĩ khrakhrak to thẽn sĩthep ne*

hwĩ   khrakhrak to   thẽ=n   s-ĩthep=ne
branch break   with go.SG=&.SS 3-stop=&.SS

'he went breaking branches and then he stopped and'
'ele foi quebrando galhos e então parou e'

(32) *akwyn nen thẽn khuthu nen amu tho thẽ.*

akwyn ne=n   thẽ=n   khu-thu   ne=n   amu   t<h>o
back do.so=&.SS go.SG=&.SS 3-load.on.back be.so=&.SS farther <3>with

thẽ
go.SG

'went back, loaded it onto his back and so carried it farther.'
'voltou, botou nas costas e assim carregou mais além.'

(33) *Tho thẽn... kôre hwĩ khrakhrak to thẽm nhithep khãm khuta.*

t\<h\>o   thẽ=n-...   [kôre   hwĩ   khrakhrak-Ø to   thẽ-m
\<3\>with go.SG=&.SS-INTS   3.ERG branch break-NMLZ with go.SG-NMLZ
nh-ithep] khãm khu-ta
E-stop   in   3-put.standing.SG

'He carried it for a while and then placed it where he had stopped breaking branches.'
'Carregou por um tempo e aí colocou onde ele tinha parado de quebrar galhos.'

(34) *Amu nen tho thẽ.*

amu   ne=n   t\<h\>o   thẽ
farther do.so=&.SS \<3\>with go.SG

'Doing so he continued carrying it farther.'
'Fazendo assim ele continuou carregando.'

(35) *Amu nen khuthun tho mon... kôre hry ro thẽm ne hwĩ khrakhrak nhithep khãm khuta.*

amu   ne=n   khu-thu=n   t\<h\>o   mo=n-...   [kôre
farther do.so=&.SS 3-load.on.back=&.SS \<3\>with go.PL=&.SS-INTS 3.ERG
hry ro   thẽ-m=ne   hwĩ   khrakhrak-Ø nh-ithep-Ø] khãm
trail with go.SG-NMLZ=&.SS   branch break-NMLZ E-stop-NMLZ in
khu-ta
3-put.standing.SG

'He did so farther, loaded it onto his back, carried it a long time and placed it where he had stopped opening the trail and breaking branches.'
'Ele continuou assim e botou nas costas, carregou muito tempo e colocou onde ele tinha parado de fazer trilha e quebrar galhos.'

(36) *Khuta nhy hõnen ndo khá tha.*

khu-ta=nhy   hõne=n   ndo khá tha
3-put.standing.SG=&.DS be.ready=&.SS eye skin rupture

'He placed it on the ground and then he (the forefather) was ready and woke up.'

'Ele colocou no chão e então ele (o antepassado) estava pronto e acordado.'

(37) *Amtysamdep ta khambrô khôt khunta nhy nen ndo khátha.*

amty s-amdep-Ø=ta   Ø-khambrô khôt khu-nta=nhy ne=n
wasp 3-be.hungry-NMLZ=NOM 3-blood   after 3-bite=&.DS be.so=&.SS
ndo khá tha
eye skin rupture

'A wasp of the *amtysamdep* species bit him to suck his his blood and he woke up.'

'Uma vespa da espécio *amtysamdep* mordeu ele para sugar o sangue e assim ele acordou.'

(38) *Tên... khátpy ra khuthun tho mo nhy ndo khá than jáwi arak anhi khãm mbaj to no.*

tên   khátpy=ra   khu-thu=n   t<h>o   mo=nhy
unexpectedly monster=NOM 3-load.on.back=&.SS <3>with go.PL=&.DS
ndo khá tha=n   jáwi   arak   anhi khãm Ø-mba-j   to
eye skin rupture=&.SS as.they.say already self in   3-hear-NMLZ with
no
lie.down.SG

'Unexpectedly, the *khátpy* monster had loaded it (the basket) on his back and was carrying it, and he (the ancestor) woke up and was already lying down listening.'

'De repente, o monstro *khátpy* tinha botado (o cesto) nas costas e estava carregando, e ele (o ancestral) acordou e já estava deitado escutando.'

(39) *"Tu âââ... khupẽ kasák, khupẽ kasák na ithát ne itho mo,"*

tu âââ khupẽ   kasák   khupẽ   kasák=na   i-thát=ne   i-tho
gosh foreigner be.evil foreigner be.evil=NFUT 1-wound=&.SS 1-with
mo
go.SG

'"Gosh... the evil monster, it was the evil monster that wounded me and was carrying me,"'

'"Nossa... o monstro malvado, foi o monstro malvado que me feriu e estava me carregando,"'

(40) *nenhy kôt hwĩ khrakhrak khôt hry ro thẽm nda ro thẽn hry jatuj khãm khutha.*

ne=nhy [*kôt   hwĩ   khrakhrak-Ø khôt   hry   ro   thẽ-m*
be.so=&.ds 3.erg branch break-nmlz along trail with go.sg-nmlz
]=nda   ro thẽ=n   hry j-atu-j   khãm khu-ta
=def[25] at go.sg=&.ss trail e-stop-nmlz in   3-put.standing.sg

'he thought so and then he (the *khátpy* monster) finished walking the trail that he had built along the broken branches and placed it (the basket) at the end of the trail.'

'ele pensou assim e então ele (o monstro *khátpy*) percorreu a trilha que ele tinha construindo ao longo dos galhos quebrandos e colocou (o cesto) no fim da trilha.'

(41) *Nenhy amu nen khwã hwĩ khrakhrak to thẽ.*

ne=nhy   amu   ne=n   kh-wã hwĩ   khrakhrak-Ø to   thẽ
be.so=&.ds farther do.so=&.ss 3-to   branch break-nmlz   with go.sg

'And then he (the *khátpy* monster) continued breaking branches.'
'E então ele (o monstro *khátpy*) continuou quebrando galhos.'

(42) *Hwĩ khrakhrak to thẽ nhy athũm... nhy nen akwyn nen thẽ.*

hwĩ   khrakhrak-Ø to   thẽ=nhy   athũm-...=nhy   ne=n
branch break-nmlz with go.sg=&.ds take.time-ints=&.ds be.so=&.ss
akwyn ne=n   thẽ
back   be.so=&.ss go.sg

'He was breaking branches, it took some time and then he went back.'
'Ele estava quebrando galhos, demorou um certo tempo e então ele voltou.'

(43) *Akwyn nen thẽn khatho.*

akwyn   ne=n   thẽ=n   k<h>atho
back   be.so=&.ss go.sg=&.ss <3>come.out.sg

'He came back and came out (of the forest).'
'Ele voltou e saiu (da floresta).'

(44) *Khathon akhum khuthun nen tho mo.*

k<h>atho=n   akhum khu-thu=n   ne=n   t<h>o
<3>come.out.sg=&.ss again 3-load.on.back=&.ss be.so=&.ss <3>with

---

[25]Relative clauses are internally headed. The head of this one is *hry*.

mo
go.PL

'He came out, loaded it again on his back and so continued taking it away.'
'Ele saiu, botou nas costas de novo e assim continuou carregando para longe.'

(45) *Tho mon kôt hry nhithep khãm khuthan amu thẽ nhy thore tho sujakhre ro no.*

t<h>o   mo=n   [kôt   hry   nh-ithep-Ø] khãm
<3>with go.PL=&.SS 3.ERG trail E-stop-NMLZ   in
khu-ta=n   amu   thẽ=nhy   thore t<h>o   s-ujakhre-Ø
3-put.standing.SG=&.SS farther go.SG=&.DS then <3>with 3-count-NMLZ
ro   no
with lie.down.SG

'He took it, left it at the place where he stopped the trail and went farther and then he (the forefather) stayed lying down counting the time.'
'Carregou, deixou no lugar onde ele tinha parado a trilha e continuou adiante e então ele (o antepassado) ficou deitado contando o tempo.'

(46) *Tho sujakhre ro no nhy athũm nhy nen akwyn khatho.*

t<h>o   s-ujakhre-Ø   ro   no=nhy   athũm=nhy   ne=n
<3>with 3-count-NMLZ   with lie.down.SG=&.DS take.time=&.DS be.so=&.SS
akwyn k<h>atho
back   <3>come.out.SG

'He stayed lying counting the time, it took some time and then he (the *khátpy* monster) came back out.'
'Ele ficou deitado contando o tempo, demorou um tempo e então ele (o monstro *khátpy*) saiu de volta.'

(47) *Akwyn swârâ khathon akhum khuthun.*

akwyn   Ø-swârâ   k<h>atho=n   akhum   khu-thu=n
back 3-towards <3>come.out.SG=&.SS again 3-load.on.back=&.SS[26]

'He came back out towards him and loaded it again on his back.'
'Ele saiu de volta pra perto dele e botou de novo nas costas.'

---

[26] Here, though the coordinating conjunction marks subject maintenance, there actually is a subject switch.

(48) *"Hyhy! Athaj nhyry ri wa thẽ."*

    hyhy ∅   athaj nhy-ry   ri=wa   thẽ
    aha FUT there do.so.NMLZ-NMLZ during=&.DS.1 go.SG

    '"Aha! While he is doing that over there I will go away."'
    '"Aha! Enquanto ele estiver fazendo isso lá eu vou embora."'

(49) *Arêkmã, arêkmã wi anhi khãm, anhi mã sumbaj to no jowi.*

    arêkmã arêkmã wi   anhi khãm anhi=mã s-umba-j   to
    soon   soon   indeed self in   self=to 3-think-NMLZ with
    no   jowi
    lie.down.SG as.they.say

    'Soon, as they say, he (the forefather) stayed lying down thinking to himself.'
    'Logo, segundo dizem, ele (o antepassado) ficou deitado pensando sozinho.'

(50) *Tho thẽn... akhum khuthun tho mon khuta.*

    t<h>o   thẽ=n   akhum khu-thu=n   t<h>o   mo=n
    <3>with go.SG=&.SS again 3-load.on.back=&.SS <3>with go.PL=&.SS
    khu-ta
    3-put.standing.SG

    'He (the *khátpy* monster) kept taking it... loaded him on his back again, took it and put it down.'
    'Ele (o monstro *khátpy*) foi levando... botou nas costas de novo, levou e depois colocou no chão.'

(51) *Kôt hry jatuj khãm khutha.*

    [kôt   hry j-atu-j   ] khãm khu-ta
    3.ERG trail E-stop-NMLZ   in   3-put.standing.SG

    'He put it down where he had stopped making the trail.'
    'Colocou no chão onde ele tinha parado de fazer a trilha.'

(52) *Akhum thẽ, akhum thẽ nhy akhum tho sujakhre mbet to no nhy...*

    akhum thẽ   akhum thẽ=nhy   akhum t<h>o   s-ujakhre-∅   mbet
    again go.SG again go.SG=&.DS again <3>with 3-count-NMLZ be.good
    to   no=nhy
    with lie.down.SG=&.DS

    'He went away again and then he (the forefather) lay down counting time with attention and...'

'Ele foi pra longe de novo e então ele (o antepassado) ficou deitado contando o tempo com atenção e...'

(53) *thẽm nda tho athũm nhy, "Hy! Kê nhyry ri wa ikatho ra" nen,*

thẽ-m=nda   t<h>o   athũm=nhy   hy kê nhy-ry
go.SG-NMLZ=NOM <3>with take.time=&.DS Ha FUT do.SO.NMLZ-NMLZ
ri=wa   i-katho   ra   ne=n
during=&.DS.1 1-come.out.SG indeed be.so=&.SS

'his trip took some time, then he (the forefather) said, "Ha! While he does so I will come out indeed,"'
'a viagem dele demorou um certo tempo, aí ele (o antepassado) disse, "Ha! Enquanto ele estiver fazendo isso eu vou sair mesmo,"'

(54) *athũm kharõ nhy nen akwyn khatho.*

athũm-∅   kharõ=nhy   ne=n   akwyn k<h>atho
take.time-NMLZ appear=&.DS be.so=&.SS back <3>come.out.SG

'a little more time passed and he (the *khátpy* monster) came back out.'
'passou um pouco mais de tempo e ele (o monstro *khátpy*) saiu de volta.'

(55) *"Hyhy! Kê nhyry ri wa thẽ."*

hyhy kê   nhy-ry   ri=wa   thẽ
aha   FUT be.so.-NMLZ during=&.DS.1 go.SG

'"Aha! While he's doing so I will go."'
'"Aha! Enquanto ele estiver fazendo isso eu vou embora."'

(56) *Khathon, akhum khuthun tho mo.*

k<h>atho=n   akhum khu-thu=n   t<h>o   mo
<3>come.out.SG=&.SS again   3-load.on.back=&.SS <3>with go.PL

'He (the *khátpy* monster) came out, loaded it again on his back and took it away.'
'Ele (o monstro *khátpy*) saiu de volta, botou do novo nas costas e levou embora.'

(57) *Akhum khuthun tho mon... kôt hry jatuj khãm khutha.*

akhum khu-thu=n   t<h>o   mo=n-...   [kôt   hry
again 3-load.on.back=&.SS <3>with go.PL=&.SS-INTS   3.ERG trail
j-atu-j   ] khãm khu-ta
E-stop-NMLZ in   3-put.standing.SG

'He loaded it again on his back, took it all the way and put it down where he had stopped the trail.'

'Ele botou de novo nas costas, levou o caminho todo e colocou no chão onde ele tinha parado a trilha.'

(58) *Hry jatuj khãm khuthan,*

    hry j-atu-j   khãm khu-ta=n
    trail E-stop-NMLZ in   3-put.standing.SG=&.SS

    'He put it down where he had stopped the trail, and'
    'Ele botou no chão onde ele tinha parado a trilha, e'

(59) *thât hwĩ khrakhrak to, khwã hry ro thẽ... nhy ary...re nhy.*

    thât   hwĩ   khrakhrak-Ø to   kh-wã hry ro   thẽ-...=nhy
    though branch break-NMLZ   with 3-to   trail with go.SG-INTS=&.DS

    ary-...-re   nhy
    for.long-INTS-little be.sitting.SG

    'was uselessly breaking branches, building a long trail, and then he (the forefather) sat for a little long.'
    'estava inutilmente quebrando galhos, construindo uma longa trilha, e então ele (o antepassado) ficou um tempinho sentado.'

(60) *Nen khatho ne... anhi ndêt khukwâj to thêk ne khathon,*

    ne=n   k<h>atho=ne   anhi ndêt   khukwâj to
    do.so=&.SS <3>come.out.SG=&.SS self   away.from monkey with

    thêk=ne   k<h>atho=n
    push.out=&.SS <3>come.out.SG=&.SS

    'He did so and then came out... Pushed the monkeys out away from him, came out, and'
    'Ele fez isso e então saiu... Empurrou os macacos para fora, para longe de si, saiu, e'

(61) *thore khẽn tha ro thẽn khuthán,*

    thore khẽn tha ro   thẽ=n   khu-tá=n
    then rock this with go.SG=&.SS 3-put.inside.SG=&.SS

    'then he brought a rock and put it inside,'
    'então ele trouxe uma pedra e botou dentro,'

(62) *khẽn tha ro thẽn khuthán,*

    khẽn tha ro   thẽ=n   khu-tá=n
    rock this with go.SG=&.SS 3-put.inside.SG=&.SS

    'he brought another rock and put it inside,'
    'trouxe outra pedra e botou dentro,'

(63) khẽn tha ro thẽn khuthán, sĩpy khukwâj ngrên hwan,
khẽn tha ro   thẽ=n   khu-tá=n   s-ĩpy   khukwâj
rock this with go.SG=&.SS 3-put.inside.SG=&.SS 3-on.top monkey
ngrê-n   hwa=n
put.inside.PL-NMLZ finish=&.SS

'he brought another rock and put it inside, and on top of them finished putting all the monkeys inside,'
'trouxe outra pedra e colocou dentro, e no topo delas terminou de colocar todos os macacos em cima,'

(64) hõnen arêkmã khukwâj itha wytin khupyn nen thẽ.
hõne=n   arêkmã khukwâj itha wyti=n   khu-py=n   ne=n
be.ready=&.SS soon   monkey this be.one=& 3-fetch.SG=&.SS do.so=&.SS
thẽ
go.SG

'he was done and then took this one monkey and so went away.'
'ele acabou e logo pegou um macaco e foi embora.'

(65) Thẽn... athũm nhy akwyn khatho.
thẽ=n-...   athũm=nhy   akwyn k<h>atho
go.SG=&.SS-INTS take.time=&.DS back <3>come.out.SG

'He went far away, it took time and he (the khátpy monster) came back out.'
'Ele foi embora para longe, demorou um tempo e ele (o monstro khátpy) saiu de volta.'

(66) Akwyn khathon khuthun, khẽn mã wikamẽn pa.
akwyn k<h>atho=n   khu-thu=n   khẽn mã
back   <3>come.out.SG=&.SS 3-load.on.back=&.SS rock to
Ø-wikamẽ=n   pa
3-be.pulled=&.SS stay.PL

'He came back out, loaded it on his back and kept being pulled down towards the rocks.'
'Ele saiu de volta, botou nas costas e ficou sendo puxado para baixo em direção às pedras.'

(67) *Khẽn mã wikamẽn pan, "Haaa! Ngrytxi thyk mbet ne khajkhit na!"*

khẽn mã Ø-wikamẽ=n pa=n Haaa ngry-txi thy-k
rock to 3-be.pulled=&.ss stay.PL=&.ss Argh beast-big die-NMLZ
mbet-Ø=ne Ø-khajkhit-Ø=na
be.good-NMLZ=&.ss 3-be.light-NMLZ=NFUT

'He kept being pulled down towards the rocks and said "Argh!" A big beast that is well dead is supposed to be light!"'
'Ele ficou sendo puxado para baixo em direção às pedras e disse "Argh!" Um animal grande que está bem morto era para ser leve!"'

(68) *"Ngrytxi thyk mbet ne khajkit na!"*

ngry-txi thy-k mbet-Ø=ne Ø-khajkhit-Ø=na
beast-big die-NMLZ be.good-NMLZ=&.ss 3-be.light-NMLZ=NFUT

'"A big beast that is well dead is supposed to be light!"'
'"Um animal grande que está bem morto era para ser leve!"'

(69) *Nenhy tho huuuh... nen sarĩn tho thẽ.*

ne=nhy t<h>o huuuh ne=n s-arĩ=n t<h>o thẽ
be.so=&.DS <3>with umpf be.so=&.ss 3-jump=&.ss <3>with go.SG

'And then he grunted and jumped and took it away.'
'E aí ele grunhiu e pulou e levou embora.'

(70) *Khuthun tho mo, tho mo... hry jatuj khãm khuta.*

khu-thu=n t<h>o mo t<h>o mo-... hry j-atu-j
3-load.on.back=&.ss <3>with go.PL <3>with go.PL-INTS trail E-stop-NMLZ
khãm khu-ta
in 3-put.standing.SG

'He loaded it on his back and took it all the way, took it all the way and put it down at the end of the trail.'
'Ele botou nas costas e levou até o fim, levou até o fim e botou no chão no final da trilha.'

(71) *Amu khwã hry ro thẽ...*

amu kh-wã hry ro thẽ
farther 3-to trail with go.SG

'He continued opening the trail...'
'Ele continuou abrindo a trilha...'

(72) Akhum hry jatuj khãm khuta.

akhum hry j-atu-j khãm khu-ta
again trail E-stop-NMLZ in 3-put.standing.SG

'He put it down again where he had stopped the trail.'
'Ele deixou de novo no lugar onde ele tinha parado a trilha.'

(73) Hry jatuj khãm khutan, amu nen hry ro thẽ.

hry j-atu-j khãm khu-ta=n amu ne=n hry
trail E-stop-NMLZ in 3-put.standing.SG=&.SS farther be.so=&.SS trail
ro thẽ
with go.SG

'He put it down where he had stopped the trail and opened the trail farther.'
'Ele botou no chão onde ele tinha parado a trilha e então continuou abrindo a trilha.'

(74) Hry ro thẽn... sĩthep ne akwyn nen khatho.

hry ro thẽ=n-... s-ĩthep-Ø=ne akwyn ne=n
trail with go.SG=&.SS-INTS 3-stop-NMLZ=&.SS back be.so=&.SS
k<h>atho
<3>come.out.SG

'He opened a long trail, stopped and so came back out.'
'Ele abriu uma trilha comprida, parou e então voltou.'

(75) Akwyn thẽn khathon kê khwã wikamẽn pan

akwyn thẽ=n k<h>atho=n kê kh-wã Ø-wikamẽ=n
back go.SG=&.SS <3>come.out.SG=&.SS also 3-to 3-be.pulled=&.SS
pa=n
stay.PL=&.SS

'He went back, came out and kept again being pulled down towards them (the rocks),'
'Ele voltou, saiu e ficou de novo sendo puxado para baixo em direção a elas (as pedras),'

(76) khẽn mã wikamẽn pan, "Haaa! Ngrytxi thyk mbet ne khajkhit na!"

khẽn mã Ø-wikamẽ=n pa=n haaa ngry-txi thy-k
rock to 3-be.pulled=&.SS stay.PL=&.SS argh beast-big die-NMLZ

mbet-Ø=ne   Ø-khajkhit-Ø=na
be.good-NMLZ=&.SS 3-be.light-NMLZ=NFUT

'he kept being pulled down towards the rocks and said "Argh! A big beast that is well dead is supposed to be light!"'
'ficou sendo puxado para baixo em direção às pedras e disse "Argh! Um animal grande que está bem morto era para ser leve!"'

(77) *"Ngrytxi thyk mbet ne khajkhit na!"*

ngry-txi thy-k   mbet-Ø=ne   Ø-khajkhit-Ø=na
beast-big die-NMLZ be.good-NMLZ=&.SS 3-be.light-NMLZ=NFUT

'"A big beast that is well dead is supposed to be light!"'
'"Um animal grande que está bem morto era para ser leve!"'

(78) *Khwã wikamẽn pa jahôt to huuuh nen sarĩn amu tho thẽ.*

kh-wã Ø-wikamẽ=n   pa-Ø   j-ahô-t   to   huuuh
3-to   3-be.pulled=&.SS stay.PL-NMLZ E-come.out.PL-NMLZ with umpf
ne=n   s-arĩ=n   amu   t<h>o   thẽ
be.so=&.SS 3-jump=&.SS farther <3>with go.SG

'He grunted his way out of being pulled down towards the rocks, jumped up and took it farther.'
'Ele ficou grunhindo sendo puxado para baixo em direção às pedras, pulou e levou mais adiante.'

(79) *Tho thẽn... tho pâj, sũrũkhwã mã tho pâj.*

t<h>o   thẽ=n-...   t<h>o   pâj   s-ũrũkhwã mã t<h>o   pâj
<3>with go.SG=&.SS-INTS <3>with arrive 3-house to <3>with arrive

'He carried it all the way and arrived home with it.'
'Ele carregou (a cesta) o resto do caminho e chegou em casa com ela.'

(80) *Sũrũkhwã me, sũrũkhwã khãm khrajê me hrõjê swârâ tho pâj.*

s-ũrũkhwã=me,[27] *s-ũrũkhwã khãm Ø-khra-jê=me Ø-hrõ-jê   swârâ*
3-house=&   3-house   at   3-child-PL=& 3-wife-PL towards
t<h>o   pâj
<3>with arrive

'At home, he brought it towards his children and wives.'
'Em sua casa, ele levou para junto dos seus filhos e esposas.'

---

[27] This was a mistake by the narrator.

(81) *Khrajê ra khathon "Haaa! Waj turê ra ngrytxi pĩn tho mo... Waj turê ra ngrytxi pĩn tho mo."*

Ø-khra-jê=ra   k<h>atho=n   haaa waj turê=ra ngry-txi
3-child-PL=NOM <3>come.out.SG=&.SS ah   must dad=NOM beast-big
pĩ=n   t<h>o   mo-...   waj turê=ra ngry-txi pĩ=n
kill.SG=&.SS <3>with go.PL-INTS must dad=NOM beast-big kill.SG=&.SS
t<h>o   mo
<3>with go.PL"

'His childen came out and (said) "Dad must have killed a big beast and brought it all the way here."'
'Seus filhos saíram e (disseram) "Papai deve ter matado um animal grande e trouxe até aqui."'

(82) *Tho thẽn... khikhre kape mã khẽn me nhy thuk nen ta nhy,*

t<h>o   thẽ=n-...   khikhre kape mã khẽn me=nhy   thuk
<3>with go.SG=&.SS-INTS house   front to rock throw.SG=&.DS thud
ne=n   ta=nhy
do.so=&.SS stand.SG=&.DS

'He carried it over, threw the rock in front of the house, it (the basket) made a '*thuk*' and stood there, and'
'Ele carregou até lá, jogou a pedra na frente da casa, ele (o cesto) fez '*thuk*' e ficou lá, e'

(83) *nenhy, "ndotê, ndotê, ndotê, ndotê" ne...*

ne=nhy   ndotê   ndotê   ndotê   ndotê   ne
be.so=&.DS be.quick be.quick be.quick be.quick do.so

'so he said "Come here, come here, come here, come here..."'
'então ele disse "Venham aqui, venham aqui, venham aqui, venham aqui..."'

(84) *"Wakhrajê nho thát, ngrytxi kukhráthá thõ kê khukhrẽ."*

wa-khra-jê   nh-o   thát ngry-txi kukhráthá thõ=kê
1INCL-child-PL E-food for beast-big do.something.with=&.DS.3.FUT
khu-khrẽ
3-eat.PL

'"For our childen's food, do something with the big beast and they will eat it."'

"'Para a comida dos nossos filhos, faça alguma coisa com o animal grande e eles vão comer.'"

(85) *"Hwararo wakhrajê re hrãm khãm sãm."*

hwararo wa-khra-jê=re Ø-hrãm-Ø khãm
yesterday 1INCL-child-PL=ERG 3-desire-NMLZ in
s-ã-m
3-be.standing.SG-NMLZ

"'Yesterday our children were hungry'"
"'Ontem nossos filhos estavam com fome'"

(86) *"Khwã ngrytxi pĩn tho mo..."*

kh-wã ngry-txi pĩ=n t<h>o mo-...
3-to beast-big kill.SG=&.SS <3>with go.PL-INTS

"'(I) killed a big beast for them and brought it all the way'"
"'(Eu) matei um animal grande para eles e trouxe até aqui'"

(87) *"Ka ndotên khwã khukhrátá thõ kê rêt thõ khrẽ."*

ka ndotê=n kh-wã k<h>ukhrátá thõ=kê
2.NOM be.quick=&.SS 3-to <3>do.something.with=&.DS.3.FUT
Ø-rêt=thõ khrẽ
3-offal=one eat.PL

"'Come quickly and do something with it and then they will eat some offall.'"
"'Venha logo fazer alguma coisa com ele e aí eles vão comer os miúdos.'"

(88) *Hrõ ra "Hy!" nen khatho.*

Ø-hrõ=ra hy ne=n k<h>atho
3-wife=NOM yes do.so=&.SS <3>come.out.SG

'His wife said "Yes!" and came out.'
'Sua esposa disse "Sim!" e saiu.'

(89) *Khathon, khukwâj rẽn ndo thẽ.*

k<h>atho=n khukwâj rẽ-n ndo thẽ
<3>come.out.SG=&.SS monkey throw.PL-NMLZ with go.SG

'She came out and was throwing monkeys (out of the basket).'
'Ela saiu e ficou jogando macacos (para fora do cesto).'

(90) *Wapãmjê thõ wê sĩmbry wê kôt khukwâj hwaj ta, tho hôt to thẽn, tho hôt to thẽn, "the!"*

wa-pãm-jê=thõ=wê   s-ĩmbry wê   kôt   khukwâj hwa-j=ta
1INCL-father-PL=one=from 3-game COP 3.ERG monkey kill.PL-NMLZ=DET
t<h>o   hô-t   to   thẽ=n   t<h>o   hô-t
<3>with pull.out.PL-NMLZ with go.SG=&.SS <3>with pull.out.PL-NMLZ
to   thẽ=n   the
with go.SG=&.SS hey!

'The game from our forefather, the monkeys that he had killed, she kept pulling out and (said) "Hey!"'
'A caça do nosso antepassado, os macacos que ele tinha matado, ela ficou puxando para fora e (disse) "Oras!"'

(91) *Khôsátxi khre khahwãrã ro ta.*

khôsátxi khre   khahwã-rã ro   ta
basket   inner.side probe-NMLZ with stand.SG

'She kept probing the inner side of the basket.'
'Ela ficou inspecionando o lado de dentro do cesto.'

(92) *"Nhintã ngrytxi jarẽn nda?"*

nhintã ngry-txi   j-arẽ-n=nda
where beast-big E-talk.about-NMLZ=DET

'"Where is the big beast he talked about?"'
'"Onde está o animal grande de que ele falou?"'

(93) *"Athaj na wa ngrytxi pĩn tho mo."*

athaj=na   wa   ngry-txi pĩ=n   t<h>o   mo
there=NFUT 1.NOM beast-big kill.SG=&.SS <3>with go.PL

'"I killed a big beast and brought all the way there."'
'"Eu matei um animal grande e trouxe até aí."'

(94) *"Ngry txire! Kôt ka sõmun khêrê?"*

ngry txi-re   kôt   ka   s-õmu-n   khêrê
beast big-ADJ can.FUT 2.NOM 3-see-NMLZ not.be

'"The beast is big! Can't you see?"'
'"O animal é grande! Você não consegue ver?"'

(95) *"Nhintã tôra ngrytxi jarẽn nda?"*

nhintã tôra   ngry-txi j-arẽ-n=nda
where though beast-big E-talk.about-NMLZ=DET

"'Where, though, is the big beast you talk about?'"

"'Onde então é que está esse animal grande de que você fala?'"

(96) *"Ngrytxi khêrê weri!"*

ngry-txi khêrê weri
beast-big not.be indeed

"'There is indeed no big beast!'"

"'Não tem mesmo animal grande nenhum!'"

(97) *"Ngry txire! kôt ka sõmun khêrê?"*

ngry txi-re   kôt   ka   s-õmu-n   khêrê
beast big-ADJ can.FUT 2.NOM 3-see-NMLZ not.be

"'The beast is big! Can't you see it?'"

"'O animal é grande! Você não consegue ver?'"

(98) *"Rik tã, ndotên wakhrajê nho thát khukhrátá thõ kê khwê rêt thõ khrẽ!"*

rik   tã   ndotê=n   wa-khra-jê   nh-o   thát
quickly indeed be.quick=&.SS 1INCL-child-PL E-food for

k‹h›ukhrátá thõ=kê   kh-wê   Ø-rêt=thõ   khrẽ
‹3›do.something.with=&.DS.3.FUT 3-from 3-offal=one eat.PL

"'Go quickly and do something with it for our children's food and they'll eat some offal!'"

"'Se apresse e faça alguma coisa para a comida das nossas crianças e aí eles vão comer alguns miúdos!'"

(99) *"Hwararo, wakhrajê re hrãm khãm sãm nhy ire ithẽm ne ire ngrytxi pĩrĩ ne tho imorõ wyráká."*

hwararo   [wa-khra-jê=re   Ø-hrãm-Ø   khãm
yesterday 1INCL-child-PL=ERG 3-desire-NMLZ in

s-ã-m=nhy   ire   i-thẽ-m=ne   ire   ngry-txi
3-be.standing.SG-NMLZ=&.DS 1.ERG 1-go.SG-NMLZ=&.SS 1.ERG beast-big

pĩ-rĩ=ne   t‹h›o   i-mo-rõ   ] wyráká
kill.SG-NMLZ=&.SS ‹3›with 1-go.PL-NMLZ   happen

"'It happened that yesterday our children were hungry, I went, killed this big beast and brought it all the way here.'"

"'Aconteceu que ontem nossos filhos estavam com fome e eu fui, matei um animal grande e trouxe até aqui.'"

(100) *"Rik athaj aj khwã khukhrátá thõ kê aj khukhrẽ."*
   rik   athaj aj kh-wã   k<h>ukhrátá thõ=kê   aj khu-khrẽ
   quickly there PL 3-to <3>do.something.with=&.DS.3.FUT PL 3-eat.PL
   "'Quick! Go there do something with it for them and so they will eat it all'"
   "'Rápido! Vão lá fazer alguma coisa com ele e então eles vão comer tudo'"

(101) *"Ngrytxi khêrê... Amne thẽn sõmu."*
   ngry-txi khêrê amne thẽ=n   s-õmu
   beast-big not.be to.here go.SG=&.SS 3-see
   "'There is no big beast... Come here and see it.'"
   "'Não tem animal grande nenhum... Venha aqui e veja.'"

(102) *Sãm thãmthã, tê, norõ thãmthã khatho.*
   s-ã-m   thãmthã   tê   Ø-no-rõ
   3-be.standing.SG-NMLZ last.long.time oops 3-lie.down-NMLZ
   thãmthã   k<h>atho
   last.long.time <3>come.out.SG
   'He was standing for a long time, oops, I mean, he was lying down for a long time and then came out.'
   'Ele ficou em pé muito tempo, quero dizer, ele ficou deitado muito tempo e então saiu.'

(103) *Swârâ thẽn, "the!" Khôsátxi khre kahrãn tên... khẽn wit nhy.*
   Ø-swârâ   thẽ=n   the khôsátxi khre   kahrã=n   tên
   3-towards go.SG=&.SS hey basket   inner.side probe=&.SS unexpectedly
   khẽn wit   nhy
   rock only be.sitting.SG
   'He went towards her and (said) "Hey!" He had probed the inner side of the basket and there were unexpectedly only rocks.'
   'Ele foi para junto dela e (disse) "Oras!" Ele tinha vasculhado o interior do cesto e inesperadamente só tinha pedras.'

(104) *"Mãn khẽn wit khrĩ!"*

mãn khẽn wit khrĩ
here rock only be.sitting.PL

'"There are only rocks sitting here!"'
'"Só tem pedras aqui!"'

(105) *Sõmun ndo tan, "Ty a... tharãm na ngrytxi thẽ!" nen,*

s-õmu-n   ndo ta=n   ty a   tharãm=na   ngry-txi
3-see-NMLZ with stand.SG=&.SS goddamn.it long.ago=NFUT beast-big
thẽ   ne=n
go.SG do.so=&.SS

'He stood there looking and said "Goddamn it! It was long ago that the big beast went away!"'
'Ele ficou ali olhando e disse "Desgraça! Faz tempo que o animal grande foi embora!"'

(106) *"Nhum nda iwê awythárá mã?" nen khô pyn, akhum atán thẽ.*

nhum=nda i-wê   a-wythá-rá   mã   ne=n   Ø-khô
who=NOM 1-from 2-protect-NMLZ be.forthcoming do.so=&.SS 3-club
py=n   akhum atá=n   thẽ
fetch.SG=&.SS again   enter.SG=&.SS go.SG

'"Who is going to protect you from me?" he said, fetched his club, entered (the forest) again and went (after the forefather).'
'"Quem que vai proteger você de mim?" ele disse, pegou sua bordina, entrou (na floresta) de novo e foi (atrás do antepassado).'

(107) *Akhum atán thẽn... kôre pĩrĩ tá mã khathon*

akhum atá=n   thẽ=n-...   [kôre   Ø-pĩ-rĩ   ] tá   mã
again enter.SG=&.SS go.SG=&.SS-INTS 3.ERG 3-kill.SG-NMLZ place to
k<h>atho=n
<3>come.out.SG=&.SS

'Entered again, went back all the way and came out to the place where he wounded him (the forefather) unconscious,'
'Entrou de novo, voltou o caminho todo e saiu no lugar onde ele tinha machucado ele (o ancestral) mortalmente,'

(108) *"Ry...a..." khô ro anhi kathwân sãm thãmthã.*

ry...a... Ø-khô ro   anhi kathwâ=n   s-ã-m
argh... 3-club with self straighten=&.ss 3-be.standing.SG-NMLZ
thãmthã
last.long.time

'"Argh..." He straightened himself with the club (against the ground) and stood there for a long time.'

'"Argh..." Ele se endireitou com a borduna (contra o chão) e ficou lá de pé por muito tempo.'

(109) *Jowi anhi tho? nenhy amu sarẽn nda mbaj khêrê, Khupyry.*

jowi   anhi tho   ne=nhy   amu   s-arẽ-n=nda
as.they.say self do.how be.so=&.DS farther 3-talk.about-NMLZ=DET
mba-j   khêrê   Khupyry
know-NMLZ not.be howler.monkey

'How is it, as they say? It was so and I don't know what else to say about this, Howler Monkey.'[28]

'Como que é, que eles dizem? Aconteceu assim e eu não sei dizer mais nada sobre isso, Guariba.'

(110) *Itha wit mẽ ra, tho nen sarẽn wit na wa khumba.*

itha wit mẽ=ra   t<h>o   ne=n   s-arẽ-n
this only people=NOM <3>with do.so=&.ss 3-talk.about-NMLZ
wit=na   wa   khu-mba
only=NFUT 1.NOM 3-know

'I know only this, that people used to tell this way.'

'Eu só sei isso, que o pessoal costumava contar desse jeito.'

(111) *Ipãm nda nen tho sujarẽn nda ne wa khumba.*

i-pãm=nda   ne=n   t<h>o   s-ujarẽ-n=nda   ne=wa
1-father=NOM do.so=&.ss <3>with 3-talk-NMLZ=DET do.so=&.DS.1
khu-mba
3-know

'My father narrated this way and I used to hear it thus.'

'Meu pai contava assim e eu costumava escutar (a história) desse jeito.'

---

[28]The narrator is talking to the linguist, whom the Kĩsêdjê nicknamed *Khypyry*.

(112) *Nenhy khátpy ra nen mẽ thõj pĩn khuthun tho mo nhy, akhum khwê thẽ.*

ne=nhy   khátpy=ra   ne=n   mẽ=thõj   pĩ=n
be.so=&.DS monster=NOM do.so=&.SS people=one kill.SG=&.SS
khu-thu=n   t<h>o   mo=nhy   akhum kh-wê thẽ
3-load.on.back=&.SS <3>with   go.PL=&.DS   again 3-from go.SG

'It was so, and so the *khátpy* monster wounded one of our people unconscious, loaded him on his back and took him far away, and he (the forefather) ran away from him.'

'Foi desse jeito, e assim que o monstro *khátpy* feriu mortalmente um de nós, botou ele nas costas, carregou ele muito longe, e ele (o ancestral) fugiu dele.'

(113) *Nenhy ne.*

ne=nhy   ne
be.so=&.DS   be.so

'Then it was like this.'
'Aí foi assim.'

Non-standard abbreviations

&	clause coordination	INTS	intensification
DS	different subject	ONTP	onomatopoeia
E	epenthetic morpheme	SS	same subject
INTJ	interjection		

References

Jacobsen, William. 1967. Switch-Reference in Hokan-Coahuiltec. In Dell H. Hymes & William E. Bittle (eds.), *Studies in Southwestern ethnolinguistics*, 238–263. The Hague: Mouton.

Nonato, Rafael. 2014. *Clause chaining, switch reference and coordination*. MIT dissertation. http://rafaeln.github.io/papers/thesis.pdf.

Santos, Ludoviko Carnasciali. 1997. *Descrição de aspectos morfossintáticos do Suyá*. UFSC dissertation.

Chapter 10

Kwaza

Hein van der Voort
Museu Paraense Emílio Goeldi

Edileusa Kwaza

Zezinho Kwaza

Mario Aikanã

1 Introduction

The story of Grandfather Fox represents a myth as told by the Kwaza people of the southwestern Amazon. Kwaza is a highly endangered isolate language with about 25 speakers. The speakers of Kwaza live in two different indigenous reserves and in a nearby village, in the southeastern corner of the Brazilian state of Rondônia, amidst a sea of deforested lands owned by big cattle ranchers and soy farmers. In one of the reserves, Terra Indígena Tubarão-Latundê, the Kwaza and Latundê (NORTHERN NAMBIKWARA) form minority populations among the Aikanã (ISOLATE). Several mixed Kwaza and Aikanã families live in another reserve, Terra Indígena Kwazá do Rio São Pedro. Despite having a very fragmented speaker community, Kwaza is still the first language of the youngest generation in two families.

This story was told by Edileusa Kwaza, who had learnt it from her late monolingual Kwaza father, Antonhão. As she told the story, Edileusa was accompanied by her partner Zezinho Kwaza. Most of the time, Edileusa and Zezinho live with their children and grandchildren in the little village outside the first reserve, and have very little contact with other Kwaza speakers. It should be considered admirable that, in spite of their Portuguese-only and often anti-indigenous environment, Kwaza is maintained as the family's home language. The story was

Figure 1: The indigenous reserves where the Kwaza live, shown in yellow.

recorded in audio and video formats in August 2014, as part of a documentation project funded through the DoBeS programme. The story has been transcribed and analyzed with the help of Mario Aikanã, a bilingual native speaker of Kwaza and Aikanã who, like most Indians of southeastern Rondônia, also has full command of Portuguese.

The story of Grandfather Fox takes place in mythological times. In those days, animals transformed themselves into humans at will. Grandfather Fox is a very smart animal who has many tricks up his sleeve. In this story, he takes advantage of a young woman after finding out about her plans for the next day. One of the lessons of this and several other traditional stories is that one should avoid speaking about one's plans for the future, so as not to attract adversity. The Aikanã also tell a mythological Fox story (chapter 11 in this volume) and, although it is quite different from the Kwaza version, it has a similar edifying message on the danger of referring to future plans. In spite of the enormous cultural and ecological changes that the Kwaza and Aikanã peoples have undergone during the 20th century, this taboo is also still very much part of their present way of life.

Kwaza is a morphologically complex, polysynthetic, suffixing language. Its word order is relatively free. Its word classes are verbs, nouns, adverbs and particles. The only obligatory part of a complete sentence is a verb, which takes inflectional suffixes expressing person and mood, in that order. Person inflections do not seem to be etymologically related to personal pronouns, which are used for disambiguation or emphasis. The person marking system distinguishes inclusive and exclusive first person plural, both inflectionally and pronominally. Third person has zero expression morphologically. There are two sets of mood inflections, distinguishing matrix clause moods such as declarative and interrogative from subordinate clause moods such as conditional, concessional, and cosubordinate. The language has a very productive arsenal of derivational suffixes, which include classifiers, directionals, valency changing morphemes, and nominalizers. Even though the language's morphological complexity is mainly located in its verb forms, nouns can also be morphologically highly complex due to recursive verbalizing and nominalizing operations. A comprehensive description of the language is van der Voort (2004).

From a linguistic point of view, the Fox story largely reflects the typical grammatical structure of traditional narratives in Kwaza. In principle, the entire story is one long sentence, each chained clause being either in a subordinate mood or in a cosubordinate mood. The story then ends with a fixed formulaic expression in a matrix mood, typically the declarative. If matrix moods are encountered inside the story they usually represent quotations, and either these are followed by a verb of saying in a cosubordinative mood or a cosubordinative mood marker is attached directly to the quoted part. Another characteristic of Kwaza text grammar is anticipatory switch-reference, which indicates that the subject — or perhaps rather the topic — to be foregrounded in the following clause is different from that of the current clause. These rules of thumb also hold for the present text, although some exceptions, indicated in footnotes, can be observed. Finally, many cases of morphological ellipsis can be found in the text, where either the verb stem or the verbal inflection is omitted. Such omitted elements can often be understood from the context, but in some cases verb stem ellipsis signals a quotative construction.

The story is transcribed in the first line in accordance with a practical orthography that was developed for use and established in 2002 by the speakers of Kwaza. The transcription is then segmented morphologically in the second line and glossed in the third line, while the fourth and fifth lines contain free translations into English and Portuguese respectively. Zezinho's responses are indicated by [brackets]. The <y> corresponds to IPA [j], and the <'> corresponds to IPA [ʔ]. The only exception to the practical orthography concerns IPA [ɛ], which is spelled here as <ɛ> instead of <ee>.

2 Hakai dariya
'Grandfather Fox'
'Vovô Raposa'[1]

(1) hakai dariya

hakai   dariya
grandparent fox
'Grandfather Fox'
'Vovô Raposa'

(2) etaitohoi tsɨwɨdɨte huruyalɛ arakate tya tsɨwɨdɨte tya huruyalɛta ta ata.

etai-tohoi   tsɨwɨdɨte huruya-lɛ arakate   tya tsɨwɨdɨte tya
woman-CLF:child girl   like-RECP young.man CSO girl   CSO
huruya-lɛ-ta ta a-ta
like-RECP-CSO CSO exist-CSO

'An adolescent girl and a young man liked one another; they liked each other, that's how it was.'
'Uma moça e um rapaz novo se gostavam muito; eles se gostavam, assim viviam.'

(3) hadeya hayanɨ̃tsɨratiwɨ toma'i'ĩta tya anãi tyarahĩta tyarahĩta tsɨlehĩ

hadeya haya-nɨ̃-tsɨ-rati-wɨ   toma=ĩ'ĩta-tya
night   day-REFL-GER-FOC-time bathe=always-CSO
a-nãi-tyara-hĩ-ta[2]   tyara-hĩ-ta   tsɨ-le-hĩ
exist-NMLZ-PROC-NMLZ-CSO PROC-NMLZ-CSO GER-FRUST-NMLZ

'Before dawn she would usually take a bath in the river, that's how she happily lived, but ...'

---

[1] Recordings of this story are available from https://zenodo.org/record/997445

'Ela costumava tomar banho no rio antes de clarear o dia, assim ela vivia feliz, porém …'

(4) *dariya tswa aretya orita tsɨwɨditewã hĩdɛ ma'ĩtɛ tomaya tyata*

dariya tswa are-tya orita tsɨwɨdite-wã hĩdɛ ma'ĩtɛ tomã-ya[3]
fox man turn-cso go.there girl-AOBJ let's.go cousin bathe-EXP

tyata
say

'Fox turned into a man and went up to the girl, saying "Let's go! Cousin, let's take a bath!"'[4]

'Raposa se transformou em um homem, e foi falando para a moça, dizendo "Vamos, minha prima, vamos banhar!"'

(5) *ta nãi waxonaryĩ wayata asata*

ta nãi wa=xona-ryĩ waya-ta asa-ta
cso like[5] take=go.pathless-CLD:area bring-cso leave-cso

'He took advantage of her and took her deep into the forest and left her there.'

'Ele então se aproveitou dela e levou ela nas profundezas do mato e deixou ela lá.'

(6) *haya damĩdita harɨkɨ tya tomã'etetya'ahĩ hɨkwɛta*

haya-damĩ-dɨ-ta harɨkɨ tya tomã-ete-tya a-hĩ hɨ=kwɛ-ta
day-want-DS-cso now cso bathe-COM-cso exist-NMLZ go=enter-cso

'At dawn he[6] would always bathe with her, so he entered the house, saying:'

'Ao amanhecer o rapaz sempre ia tomar banho com ela, aí entrou na casa dizendo:'

---

[2] The combination -*tyarahĩta* gives the preceding verbal or zero-verbalized stem the connotation 'luckily' or 'happily'.

[3] The exhortative paucal is a matrix mood. Since this is a quoted utterance, it can occur embedded in the overall cosubordinated clause chain.

[4] Background knowledge required here is that, every morning, the girl's cousin mentioned in line (2) calls her to come out and bathe in the river (as is clear from line (6)). Fox has found out about this and takes advantage by pretending to be the girl's cousin, while it is still dark.

[5] The verb root *nãi-* means 'to be like, to act thus'. Here it refers to the rape of the girl.

[6] The real young man mentioned in line (2). Note also the different subject marker on the verb stem 'to dawn', marking discontinuity of the current topic.

(7) hĩdɛ tomãya ma'ĩtɛ cwatalehĩ
     hĩdɛ   tomã-ya   ma'ĩtɛ cwata-le-hĩ[7]
     let's.go bathe-EXP cousin say-FRUST-NMLZ
     '"Cousin, let's take a bath!", but ...'
     '"Prima, vamos banhar!", mas ...'

(8) mãtyate o xɨy mãtsasi bui'oyaheredalehĩtsɨ tyatata
     mã-tyate   o   xɨy mã=tsasi
     mother-3POSS oh! you call=follow
     bui=oya-here-da-le-hĩ-tsɨ   tyata-ta
     leave=arrive-INTL-1SG-FRUST-NMLZ-RESI say-CSO
     'her mother said to him: "Oh! I thought you had called her already and that's why she has gone."'
     'a mãe falou: "O! Pensei que você já chamou ela, e que por isso ela já foi."'

(9) tsicwawata ahatyate tya mãtyate tya ka'awanihĩxotɛ tsɨwɨdɨte
     tsicwa-wa-ta   aha-tyate   tya mã-tyate   tya ka'awanihĩ-xotɛ
     begin-ISBJ-CSO father-3POSS CSO mother-3POSS CSO suffer-TR
     tsɨwɨdɨte
     girl
     'Then her father and mother started to worry about the girl,'
     'Aí, o pai e a mãe dela comecavam ficar preocupado sobre a moça,'

(10) hedutuhĩdwata
     hedutu-hĩ-dwa-ta
     lose-NMLZ-IDS-CSO
     'they understood that (she) had got lost ...'
     'eles entenderam que ela sumiú ...'

(11) cwata tsicwawata ka'awanihĩxotɛ tsɨwɨdɨte
     cwata tsicwa-wa-ta   ka'awanihĩ-xotɛ tsɨwɨdɨte
     say   begin-ISBJ-CSO suffer-TR   girl
     'it is said that they started to worry about the girl,'
     'e dizem que comecavam ficar realmente preocupado sobre a moça,'

---

[7] The combination *cwa-ta* (ISBJ-CSO) often occurs in narrations with the lexicalized meaning 'they say'/'it is said', and in some clear cases it has been glossed as such. The etymology of the verb root *tyata-* 'say to X' is not clear, but it probably contains the transitivizer (*-ta-*).

(12) *tya tsi'ahĩte a dukɨrinitenãiko a mãtyate lehĩ*

    tya   tsi'a-hĩ-te   a   dukɨri-nite-nãi-ko   a   mã-tyate
    CSO silent-NMLZ-NMLZ exist long.for-INSTR-NMLZ-INS exist mother-3POSS
    le-hĩ
    FRUST-NMLZ

    'and they lived in sadness; her mother lived longing for her daughter, but then ...'
    'e eles viviam na tristeza, e a mãe vivia sentindo saudades, mas aí ...'

(13) *tinãits*

    ti-nãi-tsɨ-re
    what-NMLZ-POT-INT

    'How is it again?'[8]
    'Como que é de novo?'

(14) *katai towɨna cẽrĩ tsãrãnũ'i'ĩta*

    katai   towɨ-na   cẽrĩ   tsãrãnũ-ĩ'ĩta
    agouti clearing-LOC peanut dig-always

    'The agouti was in the garden digging for peanuts, as always'
    'A cutia estava na roça cavocando atras de amendoim, como sempre,'

(15) *mãtyate tsɨwɨditedɨhĩ tsɨlehĩ*

    mã-tyate   tsɨwɨdite-di-hĩ   tsɨ-le-hĩ
    mother-3POSS girl-POSS-NMLZ GER-FRUST-NMLZ

    'the girl's mother, however ...'
    'mas a mãe da moça ...'

(16) *tya xudɛ'oya'i'ĩta xudɛ'oya'i'ĩta*

    tya   xudɛ=oya=ĩ'ĩta   xudɛ=oya=ĩ'ĩta
    CSO offend=run=always offend=run=always

    'said, while (the agouti was) harassing her and then running away time and again,'[9]
    'falou enquanto (a cutia estava) xingando e correndo o tempo inteiro'

---

[8] This is not part of the story. Here Edileusa's memory briefly fails. She turns to Zezinho, but then immediately picks up the thread of the story again.

[9] When one arrives at a swidden crop field, there may be agoutis scurrying around noisily as if intending to tease the visitor.

(17) tsuhũ xudɛ'oya'i'ĩta tsɨraire mãrẽritsaxata utexaraire
tsũhũ xudɛ=oya=ĩ'ĩta-tsɨ-rai-re   mãrẽritsa-xa-ta
what offend=run=always-GER-damn-INT person-2SG-CSO
ute-xa-rai-re
tell-2SG-damn-INT

'"Why do you always harass us and run? If you were a person, I'd want you to tell us ..."'
'"Para que você sempre xinga a gente e corre? Se você fosse uma pessoa, eu queria que você contasse ..."'

(18) sidɨhĩ etohoi tiryĩ wayawaredata tsi'ahɨdahĩnãrẽtsɨ tyatawasi
si-dɨ-hĩ   etohoi ti-ryĩ   waya-wa-re-da-ta
I-POSS-NMLZ child   what-CLD:area bring-ISBJ-INT-1SG-CSO
tsi'a-hĩ-da-hĩ-nãrẽ-tsɨ   tyata-wa-si¹⁰
silent-NMLZ-1SG-NMLZ-real-RESI say-ISBJ-SWR

'"where they have taken my child; I'm really sad because of this," it is told ...'
'"para onde eles levaram a minha criança; Estou muito triste por causa disso", se conta ...'

(19) yãsitya ɛta ɛta ẽryãwãna ɛta mãtiwã
yãsi-tya ɛ-ta   ɛ-ta   ẽryãwã-na ɛ-ta   mãti-wã
hear-CSO go-CSO go-CSO forest-LOC go-CSO daughter-AOBJ

'He heard it and he went and went into the forest, going after the daughter.'
'Ele ouviu e ele foi e foi no mato, indo atras da filha.'

(20) awĩydaki mãxahɨhesi ɛhɛtara wayetanĩ tyatata
awĩy-da-ki   mã-xa-hĩ-he-si   ɛhɛta-ra waye-ta-ni
see-1SG-DECL mother-2SG-NMLZ-NEG-SWR tell-IMP bring.back-1SGO-EXH
tyata-ta
say-CSO

'[He found her.] "Apparently you saw mother, so,¹¹ tell her to bring me back!" she said to him.'
'[Achou a filha.] Ela falou: "Parece que você viu mamãe. Fala para ela que me traz de volta!"'

---

[10] The switch-reference mood indicates that there will shortly be an important turn of events.

[11] At this stage, Agouti has found the daughter, and she speaks to him, using what is literally a quotative construction ('Didn't you say: "I saw mother".'). The combination *hesi* or *hehɨsi* also means 'well, so' and is used for tail-head linkage.

(21) watxidɨnãi ta mãrẽtata mãwã

watxi-dɨnãi ta mãrẽ-ta-ta mã-wã
true-manner say appear-TR-CSO[12] mother-AOBJ

"'Explain correctly to mother ...'"
"'Explica bem para mamãe ...'"

(22) mĩu arwenãdɨxalɛ sidule waidɨnãixalɛ

mĩu arwenã-dɨ-xa-lɛ si-du-le wai-dɨnãi-xa-le
chicha[13] prepare-CAUS-2SG-PREC I-BER-only good-manner-2SG-PREC

"'when you prepare it, make proper *chicha* only for me ...'"
"'quando preparar, faz chicha de verdade para mim ...'"

(23) aɨhĩ tswa dariyaxwadule tẽityadɨnãixalɛ tsukuxotɛxahĩ

ai-hĩ tswa dariya-xwa-du-le tẽitya-dɨnãi-xa-lɛ
that-NMLZ man fox-CLF:man-BER-only alone-manner-2SG-PREC
tsuku-xotɛ-xa-hĩ
chew-TR-2SG-NMLZ

"'and you mix separately for the fox-man only ...'"
"'e para o homem raposa só,...'"

(24) yerexwanũ kurakuranũ xalɛ tsukuxalɛ

yerexwa-nũ kurakura-nũ xa-lɛ tsuku-xa-lɛ
jaguar-CLF:powder chicken-CLF:powder 2SG-PREC chew-2SG-PREC

"'you mix in dog shit and chicken poop ...'"
"'você mistura bosta de cachorro e bosta de galinha ...'"

(25) tẽityadɨnãi kudɨna dokwɛdɨwayanĩxalɛ sidule

tẽitya-dɨnãi kudɨ-na do=kwɛ-dɨ
alone-manner-2SG-PREC calabash-LOC pour=enter-CAUS
waya-nĩ-xa-lɛ si-du-le
bring-REFL-2SG-PREC I-BER-only

"'you put it inside a calabash by itself and bring it to me ...'"
"'você mistura e coloque numa cabaça separada e traz para mim, e separado ...'"

---

[12] The transitivizer is probably lexicalized yielding the meaning 'to explain'.
[13] In the cultures of several indigenous peoples of Rondônia, *chicha* is a lightly alcoholic fermented beverage usually based on yam, manioc, or maize.

(26) tẽityanãi dokwɛxalɛ kataɨdule emẽ tsẽimẽ
tẽitya-nãi   do=kwɛ-xa-lɛ   katai-du-le   e-mẽ
alone-NMLZ pour=enter-2SG-PREC agouti-BER-only ø-CLF:porridge
tsẽi-mẽ
one-CLF:porridge
'"and for Agouti you separately put in maize porridge ..."'
'"para Cutia você coloque bagaço de milho,"'

(27) tẽityanãilɛ wayanĩxalɛ wayetatsɨtse tyata daheretsɨlɛ
tẽitya-nãi-lɛ   waya-nĩ-xa-lɛ   waye-ta-tsɨ-tse[14]   tyata
alone-NMLZ-PREC bring-REFL-2SG-PREC bring.back-1SGO-POT-DECL   say
da-here-tsɨ-lɛ[15]
1SG-INTL-POT-PREC
'"and you bring it to me," I think she said.'
'"e você traz isso para mim," acho que ela falou."

(28) watxile hayadɨta tsãtxa atxitxi cwata
watxile haya-dɨ-ta tsãtxa atxitxi cwata
finally day-DS-CSO scatter maize say
'And then on the next day mother (went up onto the storage platform and) dropped maize (cobs) on the ground, so ...'
'No dia seguinte a mãe (subiu no paiol e) derrubou (espigas de) milho no chão, aí ...'

(29) arwenãwata waya horomũtya wayata
arwenã-wa-ta   waya horo-mũ-tya   waya-ta
prepare-ISBJ-CSO bring finish-CLF:liquid-CSO bring-CSO
'she finished preparing the chicha and went to take it there.'
'ela aprontou a chicha e levou lá.'

(30) karẽxu katsucwata xalɛ axehĩtse
karẽxu   katsu-cwa-ta xa-lɛ   axe-hĩ-tse
dry.heartwood cross-ISBJ-CSO 2SG-PREC find-NMLZ-DECL
'"If you go across a dry log" she would meet (her daughter),'
'"Quando você travessa um pau cerno," ela ia encontrar (a filha),'

---

[14] The declarative mood is a matrix mood. Here it marks the end of a chain of quoted utterances that started with (20) and that is embedded in the general cosubordinate clause chain by *tyata*.
[15] This clause in the first person singular represents a metatextual remark by Edileusa.

(31) tsɨhĩkitya

tsɨ-hĩ-ki-tya
GER-NMLZ-DECL-CSO

'he (Agouti) having told her thus.'
'assim Cutia tinha falado.'

(32) watxile karẽxu katsutyata xareyawata axehĩko tsadwɛnɛ

watxile karẽxu   katsu-tya ta   xareya-wa-ta   axe-hĩ-tya[16]
finally dry.heartwood cross-CSO CSO search-ISBJ-CSO find-NMLZ-CSO
tsadwɛ-nɛ
onto.path-DIR:hither

'Later, crossing the dry log, they[17] then searched and got back onto the path.'
'Mais tarde, ela com a sua família toda travessaram o cerno, procuraram e sairam na estrada de novo.'

(33) itso'ɨiri tatsitswa bu'aruryĩ aruxe aihĩ tsɨwɨditewã

itso'ɨi-ri-tatsitswa   bu=aruryĩ aru-xe   ai-hĩ
liana-CLF:flat-DIR:backside put=leave place-CLF:leaf that-NMLZ
tsɨwɨdite-wã
girl-AOBJ

'There, under a huge vine, was that girl, where she had been left sitting (by Fox).'
'Alí, em baixo de um cipozeiro (Raposa) tinha deixado a moça sentada.'

(34) etaɨ etsɨratihĩ kudɨnũwata

etaɨ   e-tsɨ-rati-hĩ   ku-dɨ-nũ-wa-ta
woman have-GER-FOC-NMLZ insert-CAUS-CLF:powder-ISBJ-CSO

'The thing that a woman has[18] had been stuck in the ground ...'
'A coisa que a mulher tem estava fincado em baixo da terra ...'

---

[16] In the transcription, Mario replaced the instrumental marker -ko by the cosubordinative marker -tya.

[17] The girl's mother and the rest of her family.

[18] Her clitoris. Edileusa has skipped a part mentioned by Mario where, after Fox raped the girl, her clitoris grew and became long like a penis. The girl was then fixed to the ground with her clitoris, so that she could not get up and run away.

(35) *txe:nũ tsãrãnũ kudɨratsanũcwasi ũryĩ ũxeryĩ*

txe-nũ tsãrãnũ
close-CLF:powder soil
ku-dɨ-ratsa-nũ-cwa-si   ũryĩ ũxe-ryĩ
insert-CAUS-DIR:underneath-CLF:powder-ISBJ-SWR sit remain-CLD:area

'it was secured into the ground, underneath the soil where she remained sitting.'
'estava fixado no fundo da terra onde ela permaneceu sentada.'

(36) *harɨkɨ orita watxile kuidɨ aɨhĩ dariyaxwawã cwasi isitsɨnãixwadɨta*

harɨkɨ orita   watxile kui-dɨ   ai-hĩ   dariya-xwa-wã
now arrive.there finally drink-CAUS that-NMLZ fox-CLF:man-AOBJ
cwa-si   isi-tsɨ-nãixwa-dɨ-ta
ISBJ-SWR die-GER-SIMU-DS-CSO

'Now, when they arrived, they gave Fox that drink, and he seemed to get drunk.'
'Aí, quando chegaram eles deram aquela bebida para Raposa, e parecia que ele ficou bêbado.'

(37) *watxile duwata yeyedaratuwata ehĩtyatewã cwata*

watxile du-wa-ta   ye~ye=daratu-wa-ta   e-hĩ-tyate-wã
finally all-ISBJ-CSO dig~dig=to.after-ISBJ-CSO have-NMLZ-3POSS-AOBJ
cwa-ta
ISBJ-CSO

'Then all (the family) got together and started digging after her thing.'
'Aí, eles todos se juntaram e começavam cavocando atrás a coisa da menina.'

(38) *yewata yewata lonã yecwata oyahaɨryĩlɛ dɨcwasi*

ye-wa-ta   ye-wa-ta   lonã ye-cwa-ta   oya=haɨ-ryĩ-le
dig-ISBJ-CSO dig-ISBJ-CSO hole dig-ISBJ-CSO arrive=final-CLD:area-only
dɨ-cwa-si
cut-ISBJ-SWR

'They dug and dug a hole and dug and (by accident) cut it off at the very end ...'[19]

---

[19] As Mario explains, the part of the girl's clitoris that stayed in the ground turned later into a caecilian, known in Portuguese as "cobra-cega" (*Gymnophiona*), or an amphisbaenian worm lizard, known in Portuguese as "cobra-de-duas-cabeças" (*Amphisbaenidae*).

'Cavocaram e cavocaram um buraco e no fundo eles cortaram (acidentalmente) o finalzinho da coisa ...'

(39) cwata waye etaɨ cwata wɛ'ɨhĩ cwasi
    cwa-ta   waye   etaɨ   cwa-ta   wɛ-ɨ̃-hĩ   cwa-si
    ISBJ-CSO bring.back woman ISBJ-CSO carry-ATT-NMLZ ISBJ-SWR
    'then they took her and brought her back ...'
    'aí levaram ela e trouxeram de volta ...'

(40) etaɨ dɨcwahĩ txuhũitsɨhĩle karitsutɨ areki cwaratɨ
    etaɨ   dɨ-cwa-hĩ   txuhũi-tsɨ-hĩ-le   karitsutɨ   are-ki
    woman cut-ISBJ-NMLZ small-GER-NMLZ-only worm.lizard turn-DECL
    cwa-ratɨ²⁰
    ISBJ-FOC
    'only the woman's small cut-off part (which stayed behind) turned into a worm lizard, that is what they say.'
    'somente aquele pequeno pedaço cortado ficou para trás e virou numa cobra-cega, é que dizem.'

(41) hm
    [response from Zezinho:] 'Hm.'
    [resposta do Zezinho:] 'Hm.'

(42) cwata etaɨle wɛ axɨna cwata
    cwa-ta   etaɨ-le   wɛ   axɨ-na   cwa-ta
    ISBJ-CSO woman-only carry house-LOC ISBJ-CSO
    'Then they carried the woman home ...'
    'Aí carregaram a menina para casa ...'

(43) dariyaxwale isi mĩw kuita ta
    dariya-xwa-le   isi   mĩu   kui-ta   ta
    fox-CLF:man-only die chicha drink-CSO CSO
    'Fox got completely drunk drinking *chicha* ...'
    'Raposa ficou completamente bêbado da chicha ...'

---

[20] The story ends provisionally with the declarative matrix mood and a fixed formulaic quotative expression ('they (say)'). However, nudged by Zezinho's minimal responses, several concluding parts are added hereafter.

(44) wɛwata wasi airyĩ

wɛ-wa-ta   wa-si   ai-ryĩ
carry-ISBJ-CSO ISBJ-SWR that-CLD:area
'while they were taking her there …'
'enquanto estavam levando a moça …'

(45) hariki dariyaxwale turwetya isi mĩw kuita isihĩ tya

hariki dariya-xwa-le   turwe-tya isi mĩu kui-ta   isi-hĩ   tya
now fox-CLF:man-only heal-CSO die chicha drink-CSO die-NMLZ CSO
'Then Fox recovered from getting drunk on the *chicha*.'
'Aí, Raposa sarou da bebedeira da chicha.'

(46) kataiwãle tiryĩ oyare etai awĩyxare etai wayeware etai tyata ta

katai-wã-le   ti-ryĩ   oya-re   etai   awĩi-xa-re   etai
agouti-AOBJ-only what-CLD:area arrive-INT woman see-2SG-INT woman
waye-wa-re   etai   tya-ta   ta
bring.back-ISBJ-INT woman ISBJ-CSO CSO
'Then (he asked) Agouti: "Where has the woman gone? Did you see the woman? Did they take her back?" he said.'
'Aí, perguntou para Cutia: "Onde foi a mulher? Viu a mulher? Eles levaram ela de volta?"'

(47) kataiwãle tinãi mã'are tinãi tsotsotsi tĩcwahĩ

katai-wã-le   ti-nãi   mã-a-re   ti-nãi   tso~tsotsi
agouti-AOBJ-only what-NMLZ call-1PL.INCL-INT what-NMLZ RED~cotton
tĩ-cwa-hĩ
spin-ISBJ-NMLZ
'On Agouti … What did we use to call it? What is the thing for spinning cotton?'
'Na Cutia … Como a gente costumava chamar? Qual é a coisa para fazer linha de algodão?'

(48) towɛyasi towɛyahĩ

towɛ-ya-si   towɛ-ya-hĩ
break-IOBJ-SWR break-IOBJ-NMLZ
[response from Zezinho:] 'The thing to pierce and to break off?'
[resposta do Zezinho:] 'Aquele de furar e quebrar?'

(49) tsotsotsi'ɨyniteko tsotsotsi tĩcwaratihĩkole toweyase cwasi
   tso~tsotsi-ɨi-nite-ko   tso~tsotsi
   RED~cotton-CLF:thread-INSTR-INS RED~cotton
   tĩ-cwa-rati-hĩ-ko-le   towe-ya-se   cwa-si
   spin-ISBJ-FOC-NMLZ-INS-only break-IOBJ-CLF:anus ISBJ-SWR
   'With the thing for making yarn, with that very thing for spinning yarn, Fox poked Agouti in his ass and it broke off.'
   'Com a coisa para tecer linha, com aquela coisa mesma, Raposa enfiou na bunda do Cutia e quebrou.'

(50) cwahĩta kataɨ esinyũtorihĩ eki tsɨnãi ewahĩtsɨ
   cwa-hĩ-ta   kataɨ esinyũ-tori-hĩ   e-ki=tsɨ-nãi
   ISBJ-NMLZ-CSO agouti tail-CLF:tip-NMLZ have-DECL=GER-NMLZ
   e-wa-hĩ-tsɨ
   have-ISBJ-NMLZ-RESI
   'That is why people say Agouti has a short tail like that.'
   'Pessoal conta que é por isso que a cutia tem um rabinho curto assim.'

(51) cwata xui wadɨcwahĩki cwahĩ
   cwa-ta xui wadɨ-cwa-hĩ-ki   cwa-hĩ
   ISBJ-CSO bag give-ISBJ-NMLZ-DECL ISBJ-NMLZ
   'Then it is said he was given a crochet bag,'[21]
   'Aí a família da moça deu uma bolsa de tucum para Cutia;'

(52) xuinyẽ etuna exɨitswa unãhĩ'e nãi e kataɨ cwasi
   xui-nyẽ   etu-na   exɨitswa unã-hĩ-e   nãi e kataɨ cwa-si
   bag-CLF:leaf back-LOC fur   long-NMLZ-too like have agouti ISBJ-SWR
   'giving him a bag (made out of palm leaves) on his back, that is why Agouti also has long fur.'
   'deram a ele uma bolsa (de fibras de tucum) e assim é que a cutia tem pêlo comprido nas costas.'

---

[21] By way of thanks, the girl gave Agouti a traditional type of crochet bag (known in local Portuguese as *marico*), the yarn of which is handmade out of the fibers of the young leaves of the *wade* 'tucuma' (*Astrocaryum tucuma*) or *hakare* 'buriti' (*Mauritia flexuosa*) palm trees.

(53) etailetsɨhĩ tsi'ahĩte ata a ta tswa aure'ɨhĩ
etai-le-tsɨ-hĩ   tsi'a-hĩ-te   a-ta   a   ta   tswa
woman-only-GER-NMLZ silent-NMLZ-NMLZ exist-CSO exist CSO man
aure-ĩ-hĩ
marry-ATT-NMLZ

'Only the girl remained sad (having lost a piece of herself), married to a man,'
'Aí, somente a menina ficava na tristeza (porque perdeu um pedaço), agora casou com um homem,'

(54) harɨkɨ tswatete mãrẽritsaxwa tse cwaratihĩtsɨ
harɨkɨ tswa-tete   mãrẽritsa-xwa   tse   cwa-rati-hĩ-tsɨ²²
now   man-INTENS person-CLF:man yes ISBJ-FOC-NMLZ-RESI

'now a real human man, they say, that's the way it is told.'
'agora um homem de verdade, dizem, assim que é contado.'

(55) a'ayawɨ cwata unĩtetawata txarwa hakahĩ awɨ
a~a-ya-wɨ   cwa-ta unĩteta-wa-ta   txarwa haka-hĩ
exist~exist-IOBJ-time ISBJ-CSO converse-ISBJ-CSO first   old-NMLZ
a-wɨ
exist-time

'Speaking today about our olden times,'
'Agora, falando sobre o tempo que os velhos viviam,'

(56) tẽitya hɨhɨrwatsi tsɨwɨdɨte tyatawa mãrẽtawata cwaki cwarati
tẽitya hɨhɨrwa-tsi tsɨwɨdɨte tyata-wa mãrẽ-ta-wa-ta   cwa-ki
alone walk-MON   girl   say-ISBJ explain-TR-ISBJ-CSO ISBJ-DECL
cwa-rati
ISBJ-FOC

'they didn't let girls walk alone; they gave them advice, this is the way it is told.'
'eles não deixaram as meninas andar sozinho; eles deram conselho, assim que fizeram.'

---

[22] The last word of this sentence represents a formulaic expression that terminates the traditional story. Hereafter a few other clauses are added, in (55) and (56), explaining the norms of olden times, which also end in a formulaic expression. Then in (57) and (59) these norms are contrasted with those of the present.

(57) *txarwa txana heyahĩ*

txarwa txana he-ya-hĩ
first we.INCL NEG-IOBJ-NMLZ

'Nowadays we don't.'[23]
'Hoje, a gente não faz isso.'

(58) *hm*

[response from Zezinho:] 'Hm.'
[resposta do Zezinho:] 'Hm.'

(59) *tsɨwɨdɨte xareredɨnãiko adɨ'ata*

tsɨwɨdɨte xarere-dɨnãi-ko a-dɨ-a-ta
girl crazy-manner-INS exist-CAUS-1PL.INCL-CSO

'We let girls act crazy like that, in present day life.'
'Hoje deixamos as moças fazer bagunça, vivendo assim.'

(60) *só isso*

a-a-hĩ aɨ-hĩ-le-tse[24]
exist-1PL.INCL-NMLZ that-NMLZ-only-DECL

'That's it, just that.'
'Só isso.'

Acknowledgements

Generous funding by the VolkswagenStiftung of DoBeS (Dokumentation Bedrohter Sprachen) project nr. 85.611 is hereby gratefully acknowledged.

---

[23]Lit. 'Nowadays we aren't (given advice).'
[24]On the original recording Edileusa ended her narrative in Portuguese by saying: *só isso* 'just that/that's it'. In the transcription Mario replaced those words by their Kwaza equivalent *a'ahĩ aɨhɨletse*, in order to complete the sentence — as well as the entire story — in a declarative mood.

Non-standard abbreviations

AOBJ	animate object	INSTR	instrument nominalizer
ATT	attributive	INT	interrogative
BER	beneficiary (nominal case marker)	INTENS	intensivizer
		INTL	intentional
CLD	classifier/directional	IOBJ	indefinite object
CSO	cosubordinative	ISBJ	indefinite subject
DIR	directional	MON	monitory
DS	different subject	NEI	negative imperative
EMPH	emphatic	POT	potential
EXH	exhortative	PREC	preconditional
EXP	exhortative paucal	RED	reduplication
FRUST	frustrative	RESI	resignation
GER	gerundi(v)al	SGO	singular object
IDS	indefinite different subject	SIMU	simulative
		SWR	switch reference mood

References

van der Voort, Hein. 2004. *A grammar of Kwaza*. Berlin: Mouton de Gruyter.

Chapter 11

Aikanã

Joshua Birchall
Museu Paraense Emílio Goeldi

Hein van der Voort
Museu Paraense Emílio Goeldi

Luiz Aikanã

Cândida Aikanã

1 Introduction

The story of Fox is a myth told by different peoples of the southwestern Amazon, including the Aikanã. The Aikanã people speak an isolate language, which, with about 225 speakers out of an ethnic group of around 560, is to be considered seriously endangered. The speakers of Aikanã live in two different indigenous reserves and in several towns and villages in southeastern Rondônia, Brazil, surrounded by the deforested lands of big cattle ranchers and soy farmers. The Aikanã represent the majority ethnic group in the Tubarão-Latundê reserve, which is shared with two minority populations: the Kwaza (ISOLATE) and the Latundê (NORTHERN NAMBIKWARA). Several mixed Aikanã and Kwaza families live in another nearby reserve called Kwazá do Rio São Pedro. Although the Aikanã language is still passed on to members of the youngest generations in both indigenous reserves, knowledge of the oral and musical traditions is disappearing rapidly. In addition to the two reserves in southeastern Rondônia, there are two other reserves in the southwest and the north of Rondônia where Aikanã populations live together with other ethnic groups. The Aikanã language

Figure 1: The indigenous reserves where the Aikanã live, shown in yellow.

is neither used nor remembered in those reserves, which are located far from traditional Aikanã lands.

The Aikanã language is morphologically highly complex. Most of this complexity concerns the verb, whereas fewer morphemes are used exclusively on nouns. However, due to the availability of highly productive nominalization strategies, nouns can also be morphologically complex. Aikanã has a great number of classifier and directional-like suffixes, several valency-changing suffixes, and suffixes marking tense, modality and aspect. Frequently occurring sequences of bound morphemes may become fixed with a derived meaning that is related to that of the constituent parts.[1] There is a wealth of main clause and adverbial clause mood suffixes, and extensive clause chains can be built using a switch reference marking system similar to that of Kwaza. The person marking system involves several inflectional paradigms for subject, object, beneficiary, and reflexive functions. There are different paradigms for subject marking — some of them suffixing and one prefixing — depending on verbal classes that are not yet fully understood. Third person subjects are often unmarked. Aikanã displays a basic distinction between future and unmarked non-future tense, but there are additional past and remote future tenses. Future tense and desiderative modality canonically involve double person marking: a person marker at the end of the verb stem, just before the mood inflection, and a person marker adjacent to the verb root, which is obligatorily a first person singular or plural, expressing an embedded perspective similar to that of quotation (van der Voort 2013; 2016). Although the language isolates of Rondônia, namely Aikanã, Kanoé and Kwaza, display several similar lexical and grammatical traits, there is no compelling evidence that they should be considered genealogically related (van der Voort 2005).

The following story was told by Luiz Aikanã during his visit in June 2013 to the Museu Paraense Emílio Goeldi in Belém. The story was recorded in audio and video formats as part of a documentation project funded through the DoBeS programme. After recording, the story was transcribed, analyzed and translated into Portuguese with Luiz's help. Luiz was born in 1952 and learned this and various other stories from his grandmother, *Kwã'ĩ*. He has been living and working on the Tubarão-Latundê reserve since it was officially settled in 1973. Because of his knowledge, experience and interest, he is one of the principal sources of information on Aikanã language and culture. Additional consultation on the analysis involved Cândida Aikanã, who is a native speaker of the Aikanã language with full command of Portuguese and is also a member of the DoBeS project team.

The story of Fox takes place in mythological times, when animals transformed into humans at will. As in the Kwaza story of Grandfather Fox, Fox in the Aikanã story is very smart and knows how to trick people. Also similar to the Kwaza story, Fox leads a young woman astray (and in this case her younger sister as well) after having found out about her plans for the next day. And again, the lesson of the story is that one should avoid speaking about one's plans for the future because that will attract adversity. The Aikanã story is quite different from the Kwaza one in several respects, but it similarly conveys this warning on the danger of talking about the future, which can be considered a taboo that still

---

[1] When verb roots and suffixes enter into such a bond, person markers sometimes may intervene and therefore occur as infixes in the morphemic analysis (e.g.: lines 49, 53, 82, 108).

forms part of the present way of life of the Aikanã people despite the enormous changes that they and the other indigenous peoples of Rondônia have undergone during the 20th century.

The story is presented with a rather broad phonetic transcription on the first line, and is then segmented phonologically and morphologically on the second line. The third line contains the glosses and the fourth and fifth lines contain free translations in English and Portuguese. It is worth pointing out that description of the Aikanã language is still ongoing and the analysis presented here will be further refined as this work continues to progress. Aikanã has had a native writing tradition since the late 1980s when an orthography was developed by missionaries. This orthography is used with varying success at the schools on the reserve, in Bible translation, in a recent dictionary by Silva et al. (2013) and in the present text. The <s> usually corresponds to IPA [ts], the <x> corresponds to [tʃ], the <y> corresponds to [j], the <z> often corresponds to [ð], and the <'> corresponds to [ʔ]. Vowels following a nasal consonant are usually nasalized, but this is not marked in the orthography used here. The central vowel [ɨ] and its nasal counterpart [ɨ̃] are allophones of the phonemes /a/ and /ã/, respectively. They occur only before an [i], but since they are part of the existing orthography they are preserved here.

2 Eruerazũ kyã'apa'i

'The story of Fox'

'A História do Raposa'[2]

(1) hisa xüxü xüxüwe Kwã'ĩ kyã'arisukudiweye kyãkarekaẽ

hisa xüxü   xüxüwe   Kwã'ĩ
1SG 1SG.POSS grandmother Kwã'ĩ

kyã-are-isu-ku-diwe-ye   kyã-ka-re-ka-ẽ
speak-poor-REM.PST-1SG.BEN-PST.NMLZ-OBJ speak-1SG-FUT-1SG-DECL

'I am going to tell a story my grandmother Kwã'ĩ told me.'
'Eu vou contar o que minha avó Kwã'ĩ contava pra mim.'

---

[2] Recordings of this story are available from https://zenodo.org/record/885240

(2) *hena detyamɨi namɨi hiku'ete kuka'i'ete wareyũpɨ*
    he-na   detya-mɨi   namɨi   hiku-ete   kuka-i-ete   ware-yũ-pɨ
    then-DS woman-DIM cousin other-ALL tell-NMLZ-ALL go-DIR:close-SS
    'Once a young woman went to talk with her cousin.'
    'Daí uma moça foi falar com a prima dela.'

(3) *derinena hikiri'ikana wikere axawapata'ẽ kukaẽ*
    deri-ne-na   hikiri-'ika-na   wikere a-xa-wa-pa-ta-'ẽ
    light-PFV-DS dark-INTENS-DS peanut uproot-1PL-DIR:upwards-TR-FUT-IMP
    kuka-ẽ
    tell-DECL
    '"Let's go dig up peanuts early tomorrow morning early," the cousin said.'
    '"Vamos lá arrancar amendoim amanhã cedo," falou a prima.'

(4) *hena kadupɨi kaxata'ereĩ*
    he-na   kadupɨi   ka-xa-ta-'ere-'ẽ
    then-DS alright do-1PL-REM.FUT-HORT-IMP
    '"OK, let's do it," (the girl replied).'
    '"Está bem, vamos fazer," (a moça respondeu).'

(5) *hena hepɨ ka'yareyada eruera anapayũzadeare*
    he-na   he-pɨ   ka-'ya-re-yada   eruera
    then-DS say-SS 1SG-come-FUT-REAS fox
    anapa-yũza-de-are
    listen-DIR:next-DIR:outside-INFR
    '"Then I'll come back," (she replied), but Fox was listening through the wall.'
    '"Então vou voltar," (ela respondeu), mas o Raposa estava escutando elas através da parede.'

(6) *anapayũzadepɨ kãwãyada hikiri'ikana*
    anapa-yũza-de-pɨ   kãwã-yada hikiri-ika-na
    listen-DIR:next–DIR:outside-SS be.like-REAS dark-INTENS-DS
    'He was listening from behind the wall, it was very dark.'
    'Ele estava escutando atrás da parede bem de manhã cedo.'

(7) *derinena hikiri'ikana mẽyãpü tawĩmeata'ẽ kukaẽ*

deri-ne-na   hikiri-'ika-na   mẽ-yã-pü   tawĩ-me-a-ta-'ẽ
light-PFV-DS dark-INTENS-DS 2SG-come-IS await-2SG-1SG-FUT-IMP
kuka-ẽ
tell-DECL

'"So you come get me early morning tomorrow!" the girl said.'
'"Então você me chama amanhã cedo!" a moça falou.'

(8) *hepü hukadupɨi hepü xünehepü*

he-pü   hukadupɨi he-pü   xüne-he-pü
then-SS alright   then-SS return-3SG-SS

'"OK," the cousin said and left.'
'"OK," a prima falou, e foi embora.'

(9) *hena zune iriane*

he-na   zune iriane
then-DS night middle

'Then in the middle of the night ...'
'Daí no meio da noite...'

(10) *derikanerena mɨitü ɨitüderine*

deri-ka-ne-re-na   mɨitü ɨitü-deri-ne
day-1SG-PFV-FUT-DS only be.different-NMLZ-EMPH

'It was going to be dawn soon.'
'Estava querendo amanhecer ainda.'

(11) *yã'i eruera apa'ixüte*

yã-i   eruera apa-ixüte
come-NMLZ fox   say-REP

'Fox came, they say.'
'O Raposa veio, disseram.'

(12) *eruera yãpü*

eruera yã-pü
fox   come-SS

'Fox came.'
'O Raposa veio.'

(13) *namɨi namɨi kukana hãw heẽ*

    namɨi namɨi kuka-na hãw he-ẽ

    cousin cousin tell-DS huh say-DECL

    '"Cousin, cousin!" he called. "Yes?" she responded.'

    '"Prima, prima!" ele chamou. "Sim?" ela respondeu.'

(14) *yãw'ẽ wikere xü'iaxanapetaka'ĩwãte kukaẽ*

    yãw'ẽ   wikere

    let's.go.IMP peanut

    xü'i-a-xa-nape-ta-ka-'ĩwã-te   kuka-ẽ

    dig-uproot-1PL-DIR:forest-REM.FUT-CLF:pieces-ADMON-PST tell-DECL

    '"Let's go digging up peanuts as planned," he told her.'

    '"Vamos arrancar amendoim como combinamos," ele falou para ela.'

(15) *erünuna hikiri'ika'iwã hikiri'ikaẽ*

    erünuna hikiri-ika-iwã   hikiri-ika-ẽ

    EXPL   dark-INT-ADMON dark-INT-DECL

    '"But damn, it's still dark outside, really dark," (she replied).'

    '"Mas poxa, ainda está escuro lá fora, bem escuro," (ela respondeu).'

(16) *tawãxapü kaxatɨi kukaẽ*

    tawã-xa-pü ka-xa-ta-i   kuka-ẽ

    what-1PL-SS do-1PL-FUT-INT tell-DECL

    '"Why do we have to go now?"'

    '"Porque temos que fazer agora?"'

(17) *hinaẽ derinedupa kawaẽ*

    hina-ẽ deri-ne-dupa kawa-ẽ

    no-DECL light-PFV-CONC be-DECL

    '"No, dawn is almost here."'

    '"Não, está clareando já."'

(18) *kawãte izata'ẽ kapü kadiẽ iza'idepeta'ẽ kapü kadiẽ hẽ*

    kawãte iza-ta-'ẽ   ka-pü kadi-ẽ

    because far-REM.FUT-DECL do-SS affirm-DECL

    iza-idepe-ta-'ẽ   ka-pü kadi-ẽ   he-ẽ

    far-DIR:garden-REM.FUT-DECL do-SS affirm-DECL say-DECL

    '"It's because the garden is far away, really far away," he said.'

    '"É porque a roça fica longe, bem longe mesmo," ele falou.'

(19)   hena mamaderi hürüwanipü

   he-na   mama-deri   hürü-wa-ne-pü
   then-DS mother-3.POSS rise-DIR:up-PFV-SS

   'Then her mother awoke.'
   'Daí a mãe dela acordou.'

(20)   hena hikiri'ika'iwã tãwãmeapü kameazati

   he-na   hikiri-ika-iwã   tãwã-mea-pü ka-meaza-ti
   then-DS dark-INTENS-ADMON what-2PL-SS do-2PL-FUT.INT

   '"But it's still dark out, why are you going?" she said.'
   '"Mas está escuro ainda. Por que vocês vão fazer agora?" ela falou.'

(21)   izaderineipita'ẽ eyedupa kukadupa

   iza-deri-ne-i-pita-'ẽ   eye-dupa   kuka-dupa
   far-light-PFV-NMLZ-PROC-IMP 3PL.OBJ-CONC tell-CONC

   '"Let the sun come up first," she told them, but...'
   '"Deixa clarear mais," ela falou pra elas, mas...'

(22)   hinaẽ kapü derinedupa kawaẽ eyepü

   hina-ẽ   ka-pü deri-ne-dupa   kawa-ẽ eye-pü
   no-DECL do-SS light-PFV-CONC be-DECL 3PL.OBJ-SS

   '"No, it's already dawn," Fox said to them.'
   '"Não, está clareando já," Raposa falou para elas."'

(23)   hedupana purikɨi'eneke bubu'he'ĩwã tãwãxeapü warexatɨi kukaẽ

   he-dupana purikɨi-'ene-ke bubu-'he-'ĩwã   tãwã-xea-pü ware-xa-ti
   say-TEMP flute-COL-ALSO dance-3-ADMON what-1PL-SS go-1PL-FUT.INT
   kuka-ẽ
   tell-DECL

   'But when he said that, the girl said, "The musicians are also dancing, how shall we get past?"'[3]
   'Mas na hora que ele falou isso, a menina respondeu, "Os músicos estão dançando ainda, como é que vamos passar?"'

---

[3] At this point, men are still playing flutes and dancing, which lasts all night. In accordance with traditional custom, women are not allowed to witness the event and see or even hear the flutes, which are sacred.

(24) *hinaẽ kapü xarükanapɨire'ẽ*
 hina-ẽ ka-pü xa-rüka-napai-re-'ẽ
 no-DECL do-SS 1PL-DIR:around-CLF:forest-FUT-IMP

 '"No, we'll go around them through the brush (behind the house).'"
 '"Não, vamos desviar pelo mato (atrás da casa).'"

(25) *üre'apa'ine xarükanapɨire'ẽ kukaẽ*
 üre-apa'i-ne xa-rüka-napa-ire-'ẽ kuka-ẽ
 hide-ACT.NMLZ-LOC 1PL-DIR:around-CLF:forest-almost-IMP tell-DECL

 '"We will sneak around them," said Fox.'
 '"Vamos desviar eles escondidos," falou o Raposa.'

(26) *tãwãmeapü waremea'ĩ kukaẽ*
 tãwã-mea-pü ware-mea-'ĩ kuka-ẽ
 what-2PL-SS go-2PL-INT say-DECL

 '"How is it that you came?" the girl said.'
 '"Como é que você veio?" ela falou.'

(27) *baba hapükemukahana kãyãpü kayaẽ*
 baba hapü-ke-muka-a-na ka-yã-pü ka-yã-ẽ
 father hold-3-CLF:eye-1SG.OBJ-DS 1SG-come-SS 1SG-come-DECL

 '"Father covered my face, and then I came," (Fox said).'
 '"Meu pai segurou meu rosto, daí eu vim," (Raposa falou).'

(28) *hukadupɨi kukaẽ*
 hukadupɨi kuka-ẽ
 alright tell-DECL

 '"Alright," she said.'
 '"Tudo bem," ela falou.'

(29) *kadupɨi kaxare'ereĩ hepü hena*
 kadupɨi ka-xa-re-'ẽ he-pü he-na
 alright do-1PL-FUT-IMP say-SS then-DS

 '"Alright, then let's go," she said, and then ...'
 '"Tudo bem, então vamos," ela falou, e daí ...'

(30) *mamaderi kãwãyada tanimɨiye keapa'ẽĩ deri zãme mama'ĩ diarekaẽ*

    mama-deri   kãwã-yada tanimɨi-ye kea-pa-'ẽ deri zãme mama'ĩ
mother-3.POSS be.like-REAS sister-OBJ get-TR-IMP light today chicha
dia-re-ka-ẽ
1SG-FUT-1SG-DECL

'Her mother said, "In that case, bring your little sister. I am going to make *chicha* today."'[4],[5]

'A mãe dela falou, "Então leva sua irmãzinha, vou fazer chicha hoje."'

(31) *yoayoakuka'isuwate'ẽ*

yoa~yoa-kuka-isuwate-'ẽ
cry~cry-CLF:body-HAB-DECL

'"She is always crying."'
'"Ela fica chorando."'

(32) *deü'edika'ẽ tanimɨ̃iye kukaẽ hukadupɨi*

deü-edika-'ẽ   *tanimɨi-ye kuka-ẽ*   *hukadupɨi*
put.heavy-CLF:back-IMP sister-OBJ tell-DECL alright

'"Carry your little sister on your back," (Fox) told her. "Alright," (she responded).'
'"Leva sua irmã nas costas," (Raposa) falou. "Tudo bem," (ela respondeu).'

(33) *tanimɨideriye de'edikapü yãw'ẽ*

tanimɨi-deri-ye *deü-edika-pü*   *yãw'ẽ*
sister-3.POSS-OBJ put.heavy-CLF:back-SS let's.go.IMP

'She put her little sister on her back and "Let's go!" (she said).'
'Ela colocou a irmãzinha nas costas e "Vamos embora!" (ela falou).'

(34) *hikadepapü. hepü hikiri'ine*

hika-de-pa-pü.   *he-pü* *hikiri-'i-ne*
leave-DIR:outside-TR-SS then-SS dark-NMLZ-LOC

'She went outside. It was dark.'
'Ela saiu pra fora. Já escureceu.'

---

[4] In Rondônia, this is usually a lightly alcoholic drink based on boiled fermented maize, manioc or yams, which is prepared by women. Elsewhere it is also known as *kashiri* or *caxiri*.

[5] The form *deri* is a false start: the narrator begins to say *derinena* 'at daybreak' (lit. 'light-PFV-DS') but then corrects himself, saying *zãme* 'today'.

(35) *hikirihedupapü hidepɨidukaripü*

    hikiri-he-dupa-pü hidepai-dukari-pü
    dark-3-CONC-SS garden-3PL-SS

    'Although it was dark, they went to the garden.'
    'Mesmo no escuro, eles foram pra roça.'

(36) *bate kameyẽ'ete'i erünuna iza'iza'ĩwã kukapü iza hepü*

    bate ka-me-yẽ-'ete-'i erünuna iza~iza-ĩwã kuka-pü iza-he-pü
    where be-2SG-DUB-ALL-INT wow! far~far-ADMON tell-SS far-3SG-SS

    '"But where is it?" asked the girl. "Wow, it's still far away. It's far," he replied.'
    '"Mas onde que é?" ela perguntou. "Nossa, está longe ainda. Fica longe." ele respondeu.'

(37) *iza kukapü hete'i hũka kukaẽ*

    iza kuka-pü he-te'i hũka kuka-ẽ
    far tell-SS say-EMP in.vain tell-DECL

    '"Didn't I tell you it was far?" he said, fooling them.'
    '"Já não falei que fica longe?" falou, enganando elas.'

(38) *zamiya wãderi'ete wareyũpapü tikiri dürü'i'ete*

    zamiya wã-deri-'ete ware-yũ-pa-pü tikiri dürü-'i-'ete
    now live-NMLZ-ALL go-CLF:close-TR-SS mound sit-NMLZ-ALL

    'Then they arrived at a termite mound where he lives.'
    'Daí chegaram numa casa de cupins de barro onde ele mora.'

(39) *hena henudu ẽ perüka'i inekapü wãheyada*

    he-na henu-du-pe-rüka-'i-ne ka-pü wã-he-yada
    then-DS hole-DIR:in-CLF:round-DIR:around-NMLZ-LOC do-SS live-3-REAS

    'It's of course full of holes where he lives.'
    'Está cheio de buracos onde ele mora.'

(40) *hena hapükemukapü waredurikapaẽ*

    he-na hapü-ke-muka-pü ware-durika-pa-ẽ
    then-DS hold-3-CLF:eye-SS go-DIR:inside-TR-DECL

    'Then he covered their eyes and entered.'
    'Daí tampou os olhos delas e entrou.'

(41) *waredurikapapü*
 ware-durika-pa-pü
 go-DIR:inside-TR-SS
 'They went inside.'
 'Entraram pra dentro.'

(42) *hena kiinezũ keza iitühene'ena*
 he-na   kiine-zũ keza iitü-he-ne'e-na
 then-DS 3SG-POSS house be.different-3-ITE-DS
 'His house was very different.'
 'Daí a casa dele estava diferente.'

(43) *kawã kayaparehãyãpü kawãtena ãrüakukapederiame hena*
 kawã   ka-ya-pa-re-hãyã-pü   kawãte-na
 be.like 1SG-come-TR-FUT-1PL.OBJ-SS because-DS
 ãryüa-kuka-pe-deri-ame   he-na
 know-CLF:body-CLF:round-NMLZ-SUP then-DS
 '"He really is leading us astray," the older and somewhat more knowledgeable girl thought.'
 '"Ele falou isso só para judiar de nós," aquela que é mais sabida pensou.'

(44) *wãwã'ĩ'ikaderihame kapü hina'ĩ hina kukaẽ*
 wãwã'ĩ-'ika-deri-hame ka-pü hina-ĩ   hina kuka-ẽ
 child-INTENS-NMLZ-SUP do-SS no-NMLZ no say-DECL
 'The little child didn't worry at all, didn't say anything.'
 'A criança mais nova nem se liga, não fala nada.'

(45) *tãwãxeapü kaxa'i erükazapa'ĩ kawã dukumɨi kawãtena*
 tãwã-xea-pü ka-xa-'i   erükazapa'ĩ kawã   dukumɨi kawãte-na
 what-1PL-SS do-1PL-INT wow!   be.like ruin   because-DS
 '"How is it that we stopped here? Wow, it must be some spirit messing with us."'
 '"Como é que nós paremos aqui? Poxa, é sombração que está mexendo com a gente."'

(46) *namɨi kayareapɨite'i*
   namɨi ka-ya-re-a-pa-i-te'i
   cousin 1SG-come-FUT-1SG.OBJ-TR-NMLZ-EMPH
   '"I thought it was my cousin!"'
   '"Pensei que era minha prima!"'

(47) *he'ẽ kapü ã'apakukaẽ*
   he-'ẽ ka-pü ã-'a-pa-kuka-ẽ
   say-DECL do-SS think-3SG.REFL-TR-CLF:body-DECL
   'She went on thinking and became sad.'
   'Ela foi pensando e ficou triste.'

(48) *nake tãwã ãanaẽ kapü hina'ĩ'ẽ*
   nake tãwã ã-a-na-ẽ ka-pü hina-'ĩ-'ẽ
   COND what think-1SG.OBJ-NEG-DECL do-SS no-NMLZ-DECL
   '"What can I do? There is nothing."'
   '"Como que posso fazer? Não podemos fazer nada."'

(49) *hena'ẽ zamiya hiku is'ideri dukanuẽ hepü yoa*
   hena-'ẽ zamiya hiku ise-'i-deri d-u<ka>nu-ẽ he-pü
   quiet-IMP now other small-NMLZ-NMLZ 1SG-hungry<1SG>-DECL say-SS
   yoa
   cry
   'The little one was crying from hunger.'
   'A outra pequena estava chorando de fome.'

(50) *he'ẽ kapü kɨine hiku ti'iweke ũnenudupa*
   he-'ẽ ka-pü kɨine hiku ti'iwe-ke ũ<ne>nu-dupa
   say-DECL do-SS 3SG other grow-COM hungry<PFV>-CONC
   'The grown one also had gotten hungry but (she held on).'
   'A outra grande também estava com fome mas aguentou.'

(51) *tãwã'ãnaẽ he'ẽ yoaẽ*
   tãwã-'ã-na-ẽ he-'ẽ yoa-ẽ
   what-IMPERS-NEG-DECL say-DECL cry-DECL
   '"What can one do?" she said. "She is crying."'
   '"O que pode fazer?" ela falou. "Ela está chorando."'

(52) *eruerazũ mamaderi*
 eruera-zũ mama-deri
 fox-POSS mother-3.POSS

 'Now Fox's mother (comments):'
 'Agora a mãe do Raposa (comenta):'

(53) *dukanuẽ ũnenuxaẽ he'ẽ yoayoaredukari'ĩwã*
 d-u<ka>nu-ẽ ũ<ne>nu-xa-ẽ he'ẽ
 1SG-hungry<1SG>-DECL hungry<PFV>-1PL-DECL say-DECL
 yoa~yoa-are-dukari-'ĩwã
 cry~cry-poor-3PL-ADMON

 '"The poor dears are crying 'I am hungry, we are hungry.'"'
 '"Os coitados estão chorando 'Estou com fome, estamos com fome.'"'

(54) *tara kawhepire'ẽ eyepü kawa'ĩ*
 tara kaw-he-pi-re-'ẽ eye-(na)-pü kawa-'ĩ
 what eat-3-PROC-FUT-IMP 3PL.OBJ-(NEG)-SS be-INT

 '"Why didn't he find something for them to eat first?" (the mother thought).'
 '"Porque não procurou uma coisa pra eles comerem primeiro?" (a mãe pensou).'

(55) *kawãnunu hãemepe'eyepü kawãte'i kukaẽ*
 kawã-nunu hãe-me-pe-'eye-pü kawãte-'i kuka-ẽ
 be.like-MIR grab-2SG-CLF:round-3PL.OBJ-SS because-INT say-DECL

 '"Why the hell did you catch them?" she said to him angrily.'
 '"Então porque você pegou elas?" ela falou com raiva.'

(56) *kawayada xoakarüperekaẽ urikii hepü hikade'ẽ*
 kawa-yada xoa-ka-rüpe-re-ka-ẽ urikii he-pü
 be-REAS see-1SG-DIR:ground-FUT-1SG-DECL food say-SS
 hika-de-'ẽ
 leave-DIR:outside-DECL

 'So he said "I will look for food," and left.'
 'Então ele falou "Vou procurar comida," e saiu pra fora.'

(57) *hikadepü kapü wã'apaderi'ete yũ'eyeẽ kapü*

　　hika-de-pü　　　　ka-pü　wã-'apaderi-'ete　yũ-'eye-ẽ
　　leave-DIR:outside-SS do-SS live-ACT.NMLZ-ALL DIR:close-3PL.OBJ-DECL
　　ka-pü
　　do-SS

　　'He went outside and left for where the girls' parents lived.'
　　'Ele saiu para onde o povo morava.'

(58) *tara pu'apaderiye kuraruye kapü*

　　tara　pu-'apaderi-ye　　　kuraru-ye　ka-pü
　　what raise-ACT.NMLZ-OBJ chicken-OBJ do-SS

　　'There he got things that one raises, chickens.'
　　'Alí ele pegou coisas que a gente cria, galinha.'

(59) *düdü pu'apa'iye kikireye hãehãekepesa'eye*

　　düdü　pu-'apa'i-ye　　　kikire-ye　　hãe~hãe<ke>pe-sa-'eye
　　parrot raise-ACT.NMLZ-OBJ parakeet-OBJ grab~grab<3SG>-MAL-3PL.OBJ

　　'Pet parrots, parakeets, he grabbed them from the residents.'
　　'Papagaio, periquito, ele pegou dos moradores.'

(60) *nasunapaẽ wãderi'ete duxüpanepü hiba'eyenakedupa kapü*

　　na-suna-pa-ẽ　　　　　　　wã-deri-'ete　　　du-xü-pa-ne-pü
　　bring-DIR:hither-TR-DECL live-NMLZ-ALL DIR:in-DIR:return-TR-PFV-SS
　　hiba-'eye-nake-dupa　　ka-pü
　　give-3PL.OBJ-COND-CONC do-SS

　　'He brought those home, and entering into their residence, gave (the food) to the children, however ...'
　　'Ele trouxe de volta pra casa e entrou dentro da residência e deu (a comida) para elas, mas...'

(61) *haradukarinake*

　　hara-dukari-nake
　　not.want-3PL-COND

　　'They really didn't want anything.'
　　'Elas não queriam mesmo.'

(62) haradukarinake tãwãanaẽ kapü
 hara-dukari-nake tãwã-a-na-ẽ ka-pü
 not.want-3PL-COND what-IMPERS-NEG-DECL do-SS
 '"They didn't want anything, now what can one do?"'
 '"Não queriam, mas fazer o quê?"'

(63) yoahedukarina kapü kãwãẽ zamiya mamaderi
 yoa-he-dukari-na ka-pü kãwã-ẽ zamiya mama-deri
 cry-3-3PL-DS do-SS be.like-DECL now mother-3.POSS
 'They kept on crying as ever. And then his mother went:'
 'Ficaram chorando. Agora a mãe do Raposa falou:'

(64) tara hü'a'iye xoawe'epü tãwãmepü urikɨɨiye kamezɨi
 tara hü'a-'i-ye xoa-we'eye-pü tãwã-me-pü urikɨi-ye
 what good-NMLZ-OBJ see-3PL.BEN-SS what-2SG-SS food-OBJ
 ka-meza-i
 do-2SG.CAUS-INT
 '"Find them something good, you only bring bad stuff."'
 '"Procure um coisa boa para elas, você só traz coisa ruim."'

(65) tara dukumɨi'iye kaw'i kawã'ĩwãwã
 tara dukumɨi-'i-ye kaw-'i kawã-'ĩwã~wã
 what ruin-NMLZ-OBJ eat-NMLZ be.like-ADMON~RED
 '"They don't eat worthless things."'[6]
 '"Elas não comem coisa que não presta."'

(66) kawã'ĩ dukumɨi'iye kawxare'ẽyaremina
 kawã-ĩ dukumɨi-'i-ye kaw-xa-re-'ẽ-are-mina
 be.like-NMLZ ruin-NMLZ-OBJ eat-1PL-FUT-IMP-INFR-EMP.NEG
 '"They don't even think of eating what's worthless."'
 '"Nem pensam em comer aquilo que não presta."'

(67) hü'anɨi apaduri'iwa he'ẽ kukana
 hü'a-na-i apa-dukari-'iwa he-'ẽ kuka-na
 good-NEG-NMLZ find-3PL-ADMON say-DECL tell-DS
 '"They are suffering," she said to him.'
 '"Estão sofrendo," ela falou para ele.'

---

[6]Domestic(ated) animals are not eaten, even if the same animals would represent game in the wild context.

(68) *iza hepü*

    iza he-pü
    far say-SS

    '"Go far away," she said.'
    '"Vai longe," ela falou.'

(69) *tara hü'a'iye takepewe'eye'ẽ kukaẽ*

    tara hü'a-'i-ye   ta-ke-pe-we'eye-'ẽ   kuka-ẽ
    what good-NMLZ-OBJ shoot-3-CLF:round-3PL.BEN-IMP tell-DECL

    '"Kill something good for them!" she told him.'
    '"Mata coisa boa pra elas!" ela falou para ele.'

(70) *kadupɨi kayapitaẽ*

    kadupɨi ka-ya-pita-ẽ
    alright 1SG-go-PROC-DECL

    '"OK, then I'll go," and he left.'
    '"Está bem, já vou então," e ele foi.'

(71) *hikadepü iza izapa'apü wã'apa'i'ete hidüka'eye'i apa'ixüte*

    hika-de-pü   iza iza-pa-'a-pü   wã-apa'i-ete
    leave-DIR:outside-SS far far-TR-IMPERS-SS live-ACT.NMLZ-ALL
    h-idüka-eye-'i   apa-'ixüte
    3SG-DIR:thither-3PL.OBJ-NMLZ tell-REP

    'He left the house and went to an inhabited place very far away, they say.'
    'Ele saiu de casa e foi para uma moradia que fica bem longe, eles dizem.'

(72) *hidüka'eyepü tarawã pu'apaderiye kapü hãekepepü*

    h-idüka-'eye-pü   tara-wã pu-'apaderi-ye   ka-pü
    3SG-DIR:thither-3PL.OBJ-SS what-?[7] raise-ACT.NMLZ-OBJ do-SS
    hãe<ke>pe-pü
    grab<3SG>-SS

    'He went there far away and got what people were raising.'
    'Ele foi lá longe e pegou o que o pessoal estava criando.'

---

[7] The uninterpretable form -*wã* is apparently a slip of the tongue.

(73) kapü kẽrikukapeyada kẽriẽ kukayada
 ka-pü kẽri-kuka-pe-yada   kẽri-ẽ   kuka-yada
 do-ss linger-CLF:body-?-REAS linger-IMP tell-REAS
 'Obviously this took a while. It should take some time.'
 'Obviamente demorou um pouco. É para demorar um pouco mesmo.'

(74) ĩwã'arena kaxupane'eyãre'ẽ mamaderi hepü
 ĩwã-are-na   ka-xü-pa-ne-'eyã-re-'ẽ   mama-deri
 like.that-poor-DS 1SG-DIR:return-TR-PFV-2PL.OBJ-FUT-DECL mother-3.POSS
 he-pü
 say-SS
 '"How unfortunate, let me bring you back!" his mother said to the girls.'
 '"Coitadas! Eu vou levar vocês de volta!" a mãe dele falou para as meninas.'

(75) eruerazũ mamaderi eyepü hina'ĩ hü'anɨi'apazaẽ
 eruera-zũ mama-deri   eye-pü   hina-'ĩ   hü'a-na-i
 fox-POSS mother-3.POSS 3PL.OBJ-SS no-NMLZ good-NEG-NMLZ
 h-apa-za-ẽ
 2-find-PL-DECL
 'Fox's mother said to them, "You are suffering."'
 'A mãe do Raposa falou, "Vocês estão sofrendo."'

(76) tara kawxamɨirumia'ẽ hü'ana'i hapazaẽ
 tara kaw-xa-mɨiriu-mia-'ẽ hü'a-na-i   h-apa-za-ẽ
 what eat-1PL-DESI-2PL-DECL good-NEG-NMLZ 2-find-PL-DECL
 '"You want to eat and you are suffering."'
 '"Vocês querem comer e estão sofrendo."'

(77) kaxupane'eyãre'ẽ eyepü
 ka-xü-pa-ne-'eyã-re-'ẽ   eye-pü
 1SG-DIR:return-TR-PFV-2PL.OBJ-FUT-DECL 3PL.OBJ-SS
 '"Let me bring you back!" she said to them.'
 '"Eu vou levar vocês de volta", falou pra elas.'

(78) *hapükika'eyepü hikadepa'eyepü*
hapü-ke-ika-'eye-pü   hika-de-pa-'eye-pü
hold-3-CLF:finger-3PL.OBJ-SS leave-DIR:outside-TR-3PL.OBJ-SS
'She took them by the hand and left.'
'Ela segurou a mão delas e levou para fora.'

(79) *katemɨi nuxupane'enunu*
kate-mɨi   nu-xu-pa-ne'e-nunu
there-DIM come-DIR:return-TR-ITE-MIR
'Now they were arriving close to home again.'
'Estavam chegando perto de casa.'

(80) *anapahidepenunu mamaderi babaderi yoahedukariẽ*
anapa-hidepe-nunu   mama-deri   baba-deri   yoa-he-dukari-ẽ
hear-DIR:garden-MIR mother-3.POSS father-3.POSS cry-3-3PL-DECL
'They heard the children's mother and father crying in the garden.'
'Ouviram a mãe e o pai delas chorando na roça.'

(81) *puidepena*
pu-idepe-na
go.PL-DIR:garden-DS
'"They are walking over there ..."'
'"Estão andando por aí ..."'

(82) *ite hüridawaperekaẽ ite darüpa'eyã'ẽ eyepü*
ite   hüri<da>wa-pe-re-ka-ẽ   ite   darüpa-'eyã-'ẽ
here return<1SG.REFL>-?-FUT-1SG-DECL here stay.PL-2PL.OBJ-DECL
eye-pü
3PL.OBJ-SS
'"From here I will return and you stay put," she told them.'
'"Daqui eu vou voltar e vocês ficam," ela falou pra elas.'

(83) *hiba mama baba'i'ene yoayoahedukariẽ*
hiba mama   baba-'i-'ene   yoa~yoa-he-dukari-ẽ
this mother father-NMLZ-COL cry~cry-3-3PL-DECL
'Well, the mother and father were crying.'
'Daí a mãe e o pai estavam chorando.'

(84) *ite katemɨiyana*
 ite katemɨi yã-na
 here close come-DS
 'They were coming close.'
 'A mãe e o pai estavam chegando perto delas.'

(85) *mama baba memekuka'ana*
 mama baba bee-me-kuka-a-na
 mother father arrive-2SG-CLF:body-1SG.OBJ-DS
 '"(When you call them) "Mother, father, come to me."" (Fox's mother explained).'
 '"(Quando chama eles) "Mãe, pai, vem para cá."" (a mãe do Raposa explicou).'

(86) *wareyã'ẽyãpü pane'ẽyãta'ẽ*
 ware-yã-ẽyã-pü pane-ẽyã-ta-'ẽ
 go-come-2PL.OBJ-SS bring-2PL.OBJ-REM.FUT-DECL
 '"And when they come to you, they will take you home."'
 '"Quando chegarem, vão levar vocês pra casa."'

(87) *ite hüridawaperekaẽ hepü*
 ite hüri<da>wa-pe-re-ka-ẽ he-pü
 here return<1SG.REFL>-?-FUT-1SG-DECL say-SS
 '"Here I will return back," she said.'
 '"Daqui eu vou voltar pra trás," ela falou.'

(88) *hepü daedaedɨikasa'eyena*
 he-pü dae~dae-dɨika-sa-'eye-na
 say-SS walk~walk-DIR:remain-MAL-3PL.OBJ-DS
 'She walked back behind them.'
 'Ela voltou por trás delas.'

(89) *darüpaena darüpaẽ*
 darüpa-e-na darüpa-ẽ
 stay.PL-well-DS stay.PL-DECL
 'They stayed there for a while.'
 'Ficaram um tempo lá.'

(90) *zamiya babaderi mamaderi'i'ene kapü yoahe'ẽ*
 zamiya baba-deri   mama-deri-'i-'ene   ka-pü yoa-he-'ẽ
 now   father-3.POSS mother-3.POSS-NMLZ-COL do-SS cry-3-DECL
 'Then their father and mother were still crying.'
 'Daí o pai e a mãe delas ainda estavam chorando.'

(91) *beeyũ'eyena hepü xãyãrehãyãdukariẽ tãwĩhedukarina*
 bee-yũ-'eye-'ẽ-na   he-pü xã-yã-re-hãyã-dukari-ẽ
 arrive-DIR:near-3PL.OBJ-well-DS say-SS 1PL-come-1PL.OBJ-3PL-DECL
 tãwĩ-he-dukari-na
 await-3-3PL-DS
 'As they were getting nearby, "They are coming close to us," the children said and waited for them.'
 'Estavam indo perto deles, daí, "Estão chegando perto de nós," as crianças falaram e esperaram eles.'

(92) *hena tawĩhedupana baba baba mama mama*
 he-na   tawĩ-he-dupana baba   baba   mama   mama
 then-DS await-3-TEMP   father father mother mother
 'Then they called out, "Father! Father! Mother! Mother!"'
 'Dai elas chamaram, "Papai! Papai! Mamãe! Mamãe!"'

(93) *erüarekũyẽi hepü xoahenunu*
 erüare-kũyã-i   he-pü xoa-he-nunu
 feel.sorry-1PL.BEN-NMLZ say-SS see-3-MIR
 'The parents said, "Our poor dears!" as they saw them.'
 'Os pais falaram, "Nossas coitadas!" quando viram elas.'

(94) *darüpa'aredukarina*
 darüpa-are-dukari-na
 stay.PL-poor-3PL-DS
 'The poor kids are sitting there.'
 'As coitadas estão lá.'

(95) *erüarekumɨizɨi eyepü yoa'eyepü yoahepü*
 erüare-kuma-i-za-i   eye-pü   yoa-'eye-pü   yoa-he-pü
 feel.sorry-poor-NMLZ-ASSOC-NMLZ 3PL.OBJ-SS cry-3PL.OBJ-SS cry-3-SS
 '"You poor little things," they said to them, crying.'
 '"Coitado de vocês," falou para elas chorando.'

(96) *hepü hikuye hürükewanunu hameri*
  he-pü   hiku-ye   hürü-ke-wa-nunu hameri
  then-ss other-OBJ rise-3-DIR:up-MIR already
  'They lifted up one of the girls and were ready to go, but now ...'
  'Dai levantou uma delas para ir embora, mas...'

(97) *eruera urumekarepü hameri wãeditehe hikutehe kyã'i'apa'i*
  eruera urume-ka-re-pü   hameri wãedi te-he   hiku te-he
  fox   transform-1SG-FUT-SS already tail   have-3SG other have-3SG
  kyã-'i-'apa'i
  speak-NMLZ-ACT.NMLZ
  'One was changing into a fox and was already sprouting a tail, and the other one as well, that's what the story says.'
  'Uma estava se transformando em raposa e já estava nascendo rabo, e a outra também. É assim que a história conta.'

(98) *kawãdupa yãw'ẽ he'eyepü hapükika'eyepü*
  kawã-dupa yãw'ẽ   he-'eye-pü   hapü-ke-ika-'eye-pü
  be.like-CONC let's.go.IMP say-3PL.OBJ-ss hold-3-CLF:hand-3PL.OBJ-ss
  '"Even so, let's leave," the parents said to them, and they held hands.'
  '"Mesmo assim vamos embora," falou para elas, e segurou as mãos delas.'

(99) *pane'eyepü*
  pane-'eye-pü
  bring-3PL-ss
  'They brought them along.'
  'Levaram elas.'

(100) *keza'ete wareduxüpane'eyena kapü zamiya hena*
  keza-'ete   ware-du-xü-pane-'eye-na   ka-pü zamiya he-na
  house-ALL go-DIR:in-DIR:return-bring-3PL.OBJ-DS do-ss now   then-DS
  'They entered the house with them, but ...'
  'Entraram na casa com elas, mas...'

(101) *hameri eruera urumekareheyada kapü hina'ĩ*
  hameri eruera urume-ka-re-he-yada   ka-pü hina-ĩ
  already fox   transform-1SG-FUT-REAS do-ss no-NMLZ
  'Since they were already becoming foxes it was no good.'
  'Agora que já se transformaram em raposas, não foi bem.'

(102) *hadite'ete büxuheku'ẽ kukana*

    hadite-'ete büxu-he-ku-'ẽ   kuka-na
    shaman-ALL cure-3-1SG.BEN-IMP tell-DS

    'Father told the shaman, "Cure them for me!"'
    'O pai pediu ao pajé, "Cura elas para mim!"'

(103) *hadite wareyãpü büxühepü*

    hadite   ware-yã-pü büxü-he-pü
    shaman go-come-SS cure-3SG-SS

    'The shaman came and he cured them.'
    'O pajé veio e curou.'

(104) *arerekekukahepü*

    arere-ke-kuka-he-pü
    blow-3-CLF:body-3SG-SS

    'He blew on and cleansed the body.'[8]
    'Ele assoprou e limpou o corpo.'

(105) *keapü dupakapü*

    kea-pü dupa ka-pü
    get-SS really do-SS

    'He did it just like this.'
    'Ele fez assim mesmo.'

(106) *wɨɨwɨɨmezakukane'eta'ẽ kukaẽ*

    wɨɨwɨɨ-meza-ku-ka-ne-'eta-'ẽ   kuka-ẽ
    repeat-2SG.CAUS-1SG.BEN-TR-PFV-REM.FUT-IMP tell-DECL

    '"You must do that again for me," (the father) said to him.'
    '"Repete mais uma vez para mim," (o pai) falou pra ele.'

(107) *zamiya mama'ĩ mama'ĩkea'ẽ detyaderi'ete kukapü*

    zamiya mama'ĩ mama'ĩ-kea-'ẽ detya-deri-'ete   kuka-pü
    now   chicha chicha-3-IMP woman-3.POSS-ALL tell-SS

    '"Now make chicha!" he told his wife.'
    '"Daí faz chicha então!" ele falou para sua esposa.'

---

[8] The process of sucking and blowing away maladies is a central part of Aikanã shamanic healing and is a common practice among many lowland South American groups.

(108) *hisa zamumuye tara ari'iye takawaparekaẽ hadite kawhepü*

hisa zamumu-ye tara ãri'i-ye
1SG patawa.larva-OBJ what mamuí.larva-OBJ
ta<ka>wa-pa-re-ka-ẽ hadite kaw-he-pü
break<1SG>-TR-FUT-1SG-DECL shaman eat-3-SS

'"I am going to get some patawá and mamuí larvae for the shaman to eat."'[9]
'"Eu vou tirar coró de patauá e de mamuí para o pajé comer."'

(109) *ü'ükekukakũyare'ẽ wãwã'iye detyaderi'ete kukapü*

ü'ü-ke-kuka-kũya-re-'ẽ wãwã'i-ye detya-deri-'ete
save-3-CLF:body-1PL.BEN-FUT-IMP child-OBJ woman-3.POSS-ALL
kuka-pü
tell-SS

'"He will fix the bodies of the children for us," he said to his wife.'
'"Ele vai concertar o corpo das crianças para nós," falou para a mulher dele.'

(110) *babaderi daedaena'ĩ daedaenapü*

baba-deri dae~dae-na-'ĩ dae~dae-na-pü
father-3.POSS walk~walk-go-NMLZ walk~walk-go-SS

'Her father went walking (in the forest).'
'O pai delas foi andando (no mato).'

(111) *zamumuye takewapü*

zamumu-ye ta<ke>wa-pü
patawá.larva-OBJ break<3>-SS

'He removed patawá larvae (from the wood).'
'Ele tirou coró de patauá.'

---

[9] The indigenous peoples of Rondônia cultivate the protein-rich larvae of specific beetle species by cutting down patawa (*Oenocarpus bataua*) or buriti (*Mauritia flexuosa*) palm trees and wild papaya (*Jaracatia spinosa*, in Portuguese *mamuí*) trees, leaving them to be eaten from the inside by these larvae. After about half a year the trunks can be cracked open and the delicious larvae can be harvested.

(112) *ari'i-ye keapü*

    ãri'i-ye   kea-pü
    mamuí.larva-OBJ get-SS

    'He got mamuí larvae.'
    'Pegou coró de mamuí também.'

(113) *nusunapapü*

    nu-suna-pa-pü
    come-DIR:return-TR-SS

    'He brought them back home.'
    'Ele trouxe de volta pra casa.'

(114) *amakea'ẽ detyaderi'ete kukapü amamakezaẽ*

    ama-kea-'ẽ detya-deri-'ete   kuka-pü ama~ma-keza-ẽ
    cook-3-IMP woman-3.POSS-ALL tell-SS cook~RED-3SG.CAUS-DECL

    '"Cook it!" he told his wife, and she cooked it.'
    '"Cozinha aí!" ele falou para a mulher dele, e ela cozinhou.'

(115) *hikiririkapedupana zamiya*

    hikiri-rika-pe-dupana   zamiya
    dark-CLF:floor-CLF:round-TEMP now

    'As it was getting dark inside ...'
    'Enquanto estava escurecendo lá dentro...'

(116) *hadite tãwĩkukapü irüpü*

    hadite tãwĩ-kuka-pü   irü-pü
    shaman await-CLF:body-SS trance-SS

    'He called the shaman to enter into a trance.'[10]
    'Ele chamou o pajé para rezar.'

---

[10] In this state the shaman is sitting down on his/her bench while pulling down the invisible lines that form the net on which his/her spirit can travel, the *haditaezũ daruma* 'shaman's sling'. In order to heal, he/she performs acts such as sucking, blowing smoke, gestures of collecting, extracting, expelling, etc. The last Aikanã shaman passed away in 1985, but elderly people remember the tradition and are often able to interpret the work of shamans from other ethnic groups.

(117) *wãwã'ĩ ukikekukaku'ẽ awexü urumeẽ*

wãwã'ĩ   uki-ke-kuka-ku-'ẽ   awexü   urume-ẽ
child   clean-3-CLF:body-1SG.BEN-IMP demon transform-DECL

'"Cleanse the body of my daughter, who has transformed into a demon!"'[11]

'"Limpa o corpo da criança que se transformou em bicho do mato!"'

(118) *kukaku'ẽ kukana*

kuka-ku-'ẽ   kuka-na
tell-1SG.BEN-IMP tell-DS

'"Talk to him for me!" he said.'

'"Fala para ele para mim!" ele falou.'

(119) *hadite wareduapü*

hadite   ware-dua-pü
shaman go-DIR:inside-SS

'The shaman went inside.'

'O pajé entrou para dentro.'

(120) *wareriakapü uruhepü*

ware-riaka-pü   uru-he-pü
go-DIR:middle-SS sing-3-SS

'He went to the middle of the house and sang.'

'Ele chegou no meio da casa e cantou.'

(121) *hadite kiineke wareyũpanake büxü'ẽ hepü*

hadite   kiine-ke   ware-yũ-pa-nake   büxü-'ẽ   he-pü
shaman 3SG-COM go-DIR:near-TR-COND cure-IMP say-SS

'As soon as the shaman brought her with him, (the father) said "Cure her!"'

'Quando o pajé levou ela junto com ele, (o pai) falou "Cura ela!"'

---

[11]The *awexü* is a dangerous and powerful spirit of the forest that can transform itself into any being and is able to make people lose their mind. Especially when someone is alone in the forest or on a remote cultivated plot, the *awexü* may trick someone and lead him/her astray or directly attack and kill a person. Unexpected death and psychotic illness are often explained as the work of the *awexü*. Experiences with the *awexü* are always traumatic and accounts of them are harrowing.

(122) *arerekekukaxüne'ẽ*
arere-ke-kuka-xüne-'ẽ
blow-3-CLF:body-DIR:return-IMP

'"Blow and cleanse the body again!" (the father) said.'
'"Assopra e limpa o corpo de novo!" (o pai) falou.'

(123) *hibaye awexüye hukedurakaxüne'ẽ*
hiba-ye awexü-ye hu-ke-duraka-xüne-'ẽ
this-OBJ demon-OBJ remove-3-DIR:inside-DIR:return-IMP

'"Remove this demon from inside of her!"'
'"Tire esse bicho do mato que está dentro dela!"'

(124) *pawpawkezakaxüne'ẽ kyãkukapü*
paw~paw-keza-ka-xüne-'ẽ   kyã-kuka-pü
run~run-3SG.CAUS-TR-DIR:return-IMP speak-tell-SS

'"Make it (the demon) run away!" he said to him.'
'"Espanta o espírito para fora!" falou para ele.'

(125) *derinena zamiya deripanena*
deri-ne-na   zamiya deri-pa-ne-na
light-PFV-DS now   light-TR-PFV-DS

'Dawn came and then day came.'
'Clareou e amanheceu o dia.'

(126) *zamiya kapü kukapü daexünepü*
zamiya ka-pü kuka-pü dae-xüne-pü
now   do-SS tell-SS walk-DIR:return-SS

'"It's done," he said, and (the demon) went back to where he came from.'
'"Está pronto," ele falou e (o bicho do mato) voltou para de onde veio.'

(127) *hena wïiwïiyeye wãkanayeyepü urikïieye hürakenupapü*
he-na   wïiwïi-yeye wãkana-yeye-pü urikïi-ye hüra-ke-nupa-pü
then-DS repeat-ITE late.morning-ITE-SS food-OBJ place-3-DIR:outside-SS

'Then it had to be repeated during the day, and food was placed in the yard (for the shaman and the possessed child).'
'Daí ele fez outra vez de dia, e ele deixou comida no terreiro (para o pajé e a criança).'

(128) *kariye kawhepü*
kari-ye kaw-he-pü
that-OBJ eat-3-SS
'She ate some of that.'
'Ela comeu aquilo.'

(129) *büxühekunehe'ẽ kukapü büxühenehepü xükeakapapü*
büxü-he-ku-ne'e-'ẽ   kuka-pü büxü-he-ne'e-pü
cure-3-1SG.BEN-ITE-IMP tell-SS   cure-3-ITE-SS
xü-kea-ka-pa-pü
finish-3SG-CLF:piece-TR-SS
'"Perform the cure again for me," he said, and the shaman did so again, and finished (removing the demon's spirit from the head of the child).'
'"Cura de novo para mim," ele falou, e o pajé curou de novo, e terminou (tirando o espírito do bicho da cabeça da criança).'

(130) *taraye kawahenake xükeakapapü*
tara-ye   kaw-a-he-nake   xü-kea-ka-pa-pü
what-OBJ eat-IMPERS-3-COND finish-3SG-CLF:piece-TR-SS
'Through eating (the food) he could remove the demon's spirit (from the bodies of the girls).'
'Comendo as coisas ele tirou a alma do bicho (dos corpos das meninas).'

(131) *kapünepü zamiya kapü zamiya hü'akaxünerewaẽ wãwã'ĩ*
kapü-ne-pü   zamiya ka-pü zamiya
finish-PFV-SS now   do-SS now
hü'a-ka-xüne-re-wa-ẽ   wãwã'ĩ
good-1SG-DIR:return-FUT-2SG.BEN-DECL child
'He finished and said, "Now that it's done, your children will get well again."'
'Ele terminou e falou, "Agora que foi feito, suas filhas vão sarar."'

(132) *zare kaxünerewaẽ*
zare   ka-xüne-re-wa-ẽ
person 1SG-DIR:return-FUT-2SG.BEN-DECL
'"They will be people again for you."'
'"Vão se tornar em gente de novo para você."'

(133) *kuka'i apa'ixüte kukana*

    kuka-'i apa-'ixüte kuka-na
    tell-NMLZ say-REP tell-DS

    'This is how he spoke to the father.'
    'Assim que ele falou para o pai.'

(134) *hukadupɨi hepü*

    hukadupɨi he-pü
    alright say-SS

    '"Alright," he said.'
    '"Está certo," ele falou.'

(135) *wãwã'ĩke hina'ĩ hũka hũka eryüanahe'ẽ hukakeaderi*

    wãwã'ĩ-ke hina-'ĩ hũka hũka eryüana-he-'ẽ hũka-kea-deri
    child-COM no-NMLZ in.vain in.vain sick-3-DECL in.vain-3-NMLZ

    'The children used to be ill and were really going crazy.'
    'As crianças também não tinham sussego, viviam bagunçando.'

(136) *zamiya zɨ̃izɨ̃i eryüaxünena zamiya*

    zamiya zɨ̃izɨ̃i eryüa-xüne-na zamiya
    now correct live-DIR:return-DS now

    'But now they were behaving well again.'
    'Mas agora ficaram direitinhas de novo.'

(137) *wãwã'ĩ hikaderike hepü hü'axüneẽ*

    wãwã'ĩ-ika-deri-ke he-pü hü'a-xüne-ẽ
    child-INTENS-NMLZ-COM then-SS good-DIR:return-DECL

    'The youngest also got better.'
    'A criança mais nova melhorou também.'

(138) *hiba tiwenederi hü'axüneẽ*

    hiba ti'iwe-ne-deri hü'a-xüne-ẽ
    this grow-PFV-NMLZ clean-DIR:return-DECL

    'The older one got better.'
    'Essa mais velha melhorou.'

(139) *kyã'i apatena*
 kyã-'i   apa-te-na
 speak-NMLZ say-PST-DS
 'This is how they told it.'
 'Assim que contaram.'

(140) *dupana zarikapasapü zarikahedupana*
 dupana zarika-pa-sa-pü zarika-he-dupana
 while delay-TR-MAL-SS delay-3-TEMP
 'But a while after (Fox had abducted them)...'[12]
 'Mas um pouco depois (que o Raposa sequestrou elas)...'

(141) *hiku kapü kaxare'ẽ namɨɨderi'ika kukaderiye wareyũpü*
 hiku ka-pü ka-xa-re-'ẽ   namɨɨ-deri-ika   kuka-deri-ye
 other do-SS do-1PL-FUT-IMP cousin-3.POSS-INTENS tell-NMLZ-OBJ
 ware-yũ-pü
 go-DIR:close-SS
 'The real cousin, the one who said to do it (to get peanuts) arrived (at the girls' house).'
 'Aquela prima delas que tinha combinado com ela (arrancar amendoim) primeiro chegou (na casa das meninas).'

(142) *kaxare'ẽ ka'ĩwãte yãw'ẽ deripahãyã'ẽ namɨɨ kukaẽ*
 ka-xa-re-'ẽ   ka-'ĩwã-te   yãw'ẽ   deri-pa-hãyã-ẽ   namɨɨ
 do-1PL-FUT-IMP do-ADMON-PST let's.go.IMP day-TR-1PL.OBJ-DECL cousin
 kuka-ẽ
 tell-DECL
 '"We had agreed to do it, let's go! It's becoming day for us," the cousin said.'
 '"Vamos lá fazer o que concordamos! O dia está amanhecendo em nós," a prima falou.'

(143) *mamaderi warehikadepü keriẽ hĩzã kamezakukateare apɨɨre'i*
 mama-deri   ware-hika-de-pü   keriẽ hĩzã
 mother-3.POSS go-leave-DIR:outside-SS whoa! 2SG

---

[12] Here the narrator goes back to an earlier phase in the story, adding the part concerning the real cousin after the girls had been abducted.

```
ka-meza-kuka-te-are           apa-ire-'i
do-2SG.CAUS-CLF:body-PST-INFR say-almost-INT
```
'Her mother went outside and said: "Whoa! Aren't you the one that was going to call them?"'
'A mãe saiu pra fora e falou, "Nossa! Não foi você que chamou elas?"'

(144) *hameri'ẽ tara kawãte'i wareyãpü namɨi namɨi kukapü*

```
hameri-h-ẽ      tara kawãte-'i   ware-yã-pü namɨi namɨi kuka-pü
already-3-DECL what because-INT go-come-SS cousin cousin say-SS
```
'"Who was the one that came already and said, 'Cousin! cousin!' then?"'
'"Quem será que veio e chamou 'Prima! Prima!' naquela hora?"'

(145) *yãw'ẽ kukapü warehikadepapü hameri pa'ĩwãte*

```
yãw'ẽ         kuka-pü ware-hikade-pa-pü    hameri
let's.go.IMP say-SS   go-DIR:outside-TR-SS already
pa-'ĩwã-te
unsuccessful-ADMON-PST
```
'"Let's go!" she had said to her, but they had already left.'
'"Vamos embora!" falou para ela, mas elas já tinham saido.'

(146) *hĩzã kamezɨiare ka'ĩwãte kukaẽ*

```
hĩzã ka-meza-i-are         ka-'ĩwã-te    kuka-ẽ
2SG  do-2SG.CAUS-NMLZ-INFR do-ADMON-PST say-DECL
```
'"I thought it was you," she said to the cousin.'
'"Pensei que era você," ela falou para a prima.'

(147) *hinaẽ hisa kayana'ĩwãte kapü derinena kayata'ẽ ka'ĩwã*

```
hina-ẽ   hisa ka-ya-na-'ĩwã-te         ka-pü deri-ne-na
no-DECL  1SG  1SG-come-NEG-ADMON-PST  do-SS light-PFV-DS
ka-ya-ta-'ẽ                ka-'ĩwã
1SG-come-REM.FUT-DECL     do-ADMON
```
'"No, it wasn't me. I let it dawn first."'
'"Não foi eu não, deixei clarear o dia primeiro."'

(148) *ka'ĩwãte kawã zarena'ĩ kawã kazapasahãyãtena*

```
ka-'ĩwã-te      kawã    zare-na-'ĩ        kawã
do-ADMON-PST  be.like person-NEG-NMLZ  be.like
```

ka-za-pa-sa-hãyã-te-na
do-CAUS-TR-MAL-1PL.OBJ-PST-DS

'"So it must not have been a person that took them from us."'
'"Então não era uma pessoa que levou elas de nós."'

(149) babaderi mamaderi he'i he'i apɨixüte

baba-deri   mama-deri   he-'i   he-'i   apa-ixüte
father-3.POSS mother-3.POSS say-NMLZ say-NMLZ say-REP

'Their father and mother said this. This is what was said.'
'O pai e a mãe delas falou isso. Assim que falaram.'

(150) hepü hikirinena kawã kawã hikirinena

he-pü   hikiri-ne-na kawã   kawã   hikiri-ne-na
then-SS dark-PFV-DS be.like be.like dark-PFV-DS

'Then it got dark.'
'Daí escureceu, escureceu mesmo.'

(151) bari wareyãepü kaxata'ẽ hikiri'ikana

bari ware-yã-e-pü   ka-xa-ta-'ẽ   hikiri-'ika-na
who go-come-2SG.OBJ-SS do-1PL-REM.FUT-IMP   dark-INTENS-DS

'"When someone comes for you, saying, 'Let's do it early in the morning!'" ...'
'"Quando alguém vier para você falando 'Vamos lá amanhã cedo!'" ...'

(152) hapa'aparete'ẽ apa'i apɨixüte apa'ẽ kyãapɨisuwãẽ he'ẽ xüxüe kyã'isuwãẽ xüxüe xüxü xüxüe Kwã'ĩ

h-apa~apa-rete'ẽ   apa-'i   apa-ixüte apa-'ẽ
2SG-say~say-NEG.IMP say-NMLZ say-REP   say-DECL
kyã-apa-isuwã-ẽ   he-'ẽ   xüxüe   kyã-'isuwã-ẽ
speak-say-REM.PST-DECL say-DECL grandmother speak-REM.PST-DECL
xüxüe   xüxü   xüxüe   Kwã'ĩ
grandmother 1SG.POSS grandmother Kwã'i

'"You can't talk like that with people," my grandmother used to say.[13] Grandmother Kwã'ĩ.'
'"Você não pode falar assim com os outros," assim que falava minha avó. Vovó Kwã'ĩ.'

---

[13] Here, reference is made to the moral of the story, also mentioned in the introduction, that one should not talk about one's plans.

(153) *kariyame ãryüaka'ĩwã*
 kari-ame ãryüa-ka-'ĩwã
 this-SUP know-1SG-ADMON
 'I know just this.'
 'Só isso que eu sei.'

(154) *kawãẽ*
 kawã-ẽ
 be.like-DECL
 'That's it.'
 'É assim.'

Acknowledgments

Generous funding by the VolkswagenStiftung of DoBeS (Dokumentation Bedrohter Sprachen) project nr. 85.611 is hereby gratefully acknowledged. In addition, Luiz Aikanã's visit to the Museu Goeldi was kindly funded by the Brazilian National Science Foundation CNPq (Conselho Nacional de Pesquisa Científica) within Vilacy Galucio's project *Documentação de línguas indígenas e a sua integração no acervo digital de línguas indígenas do Museu Goeldi*. Additional comments and corrections were kindly provided by Raimunda and Mario Aikanã.

Non-standard abbreviations

ACT	action	INT	interrogative
ADMON	admonitory	INTENS	intensifier
AG	agent	ITE	iterative
COL	collective	MAL	malefactive
CONC	concessive	MIR	mirative
DESI	desiderative	PROC	procrastinative
DIM	diminutive	REAS	reason adverbial
DIR	directional	RED	reduplication
DS	different subject	REM	remote
DUB	dubitative	REP	reported past
HAB	habitual aspect	SS	same subject
HORT	hortative	SUP	superlative
IMPERS	impersonal	TEMP	temporal adverbial
INFR	inferential mood		

References

Silva, Maria Fátima S., Raimunda Aikanã, Luiza Aikanã & Luzia Aikanã. 2013. *Primeiro dicionário da língua Aikanã*. Porto Velho: SEDUC.

van der Voort, Hein. 2005. Kwaza in a comparative perspective. *International Journal of American Linguistics* 71(4). 365–412.

van der Voort, Hein. 2013. Fala fictícia fossilizada: O tempo futuro em Aikanã. *Boletim do Museu Paraense Emílio Goeldi, Ciências Humanas* 8(2). 359–377.

van der Voort, Hein. 2016. Recursive inflection and grammaticalized fictive interaction in the southwestern Amazon. In Esther Pascual & Sergeiy Sandler (eds.), *The conversation frame: Forms and functions of fictive interaction*, 277–299. Amsterdam: John Benjamins Publishing Company.

Chapter 12

Suruí of Rondônia

Cédric Yvinec

CNRS/Mondes Américains, Paris, France

Agamenon Gamasakaka Suruí

1 Introduction

This story relates one of the numerous skirmishes in the continuously warlike relations between the Suruí of Rondônia (or, according to their autodenomination, *Paiter*) and their indigenous neighbors. It is representative of the Suruí narrative genre. Suruí is a language of the Mondé family of the Tupian stock. The Suruí live in the Sete de Setembro Indigenous Land, on the border between the Brazilian states of Rondônia and Mato Grosso, near the city of Cacoal. The speakers of Suruí now number about 1,200 individuals; this population has increased steadily since the 1970s, when measles, flu and tuberculosis epidemics broke out after their first peaceful contact with the Brazilian society in 1969, causing a demographic crisis. Although the Suruí traditionally lived in just one or two villages, they are now scattered among more than 20 settlements along the boundaries of their land, which remains an island of rainforest surrounded by cattle ranchers (see Figure 1). Slash-and-burn horticulture and hunting have been replaced by coffee farming, illegal logging, and environmentalist projects. War with neighboring Indian groups and White settlers have ceased and numerous matrimonial bonds now tie the Suruí to their former enemies. Thus, although the events narrated here evoke a world vividly experienced by the generations born before the 1960s, this past is very different from the daily life of the young adults today, who form a large part of the audience of such narratives.[1]

---

[1] For general ethnographic information on the Suruí, see Mindlin (1985; 1996) and Yvinec (2011). For information on the various ways of narrating past events among the Suruí, see Yvinec (2016).

Cédric Yvinec & Agamenon Gamasakaka Suruí. 2017. Suruí of Rondônia. In Kristine Stenzel & Bruna Franchetto (eds.), *On this and other worlds: Voices from Amazonia*, 439–465. Berlin: Language Science Press. DOI:10.5281/zenodo.1008795

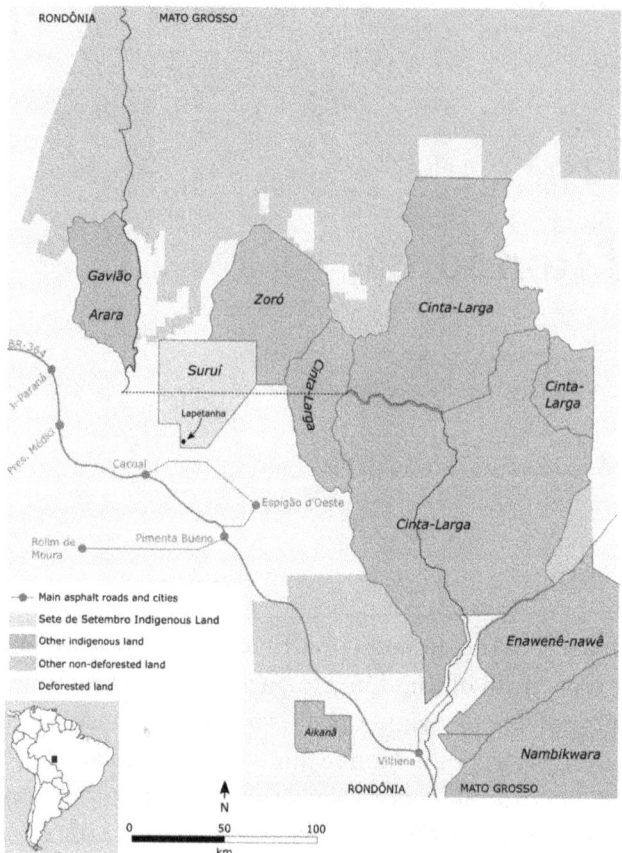

Figure 1: Present location of the Suruí (Map: C. Yvinec)

The story is 9 minutes long. It was narrated in June 2013 by Agamenon Ãamasakaka Suruí, a fifty-year-old man, one of the most powerful and respected men in the village of Lapetanha (see Figure 2). It was told to me at night, after I explicitly asked to record it. That very afternoon, Agamenon had spontaneously narrated it to his two wives, surrounded by several of his sons, daughters and nephews, while we were enjoying a break in the tedious work of picking coffee berries. The aim of the narration was both to celebrate the ancestor of his political faction and to entertain the audience, especially by singing a beautiful war song. When closely related, politically friendly adults get together, for example while sitting around a fire at night or having a rest during a collective work, they often exchange such stories among themselves. Because they are narrated over and over, their content is rarely entirely unknown to the audience.

Here, Agamenon evokes an attack on a neighboring Zoró village – a Mondé-speaking population of north-western Mato Grosso who were the Suruí's preferred enemies – that took place before the birth of all living Suruí, probably in the 1920s. The narration culminates with the song one of the warriors composed in celebration of his deeds. Indeed, it is through such songs that memory of historical events is passed down among the Suruí.

Several other stylistic features are worth noting. For the most part, the story is composed of embedded quotations of successive narrators of the event, so that it is rendered in direct first person speech, including the alleged inner discourse (thoughts) of actors. Thus, the narration paints a vivid picture of the events, intensified by the extensive use of ideophones.

Figure 2: The narrator, Agamenon G̃amasakaka Suruí (Photo C. Yvinec)

The evidential status of each embedded discourse is systematically marked, either as witnessed evidence (narration heard by the speaker from his father) or as non-witnessed evidence (narration heard by the latter from his own father, the protagonist of the event). However, in a kind of introductory summary (lines 5-8), and then again in the conclusion (lines 55–69), the narrator refers to the nature and general behavior of the main character, his grandfather.[2] Paradoxically, these parts of the story are marked as witnessed evidence, although the narrator was born years after his grandfather's death. Such deletion of non-witnessed evidentiality marking in the course of a story is common in various narrative genres, including myths. It is often due to a prioritized focus on the sequence of events rather than on the source of information. Here, on the other hand, the contrast is between a particular event (identified by a song), which needs to have its non-witnessed evidential status restated in each sentence of the description because it is painted as if it had been lived by the speaker, and general inferences that can be construed as witnessed on the basis of the lifelike description of the event. Finally, the difference between Suruí historical and mythological narratives needs to be pointed out: whereas myths are attributed to an indeterminate group of anonymous speakers, the chain of narrators of historical events is clearly established throughout the story.

---

[2]The recording situation and the absence of a Suruí interlocutor prone to ask questions and open new stories led this narrator to develop these considerations further than most narrators would do in conversational situations, and gave the story a unity that spontaneously-occurring narrations do not often have.

The transcription convention used here is mostly similar to that developed by the SIL missionaries with a group of Suruí for textbooks and Bible translation. All orthographic symbols are to be pronounced as in Brazilian Portuguese, except for the following: *g̃* is a velar nasal [ŋ] ; *h* indicates that the preceding vowel is long; *s* is a voiceless velar [x] or dental fricative [θ]; and *u* is a closed front rounded vowel [y]. The tilde, acute accent, and circumflex denote nasalization, high tone on oral vowels, and high tone on nasalized vowels, respectively. Vowels without any diacritic mark are oral vowels with low (or undetermined) tone. Suruí consonants vary in initial and final word positions, according to the preceding or following morpheme, especially in possessive noun phrases and in the construction of the object-verb group. The most frequent variations are *p~m, k~g, s~l~x, t~tx~n, d~j, m~∅*, and *w~∅*. They are reproduced in the writing convention.

Suruí typological features can be summed up as follows. The basic word orders are genitive-noun; noun-adjective; and object-verb. The subject has no strictly determined position, but tends to precede the object-verb group, and is marked by aspectual and/or evidential suffixes. There are two classes of nouns: obligatorily possessed and non-obligatorily possessed; the latter can nonetheless occur in a possessive construction, marked by the possessive prefix *-ma-*, positioned between the genitive and the noun. There are two class of verbs: transitive and intransitive. The latter can have a reflexive pronoun (which only differs from the regular pronoun in the third person) in the object position, thus aligning subjects of intransitive verbs with objects of transitive verbs. Indirect objects can appear with both classes of verbs and are marked by dative, benefactive, or ablative suffixes. Evidentiality is marked by suffixes on the subject and/or by sentence-final markers.[3] Evidentiality can be witnessed, non-witnessed, or non-declarative (a subclass of non-witnessed).[4]

---

[3] On some occasions (lines 8; 13; 60), sentence parsing contradicts the sentence-final markers, because prosody shows that the speaker extended and corrected his utterance after the sentence-final marker.

[4] Only preliminary studies are available on Suruí: on phonology, see Lacerda Guerra (2004); on syntax, see Bontkes (1985), and Van der Meer (1985), as well as the primary author's own work (Yvinec 2011: 679–691).

2 Ana omamõya G̃oxoraka ã

'This is the way my grandfather killed a Zoró'
'Foi assim que meu avô matou um Zoró'[5]

(1) *Nem, a olobde merema og̃ay ma e.*

nem a   o-sob-de   pere-ma   o-ka   ma   e
INTJ DEM.PROX 1SG-father-WIT ITER-do[6] 1SG-DAT PRF.PST SFM.WIT

'Well, here is what my father recounted to me.'
'Meu pai me contou isso.'

(2) *Nem, a, ""ana oiyã" olobiyã," olobesesob, denene.*

nem a   a-na   o-ya   o-sob-ya
INTJ DEM.PROX DEM.PROX-FOC 1SG-NWIT 1SG-father-NWIT

o-sob-e-sob   ∅-de-ee-na-ee-na-e[7]
1SG-father-NMLZ-father   3SG-WIT-ENDO-FOC-ENDO-FOC-SFM.WIT

'He said this, about my father's father: "I heard that my father said: "I did this, they say.""'[8]
'Ele falou assim, do pai de meu pai: "Eu ouvi que meu pai falou assim: "Eu fiz isso, pessoas falam.""'

---

[5]Recordings of this story are available from https://zenodo.org/record/997449
[6]The suffix *-ma* used as a verb can have many meanings, including 'to say' or 'to explain'.
[7]The combination *ee-na*, ENDO-FOC, is an adverbial locution that is pervasive in narrative speech. Its meaning is very loose and almost expletive: 'thus', 'this way', 'like this'. It emphasizes the inner links of the speech, contrasting with *i-na*, EXO-FOC, which occurs in conversations that refer to physically present objects.
[8]From this point on, the whole narration is a quotation of Agamenon's father quoting a narration by his own father, except for a few sentences (lines 5-9; 43-47; 49-50; 55-64). This embedding of quoted speech is marked at the end of almost every sentence. However, we do not reproduce it systematically in the free translation in order to lighten it a little; quotation marks only will indicate the levels of embedding. The evidential value of each level will not be reproduced either, since it remains unchanged throughout the narration: Agamenon's father's speech was witnessed (*de*, WIT), his grandfather's was not (*ya*, NWIT).

(3) ""*Nem, olobaka G̃oxoriyã" iyã" de.*
 nem o-sob-aka   G̃oxor⁹-ya   i-ya   ∅-de¹⁰
 INTJ 1SG-father-kill Zoró-NWIT 3SG-NWIT 3SG-WIT
 '"""Well, a Zoró killed my father.""''
 '"""Um Zoró matou meu pai.""''

(4) ""*Eebo oya okãyna oladeka sona olobepika sona yã" olobiyã" olobde.*
 ee-bo¹¹   o-ya   o-kãyna   o-sade-ee-ka¹²   sona
 ENDO-ADVERS 1SG-NWIT 1SG-grow 1SG-PROG.SIM-ENDO-DAT often
 o-sob-wepika   sona   a   o-sob-ya   o-sob-de
 1SG-father-avenge often SFM.NWIT 1SG-father-NWIT 1SG-father-WIT
 '"""So as I grew up, I avenged my father many times.""''
 '"""Então, quando eu cresci, vinguei meu pai muitas vezes.""''

---

[9] The word *G̃oxor*, Zoró, is a lexicalization of the locution *lahdg̃oesor*, *lahd-koe-sor*, Indian.enemy-language-ugly, 'enemy whose language is difficult to understand' – but not incomprehensible, by contrast with other neighbors, either from the Mondé family (Cinta-Larga) or not (Kawahib, Nambikwara). The Portuguese ethnonym "Zoró" is a corruption of the Suruí word. At the time of the narrated events, *G̃oxor* referred to a single population, from which are descended the two ethnic groups nowadays called Zoró and Gavião of Rondônia, who split off in the 1940s, when the latter entered in contact with rubber tappers, while the former remained in voluntary isolation until 1977 (see Figure 3). For ethnohistorical information about the Zoró, see Brunelli (1987).

[10] Quotations are marked in Suruí by an isolated subject, that is, a noun or pronoun (or the absence of it, for third person singular) with an aspectual and/or evidential suffix, to which no verbal group corresponds. Moreover, an indirect object, specifying the addressee can appear after the subject. These markers usually appear after the quoted speech and can be strung together to indicate embedding of quotations, as we see here.

[11] In Suruí narrative discourse, almost every sentence is introduced by an adverbial locution that connects it to the preceding one: *ee-bo* (ENDO-ADVERS), 'and', 'so', or 'but'; *ee-te* (ENDO-ADV), 'then', 'indeed', 'and'; *ee-tiga-te* (ENDO-SIM-ADV), 'then', 'at that time'; *a-yab-* (DEM.PROX-ENDO), 'and this', 'and the latter'. It is difficult to give a uniform translation of those discourse-linking expressions.

[12] The combination *ee-ka*, ENDO-DAT, functions as a postposition that subordinates the preceding clause as an indirect object of the verbal group of the main clause. Its meaning is either temporal or causal.

(5) *Eebo dena sona G̃oxoraka akah sone.*

ee-bo ∅-de-ee-na sona G̃oxor-aka a-kah
ENDO-ADVERS 3SG-WIT-ENDO-FOC often Zoró-kill 3.REFL-go
sona-e.
often-SFM.WIT

'So he repeatedly set out to kill some Zoró.'

'Então ele foi matar o Zoró muitas vezes.'

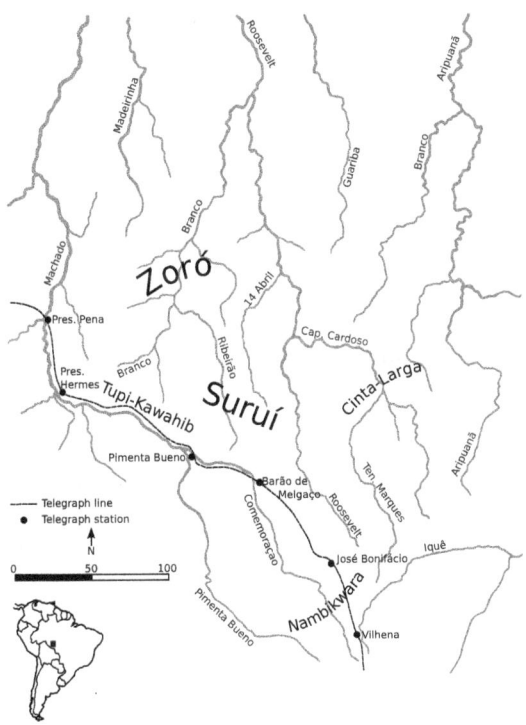

Figure 3: Approximate location of the Suruí, Zoró, and neighboring groups of the Machado-Roosevelt interfluve in the first half of the 20th century. At that time, the stations of telegraph line built by Rondon in 1914 were the only permanent colonial presence in that region. (Map: C. Yvinec)

(6) *Ayabğoy xibebiga, ikar iperedena, ihbahbağa iperedena, eyabğar iperedekena.*

a-yab-koy   xi-ibeb-iga   i-kar   i-pere-de-na
DEM.PROX-ENDO-to 3SG-track-pick 3SG-search 3SG-ITER-WIT-FOC
ihbahb-mağa i-pere-de-na   ee-yab-kar
canoe-make 3SG-ITER-WIT-FOC ENDO-ENDO-search
i-pere-de-kah-ee-na
3SG-ITER-WIT-go-ENDO-FOC

'He repeatedly searched for them and followed their tracks, he repeatedly made a canoe and set out in search of some of them.'[13]

'Ele o procurava e seguia o rastro dele, muitas vezes ele construiu uma canoa e saiu para procura-lo.'

(7) *Ayabmi aor te, ayabmi akah ihbahbtar ena te makaomi ikar.*

a-yab-pi   a-or   te[14] a-yab-pi   a-akah
DEM.PROX-ENDO-ABL 3.REFL-come ADV DEM.PROX-ENDO-ABL 3.REFL-go
ihbahb-tar ee-na   te   ma-kao-pi   i-kar
canoe-on   ENDO-FOC ADV other-dry.season-ABL 3SG-search

'Afterward he came back, and after that, during the next dry season, he would set out again on a canoe in search of some of them.'

'Depois, ele voltou, e depois disso, na próxima estação seca, ele saía de novo numa canoa para procura-lo.'

(8) *Enaitxa te iperedena sona Ğoxorkar ena sone, mater e, asobaka deke, omamõperedenene.*

ee-na-itxa   te   i-pere-de-na   sona Ğoxor-kar   ee-na
ENDO-FOC-with ADV 3SG-ITER-WIT-FOC often Zoró-search ENDO-FOC
sona-e   mater   e   a-sob-aka
often-SFM.WIT long.ago SFM.WIT 3.REFL-father-kill

---

[13] Suruí uses the third person singular pronoun (*xi-* or *i-*) to refer to the targeted enemy, but this does not mean that the Suruí warrior would have gone searching for a particular individual among the Zoró, the killer of his father. Any individual supposedly belonging to that ethnic group would be a suitable victim, and one death was still an ambitious goal for a raid. By contrast, using the third person plural pronoun (*ta-*) would have implied that the target was the whole ethnic group – but the Zoró lived in a more scattered fashion than the Suruí did. We use the plural in the free translation when it is more relevant in English.

[14] The adverbial particle *te* is almost an expletive. It is probably a weak form of the intensive adverbial particle *ter*, and often has only a prosodic function.

Ø-*de-ee-ka-e*
3SG-WIT-ENDO-DAT-SFM.WIT

o-ma-amõ-pere-de-na-ee-na-e
1SG-POSS-grandfather-ITER-WIT-FOC-ENDO-FOC-SFM.WIT

'Thus, my grandfather was always in search of some Zoró, long ago, because one of them had killed his father.'

'Assim, meu avô sempre procurava o Zoró, há muito tempo, porque aquele tinha matado o pai dele.'

(9) *Ena olobdena iwema.*

ee-na   o-sob-de-ee-na   iwe-ma
ENDO-FOC 1SG-father-WIT-ENDO-FOC DEM.EXO-do

'This is what my father said.'

'Meu pai falou assim.'

(10) *""Eebo oya xikin ã" iyã" de.*

ee-bo   o-ya   xi-ikin a   i-ya   Ø-de
ENDO-ADVERS 1SG-NWIT 3SG-see SFM.WIT 3SG-NWIT 3SG-WIT

'He said: "[My father] said: "And once I saw him."""'

'Ele disse: "[Meu pai] disse: "Aí uma vez eu o vi."""'

(11) *""Eebo oya olobg̃armeyitxa yã" iyã" de.*

ee-bo   o-ya   o-sob-karmey-itxa   a
ENDO-ADVERS 1SG-NWIT 1SG-father-younger.sibling-with SFM.WIT

i-ya   Ø-de
3SG-NWIT 3SG-WIT

'"""I was with my father's younger brother."""'

'"""Eu estava com o irmão mais novo de meu pai."""'

(12) *""Eebo oilud ena tar ã."""*

ee-bo   o-oilud   ee-na   tar ã
ENDO-ADVERS 1SG-young ENDO-FOC PRF SFM.NWIT

'"""I was already a young man."""'[15]

'"""Eu já estava moço."""'

---

[15] Men are *oilud* when they are young adults, still single, approximately between 17 and 25 years old.

(13) ““*Ete oya G̃oxoribebepemaã tar ã" iyã" de,* ““*mixağataga.*”””

   ee-te   o-ya   G̃oxor-ibeb-e-pe-maã   tar a   i-ya
   ENDO-ADV 1SG-NWIT   Zoró-track-NMLZ-path-take   PRF SFM.NWIT 3SG-NWIT
   ∅-de   mixağ-mataga
   3SG-WIT   night-go.through

   ““"That time I had followed the track of a Zoró through the night."””
   ““"Aquela vez, eu tinha seguido o rastro do Zoró durante a noite."””

(14) ““*Oker õm a.*”””

   o-ker   õm   a
   1SG-sleep NEG   SFM.NWIT

   ““"I had not slept at all."””
   ““"Eu não tinha dormido nada."””

(15) ““*Mokãyxibotorera oya xibebaã tar ã, xipemaã tar ã" iyã" de.*”

   mokãy-xibo-tor-wera   o-ya   xi-ibeb-maã   tar a
   fire-flame-carry-walk 1SG-NWIT   3SG-track-take   PRF SFM.WIT
   xi-pe-maã   tar   a   i-ya   ∅-de
   3SG-path-take   PRF   SFM.NWIT   3SG-NWIT   3SG-WIT

   ““"I had followed his track carrying a torch, I had followed his path."””
   ““"Eu tinha seguido o rastro dele, com uma tocha na mão, eu tinha seguido o caminho dele."””

(16) ““*Ete oya paitereya adihr eka, "Ãtiga meykodaatẽ ma", oya takay ena yã" iyã" de.*”

   ee-te   o-ya   pa-iter-ey[16]-ya   a-dihr   ee-ka
   ENDO-ADV 1SG-NWIT   1PL.INCL-very-PL-NWIT   3.REFL-exhaust   ENDO-DAT
   ã-tiga   mey-koda-aat-tẽ   ma   o-ya   ta-ka   ee-na
   DEM.PROX-SIM 2PL-sit.PL-ly-INCH   IMP 1SG-NWIT   3PL-DAT   ENDO-FOC
   a   i-ya   ∅-de
   SFM.NWIT 3SG-NWIT   3SG-WIT

   ““"And, as our men were exhausted, I told them: "You all should sit down here.""””

---

[16] The lexicalized locution *pa-iter* (1PL.INCL-very), 'we (inclusive of addressee) ourselves' is the ethnic autodenomination of the Suruí. Here it obviously does not refer to the whole ethnic group, but to the younger male individuals that went with the warriors to carry their provisions of food and arrows.

""""Aí, como nosso pessoal não aguentava mais, eu lhes disse: "Vocês podem sentar aquí.""""

(17) """"Eebo oyakah metota osahra, bobobob.""""
ee-bo o-ya-kah pe-tota o-sahr-a bobobob
ENDO-ADVERS 1SG-NWIT-go path-along 1SG-swift-VBLZ ID:walk.quickly
""""And I trotted away swiftly along the path.""""
""""Aí eu me fui embora rapidinho, seguindo o caminho.""""

(18) """"Ñokoy oyakah, nem, G̃oxormaarãyasade awaga ewepi yã" iyã" de.
ano-koy o-ya-kah nem G̃oxor-ma-arãya-sade a-awaga
DEM.DIST-to 1SG-NWIT-go INTJ Zoró-POSS-chicken-PROG.SIM 3.REFL-cry
ewe-epi a i-ya ∅-de
DEM.ENDO-hear SFM.NWIT 3SG-NWIT 3SG-WIT
""""I went there, and I heard the pet cock of the Zoró singing.""""[17]
""""Eu fui lá, aí ouvi o galo do Zoró que cantava.""""

(19) """"Bohb, oya osahrokabi ya" iyã" de.
bohb o-ya o-sahrokabi a i-ya ∅-de
ID:run 1SG-NWIT 1SG-swift.under.cover SFM.NWIT 3SG-NWIT 3SG-WIT
""""Quickly, I approached, ducking under cover.""""
""""Eu me aproximei rapidinho, abaixando-me para esconder-me.""""

(20) """"Äter oya xixababetâhikin a" iyã" de.
ã-ter o-ya xi-sab-abe-tâh-ikin a
DEM.PROX-very 1SG-NWIT 3SG-house-outside-stand-see SFM.NWIT
i-ya ∅-de
3SG-NWIT 3SG-WIT
""""Here, I could see their house.""""[18]
""""Aí eu vi a maloca dele.""""

---

[17] The Suruí and the Zoró used to raise various kinds of pets – mainly dogs, curassows and guans (turkey-like forest birds of the genera *Mitu*, *Penelope*, and *Pipile*) – and trust them to warn of approaching enemies. According to the Suruí, before contact, the Zoró already bred chickens that they had caught in rubber tapper settlements.

[18] The Suruí and Zoró "houses" (*lab*, non-possessed form of *-sab*) were huge, oblong, and vaulted constructions thatched with palm leaves, about 30 meters long and 5 meters high (see Figure 4). Zoró houses, in contrast to Suruí dwellings, had no bark walls but were thatched down to the ground, allowing arrows to be shot through the palm leaves.

Figure 4: A traditional Suruí house, rather small, built in 2005 near Lapetanha (Photo C. Yvinec)

(21) ''"*Yeter oytxepo!*"''

ye-ter   oytxepo
DEM.MED-very perfect

''"That's perfect!"''

''"Ótimo!"''

(22) ''"*Bohb, oya osahrokabi yã, "Ikaytxer akah ana i?*"''

bohb   o-ya   o-sahrokabi   a   i-ka-ter   a-kah
ID:run 1SG-NWIT 1SG-swift.under.cover SFM.NWIT 3SG-DAT-very 3.REFL-go

a-na   i
DEM.PROX-FOC SFM.NDECL

''"Quickly, I approached nearer, ducking under cover, and I thought: "So is he staying in this one?"'''[19]

''"Logo me aproximei, abaixado ainda, e pensei: "Será que ele fica nesta?"''

(23) ''"*Etiga te tamaawuruya waohwaohwaoh awuruya tamanikesota oğay txar ã" iyã" de.*

ee-tiga   te   ta-ma-awuru-ya   waohwaohwaoh   awuru-ya
ENDO-SIM ADV 3PL-POSS-dog-NWIT ID:bark   dog-NWIT

ta-maniga-e-sor-ta   o-ka   tar   a   i-ya
3PL-come.near.to-NMLZ-hard-VBLZ 1SG-DAT PRF SFM.NWIT 3SG-NWIT

---

[19] The Suruí, and their Indian neighbors as well, frequently left their villages for long treks in the forest, either in search of forest resources or out of fear of enemies.

∅-de
3SG-WIT

""'"But then: *Woof! Woof! Woof!* Their dog barked and did not let me come nearer to them."""'

""'"Aí, de repente: *Au-au! Au-au! Au-au!* O cachorro dele latiu, não deixando eu me aproximar mais."""'

(24) ""'"*Atãr oğay txar ã.*"""'

    a-tãr   o-ka   tar a
    3.REFL-fierce 1SG-DAT PRF SFM.NWIT

""'"It was already barking fiercely at me."""'

""'"Ele já estava brabo comigo, estava latindo demais."""'

(25) ""'"*Etiga te oya, nem, awurupami tar ã" iyã" de.*"""'

    ee-tiga   te   o-ya   nem awuru-pami tar a   i-ya
    ENDO-SIM ADV 1SG-NWIT INTJ dog-fear   PRF SFM.NWIT 3SG-NWIT
    ∅-de
    3SG-WIT

""'"And me, well, I was scared of the dog."""'

""'"Aí eu estava com medo do cachorro."""'

(26) ""'"*Eh méhk palana pagah i!" oya tar ã" iyã" de.*"""'

    eh méhk   pa-sa-a-na   pa-agah   i
    oh daybreak 1PL.INCL-PROG-DEM.PROX-FOC 1PL.INCL-dawn SFM.NDECL
    o-ya   tar a   i-ya   ∅-de
    1SG-NWIT PRF SFM.NWIT 3SG-NWIT 3SG-WIT

""'"Oh, I realized, daybreak is coming, isn't it?"""'

""'"Oh, eu percebi, já está amanhecendo!"""'

(27) ""'"*Etiga te oyakah olobğarmeyka "One te ana iwepi ner e, ba," oya ena ikay ã" iyã" de.*"""'

    ee-tiga   te   o-ya-kah   o-sob-karmey-ka   one te
    ENDO-SIM ADV 1SG-NWIT-GO 1SG-father-younger.sibling-DAT NEG ADV
    a-na   iwe-pi[20]   ter   e   ba   o-ya   ee-na
    DEM.PROX-FOC DEM.EXO-ABL very SFM.WIT father[21] 1SG-NWIT ENDO-FOC
    i-ka   a   i-ya   ∅-de
    3SG-DAT SFM.NWIT 3SG-NWIT 3SG-WIT

---

[20] The phrase *one te ana iwepi*, literally 'not this way out of that', means 'not easy'.
[21] One's father's brothers are classificatory "fathers" in the Suruí kinship terminology.

"'"So I went straight to my father's younger brother and said to him: "Father, the situation is not easy.""""

"'"Então voltei logo para o irmão mais novo de meu pai, aí lhe disse: "Pai, não é muito fácil.""""

(28) "'"Iye. "Payahrxid ewaba", te elaye, paitereykãra ejeka aye ewemiğa paitereyitxa iter" olobiya oğay a" iyã" de.

iye   pa-mayahr-sid   e-waba   te   e-sa-aye
all.right 1PL.INCL-go.away-HORT 2SG-HORT ADV 2SG-PROG-FUT
pa-iter-ey-kãra   e-de-ee-ka   aye
1PL.INCL-very-PL-retaliate.against 2SG-WIT-ENDO-DAT FUT
ewe-piğa   pa-iter-ey-itxa   ter   o-sob-ya
DEM.ENDO-seize:worry.about 1PL.INCL-very-PL-with very 1SG-father-NWIT
o-ka   a   i-ya   ∅-de
1SG-DAT SFM.NWIT 3SG-NWIT 3SG-WIT

"'"All right, my father answered, you can say: "Let's go away." I am worried about our people: because of what you did, there will be retaliations against us.""""

"'"Tá bom, disse meu pai, você pode falar assim: "Vamos embora." Estou preocupado com o nosso povo: por causa do que você fez, vai ter represálias contra nossa gente.""""

(29) "'"Ete awurusena aker õm a, waohwaohwaoh, awurusena atãr ã.""

ee-te   awuru-sa-ee-na   a-ker   õm   a
ENDO-ADV dog-PROG-ENDO-FOC 3.REFL-sleep NEG SFM.NWIT
waohwaohwaoh   awuru-sa-ee-na   a-tãr   a
ID:bark.in.the.distance dog-PROG-ENDO-FOC 3.REFL-fierce SFM.NWIT

"'"And in the distance, the dog had not fallen asleep: *Woof! Woof!* It was still barking fiercely.""""

"'"E lá, o cachorro não adormeceu: *Au-au! Au-au!* Ele ficava brabo.""""

(30) "'"Etiga te oya "Okahsidlii" oladeka, "Atemareh, ba," oya olobğarmeyka yã" iyã" de.

ee-tiga   te   o-ya   o-kah-sid-sa-i
ENDO-SIM ADV 1SG-NWIT 1SG-go-HORT-PROG-SFM.NDECL

o-sade-ee-ka   *a-ter-ma-reh*[22]   *ba*   *o-ya*
1SG-PROG.SIM-ENDO-DAT DEM.PROX-very-IMP-HORT.PL father 1SG-NWIT
o-sob-karmey-ka   *a*   *i-ya*   ∅-*de*
1SG-father-younger.sibling-DAT SFM.NWIT 3SG-NWIT 3SG-WIT

''''"But I was already thinking: "I shall go," and I said to my father's younger brother: "Wait, father!"''''

''''"Contudo eu já estava pensando: "Vou lá," e falei para o irmão mais novo do meu pai: "Espere aí, pai!"''''

(31) ''''"*Owena ite te bolakah ãsabtiga yedeiwayka mareh!*" *oya ikay ã*" *iyã*" *de.*
o-e-na   *ter*   *te*   *bo-o-sa-kah*   *a-sab-tiga*[23]
1SG-NMLZ-FOC very ADV ADVERS-1SG-PROG-go DEM.PROX-house-SIM
yed-iway-ka   *ma-reh*   *o-ya*   *i-ka*   *a*   *i-ya*
REL-master-DAT IMP-HORT.PL 1SG-NWIT 3SG-DAT SFM.NWIT 3SG-NWIT
∅-*de*
3SG-WIT

''''"Let me go and show the master of this house who I am!" I said to him."''''[24]

''''"Vou mostrar ao dono desta maloca quem eu sou!" eu lhe disse."''''

(32) ''''"*Bohb, osahror.*"''''

bohb   *o-sahr-or*
ID:run 1SG-swift-come

''''"I approached it quickly."''''

''''"Aproximei-me rapidinho."''''

---

[22] This locution is lexicalized as an interjection that means 'Wait here for me!' The plural aspect of the hortative suffix -*reh* refers to the multiple wills (those of the addressee and of the speaker) implicated in actions that require individuals to coordinate themselves.

[23] The suffix -*tiga* can have a spatial meaning, as well as a temporal one.

[24] The phrase *ã-sab-tiga yed-iway*, DEM.PROX-house-SIM REL-master, literally translates as 'the master of the place where this house stands'. This periphrastic expression can be a rhetorical device. However, it is also a way to get round the ambiguity to which the simpler construction *ã-sab-iway*, DEM.PROX-house-master, 'the master of this house,' could have given rise: indeed the latter phrase is a lexicalized expression, *labiway*, house-master, that refers to the political status of chief.

(33) ““*Awurusade atãr eamaĩ te osahrokabi.*””

awuru-sade   a-tãr   ee-amaĩ²⁵   te
dog-PROG.SIM 3.REFL-fierce ENDO-in.front.of ADV
o-sahrokabi
1SG-approach.under.cover

““"Although the dog was still fierce, I approached under cover."””
““"Embora o cachorro estivesse ainda brabo, eu me aproximei abaixado."””

(34) ““*Etiga te xiway añuma okabesahra etiga ee, mĩhnaka ana mehkap, ““Nan ariwa awuru maẽga?” bola awuruka yã”, ya ana mehkapa yã” iyã” de.*

ee-tiga   te   xi-iway   añum o-kabe-sahr-a   ee-tiga   ee
ENDO-SIM ADV 3SG-master a.little 1SG-stoop-swift-VBLZ ENDO-SIM ENDO
mĩhna-ka a-na   mehkap nan a-ariwa   awuru ma-ẽga
door-DAT DEM.PROX-FOC opening Q 3.REFL-be.noisy dog   Q-PRS
bo-o-sa   awuru-ka a   ∅-ya   a-na
ADVERS-1SG-PROG dog-DAT SFM.NWIT 3SG-NWIT²⁶ DEM.PROX-FOC
mehkap-a   a   i-ya   ∅-de
opening-VBLZ SFM.NWIT 3SG-NWIT 3SG-WIT

““"As I was running up stooping, its master half-opened the door and thought about the dog: "What is making the dog bark?"”””
““"Eu estava correndo curvado, o dono dele entreabriu a porta, e ele pensou sobre o cachorro: "O que está fazendo o cachorro latir?"”””

(35) ““*"Ah sehr awuru!" olahrikin ajeka, dik, apĩhnapoga.*””

ah sehr   awuru o-sahr-ikin   a-de-ee-ka   dik
ah ID:look.and.see dog 1SG-swift-see 3.REFL-WIT-ENDO-DAT ID:close
a-mĩhna-poga
3.REFL-door-close

““"Ah, I see, dog!" he said as he saw me running up, and: *Slam!* He shut the door."””
““"Ah, estou vendo, cachorro!" ele disse quando me viu correndo para ele, e aí: *Slam!* Fechou a porta."””

---

²⁵Here the spatial postposition *-amaĩ* has an abstract meaning of concession.
²⁶This phrase shows complex clause embedding used to express thought as inner speech: [[[*Nan ariwa awuru ma-ẽga*] *bo-o-sa awuru-ka a*] ∅-*ya*], '[[[What is making the dog bark?] I am saying this (to myself) about the dog] he said this (to himself)].

(36) ""*Turuk, awuruyakahekoy iya iõmaniga ya" iyã" de.*

turuk   awuru-sa-kah-e-koy   i-ya   i-õm-a-niga   a
ID:dodge.in dog-PROG-go-NMLZ-to 3SG-NWIT 3SG-NEG-VBLZ-SIM SFM.NWIT

i-ya   ∅-de
3SG-NWIT 3SG-WIT

""*Whoosh!* The dog dodged its way in and disappeared inside.""

""*Whoosh!* o cachorro entrou e desapareceu.""

(37) ""*Ahwob, sog, sog omador xixabapa i!*"".

ahwob   sog   sog²⁷   o-ma-de-or   xi-sab-ma-apa
ID:blow ID:set.fire ID:set.fire 1SG-PRF.PST-WIT-come 3SG-house-CAUS-burn

i
SFM.NDECL

""But I had come already and: *Puff!* I blew on my torch and: *Whoosh! Whoosh!* I set fire to his house on both sides!""

""Mas eu chegou já, e: *Puff!* Soprei na minha tocha, e: *Whoosh! Whoosh!* Toquei fogo nos dois lados da maloca dele!""

(38) ""*Etiga te etrrrk amauraã oğay ã" iyã" de.*

ee-tiga   te   etrrrk   a-ma-ur-maã   o-ka   a
ENDO-SIM ADV ID:catching.fire 3.REFL-POSS-bow-take 1SG-DAT SFM.NWIT

i-ya   ∅-de
3SG-NWIT 3SG-WIT

""It immediately caught fire and, inside, they picked up their bows to shoot at me.""

""A maloca pegou fogo logo, e, dentro, eles pegaram os seus arcos para me flechar.""

(39) ""*Oeh, amauraã doğewa i! Ã ãtigareh!" tak, tak, mãeya ñokoy, tak, mãeyka, eeerh mamugekoya" iyã" de.*

oeh a-ma-ur-maã   ∅-de-o-ka-wa   i   ã
ah 3.REFL-POSS-bow-take 3-WIT-1SG-DAT-HORT SFM.NDECL DEM.PROX

---

²⁷The repetition of the ideophone conveys the idea that the action was done twice, that is, on both sides of the house (Zoró houses had two doors).

ã-tiga-reh²⁸ tak tak ma-ey-ya
DEM.PROX-SIM-HORT.PL ID:shoot.arrow ID:shoot.arrow other-PL-NWIT
ano-koy tak ma-ey-ka eeerh
DEM.DIST-to ID:shoot.arrow other-PL-DAT ID:mortally.wounded
ma-pug-e-koe-ya i-ya ∅-de
INDF-child-NMLZ-voice-NWIT 3SG-NWIT 3SG-WIT

'"""Ah, they are picking up theirs bows to shoot at me! Let's shoot now!" I thought and I shot twice, the enemies moved away, I shot once again, and: *Arrh!* A child's voice cried out as I mortally wounded him."""'

'"""Ah, estão procurando os seus arcos para me flechar! Vamos flechá-los!" pensei, e flechei duas vezes, os inimigos se afastaram, flechei mais uma vez, e aí: *Arrh!* Uma criança gritou, mortalmente ferida."""'

(40) '""Maya maã, xitiya mamugpiekoy manáh atar ã" iyã" de.

ma-ya maã xi-ti-ya ma-pug-pi-ee-koy²⁹ manáh tar
other-NWIT take 3SG-mother-NWIT INDF-child-hear-ENDO-to insult PRF
a i-ya ∅-de
SFM.NWIT 3SG-NWIT 3SG-WIT

'"""Another had seized his bow already, and because she heard him crying, the child's mother was insulting me.""'³⁰

'"""Já um outro inimigo pegou o seu arco e, ao ouvir sua criança gritando, a mãe dela me xingou.""''

(41) '""Oya etiga te onepotê tedne G̃oxorka tar ã" iyã" de.

o-ya ee-tiga te o-tepotê ted-te G̃oxor-ka tar
1SG-NWIT ENDO-SIM ADV 1SG-shoot.arrow only-ADV Zoró-DAT PRF
a i-ya ∅-de
SFM.NWIT 3SG-NWIT 3SG-WIT

'"""But I just kept on shooting arrows at the Zoró.""''

'"""Eu fiquei flechando o Zoró.""''

---

²⁸This phrase that uses a plural hortative suffix (*-reh*) to refer to a highly individual decision and action (shooting one's arrow at the enemy) is an idiomatic construction. The plural hortative is perhaps motivated because this action requires resoluteness and self-coordination.

²⁹The locution *ee-koy*, ENDO-to, has a causal meaning.

³⁰In combat, just as in most other contexts, insults (*manáh*) scoff at the physical appearance of the addressee, especially at his or her genitals.

(42) *"Eebo oyena G̃oxorsabapa yã" iyã" de.*

    ee-bo   o-ya-ee-na   G̃oxor-sab-ma-apa   a
    ENDO-ADVERS 1SG-NWIT-ENDO-FOC Zoró-house-CAUS-burn SFM.NWIT
    i-ya   ∅-de
    3SG-NWIT 3SG-WIT

    '"'Thus I burnt down the Zoró's house."'''
    '"'Foi assim que eu queimei a maloca do Zoró."'''

(43) *Eebo omamõperedena ena G̃oxorka, xameomi ter denene, asobaka dekenene.*

    ee-bo   o-ma-amõ-pere-de-na   ee-na   G̃oxor-ka
    ENDO-ADVERS 1SG-POSS-grandfather-ITER-WIT-FOC ENDO-FOC Zoró-DAT
    xameomi ter   ∅-de-ee-na-ee-na-e   a-sob-aka
    much   very 3SG-WIT-ENDO-FOC-ENDO-FOC-SFM.WIT 3.REFL-father-kill
    ∅-de-ee-ka-ee-na-ee-na-e
    3SG-WIT-ENDO-DAT-ENDO-FOC-ENDO-FOC-SFM.WIT

    'My grandfather did this several times to the Zoró, he did it many times, because his father had been killed by one of them.'
    'Várias vezes meu avô fez isso ao Zoró, muitas vezes, porque aquele tinha matado o pai dele.'

(44) *Oilud ena alaba dena ena maiter ikay e.*

    oilud   ee-na   a-saba   ∅-de-ee-na   ee-na
    young ENDO-FOC 3.REFL-PROG.PST 3SG-WIT-ENDO-FOC ENDO-FOC
    ma-iter[31]   i-ka   e
    other-very 3SG-DAT SFM.WIT

    'He was young then, so he did it once again to them.'
    'Ele estava moço naquele tempo, aí lhes fez isso mais uma vez.'

(45) *Ayabmi dena maiter ikay e.*

    a-yab-pi   ∅-de-ee-na   ma-iter   i-ka   e
    DEM.PROX-ENDO-ABL 3SG-WIT-ENDO-FOC other-very 3SG-DAT SFM.WIT

    'And afterward, he did it once more to them.'
    'Aí depois, ele lhe fez isso mais uma vez.'

---

[31]The locution *ma-iter* (other-very) means 'more' or 'once again'.

(46) *Ayabmi dena maiter xixabapa, xixabapa tedne iperedena sone.*
 a-yab-pi   ∅-de-ee-na   ma-iter
 DEM.PROX-ENDO-ABL 3SG-WIT-ENDO-FOC other-very
 xi-sab-ma-apa   xi-sab-ma-apa   ted-te   i-pere-de-na
 3SG-house-CAUS-burn 3SG-house-CAUS-burn only-ADV 3SG-ITER-WIT-FOC
 sona-e.
 often-SFM.WIT
 'And afterward, he burnt one their houses down again, several times he just burnt a house down.'
 'Aí depois, ele queimou de novo outra maloca dele, várias vezes ele só queimou uma maloca dele.'

(47) *Omamõperedene.*
 o-ma-amõ-pere-de-na-e
 1SG-POSS-grandfather-ITER-WIT-FOC-SFM.WIT
 'My grandfather did that again and again.'
 'Meu avô fez isso várias vezes.'

(48) *""Eebo oyena G̃oxoreaka, xixabapa, olobaka deka yã" olobiyã" olobde.*
 ee-bo   o-ya-ee-na   G̃oxor-e-aka   xi-sab-ma-apa
 ENDO-ADVERS 1SG-NWIT-ENDO-FOC Zoró-NMLZ-kill 3SG-house-CAUS-burn
 o-sob-aka   ∅-de-ee-ka   ã   o-sob-ya
 1SG-father-kill 3SG-WIT-ENDO-DAT SFM.NWIT 1SG-father-NWIT
 o-sob-de
 1SG-father-WIT
 'My father said this: "My father said this: "Thus I killed the Zoró, I burnt his house down, because he had killed my father.""'
 'Meu pai falou assim: "Meu pai contou isso: "Foi assim que eu matei o Zoró, queimei a maloca dele, porque ele tinha matada meu pai.""'

(49) *Ena.*
 ee-na
 ENDO-FOC
 'It happened like this.'
 'Aconteceu assim.'

(50) *Ayabdena iwewá ikay e.*
 a-yab-de-ee-na   iwe-ewá[32]   *i-ka   e*
 DEM.PROX-ENDO-WIT-ENDO-FOC DEM.EXO-say 3SG-DAT SFM.WIT
 'And he sang to celebrate this event.'
 'Aí ele cantou para celebrar este acontecimento.'

(51) *""""Awurutihma mamekoka oğay omamibewẽtig, wẽtiga, wẽtiga ya.""""*[33]
 awuru-tih[34]*-ma   ma-meko-ka   o-ka   o-pami-be-wẽtiga   wẽtiga*
 dog-big-PRF.PST INDF-jaguar-DAT 1SG-DAT 1SG-fear-NMLZ-sound   sound
 wẽtiga a[35]
 sound SFM.NWIT
 '""""The big dog sounded its fear of a jaguar, of me it sounded it, sounded it, they say.'
 '""""O cão grande soou seu medo da onça, de mim ele o soou, o soou, ouvi falar isso.'

(52) *""""Awurutihma mamekoka oğay,""""*
 awuru-tih-ma   ma-meko-ka   o-ka
 dog-big-PRF.PST INDF-jaguar-DAT 1SG-DAT
 'The big dog, of a jaguar, of me,'
 'O cão grande, da onça, de mim,'

(53) *""""Oikin nedne loykubeyaawurutihma mamekoka oğay mamibewẽtig, wẽtiga, wẽtiga ya.""""*
 o-ikin   ted-te   loykub[36]*-ey-ma-awuru-tih-ma   ma-meko-ka*
 1SG-see only-ADV enemy-PL-POSS-dog-big-PRF.PST INDF-jaguar-DAT
 o-ka   pami-be-wẽtiga   wẽtiga wẽtiga a
 1SG-DAT fear-NMLZ-sound sound sound SFM.NWIT
 'Just at seeing me, the big dog of the enemies sounded its fear of a jaguar,

---

[32] Although the verb -*ewá* just means 'to say' or 'to talk' when it used intransitively (*awewá*, *a-we-ewá*, 3.REFL-REFL-say, 'they talk to each other'), when it is used transitively, like here, it always implies that the speech is sung.

[33] This and the two following lines were sung. Here Agamenon quoted only a sample of the song, which was actually far longer.

[34] The suffix -*tih* is often used to distinguish mythological or spiritual beings from their ordinary homonyms.

[35] Non-witnessed evidentiality is an aesthetic rule with which all Suruí sung speeches comply.

[36] This word is only used in sung speech, instead of the word *lahd*, and always with the plural suffix -*ey*.

of me, sounded it, sounded it, they say."'

'Ao me ver, o cão grande dos inimigos soou seu medo da onça, de mim, o soou, o soou, ouvi falar isso."'

(54) ""Oya iwewá ya" iyã, "ximaawurumaĩ ojehwá yã" iyã, "ena.""

o-ya   iwe-ewá   a   i-ya
1SG-NWIT DEM.EXO-say SFM.NWIT 3SG-NWIT
xi-ma-awuru-ma-aĩ   o-de-ee-ewá   a   i-ya
3SG-POSS-dog-big-CAUS-go.into 1SG-WIT-ENDO-say SFM.NWIT 3SG-NWIT
ee-na
ENDO-FOC

'I sang this, I sang that I made his big dog run in, like this."""

'Eu cantei assim, eu cantei que eu fiz que o cão grande dele se esconder dentro da casa, assim.""'

(55) *Ayabmi maite te.*

a-yab-pi   ma-iter   te
DEM.PROX-ENDO-ABL other-very ADV

'Afterward, he did it once again.'

'Depois disso, ele fê-lo de novo.'

(56) *Ayabmi denena te ena ikãyna alaba ena xixabapa akah G̃oxor ene.*

a-yab-pi   ∅-de-ee-na-ee-na   te   ee-na
DEM.PROX-ENDO-ABL 3SG-WIT-ENDO-FOC-ENDO-FOC ADV ENDO-FOC
i-kãy-na   a-saba   ee-na   xi-sab-ma-apa   a-kah
3SG-old-FOC 3.REFL-PROG.PST ENDO-FOC 3SG-house-CAUS-burn 3.REFL-go
G̃oxor ee-na-e
Zoró ENDO-FOC-SFM.WIT

'Afterward, he did it, when he grew up, he went and burnt down the Zoró's house.'

'Depois, ele o fez, quando ele cresceu, ele se foi queimar a maloca do Zoró.'

(57) *Ena asobaka eka te iperedena agõarih ikay e.*

ee-na   a-sob-aka   ee-ka   te   i-pere-de-na
ENDO-FOC 3.REFL-father-kill ENDO-DAT ADV 3SG-ITER-WIT-FOC

a-agõa-arih³⁷   i-ka   e
3.REFL-heart-lazy 3SG-DAT SFM.WIT

'Thus, because his father had been murdered, he remained merciless toward them.'

'Assim, porque seu pai tinha sido morto, ele ficou implacável contra aquele.'

(58) *Eebo dena ikãyna alaba enene, xixabapa akah e.*
ee-bo   Ø-de-ee-na   i-kãy-na   a-saba
ENDO-ADVERS 3SG-WIT-ENDO-FOC 3SG-old-FOC 3.REFL-PROG.PST
ee-na-ee-na-e   xi-sab-ma-apa   a-kah   e
ENDO-FOC-ENDO-FOC-SFM.WIT 3SG-house-CAUS-burn 3.REFL-go SFM.WIT

'And he did it again when he grew up, he went and burnt down one of their houses.'

'Ele o fez de novo quando cresceu, ele foi queimar a maloca daquele.'

(59) *Eebo dena epi xaka ene.*
ee-bo   Ø-de-ee-na   ee-pi   xi-aka ee-na-e
ENDO-ADVERS 3SG-WIT-ENDO-FOC ENDO-ABL 3SG-kill ENDO-FOC-SFM.WIT

'And afterward he killed another one.'

'Aí depois ele matou mais um Zoró.'

(60) *Xixabapa akah ñorĩ, ete "Xixabapa oğabi ma!" sadena mãeyka, ete epetimağa alaba.*
xi-sab-ma-apa   a-kah   ñorĩ   ee-te   xi-sab-ma-apa
3SG-house-CAUS-burn 3SG-go stealthily ENDO-ADV 3SG-house-CAUS-burn
o-kabi ma   sade-ee-na   ma-ey-ka   ee-te   ee-petimağa
1SG-BEN IMP PROG.SIM-ENDO-FOC other-PL-DAT ENDO-ADV ENDO-ambush
a-saba
3.REFL-PROG.PST

'He went away to burn down a Zoró house, he said to a few others: "Burn down their house for me!" and he lay in ambush.'

'Ele saiu para queimar uma maloca do Zoró, ele falou para outros seus parentes: "Queimem a maloca dele para mim!" e ele ficou emboscado.'

---

[37] The word *agõa*, 'heart', has physical and emotional meaning. When it is 'unresponsive' or 'lazy' (*-arih*), it means that one feels no compassion for someone else – which is an attitude that is not always praised, even toward enemies.

(61) *Eebo "Kağoy ena mapãri ma, palodena sona i?" xixabapa adeke, ete yakadena asabalabiĩ soeydekena pãri amauraã yakena madane.*

```
ee-bo              ka-koy ee-na      ma-pãri          ma
ENDO-ADVERS   Q-to   ENDO-FOC   INDF-make.noise   Q
palo-de-ee-na                 sona    i          xi-sab-ma-apa
someone-WIT-ENDO-FOC   often   SFM.NDECL   3SG-house-CAUS-burn
sade-ee-ka-e                    ee-te          i-sade-ee-na
PROG.SIM-ENDO-DAT-SFM.WIT   ENDO-ADV   3SG-PROG.SIM-ENDO-FOC
a-sab-alabiĩ              so-ey-de-kah-ee-na              pãri
3.REFL-house-burning   thing-PL-WIT-go-ENDO-FOC   make.noise
a-ma-ur-maã              i-sa-ee-na              ma-de-ani-e
3.REFL-POSS-bow-take   3SG-PROG-ENDO-FOC   INDF-WIT-GNO-SFM.WIT
```

'And while the house was burning up, he was watching and wondering: "Where is one making noise, is there someone?" because as one's house is in flames, one moves things about and makes noise in search of one's bow.'

'Aí, quando a maloca estava queimando, ele observava-a pensando: "Onde está quem está fazendo barulho? Será que tem alguém aí dentro?" porque, quando a maloca de alguém está em chamas, este alguém mexe as coisas e faz barulho, procurando seu arco.'

(62) *"Ãtigareh!", tap, sok, ena xaka ene.*

```
ã-tiga-reh                   tap              sok           ee-na       xi-aka
DEM.PROX-SIM-HORT.PL   ID:shoot.arrow   ID:hit.target   ENDO-FOC   3SG-kill
ee-na-e
ENDO-FOC-SFM.WIT
```

'"Let's shoot now!" he thought, he fired his arrow and hit his target, that's how he killed each one.'

'"Vamos flechar agora mesmo!" ele pensava, ele flechava e atingia o seu alvo, era assim que ele matava aquele.'

(63) *Ayabmi dena ãtiga manopetimağa, ãtiga manopetimağa, ãtiga manopetimağa, ãtiga manopetimağa.*

```
a-yab-pi                   ∅-de-ee-na                   ã-tiga
DEM.PROX-ENDO-ABL   3SG-WIT-ENDO-FOC   DEM.PROX-SIM
ma-ano-petimağa                       ã-tiga                ma-ano-petimağa
other-standing.up-ambush   DEM.PROX-SIM   other-standing.up-ambush
```

ã-tiga   ma-ano-petimağa   ã-tiga
DEM.PROX-SIM other-standing.up-ambush DEM.PROX-SIM
ma-ano-petimağa
other-standing.up-ambush

'And next to him, there was another one standing in ambush, and there another one, and there another one, and there another one.'[38]

'E aí perto dele, outro ficava emboscado, e lá mais um, e lá mais um, e lá mais um.'

(64) *Ete ãtiga manode mapa mokãyĩ, ãtiga mano, pãri dena amauraã yakade, masena, "Ãtigareh!", tap, enike.*

ee-te   ã-tiga   ma-ano-de   mapa   mokãy-ĩ
ENDO-ADV DEM.PROX-SIM other-standing.up-WIT shoot.arrow fire-inside
ã-tiga   ma-ano   pãri   ∅-de-ee-na
DEM.PROX-SIM other-standing.up noise 3SG-WIT-ENDO-FOC
a-ma-ur-maã   i-sade   ma-sa-ee-na
3.REFL-POSS-bow-take 3SG-PROG.SIM other-PROG-ENDO-FOC
ã-tiga-reh   tap   ee-na-i-ka-e
DEM.PROX-SIM-HORT.PL ID:hit.target ENDO-FOC-3SG-DAT-SFM.WIT

'Then one of them shot an arrow in the fire, and, as someone made noise in search of his bow, another one standing there thought: "Let's shoot now," and did it to that one.'

'Aí um deles flechava no fogo, aí, quando alguém fazia barulho procurando seu arco, outro que ficava lá pensava: "Vamos flechar agora mesmo," e fazia isso contra aquele.'

(65) *""Ete oyena ena yã" iyã" de.*

ee-te   o-ya-ee-na   ee-na   ã   i-ya   ∅-de
ENDO-ADV 1SG-NWIT-ENDO-FOC ENDO-FOC SFM.NWIT 3SG-NWIT 3SG-WIT

'[My father] said: "He said: "So I did it that way.""'

'[Meu pai] contou isso: "Ele contava: "Foi assim que eu fiz.""'

---

[38]Because of the size of their bows, which need to be held vertically, warriors in ambush had to wait standing upright, usually hiding themselves behind a tree trunk.

(66) ""*Eebo labdena apa ya" iyã" de, ""ewewewaya, G̃oxorsade ana apabiar awerkar anokoy ewenamg̃a enikay ã' iyã" de, ""ano agaap alap, tap""*.

 ee-bo   sab-de-ee-na   a-apa ã i-ya
 ENDO-ADVERS house-WIT-ENDO-FOC 3.REFL-burn SFM.NWIT 3SG-NWIT
 ∅-de ewewaya G̃oxor-sade a-na   a-pabiar
 3SG-WIT ID:burning Zoró-PROG.SIM DEM.PROX-FOC 3.REFL-on.all.fours
 a-werkar ano-koy ewe-nam-ka   ee-na-i-ka
 3.REFL-walk DEM.DIST-to DEM.ENDO-quantity-DAT ENDO-FOC-3SG-DAT
 ã   i-yã ∅-de ano   a-agaa-ap
 SFM.NWIT 3SG-NWIT 3SG-WIT DEM.DIST 3.REFL-belly-hole
 a-alap   tap
 3.REFL-stretch.out ID:hit.target

""'The house was burning up, the Zoró crawled on all fours and stretched out like this, and we shot at them.""'[39]

""'A maloca estava queimando, o Zoró rastejando de quatro, assim, e o flechávamos.""'

(67) *Nem, "awaĩ ikay ã" iyã" de, ""eeerh!""*

 nem a-waĩ   i-ka ã   i-ya ∅-de eeerh
 INTJ 3.REFL-shoot.arrow 3SG-DAT SFM.NWIT 3SG-NWIT 3SG-WIT ID:dying

""'One of us shot one of them, and he was dying.""'

""'Aí um de nós o flechou, e ele ficou morrendo.""'

(68) *Ena omamõdena lahdg̃a ena mater e.*

 ee-na o-ma-amõ-de-ee-na   lahd-ka
 ENDO-FOC 1SG-POSS-grandfather-WIT-ENDO-FOC Indian.enemy-DAT
 ee-na mater e
 ENDO-FOC long.ago SFM.WIT

'That's the way my grandfather treated the enemy long ago.'

'Foi assim que meu avô tratou o inimigo há muito tempo.'

(69) *Bo te.*

 bo   te
 ADVERS ADV

'That's it.'

'Foi isso.'

---

[39] The volume of the house, whose thatched roof burnt away very quickly, allowed the occupants to survive the fire, if they were not shot.

Acknowledgments

Fieldwork on Suruí in 2013 was funded by a postdoctoral fellowship from the Fondation Fyssen and by the ANR project Fabriq'Am (ANR-12-CULT-005). I would like to thank Kristine Stenzel for her careful revision of linguistic concepts and English translations.

Non-standard abbreviations

ADVERS	adversative	MED	medial
ENDO	endophoric	NDECL	non-declarative
EXO	exophoric	NWIT	non-witnessed evidentiality
GNO	gnomic		
HORT	hortative	SFM	sentence final marker
ID	ideophone	SIM	simultaneity
INCH	inchoative	VBLZ	verbalizer
ITER	iterative	WIT	witnessed evidentiality

References

Bontkes, Carolyn. 1985. Subordinate clauses in Suruí. In David L. Fortune (ed.), *Porto Velho workpapers*, 189–207. Brasília: Summer Institute of Linguistics.

Brunelli, Gilio. 1987. Migrations, guerres et identité : Faits ethno-historiques zoró. *Anthropologie et Sociétés* 11(3). 149–172.

Lacerda Guerra, Mariana. 2004. *Aspects of Suruí phonology and phonetics*. Brussels: Université Libre de Bruxelles MA thesis.

Mindlin, Betty. 1985. *Nós Paiter: Os Suruí de Rondônia*. Petrópolis: Vozes.

Mindlin, Betty. 1996. *Vozes da origem. Estórias sem escrita: Narrativas dos índios Suruí de Rondônia*. São Paulo: Atica.

Van der Meer, Tina H. 1985. Case marking in Suruí. In David L. Fortune (ed.), *Porto Velho workpapers*, 208–230. Brasília: Summer Institute of Linguistics.

Yvinec, Cédric. 2011. *Les monuments lyriques des Suruí du Rondônia : chants, événements, savoirs*. Paris: EHESS Doctoral dissertation.

Yvinec, Cédric. 2016. Bouleversements socio-économiques, transition historique et régimes d'historicité chez les Suruí du Rondônia. In Christel Müller & Monica Heintz (eds.), *Transitions historiques*, 235–246. Paris: Boccard.

Chapter 13

Ka'apor

Gustavo Godoy
PPGAS-Museu Nacional, UFRJ

Wyrapitã Ka'apor

1 Introduction

This narrative concerns an old woman who farted on a boy, making him ill. The title, a synthesis of the narrative, was proposed by Karairan (Raimundo Tembé) on the 4th of August, 2016:

(1) a'i ymanihar ke kurumĩ pynu ixo
aʔi ɪman-haɾ-kɛ kuɾumĩ ɾehɛ Ø-pɪnu i-ʃɔ
old.woman formerly-NMLZ-AFC boy at 3-fart 3-be
'A long time ago, a woman farted on a boy.'

(2) aja me'ẽ ke kurumĩ u'y sepetu ixapekwar rupi kutuk
aja-ẽ-kɛ kuɾumĩ uʔɪ-sɛpɛtu i-ʃapɛ kʷaɾ ɾupi Ø-kutuk
ANA-NMLZ-AFC boy arrow-spit 3-vagina hole by 3-pierce
'Afterwards, the boy pierced her through the anus with a wood-tipped arrow.'

The story was narrated by Wyrapitã Ka'apor, who is also known as Jamói, and recorded on the 15th of June 2014 in the village of *Xie pihun rena* (Centro Novo do Maranhão County, in the state of Maranhão). The transcription and analysis of the text were carried out by the storyteller and Gustavo Godoy, while he was conducting field research for his Master's degree in Anthropology (Godoy 2015).

Gustavo Godoy & Wyrapitã Ka'apor. 2017. Ka'apor. In Kristine Stenzel & Bruna Franchetto (eds.), *On this and other worlds: Voices from Amazonia*, 467–480. Berlin: Language Science Press.

2 The Ka'apor and their languages

The Ka'apor are an eastern Amazonian people who live in the western part of the state of Maranhão. In the 19th century, they lived in the state of Pará and, before 1800, further west in the Tocantins River basin (Balée 1994: 30–32). In 1911, the Brazilian government began the process of pacification of the Ka'apor, who were known for attacking local colonists (Ribeiro 1962); the Ka'apor population in 1928, when so-called pacification was concluded, has been estimated at 5,000 people. The current population in the Upper Turiaçu Indigenous Land is 2,300. Some Ka'apor also live among the Tembé (TUPIAN), in the Alto Guamá Indigenous Land.

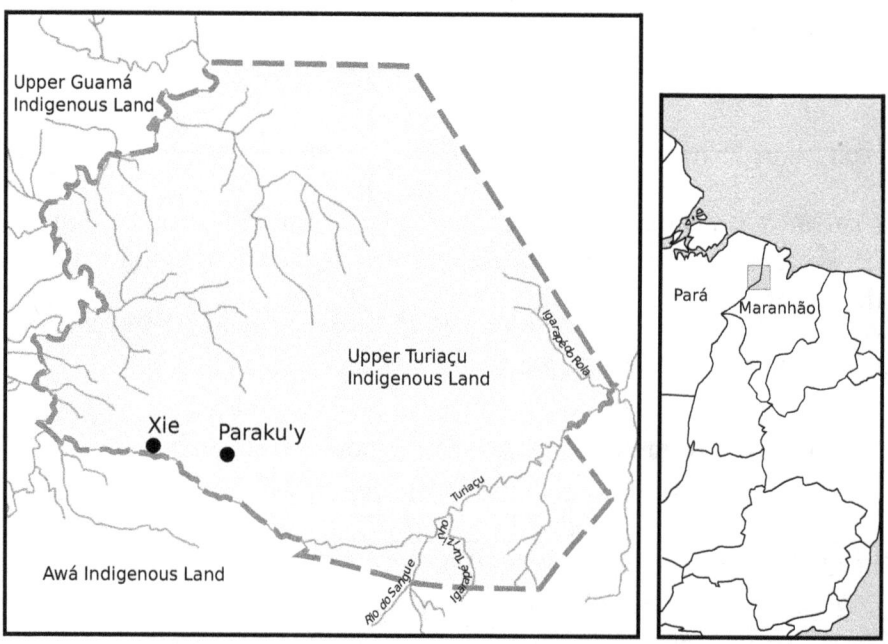

Figure 1: The Upper Turiaçu Indigenous Land and villages mentioned

The Ka'apor language is classified as belonging to the eastern branch of the Tupian family; it is part of the Tupi-Guarani set of the Maweti-Guarani sub-branch. The Ka'apor lexicon (Corrêa-da-Silva 1997; Balée 2006) shows colonial influences through the Língua Geral Amazônica (TUPIAN). Its argument marking is similar to Nheengatu (Corrêa-da-Silva 2002), which descends from Língua Geral.

Spoken Ka'apor is a vital language, actively transmitted between generations. Nonetheless, there has been a decline in the transmission of traditional genres, such as formulaic greetings and some types of songs. The Ka'apor have additionally developed a local sign language for communicating with the deaf, which has been in use since at least the 1940s (Kakumasu & Kakumasu 1988; Ferreira n.d. 1984; 2010).

3 Notes on the narrative

The theme of the narrative presented here is also found among other indigenous peoples. The Bororo (MACRO-JÊ) version tells of the origin of disease and begins with a grandmother farting on her grandson's face after he refused to submit to male initiation. The Kĩsêdjê (JÊ) version deploys a flatulent mother-in-law (Nonato 2016: 1–2). The Kuikuro (UPPER XINGUAN CARIBAN) version is very similar to that of the Kĩsêdjê (Franchetto, recordings and field notes from 1981).

While the Ka'apor and Bororo versions should be considered "serious" narratives, for the Kĩsêdjê and the Kuikuro, the theme of the flatulent mother-in-law is a feature of short and funny ("ugly") narratives. It is interesting to note the structural correspondences of the relations between the protagonists: a grandmother and grandson for the Bororo; an older woman and young boy for the Ka'apor; a mother-in-law and son-in-law in the Upper Xingu.

In the Ka'apor narrative, the eschatological event is intimately tied to the description of the behaviour of ancient killers, who were submitted to post-homicide seclusion. When the seclusion was over, the killers had to come out during the beer drinking ceremony (a drink made from the fermentation of cashews or manioc flat bread).

The plot involves four characters: a young boy (the protagonist), an elder woman (the antagonist), the youth's brother (co-protagonist) and the war chief (auxiliary). The boy grows increasingly pale (*tawa* 'yellow'), as the days go by, because of the intestinal gasses (*pɪnu*) that an old woman discharged on him. His brother grows suspicious and makes a small wooden-tipped arrow (*uʔɪ sepetu*) for the sick boy to kill the old woman. Feigning sleep, the boy stabs the arrow into the old woman's anus as she tries to fart on him once again. The malevolent woman soon falls ill and dies. The young boy confesses the homicide to the war chief (*tuʃa*), who advises him to go into post-homicide seclusion, lying down in his room (*kapɪ*). Finally, the young killer comes out during the beer drinking ceremony.

The narrative is, in fact, a reminder of this now defunct part of the beer ritual: the coming out of the killer. Furthermore, one of the four characters, the war chief, is a figure of the past.

The beer-drinking ceremony brings to an end the restrictions that fall on those who find themselves in states of susceptibility, such as the killer; its central moment is the naming ritual. In the narrative, the war chief tells the boy that he should come out after the "lifting of the children" (line 34) when the sponsors present the name of a baby. The beverage ritual is here called *akaju rıkwɛr ɲã ʔu*, "the cashew beer drinking moment" (line 37).

Figure 2: The storyteller Jamói, at the moment when the men ask about the name of his goddaughter (*tajɪr-aŋa*). Her name, *Nanã akɪr* 'unripe pineapple', is then announced.

The killer would appear in the beer drinking ceremony carrying a pack of arrows. He remained at the place of the ceremony, looking east, immobile and impassive. An old man would go towards him with words of reprobation and revenge: "Hu-Hu-Hu! You attacked your comrade! Now it is you who will be (attacked)! Now I will draw your blood!"

The old man carried a tooth (from a trahira - a fish with a big mouth and sharp teeth - or from a Brazilian squirrel) which he used to scar the killer's legs (line 42), so as to expel the morbid blood in his body (line 43). This blood contained part of the dead person. Failure to extract it would cause the killer to go mad, affected by the murdered enemy. After scarification, the killer's vulnerability would come to an end, and he could then leave his room and wander the outside world without any danger (line 45) *pɛ sɔrɔka rɛhɛ wata atu i-ʃɔ tĩ*).

4 Notes on transcription and annotation

The first line of the transcription is orthographic. The Ka'apor system of alphabetic writing is based on the phonemic analysis carried out by Kakumasu (1964); Kakumasu & Kakumasu (1988). Ka'apor has 15 phonemic consonants /p, t, k, kʷ, m, n, ŋ, ŋʷ, s, ʃ, j, ɾ, w, h, ʔ/; six phonemic oral vowels /i, ɪ, ɛ, a, ɔ, u/ and five nasal vowels /ĩ, ẽ, ã, ɔ̃, ũ/. In the orthography, the graphemes <ng, ', x, y, e, o> represent IPA /ŋ, ʔ, ʃ, ɪ, ɛ, ɔ/. The <ái, úi> sequence represent /aj, uj/.

5 A'i ymanhar ke kurumĩ rehe pynu ixo.
'A long time ago, an old woman farted on a boy'
'Muito tempo atrás, uma velha pedou em um menino'[1]

(1) ta'yn uker ou 'y pytun rahã pame ame'ẽ a'i ai pynu oho ehe je
taʔɪn u-kʷɛɾ ɔ²-u   ʔɪ   pɪtun ɾahã pamɛ amɛʔẽ aʔi   ai
child 3-sleep 3-lay.down PFV night SR   each DEI   old.woman roguish
pɪnu³ ɔ-hɔ ɛhɛ jɛ⁴
fart 3-go 3.at HSY

'Night after night, while a boy was lying (down), it is said that an old roguish woman came to fart on him.'
'Dizem que, noite após noite, quando um menino estava deitado, uma velha escrota peidava em cima dele.'

---

[1] Recordings of this story are available from https://zenodo.org/record/997433

[2] There is no number distinction in the third person prefix, glossed simply as '3'. The allomorph of this prefix in active verbs is *u-*, when the verbal root is monosyllabic and does not contain the vowel /ɔ/. If the monosyllabic root has the vowel /ɔ/, the allomorph ɔ- is used. The third person person prefix ɔ- with the auxiliary verb *-u* 'to lay down' is a exception to this rule.

[3] When the verbal root has more than one syllable, no third person prefix is attached to it. In other words, the person mark is a zero allomorph (∅).

[4] Ka'apor does not have a system with several morphemes indexing different sources of the information, as in the grammaticalized evidentials used in Kotiria realis statements (cf. chapter 5 in this volume) or the more complex evindentiality systems of other Tupian languages, such as Kamauirá, Tapirapé, and Karo. The reported evidential *jɛ* 'HSY' (hearsay or reportative modality) is the only evidential morpheme in Ka'apor. *jɛ* does not imply disbelief on the part of the speaker in relation to the content of the mythical narrative, and it occurs in almost all sentences. This contrasts with the sparse occurrence of the quotative reported evidential *-yu'ka* and its pragmatic use in the Kotiria narrative (cf. Footnote 10 of the Kotiria narrative, Chapter 5). Indeed, in Ka'apor mythological narratives, the morpheme *je* codes a diffuse source of information, more like the 'diffuse' evidential *-yu'ti* in Kotiria (cf. Stenzel 2008).

(2) *pe pytun je tĩ pe pynu oho je tĩ*

pɛ pɪtun jɛ tĩ   pɛ pɪnu ɔ-hɔ jɛ tĩ
then night HSY again then fart 3-ho HSY again

'Each night that came, she farted on him again.'
'Outra noite chegava e ela peidava de novo.'

(3) *ta'yn ukʷer ta je tĩ, ko a'i ihái ke pirok hũ je pe i'ar pe pynu hũ*

taʔɪn u-kʷɛɾ-ta   jɛ tĩ   kɔ aʔi   i-haj-kɛ pirɔk-hũ   jɛ
child 3-sleep-FUT HSY again DEI old.woman 3-skirt-AFC strip-INTENS HSY
pɛ i-ʔaɾ-pɛ   pɪnu -hũ
then 3-above-LOC fart -INTENS

'When the boy went to sleep again, the old woman took off her skirt, it is said; then (she) farted on him a lot.'
'O menino ia dormir de novo e a tal velha tirava a sua saia; então, peidava um monte nele.'

(4) *pynupynu ate ehe je*

pɪnu~pɪnu-atɛ   ɛhɛ jɛ
fart~RED-INTENS 3.at HSY

'She was really farting a lot on him.'
'Ficava peidando muito mesmo nele.'

(5) *pe oho je tĩ*

pɛ ɔ-hɔ jɛ tĩ
then 3-go HSY again

'She went again (towards the boy).'
'E ela foi de novo (até o menino).'

(6) *ta'yn ke itawa imu parahy ahy ipe je*

taʔɪn-kɛ i-tawa   i-mu   paɾahɪ-ahɪ   i-pɛ jɛ
child-AFC 3-yellow 3-brother angry-INTENS 3-DAT HSY

'The boy was yellowish (sick), his brother was very angry with him.'
'O menino estava amarelado, seu irmão ficou bravo.'

(7) *"ne tawa te ne ke ã ne jyty'ym te amõ 'y"*

nɛ-tawa-tɛ   nɛ-kɛã nɛ-jɪtɪʔɪm-tɛ   amɔ̃   ʔɪ
2SG-yellow-INTENS 2SG-AFC 2SG-lazy-INTENS another PFV

'"You are yellowish and very lazy too."'
'"Você está amarelado e está preguiçoso também."'

(8) *pandu 'ym anu ta'yn je tĩ*

    pandu-ʔɩm~anu taʔɩn jɛ   tĩ
    tell-NEG~RED   child HSY again

    'The boy didn't say anything.'
    'O menino não contava.'

(9) *pe pytun je tĩ, pe a'i [...] pytun pyter pe je*

    pɛ pɩtun jɛ   tĩ   pɛ aʔi   [...] pɩtun pɩtɛr-pɛ   jɛ
    so night HSY again so old.woman [...] night middle-LOC HSY

    'Another night, the old ... [hesitation] in the middle of the night.'
    'Então, de noite, novamente, então, a velha ... [hesitação] era no meio da noite.'

(10) *pe a'i ihon ixo je 'y*

    pɛ   aʔi   i-hɔn i-ʃɔ   jɛ ʔɩ
    then old.woman 3-go 3-AUX HSY PFV

    'Then the old woman went (towards the boy).'
    'Então a velha foi (até o menino).'

(11) *pe ihái ke musyryk je, pe ta'yn ukwer atu je Pũũũ! japũi rehe pynu je*

    pɛ i-haj-kɛ   mu-sɩrɩk jɛ pɛ taʔɩn u-kʷɛr-atu   jɛ pũũũ
    then 3-skirt-AFC CAUS-strip HSY then child 3-sleep-INTENS HSY IDEO
    i-apũi rɛhɛ pɩnu jɛ
    3-nose LOC fart HSY

    'So, (she) she raised her own skirt, the child was sleeping deeply: *Puum!* She farted in his nose.'
    'Ela levantou a saia, o menino estava dormindo bem: *Puum!* Ela peidou no nariz dele.'

(12) *pe ... pe wera uwyr tĩ, pe imu panu ipe "myja ne xoha tĩ"*

    pɛ pɛ wɛra uwɩr tĩ   pɛ i-mu   panu i-pɛ   mɩja nɛ-ʃɔ-ha
    then then light come again then 3-brother tell   3-DAT Q   2SG-be-NMLZ
    tĩ
    again

    'So ... so the light (of the morning) came again, and his brother said: "What's wrong with you?"'
    'Amanheceu de novo e o irmão perguntou: "O que está errado com você?"'

(13) *"epandu ihẽ pe rahã", pe imu pandu, "xe amõ a'i ihẽ rehe pynu ixo tĩ"*
"pytun rahã pame ihẽ rehe pynu" je; "a'erehe ihẽ ke atawa tái"

ɛ-pandu   ihẽ-pɛ   ɾahã pɛ i-mu   panu ʃɛ amõ   a?i
2SG.IMP-tell 1SG-DAT HORT so 3-brother tell DEI another old.woman

ihẽ-ɾɛhɛ pɪnu i-ʃɔ tĩ   pɪtun ɾahã pamɛ ihẽ-ɾɛhɛ pɪnu je a?ɛ-ɾɛhɛ
1SG-LOC fart 3-be again night SR   each 1SG-LOC fart HSY 3-about

ihẽ-kɛ   a-tawa   taj
1SG-AFC 1SG-yellow INTENS

'"Talk to me!" and his brother said: "The old woman is farting on me; every night she farts on me! That's why I'm turning yellow."'
'"Conte para mim!" e o irmão respondeu: "A velha está peidando em mim; todas as noites! Por isso estou amarelando."'

(14) *pe imu ... u'y ra'yr mujã ipe je, u'y sepetu, yrapar ra'yr*

pɛ i-mu   u?ɪ ɾa?ɪɾ mujã i-pɛ je u?ɪ sɛpɛtu ɪɾapaɾ ɾa?ɪɾ
so 3-brother arrow small make 3-DAT HSY arrow spit bow   small

'Then, his brother ... made a small arrow with a tip of wood and a small bow for him.'
'Então, o irmão ... fez uma flechinha para ele com ponta de madeira e um pequeno arco.'

(15) *pe ko[me'ẽ] ... pe "ejingo rahã kỹ" aja ipe je*

pɛ kɔ[mɛ?ẽ] pɛ ɛ-jingɔ   ɾahã kĩ⁵ aja i-pɛ je
so th(is)   so 2SG.IMP-shoot HORT KĨ⁵ ANA 3-DAT HSY

'So this ... so "Shoot!" he said to him.'
'Então ... "Flecha!" assim disse (o irmão) para ele.'

(16) *pe ta'yn ukwer uwyr je tĩ, pytun rahã*

pɛ ta?ɪn u-kʷɛɾ uwɪɾ je tĩ   pɪtun ɾahã
so child 3-sleep come HSY again noite SR

'The boy went to sleep again, at night.'
'O menino foi dormir de novo, de noite.'

(17) *pe a'i ai tur je tĩ*

pɛ a?i   ai   tuɾ je tĩ
so old.woman rogue come HSY again

'The old woman came again.'
'A velha chegou novamente.'

---

[5]Kakumasu & Kakumasu (1988) translate the morpheme *kĩ* as 'definitive intention'.

(18) *pe sa'e a'i ihái, xirur ke pirok hũ je ihai ai ke*

pɛ saʔɛ aʔi   i-haj ʃiɾuɾ-kɛ   piɾɔk-hũ   jɛ   i-haj   ai   jɛ
so guy old.woman 3-skirt short-AFC strip-INTENS HSY 3-skirt bad HSY

'So he ... the old woman raised her own old skirt, her pants.'
'Aí ele ... a velha levantou sua saia, sua calça, levantou alto, a sua saia surrada.'

(19) *xape ai jumupirar te'e xoty je*

i-ʃapɛ   ai   ju-mu-piɾaɾ   tɛʔɛ i-ʃɔtɪ   jɛ
3-anus bad REFL-CAUS-open free 3-towards HSY

'Her disgusting asshole opened towards the boy.'
'Seu cu nojento abriu muito na direção do menino.'

(20) *pe sa'e u'y ke hykýi je Sõõ xape kwar rupi ate jingo mondo je a'i ai ahem ate oho je*

pɛ saʔɛ uʔɪ-kɛ   hɪkɪj jɛ   Sõõ   ʃapɛ kʷaɾ rupi atɛ   jingɔ mɔnɔ jɛ
so guy arrow-AFC pull HSY IDEO anus hole in INTENS shoot throw HSY

aʔi   ai   ahɛm atɛ   ɔ-hɔ jɛ
old.woman roguish scream INTENS 3-go HSY

'So, he took the arrow and *Sõõ!* he shot it into her asshole, the arrow was stuck in her asshole. The nasty old woman screamed a lot.'
'Então, ele armou a flecha *Sõõ!* flechou bem no buraco de seu cu e a (velha) ficou com a flecha encravada. A velha foi gritando muito.'

(21) *pe a'i ai pynu 'ym je 'y amõ ku'em rahã sa'e ... amõ wera uwyr je 'y*

pɛ aʔɪ   ai   pɪnu ʔɪm jɛ   ʔɪ   amɔ̃   kuʔɛm   ɾahã saʔɛ
so old.woman roguish fart NEG HSY PFV another morning SR guy

amɔ̃   wɛɾa uwɪɾ jɛ   ʔɪ
another light come HSY PFV

'Then, the old woman didn't fart anymore; the next morning ... Another day came.'
'Então a velha não peidou mais, na outra manhã ... Chegou outro dia.'

(22) *pe pytun oho tĩ; a'i ju...ju... juwyr 'ym oho pytun rahã*

pɛ pɪtun ɔhɔ tĩ   aʔi   ju...ju...   juwɪɾ ʔɪm ɔhɔ pɪtun ɾahã
so night 3-go again old.woman [hesitation] return NEG 3-go night SR

'So, night came again; [hesitation] the old woman didn't return.'

'Veio a noite novamente; [hesitação] a velha não voltou, quando foi a noite novamente.'

(23) *pe ... pe atu u'y ipi'a kwar [rupi]⁶ upen u'am 'y*
pɛ pɛ atu uʔɪ i-piʔa kʷaɾ [ɾupi] upɛn uʔam ʔɪ
SO SO INTENS arrow 3-vagina hole [by] broke AUX.vertical PFV
'So ... So, the arrow broke in her vagina.'
'Então ... Então, a flecha quebrou no buraco da vagina dela.'

(24) *amõ ukwer rahã a'i ame'ẽ a'i ke ma'e ahy je 'y*
amõ u-kʷɛɾ ɾahã aʔi amɛʔẽ aʔi-kɛ maʔe-ahɪ je
another 3-sleep SR old.woman ANA old.woman-AFC sickness HSY
ʔɪ
PFV
'The next day, that old woman got sick.'
'No outro dia, a velha, aquela velha, adoeceu.'

(25) *pe sawa'e, ame'ẽ ta'ynuhu ukwa je*
pɛ sawaʔɛ amɛʔẽ taʔɪn-uhu u-kʷa je
so man ANA child-INTENS 3-know HSY
'That young boy already knew.'
'Aquele homem, aquele menino sabia.'

(26) *"pe'ẽ a'i ihẽ rehe pynu ixo riki ã, ame'ẽ pytun rahã"*
peʔẽ aʔi ihẽ ɾɛhɛ pɪnu i-ʃɔ ɾikiã amɛʔẽ pɪtun ɾahã
DEI old.woman 1SG in fart 3-be emphasis ANA night SR
'"That old woman was farting on me that night."'
'"Aquela velha estava peidando em mim aquela noite."'

(27) *sa'e ke pe túiha ke*
saʔɛ-kɛ pɛ tuj-ha-kɛ
guy-AFC DEI stay-NMLZ-AFC
'There was the boy.'
'Ali estava o menino.'

---

⁶Not performed in speech, but indicated in the analysis.

(28) *yman te pe a'i ke manõ je 'y*
ɪman-tɛ pɛ aʔi-kɛ manõ jɛ
lately-INTENS so old.woman-AFC die HSY
'Later, the old woman died.'
'Passou um tempo, a velha morreu.'

(29) *pe ame'ẽ ta'yn tuxa pe pandu je*
pɛ amɛʔẽ taʔɪn tuʃa-pɛ panu jɛ
so ANA child chief-DAT tell HSY
'Then, the child talked to the chief:'
'Então aquele menino falou para o tuxaua:'

(30) *"ihẽ ame'ẽ a'i ke ajukwa"*
ihẽ amɛʔẽ aʔi-kɛ a-jukʷa
1SG ANA old.woman-AFC 1SG-kill
'"I killed that old woman."'
'"Eu matei aquela velha."'

(31) *pe tuxa aja ipe je*
pɛ tuʃa aja i-pɛ jɛ
so chief DEI 3-DAT HSY
'So, the warrior chief said to him:'
'E o tuxaua assim falou para ele:'

(32) *"kawĩ, ta'ynta jahupir rahã, epandu kỹ hetaha pe"*
kawĩ taʔɪn-ta ja-hupir ɾahã ɛ-panu kĩ hɛta-ha-pɛ
beer child-PL 1PL-lift SR 2SG.IMP-tell KĨ many-NMLZ-DAT
'"Beer, when we will lift the children, talk to the people."'
'"Cauim, quando levantamos as crianças, fale para o grupo."'

(33) *"apo kapy pe te'e eju rĩ"*
apɔ kapɪ-pɛ tɛʔɛ ɛ-ju ɾĩ
now room-LOC TƐʔƐ 2SG.IMP-lay.down IPFV
'"Now, go off to your room."'
'"Agora, vá deitar no teu quarto."'

(34) *pe sa'e kapy pe túi je*
pɛ saʔɛ kapɪ-pɛ   tuj jɛ
so guy room-LOC stay HSY
'He stayed in the room (in seclusion).'
'Ele ficou no quarto (em reclusão).'

(35) *pe ... akaju rykwer ngã'u je 'y, pe sa'e uhem je 'y*
pɛ akaju ɾɪkʷɛɾ ŋã⁷-ʔu   jɛ   ʔɪ pɛ saʔɛ u-hɛm jɛ   ʔɪ
so cashew juice 3PL-ingest HSY PFV so guy 3-exit HSY PFV
'Then ... Later, after they drank cashew beer, he came out.'
'Então ... Depois deles beberem o cauim do caju, ele saiu.'

(36) *kapy ngi uhem*
kapɪ ĩ   u-hɛm
room ABL 3-exit
'He left the seclusion room.'
'Ele saiu do quarto de reclusão.'

(37) *kujã ta ke upa mupinim*
kujã-ta-kɛ   upa mu-pinim
mulher-PL-AFC all CAUS-painted
'All the women were painted.'
'Todas as mulheres foram pintadas.'

(38) *aja rahã sa'e a'e uhem ta'ynuhu, ta'ynuhu je*
aja ɾahã saʔɛ aʔɛ u-hɛm taʔɪn-uhu   taʔɪnuhu   jɛ
ANA SR   guy 3   3-exit child-INTENS child-INTENS HSY
'At this moment, the young man left the room.'
'Foi neste o momento que o jovem saiu da reclusão.'

(39) *ma'e... huwy ke*
maʔɛ   huwɪ-kɛ
hesitation blood-AFC
'And ... The blood ... '
'Ee ... Sangue ...'

---

[7] Although there is no distinction between plural and singular in the third person prefix, Ka'apor has the free pronoun ŋã to index third person plural.

(40) *upa tymã mu'i huwy ke upa muhãi je*

　　upa tɪmã muʔi　huwɪ-kɛ　upa muhãj　jɛ
　　all leg scarify blood-AFC all disperse HSY

　　'The lower part of his legs was scarified; the (bad) blood was totally dispersed.'
　　'A parte de baixo de suas pernas foram escarificada; todo o sangue (ruim) foi retirado.'

(41) *huwy ahyha ke, a'i ruwy ke ame'ẽja saka je*

　　huwɪ　ahɪ–ha-kɛ　　aʔi　　　ɾuwɪ-kɛ　amɛʔẽ-ja saka jɛ
　　blood pain-NMLZ-AFC old.woman blood-AFC DEI-ANA like HSY

　　'The evil and toxic blood, it was as if it were the blood of the old woman.'
　　'O sangue insalubre e mórbido, era como se fosse o sangue da velha.'

(42) *pe ... aja rahã katu je tĩ*

　　pɛ aja　ɾahã katu jɛ　tĩ
　　SO ANA SR　good HSY again

　　'So ... In this way he became well again.'
　　'Então ... deste jeito o jovem ficou bom.'

(43) *pe soroka rehe wata atu ixo tĩ*

　　pɛ sɔɾɔka　ɾɛhɛ wata atu　i-ʃɔ　tĩ
　　so outside by　walk good 3-be again

　　'And he was able to walk outside again.'
　　'E ele pode andar de novo tranquilamente do lado de fora.'

Acknowledgments

I thank Jamói for his teachings; he is one of my main consultants among the Ka'apor. I am also grateful to Bruna Franchetto and Kristine Stenzel for their revisions and suggestions, Luiz Costa for a first English translation of the Introduction, and Manuella Godoy, who helped me with the final details of the map. My work on Ka'apor as an MA student was supported by a grant to the Graduate Program in Social Anthropology (UFRJ) from the of Program for Continuing Academic Development (CAPES, Brazilian Ministry of Education).

Non-standard abbreviations

AFC	affected	HSY	hearsay, reported evidential
ANA	anaphora or cataphora	IDEO	ideophone
DEI	deixis	INTENS	intensifier
HORT	hortative	SR	subordinator

References

Balée, William. 1994. *Footprints of the forest.* New York: Columbia University Press.

Balée, William. 2006. Landscape transformation and language change: A case study in amazonian historical ecology. In Cristina Adams, Rui Murrieta, Walter Neves & Mark Harris (eds.), *Amazon peasant societies in a changing environment: Political ecology, invisibility and modernity in the rainforest*, 33–53. New York: Springer.

Corrêa-da-Silva, Beatriz C. 1997. *Urubú-Ka'apór - da gramática à história: A trajetória de um povo.* Brasília: Universidade de Brasília dissertation.

Corrêa-da-Silva, Beatriz C. 2002. A codificação dos argumentos em Ka'apor: Sincronia e diacronia. In Ana S. Cabral & A. D. Rodrigues (eds.), *Línguas indígenas brasileiras: Fonologia, gramática e história. Atas do I encontro internacional do grupo de trabalho sobre línguas indígenas da ANPOLL*, 343–351. Belém: EDUFPA.

Ferreira, Lucinda. 1984. Similarities and differences in two Brazilian sign languages. *Sign Language Studies* 42. 45–56.

Ferreira, Lucinda. 2010. *Por uma gramática de língua de sinais.* Rio de Janeiro: Tempo Brasileiro.

Ferreira, Lucinda. n.d. *At least two sign languages in Brazil: One among Urubu-Kaapor Indians and another in São Paulo.*

Godoy, Gustavo. 2015. *Dos modos de beber e cozinhar cauim: Ritos e narrativas dos Ka'apores.* Rio de Janeiro: Universidade Federal do Rio de Janeiro dissertation.

Kakumasu, James Y. 1964. *Urubú phonemics.* Summer Institute of Linguistics.

Kakumasu, James Y. & K. Kakumasu. 1988. *Dicionário por tópicos Kaapor-Português.* Cuiabá: FUNAI/Summer Institute of Linguistics.

Nonato, Rafael. 2016. *Noruega, Ndo ro hwêkê, Peido na cara.* Handout de comunicação dada no PPGAS-MN-UFRJ.

Ribeiro, Darcy. 1962. *A política indigenista brasileira.* Rio de Janeiro: Ministério da Agricultura.

Stenzel, Kristine. 2008. Evidentials and clause modality in Wanano. *Studies in Language* 32(2). 405–445.

Name index

Agostinho, Pedro, 28
Aikhenvald, Alexandra Y., 6, 7, 285
Andrello, Geraldo, 191

Balée, William, 468
Basso, Ellen B., 28, 30, 91, 134, 136
Bastos, Rafael, 137
Birchall, Joshua, 6
Bolaños, Katherine, 209, 277
Bontkes, Carolyn, 442
Bozzi, Ana Maria Ospina, 14
Brunelli, Gilio, 444
Bruno, Ana Carla, 9

Cabalzar, Aloisio, 191
Camargo, Eliane, 141
Campbell, Lyle, 6, 8
Cardoso, Walmir Thomazi, 282
Carneiro, Robert, 28
Castro Alves, Flávia de, 335
Cesarino, Pedro de Niemeyer, 140, 141, 160
Chernela, Janet, 191, 192
Corrêa-da-Silva, Beatriz C., 468
Crevels, Mily, 7

de Oliveira, Lucia Alberta Andrade, 190
De Vienne, Emmanuel, 181
Demolin, Didier, 195
Derbyshire, Desmond, 8
Dixon, Robert W., 6

dos Santos, Gélsama M. F., 27, 91
Dourado, Luciana, 165

Emmerich, Charlotte, 165
Epps, Patience, 1, 6, 7, 13, 191, 209, 277, 278, 283, 285, 286, 305

Fargetti, Cristina M., 165
Fausto, Carlos, 25
Ferreira, Lucinda, 469
Fleck, David W., 141
Franchetto, Bruna, 2, 8, 24, 25, 27, 30, 32, 34–36, 69, 90, 91, 134

Gabas Júnior, Nílson, 334
Galucio, Ana Vilacy, 334–336, 347
Galvão, Eduardo, 164
Gildea, Spike, 16, 335
Godoy, Gustavo, 467
Gomez-Imbert, Elsa, 194, 197, 202, 285
Guerreiro, Antonio, 135, 166
Guirardello-Damian, Raquel, 164, 165, 177, 168–172, 180

Hammond, Jeremy, 16
Haude, Katharina, 9
Heckenberger, Michael J., 25, 167

Jacobsen, William, 360

Kakumasu, James Y., 469, 471, 474
Kakumasu, K., 469, 471, 474

Name index

Kalin, Laura, 27
Kaufman, Terrence, 165
Koch-Grünberg, Theodor, 249

Lacerda Guerra, Mariana, 442
Lima, Suzi O., 27
Londoño Sulkin, Carlos D., 283

Mehinaku, Mutua, 91
Meira, Sérgio, 24
Mindlin, Betty, 439
Monod-Becquelin, Aurore, 164
Montagner, Delvair, 140
Moore, Denny, 1, 334
Murphy, Robert, 163, 166, 167
Muysken, Pieter, 6, 9

Nonato, Rafael, 359, 469

Oliveira, Melissa, 282
O'Connor, Loretta, 6

Payne, Doris L., 6

Quain, Buell, 163, 166, 167
Queixalós, Francesc, 16

Rabello, Aline Varela, 91
Ramirez, Henri, 285
Ribeiro, Darcy, 468
Rice, Keren, 2
Rodrigues, Aryon, 165, 334
Ruedas, Javier, 139

Salanova, Andrés, 1, 6, 7
Santos, Ludoviko Carnasciali, 359
Santos, Mara, 27, 30, 34
Santos-Granero, Fernando, 283
Seki, Lucy, 165
Silva, Glauber R. da, 25
Silva, Maria Fátima S., 408

Simões, Mário, 164
Stenzel, Kristine, 2, 7, 189–191, 194, 195, 197, 202, 221, 255, 270, 278, 283, 285, 471

Thomas, Guillaume, 30
Trindade, José Galvez, 190

Uzendoski, Michael, 283

Valenzuela, Pilar, 141
Van der Meer, Tina H., 442
van der Voort, Hein, 6, 7, 407
van Gijn, Rik, 9, 16
Vilaça, Aparecida, 283
Villas Boas, Claudio, 28, 163
Villas Boas, Orlando, 28, 163
Viveiros de Castro, Eduardo, 283
von den Steinen, Karl, 25, 164
Voort, Hein van der, 389

Waltz, Carolyn, 192
Waltz, Nathan E., 192
Welper, Elena, 139

Yvinec, Cédric, 439, 442

www.ingramcontent.com/pod-product-compliance
Lightning Source LLC
Chambersburg PA
CBHW081112160426
42814CB00035B/293